Beginning ASP.NET 1.0

with C#

Rob Birdwell

Matt Butler

Ollie Cornes

Chris Goode

Gary Johnson

John Kauffman

Ajoy Krishnamoorthy

Juan T. Llibre

Christopher L. Miller

Neil Raybould

Srinivasa Sivakumar

David Sussman

Chris Ullman

Wrox Press Ltd. ®

Beginning ASP.NET 1.0

with C#

© 2002 Wrox Press

Published by Wrox Press Ltd,
Arden House, 1102 Warwick Road, Acocks Green,
Birmingham, B27 6BH, UK
Printed in the United States
ISBN 1-86100-734-5

Trademark Acknowledgments

Wrox has endeavored to provide trademark information about all the companies and products mentioned in this book by the appropriate use of capitals. However, Wrox cannot guarantee the accuracy of this information.

Credits

Authors
Rob Birdwell
Matt Butler
Ollie Cornes
Chris Goode
Gary Johnson
John Kauffman
Ajoy Krishnamoorthy
Juan T. Llibre
Christopher L. Miller
Neil Raybould
Srinivasa Sivakumar
David Sussman
Chris Ullman

Additional Material
Jon Duckett
James Hart
Matt Reynolds
Dan Squier

Technical Architect
Dan Squier

Lead Technical Editor
Ewan Buckingham

Technical Editors
Alessandro Ansa
Alastair Ewins
Jake Manning

Managing Editor
Louay Fatoohi

Index
Michael Brinkman
John Collin

Production Coordinator
Abbie Forletta

Cover
Natalie O'Donnell

Proof Reader
Chris Smith

Author Agent
Cilmara Lion

Project Manager
Christianne Bailey

Technical Reviewers
Rob Birdwell
Maxime Bombadier
Daniel Cazzulino
Cristian Darie
Robin Dewson
John Kauffman
Larry Schoeneman
Marc H. Simkin

About the Authors

Rob Birdwell

Rob Birdwell makes his home in Corvallis, Oregon along with his wife and three beautiful children. He works at HP and moonlights as a musician, composer, and songwriter. He first became interested in programming when he discovered he could make a machine play one of his musical melodies. His current interests include all facets of .NET technology and especially the C# language. His hobbies include swimming, tennis, and playing his trumpet in various ensembles.

Rob would like to thank his wife, Christel, and children for their patience and support while he endeavored to make a small contribution to this wonderful book.

Matt (.MAtt) Butler

Matt Butler is lead technical brain at Left Ear Design and specializes in .NET, Windows DNA, and Java.

.MAtt went from being a homeless, starving jazz musician to a software architect holding numerous certifications, including MCSD, Sun Java Certified Programmer, BEA Certified Programmer (Java / Weblogic), and a few other miscellaneous certifications. He rode the wave of the .COM craze working on sizable profile-based search engines and transactional e-commerce applications using the Windows DNA architecture in return for 'stock options' and pizza.

.MAtt's interests include all things computer oriented (especially .NET and security), math, science, physics, spoken word, composing, and improvising introspective music.

Thanks to Daisey for being a loyal, supportive life-partner and muse and thanks to Morgan for being a wonderful daughter and talented friend. Thanks to the Left Ear crew (Matt Cribbs, James McIntosh, Jennifer Ricker, Tim Parmentier, and Brandon Stromberg) for being talented visionaries with integrity. Thanks to Gary for being a great friend and learning partner. Thanks to my family, and the people at Wrox for being so good at what they do, and, ultimately, thanks to all of the musicians with whom I have had the chance to associate with and learn from – especially my current quartet - Joseph Yorio, Sean Tarleton, Tim Stombaugh.

You can reach .MAtt at matt@biodigitalmusic.com .

Ollie Cornes

Ollie Cornes has been working with the Internet and the Microsoft platform since the early 90's. In 1999 he co-founded a business-to-business Internet company and until recently was its Chief Technical Officer.

Prior to that his various roles involved programming, technical authoring, network management, writing, leading development projects, and consulting. He has worked with Demon Internet, Microsoft, Saab, Travelstore, and Vodafone. Ollie holds a degree in computer science and is Microsoft certified.

When he's not working he spends his time devouring books on human potential and practicing Chinese internal martial arts, meditation, and healing. He also juggles fire and knives.

Chris Goode

Chris is currently an editor in the Microsoft team at Wrox. She lives in Birmingham (that's UK, not Alabama), and has a house full of old computers. Chris started programming at the age of 10 on her Atari 65XE, and has always enjoyed spending time with as much technology as possible. She has a degree in Mechanical Engineering, but decided that the engineering world wasn't for her. She's now back firmly in the world of computers, and finding that life at Wrox combines the fun stuff with the work stuff pretty well.

I'd like to thank my family for putting up with me over the years, and for buying me my first computer. Thanks to Ewan for all the time and hard work he's invested in this book, and for not objecting too loudly to my chapters. Special thanks go to James for finally popping the question, and for being so supportive.

Gary Johnson

Gary Johnson is a transplanted hillbilly currently residing in Florida. He has programmed the Web since 1995 using a myriad of technologies (mostly VB/ASP/DNA type stuff prior to .NET).

When not chained to the machine, he likes spending time with CoCo the dog or practicing the elusive art of photography. Gary would like to thank John, Nestor, Matt, and Daisey for their unwavering wonder and enthusiasm for the world.

To Diane who makes my house a home. My home is anywhere you are.

John Kauffman

John's first publications, some 20 years ago, explained sail trimming and tactics to yacht racers. He then returned to the printed page to describe his discovery of a genomic sequence in plants that could be controlled by light.

Today, he splits his time between Asia and North America where he teaches and writes for Wrox about Microsoft technologies for connecting databases to the Web. While teaching he keeps a list of students questions and mistakes, then uses that information as the basis for organizing future editions of his books. John also designed and wrote portions of *Beginning ASP Databases* and *Beginning SQL Programming*.

John dedicates his portions of the book to the master teachers from whom he has learned the art of explaining science and technology; including the faculties of science at ELCO High School and Kutztown, Millersville, Penn State, and the Rockefeller Universities

Ajoy Krishnamoorthy

Ajoy Krishnamoorthy is a consultant with over five years of experience, working in Microsoft technologies such as ASP, VB, IIS, MTS, and most recently .NET. He writes regularly for leading online publications. He received a Bachelors degree in Electronics and Communication and a Masters degree in Systems and information. He is currently working for his Masters in Business Administration at Fisher College of Business, Ohio State University. His interests include writing, hanging out with friends, and travel. He is originally from Chennai, India and currently lives in Columbus, Ohio with his wife Vidhya. He can be reached at ajoyk@ajoys.net.

This would not have been possible, without an understanding and supportive wife. Thank you Vidhya, you are the best. I also want to thank my family for their support and encouragement. Finally, thanks to Wrox Press and its wonderful people for this opportunity.

Juan T. Llibre

Juan T. Llibre is the Director of the Computer Sciences and Distance Education departments at Universidad Nacional Pedro Henríquez Ureña in Santo Domingo, Dominican Republic.

He has been a consultant to the Caribbean Export Development Agency and the Dominican Republic's Central Bank and is currently the Technical Architect for the Caribbean Virtual University, a Distance Education consortium composed of 30 Caribbean Universities, which will go online in 2002. He's also planning what he calls a "killer app" for Caribbean Tourism.

Juan has been an Active Server Pages Microsoft MCP for four years and can regularly be found in the newsgroups and mailing lists, offering advice on ASP and ASP.NET in English and Spanish.

He co-authored Wrox's *Beginning ASP 2.0* and *Beginning ASP 3.0*, and has been a Technical Reviewer for over a dozen books on ASP and its related technologies.

When he isn't writing, reviewing, seeing students and running the school, producing Distance Education courses, or hanging out with developers, he takes off to a beach hut with a high-speed connection, because "...a man must have some fun, too!"

He has three daughters, Jonquil, Anthea, and Isabelle, and two grandsons, David and Keenan.

Christopher Miller

Christopher Miller began his development in the early 1980's with Atari Basic, migrating to GW Basic, QuickBasic, and finally to Visual Basic, where he's lived and breathed, since 1992. He is currently a business consultant with cs|enlign inc. (formerly Crossoft Inc) of Pittsburgh, PA, specializing in Intranet architecture and design. He's also president of the Pittsburgh .NET User Group (http://www.pghdotnet.org).

His current projects include an adaptive intranet framework tool and other .NET-based Web Service applications. He holds a business degree from Pensacola Christian College of Florida, and all major Microsoft certifications (MCSE+I, MCSD, MCT, MCDBA).

Thanks to my wife, Stacy, for all the support. Couldn't do it without you.

Neil Raybould

Neil is working as a software developer and technical writer with cs|enlign, north of Pittsburgh, Pennsylvania. He has given several presentations on ASP and ASP.NET related topics in the Pittsburgh area. Growing up in Emporia, Virginia, Neil used lawn mowing profits in 1981 to buy a Commodore VIC-20. His current interests have progressed to include .NET and wireless applications. But, sometimes, Neil still longs for the days of CBM Basic, tape cassette drives, PEEKs and POKEs, and 3.5 K RAM.

Neil has a BS (Virginia Tech), an MBA (Duquesne University), and MCSD and MCDBA certifications.

To my wife Vicky and my daughter Abigail. You are such blessings to me. Thank you both so much for your encouragement and patience.

Srinivasa Sivakumar

Srinivasa Sivakumar is a software consultant, developer and author. He specializes in Web and Mobile technologies using Microsoft solutions. He currently works in Chicago for TransTech, Inc.

He has co-authored Professional ASP.NET Web Services, ASP.NET Mobile Controls, .NET Compact Framework and ASP.NET Security for Wrox Press and written technical articles for ASPToday.com, CSharpToday.com, .NET Developer, and others.

In his free time he likes to watch Tamil movies and list to Tamil sound tracks (Especially one's sung by Mr. S.P Balasubramaniyam).

I'd like the dedicate my section of this book to my dear sister Vijaya Ramkumar and my brother-in-law Mr. Ramkumar for their help and outstanding support. Vijaya and Ramkumar, thanks a lot for all your help. Many congratulations for your new arrival.

David Sussman

David Sussman spent most of his professional life as a developer before realizing that writing was far more fun. He specializes in Internet and data access technologies, and spends much of his time delving into beta technologies. He's just moved house, so now has no money left to add more components to his ludicrously expensive hi-fi. You can reach him at davids@ipona.co.uk.

Chris Ullman

Chris Ullman is a Computer Science Graduate who worked for Wrox for six and half years before branching out on his own. Now the father of a seven month old baby, Nye, he divides his time between being a human punchbag for Nye, trying to write extra chapters with a baby on his lap, and in rare moments of spare time, either playing keyboards in psychedelic band the Bee Men (http://www.beemen.com), tutoring his cats in the art of peaceful co-existence and not violently mugging each other on the stairs.

A selection of Chris's non-computer related writings on music, art, and literature can be found at http://www.atomicwise.com.

Table of Contents

Table of Contents

Table of Contents

Table of Contents

Introduction

ASP.NET 1.0 is the latest incarnation of Microsoft's Active Server Pages (ASP). It is a powerful server-based technology designed to create dynamic, interactive, HTML pages on demand for your World Wide Web site, or corporate intranet.

ASP.NET constitutes a key element in Microsoft's .NET Framework, providing web-based access to the immensely powerful .NET development environment. It allows us to create web applications in a new, flexible, way by encapsulating commonly used code into object-oriented controls of various kinds that can be fired by events initiated by our site's users.

ASP.NET branches out into many other technologies, such as Web Services, ADO.NET, Custom Controls, and Security. We will briefly touch upon its relationship with these fields throughout the book to provide a solid, comprehensive understanding of how ASP.NET can be used to benefit your work in a practical way.

By the end of this book you will be familiar with the anatomy of ASP.NET and be able to create flexible, secure, and robust web sites that can collect and work with information in a multitude of ways to the benefit of both yourself and your users.

What does this Book Cover?

Here is a quick breakdown of what you will find within the chapters of this book:

- ❑ **Chapter 1: Getting Started with ASP.NET** – in this first chapter we introduce ASP.NET and look at some of the reasons that you'd want to use server-side code for creating web pages and the technologies that are available to do so. This done we spend the bulk of the chapter explaining the ASP.NET installation process in detail, along with the ancillary installation of MDAC 2.7. We finish up with a simple ASP.NET example page to check that our installation is working correctly.

- ❑ **Chapter 2: Anatomy of an ASP.NET Page** – having completed the installation in the previous chapter we consider the structure of an ASP.NET page and the way that it functions in relation to the .NET Framework. We use examples to demonstrate how the page is parsed by the ASP.NET module.

❑   **Chapter 3: Forms and HTML Server Controls** – we really get to grips with ASP.NET code for the first time in this chapter, as we introduce ASP.NET server controls in relation to their HTML counterparts. We begin to demonstrate the additional functionality that they provide us with.

❑   **Chapter 4: Storing Information in C#** – having acquainted ourselves with the basics of ASP.NET controls this chapter considers the use of variables for holding data in C#. We look at how variables are implemented, what they can contain, and how they can be placed into your ASP.NET pages.

❑   **Chapter 5: Introducing XML** – complementing the previous chapter's discussion of variables, here we introduce eXtensible Markup Language (XML). We consider the implications of self-describing XML data, its plethora of uses, and its strengths and weaknesses when compared with HTML.

❑   **Chapter 6: Control Structures and Procedural Programming** – this chapter takes a whirlwind tour of the key building blocks of C# in the context of an ASP.NET page. We learn how to make our ASP.NET pages more responsive through the use of C# branching and jumping structures that enable us to control the order in which our program's statements execute.

❑   **Chapter 7: Event-driven Programming and Postback** – we cover the fundamental ideas of the event-driven way that ASP.NET works in this chapter. We learn what an event is and how it impacts on the way that we think about, and work with, ASP.NET pages. We also discuss the concept of 'postback' and how it is used to pass information between ASP.NET pages and your server.

❑   **Chapter 8: Introduction to Objects** – this chapter is the first of four dealing with the idea of objects. ASP.NET pages derive a great deal of their flexibility and power from the object-oriented way in which they are structured. This chapter lays the groundwork for a solid understanding of this technique. It introduces concepts such as properties, methods, constructors, and overloading using plentiful examples relating to real-world objects to aid your understanding.

❑   **Chapter 9: Shared Members and Class Relationships** – this chapter builds on the one before it and introduces some of the relationships it is possible to establish between objects in order to massively increase their functionality and power. In particular we consider the idea of inheritance and how an object can take advantages of the functionality of another objects simply by 'inheriting' them from it.

❑   **Chapter 10: Objects in ASP.NET** – we begin this chapter with a high-level look at the .NET Framework from an object-oriented perspective, considering some of the useful objects and namespaces that it provides us with. Before moving on to pay particular attention to the `Response`, `Request`, and `Browser` objects that provide us with a great deal of day-to-day functionality. The chapter concludes by introducing the concept of state management in .NET and discussing how and where we can store the state of our pages.

❑   **Chapter 11: Objects and Structured Data** – here we discuss the idea of collections, and how they work to hold groups of objects together as a cohesive unit that we can manipulate and organize as if it were one object. In particular we look at the use of the `Array` and `Hashtable` classes for containing information we wish to keep together (such as lists of users and their telephone numbers).

❑   **Chapter 12: Reading from Data Sources** – by this point in the book we're familiar with the basic anatomy of ASP.NET pages and object-oriented design, so we branch out to look at ADO.NET in the context of ASP.NET. Most specifically we look at the use of the Connection and Command objects for opening data sources and retrieving information into DataSets.

❑ **Chapter 13: Manipulating Data Sources** – having mastered the basics of reading data in the previous chapter we take things much further; looking in detail at the way we can manipulate the information in our DataSets, and store the results back to the data source from which they came.

❑ **Chapter 14: ASP.NET Server Controls** – this chapter explains how ASP.NET server controls derive their properties and methods from the various classes and objects that make up the .NET Framework. It explains the syntax required to make their functionality available, together with a look at the benefits that these controls can give.

❑ **Chapter 15: Reusable Code for ASP.NET** – here we consider the great benefits that can be achieved by encapsulating our code to make it more maintainable. Firstly we cover the idea of User Controls – designed to store sections of your ASP.NET code that are repeated on multiple pages of your site – before going on to consider the idea of codebehind, where the `<script>` block of our ASP.NET code is placed in its own file in order to separate the page's logic from it's presentation.

❑ **Chapter 16: .NET Assemblies and Custom Controls** – we continue the ideas of the previous chapter here. Learning how to compile a .NET assembly and use it from within our ASP.NET page, as well as how to encapsulate our business logic into a component that can be reused on other projects.

❑ **Chapter 17: Debugging and Error Handling** – no matter how careful you are things can always go wrong within your code. This chapter explains the steps you can take to minimize these occurrences and how to recover when things go wrong.

❑ **Chapter 18: Web Services** – we learn that you can expose functionality from your web site to others as a Web Service, before going on to discuss how this functionality can be discovered by other users of the Web, and the form that the data exchange takes.

❑ **Chapter 19: Configuration and Optimization** – as we near the end of the book, our discussions take a more general turn as we consider the many ways that you can streamline and speed-up your ASP.NET applications as they near completion.

❑ **Chapter 20: ASP.NET Security** – we conclude the book with a quick overview of some of the simple precautions that you can take using ASP.NET and IIS to safeguard your ASP.NET pages and ensure that they're only accessed by authorized clients in the way that you want them to be accessed.

Who is this Book For?

The purpose of this book is to teach you how to use ASP.NET to write web pages whose content can be programmatically tailored each time an individual client calls them up. This not only saves you a lot of effort in presenting and updating your web pages, but also offers tremendous scope for adding sophisticated functionality to your site. In the course of this book you will learn:

❑ What ASP.NET is

❑ How to install ASP.NET and get it up and running

❑ The structure of ASP.NET and how it sits on the .NET Framework

❑ How you can use it to produce dynamic, flexible, interactive web pages

❑ How to debug your ASP.NET pages

❑ How to secure your pages and deal with unexpected events and inputs

What do you Need to use This Book?

The only prerequisite for this book is to have a machine with the .NET Framework installed upon it. This means that you'll need to be running either Windows 2000 Professional (or better) or Windows XP.

The .NET Framework itself is available as a free download from http://www.asp.net/. It comes in two 'flavors':

❏ The .NET Framework Redistributable – the full Framework on its own. Includes everything you need to run any .NET application. Approximate size: 20Mb.

❏ The .NET Framework SDK (Software Development Kit) – the full Framework plus examples and tutorials that you can refer to in order to learn more about .NET. Approximate size: 130Mb.

This book is designed to be 'editor neutral'. So, all of the examples can be created, run and understood using a simple text editor such as Notepad. You do **not** need Visual Studio .NET in order to use this book.

Conventions

We've used a number of different styles of text and layout in this book to help differentiate between different kinds of information. Here are examples of the styles we used and an explanation of what they mean.

Code has several styles. If it's a word that we're talking about in the text – for example, when discussing a `for` loop, it's in this font. If it's a block of code that can be typed as a program and run, then it's also in a gray box:

```
<asp:Textbox id="MyTextBox" runat="server"/>
```

Sometimes we'll see code in a mixture of styles, like this:

```
private void MyButton_Click(object sender, System.EventArgs e){
  //Incredibly useful code here...
  Response.Write(MyButton.Text);
}
```

In cases like this, the code with a white background is code we are already familiar with; the line highlighted in gray is a new addition to the code since we last looked at it.

Advice, hints, and background information comes in this italic font.

Important pieces of information come in boxes like this.

Bullets appear indented, with each new bullet marked as follows:

- ❏ **Important Words** are in a bold type font.

- ❏ Words that appear on the screen, or in menus like the Open or Close, are in a similar font to the one you would see on a Windows desktop.

- ❏ Keys that you press on the keyboard like *Ctrl* and *Enter*, are in italics.

Customer Support

We always value hearing from our readers, and we want to know what you think about this book: what you liked, what you didn't like, and what you think we can do better next time. You can send us your comments, either by returning the reply card in the back of the book, or by e-mail to feedback@wrox.com. Please be sure to mention the book title in your message.

How to Download the Sample Code for the Book

When you visit the Wrox site, http://www.wrox.com/, simply locate the title through our Search facility or by using one of the title lists. Click on Download in the Code column, or on Download Code on the book's details page.

When you click to download the code for this book, you are presented with a page with three options:

- ❏ If you are already a member of the Wrox Developer Community (if you have already registered on ASPToday, C#Today, or Wroxbase), you can log in with your usual username and password combination to receive your code.

- ❏ If you are not already a member, you are asked if you would like to register for free code downloads. In addition you will also be able to download several free articles from Wrox Press. Registering will allow us to keep you informed about updates and new editions of this book.

- ❏ The third option is to bypass registration completely and simply download the code.

Registration for code download is not mandatory for this book, but should you wish to register for your code download, your details will not be passed to any third party. For more details, you may wish to view our terms and conditions, which are linked from the download page.

Once you reach the code download section, you will find that the files that are available for download from our site have been archived using WinZip. When you have saved the files to a folder on your hard drive, you will need to extract the files using a de-compression program such as WinZip or PKUnzip. When you extract the files, the code is usually extracted into chapter folders. When you start the extraction process, ensure your software (WinZip, PKUnzip, etc.) is set to use folder names.

Errata

We've made every effort to make sure that there are no errors in the text or in the code. However, no one is perfect and mistakes do occur. If you find an error in one of our books, like a spelling mistake or a faulty piece of code, we would be very grateful for feedback. By sending in errata you may save another reader hours of frustration, and of course, you will be helping us provide even higher quality information. Simply e-mail the information to support@wrox.com; your information will be checked and if correct, posted to the errata page for that title, or used in subsequent editions of the book.

To find errata on the web site, go to http://www.wrox.com/, and simply locate the title through our Advanced Search or title list. Click on the Book Errata link, which is below the cover graphic on the book's detail page.

E-mail Support

If you wish to directly query a problem in the book with an expert who knows the book in detail then e-mail support@wrox.com, with the title of the book and the last four characters of the ISBN in the subject field of the e-mail. A typical e-mail should include the following things:

❑ The **title of the book**, **last four digits of the ISBN (7345)**, and **page number** of the problem in the Subject field.

❑ Your **name**, **contact information**, and the **problem** in the body of the message.

We won't send you junk mail. We need the details to save your time and ours. When you send an e-mail message, it will go through the following chain of support:

❑ Customer Support – Your message is delivered to our customer support staff, who are the first people to read it. They have files on most frequently asked questions and will answer anything general about the book or the web site immediately.

❑ Editorial – Deeper queries are forwarded to the technical editor responsible for that book. They have experience with the programming language or particular product, and are able to answer detailed technical questions on the subject.

❑ The Authors – Finally, in the unlikely event that the editor cannot answer your problem, they will forward the request to the author. We do try to protect the author from any distractions to their writing; however, we are quite happy to forward specific requests to them. All Wrox authors help with the support on their books. They will e-mail the customer and the editor with their response, and again all readers should benefit.

The Wrox Support process can only offer support to issues that are directly pertinent to the content of our published title. Support for questions that fall outside the scope of normal book support is provided via the community lists of our http://p2p.wrox.com/ forum.

p2p.wrox.com

For author and peer discussion join the P2P mailing lists. Our unique system provides **programmer to programmer**™ contact on mailing lists, forums, and newsgroups, all in addition to our one-to-one e-mail support system. If you post a query to P2P, you can be confident that it is being examined by the many Wrox authors and other industry experts who are present on our mailing lists. At p2p.wrox.com you will find a number of different lists that will help you, not only while you read this book, but also as you develop your own applications. Particularly appropriate to this book is the aspx_beginners list.

To subscribe to a mailing list just follow these steps:

1. Go to http://p2p.wrox.com/.

2. Choose the appropriate category from the left menu bar.

3. Click on the mailing list you wish to join.

4. Follow the instructions to subscribe and fill in your e-mail address and password.

5. Reply to the confirmation e-mail you receive.

6. Use the subscription manager to join more lists and set your e-mail preferences.

Why this System Offers the Best Support

You can choose to join the mailing lists or you can receive them as a weekly digest. If you don't have the time, or facility, to receive the mailing list, then you can search our online archives. Junk and spam mails are deleted, and your own e-mail address is protected by the unique Lyris system. Queries about joining or leaving lists, and any other general queries about lists, should be sent to listsupport@p2p.wrox.com.

Getting Started with ASP.NET

ASP.NET is a new and powerful technology for creating dynamic web pages. It's a convergence of two major Microsoft technologies, Active Server Pages (ASP) and .NET. ASP is a relative old-timer on the web computing circuit and has provided a sturdy, powerful, and effective way of creating dynamic web pages for five years or so now. .NET is the new kid on the block and is a whole suite of technologies designed by Microsoft with the aim of revolutionizing the way in which programming development is conducted in the future, and the way companies carry out business. As a conjunction of the two, ASP.NET is a way of creating dynamic web pages while making use of the innovations present in .NET.

The first important thing to know about ASP.NET is that you don't need any ASP skills to be able to learn it. In fact all you need is a little HTML knowledge for building your own web pages. Knowing any ASP could in some ways be a disadvantage, because you might have to 'unlearn' some of the principles you previously held to be true. ASP.NET is a more powerful technology than its old namesake. Not only does it allow you to build dynamic web pages, but it also tailors the output in HTML to whatever browser you're using, and comes with a great set of reusable, predefined, and ready to use controls for use in your ASP.NET projects, which reduce the amount of code you have to write, so you can be more productive while programming.

So what can you do with ASP.NET? It might be easier to list what you can't, as that is arguably shorter! One of the most eye-catching things is the way you can use any programming language based in .NET, such as C#, VB .NET, or JScript .NET, to create your web applications. Within these applications, ASP.NET enables you to customize pages for a particular user, makes it much simpler now to keep track of a particular user's details as they move around, and makes storing information to a database or self-describing XML document faster and easier. You can alter the layout of the page using a visual IDE rather than having to figure out positioning within code, and even alter the contents of files on your machine (if you have the correct permissions). You can also use bits and pieces of other applications without downloading the whole application: for example, you can access a zip code verifier that is exposed by another web site, without having to download the whole of that application, or giving your users the impression that they've left your site (we'll talk more about this in the *Web Services* chapter later on). Basically, with ASP.NET the applications that you create are only limited by your imagination.

In this first chapter we'll be mainly concerned with ASP.NET's installation process. We'll start with a quick introduction to the world of web servers, dynamic web pages, and a little bit about what ASP.NET is, but what we really aim to achieve is to get you up and running a fully functional web server, with a fully functional ASP.NET installation. By the end of the chapter you'll have created a short ASP.NET test page to check that both the web server and ASP.NET are both working as intended. We'll also have a look at some of the most common pitfalls encountered, just in case things don't go as planned!

We will cover the following topics:

- ❑ Static Web Pages
- ❑ Dynamic Web Pages
- ❑ An overview of the different technologies for creating dynamic web pages, including ASP.NET
- ❑ Installing Internet Information Services (IIS)
- ❑ Installing the .NET Framework
- ❑ Testing and troubleshooting your installation

What is a Static Web Page?

If you surf around the Internet today, you'll see that there are lots of static web pages out there. What do we mean by a **static** web page? Essentially, it's a page whose content consists of some HTML code that was typed directly into a text editor and saved as an .htm or .html file. Thus, the author of the page has already determined the *exact* content of the page, in HTML, at some time before any user visits the page.

Static web pages are often quite easy to spot: sometimes you can pick them out by just looking at the content of the page. The content (text, images, hyperlinks, etc.) and appearance of a static web page is *always* the same – regardless of *who* visits the page, or *when* they visit, or *how* they arrive at the page, or any other factors.

For example, suppose we create a page called welcome.htm for our web site, by writing some simple HTML like this:

```
<html>
<head><title>A Welcome Message</title></head>
<body>
  <h1>Welcome</h1>
  Welcome to our humble website. Please feel free to view our
  <a HREF="contents.htm">list of contents</a>.
  <br><br>
  If you have any difficulties, you can
  <a href="mailto:webmaster@wrox.com">send email to the webmaster</a>.
</body>
</html>
```

Whenever any client comes to our site to view this page, it will look like this. The content of the page was determined *before* the request was made – at the time the Webmaster saved the .htm file to disk:

How are Static Web Pages Served?

OK, so let's think for a moment about how a static, pure-HTML page finds its way onto a client browser:

1. A web author writes a page composed of pure HTML, and saves it within an .htm file on the server.

2. Sometime later, a user types a page request into their browser, and the request is passed from the browser to the **web server**.

3. The web server locates the .htm page and converts it to an HTML stream.

4. The web server sends the HTML stream back across the network to the browser.

5. The browser processes the HTML and displays the page.

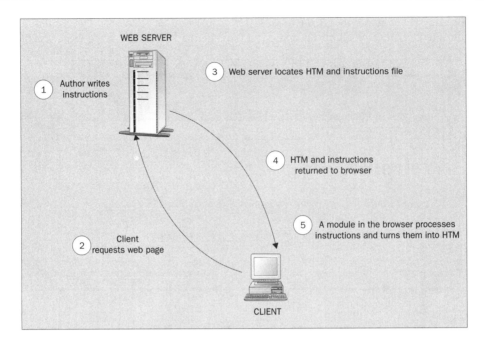

Static, pure-HTML files like `Welcome.htm` make perfectly serviceable web pages. We can even spruce up the presentation and usability of such pages by adding more HTML to alter the fonts and colors. However, there's only so much we can achieve by writing pure HTML, precisely because the content is completely determined *before* the page is ever requested.

The Limitations of Static Web Pages

For example, suppose we want to enhance our Welcome page – so that it displays the current time or a special message that is personalized for each user. These are simple ambitions, but they are impossible to achieve using HTML alone. If you're not convinced, try writing a piece of HTML for a web page that displays the current time, like this:

As you type in the HTML, you'll soon realize the problem – you know that the user will request the page sometime, but you don't know *what the time will be* when they do so! Hard-coding the time into your HTML will result in a page that always claims that the time is the same (and will almost always display the wrong time).

In other words, you're trying to write pure HTML for a web page that displays the time – but you can't be sure of the *exact* time that the web page should display until the time the page is requested. It can't be done using HTML alone.

Also, HTML offers no features for personalizing your web pages: each web page that is served is the same for every user. There's also no security with HTML: the code is there for everybody to view, and there's nothing to stop you from copying somebody else's HTML code and using it in your own web page. Static pages might be very fast, as quick as copying a small file over a network, but they are quite limited without any dynamic features.

Since we can't create our page by saving our hard-coded HTML into a file *before* the page is requested, what we need is a way to generate the HTML *after* the page is requested. There are two ways of doing this. We'll look at them both shortly, but before we go any further we need to make sure everybody is up to speed on the terminology we've introduced here.

What is a Web Server?

A **web server** is a piece of software that manages web pages and makes them available to 'client' browsers – via a local network or over the Internet. In the case of the Internet, the web server and browser are usually on two different machines, possibly many miles apart. However, in a more local situation we might set up a machine that runs the web server software, and then use a browser on the *same* machine to look at its web pages. It makes no difference whether you access a remote web server (that is, a web server on a different machine from your browser application) or a local one (web server and browser on the same machine), since the web server's function – to make web pages available to all – remains unchanged. It might well be that you are the only person with access to your web server on your own machine, as would be case if you were running a web server from your home machine. Nevertheless, the principles remain the same.

While there are many web servers available – the commonest ones being Apache, Internet Information Services (or IIS, for short) and Iplanet's Enterprise server – we're only going to talk about one in this book: Microsoft's IIS. This is because it is the only web server that will run ASP.NET. The web server comes as part of the installation for both Windows 2000 and Windows XP. IIS version 5.0 comes with Windows 2000 and IIS version 5.1 with Windows XP; however, there is very little to distinguish the two, and we shall treat them in this chapter as the same product. We'll look at how you go about installing IIS shortly, but first, let's take a look at its role in helping to create dynamic web pages.

How are Dynamic Web Pages Served?

To fully understand the nature of dynamic web pages, we first need to look at the limitations of what you can and can't do with a static web page.

Two Ways of Providing Dynamic Web Page Content

Even though, in this book, we're only going to be creating dynamic web pages using one of two very different methods, we need to be aware of the differences between these two different ways of doing things, as the underlying principles for both feature heavily throughout the book.

Client-Side Dynamic Web Pages

In the client-side model, modules (or plug-ins) attached to the browser do all the work of creating dynamic pages. The HTML code is typically sent to the browser, along with a separate file containing a set of **instructions**, which is referenced from within the HTML page. However, it is also quite common to find these instructions intermingled with the HTML code. The browser then uses them to generate pure HTML for the page when the user requests the page – in other words, the page is generated **dynamically** on request. This produces an HTML page, which is displayed in the browser.

So in this model our set of five steps now becomes six:

1. A web author writes a set of instructions for creating HTML, and saves it within an .htm file. The author also writes a set of instructions in a different language. This might be contained within the .htm file, or within a separate file.

2. Sometime later, a user types a page request into their browser, and the request is passed from the browser to the web server.

3. The web server locates the .htm page, and may also have to locate a second file that contains the instructions.

4. The web server sends both the newly created HTML stream and instructions back across the network to the browser.

5. A module within the browser processes the instructions and returns the results as HTML within the .htm page – only one page is returned, even if two were requested.

6. The HTML is then processed by the browser, which displays the page.

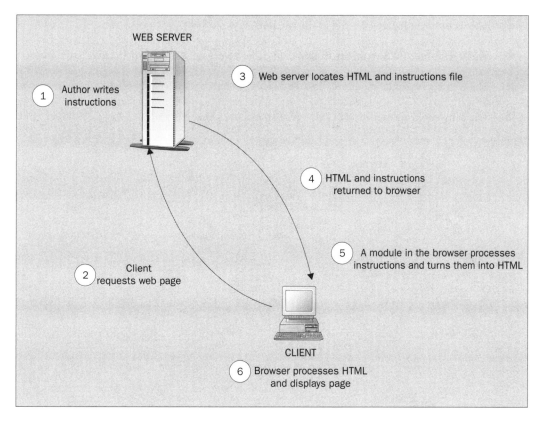

Client-side technologies have fallen out of favor in recent times, as they take a long time to download, especially if you have to download more than one file. A second drawback is that each browser interprets client-side scripting code in different ways, so you have no way of guaranteeing that if Internet Explorer understands them, Netscape Navigator or Opera will also be able to process them. Other major drawbacks are that it is a problem to write client-side code that uses server-side resources such as databases because it is interpreted at client-side. Also, client-side scripting code isn't secure and can be easily viewed with the View Source Code option on any browser, which might also be undesirable, and may compromise the security of the web site.

Server-Side Dynamic Web Pages

With the server-side model, the HTML source is sent to the web server with an intermingled set of **instructions**. Again this set of instructions will be used to generate HTML for the page at the time the user requests the page. Once again, the page is generated dynamically upon request. However, there is a subtle twist regarding where the processing of instructions is done:

1. A web author writes a set of instructions for creating HTML, and saves these instructions within a file.

2. Sometime later, a user types a page request into their browser, and the request is passed from the browser to the web server.

3. The web server locates the file of instructions.

4. The web server follows the instructions in order to create a stream of HTML.

5. The web server sends the newly created HTML stream back across the network to the browser.

6. The browser processes the HTML and displays the page.

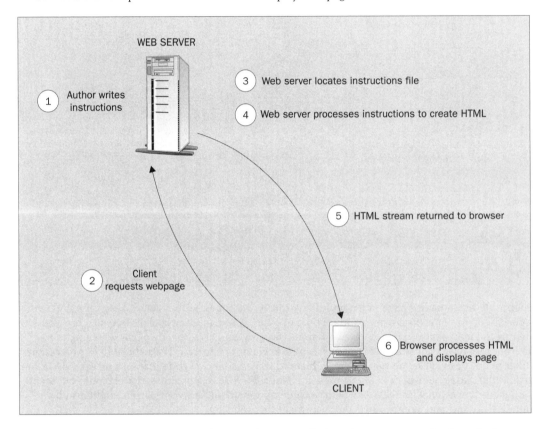

The twist is that all the processing is done on the server, before the page is sent back to the browser. One of the key advantages this has over the client-side model is that only the HTML is actually sent to the browser. This means that our page's original code is hidden away on the server, and that we can safely assume that most browsers should be able to at least have a go at displaying the generated HTML. ASP.NET, as you might have gathered, does its processing on the server-side.

While both processes for serving a dynamic web page add only a single step to the process for serving a static web page (Step 5 on the client or Step 4 on the server) this single step is crucial. In this step the HTML that defines the web page is not generated until *after* the web page has been requested. For example, we can use either technique to write a set of instructions for creating a page that displays the current time:

```
<html>
<head><title>The Punctual Web Server</title></head>
<body>
  <h1>Welcome</h1>
  In Webserverland, the time is exactly
  <INSTRUCTION: produce HTML to display the current time>
</body>
</html>
```

In this case, we can compose most of the page using pure HTML. It's just that we can't hardcode the current time. Instead, we can write special code (which would replace the highlighted line here) that instructs the web server to generate that bit of HTML – during Step 5, on the client, or Step 4, on the server – at the time the page is requested. We'll return to this example later in the chapter, and we'll see how to write the highlighted instruction using ASP.NET.

Now we're going to look at the various different technologies, including ASP.NET, and see how the logic is supported in each.

An Overview of the Technologies

You've just seen that there are also two distinct models for providing dynamic content. ASP.NET falls into the server-side model. However, we're going to look at what we consider to be the most important technologies in both models, as we will reference some of the client-side models in later chapters, particularly if we mention old-style ASP. Not all of the technologies work in the same way as ASP.NET, but they all allow the user to achieve the same endresult – that of dynamic web applications. If ASP.NET is not an ideal solution to your problems, then you might want to consider these following technologies, taking into account the following questions:

❑ Are they supported on the platform you use?

❑ Are they difficult to learn?

❑ Are they easy to maintain?

❑ Do they have a long-term future?

❑ Do they have extra capabilities, such as being able to parse XML?

❑ Are a lot of people already using them – are there a lot of tools available?

❑ Are the support, skills, and knowledge required to use them readily available?

We're now going to give a quick overview of what each one does, and in doing so, try to give you an idea of where ASP.NET (and the ASP technology that preceded it) fits in to the big picture.

Client-Side Technologies for Providing Dynamic Content

Each of these technologies relies on a module (or plug-in) built into the browser to process the instructions we talked about earlier. The client-side technologies are a mishmash of scripting languages, controls, and fully fledged programming languages.

JavaScript

JavaScript is the original browser scripting language, and is not to be confused with Java. Java is a complete application programming language in its own right. Netscape originally developed a scripting language, known as LiveScript, to add interactivity to its web server and browser range. It was introduced in the release of the Netscape 2 browser, when Netscape joined forces with Sun, and in the process, they changed its name to **JavaScript**. JavaScript borrows some of its syntax and basic structures from Java (which in turn borrowed ideas from C), but has a different purpose – and evolved from different origins (LiveScript was developed separately from Java).

For example, while JavaScript can control browser behavior and content, it isn't capable of controlling features such as file handling. In fact JavaScript is actively prevented from doing this for security reasons. Think about it: you wouldn't want a web page capable of deleting files on your hard drive, would you? Meanwhile, Java can't control the browser as a whole, but it can do graphics and perform network and threading functions.

JavaScript is much simpler to learn than Java. It is designed to create small, efficient applications that can do many things, from performing repetitive tasks to handling events generated by the user (such as mouse clicks, keyboard responses, and so on). However, JavaScript's functionality is necessarily restricted.

Microsoft introduced their own version of JavaScript, known as **JScript**, in Internet Explorer 3.0 and have supported it ever since, right up to and including IE6. It has only minor differences from the Netscape version of the language, although in older versions of both browsers the differences were more considerable.

VBScript

In Internet Explorer 3.0, Microsoft also introduced its own scripting language, VBScript, which was based on its Visual Basic programming language. VBScript was intended to be a direct competitor to JavaScript. In terms of functionality, there isn't much difference between the two: it's more a matter of personal preference – VBScript has a similarly reduced functionality. Visual Basic developers sometimes prefer VBScript because VBScript is, for the most part, a subset of Microsoft's Visual Basic language (the forerunner of VB.NET). However, it enjoys one advantage that makes it more attractive to novice programmers, in that unlike JavaScript, it isn't case-sensitive and is therefore less fussy about the particulars of the code. Although this feature has the drawback that this makes it a lot slower and less efficient.

However, the biggest drawback by far is that there isn't a single non-Microsoft browser that supports VBScript for client-side scripting. For a short while there were some proprietary plug-ins for Netscape that provided VBScript support, but these never took off. You'll find that JavaScript is much more widely used and supported. If you want to do client-side scripting of web pages on the Internet then JavaScript is the only language of choice. VBScript should only be considered when working on intranet pages where it is known that all clients are IE on Windows.

With both JavaScript and VBScript there is a module, known as a script engine, built into the browser that dynamically processes the instructions, or script, as it is known in this case.

Java Applets

Java is a cross-platform language for developing applications. When Java first hit the Web in the mid-1990s, it created a tremendous stir. The idea is to use Java code in the form of **applets**, which are essentially Java components that can be easily inserted into web pages with the aid of the <applet> tag.

Java enjoys better functionality than scripting languages, offering better capabilities in areas such as graphic functions and file handling. Java is able to provide these powerful features without compromising security because the applets run in what is known as a sandbox – which prevents a malicious program downloaded from the Web from doing damage to your system. Java also boasts strong database support through JDBC (a technology for connecting to data sources).

Microsoft and Netscape browsers both have built-in Java support via something known as the Java Virtual Machine (JVM), and there are several standard <object> and non-standard <applet> tags that are used to add Java applets to a web page. These tags tell the browser to download a Java file from a server and execute it with the Java Virtual Machine built into the browser. Of course, this extra step in the web page building phase means that Java applets can take a little while to download, and can take even longer to process once on the browser. So while smaller Java applets (that provide features such as dropdown menus and animations) are very popular on the Web, larger ones are still not as widespread as scripted pages.

Although the popularity of Java today isn't quite what some people expected, it makes an ideal teaching tool for people wishing to break into more complex languages, and its versatility makes it well suited for programming web applications.

Flash

Flash from Macromedia is a web motion graphics tool, enabling developers to create animations, interactive graphics, and user interface elements such as menus. While this might seem slightly at odds with the other fully fledged scripting and programming languages discussed here, Flash actually provides its own scripting language, ActionScript, and as a result is fast becoming the standard way of providing client-side dynamic content. It is also fully interoperable with many server-side technologies.

A plug-in enabling you to use and view Flash web pages comes as standard with most modern versions of Internet Explorer and Netscape Navigator, but can be downloaded from the www.macromedia.com if not present. The Flash tool that must be used to create Flash animations (.swf files) must be purchased from Macromedia, although a 30 day demo version is available for free.

Such is the power and versatility of Flash that it has become a popular catch-all for developers who wish to include graphics or sound. The Actionscript language it uses resembles JavaScript in many ways, which is an added advantage for developers already familiar with JavaScript. Flash files are added to HTML pages using the Flash tool. In reality the tool auto-generates an <object> or <embed> tag, which the browser recognizes and deals with appropriately.

Server-Side Technologies for Providing Dynamic Content

The server-side technologies rely on modular attachments added onto the web server rather than the browser. Consequently, only HTML, and any client-side script, is sent back to the browser by the web server. In other words, none of the server-side code is sent back. Server-side technologies have a more consistent look and feel than client-side ones, and it doesn't take that much extra learning to move between some of the server-side technologies (excepting CGI).

CGI

The **Common Gateway Interface** (**CGI**) is a mechanism for creating scripts on the server, which can then be used to create dynamic web applications. CGI is a module that is added to the web server. It has been around for quite a bit longer than even ASP, and right now a large proportion of dynamically created web pages are created using CGI and a scripting language. However, it's incorrect to assume that CGI does the same job as ASP.NET or ASP. Rather, CGI allows the user to invoke another program (such as a Perl script) on the web server in order to create the dynamic web page, and the role of CGI is to pass data – which might be supplied by the user – to the this program for processing. However, it does provide the same end result – a dynamic web application.

However, CGI has some severe shortcomings:

❏ It is not easy for a beginner to learn how to program such modules

❏ CGI requires a lot of server resources, especially in a multi-user situation

❏ It adds an extra step to our server-side model of creating dynamic content: namely, it's necessary to run a CGI program to create the dynamic page, before the page is processed on the server

What's more, the format in which CGI receives and transmits data means that the data cannot be handled in any straightforward manner by most programming languages: you need one with good facilities for manipulating text and communicating with other software. The most suitable programming languages that can work on any operating system for doing this are C, C++, and Perl. While they can more than adequately do the job for you, they're some of the more complex languages to learn. Visual Basic doesn't offer enough text handling facilities, and is therefore rarely used with CGI.

Despite this, CGI is still very popular with many big web sites, particularly those running on UNIX operating systems. It also runs on many different platforms, which will ensure its continued popularity.

ASP

Active Server Pages (**ASP**) is now dubbed 'Classic ASP', and if you see this term in the book, we will be using it to describe any ASP that isn't ASP.NET. ASP commonly relied on either of the JavaScript or VBScript scripting languages (although it was also possible to use any scripting language installed on Windows, such as PerlScript) to create dynamic web pages. ASP is a module (the `asp.dll` file) that you attach to your web server, and which then processes the JavaScript/VBScript on the web server, producing HTML, which is then sent, via the server, to the client. Processing is thus all done on the server, rather than the browser.

ASP lets us use practically any of the functionality provided by Windows, such as database access, e-mailing, graphics, networking, and system functions, and all from within a typical ASP page. However, ASP's shortcomings are that it is very, very slow. It is also restricted to using only scripting languages: it can't do all the things that a fully-fledged programming language can. Secondly, the scripting languages, being the 'junior' versions of full programming languages, took a lot of shortcuts to make the language smaller. Some of these shortcuts mean that our programs written with scripting languages are longer and more complicated than is otherwise necessary. As we're going to see, ASP.NET rectifies a lot of this by making code more structured, easier to understand, and shorter.

JSP

JavaServer Pages (**JSP**) is a technology that enables us to combine markup (HTML or XML) with Java code to dynamically generate web pages. The JSP specification is implemented by several web servers, in contrast with ASP, which is only supported under IIS, and plug-ins are available that enable us to use JSP with IIS 4.0/5.*x*. One of the main advantages of JSP is the portability of code between different servers. JSP is also very powerful, faster than ASP, and instantly familiar to Java programmers. It allows the Java program to leverage the aspects of the Java2 platform such as JavaBeans and the Java 2 libraries. JavaServer Pages isn't directly related to ASP, but it does boast the ability to embed Java code into your web pages using server-side tags. More details about JSP can be found at the official site at www.javasoft.com/products/jsp/index.html and at the JSP FAQ at www.esperanto.org.nz/jsp/jspfaq.html.

ColdFusion

ColdFusion (www.macromedia.com/software/coldfusion/) also enables servers to access data as the server builds an HTML page. Cold Fusion is a module installed onto your web server. Like ASP, ColdFusion pages are readable by any browser. ColdFusion also utilizes a proprietary set of tags, which are processed by the ColdFusion Server software. This server software can run on multiple platforms, including IIS, Netscape Enterprise Server, and Unix/Apache. The major difference is that while ASP.NET solutions are built primarily with programming languages and objects, ColdFusion utilizes HTML-like tags, which encapsulate functionality. A drawback is that the ColdFusion software doesn't come for free, and indeed you could find yourself paying well in excess of a thousand dollars for the privilege of running Cold Fusion on your web server.

PHP

PHP (originally **Personal Home Pages**, but more recently **PHP Hypertext Preprocessor**) is another scripting language for creating dynamic web pages. When a visitor opens the page, the server processes the PHP commands and then sends the results to the visitor's browser, just as with ASP.NET or ColdFusion. Unlike ASP.NET or ColdFusion, however, PHP is opensource and cross-platform. PHP runs on Windows NT and many Unix versions, and runs on the Apache web server (the free web server that commonly runs on UNIX and other related platforms). When built as an Apache module, PHP is especially speedy. A downside is that you have to download PHP separately and go through a series of quite complex steps to install it and get it working on your machine. Also, PHP's session management (the management of numerous simultaneous users) was non-existent until PHP 4, and is still inferior to ASP's even now.

PHP's language syntax is similar to C and Perl. This might prove a barrier to people with no prior programming experience, but if you have a background in either language then you might want to take a look. PHP also has some rudimentary object-oriented features, providing a helpful way to organize and encapsulate your code. You can find more information about PHP at www.php.net.

ASP.NET

So why are we looking at all these other technologies if in this book we're only going to be learning about ASP.NET? Hopefully, you'll see a similarity between the technologies, and this will aid your understanding of ASP.NET.

ASP.NET also relies on a module attached to the web server. However, the ASP.NET module (which is a physical file called `aspnet_isapi.dll`) doesn't do all of the work itself: it passes some on to the .NET Framework to do the processing for it. Rather than going into ASP.NET in this subsection here, it's time to start talking about it as a separate entity in its own right, as this is the focus of the book.

What is ASP.NET?

We're going to be asking this question a lot throughout the book, and each time we ask it, we're going to give you a slightly more in-depth answer. If we were we to give you a full answer now, you'd be overwhelmed by as-yet meaningless jargon. So, you'll probably be aware of some unanswered questions each time we describe it.

Our original definition, right at the very start of the chapter, was "ASP.NET is a new and powerful technology for creating dynamic web pages", and this still holds true. However, as you now know, it isn't the only way to deliver dynamic web pages, so let's refine our definition a little to read:

> **ASP.NET is a new and powerful** server-side **technology for creating dynamic web pages.**

Secondly, ASP.NET isn't the only thing that we're interested in. In fact, it's one of a set of technologies that comprise the **Microsoft .NET Framework**. For now, you can think of this as a giant toolkit for creating all sorts of applications, and in particular, for creating applications on the Web. When we come to install ASP.NET we will also be installing the .NET Framework at the same time, and we'll be using bits and pieces of the .NET Framework throughout the book.

How does ASP.NET Differ from ASP?

Steady on! We're just getting to this part. As we've already said, ASP is restricted to using scripting languages, mainly JavaScript or VBScript (although it can use any scripting language supported by the Windows system). We add ASP code to our pages in the same way as we do client-side script, and this leads to problems such as messy coding and restricted functionality. ASP.NET has no such problems.

First off, ASP.NET enables you to use a far greater selection of full programming languages, and also enables you to utilize to the full the rich potential of the .NET Framework. It helps you create faster, more reliable dynamic web pages with any of the programming languages supported by the .NET Framework. Typical languages supported natively are C#, VB .NET, and a new version of JScript called JScript .NET. On top of this, it is expected that third-party developers will create versions of Perl, Python and many others to work in ASP.NET. And no, before you ask, we don't expect you to know any of these programming languages. We're going to choose one language, C#, and teach you ASP.NET with it. We've chosen C#, as it's arguably the most popular of the .NET languages, and it can do pretty much anything that the other languages we mentioned can do. Lastly, and most importantly, we've chosen C# as it comes free with ASP.NET – so when you install ASP.NET, you get C# as well.

At this stage you might be thinking, "Hang on, I've got to figure out C#, then I've got to get a handle on ASP.NET – that sounds like an awful lot to learn." Don't worry; you won't be learning two languages. ASP.NET, as we said right from the beginning, is not a language – it is a technology. This technology is accessible via a programming language. What we're going to be doing is teaching you ASP.NET features as we teach you C#. So in other words, you will be creating your web pages using C# and using ASP.NET to drive it. However, before you rush out and get a C# book instead, we will be approaching the language from the angle of creating dynamic web pages only.

In summation, ASP.NET is a server-side technology that lets you use fully-fledged programming languages to create your web pages.

I'm Still Confused about ASP, ASP.NET, and C#

It's really important to get these terms separate and distinct in your mind, so before we move on to actually installing and running ASP.NET, we're going to go back and redefine them just to make sure:

- ❑ **ASP** – a server-side technology for creating dynamic web pages that only lets you use scripting languages

- ❑ **ASP.NET** – a server-side technology for creating dynamic web pages that lets you use any fully-fledged programming language supported by .NET

- ❑ **C#** – our chosen programming language for writing code in ASP.NET

Now it's time to get it all installed.

The Installation Process

Installation is going to be done in three steps. We're going to install the web server first, next we're going install the prerequisites required for ASP.NET to work, and then lastly we're going to install either the **.NET Framework Redistributable** or the **.NET Framework SDK** (both of which contain ASP.NET), and are available for download from www.asp.net.

> *SDK stands for **Software Development Kit**, and the only real difference between it and the Redistributable is the huge amounts of extra documentation and examples it supplies – 131MB compared with 21MB for it's lightweight brother.*

Anybody who is familiar with ASP might be used to it being installed automatically with the web server, and thereby doing it all in one step. This is true – classic ASP is still installed with the web server. However, ASP.NET is currently only available as a separate download. This means you will have to download ASP.NET from Microsoft's web site or from CD (if you have one). However, before you can install ASP.NET, it is necessary to have a working web server.

If you have installed IIS 5.*x* already, or have installed either the Windows 2000 Server or Advanced Server operating system, then the good news is that you can skip this section, and go straight onto the section about installing the .NET Framework. However, for the rest of us, you will have to pay careful attention to the next section.

Installing the IIS 5.x Web Server

We'll look at the installation process for IIS on Windows 2000 Professional and Windows XP Professional together as they don't differ significantly. The main difference is that Windows 2000 installs IIS 5.0, while Windows XP installs IIS 5.1. The options for installation are exactly the same; the only thing that might differ is the look of the dialog boxes.

> *It's worth noting that you cannot install IIS on Windows XP Home Edition, and therefore you cannot run ASP.NET on it. It will only work on Windows XP Professional.*

Before you install it though, it's worth noting that you might not have to do much in this initial stage, as it's possible you're already running IIS 5.x. We'll describe a process for checking whether this is the case as part of the installation process. You should also note that to install anything (not just ASP.NET, but literally anything) on Windows 2000/XP you need to be logged in as a user with administrative rights. If you're uncertain of how to do this, we suggest you consult your Windows documentation. Right let's get started!

Try It Out – Locating and/or Installing IIS 5.x on a Web Server Machine

1. Go to the control panel (Start | Settings | Control Panel) and select the Add/Remove Programs icon. The following dialog will appear, displaying a list of your currently installed programs:

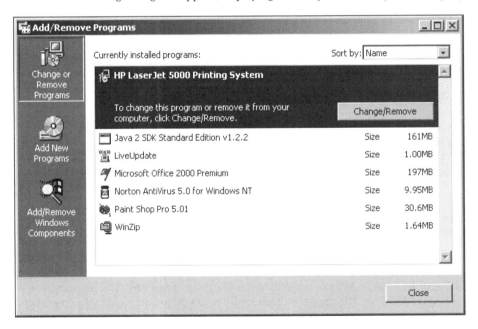

2. Select the Add/Remove Windows Components icon on the left side of the dialog, to get to the screen that allows you to install new windows components:

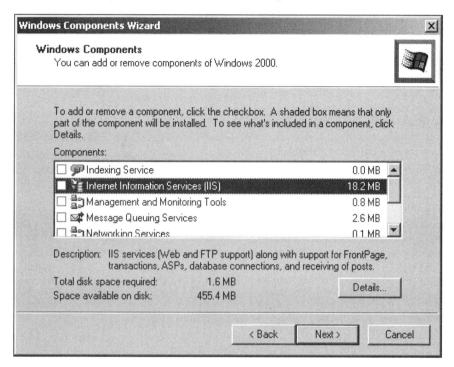

3. Locate the Internet Information Services (IIS) entry in the dialog, and note the checkbox that appears to its left. Unless you installed Windows 2000 via a custom install and specifically requested IIS, it's most likely that the checkbox will be unchecked (as shown above).

4. If the checkbox is *cleared*, then check the checkbox and click on Next to load Internet Information Services 5.x. You might be prompted to place your Windows 2000/XP installation disk into your CD-ROM drive. It will take a few minutes to complete. Then go to Step 5.

OR

If the checkbox is *checked* then you won't need to install the IIS 5.x component – it's already present on your machine. Go to Step 6 instead.

5. Click on the Details button – this
will take you to the dialog shown
here. There are a few options here,
for the installation of various
optional bits of functionality. For
example, if the World Wide Web
Server option is checked then our
IIS installation will be able to serve
and manage web pages and
applications. If you're planning to
use FrontPage 2000 or Visual
InterDev to write your web page
code, then you'll need to ensure
that the FrontPage 2000 Server
Extensions checkbox is checked.
The Internet Information Services
Snap-In is also very desirable, as
you'll see later in the chapter, so
you'll see later in the chapter, so

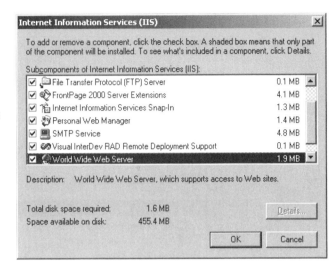

ensure that this is checked too, the other options (although checked here) aren't necessary for
this book.

> **For the purpose of this installation, make sure all the checkboxes in this dialog are
> checked. Then click on OK to return to the previous dialog.**

6. There's one other component
that we'll need to install, for
use later in this book – it's the
Script Debugger. If you scroll
to the foot of the Windows
Components Wizard dialog
that we showed above, you'll
find a checkbox for Script
Debugger. If it isn't already
checked, check it now and
click on Next to complete the
installation. Otherwise, if both
IIS 5.x and the script
debugger are already present,
you can click on Cancel to
abort the process:

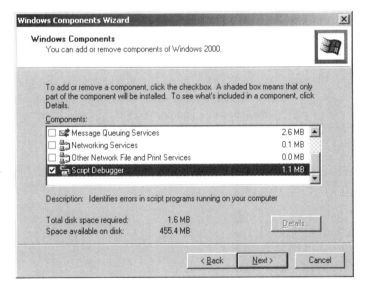

How It Works

IIS starts up automatically as soon as your installation is complete, and thereafter whenever you boot up Windows – so you don't need to run any further startup programs, or click on any short-cuts as you would to start up Word or Excel.

IIS installs most of its bits and pieces on your hard drive, under the \WinNT\system32\inetsrv directory. However, more interesting to us at the moment is the \InetPub directory that is also created at this time. This directory contains subdirectories that will provide the home for the web page files that we create.

If you expand the InetPub directory, you'll find that it contains several subdirectories:

❑ \iissamples\homepage contains some example classic ASP pages.

❑ \iissamples\sdk contains a set of subdirectories that hold classic ASP pages that demonstrate the various classic ASP objects and components.

❑ \scripts is an empty directory, where ASP.NET programs can be stored.

❑ \webpub is also empty. This is a 'special' virtual directory, used for publishing files via the Publish wizard. Note that this directory only exists if you are using Windows 2000 Professional Edition.

❑ \wwwroot is the top of the tree for your web site (or web sites). This should be your default web directory. It also contains a number of subdirectories, which contain various bits and pieces of IIS. This directory is generally used to contain subdirectories that hold the pages that make up our web site – although, in fact, there's no reason why you can't store your pages elsewhere.

❑ \ftproot, \mailroot, and \nntproot should form the top of the tree for any sites that use FTP, mail, or news services, if installed.

❑ In some versions of Windows , you will find an \AdminScripts folder, which contains various VBScript files for performing some common 'housekeeping' tasks on the web server, allowing you to stop and start services.

Working with IIS

Having installed IIS web server software onto our machine, we'll need some means of administering its contents and settings. In this section, we'll meet the user interface that is provided by IIS 5.*x*.

In fact, some versions of IIS 5.*x* provide two user interfaces, the MMC and the PWS interface. We're only going to look at one, as the other version is now obsolete. The version we will use is the **Microsoft Management Console (MMC)**, which that is a generic way of managing all sorts of services. Let's take a quick look at it now.

The Microsoft Management Console (MMC)

The beauty of the MMC is that it provides a central interface for administrating all sorts of services that are installed on your machine. We can use it to administer IIS – but in fact, when we use it to administer other services the interface looks roughly the same. The MMC is provided as part of the Windows 2000 operating system, and also comes with older Windows server operating systems.

27

The MMC itself is just a shell – on its own, it doesn't do much at all. If we want to use it to administer a service, we have to add a **snap-in** for that service. The good news is that IIS 5.*x* has its own snap-in. Whenever you need to administer IIS, you can simply call up the Internet Services Manager MMC console by selecting Start | Control Panel |Administrative Tools |Internet Services Manager.

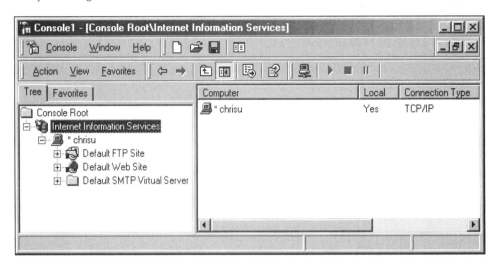

Having opened the IIS snap-in within the MMC, you can perform all of your web management tasks from this window. The properties of the web site are accessible via the Default Web Site node. We'll be using the MMC more a little later in the chapter.

Testing your Installation

The next thing to do is test the web server to see if it is working correctly, and serving pages as it should. We've already noted that the web server should start as soon as IIS has been installed, and will restart every time you start your machine. In this section, we'll try that out.

In order to test the web server, we'll start up a browser and try to view some web pages that we know are already placed on the web server. In order to do that, we'll need to type a URL (Uniform Resource Locator) into the browser's Address box, as we often do when browsing on the Internet. The URL is an http://... web page address that indicates which web server to connect to, and the page we want to view.

What URL do we use in order to browse to our web server? If your web server and web browser are connected by a local area network, or if you're using a single machine for both web server and browser, then it should be enough to specify the name of the web server machine in the URL.

Identifying your Web Server's Name

By default, IIS will take the name of your web server from the name of the computer. You can change this in the machine's network settings. If you haven't set one, then Windows will generate one automatically – note that this automatic name won't be terribly friendly; probably something along the lines of "P77RTQ7881". To find the name of your own web server machine, select Start | Settings | Network and Dial-up Connections or Start | Settings | Control Panel | System (depending on which operating system you are using – if it isn't in one, try the other) and from the Advanced menu select Network Identification. The Network Identification tab will display your machine name under the description Full computer name:

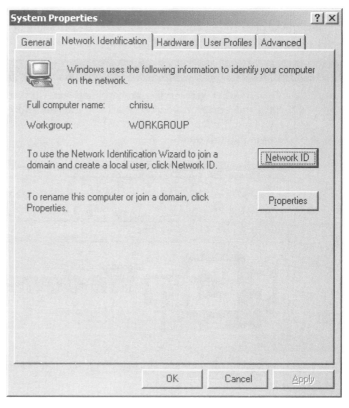

My machine has the name chrisu, and (as you can see here and in the earlier screenshot of the MMC dialog) my web server has adopted the same name. On a computer within a domain you might see something different such as WROX_UK/chrisu, if the computer was in the WROX_UK domain. However, this doesn't alter operation for ASP.NET. Browsing to pages on this machine across a local area network (or, indeed, from the same machine), I can use a URL that begins http://chrisu/...

There are a couple of alternatives if you're using the same machine as both web server and browser. Try http://127.0.0.1/... – here, 127.0.0.1 is a default that causes requests to be sent to a web server on the local machine. Alternatively, try http://localhost/... – 'localhost' is an alias for the 127.0.0.1 address – you may need to check the LAN settings (in your browser's options) to ensure that local browsing is not through a proxy server (a separate machine that filters all incoming and outgoing web traffic employed at most workplaces, but not something that affects you if you are working from home).

> **Throughout the book, in any examples that require you to specify a web server name, the server name will be shown as localhost, implicitly assuming that your web server and browser are being run on the same machine. If they reside on different machines, then you simply need to substitute the computer name of the appropriate web server machine.**

Browsing to a Page on your Web Server

Now you know the name of your web server, and that web services are running; you can view some classic ASP pages hosted on your web server by browsing to them with your web browser. Let's test out this theory by viewing our default home page:

Try It Out – Testing the Web Service

1. To verify that web services are working, start up your browser and type http://*my_server_name*/localstart.asp into the address box. (My server is named chrisu, so I typed in http://chrisu/localstart.asp.) Now press *Enter*; and (if all is well) you should get to see a page like this one:

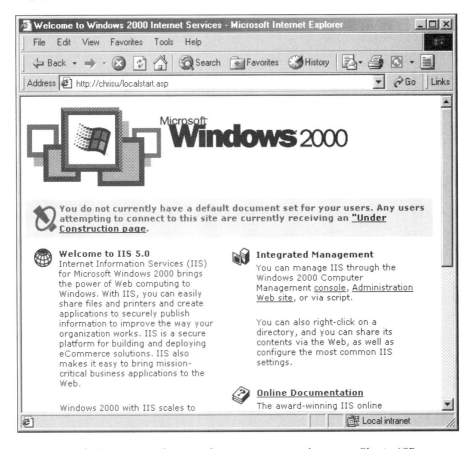

Note that the default page we see here uses the .asp extension, denoting a Classic ASP page. Support for ASP3 is provided as part of the standard IIS5.x web server program.

What Do You Do If This Doesn't Work?

If you don't get this page, then take a look at the following steps as we try to resolve the problem. If it's not working correctly, then most likely you'll be greeted with this screen:

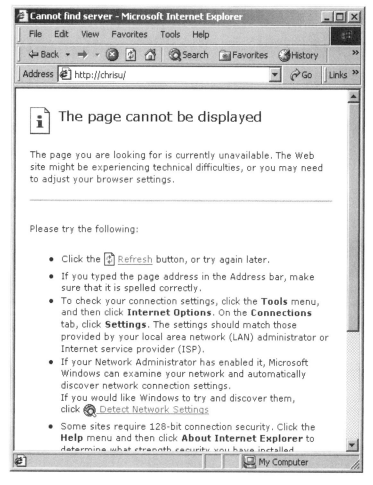

If you get this page then it can mean a lot of things. However, one of the most likely problems is that your web services under IIS are not switched on. To switch on web services, you'll first need to start the IIS admin snap-in that we described earlier in the chapter. (Select Start | Run, type MMC and hit OK, then select Open from the MMC's Console menu and locate the iis.msc file from the dialog. Alternatively, just use the shortcut that you created there.)

Now, click on the + of the root node in the left pane of the snap-in, to reveal the Default sites. Then right-click on Default Web Site, and select Start:

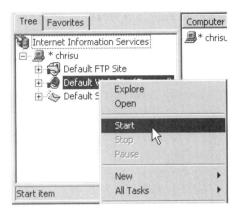

If it's still not working then here are a few more suggestions about what could be wrong, which are based on particular aspects of your PC's setup. If you're running on a network and using a proxy server (a piece of software that manages connections from inside a firewall to the outside world – don't worry if you don't have one, they're mainly used by big businesses), there's a possibility that this can prevent your browser from accessing your web server. Most browsers will give you an opportunity to bypass the proxy server:

❏ If you're using Internet Explorer, you need to go to View | Internet Options (IE 4) or Tools | Internet Options (IE 5/IE 6) and select the Connections tab. In IE 5/IE 6 press the LAN Settings button and select Bypass the proxy server for local addresses. In IE 4, this section forms part of the Connections dialog:

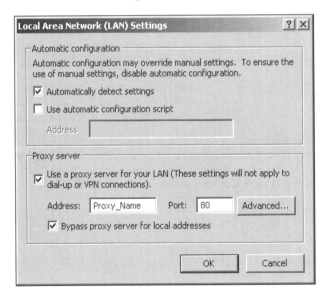

❏   If you're using Netscape Navigator (either version 4.*x* or 6.*x*) and you are having problems then you need to turn off all proxies and make sure you are accessing the Internet directly. To do this, select Edit | Preferences. In the resulting dialog select Advanced | Proxies from the Category box on the left. Then on the right, select the Direct Connection to Internet option, and hit OK. Although you won't be browsing online to the Internet, it'll allow Netscape Navigator to recognize all variations of accessing local ASP.NET pages, such as http://127.0.0.1, http://localhost, and so on.

You may hit a problem if your machine name is similar to that of some web site out there on the Internet – for example, if your machine name is jimmyd but there also happens to be a public web site out there called http://www.jimmyd.com. When you type http://jimmyd into your browser's address box, expecting to view a page on your local web server, you unexpectedly get transported to http://www.jimmyd.com instead. If this is happening to you, then you need to make sure that you're not using a proxy server in your browser settings – again, this can be disabled using the Internet Options | Connection dialog or the Edit | Preferences dialog.

Lastly, if your web server is running on your home machine with a modem, and you get an error message informing you that your web page is offline, this could in fact be a misperception on the part of the web server. This can be corrected by changing the way that your browser looks for pages. To do this, select View | Internet Options (IE 4) or Tools | Internet Options (IE 5/IE 6), choose the Connections tab and select Never dial a connection.

Of course, you might encounter problems that aren't answered above. In this case, the chances are that it's related to your own particular system setup. We can't possibly cover all the different possible configurations here, but if you can't track down the problem, you may find some help at one of the web sites and newsgroups listed later in this chapter.

Managing Directories on your Web Server

Before we install ASP.NET, we need to make one last pit stop in IIS. This is because when you come to run your ASP.NET pages, you need to understand where to place your pages, and how to make sure you have the permission to access them. As this is governed by IIS, now seems as good a time as any to investigate this.

These days, many browsers are sufficiently advanced that you can use them to locate and examine files and pages that exist on your computer's hard disk. So, for example, you can start up your browser, type in the physical location of a web page (or other file) such as C:\My Documents\mywebpage.html, and the browser will display it. However, this isn't real web publishing at all:

❏   First, web pages are transported using a protocol called HTTP – the HyperText Transfer Protocol. Note that the http:// at the beginning of a URL indicates that the request is being sent by HTTP. Requesting C:\My Documents\mywebpage.html in your browser doesn't use HTTP, and this means that the file is not delivered and handled in the way a web page should be. No server processing is done in this case. We'll discuss this in greater detail when we tackle HTTP in Chapter 2.

❏   Second, consider the addressing situation. The string C:\My Documents\mywebpage.html tells us that the page exists in the \My Documents directory of the C: drive of the hard disk **of the machine on which the browser is running**. In a network situation, with two or more computers, this simply doesn't give enough information about the web server to locate the file.

However, when a user browses (via HTTP) to a web page on some web server, the web server will need to work out where the file for that page is located on the server's hard disk. In fact, there's an important relationship between the information given in the URL, and the physical location (within the web server's file system) of the file that contains the source for the page.

Virtual Directories

So how does the relationship between the information given in the URL, and the physical location of a file work? In fact, it can work by creating a second directory structure on the web server machine, which reflects the structure of your web site. It sounds like it could be complicated, but it doesn't have to be. In fact, in this book it's going to be very simple.

The first directory structure is what we see when we open Windows Explorer on the web server – these directories are known as **physical directories**. For example, the folder C:\My Documents is a physical directory.

The second directory structure is the one that reflects the structure of the web site. This consists of a hierarchy of **virtual directories**. We use the web server to create virtual directories, and to set the relationship between the virtual directories and the real (physical) directories.

When you try to visualize a virtual directory, it's probably best not to think of it as a directory at all. Instead, just think of it as a nickname or alias for a physical directory that exists on the web server machine. The idea is that, when a user browses to a web page that is contained in a physical directory on the server, they don't use the name of the **physical** directory to get there, instead, they use the physical directory's nickname.

To see how this might be useful, consider a web site that publishes news about many different sporting events. In order to organize the web files carefully, the Webmaster has built a physical directory structure on the hard disk, which looks like this:

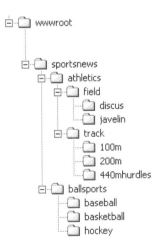

Now, suppose you visit this web site to get the latest news on the Javelin event in the Olympics. If the URL for this web page were based on the physical directory structure, then the URL for this page would be something like this:

http://www.oursportsite.com/sportsnews/athletics/field/javelin/default.asp

That's OK for the Webmaster, who understands his directory structure, but it's a fairly unmemorable web address! So, to make it easier for the *user*, the Webmaster can assign a *virtual* directory name or *alias* to this directory – it acts just like a nickname for the directory. Here, let's suppose we've assigned the virtual name javelinnews to the `c:\inetpub\...\javelin\` directory. Now, the URL for the latest Javelin news is:

http://www.oursportsite.com/javelinnews/default.asp

By creating virtual directory names for all the directories (such as baseballnews, 100mnews, 200mnews, and so on) it's easy for the user to type in the URL and go directly to the page they want:

http://www.oursportsite.com/baseballnews/default.asp
http://www.oursportsite.com/100mnews/default.asp
http://www.oursportsite.com/200mnews/default.asp

Not only does this save the user from long, unwieldy URLs – it also serves as a good security measure, because it hides the physical directory structure from all the web site visitors. This is good practice, otherwise hackers might be able to work out and access our files if they knew what the directory structure looked like. Moreover, it allows the Webmaster's web site structure to remain independent of the directory structure on their hard drive – so they can move files the between different physical folders, drives, or even servers, without having to change the structure of his web pages. There is a performance overhead to think about as well, as IIS has to expend effort translating out the physical path. It can be a pretty costly performance-wise to have too many virtual directories.

Let's have a crack at setting up our own virtual directories and permissions (please note that these permissions are set automatically if you use the FrontPage editor to create a new site – so don't use FrontPage to set up this site for you unless you know what you're doing).

Try It Out – Creating a Virtual Directory and Setting up Permissions

Let's take a quick look now at how you can create your own virtual directory. We'll use this directory to store the examples that we'll be creating in this book. We don't want to over complicate this example by creating lots of directories, so we'll demonstrate by creating a single physical directory on the web server's hard disk, and using the IIS admin tool to create a virtual directory and make the relationship between the two:

1. Start Windows Explorer and create a new physical directory named BegASPNET, in the root directory of your hard drive. For example, `C:\BegASPNET\`:

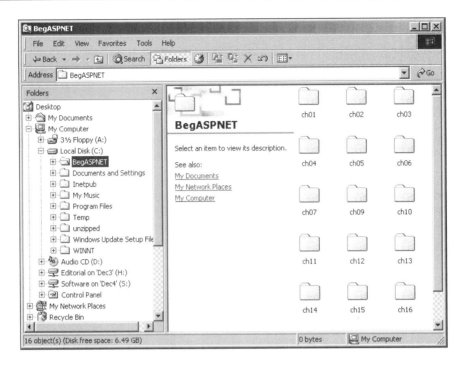

2. Next, start up the IIS admin tool (using the MMC, as we described earlier). Right-click on
    Default Web Site, and from the menu that appears select New | Virtual Directory. This starts
    the Virtual Directory Creation Wizard, which handles the creation of virtual directories for
    you and the setting up of permissions as well. You'll see the splash screen first, which looks
    like this. Click on Next:

3. Type BegASPNET in the Alias text box; then click Next:

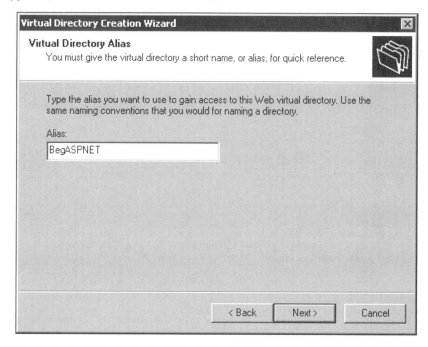

4. Click on the Browse... button and select the directory \BegASPNET that you created in Step 1. Then click Next:

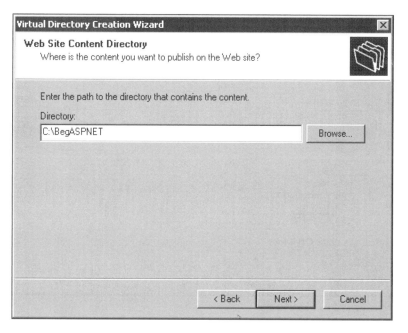

5. Make sure that the Read and Run scripts checkboxes are checked, and that the Execute checkbox is empty. Click on Next, and in the subsequent page click on Finish:

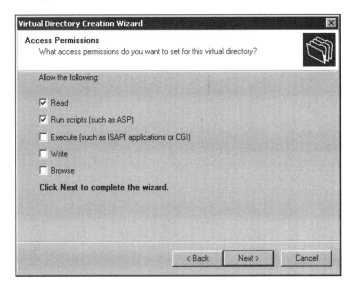

6. The BegASPNET virtual directory will appear on the tree in the IIS admin window:

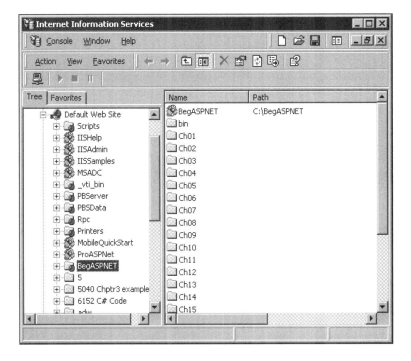

How It Works

You've just created a physical directory called `BegASPNET`; this directory will be used throughout the book to store our code examples. The download files from wrox.com are also designed to follow this structure. Within this directory we recommend that you create a subdirectory for each of the chapters in order to keep things tidy (this needn't be a virtual directory – just a physical one.)

You've also created a virtual directory called **BegASPNET**, which you created as an alias for the physical `BegASPNET` directory. If when we create Chapter 1 examples you place the ASP.NET files in the physical `C:\BegASPNET\Ch01`, directory, you can use the browser to access pages stored in this folder. You'll need to use the URL http://my_server_name/BegASPNET/Ch01/....

You should also note that the URL uses the alias /BegASPNET – IIS knows that this stands for the directory path `C:\BegASPNET`. When executing ASP.NET pages, you can reduce the amount of typing you need to do in the URL, by using virtual directory names in your URL in place of the physical directory names.

We also set the permissions `Read` and `Run` – these must be set or the IIS security features will prevent you from running any ASP.NET pages. The **Execute** checkbox is left empty as allowing others to run applications on your own machine is a sure way of getting viruses or getting hacked. We'll take a closer look at permissions now, as they are so important. If you don't assign them correctly you may find that you're unable to run any ASP.NET pages at all – or worse still, that anybody at all can access your machine, and alter (or even delete) your files via the Web.

Permissions

As we've just seen, we can assign permissions to a new directory as we create it, by using the options offered in the Virtual Directory Wizard. Alternatively, we can set permissions at any time, from the IIS admin tool in the MMC. To do this, right-click on the **BegASPNET** virtual directory in the IIS admin tool, and select **Properties**. You'll get the following dialog:

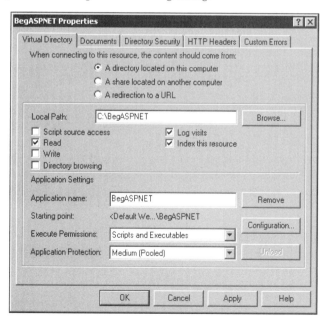

It's quite a complicated dialog, and it contains a lot of options – not all of which we wish to go into now.

Access Permissions

The four checkboxes on the left are of interest to us, as they govern the types of access for the given directory and dictate the permissions allowed on the files contained within that directory. Let's have a look at what each of these options means:

- ❏ **Script source access** – This permission enables users to access the source code of an ASP.NET page. It's only possible to grant this permission if the Read or Write permission has already been assigned. But we generally don't want our users to be able to view our ASP.NET source code, so we would usually leave this checkbox unchecked for any directory that contains ASP.NET pages. By default, all directories created during setup have Script Source Access permission disabled. You should leave this as is.

- ❏ **Read** – This permission enables browsers to read or download files stored in a home directory or a virtual directory. If the browser requests a file from a directory that *doesn't* have the Read permission enabled, then the web server will simply return an error message. Note that when the folder has Read permission turned off, HTML files within the folder cannot be read, but ASP.NET code within the folder can still be run. Generally, directories containing information that you want to publish (such as HTML files, for example) should have the Read permission enabled, as we did in our *Try It Out*.

- ❏ **Write** – If the write permission on a virtual directory is enabled, then users will be able to create or modify files within the directory, and change the properties of these files. For reasons of security, this is not normally turned on, and we don't recommend you alter it.

- ❏ **Directory Browsing** – If you want to allow people to view the contents of the directory (that is, to see a list of all the files that are contained in that directory), then you can allow this by checking the Directory Browsing option.

  If someone tries to browse the contents of a directory that has Directory Browsing enabled but Read disabled, then they may receive the following message:

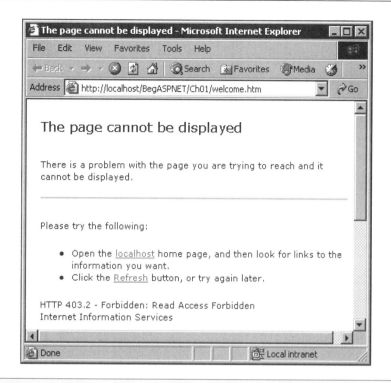

> For security reasons, we'd recommend disabling this option unless your users specifically need it – such as when transferring files using FTP (file transfer protocol), from your web site . If you don't know what FTP is then, we strongly recommend that you disable it, as you wont need it!

Execute Permissions

There's a drop-down listbox near the foot of the Properties dialog, labeled Execute permissions. This specifies what level of program execution is permitted on pages contained in this directory. There are three possible values here – None, Scripts only, or Scripts and Executables:

❑ Setting Execute permissions to None means that users can only access static files, such as image files and HTML files. Any script-based files of other executables contained in this directory are inaccessible to users. If you tried to run an ASP.NET page, from a folder with the permission set to None, you would receive the following – note the Execute Access Permission forbidden message in the page:

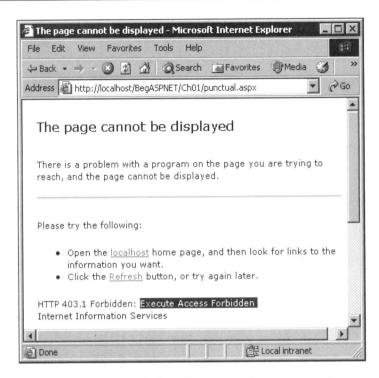

❏ Setting **Execute** permissions to **Scripts Only** means that users can also access any script-based pages, such as ASP.NET pages. So if the user requests an ASP.NET page that's contained in this directory, the web server will allow the ASP.NET code to be executed, and the resulting HTML to be sent to the browser.

❏ Setting **Execute** permissions to **Scripts and Executables** means that users can execute any type of file type that's contained in the directory. It's generally a good idea to avoid using this setting, in order to prohibit users from executing potentially damaging applications on your web server.

For any directory containing ASP.NET files that you're publishing, the appropriate setting for the **Execute** permissions is **Scripts Only**. There is one last thing about directories that needs pointing out though.

Configuring Directory Security

For the release version of ASP.NET, all ASPX pages run under a special user account with the name of **ASPNET**. For security reasons, by default this account has restricted permissions, and ordinarily this isn't a problem. However, the database samples in this chapter use Access. When updating data in an Access database, a separate file is created (with a suffix of `.ldb`), which holds the locking information. These are the details that store who is updating records, and the locking file is created and removed on demand.

The security problem we encounter is that while running pages we are running under the ASPNET account, and this account doesn't have write permissions in the samples directory. Consequently any ASP.NET pages that update the `Northwind.mdb` database will fail. Setting the write permission is simple – just follow these steps:

1. In Windows Explorer, select the BegASPNET directory, where the samples are located.

2. Using the right mouse button, select the Properties menu option, and from the Properties dialog that appears, select the Security tab:

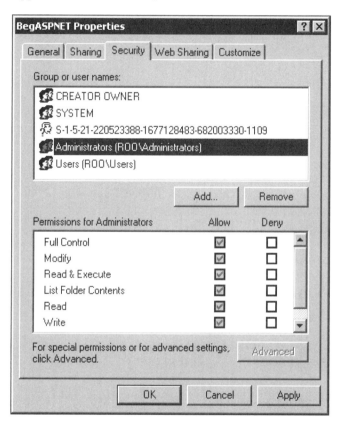

3. Click the Add button to display the Select Users or Groups dialog. In the blank space enter ASPNET and click the Check Names button. This checks the name you've entered and adds the machine name to it:

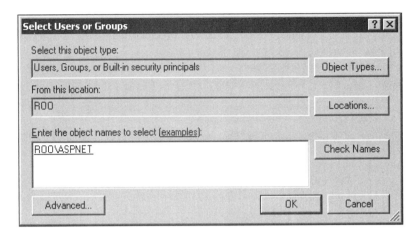

4. Click the OK button to return to the Properties dialog, and you'll see that the ASPNET user is now shown in the list of users. In the Permissions area, at the bottom of this screen, select the Write permission and tick it. This gives the ASPNET user write permission to the BegASPNet directory tree:

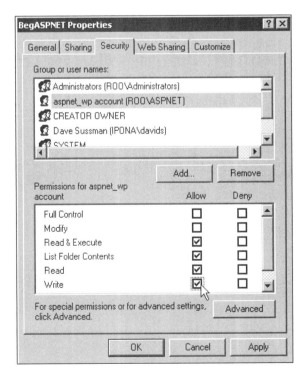

5. Click the OK button to save the changes, and to close the dialog.

This security issue is only a problem if you need write access to a directory, as both Access and our XML samples do. Most production web sites wouldn't use Access as their database store, since Access isn't designed for a high number of users. In these cases it's more likely that SQL Server will be used. Luckily, the only changes you'd have to make to the code samples shown in this chapter is to the connection string, which contains the details of how to connect to the database. The .NET SDK documentation has examples of connection strings for SQL Server.

Now you've started to familiarize yourself with IIS, you're ready to prepare your machine for the installation of ASP.NET itself.

Prerequisites for Installing ASP.NET

Before you can install ASP.NET or the .NET Framework you will need to install the Microsoft Data Access Components (MDAC) version 2.7 or later. This is a set of components that will enable you to use ASP.NET to communicate with databases and display the contents of your database on a web page. Without these components installed you won't be able to run any of the database examples in this book. This will affect examples as early as Chapter 2, so please don't skip this stage! Although you might already have an earlier version of MDAC installed (such as 2.5 if you're using Windows 2000), unless you have specifically upgraded, in all likelihood you won't have the most up-to-date version and will still need to upgrade.

The Microsoft Data Access Components is a small download (roughly 5 or 6 MB) available for free from Microsoft's site at **www.microsoft.com/data**. The installation for MDAC 2.7 is pretty straightforward, and it also comes as part of the Windows Component Update of the .NET Framework, but we'll run through it quickly just to make sure that everything is clear.

Try It Out – Installing MDAC 2.7

1. MDAC 2.7 comes as a single file MDAC_typ.exe that you will need to run. If you run this EXE file, then it will begin the installation process.

2. After agreeing to the terms of the license, there's a good chance that you will be asked to reboot your system, it will tell you this in advance:

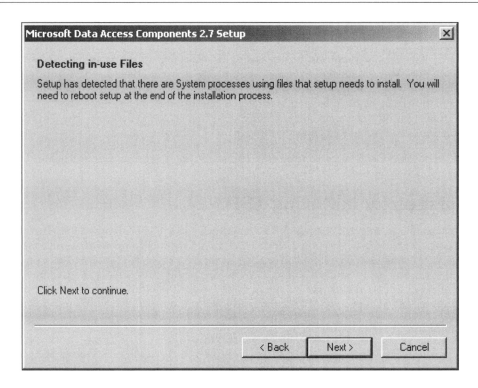

3. Then the installation process will continue without requiring further intervention, although you might have to wait for a system reboot, if one was specified earlier.

You're now ready to install ASP.NET.

Installing ASP.NET and the .NET Framework SDK

We're almost ready to install ASP.NET, but there are two important points to be made beforehand.

First, there are two different types of installation available from Microsoft's www.asp.net site, the .NET Framework SDK and .NET Framework Redistributable. Both downloads contain ASP.NET, C#, and the .NET Framework.

The **.NET Framework Redistributable** download is a smaller, streamlined download that only contains the bare bones needed for you to run ASP.NET and the .NET Framework. None of the extra documentation or samples will be included. The size differential between the two is pretty big (the Redistributable is 21MB while the .NET Framework SDK is a staggering 131MB), so unless you have the .NET Framework SDK on CD (which you can order from the Microsoft site) or broadband high-speed Internet access, you'll probably want to download the Redistributable version.

Don't worry, this won't affect your ability to run the examples in this book – everything's been written so that it will run on the .NET Framework Redistributable version of ASP.NET. While you won't have direct access to the help files, all support materials are available online at Microsoft's www.asp.net site.

Also, don't worry that you might end up replacing an existing Classic ASP installation, since ASP.NET will be installed alongside ASP and they will both continue to work with no action from us.

We'll now walk you through a typical installation of both .NET Framework Redistributable and the .NET Framework SDK. The installation process is the same for Windows 2000 and Windows XP, so once again we're only going to detail the installation process on the former. Although the wizard looks a bit different on XP, it asks for exactly the same things.

Try It Out – Installing the .NET Framework Redistributable

1. After downloading, click on the installation file (currently called dotnetfx.exe), you will be asked to confirm your intent, and then, after a short interval, you are propelled into the setup wizard:

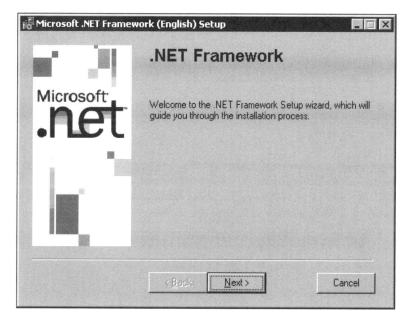

2. Click on **Next** and accept the License agreement to continue. ASP.NET will now install without further intervention:

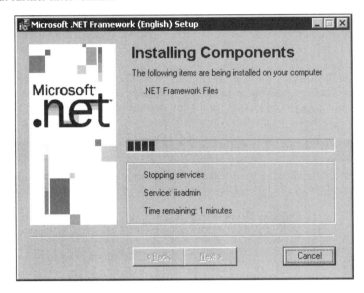

3. You will be notified when installation has finished, and unlike with MDAC 2.7, you probably won't have to reboot. You can now jump to the testing section, later in this chapter, to check everything is working.

Try It Out – Installing the .NET Framework SDK

1. After downloading, click on `setup.exe` and confirm that you do want to install NET Framework SDK package. After an interval of a few minutes, you are propelled into the setup wizard:

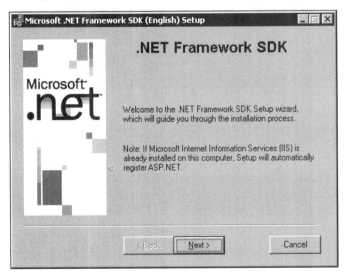

2. Click on Next and accept the License agreement to continue. The next dialog after the license agreement will ask you which different pieces of the SDK you need to install. You should check all of them, although if you're short of hard drive space, you could choose to omit the SDK_Samples or Documentation. The Software Development Kit is essential:

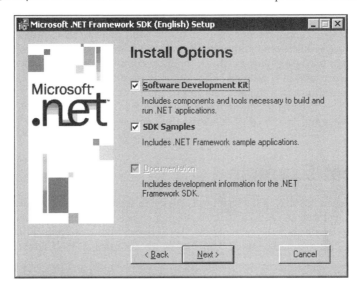

3. After clicking on Next you get to a dialog that specifies the destination folder for the different .NET Framework SDK samples and bits and pieces. You can choose to install these wherever you want. More importantly there is a checkbox at the foot of the dialog, which asks you to Register Environment Variables. This checkbox should be checked, as we will use the environment variables in later chapters:

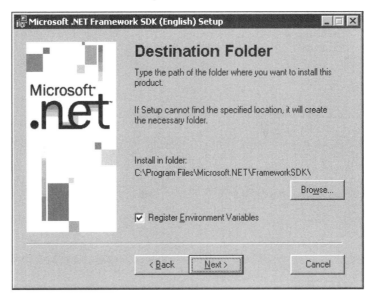

> **4.** Click on Next and the .NET Framework SDK will install without further ado. It shouldn't require a reboot.

Troubleshooting Hints and Tips

The installation process is very straightforward, and will work on the majority of machines. However, sometimes the particular configuration of your machine will prevent it from installing. Unfortunately we can't cover all of the possible eventualities, but if it doesn't work on your machine, you should check that you have enough hard disk space, as this is the most common cause of problems. Also try to ensure that the installation process isn't curtailed half way, as no installer is completely foolproof at removing all the different bits and pieces of the aborted install, and this can cause problems when you try to reinstall, and leave you needing to reformat your hard drive to get it to work correctly. Other than that, check the list of newsgroups and resources later in this chapter.

ASP.NET Test Example

OK, we've now reached the crux of the chapter, checking to see if everything is working correctly. Do you remember the punctual web server code that we talked about earlier in the chapter – in which we wanted to write a web page that displays the current time? We'll return to that example now. As you'll see it's quite a simple bit of code, but it should be more than enough to check that ASP.NET is working OK.

Try It Out – Your First ASP.NET Web Page

> **1.** Open up a text editor and type in the following code exactly as you see it, including case, as C# is case-sensitive and will reject Void instead of void, for instance:

```
<script language="c#" runat="server">
void Page_Load()
{
   time.Text=DateTime.Now.Hour.ToString() + ":" +
             DateTime.Now.Minute.ToString() + ":" +
             DateTime.Now.Second.ToString();
}
</script>

<html>
<head><title>The Punctual Web Server</title></head>
<body>
   <h1>Welcome</h1>
   In WebServerLand the time is currently:
<asp:label id="time" runat="server" />
</body>
</html>
```

We strongly suggest (and will assume throughout) that you use Notepad to code all the examples in this book, since it will always do precisely what you ask it to and no more. It's therefore a lot easier to track down any problems you're having, and is a great deal easier than troubleshooting problems caused by FrontPage or similar web page editors.

2. Save this page as `punctual.aspx`. Make sure that you save it in the physical folder you created earlier, `C:\BegASPNET\Ch01\`.

When you save the file, you should double-check that your new file has the correct suffix. It should be `.aspx`, since this is how you tell the web server that the page contains ASP.NET code. Be aware that Notepad (and many other text editors) consider `.txt` to be the default. So in the **Save** or **Save As** dialog, make sure that you change the **Save As** type to read **All Files**, or **All Files(*.*)**, or enclose the path and filename in quotes.

3. Now start up your browser and type in the following:

http://localhost/BegASPNET/Ch01/punctual.aspx

4. Click on the refresh button of the browser and the displayed time will change. In effect the browser is showing a new and different instance of the same page.

5. Now on your browser select **View Source** or similar (depending on which browser you're using) from the browser menu to see the HTML source that was sent from the web server to the browser. The result is shown below. You can see that there is no ASP.NET code to be seen, and nothing before the first `<html>` tag – the ASP.NET code has been processed by the web server and used to generate pure HTML, which is hard-coded into the HTML source that's sent to the browser:

```
punctual[1] - Notepad
File  Edit  Format  Help

<html>
<head><title>The Punctual Web Server</title></head>
<body>
   <h1>welcome</h1>
   In WebServerLand the time is currently:
<span id="time">15:10:10</span>
</body>
</html>
```

Here, you can see the HTML that was sent to the browser when I refreshed the page at 15.10:10.

6. As we mentioned before, you can expect this to work in any browser – because ASP.NET is processed on the web server. If you have another browser available, give it a go!

How It Works

Easy wasn't it? If you didn't get it to work first time, then don't rush off to e-mail technical support just yet – have a little look at the next section, *ASP.NET Troubleshooting*, first. Now let's take a look at the ASP.NET code that makes this application tick.

There is only one block of ASP.NET code (ignoring the server control – we'll look at using server controls in Chapter 3) in the whole program. It's enclosed by the <script> and </script> tags and although it does span three lines it is actually only one line of code spread over three lines, because it won't fit within the margins of the book on one line:

```
<script language="c#" runat="server">
void Page_Load()
{
  time.Text=DateTime.Now.Hour.ToString() + ":" +
            DateTime.Now.Minute.ToString() + ":" +
            DateTime.Now.Second.ToString();
}
</script>
```

The script delimiters specify which code is to be run by ASP.NET. We'll look at these in detail in the next chapter. If we ignore the <script> tags for the time being, and just think of them as ASP.NET code delimiters, then we're left with just three lines. If we further ignore the void Page_Load() and surrounding curly braces { }, which are standard to many ASP.NET programs, and which we'll be discussing in Chapter 3, we're left with this:

```
time.Text=DateTime.Now.Hour.ToString() + ":" +
          DateTime.Now.Minute.ToString() + ":" +
          DateTime.Now.Second.ToString();
```

This code tells the web server to go off and run the C# `DateTime.Now()` function **on the web server**. The C# `DateTime.Now()` function returns the current time **at the web server**. We can divide this up to return values for the hours, minutes, and seconds, using the `DateTime.Now.Time` format. We also add a `ToString`, because as it stands, we can't return a date data type, it has to be a string data type. We will look at data types in Chapter 4. Anyway we don't really want to dig into the code here, all we need to know is that the code tells the web server to go and get the system time and return it as three values, each converted to a string and separated by a colon. The resulting string looked like this:

15:39:15

The formatted string is returned as part of the `<ASP: label>` control, further down the page. We'll be looking at this control in Chapter 3.

If the web server and browser are on different machines, then the time returned by the web server might not be the same as the time kept by the machine you're using to browse. For example, if this page is hosted on a machine in Los Angeles, then you can expect the page to show the local time in Los Angeles, even if you're browsing to the page from a machine in Cairo.

This example isn't wildly interactive or dynamic, but it illustrates the way in which we can ask the web server to go off and do something for us, and return the answer **within the context** of an HTML page. Of course, by using this technique with things like HTML forms and other tools, we'll be able to build a more informative, interactive interface with the user.

ASP.NET Troubleshooting

If you had difficulty with the example above, then perhaps you fell into one of the simple traps that commonly snare new ASP.NET programmers, and that can easily be rectified. In this section we'll look at a few common errors and reasons why your script might not run. If you did have problems, maybe this section will help you to identify them.

Program Not Found, the Result of the ASP.NET Isn't Being Displayed, or The Browser Tries to Download the File

You'll have this problem if you try to view the page as a local file on your hard drive, like this:

C:\BegASPNET\Ch01\punctual.aspx

You'll also get this problem if you click on the file in Windows Explorer. If you have Microsoft FrontPage or Visual Studio .NET installed, then it will start up and attempt to help you to edit the code. Otherwise, your browser may display a warning message, or most likely it will ask you which application you wish to use to open up the ASPX file:

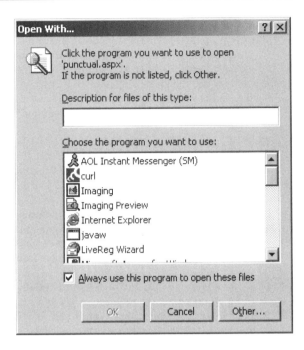

Older browsers may try to download the file:

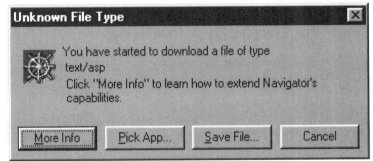

The Problem

This is because you're trying to access the page in a way that doesn't cause the ASP.NET page to be requested **from the web server**. Because you're not requesting the page through the web server, the ASP.NET code doesn't get processed, and that's why you don't get the expected results.

To call the web page through the web server and have the ASP.NET code processed, you need to reference the web server in the URL. Depending on whether you're browsing to the server across a local network, or across the Internet, the URL should look something like one of these:

http://localhost/BegASPNET/Ch01/punctual.aspx

http://www.distantserver.com/BegASPNET/Ch01/punctual.aspx

Page Cannot Be Displayed: HTTP Error 403

If you get a 403 error message, then it's probably because you don't have permission to execute the ASP.NET code contained within the page – notice the **Execute Access Forbidden Error** message at the end of the error page:

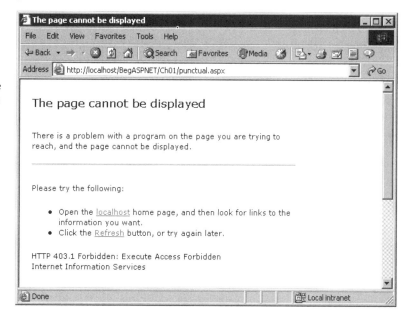

As you'll recall, permissions are controlled by the properties of the virtual directory that contains the ASP.NET page. To change these properties, you'll need to start up the IIS admin snap-in in the MMC, as we described earlier in the chapter. Find the BegASP.NET virtual directory in the left pane, right-click on it, and select Properties. This will bring up the BegASPNET Properties dialog that we met earlier in the chapter:

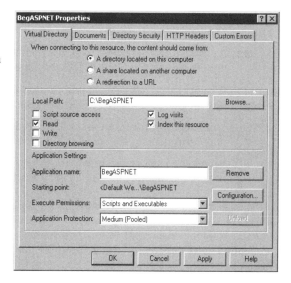

Here, you'll need to check that the value shown in the Execute Permissions box is Scripts only or Scripts and Executables –but definitely **not** None.

Page Cannot Be Found: HTTP Error 404

If you get this error message then it means that the browser has managed to connect to the web server successfully, but that the web server can't locate the page you've asked for. This could be because you've mistyped the URL at the browser prompt. In this case, you'll see a message like this:

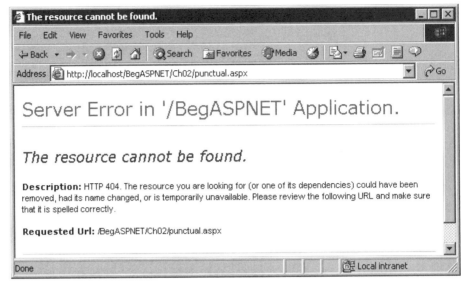

If you get this page, then you might suspect one of the following errors:

❑ A simple typing error in the URL, such as
http://localhost/BegASPNET/Ch01/punctually.aspx

❑ A wrong directory name, like http://localhost/BegASPNET/punctual.aspx instead of
http://localhost/BegASPNET/Ch01/punctual.aspx

❑ Including a directory separator (/) after the file name, like this
http://localhost/BegASPNET/Ch01/punctual.aspx/

❑ Using the directory path in the URL, rather than using the alias, such as
http://**chrisu**//BegASPNET/Ch01/punctual.aspx

❑ Saving the page as an .html or .htmfile, rather than as an .aspxfile, like this
http://localhost/BegASPNET/Ch01/punctual.htm

Of course, it may be that you've typed in the URL correctly, and you're **still** experiencing this error. In this case, the most likely cause is that you have used Notepad to save your file and that (when you saved the file) it used its default Save As Type setting, which is Text Documents (*.txt). This automatically appends a .txt suffix to the end of your file name. In this case, you will unwittingly have finished up with a file called punctual.aspx.txt.

To check if that is what happened, go to Windows Explorer, and view the (physical) folder that contains the file. Go to the **Tools** menu and select **Folder Options...**. Now, in the **View** tab, ensure that the **Hide file extensions for known file types** is unchecked, as shown here:

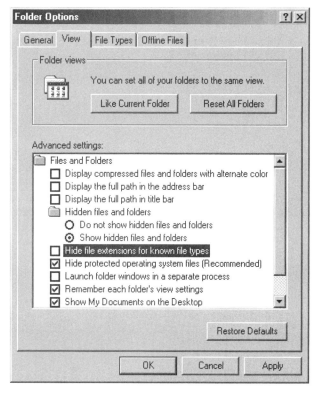

Now click **OK** and return to view your file in Windows Explorer. You may well see something like the following:

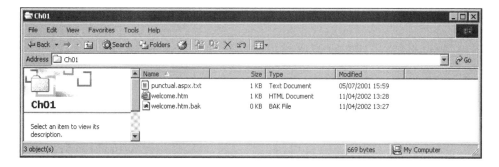

As you can see, Notepad has been less than honest in its dealings with you: when you thought that you had saved your file as `punctual.aspx`, it had inconveniently saved it as `punctual.aspx.txt`. Not surprisingly, your web server won't be able to find your file if it's been renamed accidentally. To correct the filename, right-click on it in the right pane above, select **Rename** from the drop-down menu that appears and remove the `.txt` at the end.

Web Page Unavailable while Offline

Very occasionally, you'll come across the
following message box:

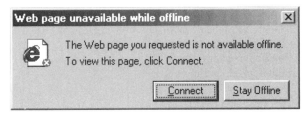

This happens because you've tried to request a page and you haven't currently got an active connection
to the Internet. This is a misperception by the browser (unless your web server isn't the same machine
as the one you're working on) – it is trying to get onto the Internet to get your page when there is no
connection, and it's failing to realize that the page you've requested is present on your local machine.
One way of retrieving the page is to hit the Connect button in the dialog; but that's not the most
satisfactory of solutions (since you might incur call charges). Alternatively, you can adjust the settings on
your browser. In IE 5/IE 6, select the File menu and uncheck the Work Offline option.

This could also be caused if you're working on a network and using a proxy server to access the
Internet. In this case, you need to bypass the proxy server or disable it for this page, as we described in
the section **Browsing to a Page on your Web Server**, earlier in the chapter. Alternatively, if you're using
a modem and you don't need to connect, you can correct this misperception by changing the way that
IE looks for pages. To do this, select the Tools | Connections option and select Never dial a
connection.

I Just Get a Blank Page

If you see an empty page in your browser then it probably means that you managed to save your
`punctual.aspx` without entering any code into it, or that you didn't remember to refresh the browser.

The Page Displays the Message but not the Time

If the web page displays the message "In WebServerLand, the time is currently" – but doesn't display
the time – then you might have mistyped the code. For example, you may have mistyped the name of
the control:

```
time.text=Hour(Now) & ":" & Minute(Now) & ":" & Second(Now)
```

and:

```
<asp:label id="hour" runat="server" />
```

The name of the control 'hour', must match the first word in the line of ASP.NET code, otherwise the
control won't be able to identify it.

I Get an Error Statement Citing a Server Error

You may get a message stating that the page cannot be displayed, and citing a server error such as:

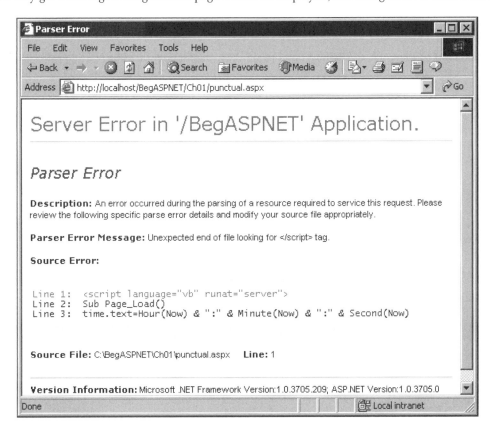

This means that there's an error in the ASP.NET code itself. Usually, there's additional information provided with the message. For example, you'd get this error message if you omitted the closing `</script>` tag on your code. To double-check that this isn't the case, use the sample `punctual.aspx` from the Wrox site at **www.wrox.com**.

I Have a Different Problem

If your problem isn't covered by this description it's worth testing some of the sample ASP.NET pages that are supplied with the QuickStart tutorials at **www.asp.net**; (it doesn't matter which installation you've got locally, you can still use these). They should help you to check that IIS has actually installed properly. You can always uninstall and reinstall if necessary, although before you do this, rebooting your server might solve the problem.

You can get support from **http://p2p.wrox.com**, which is our web site dedicated to support issues in this book. Alternatively, there are plenty of other web sites that are dedicated to ASP and ASP.NET. In fact you will find very few sites which focus on just one of the two technologies. Here are just a few:

http://www.asp.net
http://www.asptoday.com
http://www.asp101.com
http://www.15seconds.com
http://www.4guysfromrolla.com

There are lots of solutions, discussions and tips on these pages, plus click-throughs to other related pages. Moreover, you can try the newsgroups available on www.asp.net such as aspngfreeforall.

By now, you should have successfully downloaded, set up, and installed both IIS and ASP.NET, and got your first ASP.NET application up and running. If you've done all that, you can pat yourself on the back, make a cup of tea, and get ready to learn about some of the principles behind ASP.NET in the next chapter.

Summary

We started the chapter with a brief introduction to ASP.NET and to dynamic web pages in general and we looked at some of the reasons why you'd want to use a server-side technology for creating web pages. We looked at some of the history behind dynamic web pages, in the form of an overview of the other technologies. We'll expand on this very brief introduction to ASP.NET in the next chapter.

The bulk of the chapter was taken up by a description of the installation process. You *must* have installed IIS 5.0/5.1, MDAC 2.7 *and* either the .NET Framework Redistributable or the .NET Framework SDK to be able to progress further with this book, so please don't be tempted to skip parts that might not have worked. We've listed plenty of resources that will help you get everything up and running, and there's rarely a problem that somebody somewhere hasn't encountered before.

The next chapter covers the software installed with ASP.NET, the .NET Framework, and will build up in much greater detail what ASP.NET does, what the .NET Framework is, and how the two work together.

Anatomy of an ASP.NET Page

Before we get stuck into using all the fantastic features that ASP.NET has to offer, we're going to take a little time to step through the mechanics behind it. After all, we've not yet really got a fix on how ASP.NET works its magic, and although we don't need to know everything about it, it's going to be very helpful later on if we have an idea of what's going on behind the scenes.

We will be covering the following points:

- ❑ What the .NET Framework is, and what it does
- ❑ What ASP.NET is, what it does, and how it relies on the .NET Framework
- ❑ The role of the Common Language Runtime
- ❑ Core concepts of ASP.NET
- ❑ Some examples of ASP.NET and the .NET Framework in action

Since this chapter is mostly quite theoretical, I'm also including a few examples towards the end, demonstrating just how flexible and powerful ASP.NET really is.

So, first of all, let's consider the big beef behind it all – namely, the .NET Framework.

What is .NET?

I recently attended one of Microsoft's .NET road shows, and between talks, one of the speakers was giving out free software to anyone in the audience who could answer one of several simple questions. He challenged the audience by asking them to define what they thought .NET was. Tellingly, in a room full of experienced developers, not a single hand was raised. He moved on quickly, and instead chose to ask what a 'delegate' in the C# language was, and was greeted with a much larger response to this potentially much more baffling question.

You may have come across lengthy discourses from journalists and Microsoft's rival companies, claiming that even Microsoft doesn't have a clear idea of what .NET is, and it's certainly true to say that it could have been made somewhat clearer than it has been. However, accusations of it being 'vaporware' (all hype, and no substance) ring hollow if you scratch below the surface and start taking a look at the different bits and pieces that go to make it up.

In fact, **.NET** is a catchall term that embraces Microsoft's core strategy, plans, and vision for the foreseeable future. At the heart of this strategy is the **.NET Framework**, which provides the core technology that underpins it all. The Framework itself consists of several components, of which ASP.NET is just one.

.NET is designed to help solve many fundamental problems faced by programmers. Many of these issues concern rather involved programming concepts that are beyond the scope of this book – it suffices to say that it takes care of a great deal of the hard work involved in building large, reliable applications. It also blurs the line between writing applications to run locally on your own machine and writing applications that can be accessed over the Web. What's more, it doesn't bring with it all the overheads traditionally associated with 'simple' programming frameworks – that is, we don't need to write complex code in a high-powered language to get some fairly impressive speed out of our .NET programs.

In the course of this section, we'll break down this mysterious entity piece by piece, take a brief look at its main features, and consider the function of each one.

> *Since the aim of this book is to get you writing ASP.NET web applications, we're not going to try to detail every single aspect of the Framework. In many cases, all we really need to know is what its elements can do for us, and what they need from us in order to do it. Other elements provide us with important functionality, and these will merit further discussion. In this way, we hope you'll get more than a simple knowledge of ASP.NET, and also a sense for how it fits in with the .NET Framework as a whole.*

We can break down our discussion of the .NET Framework into a few specific topics:

- ❑ **MS Intermediate Language** – all the code we write is compiled into a more abstract, trimmed-down form before it's executed. Whichever .NET language is used to write the code, the trimmed code that's created from it is defined using MSIL: the Common Language of .NET.

- ❑ **The Common Language Runtime (CLR)** – this is a complex system responsible for executing the MSIL code on the computer. It takes care of all the fundamental tasks involved in talking to Windows and IIS.

- ❑ **The .NET Framework Class Libraries** – these are code libraries containing a mass of tremendously useful functionality, which we can very easily bolt into our own applications to make complex tasks much more straightforward.

- ❑ **The .NET Languages** – these are simply programming languages that conform to certain specific structural requirements (as defined by the Common Language Specification), and can therefore be compiled to MSIL. You can develop in any of the languages, such as C# or VB.NET, without any restrictions, and make programs constructed out of several of these languages.

❑   **ASP.NET** – this is how the .NET Framework exposes itself to the Web, using IIS to manage simple pages of code so that they can be compiled into full .NET programs. These are then used to generate HTML that can be sent out to browsers.

❑   **Web Services** – although not strictly part of .NET, web services are definitely enabled by .NET. They are components that can be accessed via the Web, and can be anything from news headlines, weather forecasts, stock tickers, to virus protection and operating system updates.

Before we go into detail though, we need to take a careful look at some fundamental code concepts and terminology.

From Your Code to Machine Code

As you probably know, computers understand everything in terms of binary bits – sequences of ones and zeros that represent instructions and data – hence the enthusiastic use of the word 'digital' to describe anything even vaguely related to computers. We refer to these binary instructions as **machine code**. Obviously, for most humans it's totally impractical to remember the particular sequence of ones and zeros that prints "Good Morning" (let alone one that defines a sophisticated web application) so we use programming languages as a **layer of abstraction**. We gloss over much of the possible functionality offered by the bitstream, and abstract it away as human-readable commands: many of these may even correspond to real words.

Once we've written some code in a human-friendly language, we need to convert it into machine code, and this process is called **compilation** – we literally compile the human-readable instructions into machine-readable instructions. Part of this compilation process involves hardcoding information regarding the local environment into the compiled code, so that it can make the most efficient use of all the machine resources available to it.

For many years, there's been a simple choice between two types of compilation:

❑   **Pre-compiled code** – This is code that we compile before we need to use it, so that it's ready and waiting to be executed on the hardware. This makes for very fast execution, as the compiler has the opportunity to spend time considering the full set of code, and **optimize** it to get the most out of the specific set of instructions available on the local system. However, because we've compiled it on a specific machine, we're now either tied to using it on that machine, or we need to set up another machine with the same system and all the resources that the code requires.

❑   **Interpreted code** – This code gets compiled as and when we decide to execute it. However, we don't get the performance advantages, since we have to wait for the compiler to interpret the code, and it doesn't get the chance to fully optimize the code we've written.

Introducing a Common Intermediate Language

When we write a program to run on the .NET Framework – perhaps using C# or VB.NET – we must always compile this human-readable code before using it. However, the way that .NET's compilers are designed means that this only takes us half way to the usual binary code that presents such problems of portability. In fact, they compile our code into a special format, called the **MS Intermediate Language** (**MSIL**). Some optimization can be done as part of this process, since the MSIL's structure doesn't have to be as easily human-readable as our original code. Consequently, it doesn't have to be nearly so verbose, clearly structured, or neatly arranged.

When we execute this MSIL, we pass it on to the CLR, which is the cornerstone of the .NET Framework. Just as the .NET Framework lies at the heart of Microsoft's .NET vision, the Common Language Runtime (CLR) lies right at the heart of the Framework. Its main purpose is to take care of executing any code that's been fed into it, and to deal with all the nightmarishly complex jobs that Windows and IIS require doing in order to work properly. The CLR uses another compiler – the **JIT** (**Just-In-Time**) **compiler** – to compile to true machine code, and make any last minute, machine-specific optimizations to the program, so that it can run as quickly as possible on the specific machine it inhabits.

> **MSIL is .NET's famous Common Language, and is designed to give us the best of both worlds: the structural optimization of pre-compiled code along with the portability of interpreted code.**

Most importantly, MSIL itself is not at all machine-specific, so we can execute it on any machine that has the CLR installed. In essence, once we've written some .NET code and compiled it, we can copy it to any machine with the CLR installed, and execute it there.

While the CLR currently only exists in a form that's compatible with Windows (9x, NT, 2000, and XP versions), moves are already afoot to build versions for other operating systems.

MSIL can also be generated from any human-readable language with a compatible structure. C#, VB .NET, and JScript .NET are all '.NET-compliant' languages: that is, they conform to a **Common Language Specification** that guarantees they can be faithfully compiled to MSIL. We can therefore use these and any other compliant languages *interchangeably* within our applications – once a set of files have been compiled to MSIL, they're all effectively written in the same language!

Objects, Objects Everywhere

In order to properly grasp how .NET works, you need to have at least a notional idea of what we mean when we talk about **objects**. Just about everything you come across within the .NET Framework is implemented as a software object – we can in fact describe .NET as an **object-oriented environment**. What does this mean?

An object is a self-contained unit of functionality – almost like a miniature program. It lets us (or code that we write) access and manipulate the parts of the object in simple, well-defined ways. By defining particular classes of objects (in a **class definition**) to do very specific tasks, we can define common ways of accessing or manipulating objects. Therefore we only need to create one definition for a particular task, instead of having to define each definition for each separate object individually, and thereby we can condense the code needed into a few lines.

For example, let's consider a publishing company – there are many different jobs defined within the company, such as Manager, Editor, Proofreader, and Layout Person. Once we've established the basic jobs that an Editor needs to do (edit chapters, review chapters, send chapters to authors for rewrites) we probably don't need to know all the gory details of how they do those jobs. You could simply say "Dan, please edit Chapter 2" and leave the Editor to get on with it. You might also phrase it differently though and ask, "Dan, is the chapter edited yet?", and expect the Editor to give you a response about the current state of the chapter.

This is essentially how objects make our lives as programmers easier – in this instance, there's an `Editor` class, from which template we can build an `Editor` type object called `Dan`. We can instruct the object to `Edit`, `Review`, or `Return To Author`, and we can ask it about its state: that is, whether its `EditComplete` information is set to `True` or `False`. Just to reiterate: we don't need to know *how* Dan does this – we just need to know a few specific ways in which to instruct it, and how to ask it for information.

The advantages of this type of programming are fairly obvious – we don't need to worry about how each object does its job, so it's a whole lot easier to build large, complex (but at the same time reliable) applications. We simply hook together lots of job-specific objects in simple, well-defined ways to make something large yet relatively stable.

The .NET Base Classes

One very important feature of the .NET Framework, and one that saves us from hideous amounts of tedious coding, is its **base class library**. This contains an enormous amount of ready-written code that you can include in any of your programs to simplify all sorts of useful tasks.

The base Framework classes cover a multitude of different functions. For instance, you'd expect to be able to display text, but what happens if you want to perform more specialized graphical operations such as draw a circle or a rectangle? Or add an animated image to an ASP.NET page? These functions are all provided in a number of base classes that are grouped together under a **namespace** called `System.Drawing`.

> **Namespaces are used by .NET to group together functionally similar classes. (In fact namespaces are not unique just to .NET but are found in many other languages as well.) In terms of our earlier business analogy, this is equivalent to a departmental grouping. For example, all the jobs directly involved with producing book content (`Editor`, `Author Agent`, `Project Manager`) are classified as within the namespace. `Editorial`. Likewise, jobs involving the layout and printing of the physical book (`Cover Designer`, `Illustrator`) can be classified as being within the namespace `Production`.**

To be able to use the classes contained within a namespace, we need to **import** the namespace first. We can import these classes into our ASP.NET pages, by simply adding a **directive** to the top of the file. For example, if we want to make use of all the classes defined in the `System.Drawing` namespace, we just say:

```
<%@ Import Namespace=System.Drawing %>
```

This literally *directs* the Framework to apply a specific setting to the page as a whole: in this case, importing the classes in `System.Drawing` for use in our page.

> *There are a whole variety of .NET classes, from classes that look after generating graphics to classes that help to simplify data access. We'll see some examples that rely on our importing namespaces towards the end of the chapter. After you've run them, you might try removing them and seeing what error messages are produced!*

It is then possible to use the classes in `System.Drawing`, although you will need to reference this namespace in front of each class name to uniquely indicate which class it is you want to use. So why does .NET do this? Why can't you have access to all the classes you need, all of the time? One reason is to keep your application small. The more you include in an application, the more bloated it will become, the more difficult it will be to understand, maintain, and use. So it makes sense to include only the bits you need to use, or the most commonly used classes. In fact, a selection of the most commonly used classes is included by default anyway. This concept of including classes has been a standard feature in many programming languages, such as Java, for a long time now.

The Class Browser

So how can I get a list of these pre-defined .NET classes, you might be wondering? One great tool that makes all of this more transparent is the .NET Framework class browser. This is an ASP.NET application that lists the main Framework classes defined on whatever machine it's being run from. The class browser application is available as part of the Quickstart Tutorials that are provided along with the .NET Framework SDK. If you have these installed, you'll be able to run it locally from:

http://localhost/quickstart/aspplus/samples/classbrowser/vb/classbrowser.aspx

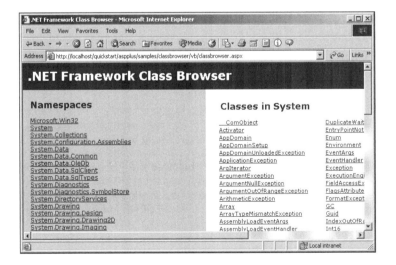

If you've only installed the .NET Framework Redistributable, then you won't have the class browser installed. It is possible, however, to access the class browser online at:

http://www.gotdotnet.com/quickstart/aspplus/samples/classbrowser/vb/classbrowser.aspx

Of course, this will list the System classes available on *that* site's web server (the standard set of base classes under the System namespace). You won't be able to browse any additional namespaces – such as custom namespaces or add-ins that you've installed – or configure the browser application. Nevertheless, you should find that it covers most of your needs. It really is a very handy tool for students and developers alike. You'll almost certainly find the class browser useful in later chapters, as much of the book will be concerned with exploring .NET's various classes.

So, we have our three sections of .NET Framework: MSIL, the CLR, and the .NET Language Base classes. But where and how does ASP.NET fit into this model?

How ASP.NET Works

For most purposes, we can simply think of ASP.NET pages as just like normal HTML pages that have certain sections marked up for special consideration. When .NET is installed, the local IIS web server is automatically configured to look out for files with the extension ASPX and to use the ASP.NET module (a file called aspnet_isapi.dll) to handle them.

Technically speaking, this module **parses** the contents of the ASPX file – it breaks them down into separate commands in order to establish the overall structure of our code. Having done this, it arranges the commands within a pre-defined class definition – not necessarily together, and not necessarily in the order in which we wrote them. That class is then used to define a special ASP.NET Page object, and one of the tasks this object then performs is to generate a stream of HTML that can be sent back to IIS, and from here, back to the client.

> *We'll take a more detailed look at various aspects of this process as we progress through the book – in particular, Chapters 10 and 14 will explore the Page object, and discuss some of the specific things it can do for us.*

For now though, we're more concerned with the immediate business of getting a page up and running. So, the first stage is to let the web server identify your web page as an ASP.NET page.

Saving your ASP.NET Files with an ASPX Suffix

In the last chapter, we defined an ASPX .NET page simply by saving some appropriate code in a file with the extension .aspx. This is important because all ASP.NET pages are identified by the .aspx suffix that is attached to the end of the filename. Only pages with .aspx will be sent to ASP.NET for processing.

Although it's possible to use `<script>` tags in an `.htm` file, anything you put between them won't be interpreted as ASP.NET code. Instead it will be sent to the browser for client-side execution, which is unlikely to work because the browser will only be expecting HTML and client-side script. If you try to include any ASP.NET code within these tags then the script will not be executed, and your web page won't perform the way you might have intended it to.

Now that we know how to identify an ASP.NET page using the extension `.aspx`, we need to consider how to identify specific sections of code within those pages.

Inserting ASP.NET Code into our Web Pages

If we place any kind of server-side code (not just ASP.NET code) within our web page source files, then we need to label it so that the server can identify it as server-side code, separate from the HTML code, and hence arrange for it to be dealt with correctly. There are three ways of placing ASP.NET code in your HTML: by using script tags, inline code blocks, or server controls. Inline code blocks (the `<% %>` delimiters) will be familiar to those who have used ASP before, but this is one place where if you are used to putting your code in one way in ASP, then you're going to have to make some changes. If you're not familiar with ASP, then this is so much the better, because script tags together with server controls are the preferred method for adding ASP.NET code.

The `<script>` Tags

The best way to delimit ASP.NET code from the HTML code in your pages is by using `<script>` tags, with the `runat` attribute set to `server`. This indicates the target host for processing the code: the web server.

> *The default when using the `<script>` tag is for the script to be executed on the browser (client-side), so if you're writing a server-side script then you must remember to specify this.*

As we know, ASP.NET itself is not a language, but a technology for creating dynamic pages. It allows us to use fully-fledged programming languages to define sections of code within our pages. The default language for coding in ASP.NET is VB.NET – to change that to define a page that uses C#, you can simply include a `Page` directive at the top of the page as follows:

```
<%@ Page language="C#" %>
```

To define some code, we can then do the following:

```
<script language="C#" runat="server">
... C# declarations go here ...
</script>
```

Since we've already specified C# as our language of choice, the `language` attribute in the above example isn't essential, and can be omitted. However, it serves to clarify which language we're using, so let's leave it in.

To define a page in a different language – VB.NET for example – you can do the following:

```
<%@ Page language="vb" %>

<script language="vb" runat="server">
... VB.NET declarations go here ...
</script>
```

In both of these snippets, all code enclosed with the `<script>` element must be in the language specified. While you can have an application with parts in more than one language, it isn't possible to mix languages in one page.

Although we can place server-side `<script>` blocks at just about any point within an ASPX, any code we put *inside* them must be **declarations**: that is, we declare sections of code that we'll be using later on, but they won't actually be executed until some other code triggers them.

A class definition is one type of declarative code – it's not code we actually want the CLR to execute as soon as it's been spotted. Rather we want to say: "here's some code that we want to use later on". We'll look at this topic in more detail when we get to Chapter 9.

The logical question is therefore: how do we trigger our page code in the first place? The solution is to use the following structure:

```
<script language="C#" runat="server">
  void Page_Load()
  {
  ... C# code goes here ...
  }
</script>
```

We won't go into detail explaining this format – suffice to say, when the page is loaded, the declarative block that we've labeled `void Page_Load()` contained within the curly braces, { and }, is triggered automatically: any code we want to run when the page starts up, we can put straight into here.

Try It Out – Inserting Server-side (ASP.NET) Code

In this example, we're only concerned with how we insert code, not with how the ASP.NET code works, so the code is quite trivial. We're just going to demonstrate how web pages are affected by the placement of ASP.NET code:

1. Using your preferred text editor, create a new document and type in the following code:

```
<html>
  <head>
    <title>Inserting ASP.NET code Example</title>
  </head>
  <body>
```

```
    Line1: First HTML Line<br />
    Line2: Second HTML Line<br />
    Line3: Third HTML Line<br />
  </body>
</html>
```

2. Save this as `message.aspx` in your test directory: if you've followed the steps from Chapter 1, this will be `C:\BegASPNET\Ch02\`.

3. Open your browser, and call up http://localhost/BegASPNET/Ch02/message.aspx:

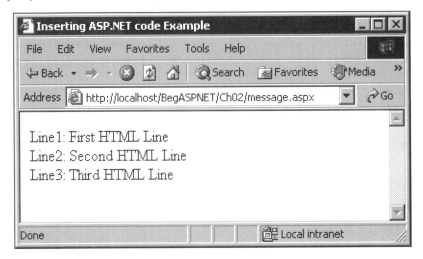

4. Now go back to the code page of `message.aspx`, and place the following code into it:

```
<script language="C#" runat="server">
void Page_Load()
{
  Response.Write ("First ASP.NET Line<br />");
  Response.Write ("Second ASP.NET Line<br />");
  Response.Write ("Third ASP.NET Line<br />");
}
</script>

<html>
  <head>
    <title>Inserting ASP.NET code Example</TITLE>
  </head>
  <body>
    Line1: First HTML Line<br />
    Line2: Second HTML Line<br />
    Line3: Third HTML Line<br />
  </body>
</html>
```

5. Save this as `message2.aspx` and view this example in your browser by typing in the URL: http://localhost/BegASPNET/Ch02/message2.aspx. You should get a similar result. However, this time we can see the results from the ASP.NET code we just added above the HTML:

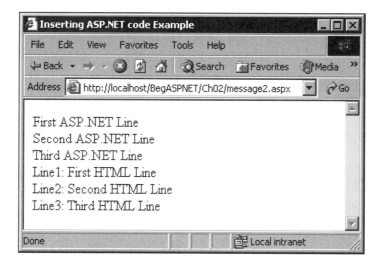

6. Now cut the code between the `<script>` tags (including the `<script>` and `</script>` tags), and paste it into the following position:

```
<html>
<head>
<title>Inserting ASP.NET code Example</title>
</head>
<body>
Line1: First HTML Line<br />
Line2: Second HTML Line<br />
Line3: Third HTML Line<br />
<script language="C#" runat="server">
void Page_Load()
{
  Response.Write ("First ASP.NET Line<br />");
  Response.Write ("Second ASP.NET Line<br />");
  Response.Write ("Third ASP.NET Line<br />");
}
</script>
</body>
</html>
```

7. Save this as `message3.aspx`.

8. Call up `message3.aspx` in your browser:

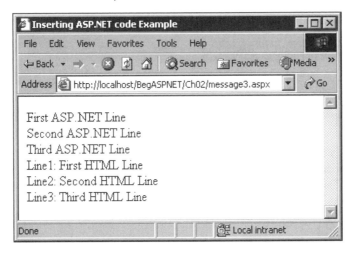

How It Works

The first thing to note is that although this is ASP.NET code, we're not actually creating a dynamic web page. All we're doing is demonstrating the order in which ASP.NET code and HTML are executed. The next point is that all three of these examples use the `.aspx` suffix – despite the fact the first page, `message.aspx`, only contained HTML code. So, as far as the web server is concerned, all three pages are ASP.NET pages. This demonstrates that HTML is treated in the same way in both pure HTML pages and ASP.NET pages.

The code in the first page just displays a number of HTML lines and some plain text:

```
<html>
<head>
<title>Inserting ASP.NET code Example</TITLE>
</head>
<body>
  Line1: First HTML Line<br />
  Line2: Second HTML Line<br />
  Line3: Third HTML Line<br />
</body>
</html>
```

When the code is parsed in your browser the lines are displayed in order, as you might expect.

In the second web page, `message2.aspx`, we have a combination of some pure HTML, some plain text, and a little server-side script. By using `runat="server"`, we specified that the following script (the highlighted lines) should be processed on the server, before the page is sent to the browser:

```
<script language="C#" runat="server">
void Page_Load()
{
    Response.Write ("First ASP.NET Line<br/>");
    Response.Write ("Second ASP.NET Line<br/>");
    Response.Write ("Third ASP.NET Line<br/>");
}
</script>
<html>
<head>
<title>Inserting ASP.NET code Example</TITLE>
</head>
<body>
Line1: First HTML Line<br/>
Line2: Second HTML Line<br/>
Line3: Third HTML Line<br/>
</body>
</html>
```

The ASP.NET code is placed within a code block called `void Page_Load()`. Whenever ASP.NET loads up a page it executes any code contained within the `void Page_Load()` block first. So if you place code in this block that spits out text to the browser, this text will always precede any text from the HTML part of the file, even if you physically put the code after the HTML lines.

> *Note also that any code placed within the `<script>` blocks must always be placed within braces and attributed a header such `void Page_Load()` otherwise it won't work.*

The ASP.NET code uses a `Response.Write` statement to display three ASP.NET lines, and as you might expect, these three lines are displayed before the HTML lines.

In the last example, we move the ASP.NET code to come after the HTML lines:

```
<body>
Line1: First HTML Line<br />
Line2: Second HTML Line<br />
Line3: Third HTML Line<br />
<script language="C#" runat="server">
void Page_Load()
{
  Response.Write ("First ASP.NET Line<br />");
  Response.Write ("Second ASP.NET Line<br />");
  Response.Write ("Third ASP.NET Line<br />");
}
</script>
```

Yet the browser still displays the ASP.NET code first.

75

This is the reason: the web server first scans the file to see if there is a `<script runat="server">` tag. If there is one, then it arranges for the `script` to be processed first. Because the ASP.NET code is in the `void Page_Load()` code block, which always runs as soon as the page is loaded, the ASP.NET output always appears first, even if the `<script>` tag is not at the top of the code page. In other words, the server takes no notice of the position of the `<script>` tag relative to other elements of the page.

There's an important lesson to be learned here: namely, that if you place ASP.NET code in the `void Page_Load()` block within the `<script>` tag, it will always be processed before the HTML code.

Inline Code Blocks (the <% %> Delimiters)

We now know how to output text to a browser using ASP.NET. Unfortunately, anything we output from ASP.NET will always precede the rest of the HTML, which is pretty awkward if we want to insert ASP.NET output anywhere else on the page. So we will now look at a couple of ways we can interweave ASP.NET output with HTML.

It's actually possible to incorporate code into our pages much more directly. If we specify a **render code block** (also known as an **inline code block**), any code it contains is executed as part of the page rendering process (this is the process by which we get our `Page` object to send back HTML for the browser to display). We can write render code blocks like this:

```
<%@ Page language="C#" %>
<%
Response.Write ("Hello!");
%>

<html>
  <body>
    Line1: First HTML Line<br />
    <% Response.Write ("First ASP.NET Line<br />"); %>
    Line2: Second HTML Line<br />
    <% Response.Write ("Second ASP.NET Line<br />"); %>
    Line3: Third HTML Line<br />
    <% Response.Write ("Third ASP.NET Line<br />"); %>
  </body>
</html>

<%
Response.Write ("Goodbye!");
%>
```

With the following result:

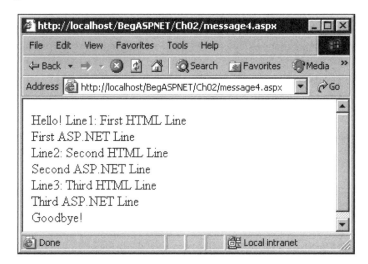

So, we can write code that executes wherever you put it, whether that's inside the HTML <head> tags, inside the <body>, or even right at the end of the page.

Server Controls

However, while this saves on keystrokes, it ultimately makes for quite intractable code. We therefore encourage you to try and find alternatives wherever possible, and we'll spend quite a lot of the next chapter looking at one particular, very powerful way of doing this: using **server controls**. Separating the ASP.NET code from the HTML not only makes the code easier to read, but means that it's a great deal easier to strip out either and reuse them in another page.

As we'll see later on in the book, we can separate code and HTML blocks even further, into separate files. For now though, for the sake of clarity, we'll keep them together.

We recommend (and will actively practice throughout the book) placing the ASP.NET code in a declarative code block near the top of the file, and just before the first <html> tag:

```
<script language="C#" runat="server">
... ASP.NET code here ...
</script>

<html>
... HTML code here ...
</html>
```

Try It Out – Interweaving ASP.NET Output with HTML

Now, you may still be wondering: "How do we intersperse static content with dynamic content if the code and the HTML are separated like this?" Let's take a quick look at how to get round this very problem. You'll soon realize that this doesn't restrict us nearly as much as you might think.

1. Enter the following code and save it as `interweave.aspx`:

```
<script language="C#" runat="server">
void Page_Load()
{
  Message.Text="The ASP.NET line";
}
</script>

<html>
<head>
<title>Inserting ASP.NET code Example</TITLE>
</head>
<body>
First HTML Line<br/>
<asp:label id=Message runat="server"/> <br />
Second HTML Line<br/>
</body>
</html>
```

2. Browse to `interweave.aspx`:

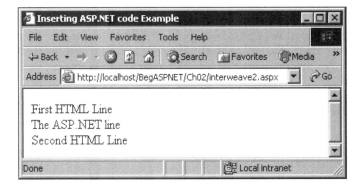

How It Works

We have solved the problems of interspersing inline code blocks with HTML markup, as all our ASP.NET code is now contained in the declarative `<script>` block at the head of the document:

```
<script language="C#" runat="server">
void Page_Load()
{
  Message.Text="The ASP.NET line";
}
</script>
```

This time, instead of having the `Response.Write` statements that send text to the browser as we did in the previous *Try It Out*, we have just one line of code in which we define the text that we want to insert – "The ASP.NET line".

The following section contains the HTML markup, but notice that we have now added a special marker (highlighted) that tells ASP.NET where to insert the text that we specified earlier in the declarative code block:

```
<html>
<head>
<title>Inserting ASP.NET code Example</title>
</head>
<body>
First HTML Line<br/>
<asp:label id=message runat="server"/> <br />
Second HTML Line<br/>
</body>
</html>
```

This marker is known as a **server control**. We will be exploring these in more detail in subsequent chapters. The `id` attribute of the server control corresponds with the line of code in the `<script>` block in which we specify the text to display. So now we can insert ASP.NET output anywhere we want on the page while maintaining a clear separation between ASP.NET code and HTML, or between content (ASP.NET code) and presentation (HTML).

ASP.NET in Action

This has been a very theory-heavy chapter, and you're probably dying for some examples now, so let's get stuck into a couple. Since we've still not looked at much ASP.NET code, we're going to throw in quite a lot of commands that won't necessarily make a lot of sense to you at this stage. However, we will break down the basic tasks that our code is performing, and you may like to refer back to this example as you progress through the book, so that you can build up a more detailed picture of what it's doing as your understanding grows.

One thing that ASP.NET makes very straightforward (particularly compared to the Classic ASP approach) is the process of binding your web page to a database.

Binding to a Database

With previous versions of ASP, binding to a database has been, quite frankly, a bit of nightmare. For most people, the key reason for using ASP, and now a key reason for using ASP.NET, is to connect a web page to a database, and to be able to browse and even update it. Prior to ASP.NET, this would have taken quite a bit of coding. A major step forward is the way that it is now possible to bind your web pages to a database using minimal amounts of ASP.NET code. ASP.NET provides a set of server controls that cut down, and almost completely eliminate, the need for separate coding.

We'll use one of the example databases provided with the .NET Framework, the grocertogo database – which is in Access format, and build a quick web page that allows us to browse the contents of the Products table, one of four tables contained with the database. If you only have the .NET Framework Redistributable then modify the lines beginning with "strConnect += "Data Source=" to point to any database you have on your system (there's a copy of grocertogo in the code download from www.wrox.com, but you'll have to alter the path name to point to where you've saved it on your system).

Try It Out – Binding to a Database

1. Open your web page editor of choice, and type in the following:

```
<%@ Import Namespace="System.Data" %>
<%@ Import Namespace="System.Data.OleDb" %>
<script language="C#" runat="server">
void Page_Load(object sender, EventArgs e)
{
  OleDbConnection objConnection;
  OleDbDataAdapter objCommand;
  string strConnect;
  string strCommand;
  DataSet DataSet1 = new DataSet();

  strConnect =  @"Provider=Microsoft.Jet.OLEDB.4.0;";

  //If you don't have the grocertogo.mdb database, then you will have to
  //change the following three lines to a different database

  strConnect += @"Data Source=C:\Program Files\Microsoft.NET\FrameworkSDK\";
  strConnect += @"Samples\quickstart\aspplus\samples\grocertogo\data";
  strConnect += @"\grocertogo.mdb;";

  strConnect += "Persist Security Info=False";

  strCommand = "SELECT ProductName, UnitPrice FROM products";
  objConnection = new OleDbConnection(strConnect);
  objCommand = new OleDbDataAdapter(strCommand, objConnection);
  objCommand.Fill(DataSet1, "products");
  DataGrid1.DataSource=DataSet1.Tables["Products"].DefaultView;
  DataGrid1.DataBind();
}
</script>
<html>
<head>
<title>Data Grid Control example</title>
</head>
<body>
<asp:DataGrid id="DataGrid1" runat="server"  />
</body>
</html>
```

2. Save this as datacontrol.aspx.

3. Open this page in your browser:

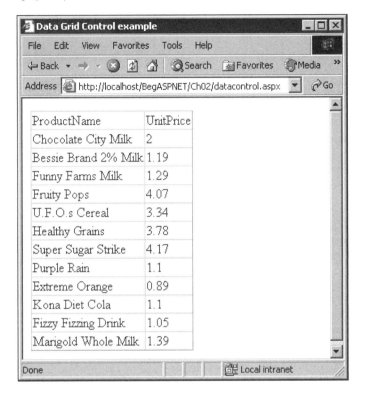

How It Works

All the ASP.NET looks quite daunting, but it's just there to supply the necessary connection and query information to the database control. We're not going to enter into a big discussion about how this control works, but we will have a quick overview of the ASP.NET that connects us to our database:

```
void Page_Load(object sender, EventArgs e)
{
  OleDbConnection objConnection;
  OleDbDataAdapter objCommand;
  string strConnect;
  string strCommand;
  DataSet DataSet1 = new DataSet();

  strConnect = @"Provider=Microsoft.Jet.OLEDB.4.0;";

  //If you don't have the grocertogo.mdb database, then you will have to
  //change the following three lines to a different database

  strConnect += @"Data Source=C:\Program Files\Microsoft.NET\FrameworkSDK\";
  strConnect += @"Samples\quickstart\aspplus\samples\grocertogo\data";
  strConnect += @"\grocertogo.mdb;";
```

```
    strConnect += "Persist Security Info=False";

    strCommand = "SELECT ProductName, UnitPrice FROM products";
    objConnection = new OleDbConnection(strConnect);
    objCommand = new OleDbDataAdapter(strCommand, objConnection);
    objCommand.Fill(DataSet1, "products");
    DataGrid1.DataSource=DataSet1.Tables["Products"].DefaultView;
    DataGrid1.DataBind();
}
```

Without breaking down the code line by line, there are three things going on that we need to discuss. These are the three things critical to our getting data back from the database. Two of them are provided by the following lines:

```
    strConnect =  @"Provider=Microsoft.Jet.OLEDB.4.0;";
    strConnect += @"Data Source=C:\Program Files\Microsoft.NET\FrameworkSDK\";
    strConnect += @"Samples\quickstart\aspplus\samples\grocertogo\data";
    strConnect += @"\grocertogo.mdb;";
    strConnect += @"Persist Security Info=False";
```

The first is the 'Provider= ' section. We don't want to explain what a provider is yet, but it is this section that tells ASP.NET what type of database we are using. In this case, we are using an Access database.

The second part is also contained within this line. This tells us where the database we wish to query with ASP.NET is physically located on the web server. In this case it is the sample database, which is installed with the .NET Framework, and should be located at:

C:\Program Files\Microsoft.NET\FrameworkSDK\Samples\quickstart\aspplus
\samples\grocertogo\data\

Because this is a long string and doesn't fit on one line it is good practice to break it up into smaller strings and concatenate them together using the + symbol as we did in the code.

The last piece of information that ASP.NET requires is to know exactly what we want from the database. The following line provides that:

```
    strCommand = @"SELECT ProductName, UnitPrice FROM products";
```

It states that we only want information about the ProductName and UnitPrice from the products parts of the database. The rest of the ASP.NET code is concerned with putting this information in a way that ASP.NET can understand. It is then displayed using the DataGrid control.

All that the DataGrid control receives is raw information in the following format "Chocolate City Milk", "2", "Bessie Brand 2% Milk", "1.19" and so on. The Data Grid control provides the display information, and creates the HTML table in which the information is presented.

Binding to a Simple XML File

It doesn't stop there either, the capabilities that ASP.NET has for connecting to databases extend to many other different data sources as well. We'll now look at how we can use the data controls to connect to a short XML document (we'll be considering XML in Chapter 5, so don't worry if you're not familiar with it).

Let's alter our example now so that we can demonstrate the flexibility of the DataGrid control, and bind it to the contents of the XML document. In fact, we'll go one step further, and create the XML document as well, and then use the control to bind to it, displaying the contents within a table, just as it would with a database.

Try It Out – Binding to a Simple XML Document

1. Open up your web page editor, and type in the following:

```
<?xml version="1.0"?>
<artist>
  <item>
    <name>Vincent Van Gogh</name>
    <nationality>Dutch</nationality>
    <movement>Post Impressionism </movement>
    <birthdate>30th March 1853</birthdate>
  </item>
  <item>
    <name>Paul Klee </name>
    <nationality>Swiss </nationality>
    <movement>Abstract Expressionism </movement>
    <birthdate>18th December 1879</birthdate>
  </item>
  <item>
    <name>Max Ernst </name>
    <nationality>German </nationality>
    <movement>Surrealism </movement>
    <birthdate>2nd April 1891</birthdate>
  </item>
</artist>
```

2. Save this as `artists.xml` in your `C:\BegASPNET\Ch02` folder.

3. Keeping your web page editor open, create a new file containing the following:

```
<%@ Page language="c#" %>
<%@ Import namespace="System.Data" %>
<%@ Import namespace="System.Xml" %>

<script language="c#" runat="server">
  void Page_Load()
```

```
    {
      string xmlFilename = @"C:\BegASPNET\ch02\artists.xml";
      DataSet newDataSet = new DataSet();
      newDataSet.ReadXml(xmlFilename);
      DataGrid1.DataSource = newDataSet;
      DataGrid1.DataBind();
    }
</script>

<html>
  <head>
    <title>Data Grid Control example</title>
  </head>
  <body>
    <asp:DataGrid id="DataGrid1" runat="server"  />
  </body>
</html>
```

4. Save this as `datacontrol2.aspx`.

5. View this on your browser; it should look like this:

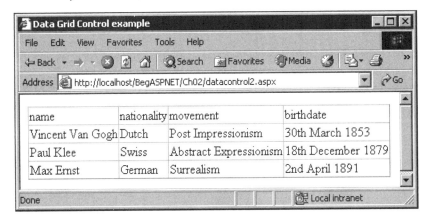

How It Works

The code in this example is much more straightforward. Our XML file is pretty much like a database table. We've kept it simple, so that you can see what is happening. `artists.xml` has three entries, for three artists. The artist's individual entry is held within a single set of item tags, structured like this:

```
<item>
  <name>Artist's Name</name>
  <nationality>Artist's Nationality</nationality>
  <movement>Artist's Movement</movement>
  <birthdate>Artist's Birthday</birthdate>
</item>
```

There are four elements: one for name, one for nationality, one for movement, and one for birthday. The data on the artists is stored between the tags. Once again, we use the `DataGrid` control to format the information as an HTML table, as once again all it receives is raw text.

The ASP.NET that connects with the XML document is much simpler than the code we used to connect with the database. It only has two purposes. The first is to provide the physical location of the XML file:

```
string xmlFilename = @"C:\BegASPNET\ch02\artists.xml";
```

The second is to read the contents of the XML document and make it available in ASP.NET code:

```
newDataSet.ReadXml(xmlFilename);
```

The rest of the code attaches the XML document data to the Data Grid control.

Summary

This chapter has been quite theory-heavy, so we've kept it quite short to prevent it becoming too overwhelming. Hopefully, your understanding of exactly what ASP.NET is has been broadened considerably. We have now seen that when we request an ASPX page from the web server:

❑ First, its contents are passed to the ASP.NET module, which parses them into a .NET-compliant class definition, and compiles this to MSIL.

❑ The `Page` class is used to instantiate an object within the Common Language Runtime, and this generates HTML that's returned to IIS, and from there sent back to the client browser.

This is quite a bit more complex than the idea of a web page being interpreted and then displayed!

Most of the hard work involved takes place within the 'black box' of the .NET Framework. This can call upon a wide range of functionality, which it makes available to our web pages.

We've also learned how to insert ASP.NET code into our web pages, and seen a quick example of one of the data controls in action. In the next chapter, we're going to look at creating HTML forms, and using client-submitted data to generate content for our web pages dynamically.

Forms and HTML Server Controls

One of the most common tasks any web developer will perform is the collecting and storing of information from the user. This could simply be a name and e-mail address, or it might range across a whole gamut of details including address, phone number, fax, credit card, and delivery address. Whatever the information you want to gather, the processing cannot be performed within the confines of HTML on the browser alone. Therefore, you need to send the information to the web server for processing. Once the web server has extracted the requisite information, an updated version of the page, or possibly on some occasions, a separate second page, is returned to the user.

Information is transmitted via web pages via a **form**, and in HTML, there are specialized tags for dealing with these. HTML forms contain a set of HTML controls, such as textboxes, checkboxes, and drop-down lists, all of which aid the passage of information from the user to the server. On top of this, ASP.NET adds its own extra controls for dealing with forms. With these, ASP.NET introduces some new concepts to the control of forms. Previously with HTML forms, for example, when you selected a particular form control, the web browser dealt with the entire handling of the form data until it was passed to the web server. However, there are now new features of the .NET Framework, such as remembering what text you've typed into a textbox, or what selection you made in a listbox between page refreshes, which is carried out on the server.

While we're going to be using some ASP.NET code to handle the interchange of form data, we won't be explaining all of the facets of ASP.NET that we will use, only those that relate directly to forms. To keep things clear, we're not going to start explaining exactly how it all works until later chapters, but by the end of the chapter, you will understand how to send information between browser and server via ASP.NET code. You'll also be introduced to some of the terminology associated with this process.

In this chapter we will cover:

- ❏ The client-server model of the web
- ❏ HTML forms and web forms
- ❏ HTML form controls
- ❏ Server Controls

Forms in the Real World

The main focus of the chapter is using forms, and implicitly, the transfer of data from the browser to the server. Before we start delving into the inner workings of the form, we'll describe a few situations in which forms would be required in the business world, to see what kind of things they are used for. If you take a look at a few commercial web sites, you'll find that forms are usually provided in the same kinds of situations, such as:

- ❏ To take information from a user. This could be for the purpose of registration, the purchase of a product, or joining an e-mail list/form/newsgroup.

- ❏ To take note of a user's preferences so that we can customize other pages in the site to include relevant information, and exclude things that don't interest them.

- ❏ To provide a questionnaire or survey on how a business may go about improving the service that it offers.

- ❏ To act as front end for a forum or newsgroup, where a user can enter and edit their text online.

These are just a few examples of some common everyday situations. In this chapter, we're just going to approach one facet of such a situation for a fictional business. This business, Feiertag Holidays, requires a web site that will allow users to view different destinations within Europe, and then browse through details of different hotels at each destination. Our forms will allow the user to select a destination and send the details of their choice to the web server. We will see how ASP.NET forms can be used to expedite the process.

One of the main advantages of using this in a typical full-blown business application is that rather than having to create a unique page for each separate destination, as might have to be done in the real world, we can create a generic page, dynamically generated by ASP.NET, which fills in details about each destination, and therefore requires a lot less coding.

However, before we get into that, it's best to take a quick overview of forms, and see the ways in which ASP.NET affects them.

Web Pages, HTML Forms, and Web Forms

With the introduction of any new technology comes new terminology and jargon. ASP.NET is no different in this respect. With ASP.NET, even the terms you use to describe a simple web page have been updated to more accurately describe the processes that are going on within them. To avoid confusion, we're going to start by defining a few familiar concepts and their ASP.NET equivalents. Let's begin with a **web page**.

Everybody reading this should know what a web page is – it's just a bundle of HTML code, made up of markup tags, nominally beginning and ending with <html> and </html> tags. The web page is placed on a machine, known as a web server, and it is the job of the web server to make that page available to all and sundry. Whether that page contains text, graphics, movies, sound, or bits and pieces of other languages/technologies or whether it was dynamically generated is of no concern to us.

An **HTML form** is a web page that contains one or more **form controls** (grouped together inside an HTML <form> element) that allow the user to enter information on the web page and send that information back to the web server. Commonly used form controls include buttons, textboxes, checkboxes, and drop-down lists. The user fills in details and presses a 'submit' button to send their data back to the web server.

Although you don't need anything more than HTML to send form data to the server, the server needs some sort of extra technology (in this case, ASP.NET) to actually *do* anything with the information it receives. HTML pages containing forms are typically saved with the suffix .html (or sometimes .htm).

ASP.NET goes one further than this and introduces a new concept, the **web form**. The web form is similar to the HTML forms we've seen before, and visually you wouldn't be able to differentiate between an HTML form and a web form, but it's what ASP.NET does behind the scenes with the web forms operation that make it quite a different entity. Firstly, the term web form refers to the grouping of two distinct blocks of code:

❏   **The HTML template** containing page layout information and ASP.NET server controls (see below). This is responsible for the presentation of the web form on the browser.

❏   **The ASP.NET code** that provides the web form's processing logic. This is responsible for generating dynamic content to be displayed within the web form. This content is typically exposed via server controls defined in the HTML presentation block.

> **Although a web form may also be an HTML form (that is, there's nothing to stop us using <form> elements inside an ASPX), remember that these two entities are defined in quite distinct terms.**

When we start using ASP.NET within our web pages, and we create a web form, we can then use a new breed of ASP.NET **server controls** within our HTML (we looked at these very briefly in the last chapter). Not only do they duplicate the functionality of many HTML elements (including the form controls), but they also do a lot more besides. A server control has the appearance of an *HTML-like* element, but actually it only marks a point in the page at which the server needs to generate a corresponding true-HTML element. The advantage this offers over an HTML control is that we can create content for the form, before returning the form to the browser, and we can generate this content from just about anywhere in our code.

> *As we've already seen, the ASP.NET code can be specified in a <script> block that may occur at any point within the ASPX file. We're keeping it at the top of the code page, to help clarify the separation of presentation and content. As we'll see in Chapter 15 though, we can ultimately place the ASP.NET code into a completely separate file (a technique known as code behind). What's important is that you recognize that when we talk about a web form, we're referring to both these sections, regardless of where they are, or how they're organized.*

So, we know that it is possible for web forms to use normal HTML form controls, but ASP.NET also comes with its own set of web form controls that are run on the server. We will be using these in preference most of the time, because they offer other advantages such as being able to remember the state of the different controls, such as what text has been typed into a textbox. These ASP.NET controls are run within specially modified HTML `<form runat="server">` tags, and are **ASP.NET forms**. There are four different terms here that we need to be clear about before we go any further:

❑ **A web page** is any page that contains just HTML (they can also contain script/other languages not covered by this book, but in this book a web page will refer to pages containing only HTML)

❑ **An HTML form** is an HTML element that contains HTML form controls

❑ **A web form** is any page that combines ASP.NET code with an HTML template

❑ **An ASP.NET** form is a form inside a web form, that contains ASP.NET server controls

Because our discussion of forms is essentially a discussion of how to transmit data from a browser back to the web server, we need to start out by considering the whole process of data transmission on the Web, so that we can put the role of forms into context. It's worth emphasizing first though that no matter which technology you use, the browser will always ultimately receive HTML.

So let's now look at how web browsers and web servers work together to make web pages available to the world.

Simple Web Theory

When we installed ASP.NET in Chapter 1, the installation was broken down into stages because we installed several different pieces of software. One of these pieces of software was the web server, whose main job is to make your web pages available to everyone. Another job of the web server is to provide an area (typically in a directory or folder structure) in which to organize and store your web pages, or whole web site.

When you use the Web to view a web page, you will automatically make contact with a web server. The process of submitting your URL is called 'making a **Request**' to the server. The server interprets the URL, locates the corresponding page, and sends back the code to create the page as part of what is called the **Response** to the browser. The browser then takes the code it has received from the web server and compiles a viewable page from it. The browser is referred to as a **client** in this interaction, and the whole interaction as a **client-server relationship**.

The term client-server describes the workings of the Web, by outlining the distribution of tasks. The server (the web server) stores, interprets, and distributes data (that is compiled into web-pages), and the client (browser) accesses the server to get at the data. **From now on, whenever we use the term client, we are just referring to the browser**.

To understand what is going on in greater detail, we need to briefly discuss how the client and server communicate over the Internet using the HTTP protocol.

The HTTP Protocol

The Internet is a network of interconnected nodes. It is designed to carry **information** from one place to another. When the user tells the browser to fetch a web page, a message is sent from the browser to the web server.

This message is sent using Hypertext Transfer Protocol (or HTTP). HTTP is the protocol used by the World Wide Web in the transfer of information from one machine to another. When you see a URL prefixed with http://, you know that the Internet protocol being used is HTTP, as HTTP is the default protocol used by web browsers. This means if we type www.wrox.com, the browser will automatically use the HTTP protocol and search for http://www.wrox.com.

The message passed from the browser to the web server asking for a particular web page is known as an **HTTP Request**. When the web server receives this request, it checks its stores to find the appropriate page. If the web server finds the page, it bundles up the HTML in an **HTTP Response**, and sends this back across the network to the browser. If the web server cannot find the requested page, it issues a response that features an appropriate error message, and dispatches *that* page to the browser.

Here's an illustration of the process, as we understand it so far:

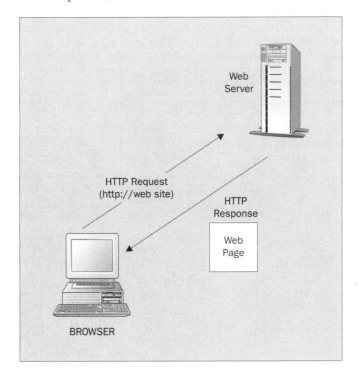

HTTP is known as a **stateless** protocol. This is because it doesn't know whether the request that has been made is part of an ongoing correspondence or just a single message, just the same way your postman won't know whether your letter is the first asking your local hi-fi company for a refund, or the fifteenth.

The reason HTTP is stateless is that it was only intended to retrieve a single web page for display. Its purpose was to handle simple transactions, where a user requests a web page, the browser connects to the requisite web server, retrieves that web page, and then shuts down the connection. The Internet would be very slow and might even collapse if permanent connections needed to be maintained between browsers and servers as people moved from one page to another. Think about the extra work HTTP would have to do if it had to worry about whether you had been connected for one minute or whether you had been idle for an hour, and needed disconnecting. Then multiply that by a million for all the other users. Instead, HTTP makes the connection and delivers the request, and then returns the response and disconnects. However, the downside of this is that HTTP can't distinguish between different requests, and can't assign different priorities, so it won't be able to tell whether a particular HTTP Request is the request of a user, or the request of a virus infected machine, that might have been set up, for instance, to hit a government web server 1,000 times an minute. It will treat all requests equally, as there are no ways for HTTP to determine where the request originated.

If a request is successful, the HTTP Response body contains the HTML code (together with any script that is to be executed by the browser), ready for the browser to use. Additional HTTP Requests are used to retrieve any other resource, such as images, dictated by the HTML code returned after the first request.

Where ASP.NET Fits in with the .NET Framework

In the last chapter, we encountered some of the major concepts involved in the .NET Framework. In this chapter, we've already gained a better understanding of how a browser sends a web page request, and how the web server sends the page back to the browser. What we're going to do now is to tie the two together, as this will help us understand what is happening when we use forms and server-side controls.

Let's sum up the five step process for delivering a web page:

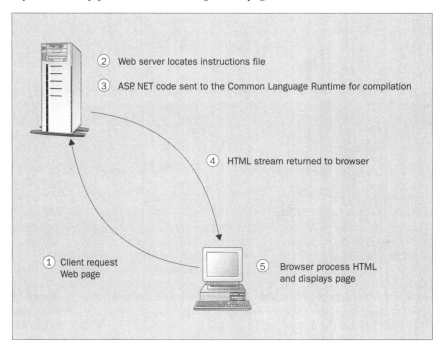

1. The client requests a web page.

2. The web server needs to locate the page that was requested; and if it's an ASP.NET page then this code will need to be processed in order to generate the HTML that is returned to the browser.

3. If the name of the web page is suffixed with .aspx, the server sends it to the aspnet_isapi.dll (which is attached to the web server) for processing. The aspnet_isapi.dll doesn't actually do much itself, it just forwards the ASP.NET code to the Common Language Runtime. We looked at what role this performs in the last chapter, and here we'll just treat it as a black box. If the ASP.NET code hasn't been compiled before, it is compiled and then executed, and pure HTML comes out at the other end. In this way the HTML is created **dynamically**.

4. The HTML stream is returned to the browser.

5. The browser displays the web page.

There are a lot of advantages to generating a page dynamically: you can return information to the user based on their responses in a form, you can customize web pages for a particular browser, you can personalize information (and utilize a particular profile for each individual), and much more beyond the static text and graphics that pure HTML returns. This is down to the fact that the code we write is interpreted at the time it is requested.

Now we have a basic understanding of how the web works, it's time to get stuck into forms. We'll begin by looking at HTML forms, as they are often much misunderstood. Also, once you know about HTML forms, the ASP.NET server controls begin to look familiar, as the HTML form controls perform many of the same functions as their server-side counterparts.

HTML Forms

In HTML, forms are important as they provide the only means by which a user can input data and send it back to the web server. The method via which this is accomplished is the <form> tag. You can use the <form> tag to specify the page you wish the data to be sent to, along with the method by which you wish to transmit the form data. Now all this changes quite dramatically in ASP.NET, but to understand it more clearly, we need to be certain of how the <form> tag works in HTML.

The <form> Tag

The <form> tag is a container tag. It is used purely to denote the set of form controls that the developer intends to use to convey information back to the server. It still needs another technology on the server side (such as ASP.NET) to be able to manipulate the form data and send it back to the user. It also adds no extra presentational features itself (the form itself is invisible).

In Netscape browsers, prior to version 6, form controls cannot be displayed without the <form> tag. In other words, all form controls, such as textboxes and radio buttons, must be placed within <form> tags, otherwise they won't be displayed at all in Netscape. On the other hand, IE and Opera can still display the form controls without the <form> tag, but if you want to send the form data back to the server, then the form controls have to be contained within a set of <form> tags. We'll take a look at the <form> tag in more detail now.

While the <form> tag supports eleven attributes (as defined by the HTML 4.01 standard), there are only two that are essential:

❑   action – specifies the web page we want to receive our form data

❑   method – specifies the HTTP method by which our form data is transmitted

The other attributes, which include name *(with which we can reference the form from client-side code) and* target *(to specify a different window or frame in which to load the returned page), are all useful in themselves. However, they're not immediately relevant to the current discussion, so we will not be looking at them here. For more information, you may want to take a look at* HTML 4.01 Programmer's Reference *from Wrox Press (ISBN 1-861005-33-4).*

The action Attribute

The first of the <form> tag's attributes, action, defines the name of the web page that will receive the form data. A typical action attribute in an HTML form might look like this:

```
<form action="nextpage.aspx" ... >
...
```

We've referenced an ASPX page here, as HTML forms have to work in conjunction with another technology. This is still an HTML form though. ASP.NET forms have a specialized set of attributes that are not part of the HTML 4.01 standard and we look at some of them later in the chapter.

When you submit a form (send it to the web server), you need to specify the name of the web page that the information will be returned to. It could possibly be the same page as the one that received the information, but for our early examples, we will be using a separate second page.

One last thing we need to say about this attribute: make sure it points to a valid page, otherwise you will generate a page error!

The method Attribute

The second attribute defines the method of transmission of the form data. There are plenty of different possible methods of transmission, but in practice, you'll only ever use two of them: GET or POST.

The GET Method

The GET method is the default, and is normally used to retrieve files from a web server. When it is used in conjunction with a <form> tag though, it **sends** the form data to the web server. Form data sent to the server is appended to the end of the URL in the form of **name-value pairs**, attached with a question mark. For example:

```
?firstname=Vervain
```

The first part of this name-value pair is the name, which acts as an identifier. The second part is the value that you wish to store. The name and value are taken automatically from a form element like a textbox or a checkbox. The name of the form element is the name used in the GET method, and the content the user has written in the form element is the value. Here 'firstname' is the **name**, while 'Vervain' is the **value**. This can be appended to the URL as follows:

```
http://www.nosuchserver.com/asppages/form.aspx?firstname=Vervain
```

The browser automatically appends the information to the URL when it sends the page request to the web server. You can add more than one name-value pair to a URL if you separate each pair with an ampersand (&). With two name-value pairs, the end of the URL might look like this:

```
?firstname=Vervain&surname=Delaware
```

As part of the URL it would look like this:

```
http://www.thereisnosuchserver.com/asppages/form.aspx?firstname=
Vervain&surname=Delaware
```

The part appended to the URL is known as a **query string**. So this is how you can still pass information between the browser and server, while leaving the HTTP body empty – it is transferred in the URL.

However, GET isn't the only method that can be used to transmit data, and indeed, when we move to ASP.NET, we'll see that GET becomes all but obsolete.

The POST Method

One disadvantage you might have discerned from using query strings is the rather public nature of their transmission. If you don't want the information sent to appear in the URL, then you will have to rely on the POST method instead. This works almost identically to the GET method, the only difference being that the form information is sent in the *body* of the HTTP Request rather than as part of the URL. This isn't any more secure though: it's just less immediately visible.

POST can also allow a greater amount of information to be transmitted. Some web servers have a limit on the amount of text you can transmit as part of a URL. Using the POST method avoids this problem. Apart from this, for all intents and purposes, the two methods provide the same functionality and level of performance. However in ASP.NET there is no choice of method of transmission, all forms will be sent to the server using the POST method. Before we look at how to return information from a form control with ASP.NET, let's do a quick tour and refresher through the many form controls that HTML offers.

HTML Form Controls

For the majority of HTML form controls, you will use the `<input>` tag to place them on the web page, and for those that have their own specialist tags, the attributes they require are broadly similar.

The HTML form controls you might use on a typical web page are:

HTML Form Control	Appearance	Description	Implementation
Textboxes	text here...	Textboxes are single line fields for typing text into	Uses the `<input>` tag, with the `type` attribute set to `text`
Text areas	Several lines of text...	Text areas are multiple line boxes for typing text into	Uses the `<textarea>` tag
Radio Buttons		Radio buttons are multiple choice buttons that allow only one exclusive answer	Uses the `<input>` tag, with `type` set to `radio`
Checkboxes		Checkboxes are single and multiple choice buttons that allow several, independent answers	Uses the `<input>` tag, with `type` set to `checkbox`
Listboxes	A B C	Listboxes are buttons that reveal a drop-down menu, from which you're allowed to select one or more options	Uses the `<select>` tag
Submit buttons	Submit Query	Submit buttons submit HTML forms to the web server	Uses the `<input>` tag, with `type` set to `submit`
Reset buttons	Reset	Reset buttons reset the contents of an HTML form that hasn't already been submitted	Uses the `<input>` tag, with `type` set to `reset`

HTML Form Control	Appearance	Description	Implementation
Normal buttons	Click here	Normal buttons trigger whatever event they are connected to	Uses the `<input>` tag, with `type` set to `button`
Password fields	∗∗∗∗∗∗∗∗∗	Password fields are like textboxes, but with one important difference: anything you type into them is disguised by an asterisk	Uses the `<input>` tag, with `type` set to `password`
Hidden fields	No visual appearance	Hidden fields are set in the HTML, and are sent along with other form data	Uses the `<input>` tag, with `type` set to `hidden`

As you can see, the `<input>` tag deals with the broad majority of HTML form controls, so we'll take a closer look at it.

The `<input>` tag has only four attributes that we will make use of:

❑   `name` – is used to identify the control in ASP.NET code.

❑   `type` – specifies which type of form control you are using. Valid options are Submit, Reset, Radio, Checkbox, Hidden, Text, Password, and Button (there are also image and file options, which fall outside of the scope of this book).

❑   `value` – not strictly necessary for all controls, but can be used to specify a default value for some button or text controls.

❑   `checked` – if you wish to pre-select a radio control, so that a particular choice is selected when the user first sees the page, you can add the CHECKED attribute to a particular `<input>` tag.

These attributes of the `<form>` tag are all you need to be able to access and manipulate form controls with ASP.NET code.

How the `<form>` Tag Works in ASP.NET

ASP.NET has a set of form controls that can be used just like their HTML form control equivalents, the main difference being that they are actually constructed dynamically on the server and then sent out. There's another difference we'll need to look at first though.

As we explained earlier when using HTML form controls, we use a modified version of the <form> tag in ASP.NET. The ASP.NET version of the <form> tag looks like this:

```
<form runat="server">
... ASP.NET form...
</form>
```

It takes only one attribute (runat="server"), which tells the web server that it should process the form itself, rather than just sending it out to the browser (which won't be able to interpret this ASP.NET-specific attribute). Even though we haven't specified the contents of the method and get attributes, ASP.NET is able to handle this itself and provide its own values. In fact all ASP.NET forms are sent by the POST method. If they are not sent by the POST method – if you try to override it – you will not be able to use the information in the form). We have a new version of the <form> tag, but how does that compare with the HTML version?

The <form> tag enables us to process form controls on the server. ASP.NET introduces its own customized versions of these controls. The ASP.NET server controls were introduced to solve many of the problems associated with the HTML form controls. For instance, if you go forward from a form on almost any web site, and then jump back again to make a correction, you will find that all of the information has disappeared. This is because HTTP is stateless, as we mentioned earlier: it has no concept of who is connecting to it, or when – it just answers requests for a connection. However, ASP.NET now takes over some of these responsibilities of looking after and persisting this data.

ASP.NET Server Controls

In this next section, we're going to be demonstrating how each of the ASP.NET server controls work, and comparing the way they are used to the way their equivalent HTML form control passed information. We'll also demonstrate how we can start achieving our ambition of separating the presentational code (HTML) from the code that provides the content (ASP.NET).

The <asp:label> Control

We'll start with a small, but very useful little control, the <asp:label> control. This control provides an effective way of displaying text on your web page in ASP.NET. It mimics the HTML <span> tag, a tag that has no effect on the text it contains, but can be used to logically group text together into sections, paragraphs, pages, or sentences. This control is actually vital to us if we want to separate our HTML from our ASP.NET code.

The <asp:label> Control Attributes

The <asp:label> control is just like any normal HTML form control in that it has a collection of attributes you can set. We won't list them all, but ones you might wish to use are:

❑   BackColor – sets the background color of the label

❑   ForeColor – sets the foreground color of the label

❑   Height – sets the height in pixels of the label

❑   id – sets a unique identifier for that particular instance of the label

❑ Text – sets the text that you want the label to display

❑ Visible – determines whether the label control is currently visible on the page: this must be either true or false

❑ Width – sets the width of the label control

If you want a full detailed list of the attributes that the <asp:label> control supports (or indeed any HTML server control), then you can use a handy tool known as the class browser, which you can run from the following URL:

http://www.gotdotnet.com/quickstart/aspplus/samples/classbrowser/cs/classbrowser.aspx
?namespace=System.Web.UI.WebControls

On the right-hand side of the page, you can find a list of all the controls, from label and dropdownlist, to checkbox and the likes. Clicking on the link for a particular control will a reveal a list of allowable attributes under the name Properties. We won't be supplying a list of attributes for the other controls, as, generally, they each support the same attributes, and this information is easily obtainable from the URL given above.

One other attribute not mentioned on the lists for any of the controls, but supported by all of them is the attribute runat, which is always set to server. This is to explicitly indicate that this particular control should be run on the server, not the browser.

<asp:label> Control Examples

To create the control with the minimum of information needed, you can just supply the runat and id attributes:

```
<asp:label id="Message1" runat="server">Hello</asp:label>
```

Placed in the context of a web page, the control might look like this:

```
<html>
<head>
  <title>Another Hello World Page </title>
</head>
<body>
  Hello
  <asp:label id="Message1" runat="server"> World</asp:label>
</body>
</html>
```

The id attribute is used to uniquely identify the <asp:label> control so you can refer to it in your ASP.NET code. The runat="server" attribute tells the server to process the control and generate HTML code to be sent to the client.

Let's look at another example. If you want to set the color of a text message to red, you could set it like this:

```
<asp:label id="Message1" forecolor="red" runat="server">Hello</asp:label>
```

Alternatively, you can use the `text` attribute. This way, everything can be contained within the opening tag, in which case you need to close the tag in the following way:

```
<asp:label id="Message1" forecolor="red"  text="Hello" runat="server" />
```

Here, we omit the closing tag, and just supply a closing / to indicate that the tag is closed. Throughout the book, if the tag doesn't enclose any content, then we will use this latter notation in preference to having a closing tag.

The `<asp:>` prefix indicates that this control is part of the set of built-in ASP.NET controls. It is possible to create custom controls, which have prefixes of the developer's choice. We will look at this later in the book.

Let's now take a look at an example of how we can use the `<asp:label>` control to display some text at requisite places within our web page. In this example, we'll assume that values of the user's name and the destination they selected on our holiday web site have already been passed across, and that all we need to do is output a message displaying confirmation that we have received the user's details.

Try It Out – Using the <asp: label> Control

1. Enter the following code in your web page editor:

```
<html>
<head>
  <title>Label Control page</title>
</head>
<body>
  <h1>Feiertag Holidays</h1>
  <br /><br />
  Thank you
  <asp:label id="Message1" runat="server" text="Chris"/>
    you have selected to receive information about
  <asp:label id="Message2" runat="server" text="Oslo"/>
.    The information pack will be sent out within the next 24 hours.
</body>
</html>
```

2. Save this as `labelcontrol.aspx`, in your test directory, and view it from your browser:

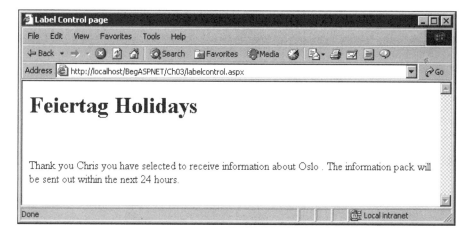

How It Works

There isn't much to explain here. Our `<asp:label>` controls fit neatly within the HTML code:

```
<h1>Feiertag Holidays</h1>
<br /><br />
Thank you
<asp:label id="Message1" runat="server" text="Chris"/>
  you have selected to receive information about
<asp:label id="Message2" runat="server" text="Oslo"/>
  .The information pack will be sent out within the next 24 hours.
</body>
```

For all intents and purposes the `<asp:label>` control could be an HTML control. The only thing that differentiates it is the fact that it is executed on the server. The only way you can note this is by checking the underlying HTML source code that is sent back to the browser:

```
<h1>Feiertag Holidays</h1>
<br /><br />
Thank you
<span id="Message1">Chris</span>
  you have selected to receive information about
<span id="Message2">Oslo</span>
  .The information pack will be sent out within the next 24 hours.
</body>
```

The `<asp:label>` controls are translated into HTML `<span>` tags, to which they are functionally equivalent.

Control Attributes

This still leaves one question unanswered though. How do we get hold of the `<asp:label>` control attributes within our ASP.NET code? Well, we can do this by adding some ASP.NET code at the head of the HTML, as in the following example. First delete the `Text` attribute at the end of both `<asp:label>` controls:

```
...
<asp:label id="Message1" runat="server" />
you have selected to receive information about
<asp:label id="Message2" runat="server" />
...
```

Now add the following ASP.NET script block before your HTML code:

```
<script language="C#" runat="server">
  void Page_Load()
  {
    Message1.Text = "Vervain";
    Message2.Text = "Madrid";
  }
</script>

<html>
<head>
  <title>Label Control page</title>
...
```

You must make sure that you type this part in exactly, using exactly the same case in the letters, otherwise it won't work. So if you typed `Void page_load()` for example instead of `void Page_Load()` then you would get an error. The same holds true for all of the examples in this chapter and indeed the book. If any example doesn't work when you first try it, check the cases are correct. This is because C# is a case-sensitive language. It can be awkward to get use to at first but once you get used to it, it will be like second nature.

So, if you run the example now, you'll see that the output has changed:

Ignore the void Page_Load() statement and it's accompanying curly braces (we'll discuss this in Chapter 7): it's the code contained within the curly braces that's important for now:

```
Message1.Text = "Vervain";
```

In the first line Message1 refers to the identity of our first <asp:label> control, while the Text attribute refers to the actual text that we wish to set. So we're saying "set the Method1 <asp:label>'s Text attribute to Vervain". The second line:

```
Message2.Text = "Madrid";
```

does just the same for the Message2 <asp:label> control, setting the text attribute to Madrid. This is reflected in the final display of our web form. This ASP.NET code has allowed us to directly influence the contents of the <asp:label> control, and set it separately, independently from our HTML code. You should also note that both lines are ended by a semi-colon. In C#, every line should be completed by a semi-colon.

So *all* of the HTML server controls are created as separate objects, which you can access with ASP.NET code. These objects allow you to reference any of the attributes of the server control as follows:

```
[ServerControl].[ServerControlAttribute]
```

So you could make the control invisible by setting the Visible attribute to false:

```
Message.Visible = "false";
```

Let's now move on to a more complex control.

The <asp:dropdownlist> Control

The <asp:dropdownlist> control is one of the best controls for demonstrating the usefulness of having a form control processed on the server side.

Before we move on to the <asp:dropdownlist> control, let's pause to look at the HTML form control equivalent. Drop-down listboxes are implemented in HTML using the <select> and <option> tags. For each option, you would have a separate opening and closing <option> tag inside the <select> tag. A listbox can be defined in HTML as follows:

```
<select name="list1">
  <option>Madrid</option>
  <option>Oslo</option>
  <option>Lisbon</option>
</select>
```

To create an ASP.NET drop-down list control that did exactly the same, you'd need to define it in the following way:

```
<asp:dropdownlist id="list1" runat="server">
  <asp:listitem>Madrid</asp:listitem >
  <asp:listitem >Oslo</asp:listitem >
  <asp:listitem >Lisbon</asp:listitem >
</asp:dropdownlist >
```

There are three important differences from the HTML form control:

❑   The `<asp:dropdownlist>` tag directly replaces the `<select>` tag

❑   The `<asp:listitem>` tag replaces the `<option>` tag

❑   The `id` attribute replaces the `name` attribute

Up until now, in all HTML form controls, the `name` attribute has been used to pass the identity of the form control to the ASP.NET code. The `id` attribute, for all but form controls, provides exactly the same function for any other HTML tags. The server-side control is therefore being brought up to date, by using the `id` attribute to perform this function, rather than the `name` attribute.

The `<asp:dropdownlist>` control has many attributes to help customize its appearance. We're not going to describe them here – once again you can find out more details using the class browser tool.

Visually, the `<asp:dropdownlist>` control is identical to the HTML drop-down list control; it's what's going on behind the scenes that is different. The best way to explain this is to look at an example. We'll create a form that asks the user to select the particular holiday destination they wish to know more about.

Try It Out – Using the <asp:dropdownlist> Control

1.   In your web page editor, type in the following:

```
<script runat="server" language="C#">
  void Page_Load()
    {
      if (Page.IsPostBack) {
      Message.Text = "You have selected " + list1.SelectedItem.Value;
      }
    }
</script>
<html>
  <head>
    <title>Drop Down List Example</title>
  </head>
  <body>
    <asp:label id="Message" runat="server"/>
    <br />
```

```
    <form runat="server">
    Which city do you wish to look at hotels for?<br /><br />
    <asp:dropdownlist id="list1" runat="server">
      <asp:listitem>Madrid</asp:listitem>
      <asp:listitem>Oslo</asp:listitem>
      <asp:listitem>Lisbon</asp:listitem>
    </asp:dropdownlist>
    <br /><br /><br /><br />
    <input type="Submit">
    </form>
  </body>
</html>
```

2. Save this as `listpage.aspx` this time, and run `it` in your browser:

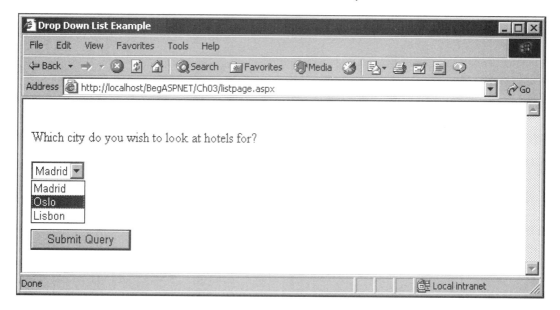

3. Select an option and click on Submit Query:

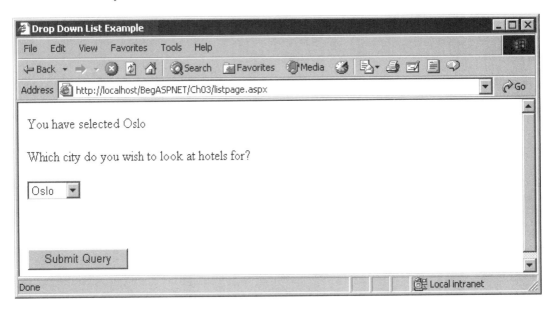

4. Now click on the View menu and select Source. You should see something like the following. Don't worry if your version isn't exactly the same – the code has been tailored to your personal browser:

```
<html>
  <head>
    <title>Drop Down List Example</title>
  </head>
  <body>
    <span id="Message">You have selected Oslo</span>
    <br />
    <form name="_ctl0" method="post" action="listpage.aspx" id="_ctl0">
<input type="hidden" name="__VIEWSTATE"
value="dDwtMTMyNTU5Mzc0Njt0PDtsPGk8MT47PjtsPHQ8cDxwPGw8VGV4dDs+O2w8WW91IGhhdmUgc2V
sZWN0ZWQgT3Nsbzs+Pjs+Ozs+Oz7NXC6yHYMc/rZZJx6p/OCXOpDklQ==" />

    Which city do you wish to look at hotels for?<br /><br />
    <select name="list1" id="list1">
      <option value="Madrid">Madrid</option>
      <option selected="selected" value="Oslo">Oslo</option>
      <option value="Lisbon">Lisbon</option>

</select>
    <br /><br /><br /><br />
    <input type="Submit">
    </form>
  </body>
</html>
```

How It Works

This is our first real look at what the ASP.NET code has been doing. As you can see, everything that has been returned to the browser has been returned as HTML code. Also, note that we are using only one page, in direct contrast to our two-page approach with HTML forms. This is because the form page submits to itself. To explain how it works, we're going to reference the source code that we can view in our browser, and compare it to our original ASPX code.

Let's start by jumping into the `<form>` section of the script. The very first thing we do with the form is set a new attribute:

```
<form runat="server">
```

This tells ASP.NET that we intend this form to be run on the server. If we compare this line to what has been returned to the browser, we can see a large difference:

```
<form name="ctrl0" method="post" action="listpage.aspx" id="ctrl0">
```

ASP.NET has generated four new attributes. The `name` and `id` attributes serve the same purpose, uniquely identifying the form, but it's the other two that are of interest. As we described earlier, HTML forms require a page to receive the form data, and a method of transmission. We didn't specify either of these in our ASPX code, so ASP.NET specified them for us. The `action` attribute actually points to the same page that we have run, so the answers are returned to our first page. It also specifies the POST method by default.

The main item on the form is the `<asp:dropdownlist>` control:

```
Which city do you wish to look at hotels for?<br /><br />
<asp:dropdownlist id="list1" runat="server">
  <asp:listitem>Madrid</asp:listitem>
  <asp:listitem >Oslo</asp:listitem>
  <asp:listitem >Lisbon</asp:listitem>
</asp:dropdownlist>
```

It's crucial to note how this is rendered. If you view the source code that's been sent back to the browser, you should see something like this:

```
<input type="hidden" name="__VIEWSTATE" value="dDwtMTg2MjQ4MjEzO3Q8O2w8aTwxPjs+O2
    w8dDxwPHA8bDxUZXh0O0Oz47bDxZb3UgaGF2ZSBzZWxlY3RlZCBMaXNib247Pj47Pjs7Pjs+Pjs+" />

Which city do you wish to look at hotels for?<br /><br />
<select name="list1" id="list1" size="4">
  <option value="Madrid">Madrid</option>
  <option value="Oslo">Oslo</option>
  <option selected="selected" value="Lisbon">Lisbon</option>
</select>
```

The second half is just a `<select>` HTML form control; this is the HTML output of a `dropdownlist`.

> *Note that it's had one of the `<option>` tags altered to reflect the selection we made before we submitting the form.*

However, it's the first line that is of particular note. This is a hidden control called __VIEWSTATE, whose value is an encoded representation of the overall state of the form (as it was when last submitted). This is used by ASP.NET to keep track of **all** the server control settings from one page refresh to another – otherwise, our drop-down listbox would revert to a static default setting every time we submitted a value.

It may not be immediately obvious how useful this can be – consider a registration form in which you have to enter a full set of personal details. If you forget to fill in a required field, and then submit the form, you may well be prompted with the same form again. Perhaps the field you missed will be highlighted, but unless the page has been very carefully coded (or is running on a sophisticated technology like ASP.NET), all the data you just entered will have to be typed in again. Thanks to __VIEWSTATE, all that data is automatically persisted through to the refreshed page, and we (as developers) haven't even to raise a finger!

We don't need to try to work out what the value contained in the `value` attribute is – it's only really designed to mean anything to ASP.NET itself. However, it's important to note that this attribute is what allows the form to keep track of the state of a server control between page moves and page refreshes. Indeed, when we ran through the example you might have noticed that even refreshing the page didn't alter the selection you'd made.

The ASP.NET Code

We've seen that the ASP.NET server control passes form data to the ASP.NET code. Now it's up to the ASP.NET code to access it. Let's take a look at how it does this now:

```csharp
<script runat="server" language="C#">
  void Page_Load()
    {
      if (Page.IsPostBack){
      Message.Text = "You have selected " + list1.SelectedItem.Value;
      }
    }
</script>
```

There are three lines of code here inside `Page_Load()`. We won't explain how the code works fully, as there are some features in it that won't be introduced until Chapter 6.

The purpose of this code is to check if a selection has been made in the listbox, and then display a message confirming the choice the user made. If they haven't made a choice, then it won't display anything in the `<asp:label>` control.

The first line of code:

```
if (Page.IsPostBack){
```

checks to see whether the page has been returned by the user before. This check involves using the Page object that we mentioned in the last chapter. The Page object keeps a record of whether or not a form has been submitted by the user in IsPostBack. If the form has been submitted, IsPostBack returns true, otherwise it returns false.

The code inside the If statement and curly braces will only be run if the form has been posted back by the user. So, if this is the first time the user has seen the form, then ASP.NET will jump the code until it encounters the next brace:

```
}
```

But, if the user has submitted the page, then the following line will be run:

```
Message.Text = "You have selected " + list1.SelectedItem.Value;
```

This line displays a customized message in the <asp:label> control about which destination the user has selected. The list1.SelectedItem.Value is the item of particular interest. The list1 identifier name is set when the server control is created. So when the <asp:label> control is created:

```
<asp:dropdownlist id="list1" runat="server">
```

then ASP.NET will enable us to use the identifier as a handle to the contents of this specific drop-down listbox control as follows:

```
list1.SelectedItem.Value
```

As list1 is unique on the page, it refers directly to our drop-down listbox. If you look up the drop-down listbox control in the class browser, you can see that the control has a SelectedItem **property** (properties correspond directly with attributes). We could reference this attribute of our drop-down listbox control as follows in our ASP.NET code:

```
list1.SelectedItem.Value
```

The SelectedItem keeps a record of which item the user has selected. The Value item returns the corresponding contents of the <asp:listitem> tag.

So given that this will return the contents of the <asp:listitem> tag for the corresponding list choice made by the user, our message is constructed as follows:

```
"You have selected " + "Lisbon"
```

109

So where does Message.Text come into all of this? Message, as you might have already noticed, is the unique identifier of our <asp:label> control. We use Message.Text to display the message, as this refers to the text that this particular <asp:label> control will display. You can find the <asp:label> control just underneath the <body> tag on our ASPX page:

```
<body>
  <asp:label id="Message" runat="server"/>
  <br />
```

In this way, we can ensure that the first time a user logs on, there is no message displayed in the <asp:label> control, as it isn't set until the page has been submitted at least once, but every time the user subsequently returns to the page, there is a message displayed. We will be looking further at how the particular if statements work in Chapter 6.

The <asp:listbox> Control

The next HTML server control that we'll look at, <asp:listbox>, is very much related to <asp:dropdownlist>. In fact, we've almost mentioned it already. Remember the <select> HTML form control that creates drop-down listboxes? Well, the <asp:listbox> is a server-side equivalent of using that <select> tag with the size attribute set to the maximum number of options possible. In fact the only difference with this control is the fact that it doesn't drop down, and that it is capable of multiple selections.

The <asp:listbox> has the following format:

```
<asp:listbox id="list1" runat="server" selection mode = "multiple">
  <asp:listitem>Madrid</asp:listitem >
  <asp:listitem >Oslo</asp:listitem >
  <asp:listitem >Lisbon</asp:listitem >
</asp:listbox>
```

There is one point of interest, however: the selectionmode attribute is used to determine whether you can select multiple or only single items from the listbox. By default, it is set to single, but you have the option to change it.

Let's take a look at a quick example, where we alter our previous example to use a listbox instead of a drop-down list control. We'll also alter it to allow multiple selections.

Try It Out – Using the <asp:listbox> Control

1. Enter the following code into your editor:

```
<script runat="server" language="C#">
    void Page_Load()
    {
  string msg = "You have selected: <br />";

    if (list1.Items[0].Selected) {
  msg = msg + list1.Items[0].Text + "<br />";
```

```
    }
          if (list1.Items[1].Selected) {
      msg = msg + list1.Items[1].Text + "<br />";
    }
          if (list1.Items[2].Selected) {
      msg = msg + list1.Items[2].Text + "<br />";
    }
      Message.Text = msg;
      }
  </script>
  <html>
    <head>
      <title>Drop Down List Example</title>
    </head>
    <body>
      <asp:label id="Message" runat="server"/>
      <br />
      <form runat="server">
      Which city do you wish to look at hotels for?<br /><br />
      <asp:listbox id="list1" runat="server" selectionmode="multiple">
        <asp:listitem>Madrid</asp:listitem>
        <asp:listitem>Oslo</asp:listitem>
        <asp:listitem>Lisbon</asp:listitem>
      </asp:listbox>
      <br /><br /><br /><br />
      <input type="Submit">
      </form>
    </body>
  </html>
```

2. Save this as `listpage2.aspx`.

3. Run this page in your browser, and use the *Ctrl*, or *shift* keys to select multiple choices:

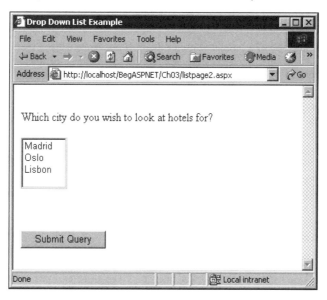

4. Click on Submit Query to see the following:

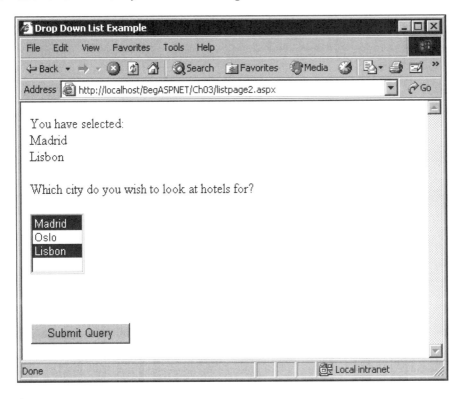

How It Works

The controls in this example have hardly changed from the previous `listpage.aspx` example. All we've done is add a `selectionmode` attribute to allow us to make multiple selections:

```
<asp:listbox id="list1" runat="server" selectionmode="multiple">
  <asp:listitem>Madrid</asp:listitem>
  <asp:listitem>Oslo</asp:listitem>
  <asp:listitem>Lisbon</asp:listitem>
</asp:listbox>
```

However, we've had to completely overhaul our ASP.NET code:

```
string msg = "You have selected: <br />";

  if (list1.Items[0].Selected) {
msg = msg + list1.Items[0].Text + "<br />";
}
    if (list1.Items[1].Selected) {
  msg = msg + list1.Items[1].Text + "<br />";
}
```

```
        if (list1.Items[2].Selected) {
    msg = msg + list1.Items[2].Text + "<br />";
    }
      Message.Text = msg;
```

In fact, we've introduced a whole new format to determine the options to display.

We use an `If` construct (we'll talk more about these in Chapter 6) to determine which items have been selected, and then use a **variable assignment** to create the display output. The first line in our code creates a `String` variable (again, we'll be looking at variables in depth very shortly). This simply declares a label 'msg' which refers to a portion in the computer's memory that we can use to hold a sequence of characters, or **string**. We set it up with a simple heading, and then add city names on the end, according to which list elements have been selected. Finally, we assign its final value (a long string of HTML) to the `Text` attribute of the `Message` label, so that it can be seen on the page.

That was a bit more complicated, wasn't it? Don't worry, it will become clearer once you've familiarized yourself with the topics in the following few chapters. For now, let's move on to some different types of control.

The `<asp:textbox>` Control

This server control is ASP.NET's version of the HTML textbox form control. In fact, it doubles up and also provides the functionality of the HTML `<textarea>` form control. Text areas are simply text boxes that feature multiple lines, thus allowing you to input larger quantities of text. The textbox control is also able to supply the functionality of an HTML form password control.

To be able to cover the remit of three HTML form controls, the `<asp:textbox>` control needs some extra attributes:

❑ textmode – specifies whether you want the control to have one line (this is the default, so we don't need to set it if we simply want one line), many lines (set it to `multiline`), or have a single line of masked content (set it to `password` if you want to conceal the text that's been entered).

❑ rows – specifies the number of rows you want the textbox to have and will only work if `textmode` is set to `multiple`.

❑ columns – specifies the number of columns you want the textbox to have. It will only work if `textmode` is set to `multiple`.

If you wish to provide any default text that appears in the control, you can either place it between the opening and closing tags:

```
<asp:textbox id="text1" runat="server">Default text here...</asp:textbox>
```

or set it in the `text` attribute:

```
<asp:textbox id="text1" runat="server" text="Default text here..."/>
```

113

Now we'll create a short example that uses the textbox control to ask for the name and address of the user, and a password as well. In HTML, this would require three different types of control: here we shall only use the one <asp:textbox> control.

Try It Out – Using the <asp:textbox> Control

1. Time to start your web page editor again and type in the following:

```
<script runat="server" language="C#">
  void Page_Load()
  {
    Message1.Text = "";
    Message2.Text = "";
    Message3.Text = "";

    if (text1.Text != "") {
      Message1.Text = "You have entered the following name: " +  text1.Text;
    }

    if (text2.Text != "") {
  Message2.Text = "You have entered the following address: " + text2.Text;
    }

    if (text3.Text != "") {
      Message3.Text = "You have entered the following password: " + text3.Text;
    }
  }
</script>
<html>
  <head>
    <title>Text Box Example</title>
  </head>
  <body>
    <asp:label id="Message1" runat="server" />
    <br />
    <asp:label id="Message2" runat="server" />
    <br />
    <asp:label id="Message3" runat="server" />
    <br />
    <form runat="server">
      Please enter your name:
      <asp:textbox id="text1" runat="server" />
      <br /><br />
      Please enter your address:
      <asp:textbox id="text2" runat="server" rows=5 textmode="multiline" />
      <br /><br />
      Please enter your chosen password:
      <asp:textbox id="text3" runat="server" textmode="password" />
      <br /><br />
      <input type="Submit">
    </form>
  </body>
</html>
```

2. Save this as textboxpage.aspx.

3. Open `textboxpage.aspx` in your browser, and type in some details:

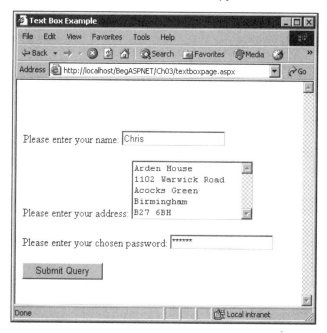

4. Click on Submit Query to see the results:

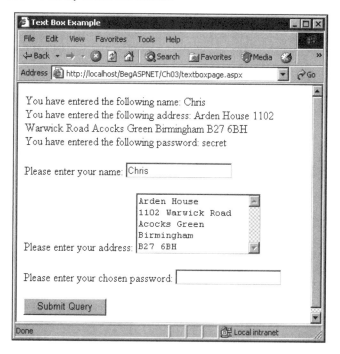

How It Works

Within the form, we have created three types of textbox control:

```
<asp:textbox id="text1" runat="server" />
<br /><br />
Please enter your address:
<asp:textbox id="text2" runat="server" rows=5 textmode="multiline" />
<br /><br />
Please enter your chosen password:
<asp:textbox id="text3" runat="server" textmode="password" />
```

The first texbox is identified as text1, and requires no other attributes other than id and runat. This is displayed as a single text field. The second control, text2, is a multiline textbox (which will render as a text area), and requires that we set the textmode attribute to multiline, so that we can set the number of rows we wish this textbox to have. Here, we have set it to five for the address. Lastly, we create a third control, text3, which we set to password with the textmode attribute. This, again, will display a single line text field, but any text typed into it is obscured by asterisks.

To display the results from three sets of controls, we have used three separate <asp:label> controls:

```
<asp:label id="Message1" runat="server" />
<br />
<asp:label id="Message2" runat="server" />
<br />
<asp:label id="Message3" runat="server" />
```

Each one of these is identified with a different id attribute. In this way, we can pass information from each of our three textboxes to a separate label control. The job of assigning text values to these three label controls falls to the ASP.NET code contained within <script> tags at the top of the page.

The code that assigns the values is very repetitive:

```
Message1.Text = "";
Message2.Text = "";
Message3.Text = "";

if (text1.Text != "") {
  Message1.Text = "You have entered the following name: " +  text1.Text;
}

if (text2.Text != "") {
Message2.Text = "You have entered the following address: " + text2.Text;
}

if (text3.Text != "") {
  Message3.Text = "You have entered the following password: " + text3.Text;
}
```

First we make sure blank values are assigned to each of the `<asp:label>` controls in the first three lines. This is because once the page has been posted back, it will display the old messages, unless we clear them.

Then for the first control `Message1`, we take the text information, and assign it to `Message1's` `text` attribute. This will display the name information. For the second control, we take the text information from the second textbox control, and assign it to the text attribute, and we do likewise for the third. Note that the line breaks from the multi-line control (second textbox control) won't display in the label on the result page. Next, we place each statement within an `if` statement. We will cover how they work in Chapter 6, but for the time being, just think of them being used to check each control individually and decide on whether to display a message depending on if the user has supplied some contents or not. So if you only entered information into the name field, only one message would be displayed. Go ahead, try it and see.

The *<asp:radiobutton>* and *<asp:radiobuttonlist>* Controls

In HTML, radio buttons are used when we need to make multiple sets of choices available, but we want the user to select only one of them. If they click on a second selection after making a first, the first selection is removed and replaced by the second. Radio buttons are implemented in HTML using the `<input>` tag, and setting the type attribute to `radio`. Every radio button on the page needs to have its own `<input type="radio">` tag. Each radio button within a particular group must have the same name attribute.

The `<asp:radiobutton>` and `<asp:radiobuttonlist>` controls work in a different way to their HTML forms equivalent. No longer do they necessarily exclude each other. In HTML radio buttons were assigned the same identifier using the `name` attribute, as below:

```
A<input name="radio1" type="radio">
B<input name="radio1" type="radio">
C<input name="radio1" type="radio">
```

This should ensure that only one radio button could be selected. However, the `<asp:radiobutton>` control actively forbids you from doing this. If you tried to set each radio button to have the same identifier with the `<asp:radiobutton>` control (remembering that HTML form controls use the `name` attribute, while HTML server controls use the `id` attribute), then you'd generate an error:

```
A<asp:radiobutton id="radio1" runat="server" />
B<asp:radiobutton id="radio1" runat="server" />
C<asp:radiobutton id="radio1" runat="server" />
```

Instead, you have to use the `<asp:radiobuttonlist>` control to get the functionality that you'd typically associate with radio buttons. The `<asp:radiobuttonlist>` works in the same way as listboxes, in that the `<asp:radiobuttonlist>` control contains a set of options that are set using the `<asp:listitem>` tag with one for each option:

```
<asp:radiobuttonlist id="radio1" runat="server">
  <asp:listitem id="option1" runat="server" value="A" />
  <asp:listitem id="option2" runat="server" value="B" />
  <asp:listitem id="option3" runat="server" value="C" />
</asp:radiobuttonlist>
```

This would look as follows:

The identifier for the whole control is set only in the id attribute of the <asp:radiobuttonlist> control, and it is this that is used to return the selected item to ASP.NET.

While you can't give the same id name to multiple radio buttons, RadioButton has a property called GroupName which, when set, will render a name attribute in the final HTML.

```
<asp:RadioButton id="RadioButton1" runat="server"
GroupName="MyGroup"></asp:RadioButton>
<asp:RadioButton id="RadioButton2" runat="server"
GroupName="MyGroup"></asp:RadioButton>
```

This will render the following HTML:

```
<input id="RadioButton1" type="radio" name="MyGroup"  value="RadioButton1" />
<input id="RadioButton2" type="radio" name="MyGroup"  value="RadioButton2" />
```

This will generate two mutually exclusive radio buttons. They have different IDs, but share the same name attribute.

We'll now create a quick example that uses a group of radio buttons to decide which destination a user has selected on an HTML form, and relays that information back to the user. We will only allow the user to select one destination.

Try It Out – Using the <asp:radiobutton> Control

1. Crank up your web page editor of choice and type in the following:

```
<script runat="server" language="C#">
  void Page_Load()
  {
    if (Page.IsPostBack)
    {
        Message.Text = "You have selected the following: " +
    radio1.SelectedItem.Value;
```

```
        }
    }
</script>
<html>
  <head>
    <title>Radio Button List Example</title>
  </head>
  <body>
    <asp:label id="Message" runat="server" />
    <br /><br />
    Which city do you wish to look at hotels for?
    <br /><br />
    <form runat="server">
      <asp:radiobuttonlist id="radio1" runat="server">
        <asp:listitem id="option1" runat="server" value="Madrid" />
        <asp:listitem id="option2" runat="server" value="Oslo" />
        <asp:listitem id="option3" runat="server" value="Lisbon" />
      </asp:radiobuttonlist>
      <br /><br />
      <input type="Submit">
    </form>
  </body>
</html>
```

2. Save this as `radiopage.aspx` and view it in your browser:

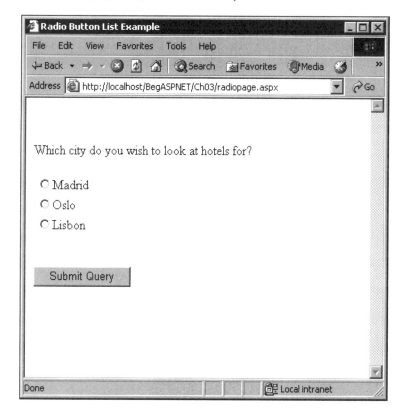

3. Select a button and click on Submit Query:

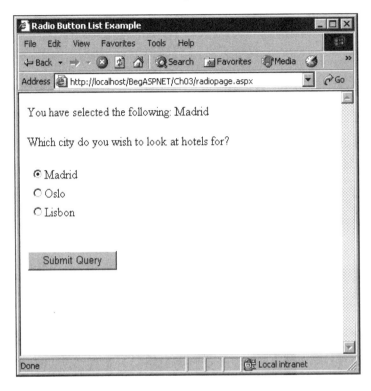

How It Works

The radiopage.aspx page has three radio buttons, for Madrid, Oslo, and Lisbon:

```
<asp:radiobuttonlist id="radio1" runat="server">
  <asp:listitem id="option1" runat="server" value="Madrid" />
  <asp:listitem id="option2" runat="server" value="Oslo" />
  <asp:listitem id="option3" runat="server" value="Lisbon" />
</asp:radiobuttonlist>
```

We have assigned each of the radio buttons their respective values, and used the
<asp:radiobuttonlist> control, to place them within the same group. We use the radio1
identifier to return them to the ASP.NET code.

In the ASP.NET code at the top of the page – delimited within the void Page_Load and curly braces – we have used the familiar three lines to return the information from the form:

```
if (Page.IsPostBack)
   {
      Message.Text = "You have selected the following: " +
   radio1.SelectedItem.Value;
   }
```

This is again used to display some plain text in the <asp:label> control, if there has been a selection made on the radio buttons. If a radio button is selected, then the message "You have selected the following: " is followed by the user's choice, which is returned by SelectedItem.Value. You should note that the line that begins Message.Text= doesn't end until the semi-colon on the second line. So in effect this is all one line. C# allows you to split lines like this, as it only considers a line to be complete when it reaches the semi-colon. This line assigns the Text attribute of the label control which is then displayed on the web form.

The <asp:checkbox> and <asp:checkboxlist> Controls

Checkboxes are similar to radio buttons, and in HTML, they were used to allow multiple choices from a group of buttons. With the <asp:checkboxlist> control it is possible to create them in groups, but unlike radio buttons, it isn't possible to restrict the user to selecting just one possible answer from a group of checkboxes: they can select as many as they like. The other fundamental difference between a checkbox and a radio button is that once you have selected a checkbox you are able to deselect it by clicking on it again.

We're not going to spend too long examining them, as most of the same principles that we followed in the <asp:radiobutton> and <asp:radiobuttonlist> examples apply.

A typical <asp:checkbox> looks like this:

```
<asp:checkbox id="check1" runat="server" />
```

If we want to use an array of checkboxes, we can contain them inside an <asp:checkboxlist> control. We need to set an id attribute for the <asp:checkboxlist> control itself, and create a <asp:listitem> control for each option inside the control:

```
<asp:checkboxlist id="check1" runat="server">
  <asp:listitem id="option1" runat="server" value="Madrid" />
  <asp:listitem id="option2" runat="server" value="Oslo" />
  <asp:listitem id="option3" runat="server" value="Lisbon" />
</asp:checkboxlist>
```

Checkboxes are typically used when you have single yes/no answers, or you wish the user to be able to make a multiple set of selections, and be able to deselect them as well.

In our next exercise, we're going to tweak our previous example, so that it uses our established holiday code to allow the user to select more than one option for a particular destination.

Try It Out – Using the <asp:checkbox> Control

1. Open up the `radiopage.aspx` and amend the code highlighted in gray, as follows:

```
<script runat="server" language="C#">
  void Page_Load()
  {
    string msg = "You have selected the following items:<br />";

    if (check1.Items[0].Selected) {
    msg = msg + check1.Items[0].Text + "<br />";
    }
    if (check1.Items[1].Selected) {
    msg = msg + check1.Items[1].Text + "<br />";
    }
    if (check1.Items[2].Selected) {
    msg = msg + check1.Items[2].Text + "<br />";
    }

    Message.Text = msg;
  }
</script>
<html>
<head>
  <title>Check Box List Example</title>
</head>
<body>
  <asp:label id="Message" runat="server" />
  <br /><br />
  Which city do you wish to look at hotels for?
  <br /><br />
  <form runat="server">
    <asp:checkboxlist id="check1" runat="server">
      <asp:listitem id="option1" runat="server" value="Madrid" />
      <asp:listitem id="option2" runat="server" value="Oslo" />
      <asp:listitem id="option3" runat="server" value="Lisbon" />
    </asp:checkboxlist>
    <br /><br />
    <input type="Submit">
  </form>
</body>
</html>
```

2. Save this as `checkpage.aspx`.

3. Open `checkpage.aspx` in your browser, and select more than one option:

4. Then click on Submit Query:

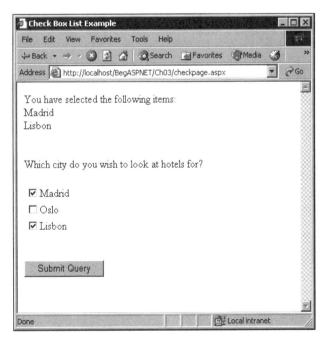

How It Works

Very little has changed with our control – all we've done is change the HTML control to an `<asp:checkboxlist>`, and then change the name of the control to reflect this:

```
<asp:checkboxlist id="check1" runat="server">
  <asp:listitem id="option1" runat="server" value="Madrid" />
  <asp:listitem id="option2" runat="server" value="Oslo" />
  <asp:listitem id="option3" runat="server" value="Lisbon" />
</asp:checkboxlist>
```

Our ASP.NET code is the same as that we used for the `listbox2.aspx` example, earlier on, except that here it refers to a checkbox rather than a listbox:

```
string msg = "You have selected the following items:<br />";

if (check1.Items[0].Selected) {
msg = msg + check1.Items[0].Text + "<br />";
}
if (check1.Items[1].Selected) {
msg = msg + check1.Items[1].Text + "<br />";
}
if (check1.Items[2].Selected) {
msg = msg + check1.Items[2].Text + "<br />";
}

Message.Text = msg;
```

As you can see, checkboxes work in a slightly different way from radio buttons. Each time you add a value, rather than replacing it, the value is added to the contents of `check1`. However, for all other intents and purposes, you use them in the same way.

> *This operation will become clearer once you're familiar with Chapters 4 and 6 in which we deal with Data and Control Structures respectively.*

One last point to note about checkboxes, though, is that you might want to treat each checkbox within a group as a separate entity, rather than have them all grouped together, in which case you could set all of them as separate `<asp:checkbox>` controls to reflect this:

```
<asp:checkbox id="check1" runat="server" Text="Madrid"/>
<asp:checkbox id="check2" runat="server" Text="Oslo"/>
<asp:checkbox id="check3" runat="server" Text ="Lisbon"/>
```

The `text` attribute here specifies the text that will appear next to the checkbox. The checkbox itself will not return a value. To find out whether it is checked or not we need to add some ASP.NET code to test if the `Checked` attribute is `true` or `false`: it will be `true` if the checkbox is checked.

Given that we've introduced a number of new concepts, in variables, we will stop here, as the subject of variables warrants a chapter in its own right. We've looked at the most basic server controls, and in order to make any more of them, we need to introduce new and more complex features.

Summary

This chapter has seen us dabble with ASP.NET code for the first time. While some of the examples might have seemed quite repetitive, it is necessary to be comfortable with how you go about handling all the different HTML server controls, as they will crop up frequently and we won't spend any time going back over how they work.

We introduced the ASP.NET server controls in preference to using the HTML form controls, and demonstrated that the server-side counterparts of many of the HTML form controls offer extra functionality over their client-side counterparts. In particular, we saw how we could use the <asp:label> control to display text and how we could use the other controls such as <asp:dropdownlist>, <asp:textbox>, and <asp:radiobutton> in place of HTML form controls.

In our next chapter, we will look at how we can store information within our ASP.NET pages, using variables.

Exercises

1. Explain the difference between an HTML form and a web form.

2. Explain the difference between <form> and <form runat="server"> and describe how each one is handled.

3. Personalize the following birthday message to the President by adding your own name and unique gift within the <script>...</script> blocks. You may want to save and run this code first to see what you're aiming for:

```
<script language="C#" runat="server">

</script>
<html>
<body>
  <h1>Happy Birthday</h1>
  <br /><br />
  <h1>Mr. President!!</h1>
<br /><br />
  I,
  <asp:label id="Message1" runat="server" text="Joe Bloggs,"/>
    wish you many happy returns. Enjoy the
  <asp:label id="Message2" runat="server" text="candy!"/>
</body>
</html>
```

4. Modify the example you just created to give the President a list of three birthday present choices to choose from. Use the <asp:checkbox> control to do this. Include a Submit button so the President knows which presents he has chosen.

Storing Information in C#

One of the most important concepts in any programming language is the ability to persist data from one command to another. Suppose we write some code that asks a user to input their name – how can we store this information long enough to use it? How do we store other types of data, such as numbers and dates? And how do we retrieve this information once stored? This can all be done using **variables**.

Variables are fundamental to programming – they enable us to assign a label to an area of memory in which we can store just about any type of information. A programming language lets you create variables, assign values to them, access their contents, and reuse those values in your code. It will enable you to perform mathematical functions, calculate new dates, manipulate text, count the length of sentences, and perform many other functions.

C# is a **strongly typed** language, which means that any variable at all will have a data type associated with it, such as a **string**, **int**, or **date**. This tells C# how to deal with the data so that numerical data will be treated as numbers, characters, letters, and words as text (even if they consist of numbers), and dates in such a way that they can be accessed as proper dates (and not just complicated long division sums such as: 5/10/2003).

In the course of this chapter, we'll be looking at each of the main data types available in C# and why you must assign each variable to a particular data type, together with the types of errors you might encounter if you don't. We'll look at some basic arithmetic operators and see how we can use them with variables, and we'll consider the most suitable data types for the kind of operation you wish to perform.

Then, we'll move on to the topic of structured data, by which means you can store your items of data in specific structures. In this chapter, we'll look at arrays, which are indexed collections of variables, and in the next, we'll introduce XML, a separate language that doesn't use variables, but provides us with another way to store structured information.

We'll look at:

- ❑ What a variable is
- ❑ Data types
- ❑ Performing simple calculations with data types
- ❑ Arrays

What is a Variable?

A **variable** is a label or reference to a container in memory that is allocated a name by the programmer. By label, we have in mind the name-tags you used to have on your clothing when you went to school. These containers in memory can be used to store pieces of information that will be used in the program. Think of variables as you might think of boxes. They're simply repositories for information that you wish to store. The variable doesn't actually contain the information, but shows you where the information can be found. However, it will look for all intents and purpose as though the variable does store the information.

For example, here are two variables – they contain a string of text and a numerical value respectively:

```
string CapitalCityOfUK;
int NumberOfStates;

CapitalCityOfUK = "London";
NumberOfStates = 50;
```

Any variable is empty until you put information into it (although the memory space is reserved while the code runs). You can then look at the information inside the variable, get the information out, or replace the information with new data. In fact, variables are essential for storing data in any computer language; C# is no exception!

Declaration

Notice that before we assigned values to each of our variables, we entered a corresponding line for each of them. These lines declare what **type** the variable is. As we hinted in our introduction, C# needs data types explicitly defining so that it knows how to deal with the contents of the variable. We define the different data types using the process of **declaration**.

Declarations are an important fact of life in programming, and in ASP.NET you should take care to declare all your variables, whether using C#, VB.NET, or JScript.NET. All variables should be declared **before** they are used within a program or web page, otherwise your program will generate an error.

In C#, a variable declaration is made by placing the name of the data type, followed by the name of the variable, separated by at least one character of white space. What this does is set aside the name, and appropriate space, for the variable in memory. Until the variable is assigned a value, it contains **nothing** (bear in mind that zero is a value, so it won't contain zero or even a blank space).

For example, the first line here declares a variable as a string type with the name strCarType; the second line assigns a string value to that variable:

```
string strCarType;
strCarType = "Buick";
```

It's also possible to declare a variable, and assign a value to it, in one line:

```
string strCarType = "Buick";
```

Also, you must note that C# is case sensitive, so the variable named `strCarType` is a different variable from `strcartype`. Also, the keywords themselves for the declarations are case sensitive too, so make sure that you type `string` and not `String`, otherwise you might find your code refusing to work.

For the time being, in this chapter we're going to stick to declaring and assigning a value as two different operations, and perform them on two lines. In later chapters, once you're happy with this, you'll see us moving to one line.

Lastly, it's also possible to declare several variables all of the same type on the same line:

```
string strCarType1, strCarType2, strCarType3;
strCarType1 = "Buick";
strCarType2 = "Cadillac";
strCarType3 = "Pontiac";
```

You can then assign each of the variables values, as we have done.

Lastly, you can go all the way and declare and assign variables of the same type on one line:

```
string strCarType1="Buick", strCarType2="Cadillac", strCarType3="Pontiac";
```

Here each variable assignment is separate by a comma, and the last one is punctuated by a semi-colon, as are all lines in C#.

Now let's put our knowledge of variable declaration and assignment to use, and look at an example. We'll take the variables we introduced at the beginning of the chapter and assign them values, then display those values within separate `<asp:label>` controls.

Try It Out – Using Variables

1. Open your web page editor and type in the following:

```
<script language="C#" runat="server">
void Page_Load()
  {
  string CapitalCityOfUK;
  int NumberOfStates;

  CapitalCityOfUK = "London";
  NumberOfStates = 50;

  Display1.Text = CapitalCityOfUK;
  Display2.Text = NumberOfStates.ToString();
  }
```

```
</script>

<html>
<head>
<title>Creating Variables Example</title>
</head>
<body>
  The contents of CapitalCityOfUk is:
  <asp:label id="Display1" runat="server" />
  <br>The contents of NumberOfStates is:
  <asp:label id="Display2" runat="server" />
</body>
</html>
```

2. Save this as `C:\BegASPNET\Ch04\variable.aspx`.

3. Open `variable.aspx` in your browser and view it; it will look something like this:

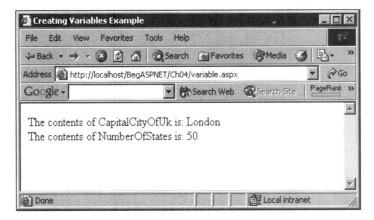

4. Now go back to the example and add the following line:

```
...
void Page_Load()
  {
  string CapitalCityOfUK;
  int NumberOfStates;

  NumberOfDaysInJuly = 31;

  Display1.text = CapitalCityOfUK;
...
```

5. Save this as `C:\BEGASPNET\Ch04\variable2.aspx` and run the example again:

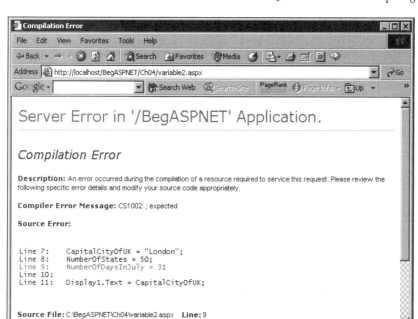

As you can see, variables cannot simply appear within your script/code – they must first be explicitly declared and then assigned. Because the variable `NumberOfDaysInJuly` hasn't been declared, an error has been generated by it.

How It Works

We've separated the code into different stages. The first section declares each of the variables we wish to use in the example:

```
string CapitalCityOfUK;
int NumberOfStates;
```

We want to use text in the `CapitalCityOfUK` variable, so we declare it as a `string`, we wish to convey numerical information in the `NumberOfStates` variable, so we declare it as an `int`.

In the next section, having declared the variables, we are now free to assign values to each:

```
CapitalCityOfUK = "London";
NumberOfStates = 50;
```

We assign the value of "London" to the CapitalCityOfUK variable. We've surrounded the value with quotes to let C# know that we are supplying a piece of text to the variable. If we wished to supply a value to a purely numerical variable, we would remove the quotation marks. This is in fact what we've done with the second variable.

In the last section, we've created two <asp:label> controls called Display1 and Display2. We then set these controls' Text values to the contents of our two variables:

```
Display1.Text = CapitalCityOfUK;
Display2.Text = NumberOfStates;
```

Our web form duly displays the contents of our variables. You might be wondering what stops the three controls from supplying the literal text CapitalCityOfUK and NumberOfStates. They're not displayed, because they're not contained in quotation marks. Anything inside quotation marks is interpreted as text. Anything not contained in them is treated as a variable, numeric value, or object.

We then went on to amend our example to add another line:

```
NumberOfDaysInJuly = 31;
```

This line looks perfectly OK, but it caused an error nevertheless – why has it done this? If we look at the line, it sets a variable called NumberOfDaysInJuly to the value 31. The problem is that we haven't declared this variable. We need to add a separate line before we used the variable in this way:

```
int NumberOfDaysInJuly;
```

If we had done this then we would have been free to use it, and the error would not have occurred.

Now we've seen just how important data types are in our ASP.NET web forms. However, we haven't discussed what the possible data types are and when you should use them. Let's look at this now.

Data Types

There are many data types in C#, which can be subdivided into two main categories: **value types** (also known as simple types) and **reference types**. The fundamental difference between the two is where and how they are stored in memory. To put it simply, there are two distinct areas of memory where variable data is stored, the **stack** and the **heap**. Space does not permit me to explain what these are and how they work, but, very briefly, the stack is used to store variable data of fixed length, whereas the heap is used to store data whose size and length can only be determined at run time and which are subject to change. For a variable on the heap, a *reference* to that data is stored on the stack. Such variables are known as reference types. By contrast, those stored on the stack are value types.

The table below lists the various categories of types that C# offers, according to whether they are value or reference types. Many of these are further discussed in this chapter, though the others are more fully described as we progress through this book:

Value Types	Reference Types
Numeric	Strings
Character	Arrays
Boolean	Classes
Structures	Interfaces
Enumerations	Objects

Numeric Types

Common numeric data types are all simple (value) types, which means that they are stored on the stack, and the amount of memory that they occupy is allocated during compilation.

Numeric types are of three types: integers, floating-point values, and decimal values. You can assign almost any number to one of these variable types providing the value does not exceed the predefined limits for the type. For whole numbers, you can use any of the three kinds of type; for fractional values you must use floating-point and decimal types. Here are some examples:

```
int IntegerNumber1;
decimal DecimalNumber2;
float FloatingPointNumber3;

IntegerNumber1 = 76;
DecimalNumber2 = -2.5356;
FloatingPointNumber3 = 3.14159;
```

This table contains a full list of predefined integer data types in C#:

Name	Description	Range	Suffix
sbyte	8-bit signed integer	-128 to 127	
short	16-bit signed integer	-32,768 to 32,767	
int	32-bit signed integer	-2,147,483,648 to 2,147,483,647	
long	64-bit signed integer	-9,223,372,036,854,775, 808 to 223,372,036,854,775,807	L or l
byte	8-bit unsigned integer	0 to 255	

Table continued on following page

Name	Description	Range	Suffix
ushort	16-bit unsigned integer	0 to 65,535	
uint	32-bit unsigned integer	0 to 4,294,967,295	U or u
ulong	64-bit unsigned integer	0 to 18,446,744,073,709,551,615	UL or LU, or any combination of cases

I'll explain what the Suffix column is about in just a moment.

There are two predefined floating point types in C#, as follows:

Name	Description	Significant Figures	Range (approximate)	Suffix
float	32-bit single-precision floating-point	7	$\pm 1.5 \times 10^{-45}$ to $\pm 3.4 \times 10^{38}$	F or f
double	64-bit double-precision floating-point	15/16	$\pm 5.0 \times 10^{-324}$ to $\pm 1.7 \times 10^{308}$	D or d

Finally the special high-precision decimal data type:

Name	Description	Significant Figures	Range (approximate)	Suffix
decimal	128-bit high precision decimal notation	28	$\pm 1.0 \times 10^{28}$ to $\pm 7.9 \times 10^{28}$	M or m

Whereas the function and range of each of the integer and floating-point data types can be determined from the tables, the decimal type does warrant some extra explanation.

The decimal type accepts numbers with up to twenty-eight decimal places. With zero decimal places, it can support numbers with a largest possible value of ± 79,228,162,514,264,337,593,543,950,335.

Suffixes

In each of the above tables, some data types have extra information in the Suffix column. C# allows you to add a letter or a combination of letters to the end of the number to tell C# what type the number actually is. The reason for this is that there is a default integer data type (int) and a default floating-point/decimal data type (double) and if there is any ambiguity as to what type the numerical value is, C# will interpret it as one of these two. Therefore if you want to specify explicitly that a value is, say, a float or a decimal, you must add the suffix to the number when it is assigned to the variable. Therefore the above variable declarations could be rewritten as:

```
int IntegerNumber1;
decimal DecimalNumber2;
float FloatingPointNumber3;

IntegerNumber1 = 76;
DecimalNumber2 = -2.5356m;
FloatingPointNumber3 = 3.14159f;
```

Character Data Types

There are just two main data types for storing text. The char type stores one character of text coded as a number. It is a fixed length data type (16-bits or two bytes) and thus is a value type.

By contrast, the string data type is able to hold any length of text from no characters at all (that is, an empty string) to many thousands of characters. Because the length is variable, it cannot be stored on the stack (as the stack is of a fixed size and could easily be filled up by a very large string). The string type is a reference type which means that only a reference to the string is stored on the stack, and the string itself is stored on the heap.

> **C# strings are enclosed in double quotes whereas char values are enclosed in single quotes. This is important, as you will receive an error message if you try to assign to a string char with the wrong type of quotes.**

Because the string type is more commonly used than char, we'll discuss it first.

The string Type

The string type will identify everything you store in it as text, even if you supply it with a mixture of text and numerical data, numerical data alone, or even date information. For example, the following code creates a string variable called CarType, with the value "Buick", a string variable called CarEngineSize, with the value "2.0", and a string variable called DatePurchased, with the value "July 4, 1999":

```
string CarType;
string CarEngineSize;
string DatePurchased;

CarType = "Buick";
CarEngineSize = "2.0";
DatePurchased = " July 4, 1999";
```

> Note that when you declare **string CarType;**, you are not instantiating a string object on the heap; rather, you are creating an object reference on the stack that does not yet refer to a **string** object.

As mentioned earlier, string values are enclosed in double quotation marks, so they can be differentiated visually from numerical values and other pieces of code. Also, note that a string containing no data, an empty string, is denoted by two double quotes with nothing in between:

```
string CarType = "";
```

Note that you can't perform mathematical functions on strings, even if their contents are purely numerical. Hence, if you try to add the two strings "12" and "14" together, as shown in the following example, you won't get the result "26" that you might have anticipated, but "1412" instead (we get 1412 here because we add Number2 to Number1 – if we added Number1 to Number2, we'd get 1214):

```
string Number1;
string Number2;
string Number3;

Number1 = "12";
Number2 = "14";
Number3 = Number2 + Number1;
```

This is because the string variable can only hold a textual representation of the number, rather than a numerical representation of it. In this last line of code we do not carry out a calculation on the two numbers, but we append the value of the Number1 text variable to the end of the Number2 text variable to create a longer string of text. This process is called **concatenation**, which we will use a lot in ASP.NET code. We shall explain the process of concatenation in more detail later in this chapter.

As a basic rule of thumb, strings are normally used for storing words or alphanumeric information – numeric information is normally stored in the appropriate numeric types. The exceptions to this rule would be any number that you can be certain that you will not perform math with, for example telephone numbers and social security numbers, which are usually better stored as strings. Also, when working with HTML or ASP.NET form data, the telephone numbers and social security numbers will always take the form of a string, and so a knowledge of how to manipulate them effectively is essential.

Note that the C# string type (small s) is simply an alias for the .NET String (capital S) class, which is part of the standard set of .NET base classes. So you can use any of these three equivalent syntaxes:

```
string myName = "Chris";

String myName = "Chris";

System.String myName = "Chris";
```

In this book, we shall be using the first of these throughout.

The char Type

The char data type is a bit of a strange one, because it stores text as a number. By this, we mean you place a single character in a variable, defined as a char, and it is stored as a 16-bit number between 0 and 65,535 representing a Unicode character.

> *Unicode is an international standard code for representing characters numerically that overcomes the problems of different encoding systems. It is language-, platform-, and program-independent. More information about Unicode can be obtained from **www.unicode.org**.*

If you were to display the contents of a char variable, you'd still see a text character, despite the manner in which it is stored. A variable using the char data type could be declared as follows – note that char data is contained within single quotes and not double quotes:

```
char Letter;
Letter = 'C';    // This would be stored as 67 (or 43 in hexadecimal)
```

If you tried to assign a character to a char variable using double quotes, you would get an error:

```
Letter = "C";    // Wrong
```

C# interprets "C" as a string, which it is, and will try to assign it to the char variable, which it cannot do.

Escape Sequences

Any character data can be stored in string and char variables, not just letters and numbers (that is character literals). An important set of characters that can be and often are contained within strings and chars are the non-printing characters such as the tab, the line feed, and the carriage return. The way of referring to and using these characters in code is to use escape sequences, which are two character combinations that are reinterpreted by C# as non-printing characters. In all cases, the first of these two characters is the backslash (\). A table containing these escape sequences is shown here:

Escape Sequence	Character
\'	Single quote
\"	Double quote
\\	Backslash
\0	Null
\a	Alert
\b	Backspace
\f	Form feed

Table continued on following page

Escape Sequence	Character
\n	Newline
\r	Carriage return
\t	Tab character
\v	Vertical tab

Note that, as the backslash is used to mark an escape sequence, a special sequence is used to represent the backslash character itself: \\. This sequence will often be used when hard-coding Windows system paths such as:

```
"C:\\BEGASPNET\\Ch04\\thisexample.aspx"
```

If you should inadvertently use single backslashes here in your string, then more than likely your code will fail, because when C# sees a \ character it always looks at the following character to determine what the escape sequence is and what character to replace it with. As only a few sequences are recognized, C# will not be able to handle the following string:

```
"C:\BEGASPNET\ch04\myfile.aspx"
```

There is however a smart way round this. If the string is prefixed with the @ character, then the entire string is interpreted as you would expect, the \ character remains a \ character and not a marker for an escape sequence:

```
@"C:\BEGASPNET\ch04\myfile.aspx"
```

This construct comes in useful if you cut and paste a system path into your code as it saves you the bother of having to double up all your backslashes, and the code is also tidier.

Another use for escape sequences is when you need to include characters that are not part of the standard character set or that cannot be typed in at the keyboard. Such characters can be referred to by their Unicode values and are represented by the following syntax:

```
\uXXXX
```

or

```
\UXXXX
```

Where XXXX are four hexadecimal numbers which uniquely define the character you want. Therefore, instead of assigning the character 'A' like this:

```
char c = 'A';
```

you can use the corresponding Unicode value for the letter A which is 0x0041:

```
char c = '\u0041';
```

Eight-digit Unicode escape codes are also recognized; they have the syntax \uXXXXXXXX or \UXXXXXXXX.

Boolean Type

A Boolean variable can only have two possible values: True or False. In C#, they are declared using the `bool` keyword and take the values of `true` and `false`, which are also keywords and therefore must always be written in lower case:

```
bool IsCSharpProgrammer = true;
bool DoesEatMeat = false;
```

However C#'s type system is very strict and will not allow you to interpret a `bool` as anything other than `true` or `false`. There is no means of reinterpreting a Boolean value as, say, 1 for `true` and 0 for `false` and, should you want to do this, you would have to use one of the integer types.

I won't say much more on the `bool` type in this chapter, as it is covered in Chapter 6, when used in conjunction with logical operators and conditional or looping operations.

The Object Type

In the table of types a few pages back, you may have noticed the `object` type in the reference type list. This is a generic type that has some very important uses in C#, though we won't see it until we look at event handling in Chapter 7. The `object` type is the base type for all data types in C# (its full name being `System.Object`), which means that it can represent any data, the identity of which can only be determined at run-time, and for that reason it is a reference type. C# has its own alias for this type and that is `object`, spelt with a small o.

Handling Dates

Handling dates is something that you will have to get to grips with as you start to program ASP.NET using C#, and for this reason we're introducing the topic at this point in our discussion. In C#, a date is stored in the `DateTime` data type which is not native to C#, but which is defined in the .NET Framework `System` namespace.

A `DateTime` variable is declared in the same way as any of C#'s native data types:

```
DateTime date;
```

However, assigning a value to the date-time variable is not a matter of supplying the date as a string. The following code will not work:

```
date = "09/19/2001";   // Will not work
```

For one thing, a `DateTime` is not stored as a string; in fact it is stored as an integer. However we cannot assign a simple integer to it:

```
date = 100;            // Will not work either
```

For one thing, we cannot directly convert an integer to a `DateTime` value, and even if we could, we would not know which integer represents the correct date. To assign a recognizable date to a `DateTime` variable we have to convert it explicitly using this syntax:

```
date = Convert.ToDateTime("09/19/2001");
```

The date here is a string formatted as mm/dd/yyyy. Note that dates are formatted differently for different part of the world, so if your Regional Settings (as set in the Windows Control Panel) specify that your dates should be in the form dd/mm/yyyy, for example, then the above conversion could fail, as the function might be attempting to create a date with a 19th month. Worse still, it could produce a valid date with month and day values swapped round. To remedy this, the above function exists in several forms, one of which takes a string as above, but another takes the day, the month, and the year as three separate parameters. We will come back to this issue as we progress through the book, as it is very important. We will also explain how to deal with situations where the parameter or parameters passed to this function cannot be converted to a date.

We have to convert it back to a string in order to be able to display it in a web page. To do this we use the `ToString()` syntax we saw earlier:

```
DisplayDate.Text = date.ToString();
```

Where `DisplayDate` refers to a hypothetical ASP.NET label control into which we store the date value.

We'll have a lot more to say on converting between types later in this chapter.

Naming Variables

As we go on, we'll look at the different types of variables, how to assign values to them, and how to use them in expressions. We'll also talk about the kinds of names you should give your variables. For example, while the variable names we've used above reflect their contents in a reasonably self-explanatory way, the meanings of the variables in the following expressions are less obvious:

```
int a;
bool varBoolean;

a = 1*10+73;
varBoolean = true;
```

They're not particularly helpful, are they? It's really up to you to find a suitable name for variables when you create them. Ideally, you should find a name that is meaningful to someone else who subsequently reads your code (especially if that someone turns out to be you, six months later). At the same time, excessively long variable names are unwieldy and easy to mistype, so you should avoid these too. If the variable names are chosen well, then the thinking behind the apparent gobbledygook in expressions like those above will become clearer. It's a good idea to make variable names descriptive even if this means making them longer. Here are some quick tips:

- ❑ `DateStart` and `DateEnd` are better than `StartDate` and `EndDate`, as these two related methods will then come next to each other in an alphabetically sorted search

- ❑ Variables like `Price`, `Name`, and `Number` are confusing because there are usually of these, such as `NameFirst`, `NameLast`, `NameSpouse`, `PriceBuyMSShares`, or `PriceSellMSShares`

- ❑ Variable names that coincide with data types aren't allowed, so:
  `int int;` would cause an error

- ❑ Avoid confusing abbreviations, such as `datFDOM` for first day of month – the acronym 'FDOM' could stand for anything

- ❑ Never use the same variable name for two different variables, no matter how sure you are that they will not conflict

You might want to check out the **Naming Guidelines in the Framework General Reference** for further tips. In most languages, the name of a variable can be almost anything you choose, but there are usually a few restrictions:

- ❑ There are usually restrictions on which characters you can use in your variable names. In C#, there are the restrictions that all variable names must begin with a letter and must not contain an embedded period/fullstop or a space. In fact you're better off avoiding symbols altogether, other than underscores, to keep your code readable and to guarantee it will work as intended. So variable names such as `.NETObject` and `Number+Number` would not be acceptable.

- ❑ Case sensitivity is another important issue. Languages such as C# or JScript.NET are both case sensitive and will interpret `counter` and `COUNTER` as two entirely different variables. For this reason, you really shouldn't create two different variables with the same name, only differentiated by case in C# or Jscript. On the other hand the VB.NET language is case-insensitive, which means that it is possible to use upper- and lower-case characters to refer to exactly the same variable. For example, VB .NET will interpret `counter` and `COUNTER` as the same variable. Even in VB.NET though you should always try to refer to variables by their exact name, taking into account case.

We'll look at case issues in a little more detail.

Case Issues

C# is a case-sensitive language so you should decide on how the casing of your variable names should be handled and then stick to this convention throughout your project. Here are some recommendations:

1. **Pascal case** for publicly accessible variables: that is, those which can be directly accessible to ASP.NET and other code. Pascal case is a convention where names consist of one or more concatenated words, each of which starts with a capital letter with all other letters in lower case. We have seen some of these already:

```
DateStart, DateEnd, PriceBuy, PriceSell, IsCSharpProgrammer, DoesEatMeat
```

2. **Camel case** for variables that can only be accessed within C# code. Camel case is the same as Pascal case except that the initial letter of the variable is lower case:

```
dateStart, dateEnd, priceBuy, priceSell, isCSharpProgrammer, doesEatMeat
```

The reasons behind these two recommendations have to do with .NET code written in C# being potentially accessible from clients written in Visual Basic .NET or another languages where casing is not important. In C#, variables such as `DateStart` and `dateStart` are different and, if both were generally available to Visual Basic .NET clients, then there could be major problems when running your code. Also because the two variables are so similar they can effectively refer to the same data. We'll see this in action when we discuss properties later on in this book.

3. Though you can use the underscore character to separate each word in a multi-word variable name such as `my_long_variable_name`, this is not recommended. Neither is the use of names consisting only of capitalized letters. However, this is a matter of personal preference and you will regularly see them used.

4. Though you cannot use C# keywords (which start with a small letter) as variable names, you can use their initially capitalized equivalents, such as `Int`, `Double`, and `Decimal`. However this practice is not recommended. In Visual Basic .NET, many of these words are keywords in their own right and Visual Basic .NET clients using your code would run into problems if you employ these as variable names in C#. Indeed, you should not use any keyword in any of the languages supported by .NET as variable names, regardless of capitalization. For a more details of all keywords to avoid, see the .NET Framework documentation.

Hungarian Notation

Naming conventions aren't compulsory, and can't be enforced, and generally it's up to the individual programmer which convention to apply. An alternative to Pascal and camel casing in known as **Hungarian notation**, which is very common in Visual Basic code and in any code that is ported from VB or Visual Basic .NET. Here a prefix denoting the type of the variable (or control) is added to the variable name itself:

```
string strName;
int intCount;
```

The principle behind this notation is that it is often useful, or essential, to be able to track the type of a variable throughout your code, especially when converting between types, and incorporating the type into the variable name itself is a good way to achieve this. However, debugging tools are becoming more and more widely used, and they keep track of each of the variables and their types themselves. As a result, Hungarian notation is not as important as it once was. However, it is still popular among programmers, and can be retained when naming Web form controls, as we shall see. In this section of the book we shall be using it for many of our variable names. These are the prefixes we shall be using:

Data Type	Prefix	Example
bool	bln	blnMember
byte	byt	bytByte
char	chr	chrChar
DateTime	dat	datToday
double	dbl	dblDouble
decimal	dec	decDecimal
float	flt	fltRate
int	int	intSalary
long	lng	lngLong
short	sho	shoShort
string	str	strTextBox

In keeping with just about everything else in life, there's also a different version of this form, called **short Hungarian notation**, which is common within Microsoft, and recommended in the MSDN .NET documentation. You can find a copy of this alternative version of the convention at:

```
http://msdn.microsoft.com/library/default.asp?url=/library/en-
us/vbcn7/html/vbconProgrammingGuidelinesOverview.asp.
```

As the longer version is more descriptive, we'll stick to using that for the time being. However, ultimately the choice of naming convention is a decision for the programmer, and every option is fine, as long as it is used consistently.

Operators

Of course, variables aren't of much use unless you can manipulate them in some way. To manipulate them, typically you'd use **operators**. An operator is a symbol that carries out a predefined operation on the operands and generates a result. If X=1+2, then X is a variable, = and + are operators, and, 1 and 2, are operands. We have already seen one or two examples of basic data manipulation using operators in this chapter, but in this section, we'll introduce the concepts more formally.

Assignment Operator

The familiar 'equals' sign (=) is probably the most common operator in computing. You've already seen it used several times to **assign** values to our variables. The variable **name** goes on the left; the variable **value** goes on the right:

```
Number1 = 2;
```

In C#, expressions are evaluated from right to left, so in the code above, the integer 2 is passed to the variable called `Number1`. You can also carry out calculations within such assignments, in which case, the expressions must be on the right-hand side of the = sign, and the final value of the expression is passed to the variable:

```
Number1 = 2 + 3;
```

A variable can also be part of the expression, including the variable on the left-hand side of the equals sign:

```
Number1 = Number1 + 3;
```

What this means is: take whatever the old value of `Number1` is, add 3 to it, and then reassign it to the `Number1` variable.

In C#, this last operation can be achieved using a more succinct syntax. The following two lines are equivalent:

```
Number1 = Number1 + 3;
```

```
Number1 += 3;
```

Where += means take the value to the left, add the value of the expression on the right and assign the result as the new value of the variable to the left. There is a similar syntax for doing other mathematical operations such as subtraction and multiplication (-=, *=, and so on).

There is an even simpler syntax when you want to add just 1 to the variable:

```
Number1++;
```

This means take the value to the left and add one to it. There is an equivalent syntax for subtracting 1:

```
Number1--;
```

Arithmetic Operations

The arithmetic operations available in C# are:

Addition	+	Division	/
Subtraction	–	Remainder/modulus	%
Multiplication	*	Negation	–

All the above operators, except one, are known as binary operators as they each require two operands:

```
Number1 = 10 + 3;
Number1 = 10 - 3;
// and so on.
```

The exception is the operator marked "Negation" which only takes one operand and is known as a unary operator:

```
NegNumber1 = -3;
```

You can also use parentheses to influence the order in which a calculation is performed. For example, in the following code we divide the variable intNumber2 by 6 and add the result to the variable intNumber1:

```
int intNumber1 = 14;
int intNumber2 = 18;
int intNumber3 = intNumber1 + (intNumber2/6);
```

First, the parentheses are evaluated: intNumber2 is divided by 6 and yields the result 3. This is added to the value of intNumber1, and the result of this (17) is assigned to the variable intNumber3.

Adding parentheses is a good idea to make your code more readable, even when parentheses may not be technically required for the evaluation to occur correctly, as in the above case (remove the brackets and you will see). This is because C# automatically evaluates the division step before the addition step. You can reverse this order by wrapping the addition step in parentheses:

```
int intNumber3 = (intNumber1 + intNumber2) /6;
```

Operator Precedence

All the operators discussed in this section are thus evaluated in this order:

Evaluated First	++, --, unary -
	*, /, %
	+, -
Evaluated Last	= ,+=, -=, *=, etc.

There are many other operators, and we'll discuss these in the coming chapters. However, let's have a go at a quick example that performs a simple tax calculation. To do this we need to create three variables, one for earnings, one for the tax percentage, and one for the total. We're going to deduct the earnings by whatever percentage the tax rate is set to, and display the output in our old friend the `<asp:label>` control.

Try It Out – Performing a Calculation on an ASP.NET page

1. Type in the following code into your web page editor:

```
<script Language="c#" runat="server">
  void Page_Load()
  {
    double dblEarn = 150;
    double dblTax = 23;
    double dblTotal = dblEarn - ((dblEarn/100)*dblTax);
    Display1.Text = dblTotal.ToString();
  }
</script>

<html>
<head>
  <title>Declaring Variables</title>
</head>
<body>
  Your total earnings after tax are $
  <asp:label id="Display1" runat="server" />
</body>
</html>
```

2. Save this as `C:\BegASPNET\Ch04\tax.aspx`.

3. View this in your browser:

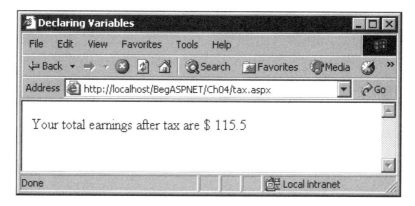

How It Works

There are only four lines of ASP.NET code in this program. The first two declare two variables, `dblEarn` for the earnings, and `dblTax` for the tax rate, and assign them values of `150` and `23` respectively:

```
double dblEarn = 150;
double dblTax = 23;
```

The third line is where the tax calculation takes place. To get our percentage, we first have to calculate what 23% of the earnings are: this is done by dividing the earnings by 100 and multiplying the result by the tax rate. Parentheses are used to indicate the order of calculation within the expression, though this is really only for the sake of readability as divisions and multiplications are carried out before subtractions:

```
double dblTotal = dblEarn - ((dblEarn/100)*dblTax);
```

The result of the calculation is stored in the variable `dblTotal` of type `double`. Finally the result is converted to a string and assigned to the `Text` property of the `<asp:label>` control called `Display1`:

```
Display1.Text = dblTotal.ToString();
```

You could calculate tax deductions for any percentage rate, and any earnings, by altering the values of `dblEarn` and `dblTax`.

Concatenating Strings

It makes sense to add integers together, using expressions such as 2 + 3, or intNumber1 + intNumber2 (as we showed above), but what happens if you wish to 'add' strings together? It doesn't make much sense to add them in the arithmetic sense – "Beans" plus "Rice" doesn't have a tangible meaning. However, C# allows us to 'add' strings together in a different sense using a process known as **concatenation**.

When two strings are concatenated, the second string is attached to the end of the first string, creating a new one. In order to concatenate two strings we use the + operator. Let's run through a few examples:

We can concatenate the strings "Helter" and "Skelter", as follows:

```
string strConcatenate = "Helter" + "Skelter";
```

Here, the result of the concatenation is the string "HelterSkelter", which will be assigned to the strConcatenate variable. You can also concatenate a number of strings within the same expression. Here, we'll concatenate three strings, one of which is a space (which is also a string, since a space is a character):

```
string strConcatenate = "Helter" + " " + "Skelter";
```

Now, strConcatenate will contain the string "Helter Skelter". You can concatenate as many string variables as you like:

```
string strFirst, strExclamationLine;

strFirst = "Never ";
strExclamationLine = strFirst + strFirst + strFirst + strFirst;
```

Then strExclamationLine will contain the line "Never Never Never Never ".

Following on from this, you can build strings using the += operator. This has a parallel meaning to that of the corresponding arithmetic operation, that is: take the value of the string on the left and append the string on the right and assign the result to the variable on the left:

```
string strFirst, strExclamationLine;

strFirst = "Never ";
strExclamationLine = strFirst;
strExclamationLine += strFirst;
strExclamationLine += strFirst;
strExclamationLine += strFirst;
strExclamationLine += "No Way";
```

strExclamationLine will then contain "Never Never Never Never No Way".

There are no other operators that you can apply to strings. Thus trying something like this is causes an error:

```
strExclamationLine = "Never Never";
strExclamationLine = strExclamationLine - "Never";   // Impossible

strExclamationLine -= "Never";                       // Also impossible
```

However there are methods of removing fragments from strings, which we'll come across later on.

Converting Between Data Types

Once a variable of a certain type is declared, you will usually want its value to be of that type for the duration of a program. For example if your interest rate is of type `float` with an initial value of 15.5, and you want to change it at some point, it is sensible for the new value to also be a `float`. You don't really want to turn it into an integer, because then you would have to drop the .5 (for an integer, by its very nature, cannot have a decimal point), and this would seriously affect the accuracy of any calculations you would make.

However, there are circumstances where conversion between types is not just advisable but essential. If you have two integers and you try to divide them, you do not want the result to be an integer as it is probable that the result would be inaccurate due to the necessity to discard all fractional data. To illustrate look at this:

```
int Number1 = 6;
int Number2 = 5;
int Number3 = Number1 / Number2;
```

What is the value of `Number3` here? It is `1`. We divided the two numbers, which amounts to `1.2`, that is certain, but the value `1.2` cannot fit into an `int` so C# has to round the number down to allow it to fit, and the result of this is that we have an inaccurate value for `Number3`.

This section will show you the various mechanisms by which C# enables you to divide two integers and get the result you expect. Here we will discuss ways of converting between all the available data types and will cover two methods already briefly explained earlier: the `ToString()` function and the various `Convert.ToXXX()` functions.

Implicit Conversion

First, however, there are certain data type conversions that require no extra work from you. Having said that, C# is very strict in what types of conversion it will process and generally speaking it will allow the conversion of types only if there is no chance at all of any data being lost as a result of the operation. To explain this consider the following:

```
int intNumber = 1000;
long lngNumber;
lngNumber = intNumber;
```

This will work because a `long` is a 64-bit signed integer and an `int` is a 32-bit signed integer, whose range lies completely within the range of a `long`, and so the value of the `int` (1000 in this case) will fit happily within the range of a `long`.

However, the following code will *not* work:

```
long lngNumber = 1000;
int intNumber;
intNumber = lngNumber;
```

The reason for this is that we are trying to put the value of a `long` into an `int`, and the range of a `long` is much greater than that of an `int`. Although the actual value, 1000, is much less than the limits of both an `int` and a `long`, the C# compiler decides that data *could* be lost in the transformation and will not allow it. In fact, if you try to compile this code, you will get this error message:

Cannot implicitly convert type 'long' to 'int'

By contrast, the first code sample will compile. This is because the conversion:

```
lngNumber = intNumber;
```

is an **implicit conversion**. We have just carried out ordinary assignment operations almost oblivious to the fact that the two types on either side of the equals sign are different, and the C# compiler seems to have overlooked this fact.

But type checking has occurred, and as I said before, C# is very fussy about which implicit conversion are permitted. Conversion from `int` to `long` is one of them. The others are shown in the following table:

From	To
sbyte	short, int, long, float, double, decimal
byte	short, ushort, int, uint, long, ulong, float, double, decimal
short	int, long, float, double, decimal
ushort	int, uint, long, ulong, float, double, decimal
int	long, float, double, decimal
uint	long, ulong, float, double, decimal
long, ulong	float, double, decimal
float	double
Char	ushort, int, uint, long, ulong, float, double, decimal

Note that long *to* int *is not there; neither is* float *to* int, *which means that if we wanted to turn our interest rate into an integer value we could not do so – well, not implicitly.*

Other data type conversions are possible but require a special syntax that takes us on to the topic of **explicit conversion**, also known as **casting**.

Explicit Conversion

When carrying out an explicit conversion, you actively tell the compiler that you want the conversion to take place, and you will take responsibility for any problems that could occur as a result. For almost all data type conversions, and in almost all circumstances, the compiler will abide by your decision and make the change. Using explicit conversions, that is, casts, you can force transformations that would not be allowed to occur implicitly. Therefore, you can force a value of a long variable into an int or a float into an int. The syntax looks like this:

```
long lngNumber = 1000;
int intNumber;
intNumber = (int)lngNumber;
```

The data type of the value to be placed in the variable to the left of the equals sign is enclosed in parentheses and placed immediately before the value that is to be converted.

For the float to int conversion, the syntax is equivalent:

```
float fltInterestRate = 15.5f;
int intNumber;
intNumber = (int)fltInterestRate;
```

In the first instance, intNumber will contain 1000, as in the end no data was lost. However, in the second instance, intNumber contains 15 as we had to lose the fractional part of the floating-point value in the transformation and as a result, the value is inaccurate and would be useless for high precision calculations involving the interest rate, though it might be useful for displaying some kind of estimated value to the user.

The problem with dividing two integers to produce the correct result can also be solved using casts. This is the original syntax that produced the wrong result:

```
int Number1 = 6;
int Number2 = 5;
int Number3 = Number1 / Number2;
```

We vary the syntax as follows:

```
int Number1 = 6;
int Number2 = 5;
double Number3 = (double)Number1 / Number2;
```

Here we declare Number3 as a double that will eventually hold the correct value of the calculation. Doing this by itself will not help us as the problem lies with the calculation and not with the assignment – you can cast an int to a double with no loss of data. Note, however, on the right-hand side of the equals sign, we have cast Number1 to a double before we carry out the division. We don't need to do the same to the Number2 variable as C# will automatically cast it to a double before it carries out the division We could have written the third line like this:

```
double Number3 = (double)Number1 / (double)Number2;
```

The result would be the same, but the first syntax is more concise and easier to read. Note that in all these examples that the cast is carried out before all other operations. This is because of operator precedence – the cast operation has very high precedence, surpassed only by manually placing operations in parentheses. Therefore this operation would not give you the result you might otherwise expect:

```
double Number3 = (double)(Number1 / Number2);
```

Here the division of the two integer values is carried out first, which produces a rounded down integer result, which is then cast to a double.

So what data types can you convert from and to? Well almost any, including totally pointless casts such as:

```
decimal d = 65m;
char c = (char)d;          // Gives you the letter A
```

However, potentially useful are conversions between signed and unsigned types:

```
uint ui = 100;
int Number = (int)ui;
```

This conversion is not available implicitly because the range of the uint does not lie completely within the range of an int. They overlap and as such data could be lost when this conversion is made. The same occurs if an int is cast to a uint.

However you cannot cast between numerical values and bool and vice versa, not even explicitly. In fact, C#'s protection of the bool type is almost impenetrable, for reasons we shall come to in Chapter 6.

Invalid Casts

We said that almost every transformation can be carried out explicitly, and those that cannot (such as to and from bool) will be revealed at compile time. However there are situations where the cast will either give the wrong result or generate a run-time error. Such errors are usually the result of an **overflow**, which occurs when the value passed to a variable as the result of a case is greater that the permitted range for that type, for example:

```
long lngNumber = 2500000000;
int intNumber = (int)lngNumber;     // An invalid cast.
                                    // The maximum int is 2147483647
```

This code will run but the value of intNumber will not be what you expect. In fact the value contained in this variable is −1794967296, which is completely wrong and would render any calculations that you carry out using the value useless from that point on. What has happened here is that the cast has succeeded but data has been lost, namely the four bytes of the long, which were discarded when the data was squeezed into the int. This could occur quite innocently as the result of a calculation producing a result that is much higher than expected, and you should prepare for this when planning your code. You should choose data types into which your data will comfortably fit, taking into account any far-reaching or bizarre situations. Usually an int suffices for most circumstances, though if you are dealing with very large numbers you should use longs and for astronomical numbers you should use doubles. Because date type overflows are unpredictable, you should use the smaller types only when you can be absolutely certain that their limit is not going to be exceeded.

However there is another way to determine whether an overflow has occurred. C# offers the checked keyword, which you can apply to your cast operation (or any other operation for that matter), which will generate a run-time error should the value exceed the maximum limit and cause an overflow. The syntax looks like this:

```
long lngNumber = 2500000000;
int intNumber;
checked
{
   intNumber = (int)lngNumber;
}
```

I've changed it slightly as the declaration of the intNumber variable doesn't need to be checked. Here the cast will fail at runtime and produce an error. We'll see shortly an introduction on how to deal with runtime errors, though a fuller description can be found in Chapter 17.

Invalid casts can also be produced if the value is less the permitted minimum value, such as assigning a negative value to an unsigned integer or a char. They do not always produce an error though you can force them to do so using checked.

Data Conversion

This is a very important area when it comes to ASP.NET programming. When data is passed into an ASP.NET page, much of it exists initially as text, such as an HTML query string, or some other type. If any calculations are to be made on any numerical data among that input, it must be first converted to numerical type. Also in order to display the result as HTML, the result has to be converted back to a string. This section covers several important aspects of data conversion that cannot be achieved using implicit or explicit casts.

String Output

Converting data to strings for output is actually very straightforward. The rules for casting to the `string` follow similar rules to those for explicit casts – there are no permitted implicit casts to `string` – though the syntax is different. Instead of using the `(string)variable` syntax, you do the following:

```
int intAge = 21;
string strAge = intAge.ToString();
```

We have seen this before during our worked examples earlier on in this chapter. You will see `ToString()` a lot when you program ASP.NET using C#, as it is the only way to pass data from C# code to, say, an ASP.NET label control. It is a ubiquitous .NET Framework base-class library function that can be applied to any data type at all, though the results may not always be what you expect. This is because `ToString()` is one of the very few functions of the ultimate base class of the .NET Framework library, `System.Object`, and is the easiest way to converting your data into strings. `ToString()` will work on integers, floating-point and decimal values, `DateTime` values and even `bool` (producing `True` or `False`). For the `DateTime` values, you can specify how the date-time data is converted by supplying an optional parameter (in parentheses, `"d"` in this case) that determines whether the string contains just the date, or just the time, or whether it contains both. You can also specify how the data is formatted as well. An example syntax is as follows:

```
datCurrentDate.ToString("d");
```

The `"d"` in parentheses tells C# to take the value of the `datCurrentDate` variable and create a string containing the date in this format:

```
mm/dd/yyyy
```

or

```
dd/mm/yyyy
```

depending on how your Regional Settings have been configured in the Control Panel.

There are lots of other date formats you can supply here, some of which are listed here:

- ❑ `D` – Gives day, month, and year in this format: "Thursday, September 20, 2001"
- ❑ `G` – Gives date and time (hours, minutes, and seconds): 09/20/2001 09:12:12
- ❑ `T` – Gives the time only (hours, minutes, and seconds): 09:12:12
- ❑ `t` – Gives the time (hours and minutes only): 09:12

A full list of formatting codes can be found in the .NET Framework documentation. Note that these formatting codes are case sensitive: `"D"` and `"d"` give very different results, as you can see.

Data Input

Converting your data input to a form on which your code can operate takes a little more explanation and a little more work. Whereas there is the ubiquitous `ToString()` function that can be applied to all types, there is no equivalent `FromString()`. This is because the input does not necessarily exist in a string format. It could be a set of objects containing data from a database, or XML data. The .NET Framework has provided us with a method of taking the crude input in whatever format it exists and converting it to any of the types discussed in this chapter. We already came across this method earlier on when we introduced the `DateTime` type. Do you recall this line of code?

```
date = Convert.ToDateTime("09/19/2001");
```

`Convert.ToDateTime` is a .NET Framework function, which takes a date as a parameter in the form of a string, in this case, and converts it to a `DateTime` type and stores it in the `date` variable.

This is not the only conversion function that is available to you. In fact there are many `Convert.To...` functions, one for each of the data types that we have looked at in this chapter and more besides; the syntax for all of these corresponds with that for the `Convert.ToDateTime()` function. The following table lists some of them:

Function	Description
`Convert.ToBoolean()`	Converts a string or other data object to a `bool` (the string must evaluate to `true` or `false`
`Convert.ToByte()`	Converts a string or other data object to a `byte`
`Convert.ToChar()`	Converts a string or other data object to a `char`
`Convert.ToDecimal()`	Converts a string or other data object to a `decimal`
`Convert.ToDateTime()`	Converts a string or other data object to a `DateTime`
`Convert.ToDouble()`	Converts a string or other data object to a `double`
`Convert.ToInt16()`	Converts a string or other data object to a `short`
`Convert.ToInt32()`	Converts a string or other data object to an `int`
`Convert.ToInt64()`	Converts a string or other data object to a `long`
`Convert.ToSByte()`	Converts a string or other data object to an `sbyte`
`Convert.ToSingle()`	Converts a string or other data object to a `float`
`Convert.ToUInt16()`	Converts a string or other data object to a `ushort`
`Convert.ToUInt32()`	Converts a string or other data object to a `uint`
`Convert.ToUInt64()`	Converts a string or other data object to a `ulong`

For the most part, this table is self-explanatory. However note that for the short and ushort types, the conversion function uses the names ToInt16 and ToUInt16. This is because the two types are both 16-bit (2-byte) integers and Int16 and UInt16 are the "official" .NET names for these two types – short and ushort are just C#'s names for them. Similarly int and uint are C#'s special names for the Int32 and UInt32 .NET types respectively, and long and ulong are C#'s names for the Int64 and UInt64 ,NET data types. In the same way, the C# type float corresponds with the Single .NET type.

So we have a set of conversion functions that enable us to take any data and change it to a type that we can work with. Does that mean we can go away and use these functions as we wish? Well, not really. These functions are powerful but they all have one major drawback – they can fail to convert your data to what you want. The reason for this is very simple. If you want to convert a string into an int, you have to supply a string that can be reinterpreted as an int. Take a look at this:

```
int myAge = Convert.ToInt32("21");
```

This code will work, because the string "21" can be transformed into an integer value of 21 and can therefore be assigned to myAge. However this code will not work:

```
int myAge = Convert.ToInt32("You're as old as you feel");
```

It will compile, as Convert.ToInt32 takes a string as input and that is what we have supplied. But the string is not interpretable as an integer, and at run-time the code will not be able to handle it. So what does it do? It aborts the running of the program and generates some data that it passes to the user to inform them that the program has aborted and why. This whole process is known as "raising an exception", and it brings us on to a very important aspect of programming, which we can only touch on here, though it is covered in more detail in a chapter of its own - Chapter 17.

What if Conversions Fail?

If you run an ASP.NET page with this line of code in it (and it doesn't matter what else there is in the page):

```
int myAge = Convert.ToInt32("You're as old as you feel");
```

The execution of the page fails and you get a Server Error page with this text in it:

Exception Details: System.FormatException: Input string was not in a correct format

This is the message generated by the .NET Framework to inform you that the string could not be converted into an int. If you scroll down the page to where more detailed information is displayed you might be able to determine the cause of the problem, though in this case, it seems to lead you on a wild goose chase. It does not actually tell you explicitly that Convert.ToInt32 failed, so the information is not that valuable to you. However all is not lost and C# offers a very neat way to deal with the exception, such that it does not cause the execution of the page to terminate immediately, and yet supplies you with information of what went wrong. This process is known as **structured error handling**.

Structured error handling is a very big topic and we can only scratch the surface here. Suffice to say that if there is any code that might just fail at run time, you wrap it in a pair of curly brackets and precede the code block with the `try` keyword:

```
try
{
  int myAge = Convert.ToInt32("You're as old as you feel");
}
```

This tells the C# compiler: "the code between the brackets might fail, so you should take some action to deal with it". So what action do you take? The action consists of a second code block prefixed with the `catch` keyword:

```
try
{
  int myAge = Convert.ToInt32("You're as old as you feel");
}
catch
{
}
```

What happens here is that if the code within the `try` block fails, the code with in the `catch` block is executed and the program is not terminated. In the above example there is nothing in the `catch` block and so nothing happens. Indeed, in this case, the code plods merrily on and you are unaware that anything did go wrong. This is almost equivalent to On Error Resume Next in Visual Basic.

However, something did go wrong and it is important the user realizes this and does something about it. There are many ways of doing this, but for the purpose of this introductory section, I'll show you just one. We will add some code in the `catch` block to tell the user that the string could not be converted to an integer:

```
try
{
  int myAge = Convert.ToInt32("You're as old as you feel");
}
catch
{
  ErrorMessage.Text = "Cannot convert this string to an integer";
}
```

Here `ErrorMessage` would be an ASP.NET label control that exists only to repost errors and does nothing otherwise. Thus we have provided a simple, meaningful message to the user informing them that the conversion failed.

With this preventative measure implemented, you can now use the `Convert.To...` functions without the fear of generating run-time errors that terminate your program.

Let's finish off this section on casts and conversions with an example illustrating much of what we have discussed.

157

Try it out – Converting between types.

1. Open up the `tax.aspx` file created earlier and made the following changes and additions:

```
<script Language="c#" runat="server">
void Page_Load() {
  string strEarn = "150";
  string strTax = "23.0";

  double dblEarn = Convert.ToInt32(strEarn);
  decimal decTax = Convert.ToDecimal(strTax);
  double dblTotal = dblEarn - ((dblEarn/100) * (double)decTax);
  Display1.Text = dblTotal.ToString();
  DateTime datNow = DateTime.Now;
  Display2.Text = " " + datNow.ToString("d");
}
</script>

<html>
<head>
  <title>Declaring Variables</title>
</head>
<body>
  Your total earnings after tax are $
  <asp:label id="Display1" runat="server" />
  <br />
  The date is
  <asp:label id="Display2" runat="server" />
</body>
</html>
```

2. Save this as `C:\BegASPNET\ch04\conversion.aspx`

3. View this in your browser:

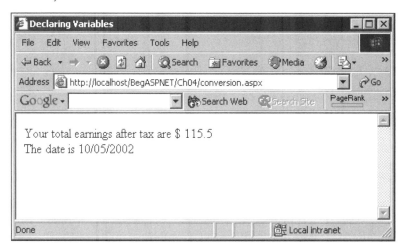

How it Works

As you can see this is just an adaptation of the `tax.aspx` example, with the date thrown in for good measure. However, the data exists initially in the form of strings not numbers, which parallels more closely what you actually get when you start importing data from, say, an HTML form:

```
string strEarn = "150";
string strTax = "23.0";
```

Then we convert the strings to numerical types:

```
double dblEarn = Convert.ToInt32(strEarn);
decimal decTax = Convert.ToDecimal(strTax);
```

The earnings value is converted to a `double` and the tax rate to a `decimal`. Now comes the exciting bit:

```
double dblTotal = dblEarn - ((dblEarn/100) * (double)decTax);
```

All the action occurs here. Lets examine it bit by bit.

```
double dblTotal = dblEarn - ((dblEarn/100) * (double)decTax);
```

The first thing that happens here is that the value of `dblEarn` is divided by 100. Here we demonstrate an implicit cast. The number 100 is an integer and it is implicitly converted to a `double` before the calculation takes place:

```
double dblTotal = dblEarn - ((dblEarn/100) * (double)decTax);
```

The result of this division is then multiplied by the tax rate stored in `decTax`. This is of the `decimal` type but must be explicitly cast to a `double` for the calculation to take place – this conversion cannot be carried out implicitly because of the risk of losing data:

(OK, we could have converted the tax rate to a `double` in the first place, but we did it this way to demonstrate an explicit cast.)

Finally the result of this calculation is subtracted from the original earnings:

```
double dblTotal = dblEarn - ((dblEarn/100) * (double)decTax);
```

Both the tax and earnings values are `double`s and so no cast is necessary here and the result is placed into a new variable of type `double`.

To be able to output the data to the ASP.NET label control, we have to convert the value of `dblTotal` to a string:

```
Display1.Text = dblTotal.ToString();
```

The final thing this code does is to create a `DateTime` object containing the value of the current system time, which is represented by `DateTime.Now`. This value is then converted to a string containing only the date, by specifying the `"d"` parameter:

```
DateTime datNow = DateTime.Now;
Display2.Text = " " + datNow.ToString("d");
```

This is then displayed as a separate ASP.NET label control:

```
<br />
The date is
<asp:label id="Display2" runat="server" />
```

We've looked at variables and the different data types they can have in some detail now, but this still leaves us with a couple of situations unaccounted for.

Constants

There will be occasions when you want a value assigned to a variable to remain constant throughout the execution of the code. A good example is statewide sales tax. This value will rarely change, yet when calculating the total of a shopping basket, you'll probably need to refer to it several times. Even if the tax is changed, you'd still only need to refer to one value, and you'd only want to update one value. To represent the sales tax you can you use something other than a variable, called a constant.

Constants are like variables except that, once they have been assigned a value, they don't change. Many programming languages provide an explicit facility for constants, by allowing the programmer to assign an initial value to them, and subsequently forbidding any alteration of that value. The main reason you'd assign a value to a constant, is to prevent its accidental alteration.

The C# syntax for declaring a constant is to place the `const` keyword before the data type in the declaration and assigning it a value all in one step:

```
const int AbsoluteZero = -273;
```

Note that constants in C# cannot be defined in the same way as C++ or VB6. In these languages, constants can be declared outside the confines and control of a class definition, that is they are global constants. In C# and other .NET languages, all constants whether global or local have to be defined within the class definition.

The naming convention for constants follows the same rules as for other variables, though commonly you will find them spelled with capital letters and using underscores to separate multiple words:

```
const int ABSOLUTEZERO = 273;
```

```
const int MAX_VALUES = 20;
```

We will not be using either of these conventions in this book.

You cannot reassign a value to a constant once it is set, however. So, if you then tried to assign another value to AbsoluteZero, such as:

```
AbsoluteZero = 0;
```

The change would be rejected and an error message produced at compile time. Constants remain in force for the duration of the code, just as variables do. It isn't possible to amend their value once they have been set. Constants make your code easier to read and maintain, as they require less updating and if you choose a self-explanatory name, they make your code easily understandable. They also give a performance increase over variables.

Structured Data Types

We've now finished discussing data types for single pieces of information, otherwise known as simple data types (or value types). Next, we're going to move on to look at how we can store related information together in one block of data from which we can extract individual items. There are several programmatic constructs that you can use to group data together. We'll concentrate, in this section, on arrays, though we'll also briefly look at the C# struct and enumeration.

Arrays

An array is basically a group of variables of the same type (any of the types discussed in this chapter and others besides), which are grouped together using a common name and which only differ by an index that is appended to that name, enclosed in square brackets. In C# an array of type string is declared as follows:

```
string [] myString;
```

This operation doesn't actually create an array, it just declares that there will be one called myString of type string but its length is undefined, as is its data.

You can have arrays of any type. They are declared in the same way:

```
int [] myInts;
```

```
DateTime [] myDates;
```

> Note that an array is a *reference type* and not value type, so when you declare an array using the above syntax, you are not creating the array itself, you are creating a reference, which will eventually refer to an actual array object.

To bring an already declared array into existence, you have to carry out a second step called initialization:

```
myString = new string[5];
```

This employs the `new` keyword that we have not come across in this book so far. What happens here is that the code takes the predefined `myString` array variable, creates five strings, and makes it possible for you the programmer to access each of them by an index specified in square brackets after the name. Each item in an array is also known as an **element**.

> **A very important note. In C#, the array indices are zero-based, which means that for an array of five strings, as above, the indices run from 0 to 4. Therefore the first string in the above array is `myString[0]` and the fifth and last string is `myString[4]`. The array element "`myString[5]`" is not defined, and if you try to reference, it you will get an error.**

As with all variables, you can declare and initialize the array in one step:

```
string [] myString = new string[5];
```

We have created an array, so how do we fill it?

This is easy. You can access each element as if it were an ordinary variable:

```
string [] strMarx = new string[5];

strMarx[0] = "Groucho";
strMarx[1] = "Harpo";
strMarx[2] = "Chico";
strMarx[3] = "Zeppo";
strMarx[4] = "Gummo";
```

You don't have to store something in each element of the array, however, and you don't even have to store data sequentially:

```
string [] strHouse = new string[5];

strHouse[1] = "Mr Jones";
strHouse[4] = "Mr Goldstein";
strHouse[3] = "Mrs Soprano";
```

In this case, the elements with indexes of 2 and 5 will contain an empty string. Indeed, all array elements are initialized with their values set to zero or equivalent, which means empty strings, zero for numerical values, and `false` for Boolean values. This means that you will not get an error if you access a previously uninitialized array element.

In C# you can declare an array and fill its elements in one step, using syntax like this:

```
string [] strHouse = new string [] { "Mr Jones", "Mr Goldstein" };
```

This creates a two-element array corresponding with the two string values contained within the curly brackets. You can also manually specify the size of the array before you fill it.

```
string [] strHouse = new string [2] { "Mr Jones", "Mr Goldstein" };
```

One drawback to this method of initialization is that you must supply the name number of values for the array elements as specified by the value in the square brackets. Lastly you don't even need to use new at all, you can declare and initialize an array just by putting a list of values in curly brackets:

```
string [] strHouse = { "Mr Jones", "Mr Goldstein" };
```

Arrays are particularly useful if you want to manipulate a whole set of data items as though they were one. For example, if you want to adjust the pay rates for a set of five employees, then the difficult way of doing it is the following:

```
int [] intEmployeePay = new int EmployeePay[5];

int intExtraPay = 10;
intEmployeePay[0] = intExtraPay;
intEmployeePay[1] = intExtraPay + 1;
intEmployeePay[2] = intExtraPay + 2;
intEmployeePay[3] = intExtraPay + 3;
intEmployeePay[4] = intExtraPay + 4;
```

What we are doing here is adding an integer (which has the same value as the array index) to intExtraPay and assigning the result to each array element in turn. This much simpler code makes use of your array structure and has exactly the same effect:

```
int [] intEmployeePay = new int EmployeePay[5];
int intExtraPay = 10;

for (int intLoop = 0; intLoop < 5; intLoop++)
{
   intEmployeePay[intLoop] = intExtraPay + intLoop;
}
```

We'll look at the for loop in more detail in Chapter 6. All you need to know at this point is that it does the same thing as the previous snippet of code, but in half the number of lines.

Now we're ready to look at a small example utilizing some of these concepts. Let's go back and adapt our textbox control example from the last chapter, so that we can store information gathered from the user in an array.

Try It Out – Using Arrays

1. If you typed in the `textboxpage.aspx` example from the last chapter, make a copy of it and amend the following lines (you can download a copy from **www.wrox.com**, as well):

```
<script runat="Server" language="C#">
void Page_Load()
{
    string[] strArrayDetails = new string[3];
    int intLoop;

    strArrayDetails[0] = text1.Text;
    strArrayDetails[1] = text2.Text;
    strArrayDetails[2] = text3.Text;

    Message1.Text = strArrayDetails[0];
    Message2.Text = strArrayDetails[1];
    Message3.Text = strArrayDetails[2];

}
</script>

<html>
<head>
<title>Text Box Example</title>
...
```

2. Save this as `textboxarray.aspx` and view it in your browser.

3. Enter some details and submit them.

4. You will see something similar to the following:

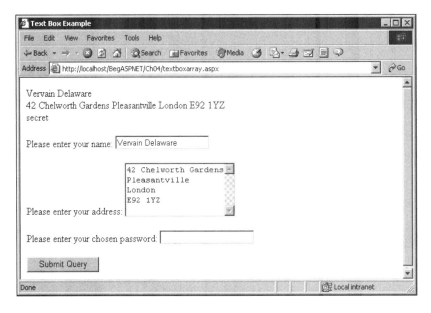

How It Works

OK, let's see what has changed. The working of the web form `textboxarray.aspx` is no different from `textboxpage.aspx` in the last chapter. It simply collects the name, address, and password. What does change is the method of storage. Instead of displaying the information we receive straight to the screen, we now store it in an array, called `strArrayDetails()`, first.

We start our ASP.NET code by declaring this as an array of string variables:

```
string[] strArrayDetails = new string[3];
```

Then we populate our array with the three items of information that the user has provided on the previous form:

```
strArrayDetails[0] = text1.Text;
strArrayDetails[1] = text2.Text;
strArrayDetails[2] = text3.Text;
```

Next we assign each of our items in the array to a respective label control, in turn:

```
Message1.Text = strArrayDetails[0];
Message2.Text = strArrayDetails[1];
Message3.Text = strArrayDetails[2];
```

The first item in the array, `strArrayDetails(0)`, contains the string value "Vervain Delaware" in this example and is displayed on the screen using `<asp:label>` control. Then `strArrayDetails(1)` is displayed, which contains the string value "24 Chelworth Gardens Pleasantville London E92 1YZ" that we assigned earlier. The last element is then displayed and the web form is complete.

Multi-Dimensional Arrays

So far, we have discussed arrays that contain just one set of data, which can be likened to a single column of data in a table. But you are not limited to this. In fact you can create arrays that can be compared to an entire table of data where each table column is represented by "columns" in the array. The use of the word "column" here is illustrative as it doesn't really describe how these complex arrays are structures, so there are two terms that are used instead, **rank** and **dimension**, which describe the structure of the array internally.

An array of rank (dimension) 2 is like a data table with columns and rows. An array of rank 3 has a three-dimensional cube-like structure. Ranks of 4 and above represent arrays that can't really be likened to anything in the human world, but you can create them and assign data to them.

However, to keep things simple let's consider an array of rank 2, the two-dimensional array. You can use such an array to store name-/value pairs, for example. Also, if you want to store a set of related information separately, such as a first and last name, a normal (one-dimensional) array would probably be unsuitable. You can achieve far better results by creating a two-dimensional array. In C#, the syntax for doing this is as follows:

```
string [,] str2DArray = new string[4,4];
```

This will set up a two-dimensional array of size 4 by 4, which can hold a total of 16 values.

> **Note that these arrays all have rows with the same number of columns. The consequence of this is that multi-dimensional arrays, declared by this syntax are also known as** rectangular arrays.

You can assign values to a multi-dimensional array by referencing each element of the array through its two-value index. For example, you could use such an array to store first and last names and phone numbers:

```
str2DArray[0,0] = "John"
str2DArray[0,1] = "Doe"
str2DArray[0,2] = "111-111-1111"
str2DArray[1,0] = "Jane"
str2DArray[1,1] = "Doe"
str2DArray[1,2] = "222-222-2222"
```

The first dimension stores the information that is related to one person, while the second dimension holds data of the same type for a different person. Let's have a look at a tabular representation of what is happening.

	Column 0	Column 1	Column 2	Column 3
Row 0	John	Doe	111-111-1111	
Row 1	Jane	Doe	222-222-2222	
Row 2				
Row 3				

The first row represents the str2DArray[0,x] set of elements, whereas the second row represents the str2DArray[1,x] set and so on, though as you can see from this representation that not all elements have values. The first column represents the str2DArray[x,0] set of elements, that is first names. From this, you can see that the content of the array element str2DArray[1,2] is 222-222-2222.

In fact, C# is not limited to arrays of one or two dimensions – the limit of the size and rank of array is probably restricted by your system's memory. However, using anything more than three dimensions is impractical, and if you find that you are having to create them, then you should think about pursuing other solutions to store your data, for example using objects.

Jagged Arrays

C# offers a means of creating a different type of multi-dimensional array, where instead of each row in the array having an equal number of columns, as in the rectangular array, the number on each row can vary from row to row. This type of array is known as a **jagged array** and is declared as follows:

```
string [][] strJaggedArray = new string [4][];
strJaggedArray[0] = new string[2];
strJaggedArray[1] = new string[4];
strJaggedArray[2] = new string[2];
strJaggedArray[3] = new string[3];
```

What you in effect get here is an array of arrays. In practice you would probably use `for` loops to do this, as we touched on earlier.

Each array element can be assigned individually like so:

```
strJaggedArray[0][0] = "John";
strJaggedArray[0][1] = "Doe";
strJaggedArray[1][0] = "James";
strJaggedArray[1][1] = "Bond";
strJaggedArray[1][2] = "007";
strJaggedArray[1][3] = "Licensed to kill";
// etc.
```

Looking this array ion a tabular format the jagged array is represented as follows, where the elements that are not defined for that particular row are marked with an X:

	0	1	2	3
0	John	Doe	X	X
1	James	Bond	007	Licensed to kill
2	...	...	X	X
3	...	...	...	X

As you can see, creating and initializing a jagged array and assigning data to its elements is a cumbersome process, and though jagged arrays can be of any rank, it should become apparent to you that even a rank 3 jagged array requires a lot of work to set it up. So be careful if you decide to use one of these kinds of arrays as you could be biting off more than you can chew. However they are useful in that instead of creating a rectangular array, which is of a fixed size with a fixed number of elements, which may or may not contain data, you can define a jagged array and only initialize rows as you need them, creating only the number of columns required to contain the data for that row. This process can save valuable system resources.

This takes us as far as we need to go with arrays and variables. We'll be using them throughout the rest of this book, so take care to understand them. Now we move on to introducing a second type of structured data that you can create in C#, something more powerful and flexible than the array – the struct.

Structs

Up until now, we have discussed simple data types such as int, double, and decimal, which only represent a single data value. C# also allows you to define types that can contain more than one data value: indeed, they can contain much more besides. These are called **complex data types**. Complex data types are based on the simple types, yet they can also incorporate other complex types to build highly complex and specialized types.

There are many complex types that are already defined by the .NET Framework. We have come across one of them already, though you probably won't have realized: the DateTime type we used to create and manipulate dates is actually a complex type. Arrays are also a complex type, built up from simple types, as we have seen. However, this section introduces us to the **struct**, which for the purpose of this introductory section, can be seen to be a container for other types, though they are much more powerful than that.

More will be said on complex data types when we come to discuss classes and objects from Chapter 8 onwards, but the struct, like the array, enables you to group together related data into a single unit and each contained item can be referenced individually. However the analogy with arrays ends here and structs are far more powerful than arrays.

❑   They can contain data of multiple types, including other complex types

❑   They can contain data other than just name-value pairs, such as methods and properties

You cannot do either of these with simple arrays.

A C# struct is declared using this syntax:

```
struct myStruct
{
    // Data in here
}
```

Between the curly brackets we can place almost anything we like. Let's adapt the Feiertag Holidays example to put its data in a struct. If you recall from the earlier array example we had an array like this:

```
string[] strArrayDetails = new string[4];
strArrayDetails[0] = Request.Form["FullName"];
strArrayDetails[1] = Request.Form["Address"];
strArrayDetails[2] = Request.Form["Sex"];
strArrayDetails[3] = Request.Form["Destination"];
```

That's all well and good, but the names of the variables do not really describe the value thy contain, and, unless the data is basically of the same kind (such as a `SoccerTeams` array containing, you guessed it, soccer teams), then for the sake of readability it would be better to reorganize the data so that its meaning can be inferred just by looking at the names of the variables. The struct enables you to do this, as the data items it contains can be individually named. A struct containing four strings that represent the same data as the above array can be defined like this:

```
struct HolidayDetails
{
   public string strName;
   public string strAddress;
   public string strGender;
   public string strDestination;
}
```

Each of the variables in the struct is known as a **field**.

Note how much meaning has been incorporated into the definition itself, which makes the data easier to find. Instead of getting or setting data by selecting an array element using an anonymous index value, you can pick it out by name: we'll show you how to do this shortly. The only thing new in this definition is the use of the word `public` before each variable declaration: this means that the variables are available for use externally – the full significance of this will be explained in Chapter 8.

Note that although we have a struct containing just strings, you could include variables of a different type altogether:

```
struct HolidayDetails
{
   public string strName;
   public string strAddress;
   public string strGender;
   public string strDestination;
   public double dblDepositPaid;
   public DateTime datDateBooked;
}
```

OK, so we have defined a struct, so how to we create one? There are two methods of achieving this. First you can declare a struct variable as you can with any other:

```
HolidayDetails myDetails;
```

where `HolidayDetails` is the name of the struct we just declared. A second method of declaration uses the new keyword:

```
HolidayDetails myDetails = new HolidayDetails();
```

The difference between the two is as follows. In the first case, all the declaration does is assign memory for each of the `struct`'s variables together on the stack. In the second case, when `new` is used, the `struct`'s variables are not just placed on the stack, they are initialized with default values of zero or equivalent: an empty string, zero for numerical values, and `false` for Boolean values.

We will come back to the `new` keyword from Chapter 8 onwards when we talk about classes and objects.

So how do you assign values to the items in a `struct`? You use the following syntax, which again we will come across much more often from Chapter 8 onwards:

```
myDetails.strName = "Vervain Delaware";
myDetails.strAddress = "42 Chelworth Gardens Pleasantville London E92 1YZ";
myDetails.strGender = "Female";
myDetails.strDestination = "Barcelona";
```

Here the period (`.`) separates the `struct` variable instance (`myDetails`) from the item variable (`strName`, `strAddress`, and so on) and the whole unit (`myDetails.strName`) acts as a single variable.

Let's put this all together in an example.

Try It Out – Using a struct

1. Open up `textboxpage.aspx` in your text editor and add the following code to the `script` block. The rest of the code stays the same:

```
<script runat="Server" language="C#">

    struct PersonalDetails
    {
      public string strName;
      public string strAddress;
      public string strPassword;
    }

void Page_Load()
{
        PersonalDetails pd;

        pd.strName = text1.Text;
        pd.strAddress = text2.Text;
        pd.strPassword = text3.Text;

        Message1.Text = pd.strName;
        Message2.Text = pd.strAddress;
        Message3.Text = pd.strPassword;

}
</script>
<html>
...
```

2. Browse to `textboxpage.aspx`, enter some data, and submit; you should receive similar output to what we had before.

How It Works

Much of the goings on in this code have been explained in the previous section. However, note that the definition of the `struct` goes outside `Page_Load()`. This is because we potentially want the `struct` to be available to all code on the page not just to `Page_Load()`. This is also why we declared each member to be `public`. The rest of the code is quite straightforward. You declare an empty `struct` variable and initialize it by assigning values to its four string members from the HTML form and use label controls to output each value back to the browser.

Enumerations

In this last section on storing variable data, we will look at the C# construct called an **enumeration**. This is a user-defined complex data type that allows a variable to have a predefined, limited set of values. To illustrate where such a construct might be useful, let's envisage an extra data field from the last *Try It Out* that contains gender information. Logically speaking, it can have one of just two values "`Male`" and "`Female`". In the above code, this is represented as an ordinary string variable, which is filled from a form textbox. Therefore it is very likely, even probable, that the variable could end up containing a value other than `Male` or `Female`, due to a typo or some rogue value being entered. So how can you limit the range of values for this variable? By using an enumeration (or in C# terms, an enum).

Enumerations are defined using this syntax:

```
enum Gender
{
   Male = 0,
   Female = 1
}
```

An enum is actually stored as an integer (by default an `int`, though you can specify another integer type). However, what makes enums special and useful is that each value for the integer can be represented by a unique textual name that you actually refer to in code. In the above example, we have defined that the integer value 0 is represented by the name "`Male`", and the value 1 by "`Female`". Looking at this from a different perspective, "`Male`" is enumerated to 0 and "`Female`" is enumerated to 1.

An enum can also be defined on a single line as follows:

```
enum Gender { Male = 0, Female = 1 }
```

Though explicitly listing each of the names that define the enumeration is mandatory, you do not have to explicitly assign integer values to them. Indeed, if you miss them out, the enumeration will automatically start at zero for the first name in the list and increase by 1 for each subsequent name. The above enumeration could be declared as follows with exactly the same result:

```
enum Gender { Male, Female }
```

171

However, if you start at a value other than zero or if you want to break the sequence of unitary increments, you have to explicitly indicate this in your enum definition:

```
enum Gender { Male = 1, Female = 5 }
```

OK, having defined an enum, how do you actually use it? Let's return to our struct example and add an enum Gender string field:

```
struct PersonalDetails
{
  public string strName;
  public string strAddress;
  public Gender optGender;
  public string strPassword;
}
```

Note that I have changed the prefix to the variable to opt as we now have a variable with two optional values rather than a string. We assign a value to this field as follows:

```
PersonalDetails myDetails;
...
myDetails.optPassword = Gender.Female;
```

What we have done here is used the textual form of the enumeration to assign the value to the field. The syntax for doing this is similar to that of accessing a struct field variable – you use the period (.) to separate the enum type (in this case Gender) from the value that you want to assign (that is Female). This method ensures that only valid values can be assigned to the field. If you try to assign a rogue value to the field, like this:

```
myDetails.optGender = Gender.Hybrid;
```

you will get an error because the value Hybrid is not defined for the Gender enum – this would have been happily accepted if we had continued to use a string variable here.

There is a second way you can assign a value to an enum variable and that is to use an integer value, which as to be explicitly cast to the corresponding enum type.

```
myDetails.optGender = (Gender)1;
```

This conversion will work for any integer value within the range of the integer type, but will only be of real use to you if the value of integer corresponds to any of the names previously defined in the enum – in this case, only the values 0 and 1.

This leaves one last form of information storage for us to discuss. `Arrays`, for all their virtues, don't hold any information about the data that they contain. To take our multi-dimensional array example, there's nothing about `str2DArray(0,0)` that tells you it contains name information at this location. It could just as easily hold an address, or a telephone number. The array structure doesn't inherently tell us anything of its data's meaning. To gather, store, and transmit data in a more 'intelligent' fashion we can use XML. This merits a chapter in its own right though, as it's more than just data storage, it's a whole new structure defined using an HTML-like format. This is to be the subject of the next chapter.

Summary

This chapter has looked at the use of variables for storing information in C#.

It really can't be stressed enough how important variables are. It is very hard to create a functional program without them. We've looked at how C# implements variables and how you go about placing them in your ASP.NET pages. We have plowed a furrow through the built-in numeric and textual data types and looked at a couple of more complex types like `string` and `DateTime` as well. We then moved on to examine how you can manipulate numbers and perform simple calculations in C#, before looking at structured data types such as arrays and structs.

In the next chapter, we will be looking at XML (Extensible Markup Language), which is a powerful means of storing structured data in a "variable-free" way.

Exercises

1. What is a variable and how is it related to data types in C#?

2. Use `string`, `int`, and `date` variables to create an ASPX file that displays your `name`, `age`, and date of birth.

3. Arrange the following into groups of `Numeric`, `Textual`, and `Miscellaneous` data types. Give an example of a value and use for each:

    int

    char

    byte

    short

    bool

    string

    long

    single

    double

    date

    decimal

4. Write an ASPX file that will multiply the values of two integer variables together. Now, modify the example to add, divide, and subtract the two numbers. After this experiment with exponential, negation, and modulus controls.

5. Create an array containing your five favorite singers. Then concatenate the elements of your array into one string, and, after the opening sentence "My 5 favorite singers are:", display them in a clear way using the <asp:label> control.

Introducing XML

We first came across the topic of **XML** (the **eXtensible Markup Language**) back in Chapter 2, when we mentioned it as a primary method of transporting data in and around .NET applications. XML is in fact one of the largest growth areas on the web, as it provides an application-independent format with which data can be shared. It requires no extras, and is completely free to use.

For this reason we're going to embark on a short digression in this chapter and introduce XML in detail, but really only touch on how it's used in conjunction with ASP.NET by the chapter's end. To get an overview about how XML fits in with Microsoft's .NET strategy, we're going to go back and describe its origins and history and the kind of things it is best suited for. We'll give a brief overview of the format of the language and how to use it. However, as we haven't discussed ASP.NET's data handling facilities in any detail and don't until Chapter 12, we won't be able to provide many working examples of XML in action, so this chapter will be quite theory heavy. Having grasped the essentials of XML you should see how invaluable it is when we come to use it in later chapters.

The topics discussed will be:

- ❏ The format of XML
- ❏ Background of XML
- ❏ Well-formed documents
- ❏ Valid documents
- ❏ Styling XML
- ❏ ASP.NET and XML

The Format of XML

One of XML's great strengths is that, unlike with a database, you don't need a separate piece of software to create an XML document, due to its plain text-based, self-describing, style. All you need is a text editor, such as Notepad.

Like the variables that we discussed in the previous chapter, XML is simply a method of storing data. However, unlike variables, XML aims to store your information in a structured manner that is easy to understand just by looking at the information itself:

```
<artist>
  <name>Vincent Van Gogh</name>
  <nationality>Dutch</nationality>
  <birthdate>30th March 1853</birthdate>
  <movement>Post Impressionism</movement>
</artist>
<artist>
  <name>Max Ernst</name>
  ...
```

You might be wondering why we don't write this as HTML:

```
<p>
  <b>Vincent Van Gogh</b>
  <br/>Dutch
  <br/><i>30th March 1853</i>
  <br/>Post Impressionism
</p>

<p>
  <b>Max Ernst</b>
  ...
```

The simple answer is 'meaning'. With the HTML version, we have lost the meaning of the information. HTML tags don't offer any extra information about our data, unlike our XML tags; and without representing the meaning in some way, we cannot search through our data or group it logically. In fact, we're committing the cardinal sin of mixing up data (our artist information) with presentation (the HTML tags) – something ASP.NET tries hard to avoid.

None of our XML tags contain any implicit styling information the way HTML tags do (that is, the HTML tag <b> makes the text bold, while the XML tag <name> doesn't have any styling information attached to it). We'll explain why that is, and how it works in this next section.

> **We will be using XML throughout the remainder of this book, so it's important that you have a good understanding of its syntax and meaning.**

Tags and Elements

Even those of us who are familiar with HTML often get the meaning of tags and elements mixed up. Just to clarify, **tags** are the angled brackets (known as delimiters), and the text they contain. Here are some examples of tags used in HTML:

❏   <p> is a tag that marks the beginning of a new paragraph

❏   <i> is a tag indicating that the following text should be rendered in italic type

❏   </i> is a tag that indicates the end of a section of text to be rendered in italic type

Elements refer to the tags **plus** their content. So, the following is an example of an element:

```
<b>Here is some bold text</b>
```

In general terms, a tag is simply a label that tells a user agent (such as a browser) how it should interpret whatever text is enclosed within the tags.

A user-agent is anything that acts on your behalf. You are a user agent working for your boss, your computer is a user agent working for you, your browser is a user agent working for you and your computer, and so it goes on.

Empty elements (such as the `<br>` element in HTML) have no content, and therefore don't have separate closing tags. When using HTML all browsers will simply allow you to specify a single opening tag, and treat that as a complete element. However, XML requires us to explicitly close all elements, so we either have to add a closing tag:

```
<br></br>
```

or use the proper condensed notation for an empty element, which is a tag like this:

```
<br />
```

The following diagram illustrates the parts of an element:

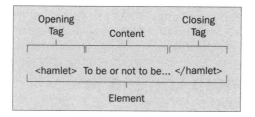

Attributes

Any tag can have an attribute. These take the form of name-value pairs (also referred to as attribute-value pairs). These name-value pairs are very similar to the ones we encountered in Chapter 3 when sending forms. In XML though, they take the following format:

```
<tagname attribute="value">
```

This is where XML is very similar to HTML. For example, in HTML 4.01 the `<body>` tag can take the following attributes:

class id	dir	lang	style	title
background	bgcolor	alink	link	vlink
text				

So, it could be defined as follows:

```
<body bgcolor="#000000" alink="#999999" link="#990099"
                        vlink="#888888" text="#999999">
```

Once again though, while the attributes in HTML have implicit meanings to the browser, to color the text and backgrounds in a certain way, for instance, an XML attribute has no implicit information. For example, the following would have no effect at all on the browser.

```
<car color="red">Chevrolet</car>
```

The attribute color is merely informational and just describes the car color. This is another example of separating out presentation from content. In our XML tags, we provide information about the type of information contained in the elements, but do not indicate any way in which this information should be displayed in the browser.

And that's pretty much all there is to the format of XML. As you can see it is similar, although not identical to HTML, but there are some fairly fundamental differences between them that need to be clarified.

Examples of Markup Languages

To do this, let's take a quick look at three markup languages, so we can see where XML fits into the big picture. We'll look at SGML, HTML, and of course XML.

SGML

Standard Generalized Markup Language (SGML) is a markup language that is used to create other markup languages. The most famous language written in SGML is HTML, which we all know and love for its use on the Web. HTML is known as an application of SGML. The problem with SGML is that it is very complicated – hence our interest in XML. XML is a simplified version of SGML, retaining much of SGML's functionality, yet initially designed for use on the Web.

Back in 1986, SGML became an international standard (ISO 8879) for defining markup languages, before the Web had even been conceived (in fact, SGML has been in existence since the late 1960s). Its purpose was to describe markup languages by enabling the author to provide formal definitions for each of the elements and attributes in the language. This allowed authors to create their own tags relating to their content. In effect, they could write their own markup language using SGML, which is exactly what happens when a new version of HTML is created. The World Wide Web Consortium (W3C) makes up the new tags, and it is up to browser manufacturers to implement them.

As a language SGML is very powerful, but with its power comes complexity, and many of its features are rarely used. It is very difficult to interpret an SGML document without the definition of the markup language, kept in a **Document Type Definition** (**DTD**). The DTD is where all the rules for the language are; after all, you cannot create your own markup language without specifying how it should be used. The DTD has to be sent with, or included in, the SGML document so that your custom created tags can be understood.

Practically speaking, this means that we have to give details of each of the elements, their order, and what attributes (and other types of markup) they can take.

HTML

As we just saw, HTML is one particular application of SGML. It describes how information is to be prepared for the World Wide Web. HTML is just a set of SGML rules and, as such, it has a DTD. In fact, there are several DTDs, for the different versions of HTML.

Being far simpler than SGML, and a fraction of its size, HTML is very easy to learn – a factor that quickly made it popular and widely adopted by all sorts of people. It was created by Tim Berners-Lee in 1991 as a way of marking up technical papers so that they could easily be organized and transferred across different platforms for the scientific community.

This is not meant to be a history lesson, but it is important to understand the concepts behind HTML if we are to appreciate the power of XML. The idea was to create a set of tags that could be transferred between computers so that others could render the document in a useful format. For example:

```
<h1>This is a primary heading</h1>
<h2>This is a secondary heading</h2>
<pre>This is text whose formatting should be preserved</pre>
<p>The text between these two tags is a paragraph</p>
```

Back then the scientific community had little concern about the aesthetic appearance of their documents. What mattered to them was that they could transfer them while preserving their meaning. They weren't worried about the color of the fonts or the exact size of their primary heading!

As HTML usage exploded and web browsers started to become readily available, non-scientific users soon started to create their own pages *en masse*. These non-scientific users became increasingly concerned with the aesthetic presentation of their material. Manufacturers of browsers used to view web sites were all too ready to offer different tags that would enable web page authors to display their documents with more creativity than was possible using plain ASCII text. Netscape was the first, adding the familiar <font> tag, which enabled users to change the actual text font as well as its size and weighting. This triggered a rapid expansion in the number of tags that browsers would support.

With the new tags, however, came new problems. Different browsers implemented the new tags inconsistently. Today we have sites that display signs saying that they are "Best Viewed Through Netscape Navigator" or are "Designed for Internet Explorer". On top of all this, we now expect to be able to produce web pages that resemble documents created on the most sophisticated Desktop Publishing systems.

Meanwhile the browser's potential as a new application platform was quickly recognized, and web developers started creating distributed applications for businesses, using the Internet as a medium for information and financial transactions.

Drawbacks of HTML

While the widespread adoption of HTML propelled the rise in the number of people on the Web, these users wanted to do an ever-increasing variety of new and more complex things, and weaknesses with HTML became apparent:

❑ HTML has a fixed tag set. You cannot create your own tags that can be interpreted by others.

❑ HTML is a presentation technology. It doesn't carry information about the structure of the content held within its tags. It is meant only for the construction of user interfaces (such as web pages).

❑ HTML is 'flat'. You cannot specify the **relationship one tag has to another tag**, so a hierarchy of data cannot be represented.

❑ Browsers are being used as an application platform. HTML does not provide the power needed to create advanced web applications, at least not to the level at which developers are currently aiming. For example, it does not readily offer the ability for advanced retrieval of information from documents marked up in HTML and it is not easy to process the data within the document, because the text is only marked up for display.

While HTML has proven a very useful way of marking up documents for display in a web browser, a document marked up in HTML tells us very little about its actual content. For most documents to be useful in a business environment, there is a need to know about the document's content. When a document contains content details, then it is possible to perform generalized processing and retrieval on that document. This means that it is no longer suitable for just one purpose – rather than just being used for display on the web, it can also be used as part of an application. Marking up data in a way that tells us about its content makes it self-describing. This means that the data can be reused in different situations. SGML made this possible, but it is now also possible with XML – which is far simpler and is rapidly gaining in popularity.

How XML Came About

The major players in the browser market made it clear that they did not intend to fully support SGML. Furthermore, its complexity prevented many people from learning it. So, moves were made to create a simplified version for use on the web, signaling a return to documents being marked up according to their content. In the same way that HTML was designed for technical papers, with tags such as the "heading" and "paragraph", there was a move to allow people greater flexibility. They wanted to create their own tags and markup languages so they could mark up whatever they wanted, however they wanted, with the intention of making it self-describing.

The W3C saw the worth of creating a simplified version of SGML for use on the Web, and agreed to sponsor the project. SGML was put under the knife and several of the non-essential parts were cut, molding it into a new language called XML. This lean alternative is far more accessible, its specification running to around a fifth of the size of the specification that defined SGML.

Creating an XML Document

XML got the name eXtensible Markup Language because it does not have a fixed format like HTML. While HTML has a fixed set of tags that the author can use, XML users can create their own tags (or use those created by others, if applicable) so that they describe the content of the element.

At its simplest level XML is just a way of marking up data so that it is self-describing. What do we mean by this? Well, as one example, Wrox Press makes details of its books available in HTML over the Web – we might display book details in HTML as follows:

```
<html>
<head>
    <title>Beginning ASP.NET 1.0 using C#</title>
</head>

<body>
<h1>Beginning ASP.NET</h1>
    <h3>ISBN 1-861007-34-5</h3>

<h4>Authors</h4>
<br></br>
<h4>Chris Ullman, .Matt Butler, John Kauffman, Rob Birdwell, Chris Goode, Gary
Johnson, Srinavasar Sivakumar, Juan Llibre, Neil Raybould, Chris Miller, Dave
Sussman</h4>

<p>US $39.99</p>

<p>ASP.NET is a powerful technology for dynamically creating web site content.
Learn how to create exciting pages that are tailored to your audience. Enhance
your web/intranet presence with powerful web applications.</p>
</body>
</html>
```

That's all you need to do if you want to put information about a book on a web page. It will look something like this:

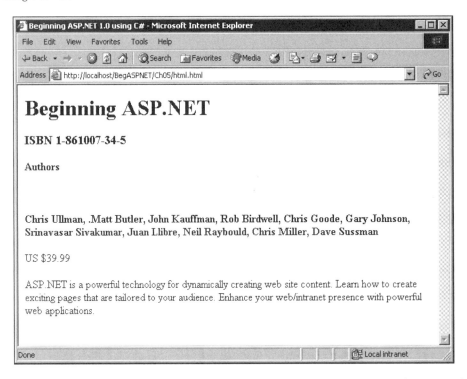

When we are building our web pages, we have lots of data in HTML, but the tags (or markup) don't give you any information about what you are displaying. There is no way that you can tell from the tags, that you are displaying, information about a book. With XML, however, you can create your own tags and make things much more clear.

So, how can we mark up the information in a more logical way, using XML? In the following *Try It Out*, we will create our first XML document that mimics the data held in the above HTML example.

Try It Out – My First XML Document

All you need to create an XML document is a simple text editor; something like Notepad will do just fine for our first example.

1. Fire up your text editor and type in the following, which we will call books.xml. Make sure you type it in exactly as shown, since XML is case sensitive and spaces must be in the correct positions:

```
<?xml version="1.0"?>
<books>
<book>
    <title>Beginning ASP.NET 1.0 using C#</title>
```

```
<ISBN>1-861007-34-5</ISBN>
<authors>
    <author_name>Chris Ullman</author_name>
    <author_name>.Matt Butler </author_name>
    <author_name>John Kauffman</author_name>
    <author_name>Rob Birdwell</author_name>
    <author_name>Chris Goode</author_name>
    <author_name>Gary Johnson</author_name>
    <author_name>Srinavasa Sivakumar</author_name>
    <author_name>Juan Llibre</author_name>
    <author_name> Neil Raybould </author_name>
    <author_name> Chris Miller </author_name>
    <author_name> Dave Sussman </author_name>
</authors>
<description> ASP.NET is a powerful technology for dynamically creating web
site content. Learn how to create exciting pages that are tailored to your
audience. Enhance your web/intranet presence with powerful web
applications.</description>
    <price US="$39.99"/>
</book>
</books>
```

2. Save the file as books.xml.

3. To open your XML file in Internet Explorer just use select **Open** from the file menu and browse to it. Alternatively, you can type in the URL Here is how our XML version of the book details is displayed when we open it in IE:

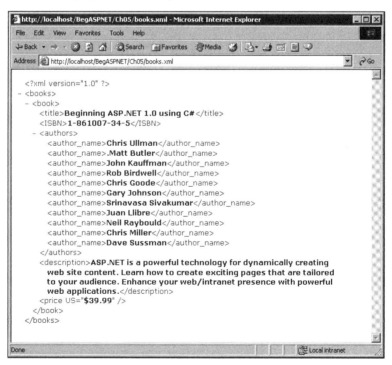

How It Works

Let's go through our code step by step and look at exactly what is happening:

```
<?xml version="1.0"?>
```

This is the XML prolog. It tells the receiving application that it is getting an XML document compatible with version one of the XML specification. Note that the XML is in lowercase and that there are no white spaces between the question mark and the opening XML. The question mark at the front denotes that this is a declaration, and not actually an XML element.

All XML documents must have a unique opening and closing tag. <books> is ours, as we have a file containing data about books:

```
<books>
  ...
</books>
```

This is known as the root element. XML tags need to have a corresponding closing tag. Unlike HTML, you cannot miss out end tags and expect your application to accept it. The only exception to this is called an **empty element**, in which there is no element content such as <br /> that we looked at earlier.

> Note that XML, unlike HTML, is case sensitive, so **<BOOK>**, **<Book>**, and **<book>** would be treated as three different tags.

Within our root element, we are describing data about a specific book, so we use an opening tag that explains what will be contained by the tag. Here we are using <book>:

```
<books>
  <book>
  ...
  </book>
</books>
```

In the same way that we made sensible opening and closing tags for the document using the <books> element, we use similarly descriptive tags to mark up more details, this time the title of the book and its ISBN (International Standard Book Number – as shown just above the bar code on the back of the book). These go inside the opening and closing <book> tags:

```
<title>Beginning ASP.NET 1.0 using C#</title>
<ISBN>1-861007-34-5</ISBN>
```

As there are several authors on this book, we'll put the list of authors in nested elements. We start with an opening <authors> tag and then nest inside this an <author_name> tag for each author. Again, these go between the opening and closing <book> tags. In this example we put them under the ISBN:

```
<authors>
    <author_name>Chris Ullman</author_name>
    <author_name>.Matt Butler </author_name>
    <author_name>John Kauffman</author_name>
    <author_name>Rob Birdwell</author_name>
    <author_name>Chris Goode</author_name>
    <author_name>Gary Johnson</author_name>
    <author_name>Srinavasa Sivakumar</author_name>
    <author_name>Juan Llibre</author_name>
    <author_name> Neil Raybould </author_name>
    <author_name> Chris Miller </author_name>
    <author_name> Dave Sussman </author_name>
</authors>
```

The fact that XML format elements are presented in a **hierarchical** structure is very important because it enables us to work with our data in a more sophisticated way, which we'll cover later.

Next, we added the description of the book. Here we are using an element called <description>, although it could equally be something like <precis>, <details>, or <synopsis>:

```
<description> ASP.NET is a powerful technology for dynamically creating web
site content. Learn how to create exciting pages that are tailored to your
audience. Enhance your web/intranet presence with powerful web
applications.</description>
```

Finally, we added the price of the book to the document. Here you can see that we are using an empty element tag, with the closing slash inside it. The currency and amount are actually held within the US attribute:

```
<price US="$39.99"/>
```

In XML, all attribute values must be contained in double quotes.

And that's all there is to it! You have just created your first XML document. It is plain text, easily human readable, and the tags describe its content and create a hierarchy of related data elements from it.

From this alone, you can tell that we are now talking about a book. Those tags that meant little in our HTML version, such as <h3> and <p>, are gone, replaced with tags describing the file's content. This makes things much more logical and it is simple to see what we are talking about.

But how does this work in a browser? We can't expect it to look at tags we've just made up and then display the information with headings and paragraphs laid out. Indeed, we saw in our last *Try It Out* that it doesn't do this. Instead, it places the tag names and the data that they contain in the browser window:

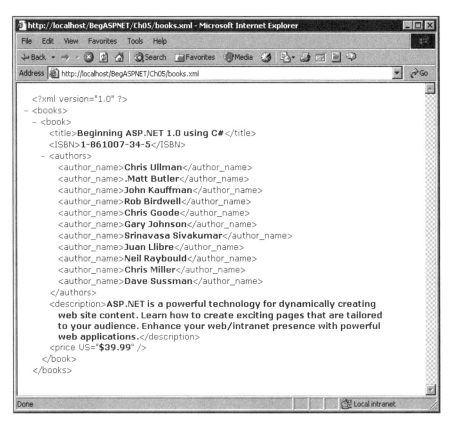

We must remember of course, that HTML is a format specifically designed for displaying information in browsers, while XML is a format concerned with marking up data to make it meaningful for any purpose. However, as we'll see later in the chapter, we can considerably improve its on-screen display with the use of **Style Sheets**.

Beyond Data Display

Up to now, it may seem as though we have been concentrating on how XML can be an alternative to HTML. Of course, XML is not an alternative to HTML – it is complementary to HTML. It is designed to abstract the data out of the HTML code, in order to make our HTML code more generic. Let's quickly expand this view and see the other effects of marking up our data as XML. We will then take a look at some of the associated specifications and techniques that you'll need to learn.

Because XML is stored and transferred as plain text it has strong advantages over most other data formats. Its pure text form is non-proprietary so it can span platforms and operating systems – any application that can read pure text can use XML. Also, the data is easy to validate. You may recall that we said SGML uses a DTD to define the rules of any markup language written with it. Well, so does XML. This means that applications can verify the structure and content of an XML file.

So, not only can XML be used as a way of presenting data that is marked up as HTML, it is equally useful for many other purposes, including:

❑ Data transfer – from the book details we could send details of orders and financial transactions, in XML, that can be understood by any platform

❑ Reusable data storage – data can be stored in plain text files rather than pre-purposed formats, such as HTML and proprietary word processor files, making it available to a far wider range of applications

This isn't to say XML is a perfect solution for all data storage. It has problems in allowing concurrent editing of the XML file; in fact it doesn't actually allow concurrent editing. So if one person starts editing a file, after a small amount of time, it will automatically be locked by the operating system. This means no one else can update it during this period. So XML won't replace databases for solutions where people are constantly updating and amending the same data. Like most technologies it has its specific strengths and weaknesses.

> *There are some XML database servers available out there, and some aren't bad, although certainly not in the league of SQL Server or Oracle, but they present a superior alternative to just using the XML file itself.*

So far we've looked at why XML was created, and discussed its structure and its similarities with HTML. Now we're going to move on to examine it in more detail. Firstly we're going to look at the kinds of documents that XML will, and won't, accept and why it is much stricter with regards to formatting than HTML.

Well-Formed vs. Valid Documents

The XML 1.0 specification lays out two types of XML document, either **well-formed** or **valid**. The distinction between the two is simple:

❑ Well-formed documents comply with the rules of XML syntax

❑ Valid documents are not only well-formed, they also comply with a DTD (Document Type Definition)

Well-Formed Documents

XML syntax is governed by the XML 1.0 specification. If you understand the specification properly you will have no difficulty in constructing a set of rules to look at a document and decide whether it is in XML or not. If it is, then it can go on for further processing, if it is not then it can be rejected. Because of the self-descriptive qualities of XML these rules can be applied equally well by either a computer or a human.

The official XML specification states well-formedness as the minimum requirement a document must satisfy in order to be considered as true XML. This specification also features a mixture of other requirements that ensure correct language terms are employed and that the document is logically coherent in the manner defined by the specification (in other words that the terms of the language are used in the right way). You can see the XML specification at http://www.w3.org/TR/2000/REC-xml-20001006. There is also a helpful annotated version available at http://www.xml.com/axml/testaxml.htm.

So, what are these rules? You'll be pleased to hear that nearly everything we need to know about well-formed documents can be summed up in three rules:

- ❑ The document must contain one or more elements

- ❑ It must contain a uniquely named element, no part of which appears in the content of any other element. This is known as the root element

- ❑ All other elements must be kept within the root element and must be nested correctly

So, let's look at how we construct a well-formed document.

The XML Declaration

This is actually optional, although you are strongly advised to use it so that the receiving application knows that it is an XML document and also the version used (at the time of writing this was the only version):

```
<?xml version="1.0"?>
```

Note that "xml" should be in lowercase. Note also that the XML declaration, when present, must not be preceded by any other characters (not even white space). As we saw previously, this declaration is also referred to as the XML prolog.

Elements

As we have already seen, the XML document essentially consists of data marked up using tags. Each start tag-end tag pair, with the data that lies between them, is an element:

```
<mytag>Here we have some data</mytag>
```

The start and end tags must be exactly the same, except for the closing slash in the end tag. Remember that they must be in the same case: <mytag> and <MyTag> would be considered as different tags.

The section between the tags that says, "Here we have some data", is called character data, while the tags either side are the markup. The character data can consist of any sequence of legal characters (conforming to the Unicode standard), except the start element character "<". This is not allowed in case a processing application treats it as the start of a new tag. If you do need to include this character, you can represent it using the entity < as follows:

```
<answer>
  <true>20 > 10</true>
  <false>20 &lt; 10</false>
</answer>
```

Note that we can only ever have one top-level element per XML document. We therefore need to place elements true and false within the element answer for this snippet to be valid as the complete body of an XML document.

Tags can start with a letter, an underscore '_', or a colon ':', followed by any combination of letters, digits, hyphens, underscores, colons, or periods. The only exception is that you cannot start a tag with the letters XML in any combination of upper or lowercase letters.

Here is another example, marking up some details for a hardware store:

```
<inventory>
    <buckets>
        <bucket>
            <make>Addis</make>
            <capacity>3 litres</capacity>
        </bucket>
        <bucket>
            <make>Metro</make>
            <capacity>2.5 litres</capacity>
        </bucket>
    </buckets>
</inventory>
```

If you think back to the three rules at the beginning of this section, you will be able to work out that this is a well-formed XML document. We have more than our one required element. We have a unique opening and closing tag: <inventory>, which is the root element, and the elements are nested properly inside the root element.

Let's have a look at some more examples to help us get the idea how a well-formed XML document should be constructed.

At the simplest level we could have either:

```
<my_document></my_document>
```

or even:

```
<my_document/>
```

To make sure that tags nest properly, there must be no overlap. So this is correct:

```
<parent>
    <child>Some character data</child>
</parent>
```

while this would be incorrect:

```
<bad_parent>
        <naughty_child>
            Some character data
</bad_parent>
        </naughty child>
```

This is because the closing `</naughty_child>` element is after the closing `</bad_parent>` element.

Attributes

Elements can have attributes. These are values that are passed to the application, but do not constitute part of the content of the element. Attributes are included as part of the element's opening tag, as in HTML. XML attribute values must always be enclosed in quote marks (either single or double quote marks are acceptable). For example:

```
<food healthy="yes">spinach</food>
```

Elements can have as many attributes as you want. So you could have:

```
<food healthy="no" tasty="yes" high_in_fat="yes">fries</food>
```

To be well-formed, however, you cannot repeat the attribute within an instance of the element. So you could not have:

```
<food tasty="yes" tasty="no">spinach</food>
```

Also, the string values between the quote marks can't contain the characters <, &, ', or ", as they can be interpreted as part of the XML tags. If you need to use these specific characters then they can be represented using CDATA sections, which we look at very shortly.

Other Features

There are also a number of other features of the XML specification that you need to learn if you want to progress to using XML frequently. Unfortunately there isn't space to cover them all here. We will, however, briefly describe a few of them.

Entities

There are two categories of entity: general entities and parameter entities. Entities are generally used within a document as a way of avoiding having to type out long pieces of text several times. They provide a way of associating a name with your text, so that whenever you need to mention it you can just mention the name instead. As a result, if you have to modify the text, you only have to do it once (rather like the benefits offered by `String` variables). A typical general entity might look like this:

```
<!ENTITY copyright "@ Feiertag Holidays, Inc., 2001">
```

You can then put the entity into the document as follows:

```
&copyright;
```

Parameter entities are only used within the DTD and for that reason we won't discuss them here.

CDATA Sections

CDATA sections can be used inside elements whenever you need to use character data. They are used to delimit blocks of text that would otherwise be considered as markup. If we wanted to include the whole of the following line, including the tags:

```
<to_be_seen>Always wear light clothing when walking in the dark</to_be_seen>
```

we could use a CDATA section like so:

```
<element>
<! [CDATA[ <to_be_seen>Always wear light clothing when walking in the
dark</to_be_seen> ]]>
</element>
```

And the whole line, including the opening and closing `<to_be_seen>` tags, would not be processed or treated as tags by the receiving application. They are often used when you have HTML tags inside your XML document, and need to prevent them from being treated as XML tags.

Comments

It is always good programming practice to comment your code – it's so much easier to read if it is commented in a manner that helps explain, reminds you about, or simply points out, salient sections of code. It is surprising how code that seemed perfectly clear when you wrote it can soon become a jumble when you come back to it. While the descriptive XML tags often help you understand your own markup, there are times when the tags alone are not enough.

The good news is that comments in XML use exactly the same syntax as those in HTML:

```
<!--I really should add a comment here to remind me about xxxxx -->
```

Of course, to avoid confusing the receiving application, you should not include either the – or -- characters in your comment text.

Processing Instructions

These allow documents to contain instructions for applications using XML data. They take the form:

```
<?NameOfTargetApplication    Instructions for Application?>
```

The target name cannot contain the word XML in any combination of upper or lowercase. Otherwise, you can create your own target name to work with the processing application (unless there are any predefined by the application at which you are targeting your XML).

In our next *Try It Out*, we will be looking at badly formed XML. We can tell a lot about whether our XML is well-formed by simply loading it into our browser. It has the ability to tell us about all sorts of errors (although it does let some slip). When you are first writing XML, it is very helpful to do this quick check so that you know your XML is well-formed.

Try It Out – Badly formed XML

1. Open up your `books.xml` file.

2. Remove the opening `<book>` tag.

3. Save the file as `bad_book.xml`.

4. Load it into an up-to-date browser, and you should see something like this:

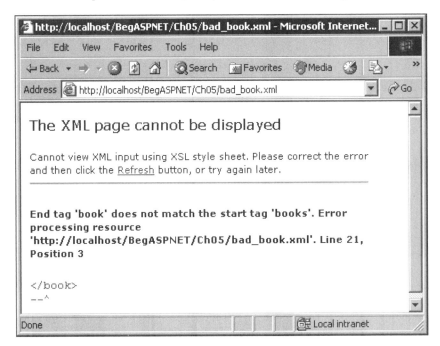

As you can see, the error message is pretty accurate. It more or less explicitly tells you that it was expecting an opening `<book>` tag. It certainly wouldn't take you long to find out what was wrong.

5. Put the opening book tag in again and change the line:

```
<title>Beginning ASP.NET 1.0 with C#</title>
```

to:

```
<title>Beginning ASP.NET 1.0 with C#<title>
```

by simply removing the slash on the closing tag.

6. Save the file again, and open it up in your browser (or simply click the Refresh button, if you have it open already). You should get a result like this:

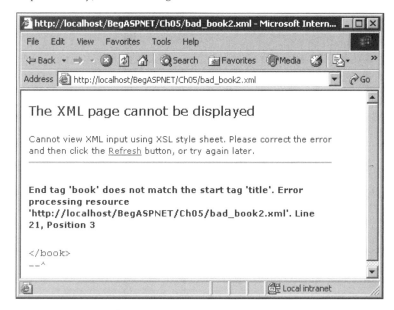

Again, we are not given the exact error, but the browser was expecting a closing `<title>` tag, which it did not receive.

7. Finally, correct the closing `<title>` tag, and remove the opening quote from the US price attribute. Save the file and refresh your browser. This time you get the exact error:

While it is not the most elegant way to test code, it certainly does help find errors quickly. If you have made more than one error, just correct your mistakes one at a time and watch the error messages change.

Valid Documents

As we mentioned earlier, valid documents are well-formed documents that conform to a DTD. When we read a book, manual or magazine article we rarely notice its structure; if it is well written then the structure will be transparent. Yet, without structure there would be no communication. We may notice headings and paragraphs, but many other aspects pass us by. For one thing this structuring makes the information in the document intelligible, either by us or to an application using it. Furthermore, it means that when a document is parsed, for example by an application, it can be checked for the presence of required portions.

There are many programs, known as parsers, available for XML. Some of these are able to validate a document against its DTD, in which case they are known as validating parsers. If the document does not follow the structure of the DTD the parser will raise an error. XML parsers are included as part of Internet Explorer 5 and onwards, and Netscape Navigator 6 and onwards, hence our need in a previous example to these versions or better.

Assuming that, in the first instance, we have an appropriate and well-planned structure for a type of document, then the resulting document instances should be logically complete with respect to its predefined structure. So, in our book example earlier we had:

❑ The unique opening and closing tags of `<books>`

❑ A `<book>` element, which encapsulates all information on a specific book

❑ Followed by a title, in a `<title>` element

❑ Then the ISBN in the `<ISBN>` tags

❑ Followed by the author, description, and price elements

If we had to exchange a lot of book information in this format, with various different people, there would be many advantages to writing a DTD (or document type definition). Such a book DTD would lay out the structure of how we expect books to be marked up, and while they're not compulsory to create XML files, they do mean that anyone following it will be able to write an XML file about books that would be valid according to our type definitions. In this manner, we could guarantee that any application using the book information, marked up according to our DTD, could understand the document. It could even do a preliminary check to ensure that the document followed our DTD in order to prevent the application showing errors if we passed in the wrong data. You could think of this as being similar to form validation for incoming and outgoing data, that is, it will define the correct elements and properties, in the same way that form fields are checked for data conforming to a specific criteria.

If we wrote an application to processes XML files that conformed to our book DTD, it would be able to process *any* files that conformed to our DTD. In which case, if Wrox had different members of staff all writing XML documents about the books, they could all follow the DTD to make sure that they were valid. Then, should other publishers adopt the same DTD, the bookstores who might make use of our XML files would be able to use the same applications to process the files sent from several different publishers.

However, it is worth noting that there are other techniques. The W3C has recently completed a set of schemas written in XML called XML Schemas.

XML Schemas

XML Schemas have several advantages over their DTD counterparts. The group working on the specification has looked at several proposals. The main ones are XML-Data and Document Content Description. Links to both can be found, with all of the submissions and specifications in progress, on the W3C site at http://www.w3.org/tr/.

There are a number of reasons why these XML Schemas will be an advantage over DTDs. Firstly, they use XML syntax rather than Extended Backus-Naur Form, which many people find difficult to learn. Secondly, if you needed to parse the schema, it will be possible to do so using an existing XML parser, rather than having to use a special parser. Another strong advantage is the ability to specify data types in XML Schemas, for the content of elements and attributes. This means that applications using the content will not have to convert it into the appropriate data type from a string. As an example, think about an application that has to add two numbers together, or perform a calculation on a date – using XML Schemas it wouldn't have to convert this data to the appropriate type, from a string, before it could perform the calculation. There will be other advantages too, such as support for namespaces, which we meet shortly. Also, XML Schemas can be easily extended, whereas DTDs cannot be simply extended once written. As XML Schemas were developed originally by Microsoft, you'll find that they are now very present within .NET. DTDs are becoming less popular, although they are certainly still very much in existence.

Even HTML has DTDs

Being an SGML application, HTML has several SGML DTDs (at the very least, a strict and loose one for each version), and the XHTML specification has an XML DTD (as opposed to an SGML DTD). XHTML is a new version of HTML that is designed as an XML application, as opposed to an SGML application. This means that you will be able to parse XHTML documents using an XML parser. You can view an HTML DTD at http://www.w3.org/TR/REC-html40/loose.dtd. According to the HTML standard you should include the following line:

```
<!DOCTYPE HTML PUBLIC "-//W3C//DTD HTML 4.01 //EN">
```

It tells the user agent the location of HTML's DTD. However, it is often left out because, practically speaking, it is not necessary and if you are using browser-specific tags, which deviate from the specification, it may cause unpredictable results.

Styling XML

So far, we have written an XML document (`books.xml`) to create a self-describing data structure about books. This is a great way to define data, as our tags clearly explain their content and are written in plain text, which is easy to transfer. However, if we are putting things up on the Web we want our pages to look good. As our earlier example showed, even in an XML-aware browser, such as IE 6, a plain XML file doesn't look that impressive:

This is because the tags that we have proposed for our book example don't say anything about how the tags should appear on the page, whereas HTML tells the browser how the data should look.

So, to make it look more attractive we must supply another file, a **style sheet**.

Why Use Style Sheets?

Unfortunately, using style sheets means that we have to use a completely separate language, in a separate file, to declare how we want our document to be presented. They do, however confer the following advantages:

❑   They improve document clarity by separating data and presentation

❑   They help reduce download time, network traffic, and server load, as one style sheet can be downloaded and can apply to many pages, rather than having the same presentational information repeated in each page

❑   They allow you to modify the presentation of several pages, by altering just one file

❑   They allow you to present the same data in different ways for different purposes

Separating rules governing how the content of a document is displayed, like < font > tags, from the content itself is greatly beneficial to our content's clarity.

With a style sheet, all of the style rules are kept in one file and the source document simply links to this file. This means that if several pages use the same type of display (which is often the case as we display an ever-increasing amount of data on web pages) we do not need to repeat the style rules in each page. The browser can download the style sheet and cache it on the client. All other pages can then use the same styling rules. This also means that should you need to change the style of your site – perhaps your company changes its corporate colors – then you do not need to laboriously change every file individually by hand, you just change one style sheet and the changes are propagated across all the pages. Indeed, conversely, it means that you can use the same data, and display it in different ways for different purposes by applying different style sheets.

Cascading Style Sheets

The Cascading Style Sheets Level 1 specification was released by the W3C in late 1996. It has been supported to a large degree in all browsers. Since 1996, a Level 2 specification has been released (May 1998), some of which has been incorporated into Internet Explorer 5 onwards, Netscape version 6, and Opera 5. In addition, at the time of writing, a third level is in progress, but nothing much in the way of this draft standard has made it even into the latest browsers.

Cascading Style Sheets are already popular with HTML developers for the same reasons that we have just expanded upon here.

CSS is a rule-based language consisting of two sections:

- ❑ A pattern matching section, which expresses the association between an element and some action

- ❑ An action section, which specifies the action to be taken upon the specified section

For CSS, this means that we have to specify an element and then define how it has to be displayed. So, if we were to develop a cascading style sheet for our books.xml file, we would have to specify a style for each of the elements that contained markup that we wanted to display.

CSS splits up the browser screen into areas that take a tree-like form, as shown in the following diagram. You can think of this much like the tree that Windows Explorer exposes:

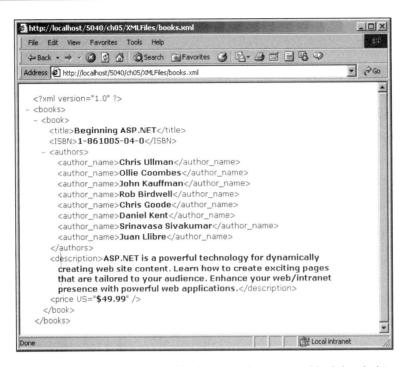

Here we have a page, with several areas. Inside the second area are a block-level object and a number of in-line objects.

> *Block-level objects are HTML elements that can contain other HTML block level elements, such as `<p>` and `<div>`, and in-line objects, while in-line objects are elements that can only contain other in-line HTML elements such as the `<b>` and `<i>` elements, and data.*

Using CSS we can specify a style for each of these. Note that the block flow object is taking up the whole line, while the others are on the same line. A block need not contain text or images that take up the whole line – it could simply contain a short title that needs to be displayed in a line of its own.

It is important to decide whether the values are to be displayed in-line or as a block. The difference is that, if they are in-line the next element will be displayed as if it were on the same line as the previous one, whereas if it is displayed as a block, each will be treated separately. We need to make this decision for each object in CSS.

While we cannot cover a full reference to CSS here you should find it fairly easy to catch on and, if you need to investigate a particular implementation, you can always check the specification at http://www.w3.org/style/css/ or in the Wrox book *HTML 4.01 Programmer's Reference* – ISBN 1-86100-533-4.

Let's try it and write a style sheet for our `books.xml` file.

Try It Out – Displaying XML with CSS

1. Start by opening up your text editor, and entering the following code:

```
title {
     display:block;
     font-family: Arial, Helvetica;
     font-weight: bold;
     font-size: 20pt;
     color: #9370db;
     text-align: center;
     }
ISBN {
     display:block;
     font-family: Arial, Helvetica;
     font-weight: bold;
     font-size: 12pt;
     color: #c71585;
     text-align: left;
     }

authors {
     display:inline;
     font-family: Arial, Helvetica;
     font-style: italic;
     font-size: 10pt;
     color: #9370db;
     text-align: left;
     }

description {
     display:block;
     font-family: Arial, Helvetica;
     font-size: 12pt;
     color: #ff1010;
     text-align: left;
     }
```

2. Save the file as `books.css`. We have now finished creating our first style sheet for XML. The only problem is that our `books.xml` file has no way of telling how it should be associated with this style sheet. So we will have to add a link to it in our original XML file.

3. To add the link to the style sheet, open up your `books.xml` file again, and add the following line between the XML prolog and the opening `<books>` element.

```
<?xml version="1.0"?>
<?xml:stylesheet href="books.css" type="text/css" ?>
<books>
```

Also if you haven't done so already, make sure you've removed the errors that you inserted into the `books.xml` *file.*

4. Open `books.xml` in your browser and you should see something like this:

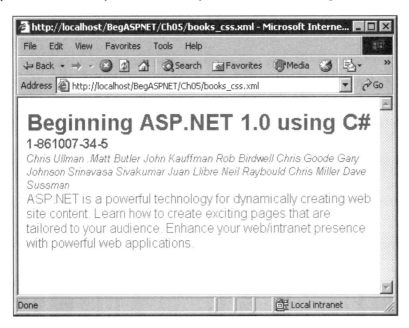

How It Works

CSS files do not need a special header, so we go straight on and declared which elements we needed to display. In this case we are just adding styling for the `<title>`, `<ISBN>`, `<authors>`, and `<description>` elements. So we add them to the file like this:

```
title {

        }
ISBN   {

        }

authors {

        }

description {

        }
```

This specifies the pattern matching section.

Having declared the elements we want to display, we must associate some action with them. So, let's see how to display the content of the `<title>` element. We want it to be displayed as a block, so within the curly brackets {} we add the directive to display the element as a block:

```
title {
      display:block;
      }
```

This simply specifies that we want to make the title a block-level element. We still need to specify the style the title should be displayed in.

> **All properties are specified with a colon delimiting the attribute and values and have a semi-colon after them. The semi-colon ending the line, should of course be very familiar as we do the same to end C# statements.**

We added a font to display the content of the `<title>` element. In the screenshot you have just seen the browser is using the Arial font. However, in case the machine using the file does not have Arial, we have allowed it to use Helvetica instead. In addition, we want it to appear in the center of the screen, in a size 20pt, bold font, and in a lilac color. So, we add some more action rules, or style elements. As you can see, these are very similar to those used for HTML:

```
title {
     display:block;
     font-family: Arial, Helvetica;
     font-weight: bold;
     font-size: 20pt;
     color: #9370db;
     text-align: center;
     }
```

We can then add some similar rules for the other element content we want to display, for example:

```
authors {
     display:inline;
     font-family: Arial, Helvetica;
     font-style: italic;
     font-size: 10pt;
     color: #9370db;
     text-align: left;
     }
```

You can see from the screenshot that the authors, despite being in separate elements in the `books.xml` file are displayed on the same line.

Finally, we included an extra line in our `books.xml` file to tell it to use the correct CSS file:

```
<?xml version="1.0"?>
<?xml:stylesheet href="books.css" type="text/css" ?>
<books>
```

The `href` attribute acts just as it would in HTML, while the `type` attribute specifies the type of style sheet that is being attached. This is an example of a **processing instruction**. You may remember us talking about them earlier in the chapter, when we were discussing XML syntax.

> **Remember that because the style sheet link is still in the XML file, the values of the attributes still need to be kept in quotation marks for the XML to be well-formed.**

While we now have a good idea of how XML works, and how to display it, we still don't know anything about how it works with ASP.NET.

Using XML with ASP.NET

We won't actually look at the mechanics of using XML in our ASP.NET pages for another couple of chapters, since we first need to properly introduce objects first.

However, it's worth pointing out that XML is used in many different ways within ASP.NET, and its usefulness should become increasingly evident as we progress through the book. As we demonstrated briefly back in Chapter 2, it can be used as a data source from which you can extract data – we'll consider this in much more detail when we get on to Chapters 12 and 13, in which we'll discuss data sources in general.

XML can also be used as a format to which you can dump database information or object state. It's used in Web Services (which we'll look at in Chapter 18) to transmit data between applications. It's also used in the various configuration files for IIS and ASP.NET (which we're going to focus on in Chapter 19). As you can see it is used for many varying purposes.

This completes our introduction to XML – even if you don't yet fully grasp its significance within ASP.NET, you should at least have some idea of what a useful, flexible, and lightweight information storage structure it can be.

Summary

In this chapter we've examined the potential of XML as a structured information storage medium. We looked at how it came into being, the job it was designed to do, and its advantages and disadvantages when compared to HTML. We moved on to look at the differences between valid and well-formed XML documents, and how you can use your web browser to provide an indication of whether a document is well-formed. We discussed elements, attributes, entities, and the various other features that make up an XML document, together with the processing instructions that you can include. We examined the creation of Style Sheets to make your XML documents more aesthetically appealing, and the advantages that this approach has over HTML, where presentation and content are combined.

In the next chapter, we will look at the basic structures that C# offers for handling variables and running programs.

Exercises

1. Explain why XML is so useful for storing data.

2. Create an XML file to hold the following employee information:

```
Company: Wrox Press

employee: Hubert Welsch
employee number: 9862
contact numbers: ext - 346
        home - 8764 35733
length of service: 2 years
department: .NET Team

employee: Paul Crick
employee number: 7461
contact numbers: ext - 399
        home - 2138 90346
length of service: 8 months
department: .NET Team

employee: Alison Freyer
employee number: 7849
contact numbers: ext - 982
        home - 7893 42769
length of service: 4 years
department: Java Team

employee: Sandra Jackson
employee number: 9862
contact numbers: ext - 222
        home - 8974 389743
length of service: 1 year
department: Finance
```

3. Create a Cascading Style Sheet to display the XML file you have just created. Use font style and alignment, and color to display the employee information in an attractive way.

4. Are the following XML documents well-formed? If not, make the necessary corrections, and explain why your corrections are important in the creation of a well-formed document:

```
<?xml version="1.0"?>
<shoppingList>
  <title>Shopping List</title>
  <items>
    <fruit items>
      <item>Rasberries</item>
      <item>Apples</item>
      <item>Oranges</item>
    </fruit_items>
    <vegetable_items>
      <item>Carrots</item>
      <item>Onions</item>
      </vegetable_items>
      <other_items>
        <item>Floor cleaner</item>
        <item>Bread</item>
        <item>Toothpaste</item>
        <item>Pasta</item)
      </other_items>
  <items>
</shoppingList>
  <Notes> Don't get cooking apples like last time and post letter to
Harold</Notes>


<?xml version="1.0">
<order>
  <salesperson>Sam Clarke</salesperson>
  <customer>Droutledge Waters</customer>
  <item>
    <description>snorkle</description>
    <quantity>37</quantity>
  </item>
  <date>
    <month>7</month>
    <day>6</day>
    <year>2001</year>
  </date>
</order>
```

5. Once you have finished with Question 4, try rearranging this information so that you can view orders that have been placed via Sam Clarke the sales person. Add another order, placed the following week, for 12 goggles, as ordered by 'Aqua Lake Enterprises'.

Control Structures and Procedural Programming

In the first few chapters of this book, we've been writing ASP.NET web forms using C# code. Up until now we've not been able to use our code for anything but the most trivial of tasks. In fact, occasionally to demonstrate points about how to populate arrays efficiently, we've had to use structures that we haven't talked about yet. You can breathe a sigh of relief now, as we're going to talk about the fundamental structures – branches, loops, and modules – that go to make up C#.

You might be wondering why we need these structures? The reason is that our ASP.NET programs, given certain conditions, need to be able to skip or repeat lines – or groups of lines. This chapter will teach you ways to change the order that the lines of your code are executed in, and how to repeat the execution of sections of code as necessary.

This chapter covers the three ways that you can use C# with your ASP.NET code to sequence the execution of your lines of code. Respectively, these are:

❑   Deciding which of two or more sections of code to run

❑   Repeating a section of code as many times as needed

❑   Jumping out of the code sequence and executing sections of code in another part of your script

Note that once again this chapter refers to using C# in our ASP.NET web forms, and hence the syntax shown in the following examples is specific to C#. You'll find that the features introduced in this chapter enable you to write much more complex ASP.NET code and the web forms you will be able to create will now begin to resemble applications, rather than static HTML pages with a few extras bolted on.

In this chapter we're going to look at:

❑   Conditional structures using `if` and `else`

❑   Conditional structures using `switch` and `case`

- ❏ `for` loops
- ❏ `do while` and `while` loops
- ❏ Functions, return types, and parameters
- ❏ Variable scope: local and global

A Quick Look at Control Structures

When programming with C#, or just about any other computer language, in ASP.NET, we have three types of structures (groups of control statements) to control the order in which the lines of code are executed. These are: branching structures, looping structures, and jumping structures. We'll now look at each of these, in turn, in more detail.

Overview of Branching Structures

Branching structures work by first performing some type of test. Based on the test results, one set of code will be executed and other sets of code will be skipped. Consider a quick real-life example. If you're in a car and pull up to a set of traffic lights, if the lights are on red, you'll have to stop the car and wait until the lights change before going. If the lights are on green, you can drive on through immediately. The course of action you take is determined by the result of the test condition (the color of the traffic light). This is pretty much how C# also handles such decisions. In fact there are two types of structure employed to help do this.

These two types of branching structures are:

- ❏ `if...else` – generally used to select one of two (or occasionally more) sets of lines to execute based on a condition to be met. A simple example: in a web page featuring news stories, we could choose whether to display the international, or the regional news headlines, depending on a user's preferences. `if` blocks are also the tool of choice for complicated comparisons, such as expressions using the terms AND, OR, and NOT.

- ❏ `switch...case` – generally used to select one (or more) sets of lines to execute from **many** possibilities. For example, in a page featuring news stories, we could choose which of several icons to include in the page next to the story, depending on whether the story was about politics, business, sport, entertainment, or technology. It might be conceivable that one story is so big that it needs to feature (or variations of it do) in two sections.

Overview of Looping Structures

Looping structures allow the same block of code to be run a number of times. Instead of skipping code – which is what the branching technique does – we **repeat** code. Back to our real-life example; you're in your car and you get to the roundabout. Now it's possible to get off at any exit, but say you're not paying attention and miss your exit, it's possible to repeat and go around the roundabout again to get to the exit. (In fact you could go around it again, and again). This is a real-world example of looping.

In this chapter we'll be studying an example where we'll use looping to generate a page for each person who is going to be staying at a hotel.

❑   `for` loops are used to repeat line(s) when, at the beginning of the repetitions, we know exactly how many repetitions we want, at the outset, or we can include some code that will generate a condition at run time to result in the loop being exited appropriately. For example, if we know there are five trucks needing a wash, we could repeat five times the set of steps involved in successfully washing a truck.

❑   `do` and `while` loops are used to repeat line(s) when we **don't** know at design time how many repetitions we want. We build into the loop a Boolean test condition, which is checked before or after each loop cycle. The loop will repeat as long as the condition is `true`. The difference between the two types of loop is that the code in the `do` loop always runs once even if the condition eventually evaluates to `false` as the test is made **after** every cycle of the loop. By contrast, in the `while` loop, the test is made **before** the loop code executes, which means that if the test initially evaluates to `false`, then the loop will not be run at all.

❑   `for...each` loops are used when we have a collection of an unknown number of items and we want to repeat the loop for every item in the collection.

Overview of Functions

Functions allow the programmer to suspend the execution of the current code to run a set of instructions in another named code block before returning to the original code. For example, we may have a block of code that outputs lines that show the customer the goods that they ordered. Whenever we want our application to display those lines, it's not an efficient use of our time or the computer's resources to re-write or copy all of that code. Instead, we just place the relevant code inside a **function** with a given name, say `ShowOrder()`. Then, we can just call the `ShowOrder()` function to show an order's details, after which execution of our original code resumes.

When to Use a Particular Control Structure

With these three classes of controls – branching, looping, and functions – we can solve virtually any programming objective in ASP.NET. The table below shows several situations we might want to program for, and suggested classes of structure that will help us achieve the desired results:

Situation	Solution	Why?
I want ASP.NET to show page A or page B.	Branching	We want to perform only one of two possible events.
I need to show the user which of several meetings they should attend. The meeting displayed is based on which department they belong to.	Branching	We want to write to the page only **one** out of several possible meeting locations.

Table continued on following page

Situation	Solution	Why?
I want ASP.NET to list each member of the club. The data about each member is held in essentially the same manner, with a name, photo, address, and other contact information.	Looping	We will be performing the same set of code (which retrieves a member's name) many times (once for each member, until we list all members).
I want to present data in a table.	Looping	We will perform the same code (make a row for a table) again and again until we have built all of the rows needed.
After placing an item that I describe in a catalog page, I want to put in a few lines of information about 'How to Order'. There will be several items across several pages that we need to do this for.	Use a function	We want to pause the main code and perform several lines of **another** set of code that describes 'How to Order'. Then we want to resume the main code. Since the 'How to Order' set of code will be performed at various times across the page, it is best to write it once and call that one piece of code as needed.
I need to calculate prices in several places on each page. The prices will be set according to input from a user form.	Use a function	We will pause building the page, jump out to execute code to calculate the price of an item, and then return to building the page using the calculated amount. Since we will calculate many prices it is best to write the formula once and have it called when needed.

Let's recap on what we've discussed so far. There are three kinds of statements that control the flow of our code's execution:

❏   Branching statements that perform a test and then execute some lines of code, but not others

❏   Looping statements that execute a set of code over and over

❏   Jumping statements that pause the execution of the current code, jump over to another set of code, and then return to where they started, sometimes bringing values back with them

Now we'll look at branching statements, and see what we can do with them.

Branching Structures in Detail

As we've already mentioned, branching controls perform some type of test. Based on the test results, one block of code will be executed and other blocks skipped.

C# offers two techniques for branching. The `if` clause is used when there are only a few choices of outcome. It is better to use `switch` statements when there are a lot of possible outcomes for one particular test.

For example, if you are making a decision on how to proceed, and have asked the user "Do you want a confirmation by telephone?", the outcome is either "Yes" (`true`) or "No" (`false`), so you would perform the branch using `if`. But if the user is asked "Do you want confirmation by telephone, fax, e-mail, voicemail, FedEx, carrier pigeon, or telepathy?" then, due to the number of outcomes, it would probably be better to use `switch`.

Before we launch into a detailed examination of how these particular branching structures are used, we need to look at some of the operators that may be used within these statements.

Comparison Operators

The comparison operators available in C# are:

Equality	`==`	Inequality	`!=`
Less than	`<`	Greater than	`>`
Less than or equal to	`<=`	Greater than or equal to	`>=`

> Note that the equality operator is a double equals "==" and not a single equals. It is very important not to use a single equals here. If you do, your code will not compile, as the single = sign indicates variable assignment, not a comparison.

Logical Comparisons Using if

The general syntax for the `if` statement is as follows:

```
if (Boolean condition)
{
  // Code in here
}
```

A Boolean condition is a statement that compares two variables or expressions and determines whether the comparison is valid (`true`) or not (`false`). For example, if `intAge` is 17, the following condition would be `true`:

```
intAge <= 18
```

whereas this one would be `false`:

```
intAge >= 18
```

The expressions on either side of the comparison operator can both be variables, or a constant and a variable (as in the above example), or expressions that evaluate to either a constant or a variable. In the C# `if` statement, the Boolean condition is enclosed in parentheses:

```
if (intAge >= 18)
```

The code following the `if` statement is run only if the condition evaluates to `true`. Note that if the code to execute comprises just a single statement, it does not need to be wrapped in curly braces, whereas multiple statements do. If the comparison operation evaluates to `false`, however, the code is not run.

To illustrate further, take a look at this:

```
if (intAge >= 18)
{
   Label.Text = "You are allowed in the club";
}
```

The message will only be displayed if the value for `intAge` is greater than or equal to 18, otherwise nothing happens.

Logical Operators

There are some special logical operators that you can use in your code to build more sophisticated Boolean conditions. In C#, they are as follows:

❑   `&&` – logical AND, which is used to join two separate Boolean conditions, and evaluates to `true` if *both* of them evaluate to `true`

❑   `||` – logical OR, which is used similarly to `&&`, except that it evaluates to `true` if *either* of the two sub-conditions evaluates to `true`

❑   `!` – logical NOT, which makes a `true` condition `false`, and a `false` one true.

Let's illustrate these with some examples:

```
if (intAge >= 18 && intAge <= 30)
{
   Label.Text = "You can join Club 18-30";
}
```

This statement uses the AND (&&) operator, which evaluates to true only if intAge lies between 18 and 30 inclusive, otherwise it is false.

```
if (intAge >= 18 || strAutomobile == "Porsche")
{
   Label.Text = "Either he is over 18 or he drives a Porsche or both";
}
```

The OR (||) operator gives you a wider range of true values. Here true is returned if intAge is greater than or equal to 18, or if strAutomobile has the value Porsche, or both.

The NOT (!) operator just negates the effect of any condition it preceeds, so:

```
if (!(intAge >= 18))
{
   Label.Text = "You're too young to join the 18-30 Club ";
}
```

means that only values of intAge less than 18 will result in the message being displayed.

This code is directly equivalent to this:

```
if (intAge < 18)
{
   Label.Text = "You're too young to join the 18-30 Club";
}
```

When you have a statement containing more than one of the logical operators, C# decides which ones to execute first according to the following simple rule, called **operator precedence**:

1. !

2. &&

3. ||

The ! operation is evaluated first, then the && operation, and finally the || operation. It is important that you remember this order of precedence as it can cause problems in your code if you are not careful. To illustrate what I mean, take the following example:

```
if (strName == "John Doe" || strAutomobile == "Porsche" && intAge >= 18)
{
   Label.Text = "Message received and understood";
}
```

What the programmer wanted here was to OR together the conditions for strName and strAutomobile, to determine whether either (or both) are equal to the values specified, and then AND the result with the evaluation of the intAge condition. The intention was to display the message "Message received and understood" only if strName is John Doe and the value for intAge is greater than or equal to 18 *or* if strAutomobile is Porsche and the value for intAge is greater than or equal to 18, *or* – of course – if all three conditions are true.

In their haste, the programmer put the OR statement first, and so does not get the desired result. The code first evaluates the && operation as follows:

```
<result> = strAutomobile == "Porsche" && intAge >= 18
```

where `<result>` represents the result of this particular Boolean operation, used here just for clarity as it never really exists as a variable in its own right. The result of this operation is then ORed with the last statement as follows:

```
strName == "John Doe" || <result>
```

The trouble with this is that you will always get a true result if strName is John Doe, regardless of what the other two values are. This means that if intAge is less than 18 then the message will be displayed, which is not what we originally intended.

To get the right result we have to put parentheses round the OR operation:

```
if ((strAutomobile == "Porsche" || strName == "John Doe") && intAge >= 18)
{
  Label.Text = "Message received and understood";
}
```

Now we get the right result and we have achieved it by forcing the code to carry out the OR operation before the AND operation.

Extending if Statements Using else if and else

As we have already seen, the basic if statement only executes its associated code if the comparison operation or operations evaluate to true. But what if we want to execute some other code when the condition is false? To do this, we use the else keyword immediately after the if block:

```
if (Boolean condition)
{
  // Code in here
}
else
{
  // more code here
}
```

The code in the `else` block, consisting of either a single statement or several within curly braces, is only executed if the `if` statement's condition evaluates to `false` – the `if` code block is ignored altogether. Conversely, in the opposite situation a `true` result will result in the `if` block being executed and the `else` block being ignored. Extending our example of our young friend trying to get into the 18-30 Club:

```
if (intAge < 18 || intAge > 30)
{
  Label.Text = "Sorry, you're ineligible to join the 18-30 Club.";
}
else
{
  Label.Text = "Would you like to join the 18-30 Club?";
}
```

So we can have code that branches two ways depending on whether a Boolean comparison evaluates to `true` or `false`. However, we can go further and include extra `if` tests, which are evaluated in order. The first one that evaluates to `true` will result in its associated block of code being executed. The general syntax is this:

```
if (condition1 == true)
{
  // Code in here
}
else if (condition2 == true)
{
  // more code here
}
else if (condition3 == true)
{
  // more code here
}
```

For example:

```
if (strAutomobile == "Porsche")
{
  Label.Text = "You are driving a Porsche";
}
else if (strAutomobile == "Lotus")
{
  Label.Text = "You are driving a Lotus";
}
else if (strAutomobile == "Lamborghini")
{
  Label.Text = "You are driving a Lamborghini ";
}
```

What happens here is that the value of `strAutomobile` is checked and if it is "Porsche" the first message is executed, if it is "Lotus", the second code block is executed and if it is "Lamborghini", the third code block is executed. If `strAutomobile` is any other value then nothing happens. A point to note here is that only one code block is executed. If the first is executed then the remainder are ignored. You can also tag an `else` block on the end, which will execute if none of the conditions evaluate to `true`:

```
if (strAutomobile == "Porsche")
{
  Label.Text = "You are driving a Porsche";
}
else if (strAutomobile == "Lotus")
{
  Label.Text = "You are driving a Lotus";
}
else if (strAutomobile == "Lamborghini")
{
  Label.Text = "You are driving a Lamborghini ";
}
else
{
  Label.Text = "Please enter which car you are driving";
  // More code
}
```

Here we checked the value of the same variable over and over again – the `switch case` construct, which we shall look at shortly, is a much tidier method of achieving this. The real power of the `if...else if...else` construct is that it can be used to check several unrelated conditions in one go, any of which (or none of which) could be `true`:

```
if (intAge >= 18)
{
  // Code here
}
else if (strAutomobile == "Porsche")
{
  // Code here
}
else if (strName == "John Doe")
{
  // Code here
}
else
{
  // Catch all code here
}
```

The Conditional or Ternary Operator

C# offers a shorthand way of doing the following `if...else` test:

```
if (conditional statement)
{
  // statement 1
}
else
{
  // statement 2
}
```

This uses a special C# construct called the **conditional operator**, which is also known as the ternary operator, as it requires three operands instead of the usual one or two. The syntax for this operator looks like this:

```
<conditional statement> ? <statement 1> : <statement 2>
```

The syntax might look a bit daunting so we'll examine it a bit by bit. The `<conditional statement>` preceding the `?` is equivalent to the `if` test and must evaluate to either `true` or `false`. Note that this statement contains no `if` keyword. For a `true` result, the single statement between the `?` and the `:` is executed, equivalent to the `if` code block, otherwise the single statement after the `:` is executed, equivalent to the `else` code block. Normally you would put the entire construct in parentheses because, in the pecking order of operator precedence, it comes well down the list (after both arithmetic and Boolean operators).

Once you get the hang of the syntax, the conditional operator can be very useful where one of two possible execution options is required for a particular situation. One common example is where you optionally add a plural ending to a string when reporting a number of items bought or sold:

```
Label.Text = "You ordered " + intBooks + " book" + (intBooks != 1 ? "s" : "") + "
from our web site.";
```

What happens here is that if the variable `intBooks` is anything other than 1, then the letter `s` is added to the word `book`, otherwise an empty string (that is nothing) is added. This would give you grammatically correct output as follows:

```
You ordered 1 book from our web site
You ordered 2 books from our web site
```

The very same result can be achieved using 4 lines of code (not counting the curly brackets).

```
Label.Text = "You ordered " + intBooks + " book";
if (intBooks != 1)
{
  Label.Text += "s";
}
Label.Text += " from our web site";
```

Comparing Strings

Up until now we have just been comparing numerical values. However, you can use the same syntax to compare two strings, although C# restricts you to equality and inequality tests such as this:

```
if (strName == "Chris")
{
    // Do something
}
```

and this:

```
if (strName != "")
{
    // Do something else
}
```

You cannot apply greater than or less than operators to strings, so you don't be tempted to try syntax such as this if you wish to determine whether a string variable occurs before the name Chris in an alphabetical listing:

```
if (strName < "Chris")
{
    // Do something
}
```

This will not work and will generate a compiler error.

A Word about Nested ifs and Indenting

if blocks, else if blocks, and else blocks do not need to contain just simple statements. They can contain if, else if, and else constructs of their own, which results in further branching of code. Placing one set of if logic within another in known as **nesting** and through it, your code can become highly versatile and powerful. There are downsides, however – if not properly thought through and planned, this can lead to all kinds of problems in your code, which may be very hard to track down without painstakingly poring over each and every line working out every possible thread of execution. If, when programming in C#, you have to use nesting of code blocks, you should always employ the practice of consistent indenting.

Indenting of code is not mandatory, by any means, though because it is so useful, editing tools such as Visual Studio .NET indent code for you automatically. Whenever you type in an opening curly brace and press *Return*, not only does the cursor move down one line but also a preset number of spaces (or a tab) to the right. Some editors go further and automatically put in the closing bracket for you at a position vertically aligned with the opening bracket and one line after where the indented cursor is positioned:

```
if (something)
{
    if (something else)
```

```
    {
    |      ← this represents the cursor
    }
  }
```

If you are using a basic text editor such as Notepad, this will not be done and you have to add the indenting yourself, which can be a drag if you cut and paste unindented code into your application, and you must then determine how the nested if blocks are actually structured – not always obvious at first glance. Indenting code using Notepad may seem like a waste of time and key clicks, but is worth it in the end, making your code much more readable and easy to follow. For this reason, all code samples in this book are indented.

Having said all this, let's move on to a more complete example illustrating the use of if. The computer "thinks" of a number between 1 and 10, and you have to guess what it is.

Try It Out – Using the if Structure

1. Open up your web page editor and type in the following:

```
<script language="C#" runat="server">
void Page_Load()
{
  int intNumber, intGuess;
  Random r = new Random();
  intNumber = Convert.ToInt32(r.Next(10)) + 1;

  if (Page.IsPostBack)
  {
    intGuess = Convert.ToInt32(Guess.SelectedItem.Value);

    if (intGuess > intNumber)
    {
      Message.Text = "<BR><BR>Guess is too high<BR>Try again, it was "
                                            + intNumber;
    }

    if (intGuess < intNumber)
    {
      Message.Text = "<BR><BR>Guess is too low<BR>Try again, it was "
                                            + intNumber;
    }

    if (intGuess == intNumber)
    {
      Message.Text = "<BR><BR>Guess is correct!";
    }
  }
}
</script>
```

```
<html>
<head></head>
<body>
<form runat="server">
  What number am I thinking of?
  <asp:dropdownlist id="Guess" runat="server">
    <asp:listitem>1</asp:listitem>
    <asp:listitem>2</asp:listitem>
    <asp:listitem>3</asp:listitem>
    <asp:listitem>4</asp:listitem>
    <asp:listitem>5</asp:listitem>
    <asp:listitem>6</asp:listitem>
    <asp:listitem>7</asp:listitem>
    <asp:listitem>8</asp:listitem>
    <asp:listitem>9</asp:listitem>
    <asp:listitem>10</asp:listitem>
  </asp:dropdownlist>
  <br>
  <br>
  <input type="submit" value="Submit guess">
  <asp:label id="Message" runat="server"/>
</form>
</body>
</html>
```

2. Save this as `C:\BegASP.NET\Ch06\ifthen.aspx`.

3. View `ifthen.aspx` in your browser:

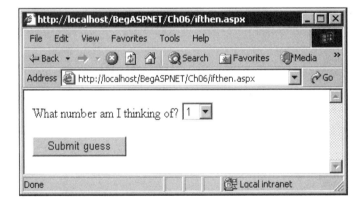

4. Choose a number and click on Submit guess:

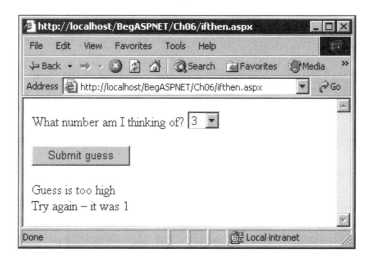

5. Carry on guessing, until you get the correct answer!

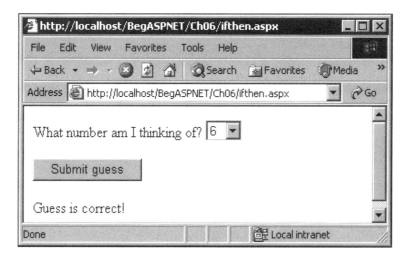

How It Works

This example starts by getting the user to enter a guess into the web form with the
`<asp:dropdownlist>` control:

```
<asp:dropdownlist id="Guess" runat="server">
  <asp:listitem>1</asp:listitem>
  <asp:listitem>2</asp:listitem>
  <asp:listitem>3</asp:listitem>
```

```
            <asp:listitem>4</asp:listitem>
            <asp:listitem>5</asp:listitem>
            <asp:listitem>6</asp:listitem>
            <asp:listitem>7</asp:listitem>
            <asp:listitem>8</asp:listitem>
            <asp:listitem>9</asp:listitem>
            <asp:listitem>10</asp:listitem>
      </asp:dropdownlist>
```

Using a drop-down list ensures that we get a valid response back from the user, as they can only choose those that we have approved and placed in the list. We can then interrogate the drop-down listbox via its name Guess, directly through the code.

It's the actual C# code that is most interesting. In our section we start by defining two variables:

```
void Page_Load()
{
   int intNumber, intGuess;
```

These two variables will respectively contain the number that we randomly generate, and the user's guess. Next, we randomly generate a number. To do this we must make use of the .NET Framework base class called Random:

```
        Random r = new Random();
        intNumber = Convert.ToInt32(r.Next(10)) + 1;
```

We have to jump ahead of ourselves here as we are employing a technique that we can only fully explain in the context of classes and objects that we don't cover until Chapter 8. For now, just accept that these two lines of code result in a random integer between 1 and 10 being generated and stored in intNumber. So we've generated our random number, we've got the guess from the user stored in intGuess, all we need to do is compare them, right?

Well, not quite: as this is a web form with just one single page, we need to check to see if the user has ever been there before. On their first arrival they won't have entered a number, and we don't want to test the random number against an empty variable.

To perform this check, we see if the Page has been posted back; if it has then IsPostback will return true. The first time we run the page, it can't have been posted back, as the user hasn't guessed yet, so it will return false and won't run the code contained within. Every subsequent time that the user has submitted a guess, IsPostBack will return true.

```
if (Page.IsPostBack) {
   ... do code inside when True...
}
```

So the first time the user accesses the page, `IsPostBack` will return `false`, and the page execution will jump to the end of the `if` statement, marked by the closing curly bracket. After this curly bracket, is a curly bracket which closes the `void Page_Load()` section, so when the program encounters this, it ends until the page loads again.

You might be wondering how ASP.NET knows which is the correct closing curly bracket, as there are several in the code. The answer is that they have been **nested** inside each other. Where there is an `if` statement inside the block of code belonging to another `if` statement, the inner `if` statement has to have a matching opening and closing brackets, before the outer block can be ended. This means that `if` blocks can be treated as completely separate self-contained entities.

Indeed all structures and functions are delimited in C# with curly brackets. If you have more opening than closing brackets, you will end up causing an error. To make sure they match, you should always indent your code as follows:

```
void Page_Load()
{
  if (Page.IsPostBack) {

    intGuess = "", so ignore all this code

  }
}
```

This makes it much easier to follow.

So having reviewed the overall structure of our code, let's have a look at what is going on inside it. The first thing we do if the `Guess` form variable is a string is to covert it to an `int`. We have already explained the reason why we need to do this in our discussion of the `Convert.To...` functions from Chapter 4. Numerical data input in ASP.NET does not initially occur with any of the numerical types, even if, as in this case, you would expect it to do so. In C#, you have to explicitly convert it to a numerical type before it can be used:

```
intGuess = Convert.ToInt32(Guess.SelectedItem.Value);
```

Now we demonstrate what we have just said about nesting prior to this example (and indenting too), for now we come to a completely separate set of `if` statements, which lie entirely within (that is, nested inside) the first `if` statement:

```
if (intGuess > intNumber)
{
   message.Text = "<BR><BR>Guess is too high<BR>Try again - it was " +
                                               intNumber;
}
if (intGuess < intNumber)
{
 message.Text = "<BR><BR>Guess is too low<BR>Try again - it was " +
                                             intNumber;
}
```

```
if (intGuess == intNumber)
{
    message.Text = "<BR><BR>Guess is correct!";
}
```

These are all ignored, unless IsPostBack has returned true. The first time around it can't return true, as the user won't have viewed the page before. Second time around, the user has submitted a guess. So, now the Page.IsPostBack test will evaluate to true, and the code inside performing three tests will be run.

Our first test checks to see whether the guess is bigger than the number:

```
if (intGuess > intNumber)
{
    message.Text = "<BR><BR>Guess is too high<BR>Try again - it was "
                                                    + intNumber;
}
```

If it is, then it sets the <asp:label> control to display a message informing the user that their guess was too high, along with the number that the user failed to guess.

Our second test checks to see whether the guess is smaller than the number:

```
if (intGuess < intNumber)
{
    message.Text = "<BR><BR>Guess is too low<BR>Try again - it was "
                                                    + intNumber;
}
```

In this case we then display a message saying that the guess was too low, and display the number.

Our last test checks to see whether the number is correct, and displays an appropriate message in our <asp:label> control:

```
if (intGuess == intNumber)
{
    message.Text = "<BR><BR>Guess is correct!";
}
```

That's all there is to this example. However, each time we play this game, a new number is generated, whether we are right or wrong. This is where the concept of state comes in. We can't get ASP.NET to remember the number, without some sort of store between page requests. We'll talk about how to do this when we come to session variables, in Chapter 10.

Conditional Statements Using switch...case

One problem of the `if` structure is that the syntax and structure can become complex and unwieldy, if you have many `else if`s and nested code blocks all providing different responses to different values of the same variable. What happens if you want to show a different page to visitors from each of five departments? What happens if you want to do a calculation based on the user providing one of twelve salary grades? Or if you have different functions for confirming an order by telephone, fax, and e-mail? All this can be achieved using multiple `else if`s, but there is a far better way of doing this, far more succinct and easier to read.

The `switch` statement takes a single variable as its argument and allows code to be run for any or all possible values of this variable, by providing code execution options that each match one or more cases. The general syntax looks like this:

```
switch (statement)
{
case option1:
  // Do something
  break;
case option2:
  // Do something else
  break;
default:
  // Do something
  break;
}
```

Before we look at `switch...case` in more detail, there are several things to note about this syntax:

- The `statement` can be anything that evaluates to any of the following types: an integer, a char, a string, or even a `bool` (though using a `bool` here is rather pointless as an `if...else` construct would be better.

- The value after each of the `case` keywords must be a constant.

- Both `case` and `default` code blocks have to be explicitly exited. The `break` keyword is normally used to mark the end of a `case` or `default` block, whereupon control passes to the next line after the `switch` statement. Other statements include `return`, `continue`, `goto case <label>`, and `goto default`.

Let's examine this further with an example. This statement carries out one of three actions depending on what is contained in the string variable `Confirmation`:

```
switch (Confirmation)
{
case "Fax":
  Message.Text = "<a href='FaxConfirmation.htm'>Fax</a>";
  break;
case "Telephone":
  Message.Text = "<a href='telephone.htm'>Telephone</a>";
```

227

```
    break;
case "Email":
  Message.Text = "<a href='Email.htm'>Email</a>";
  break;
}
```

What happens here is that the predefined and pre-assigned variable is compared to each of the values for each case and if a match if found, the code following it is run up to and including the `break`, which signifies the end of the `switch` statement, whereupon the rest of the code runs as usual. So if the value of `Confirmation` is `Telephone` then this message is displayed:

```
Message.Text = "<a href='telephone.htm'>Telephone</a>";
```

All other code is ignored. Under normal circumstances only one `case` code block is ever executed.

If a value is compared to each case in turn and no match is found, then in the above example no code is executed at all. However, you can add a block to the end of the statement that will run if no match is found and is marked with the `default:` label, which as I said just now, must also end with `break` or an equivalent statement:

```
switch (Confirmation)
{
case "Fax":
  Message.Text = "<a href='FaxConfirmation.htm'>Fax</a>";
  break;
case "Telephone":
  Message.Text = "<a href='telephone.htm'>Telephone</a>";
  break;
case "Email":
  Message.Text = "<a href='Email.htm'>Email</a>";
  break;
default:
  Message.Text = "No confirmation required";
  break;
}
```

The `default:` code block is the `switch` construct's equivalent to the `else` block of an `if` statement.

So what if you want the same code to run for more than one value? Well, C# allows you to do this using a syntax that allows you to have `case` statements that are not separated by the `break` keyword. In the example that follows, the same code runs regardless of whether a user types in yes, Yes, YES, Y, or y to confirm some action or other. The syntax for doing this is as follows:

```
switch (Confirmation)
{
case "yes":
case "Yes":
case "YES":
case "Y":
case "y":
  Message.Text = "Details will be sent.";
  break;
}
```

What we have here is a stack of case labels one after the other followed by a section of code that is run if any of the given values matches the Confirmation variable. This is the best way of achieving a single action from a set of values. You could do this using a complex if statement like this:

```
if (Confirmation == "yes" || Confirmation == "Yes" || Confirmation == "YES" ||
    Confirmation == "Y" || Confirmation == "y")
{
  Message.Text = "Details will be sent.";
}
```

But you can plainly see that the switch...case syntax is tidier.

There is an even better way for testing for the various case combinations of Yes or y, which cuts down further the number of lines of code, and that is to standardize the case of the statement which is being compared by using the ToLower() or ToUpper() method:

```
switch (Confirmation.ToLower())
{
case "yes":
case "y":
  Message.Text = "Details will be sent.";
  break;
}
```

Here, we use the .NET Framework method ToLower() to change the value of the variable being tested to all lower case, so we can then compare it to a reduced number of case labels. This enables you to test for odd case combinations such as YEs which would otherwise fail to give a match.

Although under normal circumstances you cannot execute more than one case code block at a time, you can explicitly jump from one case to another. The syntax to achieve this is as follows:

```
switch (statement)
{
case option1:
  // Do something
  if (some condition is met)
  {
    goto case option2;
  }
  break;
case option2:
  // Do something else
  break;
default:
  // Do something
  break;
}
```

What happens here is that if the value of `statement` is `option1`, the code following that `case` is executed, including the `if` test where some other condition is tested. If this evaluates to `true`, the code for the `option2` case is run as well. This is one recommended use of the C# `goto` keyword.

Another Note on Nesting and Indenting

In the same way as `if` blocks, `switch` blocks can also be nested and the same rules apply, but because there are far fewer curly brackets involved, the potential for confusion is much reduced. However, you should be careful to indent appropriately. Note also that the `case` and `default` labels are often formatted with no indenting, that is, they are positioned in the same vertical alignment as the curly brackets that contain them. However this is only a convention followed in this book. The main point to note is that the `case` and `default` code blocks *are* indented. Also code and default code blocks themselves can be enclosed in curly brackets, though that is not necessary and indeed can hinder readability – the code blocks are already delimited by the `case` (or `default`) and `break` (or equivalent) keywords.

Let's now look at an example that uses a `switch` statement to make a more detailed set of selections. In Chapter 3 we used an example that showed how the user could select a holiday from a set of destinations. We're now going to go one better and provide a brief sales pitch depending on which destination the user selects. We will use `switch...case` to decide which pitch to use.

Try It Out – Using switch...case

1. Open up your web page editor and type in the following:

```
<script language="C#" runat="server">
void Page_Load()
{
  if (Page.IsPostBack)
  {
    switch(Destination.SelectedItem.Value)
    {
      case "Barcelona":
        Message.Text = "You selected Spain's lively Catalan city";
        break;
      case "Oslo":
        Message.Text = "Experience the majesty of Norway's capital city";
        break;
      case "Lisbon":
        Message.Text = "Portugal's famous seaport and cultural hub";
        break;
      default:
        Message.Text = "you did not select a destination we travel to";
        break;
    }
  }
}
</script>

<html>
```

```
<head></head>
<body>
  <form runat="server">
  Select your choice of destination:
  <br><br>
  <asp:radiobuttonlist id="Destination" runat="server">
    <asp:listitem>Barcelona</asp:listitem>
    <asp:listitem>Oslo</asp:listitem>
    <asp:listitem>Lisbon</asp:listitem>
  </asp:radiobuttonlist>
  <br><br>
  <input type="submit" value="Submit Choice">
  <br><br>
  <asp:label id="Message" runat="server"/>
</form>
</body>
</html>
```

2. Save this as `C:\BEGASP.NET\ch06\switchcase.aspx`

3. View this in your browser:

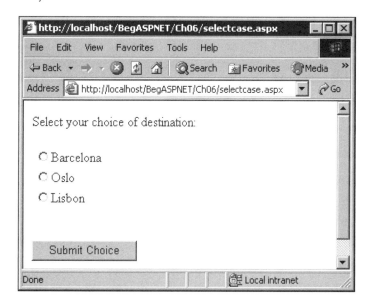

4. Make a choice and click on Submit Choice:

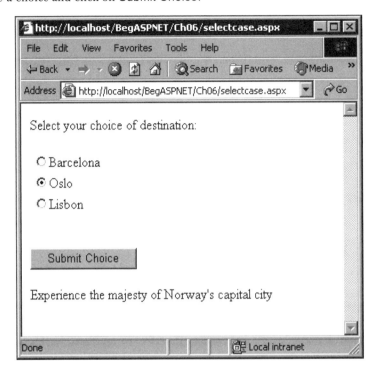

How It Works

There's a lot of code here, but it's probably simpler than the last example we looked at. We have a radio button list control, called `destination`, which allows the user to select a holiday destination:

```
<asp:radiobuttonlist id="destination" runat="server">
  <asp:listitem>Barcelona</asp:listitem>
  <asp:listitem>Oslo</asp:listitem>
  <asp:listitem>Lisbon</asp:listitem>
</asp:radiobuttonlist>
```

This is sent back by the form to the ASP.NET code.

We then use the `IsPostBack` test to see if the page has been run before, as we did in the last example. If it returns `false`, and we can skip to the end of the program and wait until the page is run again:

```
void Page_Load()
{
    if (Page.IsPostBack)
    {
        // switch case structure
    }
}
```

If has been posted back, then we take the contents of the radio button's `SelectedItem.Value` and we test the contents against various possibilities:

```
switch(Destination.SelectedItem.Value)
{
case "Barcelona":
  message.Text = "You selected Spain's lively Catalan city";
  break;
case "Oslo":
  message.Text = "Experience the majesty of Norway's capital city";
  break;
case "Lisbon":
  message.Text = "Portugal's famous seaport and cultural hub";
  break;
```

As our page contains one question with three options, we deal with all of these possibilities within our `switch` statement. So if we have selected **Oslo**, then only the code in the `case "Oslo"` section will be run.

There is a default clause at the end whose code should never be executed as the only values that the form variable can take have already been catered for. However this has been put in as a precaution, as good programming practice:

```
default:
  message.Text = "you did not select a destination to travel to";
  break;
}
```

There is one drawback of `switch` statements though. When determining the action to take for a range of values, you cannot use any of the comparison operators, so you cannot do this:

```
switch (value)
{
case value < 0:  // Invalid syntax
```

So either you have to do some work to make sure that the value you want to compare is constant at the time the `switch` statement runs, or you have to add stacked `cases` for a range of values or return to logical structures using `if`.

OK, we have finished our discussion of the two kinds of decision-making structure, now it's time to move on to some looping structures.

Looping Structures in Detail

C# offers four types of looping structures: `for`, `do...while`, `while`, and `foreach...in`, which all repeatedly execute a code block but are used for different purposes, although there is much overlap.

When you require one of these structures, it's advisable to decide which to use depending on whether you know in advance how many loops you want to execute. If you **can** determine the number of loops at the point where your program is about to begin the loop (for example, if the loop will always be performed exactly ten times, or if the number of loops stored in a variable), then use `for`. If you **do not** know ahead of time how many loops you want to perform, and will have to decide after each cycle whether to continue, then I suggest using either the `while` or the `do...while` loop.

The for Loop

The `for` loop is arguably the most complicated of the looping types but is the most commonly found. In C#, the general syntax looks like this:

```
for (<initializors>; <expression>; <iterators>)
{
  // Code in here
}
```

Where:

- ❏   `<initializors>` is usually a loop counter set at its initial value. There can be more than one initializor, in which case they are specified in a comma-separated list.

- ❏   `<expression>` is a Boolean condition, which has to evaluate to `false` to exit the loop.

- ❏   `<iterators>` is a means of changing the loop counter either by increasing or decreasing it. Again there can be more than one of these, specified in a comma-separated list.

A semicolon must separate each of these three parameters and the whole statement must be wrapped in parentheses. Following the `for` statement is the code to be repeated, which should be wrapped in curly brackets if there is more than one statement in the repeating block.

Here is a simple example to get started. Imagine in our holiday application that we need an age declaration from each person going, as some of the adventure holidays require participants to be over (or under) a certain age. The company requires each user's signature to be handwritten. To do this, the user has to log in to the company's web site, get the sign-in sheet, and print it. Now, imagine we needed a sheet for five people; this code could be used to do it:

```
Message1.Text = "";
for (int intCounter = 0; intCounter < 5; intCounter ++)
{
  Message1.Text += "Attendee Name _____" +
      "<br /><br />Attendee Age _____<br /><br /><hr /><br />";
}
```

This is how it works. In order to keep count of loop cycles (also known as iterations) we define a variable called `intCounter` in the `for` statement itself. The loop runs and will keep on running while the value of the counter is less than or equal to 5 (as specified by the test condition) and each cycle of the loop results in the counter being incremented by 1. As the loop progresses, a text string is built containing repeating text strings. As we are using the concatenation (+=) operator, we have to set the string to an empty string before the loop starts, or we would add the text to what was already there. The output for this code is shown here:

This simple first example assumes that we would always have five attendees. What if that number varied? In that event, we could have a first web page that asked for the number of attendees, and then use that number to determine how many lines to print. We can use `for` loops to do this because, at the point when we start the loop, we know how many attendees there are.

If we assume that the text field, called `numberAttendees`, contains the number of attendees input by the user, then the responding page can grab the user's data from the field named `numberAttendees` and place it into the variable called `number` (explicitly converting it to an `int` in the process). Then we can begin the `for` loop. This time we don't go through exactly five cycles. Rather, we go through the number of cycles specified by `numberAttendees`. Our sign-in sheet is now usable for any number of attendees:

```
numberAttendees = Convert.ToInt32(NumberAttendees.SelectedItem.Value);
Message1.Text = "";
for (int intCounter = 0; intCounter < number; intCounter ++)
{
  Message1.Text += "Attendee Name _____" +
      "<br /><br />Attendee Age _____<br /><br /><hr /><br />";
}
```

OK – let's go and create a version of this example that takes a number from the user and supplies the requisite number of signature/age sections to declare:

Try It Out – Using for Loops

1. Open your web page editor and type in the following:

```
<script language="C#" runat="server">
void Page_Load()
{
  int number, counter;
  if (Page.IsPostBack) {
    number = Convert.ToInt32(NumberAttendees.SelectedItem.Value);
    Message1.Text = "";
    for (counter = 0; counter < number; counter ++)
      {
        Message1.Text += "Attendee Name _____<br /><br />" +
            "Attendee Age _____<br /><br /><hr /><br />";
      }
  }
}
</script>

<html>
<head>
<title>Loop Example</title>
</head>
<body>
<form runat="server">
Enter the number of attendees (max 6):
<br>
<br>
<asp:dropdownlist id="NumberAttendees" runat="server">
  <asp:listitem>1</asp:listitem>
  <asp:listitem>2</asp:listitem>
  <asp:listitem>3</asp:listitem>
  <asp:listitem>4</asp:listitem>
  <asp:listitem>5</asp:listitem>
  <asp:listitem>6</asp:listitem>
</asp:dropdownlist>
<br>
<br>
<input type="submit">
<br>
<br>
<asp:label id="Message1" runat="server"/>
</form>
</body>
</html>
```

2. Save this as `C:\BEGASP.NET\ch06\loop.aspx`.

3. Open `loop.aspx` in your browser:

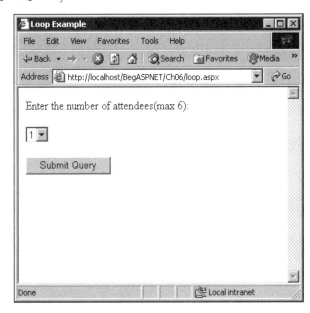

4. Select a number and check the sheet that appears looks like the next screenshot:

How It Works

In this example we selected 2 from the drop-down box, and two sections for signatures were displayed. The program required just one piece of information from the user in order to create the page:

```
<asp:dropdownlist id="numberAttendees" runat="server">
  <asp:listitem>1</asp:listitem>
  <asp:listitem>2</asp:listitem>
  <asp:listitem>3</asp:listitem>
  <asp:listitem>4</asp:listitem>
  <asp:listitem>5</asp:listitem>
  <asp:listitem>6</asp:listitem>
</asp:dropdownlist>
```

To limit it to a sensible number, we decided to impose a maximum of 6. This control passed the information across under the name `numberAttendees`.

The C# code only required two variables. The first to hold the number supplied by the user, the second to hold the counter for the loop:

```
void Page_Load()
{
  int number, counter;
```

Before we could use the loop to display the sections for signatures, we had to check to see whether this was the first time the user had accessed the page, by checking `Page.IsPostBack`. If it was `false`, we would skip the contents, jump to the end of the program, and wait for the user to submit a value:

```
  if (Page.IsPostBack) {
    Loop Structure
  }
}
```

Inside this branching structure, if there is a number in the `numberAttendees.SelectedItem.value`, this must be the number the user supplied, so we convert it to an `int` and assign it to our `number` variable:

```
        number = Convert.ToInt32(NumberAttendees.SelectedItem.Value);
```

Next we blank the contents of our `<asp:label>` control:

```
        Message1.Text ="";
```

Without this if someone used this example once, it would work, but then each time the user made a second or third selection, they'd get a whole new set of signature spaces added on top of the ones they had earlier.

Now we can create a loop starting with the counter at zero, and incrementing it for each cycle of the loop:

```
for (counter = 0; counter < number; counter ++)
{
  message1.Text += "Attendee Name _____<br /><br />" +
          "Attendee Age _____<br /><br /><hr /><br />";
}
```

Each time the loop is executed, and while the loop counter is less than the value of number, the <asp:label> control has an extra section added to its Text value. When the number of the loop in counter equals the value of number, the loop ends and the code resumes execution at the first statement following the closing bracket.

The while Loop

We briefly mentioned the while loop earlier in the chapter. You may remember that it's used where the number of iterations it has to carry out is unknown when the loop begins. A Boolean test is made at the beginning of each cycle. So, on each loop it performs a test and continues looping as long as the specified condition is true.

The syntax looks like this:

```
while (condition)
{
  // looping code here
}
```

There is a serious trap that every novice programmer (and plenty of more experienced ones, too!) falls into: if you start a loop and do not provide a means for it to stop, then it will continue forever in an infinite loop.

Most current servers will eventually cut off a given ASP.NET page, since the server needs to attend to other visitors and must optimize its resources. If a page seems to be hung and not loading properly, it could be due to an infinite loop, which can effectively cause the web server not to respond to page requests.

The while loop is perfect for some tasks where it is impossible to know how many times you are going to have to execute it beforehand. For example, we could write a page that simulates rolling a die (by coming up with a random number between one and six) – and keeps rolling it until it gets a six. However, we don't know – at the time of writing our ASP.NET code, or even before we first roll the die – how many times we'll have to roll the die to get a six. So, for example, we could write:

```
Random r = new Random();
int diceRoll = 0;
while (diceRoll != 6)
{
  diceRoll = Convert.ToInt32(r.Next(6)) + 1;
  message1.Text = message1.Text + "Rolled a: " + diceRoll + "<br />";
}
```

The code begins by setting up a variable: `diceRoll` that will track the value of our last dice roll. When we declare it, we initialize it to zero at the same time. We have to do this because we immediately test its value in the `while` statement, and if it were to have no value, the code would not compile because the `diceRoll` variable was unassigned at the point that it was used.

Next, we begin the loop. In order to avoid an infinite loop, we have to make sure that the loop can end by providing a way for the `diceRoll` variable to equal 6. We do this by rolling the die (or more truthfully, by creating a random number between 1 and 6 using the random number generator we met earlier) and storing the value in `diceRoll`. Then we print some text from within the loop.

After the loop has executed once, the test is executed again, this time using the value rolled inside the loop. If it is not a six, then the loop is run again. If it is a six, then the loop exits.

Let's put this code into an example.

Try It Out – Using while

1. Open your web page editor and type in the following:

```
<script language="C#" runat="server">
void Page_load()
  {
    Random r = new Random();
    int diceRoll = 0;
    while (diceRoll != 6)
    {
      diceRoll = Convert.ToInt32(r.Next(6)) + 1;
      message1.Text = message1.Text + "Rolled a: " + diceRoll + "<br />";
    }
  }
</script>

<html>
<head>
<title>Do Loop Example</title>
</head>
<body>
  <asp:label id="message1" runat="server"/>
</body>
</html>
```

2. Save this as `C:\BEGASP.NET\ch06\whileloop.aspx`.

3. View this in your browser:

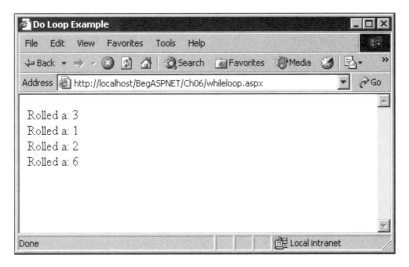

How It Works

We started by declaring random number, and variable to hold our dice roll number:

```
void Page_load()
  {
    Random r = new Random();
    int diceRoll = 0;
```

Then we run the loop. If the last dice roll was anything other than a six, we want to roll again, so we use the inequality operator to tell C# to keep running the loop, so long as the dice roll is not equal to six. We do this because we want the loop to stop once we have a six:

```
while (diceRoll != 6)
  {
    diceRoll = Convert.ToInt32(r.Next(6)) + 1;
    message1.Text = message1.Text + "Rolled a: " + diceRoll + "<br />";
  }
}
```

When `diceRoll` equals 6, it will stop, and not execute the contents of the loop, instead jumping on to the next statement, beyond the loop. In this case it is:

```
}
```

and this will end the C# code.

Note that it is possible for this code to enter an infinite loop – it is, however, very, very, unlikely that the computer will keep on selecting random numbers forever without selecting a six at some point...

The do...while Loop

You're not restricted to having the condition at the beginning of your loop. If you want your condition at the end, that is possible too, thanks to the do...while syntax:

```
do
{
  // looping code here
} while (condition);
```

Once thing you should note about this syntax is the semicolon after the while statement. It is required for the code to compile and is easily forgotten, if, say, you are converting a while loop into a do...while loop.

So, if you go back to the previous example, you can amend it as follows:

```
void Page_load() {
  Random r = new Random();
  int diceRoll;
  do
  {
    diceRoll = Convert.ToInt32(r.Next(6)) + 1;
    message1.Text = message1.Text + "Rolled a: " + diceRoll + "<br />";
  } while (diceRoll != 6);
}
```

Note that you do not have to assign a dummy value to the diceRoll variable before the loops runs. This is because the variable is set during the first (and possibly only) run of the loop and is tested afterwards.

If you save your amended whileloop.aspx file as dowhileloop.aspx, you will see exactly the same sort of output (but with different numbers, naturally):

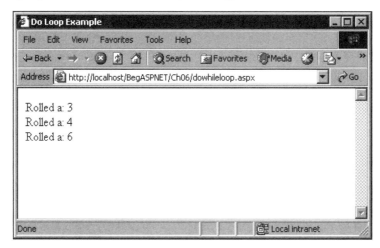

The foreach Loop

Last, but not least is a cousin of the `for` loop, the `foreach...in` loop, though the similarity lies more in the keywords, than in the behavior. It is used to iterate though the items in a collection and carry out some action on each item in turn. Here is its syntax:

```
foreach (object obj in collection)
{
  // Operate on each obj object
}
```

What happens is that a temporary variable is created, which will contain each item in turn. This object should be of the type corresponding to the objects in the collection, though if you don't know the actual type of the objects in the collection, you can use the generic `object` type instead. We have come across this type briefly in Chapter 4, and we will see it much more often from the next chapter onwards, so just think of it as a general type that can represent anything. With the temporary variable declared, we then point it to the collection we want to iterate through using the `in` keyword.

Note though that the code containing the `foreach` block has no counter, neither does it have a test condition so it cannot know, even at run time, how may items are in the collection nor is there any built-in mechanism for exiting the loop. However the collection itself knows how big it is, and so it and not the `foreach` block will determine when the loop ends. We'll meet collections, later, in Chapter 11. For now, you can think of them as being groups of objects.

Break and Continue

To finish off this section we have to ask ourselves two questions: "How do you abort a loop?" and, "How can you abort a particular loop iteration and start the next one?" These two actions can be applied to any of the looping structures explained earlier, and in C# they are very easy to do.

You can abort a loop by using the `break` keyword:

```
while (condition)
{
  if (something else is true)
  {
    // exiting code
    break;
  }
}
```

This breaks out of the loop at the `break` statement, and the program resumes at the statement immediately after the loop. This is a useful method of exiting a loop where no test condition can be found to evaluate to `false` and thus exit normally. The use of `break` will always be within an `if` or a `switch` statement.

For nested loops, `break` will only exit the innermost loop – the outer loop will iterate as normal and the inner loop will again run for the next iteration of the outer loop.

To cut short an iteration and proceed with the next iteration, use the `continue` keyword:

```
while (condition)
{
  if (something else happens)
  {
    // code
    continue;
  }
}
```

This is a much gentler way of skipping code. Only the lines that follow up to the end of the current loop cycle are skipped. The use of `continue` will always be from within either an `if` or a `switch` statement.

This ends our discussion on the methods of looping in code. Now, we turn our attention to the equally important jumping structures.

Functions in Detail

As you write more ASP.NET code, you'll find that you want to use the same code in more than one place. ASP.NET allows you to write code once, then run it as many times as needed to support the main body of your code. These mini-programs are called functions. We want ASP.NET to jump away from execution of the main body of code, run through the commands specified in a function and then return to the task of executing the main body of code.

> **Now for some terminology. In C#, functions are also known as methods. The use of one term or the other is often a matter of personal preference though you will find some situations where one is favored over the other. We will point these out as we come to them in our discussion. For now, we shall use the term function.**

For example, you may have some code to insert lines of text about how to contact the Sales Department. If you would like to have these show up in various places on the page, but want to avoid having to rewrite the code separately each time, you can put them into a function, then whenever you want the code to run you can invoke the function, rather than rewrite the code.

So what are the benefits of using these structures?

Defining Functions

We are not introducing anything new here at all. In fact, right from the very start of this book we have been using functions and we have referred to them as such – `Page_Load()` function, `ToString()` function, `Convert.ToDateTime()` function, and so on. Now we shall explain them more fully.

The simplest syntax for a function is as follows:

```
<return type> <function name> ( <optional parameters> )
{
  // code here
}
```

There are other syntax forms, which we'll discover as we progress through the book. For now, let's discuss what each of the above elements means.

Return Types and Parameters

Once the function has done its calculations, it may report the results back to the calling code. C# does this by defining a return type as part of the function definition and includes the return keyword in the function body followed by a value or a variable of the corresponding return type:

```
string MyFunction()
{
  return "OK";
}
```

Here we have defined a function called MyFunction, with no parameters, which returns a string. Inside the body of the function, delimited by curly braces, the function returns a string with the value "OK". This is a rather useless C# function, though all the essential ingredients are there.

If you want to include parameters, you do so like this:

```
string MyFunction(string Name, string Age)
{
  return "OK";
}
```

This is the simplest method of defining parameters. Each parameter consists of two parts, the type of the parameter and the name of the parameter. The parameters are separated by commas.

The naming convention for functions and parameters follows the same rules as for variables: they should describe what they are intended to do and what data they will contain, to make it easy for other people to follow your code.

Return types can be any of the data types that you came across in Chapter 4 as well as any user-defined types that you may have defined. There is, however, a special return type that is used where no return value is supplied – the keyword void. We have seen this a lot in this book:

```
void Page_Load()
{

}
```

Note that if you specify a function as returning void, you do not need the return keyword.

Calling Functions

You call a function that returns void by just typing its name followed by an opening parenthesis, a comma-separated parameter list and a closing parenthesis:

```
MyVoidFunction("Hello");
```

For a function that does return a value you can (but you don't have to) provide a variable to contain this value:

```
string ReturnValue;
ReturnValue = MyFunctionWhichReturnsAString();
```

Of course you can declare and assign your variable for the return value in one go:

```
string ReturnValue = MyFunctionWhichReturnsAString();
```

We can also incorporate our function in a more complex statement, for example where a return value is used in a calculation:

```
double payment = 15 * GetInterestRate() / 100;
```

Here, `GetInterestRate()` returns a `double`. You can also change the type of the return value by applying a cast to the function call itself:

```
decimal payment = 15 * (decimal)GetInterestRate() / 100;
```

Passing Parameters by Value

When we call functions, we need to understand a little more about what's actually happening when we pass parameters to them. By default, simple data values are passed to functions **by value**. This means that when the parameter variables are created inside the function, they are all set up to have the value that was passed in. This may seem like it goes without saying, but there are some subtle consequences. Effectively, it means that inside a function, we are working with a *copy* of the original data. Look at the following code:

```
void Increment(int Number)
{
  Number++;
}

void Page_Load()
{
    int A = 1;
    Increment(A);
    Message.Text = A.ToString();
}
```

This function takes an integer as a parameter and increments it. However, when we use this function from our Page_Load() function, we pass in a variable containing the number 1, but when we display the contents of this variable, we find it hasn't been incremented. Why is this? It is because only the **value** of our variable was passed.

When Increment(A) is called in the above code, the value stored in the variable A (which is 1) is copied into a new variable inside the Increment() function, called Number. The Increment() function then adds one to the value stored in this variable – but the value stored in A is left untouched.

Passing by value means that a copy is made for the function to play with, and the value of the original variable in the calling code is left untouched.

Passing Parameters by Reference

So what should you do if you do want the calculation within your function to affect the content of the variable in the calling code? That is when you should pass the parameter **by reference**. It is possible to pass data by reference by making a small change to the beginning of the function definition. Objects are a little different; they are known as reference types, and the default behavior is for them to be passed by reference, not by value. We'll look at what this means in a moment. First, let's amend our Increment() code to use pass-by-reference:

```
void Increment(ref int Number)
{
  Number++;
}

void Page_Load()
{
  int A = 1;
  Increment(ref A);
  Message.Text = A.ToString();
```

All we need to add to the function is the ref keyword before the parameter but we must also use the ref keyword in the function call. Now we find that the function actually works the way we expect. What happens now is that when the Increment(A) call is made, instead of a copy being taken of the value stored in A, the variable in the function is set to 'point' to the same piece of data represented by variable A – that is, a reference to variable A is created in the Number variable inside the function. This way, whenever the code inside the function makes a change to the Number variable, it is also changing the data in the A variable.

As mentioned above, this behavior is the default behavior for objects, which are also known as reference types. Look at the following function:

```
void AddLineToLabel(Label Target, string Line)
{
  Target.Text = Target.Text + Line + "<BR>";
}
```

This function takes two arguments: a target label control (a label is just an object, so it is a reference type), and a string. The idea is that it will add the supplied string to the supplied label control, followed by an HTML line break tag.

Now we can call this function using code like this:

```
<script language="c#" runat="server">

...
void Page_Load()
{
  AddLineToLabel(Message, "Hello World");
}
</script>

<html>
...
<body>
  <asp:label id="Message" runat="server"/>
</body>
</html>
```

The important lines are highlighted. We've declared a label control called `Message`. We can call our function within the `Page_Load()` function, passing in the `Message` label object and a string we want it to contain. However, we said before that data passed in as parameters is passed by value (unless specified using `ref`), which means that a copy of the value is made to use within the function. Does this mean that, in our function, it will attempt to add text to a copy of the actual label on the page and not the real label? Well, running this page shows this is not the case. In fact, when you pass an object instance as a parameter to a function, it is the not the object itself that is copied. It is the reference to that object that is copied, and therefore it will point to the same object on the heap.

out Parameters

A powerful feature of C# is the ability for a single function to return more than one value to the calling code. We have already discussed the return value. However, only one return value can be returned per function call, and any other values you might want a function to provide have to be assigned to special function parameters. Recall that ordinary parameters are read-only, whereas `ref` parameters are able to modify the values of the parameter – in effect, it is a read-write parameter. The third type of parameter is one where the value is unset before the function is called, is set while the function code is running, and can be used thereafter. As far as the called function is concerned, the parameter is write-only when it receives it.

In C# such as parameter is called an `out` parameter and is specified using the `out` keyword, both in the function definition and in the function call. We can change the previous example to illustrate this:

```
string SetNumber(out int Number)
{
  Number = 10;
  return "OK";
}
```

```
void Page_Load()
{
  int A;
  string ReturnValue = SetNumber(out A);
  Message.Text = A.ToString();
  Message.Text += "<br/>" + ReturnValue;
}
```

First, take a look at `Page_Load()`. We create a variable called `A` but do not initialize it. This is important because the function does this job for us. (We can, if we want to, initialize the variable first, but the function will then overwrite its value.) Next we create a string to hold our return value for the `SetNumber()` function and we call it passing the unassigned variable preceded by the `out` specifier. Then we output a message containing the two values.

Now for the function itself. We've redefined it to return a string as well as the `out` parameter to demonstrate that you can return two values from the same function. Also, the original function returned `void`, and it seems a bit pointless to have a `void` function use an `out` parameter – you could just as easily use a return value. All this function does is set the parameter and exit. However, if you run the code you will see both values displayed in the ASP.NET label control.

This example will take the date that the user checked out a book, use a function to calculate the date the book should be returned on, and then display this to the user. We don't want to alter the checkout date in any way in our function so we will pass our parameter by value.

Try It Out – Using Functions

This example will take the date that the user checked out a book, use a function to calculate the date the book should be returned on, and then display this to the user. We don't want to alter the checkout date in any way in our function so we will pass our parameter by value.

1. Open up your web page editor again and type in the following:

```
<script Language="c#" runat="server">
  void Page_Load()
  {
    DateTime DueDate;
    DateTime CheckOutDate;
    CheckOutDate = DateTime.Now;
    DueDate = FindDueDate(CheckOutDate);
    message1.Text = "<br>Your books were checked OUT on " + CheckOutDate;
    message2.Text = "<br>Your books are due on " + DueDate.ToString("d");
  }

  DateTime FindDueDate(DateTime CheckOutDate)
  {
    return CheckOutDate + TimeSpan.FromDays(14);
  }
</script>

<html>
<head>
<title>Sample Function Page</title>
```

```
  </head>
  <body>
    <h2>Thank you for using the On-Line Library.</h2>
    <asp:label id="message1" runat="server"/>
    <asp:label id="message2" runat="server"/>
  </body>
  </html>
```

2. Save this as `C:\BEGASP.NET\Ch06\function.aspx`

3. View this in your browser:

How It Works

Within our code there are two functions. One is `Page_Load()` which we have seen many times before, and the other is called from within the `Page_Load()` function. We'll start by looking at our function:

```
DateTime FindDueDate(DateTime CheckOutDate)
{
    return CheckOutDate + TimeSpan.FromDays(14);
}
```

It performs the relatively mundane task of adding 14 days to the date supplied by the user. The only problem is the little matter of how you carry out date arithmetic. We can use a very handy .NET Framework base-class function we haven't met before. `TimeSpan.FromDays()` takes a `double` as a parameter and returns a variable of the `TimeSpan` data type representing the number of days in a form that can be added to a `DateTime` variable. The `TimeSpan` and `DateTime` types are very similar and such operations are permitted, although directly adding a `double` to a `DateTime` is not. The sum of these two values is then returned.

To see how `CheckOutDate` is created, let's look at our main function. We start by declaring two variables, both of type `DateTime`. The first is the date returned by the function, the date we have to return the book by, the second is the date we checked the book out on:

```
void Page_Load()
{
  DateTime DueDate;
  DateTime CheckOutDate;
```

The checkout date is taken from the system time, given by `DateTime.Now`:

```
  CheckOutDate = DateTime.Now;
```

Next we run our function, and assign the value returned by it to the variable `DueDate`:

```
  DueDate = FindDueDate(CheckOutDate);
```

Lastly, we use two `<asp:label>` controls to display the checkout date and the date we must return the books by:

```
  message1.Text = "<br>Your books were checked OUT on " + CheckOutDate;
  message2.Text = "<br>Your books are due on " + DueDate.ToString("d");
}
```

Note that in the last line of code, we use the special version of `ToString()` specific to the `DateTime` type and specify the `"d"` parameter option to return the formatted date, stripping out the time included in `DueDate` – we don't want our client to be tied to a certain time to return their library book, do we?

Variable Scope

Before we looked at our function example, we briefly discussed the concept of passing variables as parameters to functions and saw that it is possible for a variable to have one value inside a function and another value outside it. In other words, if you modify the variable within the function, any changes to its value are not reflected when you subsequently access the same variable in the calling code. The original value of the variable is retained.

This is the situation that occurs when you pass a variable by value, and we have said that when this happens, a copy of the variable is made, which comes into existence when the code in the function starts executing and ceases to exist at the end of the function. When the original variable is called in subsequent code, it contains the same value as it had before it was passed to the function – the value of the copied variable is lost, because once outside the function, the copied variable no longer exists.

The *copied* variable is said to have **scope**. Scope refers to the area of code over which a variable is valid. A variable that exists only within a function, and cannot be used outside that function, is said to have **local scope**. However, a variable whose value is available not just to the calling code but also to any functions that might be called is said to have **global scope**. The idea that a variable can be valid only for part of a page, and not have any influence over the rest of the page, is a powerful one, and confers certain performance enhancements. The .NET runtime only has to track it for a short amount of time, rather than the whole lifetime of a page, so it consumes fewer resources because when the function that uses the variable has finished, the memory is freed up.

Local Variables

So let's have a look at variables that only exist within the confines of a function. On the surface this can look very complex, but it is really quite straightforward when you look at it closely. Consider two variables, both named `Different`. We'll try to assign different values to these two variables:

```
string Different;

Different = "Hello, I'm variable one";
Different = "Hello, I'm variable two";
```

If you output the value of `Different`, you'd find that it contained the string "Hello, I'm variable two". We've created one variable, and assigning a new value to it leads to any previous value being overwritten.

This isn't the case when you declare the variable in two different functions. If you defined `Different` twice in two different declarations, then you'd see a different result:

```
void FunctionNumber1()
{
  string Different = "Hello, I'm variable one";
}

void FunctionNumber2()
{
  string Different = "Hello, I'm variable two";
}
```

If you output the value of `Different` in `FunctionNumber1()`, then you'd see Hello, I'm variable one. If you output the value of `Different` in `FunctionNumber2()`, you'd see Hello, I'm variable two. However, if you then go back and run `FunctionNumber1()` again, you'd get Hello, I'm variable one again. This is because they are two completely different variables, although they share the same name.

These variables are known as **local variables**, because they are local to the function that created them. Outside that function, the local variable has no value: this is because the lifetime of the variable ends when the function ends. As these local variables are only active for the lifetime of a function, ASP.NET doesn't have to worry about keeping track of them over a whole page. Once the function exits, the variable's lifetime is over, thus freeing memory, and consequently increasing performance. You cannot create a variable twice within the same scope, that is, you cannot have two variables within the same scope (the same function) that share the same name.

Block-Level Variables

There is another type of scope, known as block-level scope. Block-level scope means that a variable defined inside a block of code only exists while the flow of execution is within the curly brackets, { and }, that delimit that block. The code block can be an if, else if, or else block, a switch block, any of the looping structures, or try and catch blocks.

A variable declared within a block can be used only within that block. In the following example, the scope of the variable strBlockLevelVariable is the block following the if, so this variable can no longer be referenced when execution passes out of the block:

```
if (intCheck == true)
{
   string strBlockLevelVariable = "Very Short Lived!";
}
Message1.Text = strBlockLevelVariable;  // Get error
```

You would get a compilation error since the strBlockLevelVariable is not defined outside the if block. The advantage of declaring block-level variables is that you can use less memory, in that if the Boolean test evaluates to false, the block-level variable is not created. Conditionally creating variables in this way can also boost performance. However you must make sure that you do not need to use the variable once you leave the block, as the variable then becomes undefined. Be careful, because it is very easy to declare a variable inside a block, and then try to access it outside the block scope. For this reason, it is a good idea to declare any procedure-level variables you use within your code at the very top of the procedure before the actual code of the procedure.

Now, let's take a look at how to use two procedure-level local variables. To demonstrate that they are local we'll make them share the same name during our ASP.NET program.

Try It Out – Creating Procedure-level Local Variables

1. Start your favorite editor and create the following program:

```
<script Language="c#" runat="server">
  void Page_Load()
  {
    message1.Text="";
    message1.Text+="<BR />Calling Function 1...";
    Function1();
    message1.Text+="<BR />Calling Function 2...";
    Function2();
    message1.Text+="<BR />Calling Function 1...";
    Function1();
  }
  void Function1()
  {
    string Different =
               "<i>Hello I'm the variable Different in Function 1</i>";
    message1.Text+= Different;
  }
  void Function2()
  {
    string Different =
```

```
                        "<b>Hello I'm the variable Different in Function 2</b>";
        message1.Text+= Different;
      }
</script>
<html>
<head>
<title>Scope</title>
</head>
<body>
<asp:label id="message1" runat="server"/>
</body>
</html>
```

2. Save the program as `C:\BEGASP.NET\ch06\local.aspx`

3. Execute it in your browser of choice:

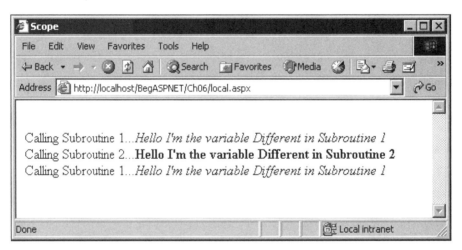

How It Works

This program contains two almost identical functions:

```
void Function1()
{
 string Different = "<i>Hello I'm the variable Different in Function 1</i>";
 message1.Text+= Different;
}
void Function2()
{
 string Different = "<b>Hello I'm the variable Different in Function 2</b>";
 message1.Text+= Different;
}
```

However, each of the variables named `Different` is declared and assigned a value within the confines of its respective function, and so doesn't exist outside the context of that function. We surround the contents of the variable in `Function1` with `<i>` tags, and the contents of the variable in `Function2` with `<b>` tags to clearly differentiate them. Neither variable interferes with the running of the other, despite the fact that they both have the same name.

If you asked the ASP.NET program to print the value of `Different` from **outside** either of these functions, it would return an error saying that variable hasn't been declared or is out of scope.

In our main program, we call these functions alternately:

```
void Page_Load()
  {
    message1.Text="";
    message1.Text+="<BR />Calling Function 1...";
    Function1();
    message1.Text+="<BR />Calling Function 2...";
    Function2();
    message1.Text+="<BR />Calling Function 1...";
    Function1();
  }
```

Hence we can see that the value of `Different` in `Function1()`, is not affected by the value of `Different` in `Function2()`. Once again we stress that unless you deliberately intend for some reason to name both variables the same, for readability's sake alone, you should give all your variables unique names.

Global Variables

So, if variables created in functions are local to the function that created them, how do you go about ensuring that the value of one variable persists from one function to the next, when you need it to? In other words, how do you extend the lifetime of your variables? The answer comes in the form of global variables. These are variables that are declared **outside** functions (but inside class definitions and ASP.NET `<script>` blocks).

The lifetime of a global variable stretches from the start of the ASP.NET page right through to the very end of the page, and spans any functions created within the script. In comparison, local variables contained within a function are destroyed when the function is exited, and hence the memory space is saved. It's a good idea to use local variables wherever possible, because it can make things easier to read, helps avoid bugs in code, and improves performance. However, there are times when you want to use the same variable throughout many different functions.

Try It Out – Using Global Variables

Let's see how we can amend our previous program to include a global-level variable. We're going to simply add a new global variable to the program and then display it from inside and outside the functions.

> **1.** Load up the previous program, `local.aspx`, in your preferred web page editor and add the following lines:

```
<script language="C#" runat="server">

string Global ="<br><u>Hello I'm a persistent global variable</u>";

void Page_Load()
{
    message1.Text="";
    message1.Text+= Global;
    message1.Text+="<BR />Calling Function 1...";
    Function1();
    message1.Text+="<BR />Calling Function 2...";
    Function2();
    message1.Text+="<BR />Calling Function 1...";
    Function1();
}


void Function1()
{
 string Different = "<i>Hello I'm the variable Different in Function 1</i>";
 message1.Text+= Different;
 message1.Text+= Global;
}


void Function2()
{
 string Different = "<b>Hello I'm the variable Different in Function 2</b>";
 message1.Text+= Different;
 message1.Text+= Global;
}

</script>
<html>
<head>
<title>Scope</title>
</head>
<body>
<asp:label id="message1" runat="server"/>
</body>
</html>
```

2. Save it this time as `C:\BEGASP.NET\ch06\global.aspx`

3. Run this program in your browser.

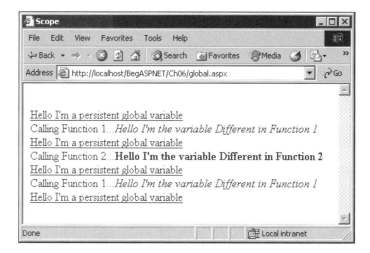

How It Works

We've not changed our original program much; the most important new feature is the global variable, `Global`, which is declared and initialized outside all of the functions as follows:

```
string Global ="<br><u>Hello I'm a persistent global variable</u>";
```

We first display this string from the `Page_Load()` function, the second time from within `Function1()`, the third time from within `Function2()` and the final time from within `Function1()`. Each time, the variable is displayed using the following code, so there's no trickery of any sort:

```
message1.Text+= Global;
```

The output shows how global variables and local variables can be used side by side in any ASP.NET program. In fact you can use both procedure-level local variables and block-level local variables together, but just be sure to remember what kind of scope each has!

Summary

This chapter has been a whirlwind tour through the key building blocks of C#. The three main structures we looked at were branching structures using `if...else` and `switch...case`, looping structures (`for`, `do...while`, `while`, and `foreach`), and functions. These enable us to control the execution of ASP.NET programs by making decisions about which particular branch to take, by repeating a piece of code several times, or by being able to jump out of a function and into another, whenever required.

Together with the last few chapters, this gives us a solid grounding in most of the C# coding basics. In the next chapter we will be looking at events and how they are used in ASP.NET programming. They will fundamentally alter the way in which you view your programs in ASP.NET and even how you write them.

Exercises

1. For each of the following Boolean expressions, say for what values of A each of them will evaluate to *true* and when they will evaluate to *false*:

   a. `!(A > 0 && A < 5)`

   b. `A > 1 && A < 5 || A > 7 && A < 10`

   c. `A < 10 || A > 12 && !(A > 20)`

2. Suggest a loop structure which would be appropriate for each of the following scenarios, and justify your choice:

   a. Displaying a set of items from a shopping list, stored in an array

   b. Displaying a calendar for the current month

   c. Looking through an array to find the location of a specific entry

   d. Drawing a chessboard using an HTML table

   Write an ASP.NET page to perform one of these tasks.

3. Write a function that generates a random integer between two integer values passed as parameters. Build an ASP.NET page that allows you to enter the lower and upper limits, and generates a set of random numbers in that range.

4. Suggest a situation when you might want to pass variables into a function by reference. Write an ASP.NET page to illustrate your example.

The solutions to these exercises are available at http://p2p.wrox.com

Event-driven Programming and Postback

One of the most important features of ASP.NET is the way it allows you to use an event-driven programming model. This isn't a new thing as the Windows interface itself is an event-driven environment. What this means is that nothing happens under Windows unless it is in response to something (an event) that Windows has detected. Example of such events could be a user clicking on a desktop icon, pressing a key, or opening the Start menu. ASP.NET works in a similar manner.

In ASP.NET web forms rely on events to trigger the running of code housed in special functions called **event handlers**. As we've just mentioned, this is nothing new, it's been possible to run small sections of client-side code on the user's browser with HTML for a long time. What ASP.NET is doing differently is using **postback**, where additional information is sent back to the server for processing, rather than doing it entirely on the client-side browser. This postback means that information can be sent back to the server whenever an event is triggered by the user. This is a very powerful concept, as it means we can do things like remembering which option in a list was selected, or what information a user typed into a textbox, between page submissions. We've already seen these features in action in Chapter 3, but so far we've only hinted at what has been going on – now we're going to look at it in more detail.

The event-driven nature of ASP.NET, however, doesn't just stop there. It allows us to completely modularize our code into separate functions, which are only run when a specific situation requiring them has arisen. We're going to see how ASP.NET can pass back information to the user, in response to particular events being generated, in a whole new way. This will enable us to create web forms that not only look different from the ones we have seen in previous chapters, but are faster, more efficient, and work in a more logical way.

In this chapter we'll look at:

- ❑ What an event is
- ❑ What event-driven programming is
- ❑ ASP.NET 'generic' events
- ❑ HTML events
- ❑ ASP.NET server control events
- ❑ The ASP button control
- ❑ Server-side processing of events
- ❑ How the event-driven programming model changes the way in which we program

What is an Event?

Let's start by defining exactly what an event is in the real world. For example, a fictional employee, Joe, sits in Marketing doing his Sales job, talking to contacts. He can receive information in two ways, one is via the phone, to say things like "We need to restock ten cans of jumping beans". When the phone rings, this is an event that he can respond to. He'll answer the phone and take appropriate action, such as sending out an extra ten cans of beans. So an event is just something that happens that can be detected and reacted to.

Extending our example further, Joe can also receive news via e-mails, such as a new policy from the boss, meaning he has to put $1 on all canned goods. This is a different event. Joe can also react to the event in any way he chooses. He can phone the stores and say "I'm afraid, I've got to charge you $1 extra for the cans of jumping beans", or he could say, "Stuff it, boss! We charge too much for our beans already, I'm quitting". So the way that events are responded to is variable, and determined by the individual person, or object.

So, you can break down our event-driven environment into three chronological sections:

- ❑ An events occurs – for example the phone rings
- ❑ The event is detected by the system – Joe hears the phone
- ❑ The system reacts to the event – Joe answers the phone

In an operating system such as Windows events occur in a very similar manner. A user clicks the mouse. The mouse sends a message to the Operating System. The Operating System receives the message from the mouse, and generates an `onclick` event. This event is detected by the Operating System and appropriate action taken, such as displaying a menu or highlighting a piece of text.

What is Event-driven Programming?

Event-driven programming fundamentally changes the nature of the programming model. We leave behind the idea of sequential pages being processed on a server, and confront instead a proper event-driven program, where the server responds to events triggered by the user. This may all sound like gobbledygook at the moment, but bear with us. All we mean by this is that before event-driven programming your programs would execute from top to bottom, like this:

```
Line 1
Line 2
Line 3
Line 4
```

Broadly speaking 'traditional' programming languages (those over ten years old) will start with the first line of your code, process it, move on to the second line, process that, and then move on to the third. Even when functions are used it doesn't change the order of execution a great deal – as one procedure calls another, which calls another, and so on. So there is still an ordered sequence of execution.

The concept of event-driven programming changes all of this – with events, this sequential way of doing things is no longer appropriate. Consider the Windows operating system again. Windows doesn't execute in a sequential fashion. If you click on a menu, you expect the menu to appear instantly, if you double-click on an icon, then you expect the corresponding program will run immediately, you don't want to have to wait for Windows to finish whatever it is doing first. Indeed, you don't have to because the Windows interface is event-driven and able to react to an event to create a new thread, and thereby perform things as soon as the user clicks on an icon or chooses a menu selection. Under the covers, Windows is waiting for an event to occur. As soon as one does it will take the appropriate action to deal with that event.

Without events a lot of Windows programs couldn't run. Windows doesn't run Word, Notepad, or the Calculator by itself, as part of a sequential series of executions, it only loads them when the user requests them. This same principle of programming is being used in ASP.NET. Typically the code in your web page (not HTML code, but client-side scripting) will be run by the browser, and will react to your mouse-click by itself. However with ASP.NET, the processing of events is shifted to the server.

ASP.NET Events

Everything in ASP.NET comes down to objects, and in particular the `page` object we mentioned in Chapter 2. Each web form you create is a page object in its own right. You can think of the entire web form as being like an executable program whose output is HTML. Every time a page is called the object goes through a series of stages – initializing, processing, and disposing of information. Because the `page` object performs these stages each time the page is called they happen every time a round trip to the server occurs. Each one of these stages can generate events, in the same way that clicking a mouse button can in Windows.

What happens in ASP.NET is that as you view your ASP.NET web form, a series of events are generated on your web server. The main events that are generated are as follows:

❑ `Page_Init` – occurs when the page has been initialized. You can use the function `void Page_Init()` associated with it to run code before .NET does certain automatic actions, such as displaying controls on the page. It works in the same manner as `Page_Load`, but occurs before it.

❑ `Page_Load` – occurs when the whole page is visible for the first time (that is, when the page has been read into memory and processed), but after some details about some of the server controls may have been initialized and displayed, by `Page_Init`.

❑ Control Events are dealt with – once the ASP.NET server controls have loaded they can respond to click events, the changing of a selection in a list or checkbox, or when a control is bound to a data source. *They are only dealt with when the form is posted back to the server* – we look at this later in the chapter.

❑ `Page_Unload` – occurs once the control events in a page have been dealt with, and is an ideal place to shut down database connections, and the like. It isn't compulsory to do this, as .NET will perform these operations for you, but it is good practice to tidy up your code, and the function attached to this event is the best place to do it.

> In addition, there is a set of events that the **Page** object supports that are not always fired, such as **PreRender**, which is generated just before the information is written to the browser and allows updates to be made to the page. There is also the **Error** event that occurs whenever an error is generated on the page and the **CommitTransaction** and **AbortTransaction** events which are fired whenever a transaction is about to be started or canceled.

We've already said that when a `page` object is first instantiated it is completely blank. Every time you submit a page, you instantiate a new version of the `Page` object, even if you continually submit the same page. This is because of the **statelessness** of the HTTP protocol. In Chapter 3 we talked about this fact, and how it means that when the browser makes a connection to the server with a request for the page, the web server searches for the page and either returns a page or appropriate status message, and then shuts down the connection. Everything you wish to do with the page must be performed within this series of stages, before the connection is closed.

What we're getting at here is that each `Page` object is entirely separate: each time you refresh details or submit information to the same web page, as far as the web server is concerned, it is a brand new page and is treated as such. There is **no persistence** of information between pages, and this has to be handled using other means that we will see in later chapters. However ASP.NET is able to use certain aspects of the ASP.NET server controls to remember the state of information contained within the controls.

To keep things simple, we're going to leave looking at Control Events until a little later in the chapter, and first concentrate on getting a solid understanding of the three events that ASP.NET will always call in the lifetime of a page. As we mentioned before, they are `Page_Init`, `Page_Load`, and `Page_Unload`.

As we've already mentioned, if you want code to execute on your page before anything else occurs, then you need to associate it with the `Page_Init` event:

```
<script language="c#" runat="server">
void Page_Init()
{
      ... code here ...
}
</script>
```

Alternatively, if you want to perform actions, *after* the page has been loaded, *but* before the user has had a chance to submit any information, then the `Page_Load()` event should be used:

```
<script language="c#" runat="server">
void Page_Load()
{
      ... code here ...
}
</script>
```

We've used the `Page_Load()` function for all of our examples so far in this book to make sure that the code that we are writing gets run, although we could just as easily have placed it in the `Page_Init()` function.

To clarify this concept, once again, `Page_Load` is an event that is triggered every time your web form is loaded, and it calls the `void Page_Load()` function. So what's really happening is when the page is loaded, the event is triggered; ASP.NET then detects the event and runs the contents of the function associated with it.

If we look at the following code, we can see:

```
<script runat="server" language="c#">
void Page_Load()
{
      Message1.text = "This is text that is only displayed once the Page_Load()
      event has been triggered.";
}
</script>
<html>
<head>
<title>Event Driven Page</title>
</head>
<body>
<asp:label id="Message1" runat="server" />
</body>
</html>
```

This ASP.NET code is only triggered in response to the `Page_Load()` event occurring. What happens if we take our code and put it into a different function? The answer is that the code will now only run when another event is triggered and calls the new function, or if the function is called from elsewhere in our ASP.NET code.

For example, you could move the code that displays the text into a separate function, called `Function_1()` instead:

```
<script runat="server" language="c#">
void Function_1()
{
  Message1.text = "This is text that is only displayed once the Page_Load()
  event has been triggered.";
}
</script>
...
```

Now, if you went back to the example, and changed the code in this way it wouldn't work properly anymore, as this code would no longer be run whenever the page opened. However you can fix this by calling `Function1()` from `Page_Load()`:

```
<script runat="server" language="c#">
void Page_Load()
{
  Function1();
}
void Function_1()
{
    ...
}
</script>
```

This is common practice when programming events as it keeps the event handling code as simple as possible and the same functionality can be called from any event handler.

This describes where `Page_Init` and `Page_Load` are triggered, but that still leaves us with the `Page_Unload` event. Like the other two this will occur every time a page is sent and before the user gets to use the page, of course, but the main difference is this event occurs after all of the ASP.NET code in the page has been executed and has completed its tasks. The `Page_Unload` event occurs after all other tasks have been performed, but remember as these events are performed as a **single discrete action** on the server, the `Page_Unload` will already have been performed by the time the user gets to see the page.

The only function of this final event is to give you the chance to perform housekeeping actions such as closing down objects, before the page is sent back to the user. As `Page_Unload` is performed after the rest of the ASP.NET has been completed, it is not possible to use controls or ASP.NET statements to output any content or send HTML in the associated `Page_Unload()` function either. Typically, not much else is done other than the previously mentioned housekeeping and tidying tasks in `Page_Unload()`.

This gives you a good idea of the sequence of steps that ASP.NET runs through when you request a page. However, between a page being loaded and it being unloaded there is the potential for the user to generate an event by clicking a button, changing a listbox, and so on. These are the events that we are interested in as they can be generated by elements on the ASP.NET form. These events are associated with particular ASP.NET server controls. And you can set and trigger them in the same way that we've already seen.

Events in HTML

Before we launch into more detail of how these events work in ASP.NET, it helps to look at the way that they are dealt with by HTML.

For those used to writing HTML pages, to understand the advantages of using ASP.NET event handlers, you first need to see how HTML does it. In a form, HTML will usually use the `<input>` tag with the type attribute being set to `Submit` to create a submit button, in order to send the form's data. However, if you wanted to create a button but didn't wish to send the contents of the form to the server for processing, you'd need to use the HTML `<input>` tag again, but this time setting the type attribute to `button`. This button wouldn't do anything at all at the moment: to get it to react to an event you'd need to add some more code to the `<input>` tag. Typically HTML will use a combination of a form and a small piece of client-side script to achieve this. The client-side script is placed in a special event attribute of a HTML tag and the tag is placed inside the form as usual.

This is best demonstrated with an example. We're going create a page with a button that displays a message when the user presses it. Don't worry: you don't need to know any client-side script for this example. But you must be using a modern browser, IE 4 and upward, Netscape 6 and upward, or Opera 5 and upward.

Try It Out – Handling an Event in HTML

1. Open up your web page editor and type in the following:

```
<html>
<head>
<title>HTML Event Example</title>
</head>
<body>
<form>
<input type="button" value="Click Me" onclick=
                                "alert('You have raised an event!')">
</form>
</body>
</html>
```

2. Save it as `htmlevent.htm` (note the HTM suffix; this isn't an ASP.NET web form).

3. View it in your browser and click on the button:

How It Works

This is an example of a built-in HTML event, known as an **intrinsic event**. These events are supported by nearly every HTML tag you care to mention, from <body> to <img> and, of course, as in this example <input>. Below is a list of some of the events that it is possible for a browser to react to:

❑   onmouseup – occurs when a mouse button is released while clicking over an element

❑   onmousedown – occurs when a mouse button is pressed and held while clicking over an element

❑   onmouseover – occurs when a mouse is moved over an element

❑   onmousemove – occurs when a mouse moves over an element

❑   onclick – occurs when a mouse is clicked over an element

❑   ondblclick – occurs when a mouse is double-clicked while hovering over an element

❑   onkeyup – occurs when a key is released over an element

❑   onkeypress – occurs when a key is pressed and released over an element

❑   onkeydown – occurs when a key is pressed and held down while over an element

In our extremely simplistic program we have just created a form with a single button:

```
<form>
<input type="button" value="Click Me" onclick=
                                    "alert('You have raised an event!')">
</form>
```

The `<input>` tag is set to have a `type` of `button`, so when the button is clicked it isn't automatically submitted. Next, we use `onclick`. Inside this event attribute there is a little bit of JavaScript code that brings up a dialog box with a message (**alert**) in it. The code inside the `onclick` attribute is known as an **event handler**. An event handler is simply a section of code that manages a suitable response to the event, just like the `void Page_Load()` function does.

We could change the code so that our button reacts to a different event; here we've changed it to the `onmouseover` event:

```
<form>
<input type="button" value="Click Me" onmouseover=
                              "alert('You have generated an event!')">
</form>
```

If you go back and change your code, it will now react if you move your mouse over the button, rather than having to click on it. The event handling code is just the same. You could also amend your code so that your button can respond to several events:

```
<form>
<input type="button" value="Click Me" onclick=
                      "alert('You have generated a click event!')"
                              onmouseover=
                      "alert('You have generated an event by hovering!')">
</form>
```

The reason we're talking about how HTML does this is because ASP.NET does it in a very similar way, and this provides a good introduction. We'll go on to look at how ASP.NET handles these kinds of events now.

Server Control Events in ASP.NET

ASP.NET, like client-side scripting, enables you to use events, such as `onclick` and `onchange` within your server-side controls, and then write ASP.NET code that 'reacts' to them in any .NET language. This is a major advantage as you don't have to rely on a modern browser to get these events to work – we mentioned previously that forms in ASP.NET have more versatility, and that's because you can provide complex event handling even on the oldest of browsers. This is because, while the browser used to deal with the events in HTML, in ASP.NET the web server deals with them and sends pure HTML back to the browser. Better still, it adds device independence, in addition to browser independence to the code.

You can add events to ASP.NET controls, in exactly the same way that you would add them in HTML to client-side controls. In ASP.NET an `onclick` event for a button control might look like this:

```
<asp:button id="button1" text="Click me" onclick=
                              "ClickEventHandler" runat="server" />
```

As `onclick` is a client-side event, it can only be used server-side with `asp:` controls Here we supply the name of a function in the `onclick` event attribute. This function name will be mapped directly onto a function with the same name found in your script code:

```
<script language="C#" runat="server">
void ClickEventHandler(object Sender, EventArgs e)
{
  //... ASP.NET code here...
}
</script>
```

If you haven't provided a function with the same name, then the code won't compile, as it has to have a matching event. The code will only be run when the name of the function in the server control attribute matches the name of a function in your code. You can call the function whatever name you want, as long as you are consistent in using the same name in the server control and within the `<script>` elements.

The arguments we provide for this event handler are used to let the calling event pass information to the handler. The first of these – `Sender` – provides a reference to the object that raised the event, while the second – e – is an event class that captures information regarding the state of the event being handled and passes an object that's specific to that event. More on these parameters shortly, but let's first consider the different events available to us.

ASP.NET web controls have a reduced set of events (compared to HTML) that can be added to controls as extra attributes. These are as follows (note that these event names aren't case sensitive):

Event name	Description
onLoad	Occurs when the control has loaded into the `Page` object.
onUnload	Occurs when the control has been unloaded from memory.
onClick/onCommand	Occurs when a mouse button (or similar) is clicked when hovering over the `<asp:button>` control after the form has been submitted to the server. Only the `<asp:button>` and `<asp:imagebutton>` server control have these events The difference between the two event is that `onCommand` is used when the button is associated with a command (such as sort) and `onClick` when the button is not associated with any command and just used to submit form data.
onInit	Occurs when the control is first initialized.
onPrerender	Occurs just before the control is rendered.
Disposed	Occurs when the control is unloaded from memory.
DataBinding	Occurs when the control binds to a data source.

In addition to this, we also have the following events that can't be handled by the user in an event handler, but that occur in ASP.NET and cause it to amend the contents of ViewState. (They can also be handled as client-side events):

Event name	Description
SelectIndexChanged CheckChanged TextChanged	Occur when the contents of a control have been altered, such as a checkbox being clicked, or a list item being selected. They only apply to the appropriate controls, such as list items, checkboxes and textboxes.

The large difference between HTML controls and ASP.NET server controls is the way they're dealt with. With HTML form controls, when the event is raised, the browser deals with it. It will sit around waiting for a user to click on the page or move their mouse. But, with server-side controls, the event is raised by the browser, but instead of being dealt with by it, the client raises a trigger telling the server to handle the event. In fact, the server only generates a single form postback event, which occurs when you click on the ASP.NET `button` control. Anything else that might have been done in the page is packaged up within this single event. So if you've checked a radio button and chosen an item from a listbox, this information is recorded when you send the form.

It doesn't matter what kind of event was raised, the client will always return this single postback event to the server. However, some events are impossible to deal with on the server, such as key presses or mouseovers, so there are no equivalent ASP.NET events for these. They will not be passed on to the server and have to be handled by the client. In fact, this is a very powerful technique: we can have client-side events on a server-side control. The server-side ones will be handled by the server, but the client-side ones will be handled by the client. The reasons for this are simple.

With HTML and client-side scripting, your browser will wait for you to click on a control. It can sit around all day waiting for you if you keep the same page open. This can't happen in ASP.NET, because as mentioned previously, HTTP only allows you to open a connection, get a page, and close that connection. Similarly, the server cannot keep a copy of `Page` object open on the server, on the off chance that you might submit details to the page at a later point. Rather, the whole set of events, corresponding to the changes you have made to the page, have to be dealt with in a single discrete action. The `Page` object is initialized, the page is loaded, and the control events are then bundled up into a postback event and dealt with – the page is then unloaded. This means you can deal with the server-side events, but return your code to the browser, which can then react to the client-side events that require more instant responses. So, to go back to the `OnTextChanged` event, here you have a server-side event that ASP.NET reacts to. It can amend the contents of a textbox control, via ViewState, using this. However, you might want the browser to actually examine the code contained within and react to what the user has typed to stop them submitting details in the first place – such as if they tried to type in letters, rather than numbers, in a text field asking their age.

The advantage of passing events to the server is that it adds better structure to your code, because you can separate out the event handling code in your ASP.NET applications entirely. There are some disadvantages too, though – wherever possible it's a good idea to do client processing, to offload work from central server CPUs to improve performance.

So, if the majority of events can still only be handled by the browser, what events are handled on the server? Well there is one ASP.NET server control in particular that can be used to send this postback information as part of the form data – this is the ASP.NET `button` control.

The ASP.NET button Server Control

There is one ASP.NET server control in particular, that we need to look at, which can be used to react to events. This control performs the equivalent functionality of setting the `<input>` tag type to "submit" in HTML. This is the `button` control, and the reason we haven't looked at it before is that you need to know a little about how events work to be able to make any decent use of it.

The button control has the following format:

```
<asp:button  id="id_name" event="event_handler_name" runat="server" />
```

You can use it to create a simple `<input type="submit">` element, and respond to a set of events we looked at earlier:

- `onInit`
- `onPrerender`
- `onLoad`
- `onClick`
- `onUnload`
- `onCommand`
- `Disposed`
- `DataBinding`

If we're going to get our page to respond dynamically, we need to use one of the events capable of doing this – `onClick` (`onCommand` being the other).

This example contains three ASP.NET HTML server controls. The first is a checkbox to register a user's choice, the second is a button that will raise the event, and the third a label control. As we've mentioned earlier in the book, you can't render dialog boxes directly in ASP.NET – to display information dynamically you have to use the `label` control.

This next example asks the user for some information about whether they wish to receive further information from a company. It will display a message appropriate to the user's response depending on whether they checked the checkbox or not.

Try It Out – Using the ASP.NET Button Server Control

1. Open up your text editor and type in the following code:

```
<script language="C#" runat="server">
  void ClickHandler(object Sender, EventArgs e)
  {
    if (ExtraInfoBox.Checked) {
      Message.Text = "<br /><br />You will hear from us shortly";
```

```
    }
    else {
      Message.Text = "<br /><br />You will not receive any further"
                                    + " information from us";
    }
  }
</script>

<html>
  <head>
    <title>Server-side event processing example</title>
  </head>
  <body>
    <form runat="server">
      <asp:CheckBox id="ExtraInfoBox" Text=
                "Click here to receive extra information" Runat="server" />
      <br /><br />
      <asp:Button id="Button1" Text="Click Here to Submit"
                                    onclick="ClickHandler" runat="server"/>
      <asp:Label id="Message" runat="server"/>
    </form>
  </body>
</html>
```

2. Save this as `event.aspx`.

3. Run the code in your browser:

4. Check the box and click on the "Click here to Submit" button. An appropriate message is displayed:

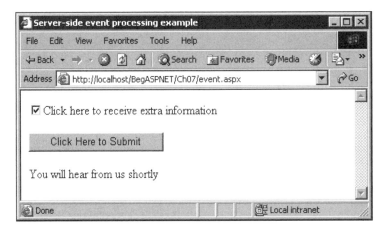

How It Works

We're simply taking the event raised when a user clicks on the button and running a short passage of ASP.NET code. Our function `ClickHandler` is the event handler specified in the `onClick` event attribute. This event handler examines the checkbox in the example and displays a different message in the `label` control depending on whether or not the checkbox has been selected. This is our event handler/function code:

```csharp
<script language="C#" runat="server">
  void ClickHandler(object Sender, EventArgs e)
  {
    if (ExtraInfoBox.Checked) {
      Message.Text = "<br /><br />You will hear from us shortly";
    }
    else {
      Message.Text = "<br /><br />You will not receive any further"
                                    + "information from us";
    }
  }
</script>
```

This code will display an appropriate message depending on whether the contents of the `ExtraInfoBox` checkbox control has been activated or not. The crucial difference from all of the other examples we have looked at so far is that, instead of the automatically generated `Page_Load` event, we are using our own customized event. This means our code is only run when the click event happens. If nobody clicks on the button then nothing happens.

Another important point to notice about the click event handler code placed at the top of the page is that it requires two parameters. Up to now our `Page_Load` event has required no parameters, because we didn't need to pass information to it. You can use parameters here in just the same way as you would with normal functions, but you should be aware that there are special reasons why events require parameters.

Each event that is generated also generates information about itself – such as which control it was generated by. To be able to use this information within your function you need to pass in two parameters. The first of these has type `object` and is named `Sender`, the second is of type `EventArgs` and is named `e`, although they can be given any names. Both of these parameters are passed to any server-side event that can be raised by ASP.NET. They're important because they pass information to ASP.NET about which HTML element generated that event, what type of event was generated and other informative details about the event, and allow you to use and manipulate these values within your ASP.NET code.

When an event is generated a corresponding object is passed as the `Sender` parameter. This contains information about the object that is sending the information about the event. The second parameter `e` contains a set of related information – such as data about which class the event is a member of. It's still too early to deal completely with what is happening here, as you won't understand it without a thorough understanding of objects (which we cover in Chapter 8), but it should be a little clearer when we come to talk about it again in the next couple of chapters. All you need to know is that parameters pass details to a function about the specific event that has been generated. Every function/event handler works in the same way, whether raised by ASP.NET or by the programmer, and must be passed these 'generic' parameters.

But this isn't the only information that is passed. The data contained within the form is also passed at the same time by ASP.NET, when an event function is called with the ASP button control:

```
asp:Button id="Button1" Text="Click Here to Submit" onclick="ClickHandler()"
                                                     runat="server"/>
```

In this model, when the user submits the form. The form data is sent, not using the `<Input type="submit">`, but by the ASP `Button` server control. This control generates an event, which calls our function as an event, and by passing two parameters (`object Sender`, `EventArgs e`) you are able to use all of the form data directly on your page. This is postback.

We're now going to move on and consider the process of postback in more detail.

Event-Driven Programming and Postback

A big issue throughout this book so far has been the postback architecture. You may not have noticed this, as we've not focused on it or explained it until now. Postback is the process by which the browser posts information back to the server telling the server to handle the event, the server does so and sends the resulting HTML back to the browser again. Postback only occurs with web forms, and it is only server controls that post back information to the server.

ASP.NET doesn't look after the processing of all events, as it is still necessary to handle some events (such as `onmouseover`) on the client side, as the server couldn't possibly react to them in time.

But the great advantage of processing some events on the server is that you don't have to rely on a particular browser to recognize your client-side script, and you can send back extra information – for example, the state of a particular control – to help influence you decision. This is something fundamentally different from what happens in HTML. Let's just demonstrate this now with an example:

Try It Out – Demonstrating HTML's Lack of Postback

1. Open your web page editor and type in the following:

```
<html>
<head>
  <title>HTML Event Example</title>
</head>
<body>
<form method="get">
Select either A, B or C and click the button at the bottom<br/>
<br/>
A<input type="radio" value="a" name="test"><br />
B<input type="radio" value="b" name="test"><br />
C<input type="radio" value="c" name="test"><br /><br />
<input type="submit" value="Click Me" onclick="
                              alert('You have generated an event!')">
</form>
</body>
</html>
```

2. Save this as `htmlevent2.htm`, making sure you remember the HTM suffix again.

3. View this in your browser and click on a choice:

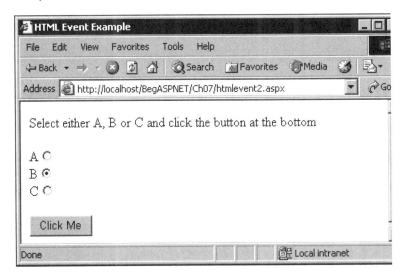

4. Now click on the Click Me button – after receiving a dialog saying that you have generated an event you will see the following:

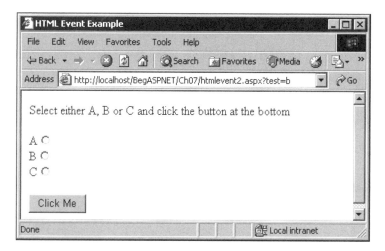

Your selection has disappeared!

How It Works

There isn't anything unusual happening in our HTML form. Though you should note that, as we've omitted the action attribute of the form, it will post the data to back to itself:

```
<form method="get">
Select either A, B or C and click the button at the bottom<br/>
<br/>
A<input type="radio" value="a" name="test"><br />
B<input type="radio" value="b" name="test"><br />
C<input type="radio" value="c" name="test"><br /><br />
<input type="submit" value="Click Me" onclick="
                                alert('You have generated an event!')">
</form>
```

As you can see from the URL, a querystring has been appended to submit the information:

```
http://localhost/5040/ch07/htmlevent2.htm?test=b
```

However, when we go back to the page, our selection has disappeared. This is the normal behavior for HTML. However ASP.NET can improve upon this, as we shall see. Let's adapt our previous example to use an ASP.NET server control instead:

1. Type the following into your page editor:

```html
<html>
<head>
  <title>Postback Event Example</title>
</head>
<body>
<form runat="server">
  Select either A, B or C and click the button at the bottom<br/>
<br/>
<asp:radiobuttonlist id="test" runat="server">
<asp:listitem id="option1" value="a" runat="server" />
<asp:listitem id="option2" value="b" runat="server" />
<asp:listitem id="option3" value="c" runat="server" />
</asp:radiobuttonlist>
<br /><br />
<input type="submit" value="Click Me" onclick=
                                   "alert('You have generated an event!')">
</form>
</body>
</html>
```

2. Save this as `postback.aspx`.

3. View this in your browser, select a choice and click on the button:

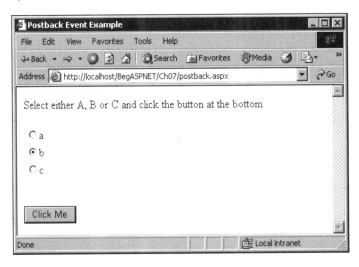

This time your choice is remembered.

How It Works

This is an example of the concept of postback in action. Click on View Source in your browser to view your code – because of differences between machines and browsers your code won't look exactly like this, but it will be pretty similar:

```
<html>
<head>
  <title>Postback Event Example</title>
</head>
<body>
<form name="ctrl0" method="post" action="postback.aspx" id="ctrl0">
<input type="hidden" name="__VIEWSTATE" value="dDw0MDk5MTgxNTU7Oz4=" />

Select either a, b or c and click the button at the bottom<br/>
<br/>
<table id="test" border="0">
  <tr>
    <td>
      <span value="a">
        <input id="test_0" type="radio" name="test" value="a" />
        <label for="test_0">a</label>
        </span>
    </td>
  </tr><tr>
    <td>
      <span value="b">
        <input id="test_1" type="radio" name="test" value="b"
                                                    checked="checked" />
        <label for="test_1">b</label>
        </span>
    </td>
  </tr><tr>
    <td>
      <span value="c">
        <input id="test_2" type="radio" name="test" value="c" />
        <label for="test_2">c</label>
        </span>
    </td>
  </tr>
</table>
<br /><br />
<input type="submit" value="Click Me" onclick=
                              "alert('You have generated an event!')">
</form>
</body>
</html>
```

The `<asp:radiobuttonlist>` control has been turned into its equivalent `<input>` controls and has been formatted as part of a table. Also the event attribute is no longer specified in the input tag. However, the largest change is the addition of the hidden `VIEWSTATE` control:

```
<input type="hidden" name="__VIEWSTATE" value="dDw0MDk5MTgxNTU7Oz4=" />
```

Information about the state of the form is sent back in an associated hidden control, called `__VIEWSTATE`. This information is generated by ASP.NET. In fact the information contained within `__VIEWSTATE` control in the value attribute is actually an encrypted version of the old state of the form. ASP.NET is able to look at the old version and compare it to the current version. From this it knows how to persist the state of ASP.NET server controls between page submissions. If there are differences, such as a different radio button being selected, then internal events are generated by ASP.NET in response to this and it deals with it appropriately, to create a 'current' version of the form. This `__VIEWSTATE` control is crucial to ASP.NET being able to remember the state of controls between page submissions, without actually maintaining a page object or HTTP connection throughout.

ASP.NET has used this postback information about the state of the page to create a new version of it, with the state of the corresponding controls being remembered. This can be used by the browser in future iterations of the page, but is never displayed again. So postback works by using only HTML tags and controls, which contain information that can be interpreted by ASP.NET.

The IsPostBack Test

Before we leave postback though, let's go back to something we introduced in Chapter 3, the `IsPostBack` test. This was used to see whether a user had returned a form, together with data, or whether it was the first time the form had been displayed. Now you can see that our `IsPostBack` test is just checking to see whether any postback information has been generated by an event. If it hasn't then this test generates `false`, otherwise it generates `true`. The `postback` test has to be used in conjunction with a particular page, so the following syntax is used:

```
if (Page.IsPostBack) {
```

This is only used with ASP.NET forms but it makes the process of forms posting back to themselves much simpler.

Changing the Way we Program on the Web

Throughout this chapter, we've been referring to `void Page_Load()` as just another function, and indeed this is all it is. But it is slightly different in that ASP.NET automatically calls this function for us. As virtually all ASP.NET code is placed in functions, we rely on the event associated with this code to kick-start our applications.

In order for ASP.NET to handle other events, you'll need to create your own event handlers, using your own functions. These functions will be called by event attributes of the HTML server controls, such as `onclick`. When you call these functions you are able to pass information about the event by which they were called using the event parameters we discussed earlier.

In fact all programming in C# is event-driven and object-oriented, it's just a case of whether:

❑ ASP.NET raises the event, as is the case with `Page_Load()` or `Page_Init()`

❑ The user of the web page raises it by clicking on a button and raising an associated handler

Whichever is the case, they both operate in the same way, causing the program to break from whatever it was doing and move to the requested function.

We're going to look at an example that draws all of the things we've looked at in the chapter together and utilizes this new way of doing things. It contains two textboxes to take information from the user, and will perform a calculation depending on whether the user selects an add, subtract, divide, or multiply button.

Try It Out – Event-driven Example

1. Open up your web page editor and type in the following:

```
<script runat="server" Language="c#">
  void Add(object sender, EventArgs e) {
    try
    {
      double d = Convert.ToDouble(tbxInput1.Text) +
                 Convert.ToDouble(tbxInput2.Text);
      lblAnswer.Text = d.ToString();
    }
    catch
    {
      lblAnswer.Text = "An error occurred";
    }
  }
  void Subtract(object sender, EventArgs e) {
    try
    {
      double d = Convert.ToDouble(tbxInput1.Text) -
                 Convert.ToDouble(tbxInput2.Text);
      lblAnswer.Text = d.ToString();
    }
    catch
    {
      lblAnswer.Text = "An error occurred";
    }
  }
  void Factor(object sender, EventArgs e) {
    try
    {
      double d = Convert.ToDouble(tbxInput1.Text) *
                 Convert.ToDouble(tbxInput2.Text);
      lblAnswer.Text = d.ToString();
    }
    catch
    {
      lblAnswer.Text = "An error occurred";
```

```
      }
    }
    void Ratio(object sender, EventArgs e) {
      try
      {
        double d = Convert.ToDouble(tbxInput1.Text) /
                   Convert.ToDouble(tbxInput2.Text);
        lblAnswer.Text = d.ToString();
      }
      catch
      {
        lblAnswer.Text = "An error occurred";
      }
    }
  }
</script>
<html>
  <form runat="server">
    <asp:textbox id="tbxInput1" runat="server" />
    <asp:button id="btnAdd" runat="server" text=" + " Onclick="Add" />
    <asp:button id="btnSubtract" runat="server" text=" - "
                                              Onclick="Subtract" />
    <br/>
    <asp:textbox id="tbxInput2" runat="server" />
    <asp:button id="btnFactor" runat="server" text=" x " Onclick="Factor" />
    <asp:button id="btnRatio" runat="server" text=" ÷ " Onclick="Ratio" />
    <br/>
    <b>Answer = <asp:Label id="lblAnswer" runat="server" /></b>
  </form>
</html>
```

2. Save this as `eventdriven.aspx`.

3. View it in your browser:

4. Enter two numbers into the text fields and select the multiply button to perform a calculation:

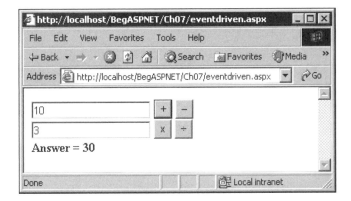

5. You will see the answer displayed for your particular operation. Go back, alter the numbers, and click a different button, such as subtract:

Only the operation corresponding to the button clicked was performed.

Please note that if you don't enter a number into one or other of the boxes before selecting an operator, you will cause an error. We intercept this error in the code, and just display an appropriate error message.

How It Works

This example works by using event-driven programming, as we outlined previously. We have created four separate functions, `Add()`, `Subtract()`, `Factor()`, and `Ratio()`.

```
<script runat="server" Language="c#">
  void Add(object sender, EventArgs e)
  {
    try
```

```
        {
          double d = Convert.ToDouble(tbxInput1.Text) +
                  Convert.ToDouble(tbxInput2.Text);
          lblAnswer.Text = d.ToString();
        }
        catch
        {
          lblAnswer.Text = "An error occurred";
        }
      }
      void Subtract(object sender, EventArgs e)
      {
        try
        {
          double d = Convert.ToDouble(tbxInput1.Text) -
                  Convert.ToDouble(tbxInput2.Text);
          lblAnswer.Text = d.ToString();
        }
        catch
        {
          lblAnswer.Text = "An error occurred";
        }
      }
      void Factor(object sender, EventArgs e)
      {
        try
        {
          double d = Convert.ToDouble(tbxInput1.Text) *
                  Convert.ToDouble(tbxInput2.Text);
          lblAnswer.Text = d.ToString();
        }
        catch
        {
          lblAnswer.Text = "An error occurred";
        }
      }
      void Ratio(object sender, EventArgs e)
      {
        try
        {
          double d = Convert.ToDouble(tbxInput1.Text) /
                  Convert.ToDouble(tbxInput2.Text);
          lblAnswer.Text = d.ToString();
        }
        catch
        {
          lblAnswer.Text = "An error occurred";
        }
      }
</script>
```

Note that in all four functions we have used `try...catch` *to deal with any input (such as letters or a blank textbox) that cannot be converted to a* `double`. *See Chapter 4 for a reminder on how this works.*

These functions are called by the four ASP.NET button controls we have created:

```
<asp:button id="btnAdd" runat="server" text=" + " Onclick="Add" />
<asp:button id="btnSubtract" runat="server" text=" - " Onclick="Subtract" />
...
<asp:button id="btnFactor" runat="server" text=" x " Onclick="Factor" />
<asp:button id="btnRatio" runat="server" text=" ÷ " Onclick="Ratio" />
```

Each button has a symbol corresponding to its equivalent mathematical operation, and it calls that relevant function. All four functions work in an identical way. Let's look at Add() more closely:

```
void Add(object sender, EventArgs e)
{
  try
  {
    double d = Convert.ToDouble(tbxInput1.Text) +
               Convert.ToDouble(tbxInput2.Text);
    lblAnswer.Text = d.ToString();
  }
   catch
  {
    lblAnswer.Text = "An error occurred";
  }
}
```

This is called by the onclick attribute of btnAdd, and is passed the two generic parameters. These parameters allow it to access the two textboxes, which contain the numbers that the user entered:

```
<asp:textbox id="tbxInput1" runat="server" />
  ...
<asp:textbox id="tbxInput2" runat="server" />
  ...
```

The first textbox is called tbxInput1, so we can reference it as tbxInput1, and reference its contents by referring to its Text attribute. The second textbox is tbxInput2 and can be referenced similarly. In order to carry out a mathematical operation on these values, which are imported from the ASP.NET page as strings, they have to be converted to doubles, a process which can fail, which is why the conversion operations are wrapped in special error handling code.

The sum of the two values is converted back into a string and stored in the Text attribute of the lblAnswer control. This information is displayed on our screen. The other three functions work in the same way, and will only be executed if the particular button associated with them is pressed.

In this way ASP.NET can react in a different way to each of the buttons on the page, while making use of the same data. We'll be coming across events a lot more throughout the book and expanding on our understanding of them in later chapters, but for now this gives you the necessary foundations on which to base your understanding of them.

Summary

We've kept this chapter short, as we want to focus on the main points that are central to the event-driven way in which ASP.NET works. It generates a set of events, which occur whenever a web page is initialized, loaded, and unloaded on the server. During this sequence, ASP.NET can also react to other events that may have been generated by the server controls. The code needed to react to these events is placed in event handlers. By passing two generic parameters to these event handlers, you are able to use all of the form data

Event-driven programming is something utilized in ASP.NET and something that fundamentally alters the way in which pages/web forms are created. You might create a web form with several sections of code, some of which are never executed, while others will be executed constantly. When web forms are created you now need to think which events will occur, and how to make your pages react to them.

In the next chapter we move on to the concept of objects and see how everything in ASP.NET, including events, is in fact just an object. This will fundamentally alter, yet again, the way in which we create our ASP.NET web forms.

Exercises

1. Explain why event-driven programming is such a good way of programming for the Web.

2. Run the following HTML code in your browser (remember to save the page with an `.htm` extension). Now translate the HTML into a set of ASP.NET server controls so that the information entered into the form is maintained when the submit button is clicked. Add a function to the button to confirm that the details entered were received:

```
<html>
<head>
  <title>HTML</title>
</head>
<body>
  <form>
    <h4>Please enter your name:<h4>
    <input type="text"><br /><br />
    <h4>What would you like for breakfast?<h4>
    <h4>Cereal<input type="checkbox"><h4>
    <h4>Eggs<input type="checkbox"><h4>
    <h4>Pancakes<input type="checkbox"><h4><br />
    <h4>Feed me:<h4>
    <h4>Now<input type="radio" name="test"><h4>
    <h4>Later<input type="radio" name="test"><h4>
    <input type="submit" value="Thank you!">
  </form>
</body>
</html>
```

3. Add a `Page_Load()` event handler to the ASPX code you have just created that confirms the selections made, in the following format:

Thank you very much ____

You have chosen _____ for breakfast. I will prepare it for you _____

4. Create a very basic virtual telephone using an ASPX file that displays a textbox and a button named 'Call'. Configure your ASPX file so that when you type a telephone number into your textbox and press 'Call', you are:

❑ Presented with a message confirming the number you are calling

❑ Presented with another button called 'Disconnect' that, when pressed, returns you to your opening page, leaving you ready to type another number.

5. Using the `switch` construct, associate three particular telephone numbers with three names, so that when you press the 'Call' button, your confirmation message contains the name of the person you are 'calling' rather than just the telephone number.

The solutions to these exercises are available at http://p2p.wrox.com, and with the code download on www.wrox.com.

Introduction to Objects

"Computers only become something when given a special application. Ditto Lego. Lego's discrete modular bricks are indestructible and fully intended to be nothing except themselves."

– excerpt from "Microserfs" by Douglas Coupland (HarperCollins, 1995)

In previous chapters we've seen how we can hook up various statements and control structures in ASP.NET and use them to generate individual dynamic web pages. However, as your web pages (and ultimately web applications) become more complicated, your code will gradually become more difficult to understand; consequently it will become more difficult to maintain, and you'll wonder whether it was worth all that hard work in the first place.

What's more, all the functionality we've implemented in our pages so far is tied to a specific page, which make it difficult to reuse this logic elsewhere without going to the trouble of cutting and pasting (and making any subsequent modifications) in every separate file you want to support it.

In this chapter, we're going to start learning how we can get round these problems by writing more modular code. We're going to look at one of the core concepts of .NET – **objects** – and here are some of the questions we'll answer:

- ❑ How and why you should organize your code
- ❑ How to use components to organize your code
- ❑ What **objects** and **classes** are, and how to use them as components
- ❑ How to use objects

The entire .NET Framework (including ASP.NET, ADO.NET, Windows Forms, and everything else you're likely to come across) is based on objects. Whenever you write any sort of program for .NET, you're actually working with objects – whether or not you realize it. Since we're going to be seeing a lot of these objects in the course of the book, it's absolutely critical that you have solid understanding of the topics we discuss in this chapter.

Organizing Your Code

In very simple applications (as we've seen in the opening chapters of this book), any given task may only ever be performed once – larger applications may require the same task be performed many times over by different parts of the application. Instead of rewriting that code over and over, it's much more efficient to identify such tasks, and reuse code as much as possible.

❑ If we reuse code, there is less to write overall, so we can develop our application more quickly.

❑ If we reuse code, the final application will be smaller, and therefore will probably have fewer bugs. Indeed, debugging the application should be easier anyway, because there will be fewer lines of code to wade through.

Consider an ASP.NET web application that stores data in a database. Connecting to the database and retrieving data are tasks that the application performs. Using techniques we've learned so far, we'd need to repeat every line of the code required to perform these tasks in every page that required database access. As soon as we wanted to change the application's database system, we would have to change the database access code in every single page. In a large application, this could amount to hundreds or even thousands of pages that we'd have to update.

There are two reasons why such a change is a problem. Firstly, the changes are tedious and time consuming to make. We all know that "time is money", and the developer's time could be better spent improving the application. Secondly, the more code a developer changes, the more risk there is of introducing new errors.

Both these problems can be avoided if, instead of repeating the same code in many different parts of an application, the code is written once and accessed by the different parts of the application as and when they need it.

Of course, there is some extra work involved in making your code reusable: each block of code must be designed to meet the requirements of each part of the application that will use it. You therefore need to design applications with this in mind, so that you don't wind up asking your recycled code to do something slightly different each time it's called.

> **Efficient reusability stems from good planning, and while this may entail a little more work initially, it can pay enormous dividends as your application grows.**

If we now consider a typical web site that uses dynamically generated pages, maintenance often falls to two specific people to undertake:

❑ the **designer**, whose role is to maintain the **presentation** (graphics, layout, interface – commonly summarized as 'look and feel') of the site

❑ the **developer**, who is responsible for the **functionality** or **logic** of the application, providing code to manage database access and business rules for example

Some situations may see a clear separation between these roles – others may entail some overlap between them. The key point is that when you're thinking about the design of the page you don't want to have to worry about the .NET code that provides its functionality. Designers typically want to treat a task like database access as a 'black box' – that is, you put something simple in and get something simple out, but don't need to know what happens in between. Likewise, as a developer, you probably don't want to worry about the details of how your data is going to be displayed.

This separation of roles leads us to a practical organization of an application into **layers** or **tiers**, and as we progress through the book we'll see this arrangement made more and more explicit.

We've already been structuring our code to separate logic (`<script>` blocks) and presentation (`<html>` blocks). Fortunately, ASP.NET makes it very easy for us to do this, thanks to its use of objects. We're now going to take a proper look at the notion of objects, and see how we can use them to organize our code to the best possible extent.

So, What's an Object?

A **software object** is simply a bundle of code that describes some sort of real-world object. It might be a physical object (such as a book or a person) or an abstract object (like a number). Anything that exists in the real world can be represented in some fashion as a software object.

> **Typically we don't use the term 'software object', but simply talk about an 'object'. We call the idea of using objects in software 'object orientation', sometimes known as OO, or OOP for 'Object-Oriented Programming'.**

It's human nature to think about the world in terms of objects – in other words, we break it down into smaller units, each of which is a self-contained entity to which we can assign a name. Each has its own particular attributes, and can engage in various activities with other objects around it.

We can consider a car as one example of an real-world object – we can name it ("this is a car"), we can clearly separate it from other entities in the real world ("a fish is not a car"), we can list its attributes ("this car is blue"), and list the actions it can perform ("this car can start, stop, and change gear"). We can even describe relationships between it and other objects ("a person can drive the car", "the car has four wheels", "the car is an automobile").

> **Objects can be physical (like a car, which we can touch) or abstract (like a specific route between two points, which exists as a well-defined entity, but has no physical element).**

Let's start out by taking a close look at our car example. Many of the code samples in this chapter are going to see us developing a software object that represents a car – this could be used in an application that simulates traffic flow – and it doesn't take too much imagination to think of a few related examples of real-world objects that we might also consider modeling as objects:

- ❑   the **car** itself
- ❑   the **factory** that produced it
- ❑   the **wheels** on the car
- ❑   the **brake** pedal
- ❑   the **engine**

Of course, these are all physical objects. We might also want to consider abstract objects, such as the car **manufacturer**. (While it's hard to get a physical grip on something like General Motors or Ford, it still exists as a well-defined legal entity.) All of these real-world objects are well defined and self-contained, with state (what they *are*) and behavior (what they *do*). For example:

- ❑   the **car** is *blue* and can *accelerate*
- ❑   the **factory** is *in Germany* and *makes cars*
- ❑   the **wheels** are *fully inflated* and can *turn round*

When we talk about a **software object**, we're referring to a special sort of software construct that bundles together data and functions in a self-contained unit. By doing so, we can represent these real-world objects as software objects, with state represented by the object's **properties** (data stored in the object) and behavior represented by its **methods** (object-specific functions). In the next few sections, we'll take a look at how we might settle on a suitable representation, what we can do with an object once we've defined it, and why it makes our lives so much easier.

Perhaps we want to write a program that simulates traffic in a city – it's natural to think about modeling it in terms of objects. For example, we'll frequently want to reuse code that describes "a car", "a route", "a traffic light" and establish interactive relationships between these blocks of code.

Object-Oriented Programming (OOP) gives us a very elegant and powerful way to reuse code, and in the course of the chapter, you'll see that it also has the following benefits:

- ❑   It appeals to the way humans think
- ❑   It helps us write code more efficiently
- ❑   It helps us write simpler code
- ❑   It helps us write code that's easier to change later
- ❑   It helps us write more reliable code
- ❑   It helps us write more comprehensible code

The Microsoft developers who built the .NET Framework have defined a massive collection of objects, and the Framework's entire set of functionality is built around these in one way or another. Whenever we write a program in .NET, we're actually just hooking together various objects so that they can do something useful for us. In fact, objects lurk quietly behind every one of the elements we've seen so far – among hundreds of different ready-built object types are form `buttons`, labels, basic variable types `int`, `bool`, and `string`; even the web page itself has an object to describe it.

Abstraction – Modeling the Real World

When we write code using objects, we do it by breaking our large complex program down into lots of smaller easily understandable pieces. Then we can spend more time thinking about how each of these objects talks to each of the others. If we are thinking on this slightly higher level we can forget the details of how any particular object works. The benefit of this is that our program is much easier to understand because we do not need to keep the whole thing in our heads at once.

For example, think about a car. A car is a complex beast with many hundreds or even thousands of parts. If you considered every single part, and tried to take in the detailed nature of how each one interacted with all the others, you'd probably find yourself with quite a headache – even if you'd spent the last 30 years designing cars, there would probably be plenty of elements (the CD player or the GPS system, for example) that you'd simply not worry about, as long as they did their specific job properly.

On a high level, we know what a car is for, we know what to expect of it, and we know what it can do for us. We can name the most important parts of a car: the engine, the wheels, the pedals, and so on. Once we can get away from the 'nuts and bolts' level and consider the car in terms of these large pieces, most of the problem of complexity just vanishes. In practice, you don't need to know the precise mechanics of the braking system in order to bring the car to a halt – you simply press the pedal and the car slows down.

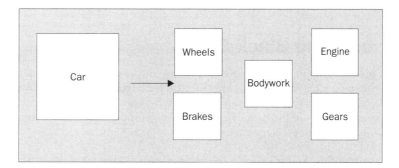

Breaking programs up in this manner has a similar effect – we can make use of each piece in an application without worrying too much about the details of how that piece works. It also means that if we have a problem in one part of the system, we don't need to worry about the details in any other part of the system, since each one can be treated as a discrete unit. Again, in practice, you don't need to know how the drive shaft works in order to fix a flat tire.

When we design an object, we are generally looking to implement some complex or frequently used functionality, and expose the simplest possible useful interface. Developers who then use the object should have just enough control to do what they need to do with it – but beyond that, we want to hide as many operational details from them as possible. This is a process known as **abstraction**.

The details that we abstract away can be separated into to main categories:

❑ Details that **aren't relevant** or **appropriate** to the particular situation we're modeling – if we designed a 'person' object to represent someone registered on our web site, we'd want it to incorporate details that were relevant to our particular line of business. It's unlikely that a bookshop site would require this object to describe 'hair color', whereas a dating service might well want it to. Likewise, we might incorporate 'shift up a gear' and 'shift down a gear' functionality into our car object – we **don't** want to let it 'change to 5th gear', as there's no telling what that might do to the gearbox (particularly if we'd just come out of 1st).

❑ Details that are **implicit**, either to the specific situation, or in the functionality that *is* exposed – if the person object can tell you about 'date of birth', there's little point in having it tell you about 'age' as well, since you can deduce one from the other. Perhaps we're just considering cars that are being driven on the freeway – we don't need to specify whether or not the car has wheels, since it's a safe bet that we won't be considering any flying cars (not for a while at least...).

Ultimately, we need to be able to make an informed decision as to what features each object needs to describe. As we'll see in a moment, these 'features' break down as things that the object *is*, and things that the object can *do*. The important thing is that once we've established the main blocks that make up our model, we can treat each one as a black box. Provided it's been well designed (as appropriate to the needs of our situation) we only need to give it a valid input to receive a valid output – we don't need to worry about exactly what processing has occurred.

Encapsulation – The Black Box

Once we have a model of the main objects we want to use in our program, we need to know about their most important characteristics. When we do this we treat each one as a black box, and simply consider what we want the object to do for us – we can largely ignore *how* it will do that. This helps us to focus on the most important aspects of the problem, rather than getting dragged into every minute part of the overall functionality right from the very start.

As an analogy, consider this. You're taking a friend out for lunch, but when you get to the parking lot where you've left your car, you find a rogue engineer stood in front of pile of several thousand pieces of metal and plastic – he helpfully points out that you'll have to reconstruct your automobile before you can drive it anywhere. The chances are that (once you'd called the police) you'd try and get a ride from your friend, whose own car is nearby and still in one piece.

However if the same engineer handed you a set of keys and pointed to a nearby BMW Z3, you might well jump in, and more than likely be able to pop the key in the ignition, start the engine, and put it in gear before driving off for an afternoon on the road. The point is, you don't need to understand how the raw components of your car fit together in order to drive it.

When we're using objects, their essential characteristics are what matter, not how they work underneath, which means we have a great deal less to think about. Since .NET provides hundreds of ready-built objects for us to use, there's less work for us to do too.

There's just one question we haven't answered: how do we actually apply this to software objects?

Object Properties

Let's look more closely at our car example. If we were going to specify a car as an object, we'd expect it to be able to be able to tell us about itself:

❑ How fast is the car moving?

❑ What color is it?

❑ Is the engine running?

❑ How long is the car?

❑ What's the number/license plate?

❑ How many doors are open?

Attributes like these (by which an object exposes itself to the outside world) are called **properties**.

Object Methods

It's also important to look at the things our object ought to *do* for us:

❑ Change gear

❑ Steer right/left

❑ Accelerate

❑ Brake

❑ Start engine

❑ Stop engine

Actions like these that we expect an object to perform are called **methods**. You can think of them as being similar to verbs – "doing" words. Methods should always correspond to things that the object can *do to* or *do with* its properties. For instance, a 'change gear' method is only useful if our car object has a 'gear number' property for it to modify. Likewise, well-chosen methods should relate specifically to the object that contains them. For example a 'take off' method would not fit in terribly well with our Car object, as it clearly doesn't fit in with what a car does.

The process of packaging up functionality in an object by specifying these essential characteristics and behaviors is called **encapsulation** – this is the fundamental feature of an object-oriented system that supports the process of abstraction. Once we encapsulate functionality within an object, we can treat it as a perfectly self-contained whole and only consider its most important properties (data held within the object) and methods (blocks of code that can use and/or modify that data). We can then focus on how our object interacts with other code and forget about how it works inside: never again will we need to hold the entire application in mind at once.

So, once we have a car object, we can ask it to do things for us without needing to know how it does it. Since .NET provides us with so many useful, ready-built objects, we can pick and choose from them according to what we want them to *do* for us; as long as we know what methods and properties they expose, we don't need to worry about how they work underneath. Effectively, Microsoft has built half our web site for us already, and in the next chapter we'll specifically look at each of the main objects that underpin all our ASP.NET web pages. Before that though, we're going to introduce you to the basic mechanics of defining, creating, and using objects.

Using Objects

So, now that we have some idea why objects can be useful to us, how are we going to work with them in the context of a web page? First, we need to consider where they come from.

Where do Objects Come From?

Before we ask .NET to create an object, it has to find out what how that object works, and what it is supposed to look like. If we want to create a brand new type of object, we need to start out by defining a blueprint for that object, which we call an **object class definition** (or more usually, just a **class**). This must describe *everything* there is to know about how any object of that type works, both internally and externally.

When we actually create an object – a specific **instance** of the class – the .NET Framework takes this blueprint and uses it as a template for the new object. For example, if we'd defined a class called Car, we could then use it to create several Car type objects:

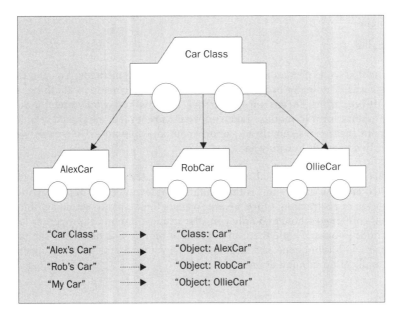

The diagram shows how we might create (the technical term is **instantiate**) three separate objects from a single class. In this case, we call them AlexCar, RobCar, and OllieCar, denoting the fact that they represent three different cars belonging to three different people. We might choose to set the color property on Alex's car object to "red" – even if we then set the same property on Rob's car object to "yellow", Alex's car would stay red.

Just to give you an idea of precisely how simple it is to do this, here's a snippet of code that instantiates all three objects and assigns them properties. We'll assume for now that we've already defined the Car object, and we'll see how we can do that in a moment:

```
Car AlexCar, RobCar, OllieCar;

AlexCar = new Car();
RobCar = new Car();
OllieCar = new Car();

AlexCar.Color = "red";
RobCar.Color = "yellow";
OllieCar.Color = "blue";
```

Defining a class

It's very easy to define a class in ASP.NET, and it's not dissimilar to how we declared variables and functions in the last couple of chapters. In fact, variables and functions play a crucial role in our class definitions, since we use them both in defining methods and properties. Let's take a look at how we might define our Car class – for now, we'll consider just two properties, Color and Gear, and one method, ChangeGear().

We start out by declaring that we want to define a public class called Car:

```
Public class Car
{
```

The fact that we specify the **visibility** of this class as Public means that we'll be able to use it from anywhere in our code. There are other options available (Private and Protected), which can be used to restrict use of the class to specific parts of an application – this doesn't really become an issue until we look at defining classes within classes, so we'll leave further discussion until the next chapter, when we look at this topic.

Our next step is to declare a couple of variables: a string to denote the color of the car object, and an integer denoting the gear it's currently in:

```
private string color;
private int gear;
```

Now, it's important to note that these variables do *not* comprise the class properties – there's more to properties than that. These are simply private variables that will be held within each instance of a `Car` type object; they will only be visible to code that's part of *that particular object*.

Elements within a class or object are generically referred to as **members**, and the full technical name for these particular variables is **private instance data members**: they represent *data*, and are *private* within each *instance* of the class. It's common practice to name private members in camelCase, that is with an initial lower case letter and a capital for the start of each word.

> **We can define the overall state of an object by considering the values of all its data members. If the data members within two instances of the same class all have identical values, we can say that the objects have identical state.**

We're now ready to expose our first property. This is also declared with `public` visibility, which means that we'll be able to access this property (called `Color`) from outside the object:

It is common practice for the property to have the same name as the private variable that it refers to, only written in PascalCase, that is with an initial capital letter.

```
public string Color
{
get
{
  return color;
}
set
{
  color = value;
}
}
```

As you can see, we're now using the private data member `color` (which, as we know, holds a string describing the color of each `Car` instance) and specifying two sub-blocks: `get` and `set`. These are actually special methods that let us define the code that's used to respectively retrieve values from the private member and set values on it. They're known technically as **accessor methods**, since they grant us *access* to the object's private members.

Accessors are a much better way to expose an object's data members than letting users manipulate them directly. Apart from helping us specify certain properties as providing only read (or write) access, they give us the ability to write custom code that is executed whenever the property is accessed.

So, whenever we try to retrieve (that is, 'get') the property value, the code we've defined between the curly brackets following the `get` keyword will be executed, and the value specified in the final `return` statement is the value our calling code gets back. In this case, we simply return whatever value happens to be stored in `color` at the time.

In this case, we just want to get and set the contents directly, so we use the return statement to get the private value:

```
get
{
  return color;
}
```

Likewise, when we try to assign (that is, 'set') a new value to the property, we run the code defined in the curly brackets after the set keyword. In this case, the parameter value is assigned to the local string value, and we use value to assign this data to the private member:

```
set
{
  color = value;
}
```

When we talk about a property, we're actually referring to the object-specific data that's exposed by these two accessor methods. In this case, that's the *value* of the private member color – take note: that's not the variable itself, but just the data it contains.

For our next property, Gear(), we will illustrate another feature of properties, which demonstrates more of what we can do with them. Instead of defining both get and set accessors, which enable you to read and set the values of the property as you would for any other variable, you can restrict your user's access to the property's value by defining just one of the two accessors.

A read-only property is defined by simply defining a get accessor as follows:

```
public int Gear
{
  get
  {
    return gear;
  }
}
```

What's the point of this then? Now we can only *look* at a Car object's Gear property, and have no way to change it. Well, as we mentioned earlier on, one of the advantages of using objects is that we can hide away any functionality that we deem inappropriate. If we simply exposed the gear integer to the outside world as a property, we could easily set it to any integer value. However, that would break our model, insofar as there's not much we can usefully say about a car that's supposedly in 1,739th gear (apart from expressing a little skepticism). What's more, we'd like to protect the gearbox from too much wear and tear, so we're restricting our drivers to incremental gear changes – that is, one gear up (or down) at a time.

This is where our method definition makes an appearance. It's literally just a function that takes a single parameter and uses it as the basis for performing operations on the private member gear. What's more, it can take a look at the modified value of gear, and ensure that it's maintained within certain constraints. We've decided to model a 5-gear car, so (assuming that 'neutral' is represented by a zero value, and 'reverse' by a negative one) we constrain it between values of −1 and +5:

```
public void ChangeGear(int direction)
{
if (direction < 0)
  gear --;
if (direction > 0)
  gear ++;
if (gear > 5)
  gear = 5;
if (gear < -1)
  gear = -1)
}
```

When we call this method, we'll need to specify a single integer parameter – if that's positive, we move up one gear; if it's negative we move down one gear. If either of our constraints is breached, the gear number is set to the constraining value.

All we then have to do is mark the end of our class definition:

```
}
```

In order to use this class definition in an ASPX file, we simply need to place it in a declarative code block (that is, inside the body of a <script runat="server"> element). However, before we do that, let's take a quick look at how we're going to use our new class. We need to start out by creating an **instance** of the class – that is, we have a blueprint for our Car – now we need to find out how to use it to make an *actual* Car object.

Creating Objects

The process of creating an object from a class definition is called **instantiation**, and we do it in much the same way as we do with variables of the built-in types (string, int, and so on). We can break the process down into two stages: declaration and initialization.

We declare an object in exactly the same way as we declare a variable. For example, to declare a Car type object called AlexCar, we can do it like this:

```
Car AlexCar;
```

However, if we were now to try to use it, we'd find ourselves in a spot of bother – let's consider why.

When you declare a type like an `string` or an `int` you can use it straight away, as the memory for **value** types such as these is allocated during compilation. However, we're talking about class instances here (which are **reference** types). A reference is created on the stack during compilation: this reference will eventually refer to an object instance created on the heap at run time. At this point in our code, however, there is no object instance, and if you try to access any methods or properties you will get an error message.

We therefore need a second line of code to actually create a slot in memory for our object. We use the `new` keyword to actually *initialize* the `Car` object:

```
Car AlexCar;
AlexCar = new Car();
```

So, the first line specifies a label that we'll use to point to the `Car` object, while the second actually creates the `Car` object for us. We can squash the two statements into one:

```
Car AlexCar = new Car();
```

We now have the means to create a fully functional, if rather simple, `Car` object.

> **Note that all classes are reference types. This means that when you declare a variable of a class type, you don't create the class, but just a reference that exists on the stack. The object itself is created using the `new` operator as shown above. At this point the object instance (or class instance) is created by the .NET Framework on the heap. Only then can its properties be accessed and its methods called.**

> **Note that if you create a *local* variable of either a value or reference type, then you must initialize it before you use it, otherwise you will get a compiler error. Variables that are members of a class instance are automatically initialized with default values.**

Setting Objects to null

We have mentioned that .NET can provide default values for value types when they are declared, that is zero for numerical types and `false` for `bool`s, and `""` for `string`s. So what is the equivalent default value for an object type or any other reference type for that matter?

The answer to this question is that a reference to a non-existent object has a value of `null` – a literal defined by C# for this very purpose. `null` is not an object, neither is it a physical memory location. It is a temporary value for an object that has not been instantiated and if you try to access methods and properties of such an object variable, you will get a run-time error:

System.NullReferenceException: Value null was found where an instance of an object was required.

You have to be careful when you access object instances, as you have to safeguard yourself against accidentally accessing a **null reference**. In fact, we have already seen code that achieves this in Chapter 4 where we first came across null. In those code examples, a test was made to see whether or not a form variable contained any value:

```
if (Request.Form["data"] != null)
{
    // Code runs if form variable contains data, that is, it is not null
}
```

When an ASP.NET page receives a form, the data it contains is not in the form of strings but as an array of objects and so testing for an empty string or a zero value is not appropriate, and you have to test for nulls.

We can also set an object variable to null when we first declare it:

```
Car AlexCar = null;
```

Or when we have finished with the object instance but want to keep the variable for future use:

```
AlexCar = null;
```

Using Methods and Properties

We use an object's methods to tell it to do things, and its properties expose information about its state, or what it *is*. It's very easy to make a method call – simply state the name of the object whose method you want to call, add a period, add the name of the method, and add a pair of brackets. If the method requires you to specify any parameters, you can add them inside the brackets, separated by commas.

If we want our to make our AlexCar object change up a gear, we should be able to forget about the gearbox and all its inner workings, and simply tell it to do what we want in the form of a very simple command. In this case, we'd call the ChangeGear() method with a positive parameter as follows:

```
AlexCar.ChangeGear(+1);
```

The syntax used to make a method call is just like what we used in the last chapter to call a method or function, except that we need to specify a particular object name before the method name, so that it's clear which object's method we wish to call.

In fact, all the calls we looked at in the last chapter were actually method calls themselves. Since all those methods and functions were defined as part of the declarative code block (between <script> tags) but not within an explicit class declaration, they were incorporated as methods on the underlying Page object. However, since all our page code also resides in this object, we can call these local methods without specifying an object beforehand.

As well as asking the object to perform actions for us, we can find out about its current state by means of its properties. These allow us to access and modify the data within the object – we access them using the same dot notation as we did to make method calls – but don't require us to use parentheses after their names. For example, we could set the color of the car using this statement:

```
AlexCar.Color = "Turquoise";
```

Alternatively, if we wanted to assign the color of Alex's car to a string variable, we could write some code like this:

```
string strCarColor;
strCarColor = AlexCar.Color;
```

> **Remember, an object's properties don't necessarily map one-to-one with the data stored inside it. In some cases, our accessor methods (by means of which the properties are exposed) may expose data that's based on the information held in several different private members. It may even be that the information exposed originates in an external data source, such as a file or database.**

Try It Out – Working with a Car Object

In this example we'll place our `Car` class definition within an ASP.NET page and use it to create an object called `MyCar`. We'll then set the object's `Color` property to `"Yellow"`, and display that color on the page by reading it back out of the object.

1. Create a file called `car_object1.aspx`, and type in the following code:

```
<%@ page Language="c#" runat="server" %>
<script runat="server">
public class Car
{
  private string color;
  private int gear;
  public string Color
  {
    get
    {
      return color;
    }
    set
    {
      color = value;
    }
  }
  public int Gear
```

```
    {
      get
      {
        return gear;
      }
    }
    public void ChangeGear(int Direction)
    {
      if (Direction < 0)
        gear--;
      if (Direction > 0)
        gear++;
      if ( gear > 5)
        gear = 5;
      if ( gear < -1)
        gear = -1;
    }
  }
  void Page_Load()
  {
    Car MyCar = new Car();
    Response.Write("<b>New object 'MyCar' created.</b>");
    Response.Write("<br/>Color: " + MyCar.Color);
    Response.Write("<br/>Gear: " + MyCar.Gear);
    MyCar.Color = "Black";
    MyCar.ChangeGear(+1);
    Response.Write("<br/><b>Properties updated.</b>");
    Response.Write("<br/>New color: " + MyCar.Color);
    Response.Write("<br/>New gear: " + MyCar.Gear);
  }
</script>
```

2. Save the file and call it up in your browser – here's what it looks like:

How It Works

Our first block of code defines our public `Car` class, as we described earlier. The first thing we do in here is to declare our private members, variables `color` and `gear`, that will store each of our `Car` objects' internal data:

```
<%@ page Language="c#" runat="server" %>
<script runat="server">
public class Car
{
  private string color;
  private int gear;
```

Next, we define the public property `Color()`, so that when we come to use a `Car` object, we can read values straight from its private member `color` (courtesy of `get`) and assign values to it (thanks to `set`):

```
public string Color
{
  get
  {
    return color;
  }
  set
  {
    color = value;
  }
}
```

Our next property `Gear` is a read-only property; it therefore has just one accessor method, `get`, so that we can read the value of `gear`, but can't assign values to it directly:

```
public int Gear
{
  get
  {
    return gear;
  }
}
```

However, the method `ChangeGear()` lets us modify `gear` by increments – we specify an integer parameter called `Direction`, and depending on whether it's positive or negative, we move the car up or down a gear. We don't want it getting carried away, so we check to see if `gear` is too high or low to make sense in the context of our model; if it's out of range, we simply pull it back into range again:

```
public void ChangeGear(int Direction)
{
  if (Direction < 0)
    gear--;
  if (Direction > 0)
```

```
    gear++;
  if ( gear > 5)
    gear = 5;
  if ( gear < -1)
    gear = -1;
  }
}
```

That's our class defined – now to make use of it. Since we want to demonstrate how the object's properties change over time, we've put all our code into the `Page_Load` sub, where we know it will be executed in sequence. As we know, using `Response.Write()` like this isn't really the best way to write ASP.NET pages. In this case, though, it helps us to demonstrate what's happening to the object as we progress through the code.

We start off by creating a `Car` type object called `MyCar`, and generating a message to that effect:

```
void Page_Load()
{
  Car MyCar = new Car();
  Response.Write("<b>New object 'MyCar' created.</b>");
```

Next, we use properties `Color` and `Gear` to access information from the object, and then write it out to the browser along with appropriate captions:

```
  Response.Write("<br/>Color: " + MyCar.Color);
  Response.Write("<br/>Gear: " + MyCar.Gear);
```

We now assign the string `"Black"` to the `Color` property; and use the `ChangeGear()` method with a positive parameter to move up a gear. Note that even if we'd specified `ChangeGear(+10)`, the gear number would still only have gone up by one:

```
  MyCar.Color = "Black";
  MyCar.ChangeGear(+1);
  Response.Write("<br/><b>Properties updated.</b>");
```

Finally, we write out the new property values, so that we can see how they've changed:

```
  Response.Write("<br/>New color: " + MyCar.Color);
  Response.Write("<br/>New gear: " + MyCar.Gear);
}
</script>
```

We've now seen a very simple demonstration of how we can define a class, create an object, and then use and manipulate its public members (that is, the object's properties and methods).

> *You may have spotted that the* `Response.Write()` *mechanism we've been using to send text to the browser actually takes the form of an object method call.* `Response` *is actually the name of an object used by ASP.NET to work with the HTTP Response stream – the stream of data that's sent from the web server to a client browser, carrying all the page information (including all the HTML source) that's used to make up the web page you end up seeing displayed.*
>
> `Response` *is actually an instance of the* `HttpResponse` *class, and* `Write()` *is one of the methods defined by this class. We're going to take a much more detailed look at* `Response` *(and other important ASP.NET objects) in the next chapter.*

That's all well and good as a demonstration, but we haven't really seen much practical benefit so far. It seems like an awful lot of trouble to go to just to bundle a few values together. That's partly because we don't have a specific use in mind for our `Car` object; we selected it simply because it's a familiar real-world object that has lots of complex functionality to model. As such, it's great for making a conceptual start, but not really terribly useful until we perhaps decide to build some kind of a driving simulator.

Let's look at another example, which might be a little more useful in the context of a simple web application – a calculator.

Try It Out – Creating a Calculator Class

In this section, we're going to start building a class called `Calculator` that will enable us to perform simple operations on user-supplied values. Just like a real calculator, one of our `Calculator` objects should be able to maintain a 'working value', and let us perform sequences of operations (add, subtract, multiply, divide) on that, as required. So, we need the following public members:

❑ Properties – `CurrentValue`

❑ Methods – `Add`, `Subtract`, `Multiply`, `Divide`, `Clear`

We'll also need a private data member, which we'll call `_current`, to hold the data we'll expose via the `CurrentValue` property.

1. Create a new file in your test directory. The first thing we need to do is define the `Calculator` class, so add the following code:

```
<%@ page Language="c#" runat="server" %>
<script runat="server">
  public class Calculator
  {
    private double currentValue;
    public double CurrentValue
    {
      get
      {
        return currentValue;
      }
```

```
      }

      public void Add(double addValue)
      {
         currentValue += addValue;
      }

      public void Subtract(double subValue)
      {
         currentValue -= subValue;
      }

      public void Multiply(double multValue)
      {
         currentValue *= multValue;
      }

      public void Divide(double divValue)
      {
         currentValue /= divValue;
      }

      public void Clear()
      {
         currentValue = 0;
      }
   }
```

2. Now we add some operations to be executed when the page is loaded:

```
void Page_Load()
{
   Calculator MyCalc = new Calculator();
   Response.Write("<b>Created a new Calculator object.</b><br/>");
   Response.Write("Current Value = " + MyCalc.CurrentValue);

   MyCalc.Add(23);
   Response.Write("<br/><b>Added 23 - MyCalc.Add(23)</b><br/>");
   Response.Write("Current Value = " + MyCalc.CurrentValue);

   MyCalc.Subtract(7);
   Response.Write("<br/><b>Subtracted 7 - MyCalc.Subtract(7)</b><br/>");
   Response.Write("Current Value = " + MyCalc.CurrentValue);

   MyCalc.Multiply(3);
   Response.Write("<br/><b>Multiplied by 3 - MyCalc.Multiply(3)</b><br/>");
   Response.Write("Current Value = " + MyCalc.CurrentValue);

   MyCalc.Divide(4);
   Response.Write("<br/><b>Divided by 4 - MyCalc.Divide(4)</b><br/>");
```

```
        Response.Write("Current Value = " + MyCalc.CurrentValue);

        MyCalc.Clear();
        Response.Write("<br/><b>Cleared - MyCalc.Clear()</b><br/>");
        Response.Write("Current Value = " + MyCalc.CurrentValue);
    }
</script>
```

3. Finally, save the page as `calculator_object.aspx` and point your browser to it. You'll see something like this:

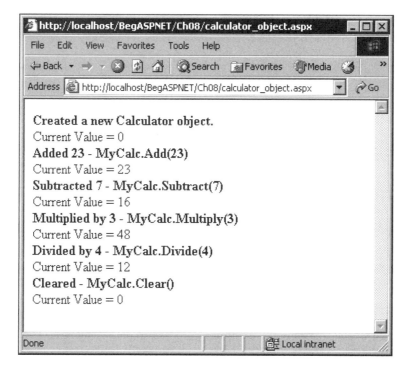

How It Works

What we've done here is conceptually very similar to what we did when with the `Car` class: we started off by defining a class, and used it to instantiate an object, which we then manipulated in a number of different ways via its public members. In this case, we only have access to the object's innards via five methods – the only property on the `Calculator` object is read-only:

```
<%@ page Language="c#" runat="server" %>
<script runat="server">
  public class Calculator
  {
    private double currentValue;
    public double CurrentValue
    {
```

```
        get
        {
          return currentValue;
        }
    }
```

Notice that we've used the `public` keyword again – this tells .NET that anyone with an instance of `Calculator` is allowed access to the `CurrentValue` property (even if it is limited to read-only). If we were to replace `public` with `private`, `CurrentValue` would only be available to other properties and methods within the same object.

Our first method `Add()` will add a specified `double` to the current value held in `currentValue`. The next three perform various other operations in the same way:

```
public void Add(double addValue)
    {
      currentValue += addValue;
    }

    public void Subtract(double subValue)
    {
      currentValue -= subValue;
    }

    public void Multiply(double multValue)
    {
      currentValue *= multValue;
    }

    public void Divide(double divValue)
    {
      currentValue /= divValue;
    }
```

The final method `Clear()` simply resets our `currentValue` data member back to zero:

```
    public void Clear()
    {
      currentValue = 0;
    }
  }
```

Now we define the usual `Page_Load()` subroutine, in which we instantiate an object based on our `Calculator` class:

```
  void Page_Load()
  {
    Calculator MyCalc = new Calculator();
    Response.Write("<b>Created a new Calculator object.</b><br/>");
    Response.Write("Current Value = " + MyCalc.CurrentValue);
```

Each of the next few blocks of code calls one of the object's (rather self-explanatory) methods, and writes out the current value once the method call's completed:

```
          MyCalc.Add(23);
          Response.Write("<br/><b>Added 23 - MyCalc.Add(23)</b><br/>");
          Response.Write("Current Value = " + MyCalc.CurrentValue);

          MyCalc.Subtract(7);
          Response.Write("<br/><b>Subtracted 7 - MyCalc.Subtract(7)</b><br/>");
          Response.Write("Current Value = " + MyCalc.CurrentValue);

          MyCalc.Multiply(3);
          Response.Write("<br/><b>Multiplied by 3 - MyCalc.Multiply(3)</b><br/>");
          Response.Write("Current Value = " + MyCalc.CurrentValue);

          MyCalc.Divide(4);
          Response.Write("<br/><b>Divided by 4 - MyCalc.Divide(4)</b><br/>");
          Response.Write("Current Value = " + MyCalc.CurrentValue);

          MyCalc.Clear();
          Response.Write("<br/><b>Cleared - MyCalc.Clear()</b><br/>");
          Response.Write("Current Value = " + MyCalc.CurrentValue);
      }
   </script>
```

Once again, we've used `Response.Write()` to display a running tally, so that we can see how each of our operations affects the `MyCalc.CurrentValue` property. In practice though, we'd endeavor to find a cleaner way to present the data, probably using a variety of ASP.NET controls to separate our code (responsible for dynamic content generation) from the presentation structure (using pure HTML and control elements to mark where we want our dynamic content placed).

Initializing Objects with Constructors

So far we've glossed over a few technicalities that arise when we're creating objects. One of these is the matter of initialization: we'll often define object properties that need to have well-defined values at all times. Perhaps we're modeling a bookstore – each `Book` object we create will need to have a well-defined `Title` property, as well as an `ISBN` property.

We *could* just leave it to trust that every time someone using our class made a `new Book()`, they'd follow it up with statements like:

```
      Book.Title = "Beginning ASP.NET 1.0 with C#"
      Book.ISBN = 1861007345
```

In fact, trusting the user should be the very last thing we want to do. Many of the advantages of using objects stem from the fact that they let us prevent users getting so much as a chance to break their functionality. The other problem we might face is that properties such as these are likely to be defined as read-only – after all, we shouldn't allow users to rename a Book object when the physical book it represents doesn't let us do so.

As far as our bookstore is concerned, a book without a name and ISBN is useless. Consequently, a Book object that doesn't have well-defined properties Title and ISBN is a *broken* book object. So how do we get round this? We follow the example of our real life book: we make sure that the relevant internal members are given appropriate values when the object is created – that is, we initialize these private members as part of the instantiation process.

We can do this by defining a special class method that will be called whenever we construct an object. As you'll recall from our earlier discussion, we can break the process of instantiation down into two stages:

```
Car AlexCar;                    'declaration
AlexCar = new Car();            'initialization
```

The second of these stages is responsible for setting up the object in memory, and will call on a **constructor** method for that object to do the necessary work. Constructors normally just work behind the scenes, and we don't need to know what they're doing – we just trust them to get our objects ready for use, and to set their data members to sensible values.

However, we can also make use of constructors explicitly – when we specifically want to initialize an object's data members (that is, specify how we want the object to be set up). We can tap into this process by simply defining a class method called new(). Whenever we construct an object using the new keyword, .NET will look out for a definition of this method within the class. If one exists, it will automatically execute any code we've placed inside it as a part of the construction process.

Try It Out – Initializing Book Properties

In this example we're going to create an object called MyBook from a brand new Book class, within which we'll define a constructor method so that it's automatically initialized with values for title and isbn.

1. Open up your editor and type in this code:

```
<%@ page Language="c#" runat="server" %>
<script runat="server">
public class Book
{
  private string title;
  private int isbn;
  private decimal price;
  public Book()
  {
    title = "Beginning ASP.NET 1.0 withC#";
    isbn = 1861007345;
  }
```

```csharp
public string TitleInfo
{
   get
   {
      return title + " <i>[ISBN: " + isbn + "]</i>";
   }
}

public string Title
{
   get
   {
      return title;
   }
}

public int Isbn
{
   get
   {
      return isbn;
   }
}

public decimal Price
{
   get
   {
      return price;
   }
   set
   {
      price = value;
   }
}
}
```

2. We now add some code that will create and use the object when the page is loaded:

```csharp
void Page_Load()
{
   Book MyBook = new Book();
   Response.Write("<b>New book 'MyBook' created.</b>");
   MyBook.Price = 39.99m;
   Response.Write("<br/>Title info: " + MyBook.TitleInfo);
   Response.Write("<br/>Price: $" + MyBook.Price + "<br/>");
}
</script>
```

3. Now save the file in your test directory as `book_object.aspx`, and call it up from your browser – you should see this:

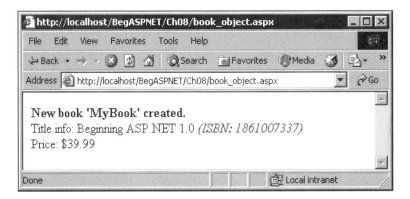

All well and good – that is, until we want to create an object that represents a different book. Because of the way we've defined our constructor, we've effectively hard-coded this specific book information into our class definition, and in doing so, radically reduced the potential usefulness of the class. Unless the bookstore's business plan relies solely on the runaway success of this one book, we are going to need a little more flexibility.

In fact, this isn't an enormous problem:

4. Update the constructor method as follows:

```
public Book(string newTitle, int newIsbn)
{
  title = newTitle;
  isbn = newIsbn;
}
```

5. Now add appropriate parameters to the line where the `Book` object was created in `Page_Load()`:

```
void Page_Load()
{
Book MyBook = new Book("Beginning ASP.NET 1.0 with C#", 1861007035);
  response.write("<b>new book 'MyBook' created.</b>");
  ...
}
```

6. If you run the example again, you'll see exactly the same results. However, if you now add the following lines to `Page_Load()`, you'll see that we now have much more flexibility:

```
void Page_Load()
{
```

```
Book MyBook = new Book("Beginning ASP.NET 1.0 with C#", 1861007345);
Response.Write("<b>new book 'MyBook' created.</b>");
MyBook.Price = 39.99m;
Response.Write("<br/>Title info: " + MyBook.TitleInfo);
Response.Write("<br/>Price: $" + MyBook.Price + "<br/>");

Book AnotherBook = new Book("Professional ASP.NET 1.0 SE", 1861007035);
Response.Write("<b>new book 'AnotherBook' created.</b>");
AnotherBook.Price = 59.99m;
Response.Write("<br/>Title info: " + AnotherBook.TitleInfo);
Response.Write("<br/>Price: $" + AnotherBook.Price + "<br/>");
        }
</script>
```

7. Call up the page one last time, and you should see information displayed on both books:

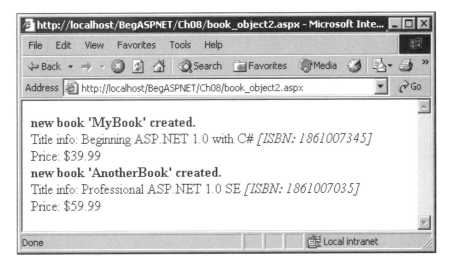

How It Works

The most important sections in this example are the Book class constructor, and the statement we use to instantiate an object from that class. Any code we place inside the constructor method gets executed as and when a new Book type object is created:

```
public Book(string newTitle, int newIsbn)
{
  title = newTitle;
  isbn = newIsbn;
}
```

By using parameters as part of the constructor method call, we can specify how we want each object to be initialized as a part of the statement we use to instantiate it:

```
Book MyBook = new Book("Beginning ASP.NET 1.0 with C#", 1861007345);
```

Now that these values are set for the new object, they can only be accessed via ReadOnly properties such as MyBook.Title, MyBook.Isbn, or MyBook.TitleInfo (which returns an HTML string containing both the title and ISBN for the appropriate book in a standard format).

Overloaded Methods

When we write methods and subroutines that take parameters, it's important to account for all the different combinations of parameters we might want them to accept. If we consider the constructor method that we defined in the last example, perhaps we need the option to specify a subtitle for the book as part of the instantiation. We want to keep it separate from the main title (since the subtitle may be long and too unwieldy to display comfortably on the web site), but can't guarantee that we'll need to specify it for every book. In fact, most books won't require its use at all. The obvious solution is to add it to the class as follows:

```
<%@ page Language="c#" runat="server" %>
<script runat="server">
public class Book
{
  private string title;
  private int isbn;
  private decimal price;
  private string subtitle;
  public Book(string newTitle, int newIsbn, string newSubtitle)
  {
    title = newTitle;
    isbn = newIsbn;
    subtitle = newSubtitle;
  }

  public string Subtitle
  {
    get
    {
      return subtitle;
    }
  }
}
```

That's absolutely fine, assuming we have a list of keywords to assign:

```
Book ABigBook As new Book("Professional Linux Programming", 1861003013, _
    "Databases, PostgreSQL, MySQL, LDAP, security, device drivers, " +
    "GTK+, GNOME, Glade, GUI, KDE, Qt, Python, PHP, RPC, " +
    "diskless systems, multimedia, internationalization, CORBA, PAM, " +
    "RPM, CVS, Flex, Bison, Beowulf, Clustering, ORBit, MPI, PVM, " +
    "and XML");
```

Even if we don't, we can always just specify an empty string:

```
Book AnotherBigBook = new Book("Professional C#", 1861004990, "");
```

However, this opens us up to another 'can break, will break' situation. Since most of the books aren't going to require users to specify the last parameter, it's quite possible that sooner or later someone will forget to include it – the class will have all the information it needs to fully instantiate an object, but the method call's **signature** will be incorrect, so it won't work.

> When we talk about a method's signature, we're referring to the specific combination of parameter types that the method definition is designed to accept. If two methods both accept the same number and type of parameters in the same order then we can say that they have the same signature. If we call a method specifying the wrong number or type of parameters, then the call will fail because the signature is wrong.

Fortunately, there's a quick way out. We simply define *another* constructor method – one that takes just two parameters (as this one did in the first place). We then have:

```
public Book(string newTitle, int NewIsbn)
   {
      title = newTitle;
   isbn = newIsbn;
   }

public Book(string newTitle, int newIsbn, string newSubtitle)
{
   title = newTitle;
   isbn = newIsbn;
   subtitle = newSubtitle;
}
```

Basically, we now have two constructor methods with the same name on our Book class – the only difference lies in their signatures. Fortunately, this is enough for .NET to distinguish between them, and we can safely use either form.

It's actually very common to find objects with several constructors, each having a different signature. For example, if you use the Class Browser (which we looked at briefly in Chapter 2) to take a look at the methods available on the System.DateTime class, you'll see that it actually contains *seven different* constructor methods:

Class System.DateTime

Constructors

Visibility	Constructor	Parameters
public	DateTime	(Int64 ticks)
public	DateTime	(Int32 year , Int32 month , Int32 day)
public	DateTime	(Int32 year , Int32 month , Int32 day , Calendar calendar)
public	DateTime	(Int32 year , Int32 month , Int32 day , Int32 hour , Int32 minute , Int32 second)
public	DateTime	(Int32 year , Int32 month , Int32 day , Int32 hour , Int32 minute , Int32 second , Calendar calendar)
public	DateTime	(Int32 year , Int32 month , Int32 day , Int32 hour , Int32 minute , Int32 second , Int32 millisecond)
public	DateTime	(Int32 year , Int32 month , Int32 day , Int32 hour , Int32 minute , Int32 second , Int32 millisecond , Calendar calendar)

In this case, the different signatures reflect different ways (and different levels of accuracy) in which we may want to specify a date and time. We can use a single `long` value to specify the number of ticks (100 nanosecond units – that is, 10,000,000 ticks make one second) between midnight on January 1st in the year 1C.E. and the time we wish to specify. This helps us if we need to make very accurate measurements over short periods of time, as we might want to do when examining the performance of the server. For more pedestrian use of the `DateTime` object, we can opt to specify three `int` values for the year, month, and day. Or, if we want the time as well, we can specify that down to the second, or even down to the millisecond. There's also the option to specify a `Calendar` object that contains details on how dates are divided (as weeks, months, years, which are different for different cultures).

Effectively, Microsoft has defined seven *different* constructors that happen to share the same name. Depending on how we want to use the `DateTime` object we're instantiating, we can choose the most appropriate one, without having to remember seven different constructor method names. We describe this process as **overloading** the constructor. Note that it is the difference in the parameter list within the method signature that determines which version of the method will be called.

> **When we overload an object method, the main proviso is that each version of that method should have a different signature.**

In fact, we can apply this principle to any method calls we define on an object. If we have a class that defines two methods that basically do the same thing, but use different parameters to do so, we might want to consider using just one name for both of them. Consider our `Car` class for a moment. It already features a `ChangeGear()` method, whose signature is of the form:

```
ChangeGear(int direction)
```

Perhaps we now decide to offer users the opportunity to specify "up" or "down" as parameters, which will move the gear incrementally up or down respectively. Our initial approach might be to define a brand new method – ChangeGearUsingWords(string Direction). That should work just fine, but it's going to be a pain for a developer using it to have to remember to use the new method name. It's surely far better to overload the original method, so that it's simply a matter of choosing between a string and an integer for the parameter. We can do this as follows:

```
public void ChangeGear(int Direction)
{
  . . .
}

public void ChangeGear(string Direction)
{
  . . .
}
```

> *While it's quite possible for ASP.NET to figure out what's going on here without the keyword (as with type conversion, it won't actually complain at all unless you have the 'Strict' option turned on) it's worth including nevertheless, simply so that it's clear to anyone looking at your code – including yourself – that these methods have been overloaded.*

We can now call the method as MyCar.ChangeGear("up") or MyCar.ChangeGear("down"), and it will do exactly what we'd expect. What's more, the old technique MyCar.ChangeGear(+55) still works as well, so we don't break any code we've already written to use *that* form.

Using one name for several similar actions is often far more convenient to programmers than having five very similar methods with different names. Overloading can therefore make life a great deal easier for developers.

Try It Out – Using an Overloaded Constructor

In this example we're going to use some of the constructors defined on the Framework class System.DateTime. We'll create four separate objects from the same class, using a different constructor each time. Each time, we'll display the resultant setting. First, we'll create a DateTime object using its default constructor; next we'll use a constructor that lets us specify a particular date; third, we'll use a constructor that lets us specify the time as well, and finally, we'll just specify a few million ticks, to see how they work in practice.

1. Open up your editor and type in this code:

```
<%@ Page Language="c#" %>
<script runat="server">
  void Page_Load()
  {
    DateTime myDateTime1 = new DateTime();
    Response.Write(myDateTime1);
    Response.Write("<br />");

    DateTime myDateTime2 = new DateTime(1972,11,4);
    Response.Write(myDateTime2);
    Response.Write("<br />");

    DateTime myDateTime3 = new DateTime(1972,11,4,14,5,0);
    Response.Write(myDateTime3);
    Response.Write("<br />");

    DateTime myDateTime4 = new DateTime(260000000);
    Response.Write(myDateTime4);
    Response.Write("<br />");
  }
</script>
```

2. Save the file in your test directory as `datetime_constructor.aspx`.

3. Open up your browser and view the file; you should see something like this:

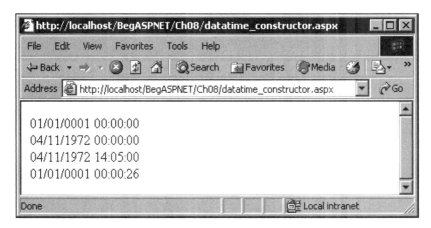

Note that the first line shows "01/01/0001 00:00:00", which is the default 'zero' date and time that the object uses if we do not specify anything else.

How It Works

First time around, we simply instantiate the object using its default constructor. Since it's a basic system object, we don't *need* to specify brackets after the class name, but we do so here for clarity:

```
DateTime myDateTime1 = new DateTime();
```

With the second `DateTime` object we pass three parameters to the constructor: integers representing year, month, and day respectively:

```
DateTime myDateTime2 = new DateTime(1972, 11, 4);
```

We now create our third `DateTime` object and pass it six parameters, specifying not only the date but also the time. The last three parameters are integers representing hour, minutes and seconds:

```
DateTime myDateTime3 = new DateTime(1972,11,4,14,5,0);
```

Finally, we specify 260 million ticks, which equate to 'zero' plus twenty-six seconds:

```
DateTime myDateTime4 = New DateTime(260000000);
```

As we'd expect, the time shows up as 00:00:26 on January 1st in the year 1C.E.

Try It Out – Using an Overloaded Method

Let's look at a worked example of overloading one of our own methods. While we're at it, we're going to give our `Car` class a single constructor method, so that `Car` objects can be defined with a specific color.

1. Open up our earlier sample `car_object1.aspx`, and modify it as follows:

```
<%@ page Language="c#" runat="server" %>
<script runat="server">
public class Car
{
  private string color;
  private int gear;
  public string Color
  {
    get
    {
      return color;
    }
    set
    {
      color = value;
    }
  }
  public int Gear
```

```
  {
    get
    {
      return gear;
    }
  }


  public void ChangeGear(int direction)
  {
    if (direction < 0)
    gear -= 1;
    if (direction > 0)
    gear += 1;
    if (gear > 5)
    gear = 5;
    if (gear < -1)
    gear = -1;
  }


  public void ChangeGear(string Direction)
  {
    if (Direction.ToLower() == "down")
      ChangeGear(-1);
    if (Direction.ToLower() == "up")
      ChangeGear(+1);
  }

  public Car()
  {
    color = "Cold gray steel";
  }
}

void Page_Load()
{
  Car MyCar = new Car();
  Response.Write("<b>New object 'MyCar' created.</b>");
  Response.Write("<br/>Color: " + MyCar.Color);
  Response.Write("<br/>Gear: " + MyCar.Gear);
  MyCar.Color = "Black";
  Response.Write("<br/><b>Properties updated.</b>");
  Response.Write("<br/>New color: " + MyCar.Color);
  Response.Write("<br/>New gear: " + MyCar.Gear);

  MyCar.ChangeGear("up");
  Response.Write("<br/><b>Shifted 'up' one gear.</b>");
  Response.Write("<br/>New gear: " + MyCar.Gear);

}
</script>
```

2. Now save this in your test directory as `car_object_overload.aspx`, and call it up in your browser:

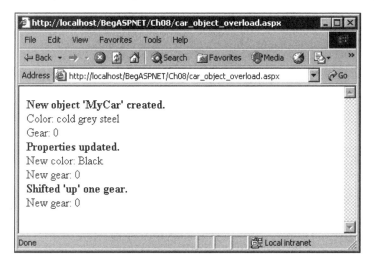

How It Works

We'll start by taking a look at the class definition, where we can see the original version of the method, which takes an integer parameter:

```
public void ChangeGear(int direction)
{
   if (direction < 0)
     gear -= 1;
   if (direction > 0)
     gear += 1;
   if (gear > 5)
     gear = 5;
   if (gear < -1)
     gear = -1;
}
```

Next we define a new subroutine that gives us a new way to do the same thing. Note that we *might* have just done it as follows, using a near copy of the code in our original method, with just three differences:

```
public void ChangeGear(string Direction)
{
   if (Direction.ToLower() == "down")
     gear--;
   if (Direction.ToLower() == "up")
     gear++;
   if (gear > 5)
     gear = 5;
   if (gear < -1)
     gear = -1;
}
```

However, it should be quite obvious that this is unnecessary – what's more, it opens up a whole new set of potential problems. Just imagine what would happen if we decided to change the top gear specified, but only remembered to update it in the first method. Perhaps ChangeGear(string) would now max out at 6, while ChangeGear(int) still stopped at 5. The two overloaded methods would behave differently, when they clearly should not.

For these reasons, you're encouraged to do all you can to reuse code at every level, and that's what we've actually done:

```
public void ChangeGear(string Direction)
{
  if (Direction.ToLower() == "down")
    ChangeGear(-1);
  if (Direction.ToLower() == "up")
    ChangeGear(+1);
```

This clearly requires less original code, and keeps all our bounds checking in one place.

We now add a very simple constructor, so that color is never left undefined:

```
public Car()
{
  color = "Cold gray steel";
}
```

Finally, we add a call to our new version of the MyCar.ChangeGear() method: the first one still passes an integer parameter (moving the gear up from 0 to 1), while the second passes the string "up" which moves it into second gear:

```
MyCar.ChangeGear("up");
  Response.Write("<br/><b>Shifted 'up' one gear.</b>");
  Response.Write("<br/>New gear: " + MyCar.Gear);
```

Operator Overloading

This section introduces you to a feature of C# that can add more power to your classes and objects. We have previously spoken about function overloading, which provides the ability to define several functions with the same name but different in the number and/or types of parameters, and a similar procedure can be applied to operators. By default, operators are defined to carry out one particular task. For instance, the addition (+) operator is used to add two numbers together to produce a sum, like so:

```
int intSum = intNumber1 + intNumber2;
```

and:

```
double dblSum = dblNumber1 + dblNumber2;
```

In the first instance, + means: "Add the value of the integer `intNumber2` to that of the integer `intNumber1`." A similar description to this can be applied to the second of the two statements above. It might seem that the + operator can only be applied to numbers, but this is not the case.

C# allows you to redefine what the + operator is able to do using a special function called an **operator overload**, which enables you to apply 'addition' to types other than integer or floating point. Indeed we have already seen something like this once before in this book, in Chapter 6 to be precise, though you will not have realized it. Have a look at this code:

```
DateTime FindDueDate(DateTime CheckOutDate)
{
    return CheckOutDate + TimeSpan.FromDays(14);
}
```

The syntax involves the use of a + operator that is doing something quite different from adding two simple numeric values. On the left side of the + is a variable of the `DateTime` type, called `CheckOutDate`. On the right-hand side is a function call that returns a `TimeSpan`, a special data type that can be used to add date-time components (such as days) to `DateTime` values.

So, what does the + mean in this code example? You can interpret its action as follows: "Take a `TimeSpan` value (returned from the `FromDays()` method) representing 14 days, and add it to the value of the `DateTime` variable called `CheckOutDate`." Clearly the + does far more than just add two numbers. It has been redefined so that values of `DateTime` variables can be modified by adding days, weeks, months, and so on, in other words it has been **overloaded**.

The general syntax for defining an overloaded + operator looks like this:

```
public static ClassType operator + (object lhs, object rhs)
{
    ClassType c;
    // Code here to implement an addition-type operation
    return c;
}
```

Let's examine this syntax a little bit more closely as all operator overloads are defined in a similar way.

Ignore, for the time being, the `public static` part – basically that means that they should be generally available to external code without the need to create any specific instances of the class (more on this in the next chapter). Next you have a return type, in which you store the result of the operation. This will vary for different operators: for the + operator you have to have a predefined object type here, usually the same as the class for which the operator overload is defined, in this case `ClassType`. The `operator` keyword tells the C# compiler that the following symbol represents the operator that is to be overloaded. After the operator symbol are the operands in parentheses. There can be one or two operands depending on the operator. The + operator requires two operands – it is known as a **binary operator**. On the other hand, **unary operators** (such as the NOT operator (`!`)) require only one. For binary operators, one or both of the operands must be a `ClassType`, whereas for the unary operators, the single operand must be a `ClassType`.

The subsequent code, delimited by curly brackets, is what runs whenever the compiler comes across the + operator in code and the types of each operand are as defined. The structure is like any other function in that you must create and return an instance of the ClassType. What happens in between is entirely up to you. Often you will include some bounds checking or validating code. Alternatively, you could use overloads to manipulate individual data members of your class, which might be of ordinary numerical types.

However you should try to make sure that the action carried out by the overloaded operator bears some resemblance to the default definition for that operator. When applied to DateTime variables, the meaning of + can be intuitively understood – you are adding days, weeks, or whatever to the DateTime value. The same holds for the subtraction (-) operator, which has been overloaded to allow the subtraction of days, weeks, etc. from DateTime values. However, for the other arithmetic operators, *, /, and %, applying these to DateTime values provides no obvious meaning or realistic application – you can't multiply or divide dates – therefore, these have not been overloaded.

These are some of the operators that can be overloaded:

Type	Unary	Binary
Arithmetic:	– (negation)	+, – (subtraction), *, /, %
Boolean	! (NOT)	& (AND),	(OR)
Comparison		==, != , <, >=, <=, >

There are other operators that you can overload, but this list covers those you might employ most frequently. Note that you cannot overload the Boolean comparison operators && and ||, though you can achieve the same effect by overloading the & and | operators which are used to perform bitwise operations. (For a description on what bitwise operations are and how to carry them out, check out *Beginning C#* ISBN 1-86100-758-2.)

Note also that you cannot overload the assignment operator (=), though if you overload the + operator, that affects how the += operator works. Here's an example:

```
CheckOutDate += TimeSpan.FromDays(1);
```

What this is doing can be described in this way: "Take the value of the DateTime variable to the left of the assignment operator, CheckOutDate, append the TimeSpan representing one day (*using the overloaded + operator*) and assign it back to CheckOutDate." What this means that the overload of + is automatically applied to the += operator, and therefore there is no need for a separate overload of +=, which C# doesn't actually allow.

An Example of Operator Overloading

Let's apply some simple operator overloading concepts to our Car class. This requires a bit of prior planning as we want the operators to mean something when applied to instances of the class. For example, what might the following syntax mean?

```
Car Car1 = new Car();
Car Car2 = new Car();
Car Car3 = Car1 + Car2;
```

Well, unless you are in the business of renovating old vehicles from parts of others, not much. The other arithmetic operators, when applied to cars, are also meaningless; you cannot subtract them, multiply them, divide them or get their modulus. So the arithmetic operators cannot be meaningfully applied to Car objects, and there is no point in defining operator overloads for them.

However that does leave us with the comparison operators. You can certainly compare two cars, such as their colors, sizes etc., so this syntax, when applied to Car objects, is meaningful:

```
if (Car1 == Car2)
```

Before we move on, there are a few rules that must be obeyed when dealing with overloaded comparison operators.

- ❏ They must return a bool

- ❏ They must be implemented in pairs: == with !=, < with > and <= with >=

For this example we are going to compare two Car objects for equality or otherwise, which means overloading both == and !=.

When you compare two cars, you compare each of the features of the car, and equality (or equivalence) is determined if and only if the relevant features of the car have been individually compared (for example, the color, the size, the engine capacity, and the model). If any of these properties is not the same for the two cars, then they are not equivalent.

The same criteria can be applied to our Car class where we have only two properties to compare: Color and Gear. This is the code for the == overload:

```
public static bool operator == (Car Car1, Car Car2)
{
  if (Car1.Color == Car2.Color && Car1.Gear == Car2.Gear)
  {
    return true;
  }
  else
  {
    return false;
  }
}
```

What happens here is that the values for both the Color properties for the two Car objects are compared and combined (with the AND operator) with the comparison of the two values of each of the Gear properties. If the result of this entire operation is true, then that is returned, otherwise false is returned.

To finish, we must implement the != overload as follows:

```
public static bool operator != (Car Car1, Car Car2)
{
   return !(Car1 == Car2);
}
```

What this does is apply the NOT operator to the result of comparing the two Car objects using the previously defined == operator. This practice is quite common when defining each pair of comparison operators, where one contains all the code and the other just reverses the result of the first. You could as an alternative define the != overload more fully like this:

```
public static bool operator != (Car Car1, Car Car2)
{
   if (!(Car1.Color == Car2.Color && Car1.Gear == Car2.Gear))
   {
      return true;
   }
   else
   {
      return false;
   }
}
```

More on Operator Overloading

It may come as a surprise to you that you can overload operators in the same way as you can ordinary functions. The rules for doing this are the same: you should use the same name (obviously for operators!) and the *types* of parameters should be different for each one. As the operators are themselves either unary or binary, and that definition cannot change, the *number* of parameters must remain the same for all overloads.

We can use features of the DateTime structure to illustrate this. Unlike the addition overload, the DateTime's subtraction (-) overload has two forms. The first parallels the + overload, only it subtracts a TimeSpan variable from a DateTime variable to produce a DateTime value:

```
public static DateTime operator - (DateTime dt, TimeSpan ts)
{
   // Implementation
}
```

The second subtracts two `DateTime` values to produce a `TimeSpan` value:

```
public static TimeSpan operator - (DateTime dt1, DateTime dt2)
{
  // Implementation
}
```

Which of these is actually executed depends on what type of `DateTime` value you actually require. If, say, you wanted to implement some code to send a reminder to someone one hour before some event is to take place, then you would use the first overload as follows:

```
DateTime Reminder = EventTime - TimeSpan.FromHours(1);
```

If you wanted to calculate how long an event lasted, you would use the second operator overload to get the time span between the start and the finish of that event:

```
TimeSpan TimeInterval = EndTime - StartTime;  // Both DateTime values
```

Summary

In this chapter we've covered quite a few subject areas and many of those have involved new concepts and definitions of words. Here are the core object-oriented concepts we looked at:

❑ **Abstraction** – when we're traveling through an ASP.NET project, think about what objects you'll need and what their most important characteristics and behaviors are.

❑ **Encapsulation** – every object is a black box that is supremely good at one thing. .NET provides literally hundreds of ready-built objects for us to use.

❑ **Classes** – we create objects from classes, which we can think of as templates for making objects.

We then looked at practical examples using different features of objects and using them in different ways. Here are the areas where we looked at example ASP.NET pages:

❑ **Instantiating objects** – creating objects from classes, just like using a cookie cutter to cut out cookies. We saw how we create and instantiate objects using an expression like this: `Dim myCar As New Car()`.

❑ **Methods** – we ask objects to perform actions for us by calling their methods. We call methods like this: `myCar.StartEngine()`.

❑ **Properties** – we can look at and change information inside objects using their properties. We use properties like this (within the `get` and `set` code blocks): `color = myCar.Color`.

❑ **Constructors** – when an object is created the object's constructor method initializes it. This is particularly useful to us when we want to initialize an object with specific values; we pass parameters to the object when it is created.

❑ **Overloading** – methods are often overloaded so that they can be called using different parameters according to what we want to use them for. We saw how to create a `DateTime` object by passing its constructor various different combinations of parameters. We also saw how to overload the `ChangeGear()` method on our `Car` class so that it could take either a string or an integer parameter.

Exercises

1. Explain the following terms in your own words, and give one example of how each one might be applied in the context of a simple object-oriented holiday booking application:

❑ Object

❑ Class

❑ Property

❑ Method

2. Explain what classes we might want to define in order to model each of the following real-world scenarios, along with the members we'd expect them to have. If there is more than one possible solution, explain what additional information we require to establish which one will be most suitable:

❑ Purchasing items at a supermarket checkout

❑ Enrolling on a college course

❑ Maintaining an inventory of office equipment

3. Extend our `Car` class example to demonstrate on the browser that the value of the object's `Gear` property is restricted to a range of values between -1 and +5. Explain in your own words why it's a good idea to define functionality in method overloads that relies on calling an existing version of the same method.

4. We may want to display the `Price` property of a `Book` object in a currency other than US dollars. Define a new property `ConvPrice`, whose accessor method `get` takes two parameters denoting a currency symbol and a conversion rate, and returns the book price in the appropriate currency.

❑ Of course, this isn't quite how book prices are calculated for an international market, with additional factors such as local taxation playing a part in the total cost. Normally, separate prices are listed for the main countries in which a particular book will be sold. Update the book class again, so that we can specify three different prices for each object.

❑ Define additional data members for these extra prices, and a property called `LocalPrice` that lets us specify a country code parameter (`"US"`, `"UK"`, `"Can"`, for example) to denote which country's pricing value we want to `get` or `set`. Prices should still be stored internally as `decimal` variables. Overload the `get` accessor method so that we can optionally specify a currency symbol for display with the price.

Shared Members and
Class Relationships

Now that we've introduced the basic concepts behind objects and how to use them in isolation, we can start considering some of the ways in which they might be associated as part of a bigger picture – that is, how objects can relate to one another.

The most obvious relationship between two objects originates in something we *do* with one object in the process of dealing with another – that is, a behavioral relationship. For example, if we specify one object as a parameter in a method call on another object – the second object *uses* the first in order to execute that method. However integral it is though, the relationship is temporary one – as soon as the method call is complete, the objects have nothing more to do with each other.

We must also consider some more lasting relationships – structural relationships that play a permanent role in defining both an object's internal architecture and its behavior. Perhaps we define a member that applies to all objects in a particular class and not to any one in particular. Alternatively, we might consider a class data member whose type is defined by a different object class, or a new class that duplicates the functionality of an existing one but then expands upon it.

There's also the issue of functionality that can't be applied to any specific object – for example, a property that exposed the total number of Car objects we'd instantiated, or performed an operation on them all at once.

In this chapter, we're going to look at three particular relationships between objects:

❑   Member sharing – members defined on the class as a whole, and not on any specific object

❑   Object containment – one object type used as a data member inside another

❑   Object inheritance – one class based on another

Shared Members

So far, all the properties and methods we've looked at only have any meaning when applied to a specific object instance. In the last chapter, we demonstrated how separate objects were typically independent of one another, and that a method called on one would leave another totally unaffected – each is technically referred to as an **object instance member** (thereby giving us **object instance properties** and **object instance methods**).

However, there may be occasions when we want to share functionality between objects of a particular type. We may want to define methods and properties that apply to the class as whole, and aren't tied to a specific object: **shared members** (sometimes also referred to as **static members**) let us do just this.

Perhaps we want to keep track of how many Car objects we've created – we want a shared property called Count that can return this value, which is going to be independent of any particular object. Alternatively, we might want to implement a shared method called ChangeColor(), which can be called once to set all our car objects' color properties to "Black".

Shared Properties

As we've seen, we use the following syntax to access an object instance property:

```
<object>.<instanceproperty>
```

We can use exactly the same syntax to access a shared property:

```
<object>.<sharedproperty>
```

However, since the property applies to all objects of that class, we don't need to specify any particular instance; rather we can specify the relevant class name like this:

```
<class>.<sharedproperty>
```

> A shared (or static) member is one that operates across all instances of a class. It can be accessed via the object class itself as well as any specific instance of that class.

Try It Out – Using a Shared Property

Let's make a new class called User, which we might use to represent registered visitors to our site. We won't define any functionality except for a shared property called Count, which we can use to keep track of how many User objects we've created. In this example, we'll create three instances of the User class and display the value of the shared property as we go.

Since this is just a demonstration, and we want to look at how our page settings evolve over time, we're going to use Response.Write to output data directly to the HTTP Response stream.

1. Create a file called counting.aspx in your test directory, and add the following code:

```c#
<%@ page Language="c#" runat="server" %>
<script language="c#" runat="server">
  public class User
  {
    static private int count;
    static public int Count
    {
      get
      {
        return count;
      }
    }
    public User()
    {
      count++;
    }
    static User()
    {
      count = 0;
    }
  }
  void Page_Load()
  {
    Response.Write("User Count = " + User.Count);
    Response.Write("<hr/>Creating User Alex.");
    User Alex = new User();
    Response.Write("<br/>User Count = " + User.Count);
    Response.Write("<hr/>Creating User Rob.");
    User Rob = new User();
    Response.Write("<br/>User Count = " + User.Count);
    Response.Write("<hr/>Creating User Jake.");
    User Jake = new User();
    Response.Write("<br/>User Count = " + User.Count);
  }
</script>
```

2. Open up your browser and view the file. Here's what it looks like:

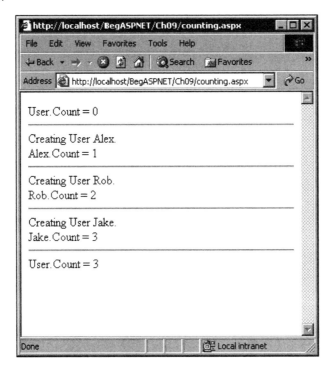

How It Works

We start off by defining our class User, with a private shared member called count. Note the naming convention we use. We'll use this variable to keep track of the total number of User objects we've created:

```
public class User
    {
    static private int count;
```

We now expose the private variable via the shared property Count. Since we don't need to edit the object count:

```
static public int Count
    {
      get
      {
        return count;
      }
    }
```

The ordinary class constructor simply increments the `count` variable:

```
    public User()
{
    count++;
}
```

Next we come to something that we've not encountered before, known as a **static constructor**. This special type of constructor is used to initialize the values of static variables and optionally to do some additional bounds checking or validation of the variable's value:

```
static User()
    {
        count = 0;
    }
```

We use `Page_Load` to generate some output for the browser to display, and track the status of our shared property as we create a number of `User` objects:

```
void Page_Load()
{
    Response.Write("User Count = " + User.Count);
    Response.Write("<hr/>Creating User Alex.");
    User Alex = new User();
    Response.Write("<br/>User Count = " + User.Count);
    Response.Write("<hr/>Creating User Rob.");
    User Rob = new User();
    Response.Write("<br/>User Count = " + User.Count);
    Response.Write("<hr/>Creating User Jake.");
    User Jake = new User();
    Response.Write("<br/>User Count = " + User.Count);
}
```

Take special note of the first line – we're able to use the `Count` property even before we've instantiated any `User` objects. We can then access it from any of the `User` objects we subsequently make, but the value stays independent of the source; we get the same `Count` value, no matter where we look at it from.

Shared Methods

In just the same way we can define shared methods, whose functionality is common to all objects of the same type.

We use a shared method in just the way you'd expect (that is, just like a normal 'object instance' property), only once again we have the option to call it on the class as a whole, rather than on one specific object:

```
<classname>.<methodname>(...)
```

As with our shared properties, we don't even need to create an instance of the class to make use of the method call. There are plenty of useful examples of shared methods in .NET, some of which we've been using already. For example, all constructor methods are shared by definition – they can't be object instance methods, since you don't actually *have* an object on which to make a object instance method call *until* you've called new().

One very good example of a .NET class that makes use of shared methods is System.Math. In fact it doesn't feature any public instance members at all – even its constructor is private, so it's impossible (and indeed quite pointless) to instantiate an object of type Math. However, the methods it does expose allow us to perform all sorts of useful mathematical operations, as well as providing us with a couple of useful constants (the exponential constant E and the 'circumference/diameter of a circle' ratio PI). Let's take a look at a few things we can do with this class.

Try It Out – Using Shared Members on the System.Math Class

Let's look at another example using some more shared methods of the Math class. In the example we're going to use the methods of the Math class to find the square, absolute value, and logarithm of a number entered into a textbox.

1. Open up your editor and type in the following code:

```
<%@ page Language="c#" runat="server" %>
<script language="c#" runat="server">
  void Page_Load()
  {
    pi.Text = Math.PI.ToString();
    exp.Text = Math.E.ToString();
  }
  void Update(object sender, EventArgs e)
  {
    try
    {
      double dblInput = Convert.ToDouble(input.Text);
      sqrt_input.Text = dblInput.ToString();
      sqrt_result.Text = Math.Sqrt(dblInput).ToString();
      abs_input.Text = dblInput.ToString();
      abs_result.Text = Math.Abs(dblInput).ToString();
      log_input.Text = dblInput.ToString();
      log_result.Text = Math.Log10(dblInput).ToString();
    } catch {
      sqrt_result.Text = "";
      abs_result.Text = "";
      log_result.Text = "";
      errormessage.Text = "Error occurred in input";
    }
  }
</script>
<html>
  <body>
    <hr />
    Pi = <asp:label id="pi" runat="server" /><br />
```

```
      Exponential Constant = <asp:label id="exp" runat="server" />
      <hr />
      <form runat="server">
      Input = <asp:textbox id="input" runat="server" />
      <asp:button text="Submit" runat="server" onclick="Update" />
      </form><hr />
      Square root of <asp:label id="sqrt_input" runat="server"/>
      = <asp:label id="sqrt_result" runat="server" /><br />
      Absolute Value of <asp:label id="abs_input" runat="server"/>
      = <asp:label id="abs_result" runat="server" /><br />
      Logarithm of <asp:label id="log_input" runat="server"/>
      = <asp:label id="log_result" runat="server" /><br />
      <asp:label id="errormessage" runat="server" /><br />
  </body>
</html>
```

2. Save the file in your test directory as `math.aspx`.

3. Open up your browser and enter a positive value in the textbox. Hit the Submit button, and you should see something like this:

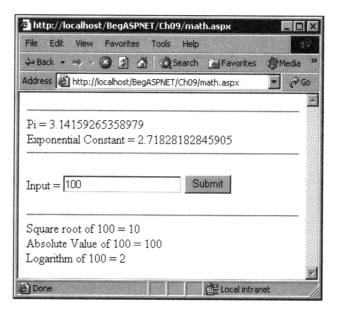

4. Now try this again, but using a negative value for the input:

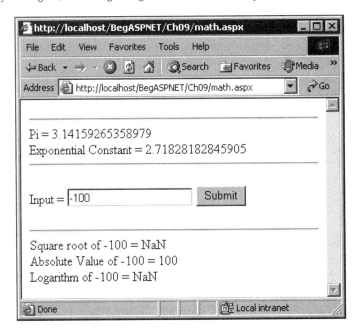

How It Works

We start off by setting up label text for the two constants exposed by the Math object:

```
<%@ page Language="c#" runat="server" %>
<script language="c#" runat="server">
  void Page_Load()
  {
    pi.Text = Math.PI.ToString();
    exp.Text = Math.E.ToString();
  }
```

Now we define a function with which to update various other labels according to what's been entered in the textbox called input. We convert that from a string to a double, and use it as a parameter in each of three calls to shared methods on the Math class; the results are assigned as text on the appropriate labels:

```
void Update(object sender, EventArgs e)
{
  try
  {
    double dblInput = Convert.ToDouble(input.Text);
    sqrt_input.Text = dblInput.ToString();
    sqrt_result.Text = Math.Sqrt(dblInput).ToString();
    abs_input.Text = dblInput.ToString();
```

```
         abs_result.Text = Math.Abs(dblInput).ToString();
         log_input.Text = dblInput.ToString();
         log_result.Text = Math.Log10(dblInput).ToString();
      } catch {
         sqrt_result.Text = "";
         abs_result.Text = "";
         log_result.Text = "";
         errormessage.Text = "Error occurred in input";
      }
   }
}
</script>
```

We define the presentation code, starting off by presenting our two constants:

```
<html>
  <body>
    <hr />
    Pi = <asp:label id="pi" runat="server" /><br />
    Exponential Constant = <asp:label id="exp" runat="server" />
    <hr />
```

We specify a form control, in which we place the textbox (for user input) and button (with which we can raise an Update event, and call the corresponding function):

```
<form runat="server">
Input = <asp:textbox id="input" runat="server" />
<asp:button text="Submit" runat="server" onclick="Update" />
</form><hr />
```

Finally, we use some more label controls to display the results of our efforts:

```
Square root of <asp:label id="sqrt_input" runat="server"/>
= <asp:label id="sqrt_result" runat="server" /><br />
Absolute Value of <asp:label id="abs_input" runat="server"/>
= <asp:label id="abs_result" runat="server" /><br />
Logarithm of <asp:label id="log_input" runat="server"/>
= <asp:label id="log_result" runat="server" /><br />
<asp:label id="errormessage" runat="server" /><br />
  </body>
</html>
```

Now that we've looked at how useful an individual class can be on its own, without any pesky objects stealing the limelight, let's start thinking about some of the ways in which different classes can be used to work together.

Class Relationships

Let's consider our car model again, and some of the objects we might associate with it; we might identify the following relationships:

- ❏ A Key *starts* a Car
- ❏ An Engine *powers* a Car
- ❏ A Person *drives* a Car
- ❏ A Driving Test *requires* a Car

For the rest of this chapter, we're going to explore three types of relationship that each play very significant roles in an object-oriented system:

- ❏ One class *using* another
- ❏ One class *containing* another – for example, a Car contains an Engine
- ❏ One class *inheriting* functionality from another – for example, FlyingCar might inherit from Car

We already know that objects are designed to make our lives easier – as we're going to see, these relationships enable objects to permeate every level of a program, and even form the basis of the programming environment in which we write it.

Association – 'Uses A'

Let's start out by considering the simplest and most fleeting relationship between object classes – one class *using* another. An object of class (A) might use class (B) in either one of the following ways:

- ❏ A member defined on class A receives, creates, and/or returns an object of class B
- ❏ Class A defines a data member as an object of class B

It's possibly a little clearer to define the relationship in terms of what it isn't:

> **If an object of class A can perform its full set of functionality while having absolutely no awareness of class B, we can safely say that class A *does not use* class B.**

Let's start by looking at some ways in which we might want to use one object in a method call on another.

Let's imagine a lending library whose inventory/membership system features one object type to represent individual account-holders at the library (class Account), and another to represent individual books, magazines, CDs etc. that may be borrowed (class Item). Supposing the Account class defines a method called Borrow() – when a visitor borrows a book (or whatever), we simply call this method on the relevant Account object.

Of course, we want to uniquely identify the book that this person has borrowed, and store this data inside their `Account` object (so that we can keep track of how much they currently have on loan). We don't need to store every bit of information we have on the book, perhaps just an ISBN and a copy number. Instead of submitting these values (or finding suitable equivalents if they're borrowing a magazine or CD) we can simply pass in the appropriate `Item` object, and code the `Borrow()` method to get whatever information it needs from that `Item`'s `public` properties.

As another example, let's return to our `Car` object from the last chapter: suppose we extend it to support methods `Start()` and `Stop()`. We don't just want anyone to be able to start the car, so we could design the former method to accept a single parameter – an object of class `Key`. We could compare a property on this object against a new private `Car` member representing the ignition, and assuming they matched, start up the engine. If there is no match, we've clearly specified the wrong key, so the car won't start for us.

Let's take a look at how we could code this.

Try It Out – Using a Key object to Start() up a Car object

1. Continuing the car theme of this and the last chapter, create a file called `car_object.aspx` and enter the following code:

```
<%@ page language="C#" runat="server" Debug="true"%>

<script runat="server">

  public class Key
  {
    private int shape;
    public Key(int newshape)
    {
      shape = newshape;
    }

    public int Shape
    {
      get
      {
        return shape;
      }
    }
  }
```

2. Now, add the following new `Car` class definition:

```
public class Car
  {
    private string color;
    private int gear;
    private int ignition;
```

```
      private bool engineRunning;
      private static int count = 0;
      public Car(int IgnitionShape)
      {
        color = "Cold gray steel";
        ignition = IgnitionShape;
        count += 1;
      }

      public static int Count
      {
        get
        {
          return count;
        }

      }

      public string Color
      {
        get
        {
          return color;
        }
        set
        {
          color = value;
        }
      }

      public int Gear
      {
        get
        {
          return gear;
        }
      }

      public string IsRunning
      {
        get
        {

          if (engineRunning)
          {
            return "The engine is running.";
          }
          else
          {
            return "The engine is not running.";
          }
        }
      }
```

```
      public void ChangeGear(int direction)
      {
        if (direction < 0) gear -= 1;
        if (direction > 0) gear += 1;
        if (gear > 5) gear = 5;
        if (gear < -1) gear = -1;
      }

      public void ChangeGear(string direction)
      {

        if (direction == "down")
        {
          ChangeGear(-1);
        }
        if (direction == "up")
        {
          ChangeGear(+1);
        }

      }
      public void Ignition(Key IgnitionKey)
      {
        if (IgnitionKey.Shape == ignition) engineRunning = true;
      }
      public void EngineOff()
      {
        engineRunning = false;
      }

    }
```

3. Finally, we have the new `Page_Load` block as follows:

```
public void Page_Load()
  {
    Key AlexKey = new Key(0987654321);
    Key RobKey = new Key(1861005040);
    Key MyKey = new Key(1234567890);

    Car MyCar = new Car(1234567890);
    Response.Write("<b>New object 'MyCar' created.</b>");


    Response.Write("<br/>Color: " + MyCar.Color);
    Response.Write("<br/>Gear: " + MyCar.Gear);

    MyCar.Color = "Black";
    MyCar.ChangeGear(+1);
    Response.Write("<br/><b>Properties updated.</b>");

    Response.Write("<br/>New color: " + MyCar.Color);
```

```
    Response.Write("<br/>New gear: " + MyCar.Gear);

    MyCar.ChangeGear("up");
    Response.Write("<br/><b>Shifted 'up' one gear.</b>");

    Response.Write("<br/>New gear: " + MyCar.Gear);

    Response.Write("<hr/>Attempting to start MyCar with AlexKey: ");
    MyCar.Ignition(AlexKey);
    Response.Write(MyCar.IsRunning);

    Response.Write("<hr/>Attempting to start MyCar with RobKey: ");
    MyCar.Ignition(RobKey);
    Response.Write(MyCar.IsRunning);

    Response.Write("<hr/>Attempting to start MyCar with MyKey: ");
    MyCar.Ignition(MyKey);
    Response.Write(MyCar.IsRunning);
    Response.Write("<br/>Attempting to stop MyCar: ");
    MyCar.EngineOff();
    Response.Write(MyCar.IsRunning);

  }
</script>
```

4. Save the file in your test directory, and call it up from your browser – you should see this:

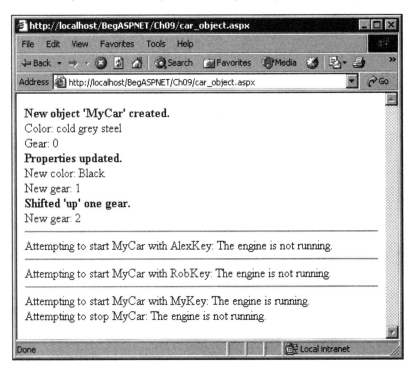

How It Works

As we covered the operation of this example in the previous chapter, we'll just look at the most important aspects of it here. We start off by adding a new class definition to our web form. This provides a template for our Key objects, and exposes a single read-only property called Shape; this is an integer value that we use to represent the precise shape of the car key we're modeling. Since a key works by applying one of many possible shapes to some kind of lock mechanism (in this case, the ignition), we're modeling it as an integer value in the range defined by the int data type (-2,147,483,648 to 2,147,483,647), representing any one of 4,294,967,296 unique key shapes:

```
public class Key
{
  private int shape;
  public Key(int newshape)
  {
    shape = newshape;
  }

  public int Shape
  {
    get
    {
      return shape;
    }
  }
}
```

We now declare a private integer variable ignition on the Car class. We'll use this to hold a value that represents the unique key shape required to start the engine. We can then compare the two to discover whether the right key has been used. We also declare a private Boolean variable called engineRunning, which we'll use to represent the state of the engine:

```
public class Car
  {
    private string color;
    private int gear;
    private int ignition;
    private bool engineRunning;
```

We amend our Car class constructor, so that each new object is defined with a specific ignition setting, submitted as an int parameter:

```
public Car(int IgnitionShape)
    {
      color = "Cold gray steel";
      ignition = IgnitionShape;
      count += 1;
    }
```

Next, we add a string property called `IsRunning`, which will tell us whether the engine is running or not. Rather than directly exposing the private data member `isRunning`, we use it as a condition in the property's `get` method to determine an appropriate message as a `return` value:

```
public string IsRunning
  {
    get
    {

      if (engineRunning)
      {
        return "The engine is running.";
      }
      else
      {
        return "The engine is not running.";
      }
    }
  }
```

Now for the crux of the example: an `Ignition()` method on the `Car` class, which takes a `Key` object as its one parameter. We use `IgnitionKey` as a label to refer to this object, and read its `Shape` property in the usual way. As we've noted, the particular shape of a car key is represented as an `integer` (effectively representing any one of 4,294,967,296 possible shapes), and the car's ignition is represented likewise. If the two match up, then `engineRunning` is set to `true`, and the car has been started successfully. Otherwise, nothing happens at all:

```
public void Ignition(Key IgnitionKey)
  {
    if (IgnitionKey.Shape == ignition) engineRunning = true;
  }
```

There's no such condition attached to switching off the engine, so we use the method `EngineOff()` to unset `engineRunning` no matter what:

```
public void EngineOff()
  {
    engineRunning = false;
  }
```

Now we add some code to `Page_Load` that will make use of this new functionality. We start by instantiating three `Key` objects, each with different shapes:

```
public void Page_Load()
  {
    Key AlexKey = new Key(0987654321);
    Key RobKey = new Key(1861005040);
    Key MyKey = new Key(1234567890);
```

We instantiate a `Car` object (called `MyCar`), whose ignition is set with the same value used to describe the shape of `MyKey`:

```
Car MyCar = new Car(1234567890);
Response.Write("<b>New object 'MyCar' created.</b>");
...
```

We apply each of the `Key` objects to `MyCar.Ignition()`, and find (predictably enough) that only one of them works:

```
Response.Write("<hr/>Attempting to start MyCar with RobKey: ");
MyCar.Ignition(RobKey);
Response.Write(MyCar.IsRunning);

Response.Write("<hr/>Attempting to start MyCar with MyKey: ");
MyCar.Ignition(MyKey);
Response.Write(MyCar.IsRunning);
Response.Write("<br/>Attempting to stop MyCar: ");
MyCar.EngineOff();
Response.Write(MyCar.IsRunning);

}
```

Note that when we call the `Ignition()` method, we can't simply submit an `int` like this:

```
Ignition(1234567890)
```

The parameter *must* be a `Key` object, and its `Shape` property is always what's used to test against the ignition.

Of course, this is quite a trivial example, and still some way off perfection: for example, we'd ideally automate the key instantiation process, so we don't have to explicitly create two objects for each `Car` we make. What's more, it doesn't really show off all the advantages of passing objects rather than standard data types.

However, if you consider the reasons we looked at in the last chapter for using objects in the first place, you should get an idea of why this approach is a good thing. Classes `Key` and `Car` both *encapsulate* the `Shape` functionality, so that any code using a `Key` to call the `Car.Ignition()` method **doesn't need to know anything about how either works**. So, for example, if we decided to change the way we represent key shape (perhaps use a `Long` instead), any code that used the `Key` object to start the car would remain unaffected.

Containment – A 'Has a' Relationship

Earlier on, we identified two possible ways for one object to be *used* by another; the first involved submitting one object as a method parameter in a call on the other object, and we've just looked at one way in which that might be used. The association between objects is brief, lasting only as long as the method call.

The second describes a somewhat more involved association, often referred to as **containment** (also known as *composition* or *aggregation*). This is a very powerful object-oriented technique, by which we can define the data members of one class as objects derived from another class. For example, our Car class might define a private member of type Engine (another new class, designed to represent the car's engine). We could then say that the Car class (and every Car type object we instantiate from it) contains an Engine object.

So, why is it great to have one object within another? The answer's quite simple: it helps us to define complex classes using simpler, existing ones, and therefore provides us with a frequently useful way to reuse code.

> **When some class A defines a data member of class B, we can say that an object of class A contains an object of class B.**

Containment is often described as a 'has a' relationship – in many cases, we can take the names of a class and object that's contained within it, place the words 'has a' between them, and find that it's a valid statement.

> *In fact, it's often worth trying out a few others as well, such as 'contains', 'is composed of', 'comprises', and 'consists of'. If any of these fit the bill, then you're probably looking at a sensible use of containment.*

When you establish your overall object model, this should prove helpful in identifying which objects should contain which other objects. If we apply this to our car example we might get:

❑ A car has an engine

It's reasonable to use an engine object as a data member within the car class. On the other hand:

❑ An engine has a car

doesn't really make any sense.

Let's assume we've defined an Engine class, whose properties include SerialNo, Rpm, Name (which is set by the constructor), and IsRunning, and whose methods include SwitchOn and SwitchOff. We might use an Engine object like this to replace our private Boolean engineRunning, so that our Car class becomes a little richer in useful detail.

> *We won't show you how to define the Engine class here, as its particular implementation details really aren't important to the present discussion. If you want to test the code below, a simple class definition featuring a single constructor method should be quite adequate.*

Consider this new code for the `Car` class that could expose an engine object:

```
public class Car
{
  private string color;
  private int gear;
  private int ignition;
  private Engine engine;
  ...
public Engine objEngine
{
  get
  {
    return engine;
  }
  set
  {
    engine = value;
  }
}
}
...
```

We could now create a new `Car` object, and set this property with a new `Engine` object:

```
Car ShumaCar = new Car();
ShumaCar.objEngine = new Engine("Ferrari 050 V10");
```

The `SchumaCar` object now contains an actual object of type `Engine` (whose `Name` property is the string `"Ferrari 050 V10"`) and we can access this directly via the property `ShumaCar.MyEngine`. Since this exposes the contained `Engine` object in its entirety, we could examine the engine's `Name` property using the expression:

```
Engine_Name = SchumaCar.MyEngine.Name
```

We could also make method calls on the `Engine` object in a similar fashion:

```
Engine_Name = SchumaCar.MyEngine.SwitchOn()
```

Of course, this gives us all the functionality we'd expect from the `Ignition()` method on the `Car` object itself. In fact, it exposes rather more than we'd like, since we now have direct access to the engine, we're in a position to start it up without a key – effectively 'hotwiring' the car!

What we ought to have done in this case, is to make the `Engine` object a private member of the `Car` class (as we did with the original `engineRunning` Boolean) and access its functionality via `Car` methods and properties. However, what this example has shown us is that when we do want direct access to objects inside objects, it's really not hard at all.

Containment in .NET

As we've noted already, the .NET Framework features many, many objects, and we're going to take a look at some of the most intrinsically important ones (in the context of working with ASP.NET pages, that is) in the next chapter. As you'll see, using objects as class properties is an extremely widespread practice, strictly speaking, just about *everything* we see in .NET is an object (including all our data types: `int`, `string`, `bool`, and so on), so it's actually fair to say that it's fundamental to object-oriented programming in .NET.

Before we try to take on *all* of these important .NET objects, let's consider just one of them, and see how it exposes information to us via a contained object.

In the next example we're going to look at some of the properties of the `Browser` object that ASP.NET provides for us – this is exposed as a property of the intrinsic object `Request`, which we'll look at in much more detail in the next chapter. For now, suffice it to say that `Request` is a `System.Web.HttpRequest` type object (that is, based on a class called `HttpRequest`, as defined in the .NET namespace `System.Web`). This object is instantiated as a standard part of the web form execution process, and is used to hold all the information from the HTTP Request that our browser submitted to the server.

The `Request` object's properties are used to expose the data submitted in the current HTTP Request. One of the public members this class supports is a property called `Browser`, and this exposes an object of type `HttpBrowserCapabilities`, which is also defined in the `System.Web` namespace. This object is used specifically to expose data in the HTTP Request pertaining to the client browser – it supports properties that include `Browser` (the type of browser being used), `Version` (the browser version), `Frames` (whether or not the browser supports frames), and plenty more besides.

Try It Out – Using Contained Objects

We're now going to use `Request` and `Request.Browser` to tell us a few things about our browser software:

1. Open up your editor and type in this code:

```
<%@ Page Language="c#" %>
<script runat="server">
  void Page_Load()
  {
    lblRequestType.Text =     Request.RequestType;
    lblAOL.Text =             Request.Browser.AOL.ToString();
    lblJavaScript.Text =      Request.Browser.JavaScript.ToString();
    lblBrowserType.Text =     Request.Browser.Type;
    lblTableSupport.Text =    Request.Browser.Tables.ToString();
  }
</script>
<html>
  <body>
    Request type : <asp:label id=lblRequestType runat="server" /><br />
    AOL : <asp:label id=lblAOL runat="server" /><br />
    JavaScript : <asp:label id=lblJavaScript runat="server" /><br />
    Browser : <asp:label id=lblBrowserType runat="server" /><br />
    Tables : <asp:label id=lblTableSupport runat="server" />
  </body>
</html>
```

2. Save the file as `containment.aspx`.

3. Call up your browser and view the file. Here's what it looks like in Internet Explorer 6:

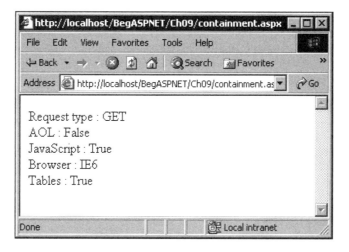

How It Works

One of the first lines in the page is a statement that accesses a property called `RequestType` on the `Request` object; this tells us whether the page was requested using a `GET` or `POST` method. The value it sends back is assigned to the label control `lblRequestType`:

```
lblRequestType.Text = Request.RequestType;
```

Subsequent information comes from one level deeper, from within the `Browser` object, which is contained by the `Request` object:

```
lblAOL.Text =           Request.Browser.AOL.ToString();
lblJavaScript.Text =    Request.Browser.JavaScript.ToString();
lblBrowserType.Text =   Request.Browser.Type;
lblTableSupport.Text =  Request.Browser.Tables.ToString();
```

Notice how we reference the `Request` object, and then use a period to specify the `Browser` property on that object. This `Browser` property returns an `HttpBrowser` type object, and this is usually referred to as the `Browser` object. This object exposes its own properties, which we access in the same way: simply add a period, followed by the name of the property.

For example, we can see that the `Request.Browser.Type` property returns a string denoting what browser we're using – in this case, it's Internet Explorer 6, so it returns `"IE6"`.

There's one more type of class relationship we need to look at before properly delving into all the .NET classes and how they work. What if we have an existing class that defines a set of fantastically useful functionality, but seems to be missing one or two little features that we need to make use of it?

Inheritance – 'Is A'

Let's assume that we have accurately and thoroughly modeled all of the essential features of our `Car` class; we've implemented it, tested it rigorously, and found to be bug free – perhaps it's now being used in a number of different applications.

However, a new scientific breakthrough has made the long-touted "flying car" a practical reality, and we wish to model these beautiful airborne machines as well. Now it turns out that the only feature of a flying car that we need to model (above and beyond those we've already modeled for a normal car) is its altitude, as well as providing methods to let us control its vertical motion. All the other features we need to describe a car are the same as those that we've already programmed for the `Car` class; although the flying car is a wonder to behold, it's fundamentally *still* a car.

This new `FlyingCar` class is going to need some methods that the `Car` class simply doesn't implement:

❑   `Ascend()`

❑   `Descend()`

We're also going to need an extra property:

❑   `Altitude`

How might we approach this new requirement for a `FlyingCar` class? If we didn't know anything about object-oriented programming, we might try one of the following approaches:

Add Redundancy to the Original Class

Simply add an altitude property and vertical steering methods to our `Car` definition, and simply leave these attributes empty when they aren't applicable. We could also track whether these attributes were applicable to a given `Car` object, by adding a `bool` data member denoting whether a specific car can fly:

```
public class Car
{
  private string color;
  private int gear;
  private int ignition;
  private Engine engine;
  private bool canFly;
  ...
```

Of course, any new methods we wrote for this class would need to take account of its value, and this results in convoluted code, which is difficult to debug and maintain.

Define a Near Duplicate Class

We could create a new FlyingCar class by duplicating the contents of class Car class and adding the extra features we require to this copy. Of course, this would be terribly inefficient, as most of our code would then be identically defined in two places. What's more, if we wanted to modify the internal functionality of the Car at some later date, then we'd have to make the same changes in both classes.

Strictly speaking, either of these two approaches would work, but either way, the inherent redundancy in the code would make them far more difficult to maintain. What's more, they really break down quite horribly when you consider adding a third, fourth, or even a fifth type of 'special' Car.

Define a New Class that Inherits Functionality from the Original Class

Fortunately, we have another alternative – we can solve this problem by taking advantage of **inheritance**, a powerful object-oriented mechanism, by which we can define a new class solely in terms of the differences (in terms of the functionality it supports) between it and another existing class.

We can therefore define a FlyingCar as a special type of Car with three extra members that normal Cars have no need for:

```
public class FlyingCar : Car
{
  private int pressure;

  public int Altitude
  {
    get
    {
      return PressureToAltitude(pressure);
    }
  }
  private int PressureToAltitude(int Pressure)
  {
    ...
  }
  public void Ascend()
  {
    ...
  }
  public void Descend()
  {
    ...
  }
  public FlyingCar(int IgnitionShape) : base(IgnitionShape)
  {
  }
}
```

There are two new things in this code that we need to explain. First we signify that we are using inheritance in the class definition itself. The syntax for achieving this is to append the class to be inherited from, the **base class**, to the new class, the **derived class** or a **subclass**, and separate the two with a colon.

```
public class FlyingCar : Car
```

The rest of the code looks much like what we have discussed so far: we define a private variable, a public read-only property and some methods. When we come to the class constructor we have some syntax we have not seen before:

```
public FlyingCar(int IgnitionShape) : base(IgnitionShape)
{
}
```

We use this syntax because, although we want the FlyingCar constructor to have a parameter, the base-class Car constructor also has a parameter. This leads us to some important facts about how objects that inherit from each other are instantiated. Though in this code we would only create a FlyingCar object, according to the way inheritance works, we have to call the constructors of the base class as well. Indeed we have to call the constructor of the base class's base class and so on all the way up the ultimate base class which is the .NET Framework's System.Object base class. So when you create an object, more than one constructor is called and if any of the other constructors require parameters, then they have to be specified as well. If you were to try to run this code without the ": base(IgnitionShape)" code snippet, you would get an error:

No overload for method 'Car' takes '0' arguments

What it is trying to do is call the constructor of the Car class with no parameters and there isn't one. There are several ways to fix this. First you could add a parameterless constructor to the Car class:

```
public Car()
{
}
```

This is all well and good for this example where the Car class code is at our disposal, but say we are deriving from a base class whose source code is not available. This is not an unlikely scenario. You cannot assume you can tinker around with base classes like this. Also, though the code will compile, it might not work as expected since the parameter value you should have supplied might have set the value of a vital piece data in your code, which would otherwise be unset, as is the case here. So unless you know how your base class is structured and how by calling a parameterless constructor you can set any critical data values, you cannot use this method.

By far the best solution is to tell the derived class constructor which base class constructor you want to call and pass any parameters up to it, if there are any.

```
public FlyingCar(int IgnitionShape) : base(IgnitionShape)
```

The section of code from the colon onwards means this: "When you create a FlyingCar object, call up the constructor of the base class passing the value of the IgnitionShape parameter to it." This code will compile now as the Car class's only constructor takes an int as its only parameter.

The benefit of calling all these constructors is this: when you create a `FlyingCar` object, you also get all the `Car` object functionality for free (and also `System.Object` functionality too, which includes the ubiquitous `ToString()` function). You can see now that by only adding a relatively small amount of code, you have added much greater power to your class.

Terminology for Inheritance

The `Car` class from which we've derived `FlyingCar` (meaning we inherited from) is usually referred to as the **base class** (or sometimes as the **parent class**, **superclass**, or **supertype**), whereas `FlyingCar` can be referred to as a **subclass** of `Car` (or alternatively as a **child class**, **derived class**, or **subtype**).

> **Inheritance is often referred to as establishing an 'is a' relationship between two classes: if we can say that class A (in this case the `FlyingCar`) 'is a' particular variety of class B (the `Car`), then it makes sense to model A by deriving from B:**

Note that anything that we can say about a base class must also be true about all of its subclasses.

❑   A `Car` has an engine, so a `FlyingCar` has an engine

❑   A `Car` has a gearbox, so a `FlyingCar` has a gearbox

❑   A `Car` steers left and right, so a `FlyingCar` steers lefts and right

One simple but effective test for the legitimacy of inheriting from a class is as follows:

> **If you can say anything about a base class A that cannot be said about a proposed subclass B, then B is not really a valid subclass of A.**

Of course, the converse is not true. A subclass is a special case of its base class, so it is quite legitimate to say something like "a `FlyingCar` can fly up and down, whereas a `Car` cannot" without compromising the model.

So, when we want a class that has the features and functionality of an existing class, but with some additional features, we can use **inheritance** to create a new object type that supports both. When an object of type A can be treated as a specialized version of another object of type B, we can say that class A is derived – or **inherits** – from class B. Objects of type A will support all the methods and properties supported by objects of type B, as well as any additional members that have been defined in A.

Some object-oriented systems allow you to inherit from more than one class (a process known as multiple inheritance). However, this is not the case here: a .NET class can only directly inherit functionality from one other class. However, the inheritance may have many layers – that is, the ancestor class may itself inherit from another class, which may inherit from yet another, and so on.

The Pros and Cons of Inheritance

Inheritance is one of the most powerful features of an object-oriented system, because:

❏ **Derived classes are much more succinct than they would be without inheritance.** Derived classes only define what it is that makes them different from their ancestor class. A flying car is simply a car that can also move vertically.

❏ **We can reuse and extend tested code without modifying it.** We make our new class FlyingCar without disturbing the original Car class definition in any way. Any other code that relies on Car objects will be unaffected by the existence of FlyingCar, so we avoid having to retest existing sections of our application.

❏ **You don't need the source code for a class in order to derive a new class from it.** As long as you have the compiled version of a class, the inheritance mechanism works just fine; you therefore don't require the original class definition in order to extend it. You can often save a lot of time and effort by finding an existing class (a system class, or third-party offering) that does much of what you need, and then deriving a subclass from it. You simply need to add the features you want for your own purposes.

❏ **Classification is the natural way for humans to organize information.** As we've already noted, it makes sense to organize our software along the same lines as those along which we think. Our code is therefore much more intuitive, and consequently easier to maintain and extend.

Bear in mind though: overusing inheritance can make programs more complex than they need to be. It's just as important to know when *not* to use inheritance as it is to know when and how to use it in the first place. If you use it inappropriately and your program breaks down as a consequence, you may well find yourself having to rewrite large quantities of code just to get back to where you started. Use it sparingly, and use it wisely.

System.Object – The Ultimate Base Class

Every class (and therefore every object) in .NET ultimately inherits from a class called Object, defined in the System namespace, which provides us with a small set of standard properties and methods that it's useful for all objects to support, regardless of what type they are.

Class System.Object

Constructors

Visibility	Constructor	Parameters
public	Object	( )

Methods

Visibility	Return	Name	Parameters
public static	Boolean	Equals	(Object objA , Object objB)
public	Boolean	Equals	(Object obj)
public	Int32	GetHashCode	( )
public	Type	GetType	( )
public static	Boolean	ReferenceEquals	(Object objA , Object objB)
public	String	ToString	( )

Hierarchy
System.Object

For example, one of the properties it supports is called GetType. This exposes an object of class Type, whose FullName property is a string naming the class (or type) of the object on which we're calling it. The simplest way to see this in action is to take a look at the string returned for an object type object:

```
object obj = new Object;
Response.Write(obj.GetType().Fullname);
```

If you add this code to the logic in a web form, you'll see the following result:

System.Object

That's all well and good. Now let's try the same with another type of object:

```
int value = 0;
Response.Write(value.GetType().FullName);
```

If you use this code in your web form, you'll see the following result:

System.Int32

This is the system class that .NET uses internally to work with int variables. In fact, whenever you're working with an int, you're effectively working with an Int32 type object.

Let's try this one more time, using an object based on our Car class:

```
Car MyNewCar = new Car(1234);
Response.Write(MyCar.GetType().FullName);
```

If you put this code into a web form (along with the Car class definition, of course), and save it in a file called car_gettype.aspx, you should see something like this:

ASP.car_gettype_aspx+Car

There are some important things to note here:

❑ We've successfully used a property called GetType() on the MyCar object, even though it's not specified in the class definition.

❑ The full name of the type we get back consists of three parts, denoting:

❑ The ASP namespace – this is the standard namespace used to hold the page classes that are generated automatically from ASPX files

❑ The name of the page class – this is based on the name of the actual ASPX file being used; in this case, my web form was saved as car_gettype.aspx

❑ The name of the user-defined class – in this case, Car

In fact, only the first point is of immediate concern to us: we've demonstrated one of the features that the `Car` class has *automatically* inherited from the `object` class. We don't need to define a `GetType` property; it's simply there, ready and waiting, no matter how little code we've put in our own class.

> *The second point is less relevant to our present discussion, but interesting nevertheless, as it digs a little further into how ASP.NET works under the covers. As we know, all the code we're writing in our pages is actually C# code; it's only when we put it together with HTML and server controls (and expose all this from an ASPX file on the web server) that we get a proper web form. This reveals a little of the structure of the page class, which makes substantial use all of these class relationships, and some more besides.*

Try It Out – Using Inheritance to Create a Scientific Calculator Class

To round off our discussion of inheritance, we're going to look at using it to beef up the functionality of the simple calculator class we defined in the last chapter. We're going to define a `ScientificCalculator` class, which will support all the functionality of `Calculator`, but with an additional method `SquareRoot`.

This is a fairly typical example of inheritance – we take the base behavior of something we already have and roll in our own functionality without much effort at all.

1. Make a copy of the `calculator_object.aspx` file from the previous chapter and call it `sci_calculator_object.aspx`.

2. Now open up the file, and add the following highlighted code to the `<script>` block:

```
<%@ page Language="c#" runat="server" %>
<script language="c#" runat="server">
  public class ScientificCalculator : Calculator
  {
    public void SquareRoot()
    {
      double root = Math.Sqrt(CurrentValue);
      Clear();
      Add(root);
    }
  }

  public class Calculator
  {
    private double current;
    ...
  }
</script>
```

3. Modify/add the following highlighted code in the `Page_Load` sub:

```
void Page_Load()
  {
    ScientificCalculator MyCalc = new ScientificCalculator();
    Response.Write("<b>Created a new ScientificCalculator object.</b><br/>");

    Response.Write("Current Value = " + MyCalc.CurrentValue);

    MyCalc.Add(23);
    Response.Write("<br/><b>Added 23 - MyCalc.Add(23)</b><br/>");
    Response.Write("Current Value = " + MyCalc.CurrentValue);

    MyCalc.Subtract(7);
    Response.Write("<br/><b>Subtracted 7 - MyCalc.Subtract(7)</b><br/>");
    Response.Write("Current Value = " + MyCalc.CurrentValue);

    MyCalc.Multiply(3);
    Response.Write("<br/><b>Multiplied by 3 - MyCalc.Multiply(3)</b><br/>");
    Response.Write("Current Value = " + MyCalc.CurrentValue);

    MyCalc.Divide(4);
    Response.Write("<br/><b>Divided by 4 - MyCalc.Divide(4)</b><br/>");
    Response.Write("Current Value = " + MyCalc.CurrentValue);

    MyCalc.SquareRoot();
    Response.Write("<br/><b>Square root - MyCalc.SquareRoot()</b><br/>");
    Response.Write("Current Value = " + MyCalc.CurrentValue);

    MyCalc.Clear();
    Response.Write("<br/><b>Cleared - MyCalc.Clear()</b><br/>");
    Response.Write("Current Value = " + MyCalc.CurrentValue);
  }
```

4. Save the file, and check your browser – you should see this:

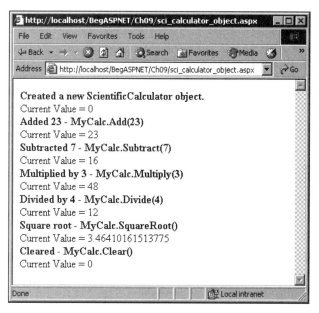

How It Works

We start off by defining our new class `ScientificCalculator`. To tell .NET that we want it to inherit functionality from another class, we simply add a colon to the end of the opening statement, followed by the name of the base class – in this case, `Calculator`. We then define our new method, in the normal way:

```
public class ScientificCalculator : Calculator
{
  public void SquareRoot()
  {
    double root = Math.Sqrt(CurrentValue);
    Clear();
    Add(root);
  }
}
```

You might be wondering why we don't just assign `current` with the result of the `Math.Sqrt()` operation that we use to calculate the square root. The answer's actually quite simple: `current` is defined as a private member of the `Calculator` class, and is therefore, invisible to any code outside that class – and that includes the `ScientificCalculator` subclass.

You could get round this problem by changing the access modifier from `private` to `protected` for the `current` member of the `Calculator` base class:

```
protected double current;
```

This would allow all derived classes to use the variable but not external code. However this requires you to have access to the base class source code which we do not necessarily have, and as I said before, I say again, though slightly more forcefully: hands off all base class code!

In addition changing the access modifier to allow more access presents a security problem in that potentially sensitive data could then be accessible through inheritance. Therefore when you are designing a class from which you want to derive other classes and you want to restrict access to certain data, you have a choice. You can mark the variables `private`, which will prevent any other class (derived or otherwise) from accessing them, or mark them as `protected`, which means that derived classes can access their values as if they were public, and can be useful if you want to share certain data between related classes.

OK, so let's heed the warning above and not modify the `Calculator` class at all. We have to calculate the square root without directly using the `current` variable, and to do this we apply any results via the public methods already exposed by the `Calculator` class. This isn't too tricky – we can simply `Clear()` the existing value and then call `Add()` passing in our result as the parameter.

In the `Page_Load()` method, we start by creating an instance of our derived class:

```
ScientificCalculator MyCalc = new ScientificCalculator();
Response.Write("<b>Created a new ScientificCalculator object.</b><br/>");
```

Then we call each function in turn, using the same object instance `MyCalc` to call them regardless of whether the functions themselves are in the `Calculator` or `ScientificCalculator` class, thus once again demonstrating the power of inheritance.

Note also that in this example we have not had to define any constructors at all, either for the base class or for the derived class. .NET is able to figure out from this that we want to create a `ScientificCalculator` object, which then requires all the base class constructors to be called in turn right up to `System.Object`. With no constructors defined, default constructors are used for all objects.

```
Response.Write("Current Value = " + MyCalc.CurrentValue);
```

The Limitations of Inheritance

As we said before, you can only inherit from one class, and this is really the only limitation when it comes to inheritance (and there is a way round this as explained in the next section). However there is one exception to this rule that you cannot get round; if you mark a class as `sealed` when you define it, then you cannot inherit from this class and you will get a compiler error if you try:

```
public sealed MyUninheritableClass
{
   ...
}
```

Advanced Inheritance Concepts

C# enables you to create special classes whose functions and properties can only be used by derived classes. Indeed, these classes are defined as being **uninstantiable**, by which I mean, you cannot create instances of them using the `new` operator. There are two types of these classes, as described below:

❑ **Abstract classes (or abstract base classes)**. These are ordinary classes, which are marked with the `abstract` keyword when they are defined. They can contain properties, functions, constructors and all the other features of ordinary classes, with one extra feature not found elsewhere: **abstract methods**, which are basically function headers with no implementation, which the derived classes must provide.

> Note that we have used the word function a great deal in this book. However in this section we will use the word *method* a lot more. In C# the two terms have much overlap regarding their meaning and use. We talk about "function overloading" and "function calls" (though "method calls" is an acceptable alternative). In this section we discuss "abstract methods" and "interface methods" which is the more usual terminology in this context, hence the abrupt change in terminology.

❑ **Interfaces** are a special type of abstract class, specified using the `interface` keyword and not the `class` keyword in their definition. They can contain properties and methods, though the methods can only be abstract methods, and as such any class that derives from the interface must implement them all.

> We have said that a class may only inherit from one base class. However a class can derive from zero or more interfaces, so long as each and every method defined by the interface is implemented.

Both these types of class are used when a generic class is required that would be of no use or value in itself, but which would augment the functionality and power of any classes derived from it. To illustrate what I mean, take the `Car` class that we have developed in the last two chapters. At the moment, it is a standalone class containing in itself all the functionality it needs. However if we should define a `Truck` class, you would find that it would have a parallel set of properties and functions associated with it: in fact everything that we have defined as applying to a `Car` object (`Color`, `Gear`, `IsRunning()`, `Ignition()` and so on) also applies to the `Truck` object. This would mean we would duplicate much of that code when defining the `Truck` object.

A better object-oriented function of defining two different objects with the same base functionality is to define a third a generic object, say, `Vehicle`, and derive `Car` and `Truck` from that:

```
public class Vehicle
{
    ...
}

public class Car : Vehicle
{
    ...
}

public class Truck : Vehicle
{
    ...
}
```

The above code snippet demonstrates C#'s inheritance syntax. We first define the 'shell' of a base class called `Vehicle` and then declare two classes `Car` and `Truck` that derive from `Vehicle`. No keyword is used here to indicate inheritance, just a colon.

So what would the nature of the `Vehicle` class be? There are several options here.

❑ It can contain all the functionality common to both trucks and cars, leaving specific functionality for the derived classes – this follows the same principles as the ordinary inheritance already discussed for the `Car` and `FlyingCar` classes.

The advantage of this is that once you have defined the functions, you can use them again and again in all the different objects. The disadvantage is that the functionality might need to be subtly (or substantially) different for each derived class. No one would say that you drive cars, trucks, airplanes and other vehicles in exactly the same way, so a `Drive()` function might have to be different for each class.

❏　You put the function definitions in the base class and implement them in the derived classes.

We have already said that this is where abstract classes and interfaces come in, and we'll look at how this happens in just a moment. However, there is a third option open to you:

❏　Implement a default implementation of a function in the base class and then, if required, add a modified implementation of the same function in the derived class, which replaces or overrides the default implementation.

This is a very powerful hybrid of the first two options and is available through any class (whether abstract or not). To do this, you first define a **virtual function** in the base class and **override** it in the derived class. A virtual function is just an ordinary function that can (but doesn't have to) be overridden by a derived class. Similarly an overridden function is just an ordinary function that just happens to be a different version of a function of the same name and the same signature in the base class.

OK, enough of the theory. How do we code this using some or all of the options laid out above?

Virtual Functions

Let's suppose we have a class `Vehicle` that has two functions `Drive()` and `SlowDown()`.

```
public class Vehicle
{
  public bool Drive()
  {
    // implementation
  }

  public bool SlowDown()
  {
    // implementation
  }
}
```

We could leave this as is and let the derived `Car`, `Truck`, and `Airplane` classes just call them without modification. Though this is fine for `SlowDown()`, in that slowing down is the same for a car, a truck and an airplane, we have indicated that there are differences in the way that `Drive()` will work for these classes. So applying the last of the options, we can declare the `Drive()` function to be virtual as follows:

```
public class Vehicle
{
  public virtual bool Drive()
  {
    // implementation
  }
```

The `virtual` keyword tells the compiler that this function could be overridden in a derived class, though it doesn't have to be. So, say we put in an implementation of `Drive()` that applies to cars, it can be called without modification by `Car` objects, and while it doesn't completely match the way that a truck is driven, it would be completely inappropriate to the way airplanes are "driven" – in English we don't even use the word "driven" for airplanes! However for the purpose of this discussion, let's define a brand new `Drive()` function for the `Airplane` class. It will be declared as follows:

```
public class Airplane : Vehicle
{
  public override bool Drive()
  {
    // specific implementation for airplanes
  }
```

The `override` keyword tells the compiler that we don't want the default implementation but we are using this version instead.

However, if you are deriving from a base class (where you do not have access to the code) and you just happen to use a function of the same name and signature as that of a non-virtual function of the base class, you're stuck! You will get a compiler error if you try to use the function as it is already defined for the class through inheritance, and you cannot use `override` as the base class function is non-virtual. Fortunately, C# offers a cool way out of this predicament. You can hide (not override) the unwanted base class function using this syntax:

```
public class MyClass : MyBase
{
  public new bool DoIt()
  {
    // new implementation of code for DoIt
  }
```

This assumes that `MyBase` has a function called `DoIt()` with no parameters that returns a `bool`. Whenever `DoIt()` is called from a `MyClass` instance, then this code is run and not the version from the base class. However does this mean that the base class version of this function is inaccessible from the derived class? Similarly, once a virtual function is overridden, is the original implementation unavailable? Well, the answer is "no" on both counts, you can get at the original function using syntax like this:

```
base.DoIt();
```

or:

```
base.Drive();
```

What this means is that the base class function of this name is called instead of the derived class version. Note that `base` is a keyword and not a class type or class instance, so this syntax will work for any base class.

Referring to the Current Object – The this Reference

We have seen how to refer to the base class using the base keyword. We can also refer to the current object instance in your code using the C# keyword this. Say a function requires an object of a certain type as its parameter:

```
void MyFunction(ClassType c)
{

}
```

and you call this function from your code. If you pass this as the parameter, then the actual object can be of the type ClassType or any inherited class:

```
MyFunction(this);
```

There are other uses of this, but the above is the most common.

Abstract Classes and Interfaces

So if we want our generic vehicle class to be an abstract class rather than an ordinary class, what changes do we need to make and what benefits can we get? First we declare it abstract as follows.

```
public abstract class Vehicle
{
  public bool Drive()
  {
    // implementation
  }
  public bool SlowDown()
  {
    // implementation
  }
}
```

The addition of this one keyword changes everything. Up until now, Vehicle objects could be instantiated using new. Now they cannot. The rest of the code can remain unchanged. Both virtual and non-virtual functions can be called by derived classes without any trouble. However, with an abstract class, we can go further and define abstract methods. These consist of method signatures and nothing else, like this:

```
public abstract class Vehicle
{
  public abstract void SetSpecificVehicleProperties();
```

Note the semicolon at the end of the line and the absence of curly brackets that would form part of the implementation.

The outcome of adding this line is that all derived classes must implement this function, in addition to anything else:

```
public class Car : Vehicle
{
  public override void SetSpecificVehicleProperties()
  {
    // Specific Car implementation here
  }
}

public class Truck : Vehicle
{
  public override void SetSpecificVehicleProperties()
  {
    // Specific Truck implementation here
  }
}
...
```

You would use abstract methods to force derived classes to implement versions of the method appropriate to their classes, which can be similar or totally different from each other. The only things these function implementations have in common are the number and type of parameters and the return value. Note how the implementations are all marked by the `override` keyword. This is because abstract methods are also virtual methods – indeed they have to be if they are to be of any use.

So, having defined one abstract method, we could go all the way and make all of the methods of the `Vehicle` class abstract:

```
public abstract class Vehicle
{
  public abstract void SetSpecificVehicleProperties();
  public abstract bool Drive();
  public abstract bool SlowDown();
}
```

What we now have is a class that cannot be instantiated and for which all derived classes must implement all methods. This is no class in the ordinary sense of the word. What we have now is an **interface**. In fact, an interface could be basically described as an abstract class with abstract members (by which we mean methods and properties – you can have abstract properties, which are overridden in exactly the same way as methods). However we don't have an interface in the strict C# sense, in that it is still defined as a class, which means that the derived classes can only inherit from this class and no other.

To turn it into a proper interface requires some changes to the syntax, as follows:

```
interface IVehicle
{
  void SetSpecificVehicleProperties();
  bool Drive();
  bool SlowDown();
}
```

We have removed all instances of "abstract" since interfaces are by definition abstract. We have replaced the class keyword with the interface keyword, which completely changes the nature of what we have created. Now the functionality of the interface can be inherited by a class along with its base class (and other interfaces). We have also removed all instances of the "public" keyword since interfaces have to be publicly accessible to be of any use, as are their methods and properties. We've also changed the name of the interface by prefixing a capital I. This is the convention for interfaces as it makes them immediately identifiable, though it is not mandatory. We have said that interfaces can have properties as well as methods. This is how you would define a read/write property:

```
interface IVehicle
{
  void SetSpecificVehicleProperties();
  bool Drive();
  bool SlowDown();
  string Name
  {
    get;
    set;
  }
}
```

Once again there is no implementation. The line get; signifies that you can read from this property; and set; informs you that you can write to it – you can miss either of these out to get read-only or write-only properties.

Interfaces are very useful if you have some functionality that could be used by a wide range of classes: just look up the .NET Framework documentation, and see how many classes implement ICloneable! However don't put too much functionality into an interface, since any class that uses it must implement all methods and properties. An interface with ten methods and properties requires a lot of work from the programmer; a hundred would mean that your interface would probably never be used. Interfaces have to be carefully planned, and it is better to have ten interfaces offering one method each (ICloneable offers just one method called Clone()) than to have one interface offering ten. Also, interfaces can inherit from other interfaces (though obviously they cannot inherit from classes) which enables you to develop a hierarchy of interfaces where the base interface has general functionality on offer, while derived interfaces provide more specific functionality.

Converting between Object Types

In Chapter 4, we discussed in depth how to convert between different data types, summarized as follows:

1. We can carry out certain conversions implicitly such as an int to a long:

```
int intValue = 2;
long lngValue = intValue;
```

2. Many of the conversions we cannot carry out implicitly (such as `long` to `int`), we can specify by explicitly prefixing the variable we want to convert with the type in parentheses; such a conversion is usually called a **cast**:

```
long lngValue = 2;
int intValue = (int)lngValue;
```

We also looked at how to convert values to a string, and from a string (or another object) to one of the common numerical types using the `Convert.To...` series of functions. In this section we will look at ways of converting an object of one type to an object of another type.

Implicit Conversions

As with simple types, you can carry out implicit conversions between object types. However, if you think the rules were strict for the implicit conversion of simple types, they are positively stifling for objects. The fundamental principle for allowing implicit conversions is that there must be no risk of any data being lost. For simple types, the application of this is easy to understand: you can convert one type to another only if the range of the type being converted from will fit inside the range of the type being converted to, thus allowing `int` to `long`, and `float` to `double` conversions. For objects, though – which by their very nature are going to contain members of different types, including other object types and complex types – it is highly improbable that the conversion between one object and another will result in no data being lost. Therefore according to this definition, implicit conversions of objects are impossible.

However, there is another criterion that can be applied to objects, relating to inheritance. We have made much of the "is-a" relationship between a derived class and its base classes: a `FlyingCar` is a `Car`, and a `Car` is a `Vehicle`. Can this be extended to enable the objects themselves to be converted from one to another? The answer to this is yes, under certain circumstances.

So, taking our `Car` class and its derived `FlyingCar` class, you can covert a `FlyingCar` object to a `Car` object using code like this:

```
FlyingCar MyFlyingCar = new FlyingCar(1234567890);
Car MyNewCar = MyFlyingCar;
Response.Write(MyNewCar.GetType().FullName);
```

What we do here is create an instance of the derived class, assign it to a variable of the base class type and output the type of the latter. If you run this code, you get a surprising result:

ASP.test_aspx+FlyingCar

It seems that nothing has happened at all – the `Car` object is still, apparently, a `FlyingCar` object! Behind the scenes, the reference to the object has been changed so that it does not point to the `FlyingCar` object, but to its contained `Car` object. Remember that we said that all `FlyingCars` are `Cars`? As far as objects are concerned, `FlyingCar` objects contain their own `Car` objects, and what the conversion has achieved is to provide a reference to this embedded object. The `FlyingCar` object still exists, hence no data has been lost, so the original principle still holds, but now you cannot access the methods and properties unique to it, only those of the `Car` object.

In this diagram, the `FlyingCar` object is represented as a rectangle with a `Car` object as a second embedded rectangle. When you convert the `FlyingCar` to a `Car`, in effect what you are doing is shifting the focus from the outer rectangle representing the `FlyingCar` object with its embedded `Car` object to the inner rectangle representing only the embedded `Car` object. This means that you can access the `Color` property and call the `ChangeGear()` method but the `Altitude` property and `Ascend()` methods are no longer available.

Does it follow then that you can recover access to the `FlyingCar` object from its embedded `Car` object? Indeed this is so, only the conversion has to be done explicitly.

Explicit Conversions

Explicit conversions (or **casts**) between objects use the same syntax as those for simple types. You prefix the object instance with the type you want to convert to, enclosed in parentheses. However, as with implicit conversions, there are limits to the objects you can convert to, even explicitly. We have just said that you can recover access to a derived class that has been previously cast to its base type. You do this using an explicit cast as follows:

```
FlyingCar MyRecoveredFlyingCar = (FlyingCar)MyNewCar;
```

As with the implicit conversion already described, what we are actually changing here is the object reference. The original object, `MyNewCar`, was in fact a `FlyingCar` all the time, though because it has previously been cast to a `Car` type, only the `Car` object's methods and properties were accessible. Now the object reference has been reset to point to the external, containing `FlyingCar` object.

However, this is as far as explicit conversions go when converting between objects (other than those that are defined separately, and we shall come to these in just a moment). If the `MyNewCar` object had been created as a `Car` object in the first place, and you tried the very same line of code as above:

```
Car MyNewCar = new Car(1234567890);
FlyingCar MyRecoveredFlyingCar = (FlyingCar)MyNewCar;
```

371

you would get a runtime exception. This is because you cannot force a base type to be reinterpreted as a derived type. This is not allowed, even explicitly, because you would not be losing information by doing this, you would actually be *gaining* information, information for which no memory has been allocated. There is no way of adding the extra methods and properties unique to the derived class to the reinterpreted base class object, so this type of conversion is not allowed using casts. However, you can convert a base class object to a derived class instance using the longhand method of creating a derived class object and assigning values to all the properties one by one from the corresponding properties of the pre-existing base class object:

```
BaseClass b = new BaseClass();
b.PropertyA = ValueA;
b.PropertyB = ValueB;

DerivedClass d = new DerivedClass();
d.PropertyA = b.PropertyA;
d.PropertyB = b.PropertyB;
```

Boxing and Unboxing

We have shown that, within strict limits, you can convert between base and derived class objects. However a similar principle can be applied when converting between value and reference types. By reference types we are not talking about strings – we have covered these already. Here, we are talking about generic objects. Recall from our earlier discussions that the C# object type, an alias for the generic System.Object type, is a general purpose object, which can represent anything at all, and that includes value types such as ints, and doubles.

The term **boxing** is used to describe the process of converting a value type to a reference type, specifically an object type. However, this is not as simple as it appears. The memory allocated at compile time to an int is on the stack whereas the memory that is allocated at run time to an object is on the heap. When you box a variable, what you are in effect doing is taking it from the stack, copying it, and then placing the copy on the heap wrapped up as an object, leaving a reference to the object on the stack (along with the original variable, which remains). This is quite a severe change, though C# allows you to do it implicitly, as shown:

```
int x = 2;
object o = x;
```

This parallels what we have already seen when implicitly converting from a derived type to a base type. The object type represents the ultimate base type and like all .NET types, int represents a derived type called System.Int32.

So why would you do this? Well, you might have a variable in your code that is an int type (or any value type) that you need to pass to a function that requires an object type (or any reference type) as a parameter. Or, you might have an integer value that must be stored as an object type.

Say we have a hashtable that stores data on how many hits our web site receives. (For those who don't know, a hashtable is a kind of array, which stores data as key-value pairs – more on this in Chapter 11.) The hashtable's keys will be URLs, whereas the corresponding values would be integers, which have to be boxed in order to store them in the hashtable:

```
HashTable ht = new HashTable();
ht["http://www.wrox.com"] = 250;
ht["http://p2p.wrox.com"] = 175;
```

So once a variable has been boxed, is that the end of the story? Can it be converted back to a value type and its value placed on the stack? Well, of course it can. The reverse process of converting a variable of a reference type, that is `object`, back to a value type is called **unboxing**.

To unbox a variable, you just explicitly cast it back to the original type, whose value will be assigned to a variable on the stack, which can be either the original variable (which has been there all along and is not affected by any changes made to the boxed variable), or a brand new variable. This is illustrated in this code snippet:

```
int i = 20;
object o = i;
Response.Write(o.GetType().FullName);
Response.Write("<br/>");
i = 21;
int j = (int)o;
Response.Write("Value of original variable: " + i);
Response.Write("  Value of variable that was boxed: " + j);
```

An integer is assigned a value of 20 and then boxed. The `GetType()` function is called on the boxed variable to get its type and write it out, after which the original integer variable is modified. Then, a new integer variable is created and is assigned the value of the unboxed object instance using an explicit cast. Finally, the values of both integers are displayed. The output of this code is as follows:

System.Int32
Value of original variable: 21 Value of variable that was boxed: 20

The first line of output confirms that the boxed variable is still an `int` even though it is on the heap and not the stack at this point. The second line of output shows us that the original integer variable has persisted all the way through the operation and that only a copy of it was boxed.

To complete our hashtable example, we can unbox the values of the data stored there using syntax like this:

```
foreach (int item in ht.Values)
{
    // Use the int value item
}
```

Here the values contained in the hashtable are unboxed and assigned to the temporary variable `item`, which can then be used within the loop code to populate an integer array for example.

User-Defined Conversions

We have shown how to convert a derived class type to its base type and back again. We have shown how to convert a value type to a reference type and back again. Is that the end of the story as far as converting between object types is concerned?

This section introduces the final method of converting between two object types, the **user-defined conversion**, or **user-defined cast**. These are special functions that parallel operator overloads (and have a very similar syntax), and enable you to redefine how the C# casts operate:

```
Car MyCar = MyObject;              // implicit

Car MyCar = (ClassType)MyObject;  // explicit
```

There are certain rules that must be adhered to when dealing with user-defined casts:

- ❏ If you want to define an implicit cast, that is, one that does not require the type be prefixed in brackets, you have to specify this in the definition, otherwise the code will not compile.

- ❏ If you want to define an explicit cast, this has to be specified as well.

- ❏ You cannot define casts between objects where one is inherited from the other. The reason for this is that you can use the predefined mechanism, already explained, to convert a derived type to its base type and back again. However, this restriction also holds for converting an instance of a base type to a derived type; this type of cast is not possible at all.

- ❏ Casts can be defined between object types that are *not* inherited from one another. These can be completely unrelated classes or two classes with a common base class.

Let's illustrate this using the simple object hierarchy we looked at earlier. We have a Vehicle base class (which could also be an interface) and three derived classes Car, Truck, and Airplane. We have seen that we can cast up the hierarchy from Car to Vehicle and back again without needing to write any extra code. We also know that instantiable (that is non-abstract) Vehicle objects cannot be cast to any derived types. However, what if you have a Car object and you really want a Truck object? From the guidelines above, we can see that conversion between these two classes is possible using user-defined casts, and they do not inherit from one another. So how do we do it?

Coding user-defined casts requires planning. For example do you want implicit conversions such as:

```
Car MyCar = new Car();
Truck MyTruck = MyCar;
```

Or would you require explicit conversion:

```
Car MyCar = new Car();
Truck MyTruck = (Truck)MyCar;
```

Note that for the sake of simplicity, we have assumed a no-parameter constructor for the Car class in this section

The choice is up to you, but as with operator overloads, you have to decide whether such a conversion is meaningful, and if so, we have to go on to determine whether the conversion can be done automatically (that is implicitly) or whether you discern a risk in such a conversion, which would mean that you would require explicit conversion. For classes that are similar but not identical, you might decide on the former option. For classes where the conversion would result in much data being lost, then you might choose the latter option. Therefore, for classes whose structure and purpose are very different, you would be wise to choose the latter option. So let's look more closely at our three classes to assess the options:

❑   Car to Truck – meaningful and not risky

❑   Truck to Car – meaningful but risky, there could be data loss

❑   Car to Airplane – meaningless

❑   Truck to Airplane – meaningless

❑   Airplane to Car – meaningless

❑   Airplane to Truck – meaningless

So for the sake of illustration, we are going to define two casts, an implicit cast from Car to Truck and an explicit cast from Truck to Car.

The implicit cast is defined as follows:

```
public static implicit operator Truck (Car objCar)
{
  Truck t = new Truck();
  // Code here
  return t;
}
```

This can be placed in either the Truck or Car class definitions, but not both, because they would have the same signature. The compiler won't know which one to call and so will produce an error. For this reason, casts between one given object and another cannot be overloaded.

Note the similarity between this and the operator overload syntax that we discussed in the previous chapter. Once again, user-defined casts have to be declared public and static in order for them to be accessible to external code without the need to create a class instance. The implicit keyword tells the compiler that the cast being defined can be an implicit one (though it can be called explicitly as well). The operator keyword tells the compiler that the object type that follows is the destination type for the cast object. The single parameter in brackets is the object whose type is undergoing the cast operation. In the function body, an object instance of the destination type has to be created, and after any code has been run, this object is returned.

What happens in this code is completely up to you – the only requirement is that the appropriate object type is returned. A typical use of such a conversion would be to transfer member data between the old type and the new, filling fields with common (that is inherited) or compatible values:

```
public static implicit operator Truck (Car objCar)
{
  Truck t = new Truck();
  t.Color = objCar.Color;            // Common (inherited) or compatible
  t.EngineType = objCar.EngineType;  // property values
// etc.

  return t;
}
```

and to assign default values to the properties of the destination object that are not found in the original object, or to call methods on the destination object to fill up certain property values:

```
public static implicit operator Truck (Car objCar)
{
  Truck t = new Truck();
  t.Color = objCar.Color;
  t.EngineType = objCar.EngineType;
  t.LoadCapacity = 100;              // Property unique to Truck objects
  t.ChangeGear(0);                   // Method call (put gear in neutral)
// etc.
  return t;
}
```

To invoke this cast you would use direct assignment like this:

```
Car MyCar = new Car();
Truck MyTruck = MyCar;
```

Explicit casts are defined in a very similar way, only they use the explicit keyword instead of the implicit keyword:

```
public static explicit operator Car (Truck objTruck)
{
  Car c = new Car();
  c.Color = objTruck.Color;
  c.EngineType = objTruck.EngineType;
  c.ChangeGear(0);
// etc.
  return c;
}
```

Other than that, the code has a similar structure to that of an implicit cast. However there is one thing further to note – if you try to use an explicit cast implicitly the compiler will generate an error.

To invoke this cast you would use syntax like this:

```
Truck MyTruck = new Truck();
Car MyCar = (Car)MyTruck;
```

Employing user-defined casts can be risky, especially if you are using a predefined class as one of your objects and you don't really know what object types you are dealing with. It is best to use structured error handling (`try...catch`) when you come to use your casts to deal with any run-time errors that might occur. See Chapter 17 for more details on this.

Summary

In this chapter we've looked at some of the relationships it's possible to establish between object classes, and considered both the principles behind them and how we use them in our ASP.NET pages. While objects are by no means a universal panacea for all our problems, they can help us enormously in our endeavors to write robust, organized code, and to do so quickly and efficiently.

❏ **They appeal to the way humans think**. It's quite intuitive to build pages using objects with names such as `DateTime`, `Page`, `Button`, `Label`, and `Browser`. These words describe concepts we're already familiar with, and we can work with them in a way that is natural to us.

❏ **They help us write simpler, more efficient code**. Once we have broken a complex application into units of encapsulated functionality, we can more readily focus on specific problems, rather than trying to take on board the application as a whole. This increased focus helps us to write code faster, since there's less for us to think about at any given time. Furthermore, each unit is likely to consist of simpler program code than it would otherwise.

❏ **They make it easier to reuse code**. By building an application up from self-contained, task-specific pieces, we are more likely to be able to reuse these pieces in other contexts. The .NET Framework is a great example of reusing objects – we can write robust, efficient web forms faster, since the Framework provides us with so much ready-built functionality.

❏ **They help us write code that's easier to change later**. We find that when an application has grown, although it becomes more complex, the fact that it still consists of a set of objects that work together means we can more easily locate the objects that need changing.

❏ **They help us write more reliable code**. Since objects are both self-contained and well defined, it's relatively easy to write code to test them thoroughly. Once an object has been thoroughly tested, we can reuse it many times without having to worry about its robustness.

❏ **They help us write more comprehensible code**. If you break down your program's functionality in a logical, systematic fashion, and model it on identifiable real-world entities, other users should find it relatively easy to figure out what each object does. In an ideal situation, a newcomer to your application can establish a simple understanding of how it works based on just a brief exposure to the code.

It's often useful to create methods or properties that are shared between all the objects created from a specific class. These are called shared methods or shared properties and we use them by referencing the class name instead of the object name – for example: `numberOfUsers = User.Count`.

It's very common in .NET for an object to contain another object. This happens because a property on one object returns another type of object. When this happens we can use a special syntax to keep code tidier: `ObjectA.ObjectB.ObjectC.SomeMethod()`.

Every class defined in .NET inherits from `Object`, whose properties and methods are therefore available on all objects. Each class has its own methods and properties, but also gets a few for free, courtesy of the `Object` class. These include the `GetType` property, which tells us what type the object is. This can be used on objects of any class, even those we define ourselves for which we have not defined a `GetType` member.

Now we have looked at object-oriented programming in general, and a few specific classes that .NET provides, the next chapter will explore some of the useful objects that ASP.NET makes available to our web forms.

Exercises

1. Name three different types of class relationship, and give examples of when it would be appropriate to use each one.

2. Create an ASP.NET page that displays the current date and time using the shared property `Now` of the `DateTime` class.

3. Define an `Account` class for library users that has a `Borrow()` method, and an `Item` class that represents a library book with properties `Title` and `ISBN`. Code the `Borrow()` method so that it gets the title and ISBN of the borrowed book from the `Item` object.

4. Define an `Engine` class, whose properties include `SerialNo`, `Rpm`, and `Name` (to be set by the class constructor), and whose methods include `SwitchOn` and `SwitchOff`. Now integrate it with the `Car` class so that you can access these properties and methods from instances of the `Car` class.

5. Using inheritance, define a `FlyingCar` class that has an `Ascend()` method, a `Descend()` method and read-only property that returns the altitude of the flying car.

Objects in ASP.NET

The bulk of the .NET Framework consists of a huge library of object classes, and just about anything we do in ASP.NET will make substantial use of objects that have been defined by these classes. One of the dominant characteristics of .NET is that it defines everything – from intrinsic variables, right up to full-blown applications – as explicit objects.

The Framework includes literally hundreds of classes, which is great for us, as it means we have a tremendous amount of ready-made functionality on tap. That means we have less code to write, and can do things quicker and more easily. Don't be put off by the number of classes there are to learn; some may already be familiar to you and the rest will just take a little time, but it's worth it!

The classes provided help us out with a whole host of different tasks: working with files, XML data, databases, web pages, monitoring web site performance, generating random numbers – in fact it's almost a case of 'you name it, there's a class for it'. We're going to be spending most of the rest of the book getting to know the objects you're most likely to use with ASP.NET, what they are, and what we can do with them.

For now, we're going to focus specifically on the objects that are central to how ASP.NET functions. In doing so, we will start to crystallize your understanding of how ASP.NET hangs together, and how you can get the most out of it when developing web applications. In the course of the chapter, you'll learn about:

- ❑ Namespaces and finding classes in .NET
- ❑ The Page class, and some of the useful things it enables us to do – such as redirecting visitors to other pages, and finding out about the browser your visitor is using
- ❑ ASP.NET applications and application state – what web applications are, and how to store commonly used pieces of information centrally in a web site
- ❑ ASP.NET sessions and session state – looking at how a shopping basket system might work, and saving visitors' preferences

Namespaces

Some of the many classes that .NET includes provide the fundamental building blocks of .NET programming (basic data types like `System.String` and `System.Bool`, classes that let the user manipulate files, and so on), while some relate specifically to web development, and others to developing Windows applications. Many more are potentially useful in any number of situations (supporting features such as security and localization).

> **Localization is the process of 'translating' the language used in the user interface of a computer program to different languages and dialects.**

Before we start looking at the most important web development objects, let's consider how we go about finding the classes we need. The .NET Framework uses a rather neat naming scheme to organize all its classes: **namespaces**. A namespace is a group of similar classes. For example, if you wanted to find classes that let you connect to a database, you'd look for classes that are listed as being in the `System.Data namespace`. If you want to look for classes that let you build web pages, look for classes listed as being in the `System.Web` namespace. Both of these namespaces are contained within the general `System` namespace. These particular namespaces contain classes that can be used to implement input/output processes (`.IO`) and web (`.Web`) development respectively.

> *The names of namespaces are usually quite short, but always very accurate in describing what classes they contain. For example, the `System.XML` namespace contains classes to do almost anything you can think of with XML data.*

Namespaces are arranged hierarchically, with `System` at the root; `System` contains all the classes that define the fundamental building blocks. For example, the definition of `bool` and `string` types are in the `System` namespace, as they can be used within all namespaces. The `System.Web` namespace contains generic classes for building web sites, while `System.Web.UI` has classes for building pages from user interface components like buttons. When we want to program HTML buttons, we'll use a much less widely used class, way down in `System.Web.UI.HtmlControls`. You can see how the hierarchy flows.

> **As a rule, classes at the top of the tree are highly generic, while those towards the bottom are highly specialized.**

Think about how postal addresses work across the world, and how they relate to individual houses or offices. In our case, the things we're trying to locate are classes (houses), and we work out where they are by using namespaces that describe their location (postal addresses).

When we reference a class in a namespace, we use this syntax:

```
<namespace name>.<class name>
```

For example, the class we use to work with files is called `File`, and it lives in the `System.IO` namespace, so we reference it like this:

```
System.IO.File
```

We can then extend that to reference methods, or properties, of the class (the following code is a simplified version of how to open a file, but for now, let's just get hold of the concept):

```
System.IO.File.Open("filename.txt")
```

In some places, you'll see the C# keyword `Import` used to import a namespace to a file, so that we can reference the class name directly. For example if a page imports the `System.IO` namespace, it can reference the `File` class without explicitly prefixing it with the namespace:

```
File.Open("filename.txt")
```

There are three main reasons why Microsoft has arranged the .NET classes into namespaces in this way:

❑ **Organization** – There are far too many classes to usefully put in a list. Since the namespaces are organized hierarchically, it's quite easy (and intuitive) to browse through them and find out what's available (in the .NET documentation or on the Microsoft Developer Network web site at http://msdn.microsoft.com). If we know about a class that resides in a particular namespace, we can be pretty sure that similar classes are also held in that namespace. This means we can easily find classes related to one we're already using, as well as seeing what other functionality .NET provides in that area.

❑ **Universality** – One of the biggest hazards of object-oriented programming on a large scale is the possibility that two different classes of a type of object will be mistaken for one another. As you might recall from the last chapter, we had to import the `Cars` namespace before using the `Car` class. Supposing there was already a base class called `Car` in the `System.Web.Util` namespace; as long as we don't import that namespace as well, there is no room for ambiguity when we come to say `Car MyCar = new Car()`. Sooner or later, we may well want to start creating our own – so .NET doesn't just have to manage Microsoft's classes, but any that we create as well.

❑ **Ease of use** – By default; we must reference classes using a full namespace hierarchy. However, as we said above, once we import a namespace, the classes within it can be referenced simply by name. Since the classes are arranged in logical function-specific groups, we can usually get away with importing a few namespaces, and then referencing all the classes by name only. You only have to try working with the classes in `System.Security.Cryptography` (for example) to appreciate how much typing this can save you!

Use of namespaces in .NET stems from their use in XML schemas: many situations require the structure of an XML document to be well-defined (in the same way that we need to know the methods and properties of an object) in order for software to usefully interact with it. See www.w3.org/TR/REC-xml-names for more details.

Namespaces for ASP.NET

All the web-related classes (forming the backbone of everything we do in ASP.NET) are grouped together in (and below) the `System.Web` namespace. While the most important ASP.NET classes are held in the `System.Web` namespace, we're going to be using plenty of classes from other namespaces in the course of the book. These, then, are the namespaces that we'll make most use of when building web sites with ASP.NET:

❑ `System.Web` – This provides a large range of classes that help us build web sites. `System.Web` is imported automatically into any ASPX file you run, and the classes it holds are responsible for virtually all of the web-based functionality we've seen so far – more on these shortly.

❑ `System.Web.UI` – This provides classes that represent the controls we use to build web pages, for example HTML elements, buttons, labels, calendars and dropdown lists. We were actually using some of the `System.Web.UI` classes in Chapter 3, when we looked at web forms. We'll see them again in Chapter 14, when we look at server controls.

❑ `System.IO` – As we saw earlier, this namespace provides classes we can use to work with files.

❑ `System.Collections` – Holds various collections classes. Collections are objects that contain lists of other objects; we'll take a look at them more closely in the next chapter.

❑ `System.Diagnostics` – This namespace holds classes that can help us diagnose problems when things go wrong. We'll see more of this in Chapter 17.

❑ `System.Data` – We use classes in this namespace to work with data and databases. We'll come across these classes in Chapter 12 and Chapter 13.

❑ `System.Globalization` – Classes in this namespace help us to create globalized web sites that can work in different parts of world.

❑ `System.Drawing` – The classes in this namespace offer us graphical functions, so that we can dynamically generate images.

❑ `System.XML` – This namespace is home to a number of classes for working with XML data.

These are still just a small proportion of the overall set of base classes in the .NET Framework – to fully document them all would be a mammoth undertaking. The focus of this chapter will be specifically on the classes within the `System.Web` and `System.Web.UI` namespaces. We're going to start off by looking at the class used to help define the 'magic object' that lurks quietly behind every ASP.NET page we see.

The Page Class

To understand the role of the `Page` class, it's important to have a picture of what's going on when we request an ASP.NET page from the web server. As we know, IIS hands over most of the hard work involved to the .NET Framework.

When a browser initially calls up an ASP.NET page, IIS recognizes that this is an ASPX file request, and lets the ASP.NET module (`aspnet_isapi.dll`) deal with it. The `aspnet_isapi.dll` places the ASPX file we request into a new class definition. This new class is defined in a namespace called `ASP`;

so the contents of a file called `mypage.aspx` end up in a class called `ASP.mypage_aspx`.

The easiest way to see this class definition is to actually break the code in your ASPX file. By default, the error message presented will give you the option to View Compilation Source, *and this compilation source, in our example above, would be a file called* ASP.mypage_aspx.

The new `ASP` class is then instantiated as an object in the CLR. A render method is then called on our new object, that returns appropriate HTML via the `aspnet_isapi.dll` to IIS, which then sends the HTML to the client that originally made the request. We can see this process taking place in the diagram below:

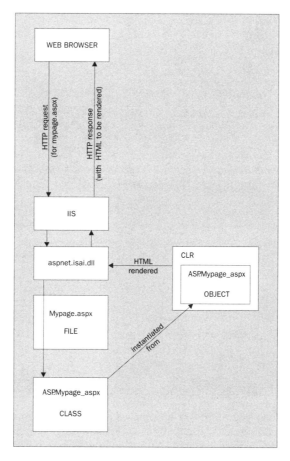

So that's how .NET gets us from an ASPX file on the server to an HTTP Response full of useful HTML. What we haven't mentioned is the fact that our `ASP` class inherits from the `Page` class. This means that our ASP.NET page has access to the useful functionality that the `Page` class provides.

The `Page` class lives in the `System.Web.UI` namespace, (`UI` refers to 'User Interface', which is what users of our web site see on the page constructed from HTML). Let's update our diagram to incorporate this important aspect:

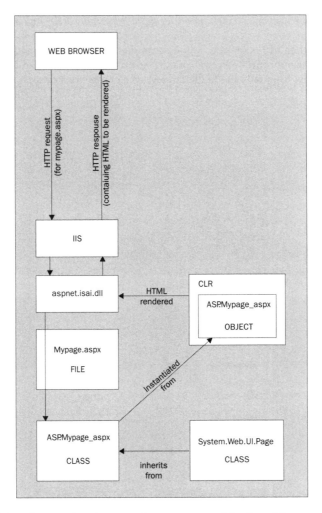

The `Page` class is like a fairy godmother, as it brings us a wealth of useful properties and methods that we can use on our ASP.NET pages. It also gives us access to a range of other objects created from classes in the `System.Web` namespace, and we'll be looking at these later on in this chapter. To whet your appetite, here is just a small selection of the things it enables us to do:

- ❑ Redirect users to another page
- ❑ Find out about the web browser our visitor is using
- ❑ Find out what web site the person was on before they came to ours
- ❑ Personalize pages for our visitors

❑   Store commonly used information centrally

❑   Find out exactly what web address the person typed in to get to our web page

Now let's look at the first item on the above list in more detail.

Redirecting the User to Another Page

Sometimes when we build a web page, we want to automatically send the user to another page. For example, if an unauthenticated user tried to access a password-protected page on a web site, we'd want them to be redirected to a page where they are asked to sign in and provide a password.

The Page object has a property called Response. We have come across the Response property a few times in the book, but in this chapter, we'll learn a little more about how it actually works. When called, the Response property returns an object of the type HttpResponse. This features a method called Redirect that we can use to send the user off to another page; we just pass it a string representing the web address of the new page.

For example, we could create a very simple ASP.NET page (redirect.aspx) that automatically redirects us to the Wrox web site:

```
<%@ Page Language="c#" %>
<%
  Response.Redirect("http://www.wrox.com/");
%>
```

At the moment, we're focusing on the Redirect method, but we will look at the Response object in more detail shortly.

Let's look at a slightly more useful example.

Try It Out – Navigating with a Drop-down List

In this example, we're going to display a drop-down list that shows some web sites and a button, both of which will be created using server controls. When we select one and click the Go button, we'll be taken to the web site we have chosen.

1.   Open up your editor and type in the following code:

```
<%@ Page Language="c#" %>
<html>
  <body>
    <form id="WebForm1" method="post" runat="server">
      <asp:DropDownList id=MyDropDownList runat="server"/>
      <asp:button id=MyButton runat="server" Text=""/>
    </form>
  </body>
</html>
```

2. Save this file as `navigator.aspx`. If you call up the file from your browser at this stage, you'll see this:

We can see that both the drop-down list and the button are shown, although both are rather small, as we haven't added any items yet!

3. Let's add some code to do that – update the code as marked:

```
<%@ Page Language="c#" %>
<script Language="c#" runat="server">
  void Page_Load(object source, EventArgs e)
  {
    if (!(IsPostBack))
    {
      MyButton.Text = "OK";
      MyDropDownList.Items.Add("http://www.microsoft.com");
      MyDropDownList.Items.Add("http://www.wrox.com");
      MyDropDownList.Items.Add("http://msdn.microsoft.com");
    }
  }
</script>
<html>
  <body>
    <form id="WebForm1" method="post" runat="server">
      <asp:DropDownList id=MyDropDownList runat="server"/>
      <asp:button id=MyButton runat="server" Text=""/>
    </form>
  </body>
</html>
```

View the file again in your browser, and you'll see that the button now says **OK** and the drop-down list contains three items describing three web site addresses:

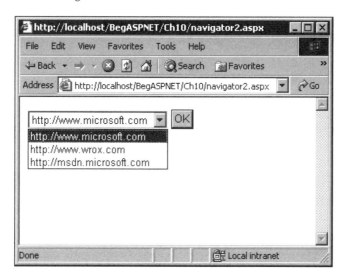

4. Now we have a page that looks the way we want, but if we select a web site from the list and click **OK**, nothing happens. Let's fix that now; add the marked code:

```
<%@ Page Language="c#" %>
<script Language="c#" runat="server">
  void Page_Load(object source, EventArgs e)
  {
    if (!(IsPostBack))
    {
      MyButton.Text = "OK";
      MyDropDownList.Items.Add("http://www.microsoft.com");
      MyDropDownList.Items.Add("http://www.wrox.com");
      MyDropDownList.Items.Add("http://msdn.microsoft.com");
    }
  }
  public void Click (object sender, EventArgs e)
  {
    Response.Redirect(MyDropDownList.SelectedItem.Text);
  }
</script>

<html>
  <body>
    <form id="WebForm1" method="post" runat="server">
      <asp:DropDownList id=MyDropDownList runat="server"/>
      <asp:button id=MyButton runat="server" OnClick="Click" Text=""/>
    </form>
  </body>
</html>
```

5. Save the page, and open it in your browser again, and you'll find that when you select an item and click **OK**, you'll be taken to the web site you selected.

389

How It Works

Let's take a quick look through the code we've just added. First of all, we create a drop-down list and a button:

```
<asp:DropDownList id=MyDropDownList runat="server"/>
<asp:button id=MyButton runat="server" OnClick="Click" Text=""/>
```

Next, we make sure this is the first time the page has been viewed:

```
if (!(IsPostBack))
{
```

We added this check because the page is reloaded every time the OK button is clicked, to carry out our Redirect method. In effect, this means that without this test each time we press the button another three duplicate items would appear in the drop-down list, as they would be reloaded. After this, we have a statement that adds the text OK to the button:

```
MyButton.Text = "OK";
```

In fact, we could just as easily do this by including a value attribute (Text="OK") in the <asp:Button> line. In this case, we chose to use a line of code to do it, as it's a nice simple demonstration of how we can manipulate a button using code.

Then we add three items to the drop-down list using the Add method, which takes a string as a parameter:

```
MyDropDownList.Items.Add("http://www.microsoft.com");
MyDropDownList.Items.Add("http://www.wrox.com");
MyDropDownList.Items.Add("http://msdn.microsoft.com");
```

Moving on, the first change we made was to add an **event handler** to the button definition. What we're saying is "When someone clicks here (which causes an event), execute the specified function (handle the event)."

```
<asp:button id=MyButton runat="server" OnClick="Click" Text=""/>
```

Next, we added the event handler itself, the Click() function, which starts off like this:

```
public void Click (object sender, EventArgs e)
{
```

The important things to notice here are that, firstly this is a function, and secondly that it is called Click(). Of secondary importance are the parameters that are passed to the function. Nearly all event handlers in the .NET Framework take these two parameters. The first parameter is a reference to the control or object that actually fired the event. The second parameter is a reference to an object that gives extra information about the event itself. In our case, sender will be the button object that the user clicked and e will be blank, because no extra information is passed through with this event.

Next you can see the `Response.Redirect()` method call, just like we used in the last example, except this time, we're passing it a string parameter that we obtain by using the `Text` property on the selected `MyDropDownList` item:

```
    Response.Redirect(MyDropDownList.SelectedItem.Text);
}
</script>
```

This example was a pretty good demonstration of ASP.NET pages that use some objects and work with events; we'll be doing a lot more of this throughout the rest of the book.

Now we've seen the .NET Framework from a high level, and we've seen how to use the `Redirect()` method of the `HttpResponse` class.

The `HttpResponse` provides a way for the page to communicate with the browser. It is commonly used to send HTML code back to the browser and, as in this case, tell the browser to load a different page. We can get hold of an instance of `HttpResponse` through the `Response` property of the `Page` class.

Let's look at the `Response` object and its cousins in the `System.Web` namespace in a little more detail.

ASP.NET Core Objects

In this section, we'll look at what are perhaps the most important objects in ASP.NET:

- ❑ `Request` – gives us access to information about the person or process requesting the web page

- ❑ `Response` – provides a way for us to accurately control how the Response is sent back to the person who made the Request

- ❑ `Server` – provides a range of useful web-related utilities

- ❑ `Application` – implements a useful site-wide storage location for frequently used information

- ❑ `Session` – makes it possible for us to store information for each user's session, for example, a shopping cart

These objects are fundamental to how ASP.NET operates, and also to how we make use of ASP.NET's features. Before we look at the objects themselves and the facilities they provide, let's see how ASP.NET makes these objects available to us.

Each of the objects (`Request`, `Response`, and so on) is created from a class. For example, although we refer to the `Response` object, it is created from the `System.Web.HttpResponse` class. The reason we call it the `Response` object is because the specific instance of the `HttpResponse` class that we're interested in is accessible using a property of our `Page` object called `Response`.

Remember the diagram we looked at when we were seeing how the `Page` object fitted into the process of retrieving an ASPX page? Let's look at the lower part of that diagram again to see exactly how the `Response` object is called. Say our file, `mypage.aspx`, contains a `Response.Redirect` command – this is how it would be accessed:

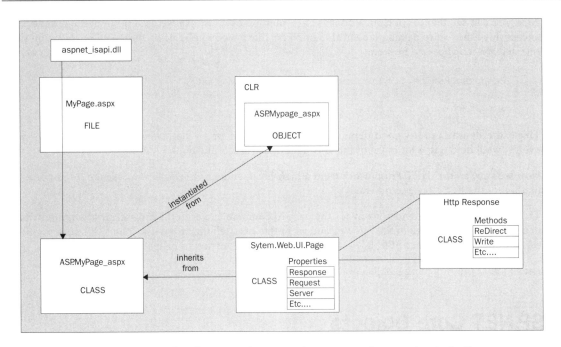

You can see in the diagram that the `Page` class provides a range of properties, including `Response`, `Request`, and `Server`. When we access the `Response` property, it returns an object of the type `HttpResponse`. We can then use methods from that object, such as `Redirect()`.

What this means is that, because there's no work to do in locating the relevant object, we can use a very simple statement to access methods and properties on an `HttpResponse` object (or any of the others) directly from our ASP.NET page.

Now we know how to get at these objects, let's find out what they can do for us.

Request Object

When someone opens a web browser and requests a web page from our site, our web server receives an HTTP Request that contains a whole load of information about the user, their PC, the page, and their browser. As we noted in the last chapter, all that information is neatly packaged up and made available to us in the `Request` object.

This means that, rather than being concerned with finding bits of information from all over the place, everything related to that single HTTP Request is provided in a single object, which contains a series of methods and properties we can use to find out what we need to know. The `Request` object is effectively passing a message to us from the person's web browser saying, "Here's who I am, and here's what I want."

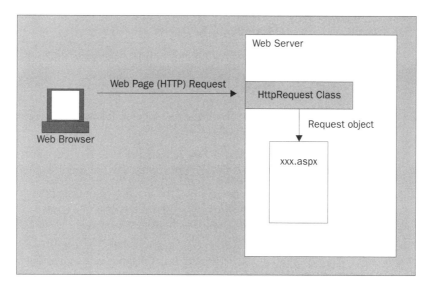

We've already looked briefly at this object and its `Browser` property – let's take a look at the rest of the properties that are returned as part of the `HttpRequest` class:

Property	Description
ApplicationPath	Tells us which folder of our web application the requested page lives in.
Path	Is the same as `ApplicationPath` in that it returns the full web address path to where our page is, but also includes the page's filename.
PhysicalApplicationPath	Returns the full path to our page, but on our physical disk, not as a web address.
Browser	Provides access to the `Browser` object that is hugely useful in finding out about the visitor's web browser software and its capabilities.
Cookies	This property lets us see the cookies that the visitor may have from previous visits to our site. We'll look at cookies later in the chapter.
IsSecureConnection	Whether the HTTP connection is using encryption (in most cases it won't be).
RequestType	Whether the Request was a GET or POST request.
QueryString	Returns any parameters that have been passed to the page using GET.

Table continued on following page

Property	Description
Url	Returns the complete address as submitted by the browser.
	To display the web address held by the Uri object as a string, we use its method ToString().
RawUrl	Like Url, but the protocol and domain name are omitted from the beginning.
	(So if http://www.wrox.com/article.aspx is returned by Url, RawUrl returns /article.aspx.)
UserHostName	Returns the name of the machine requesting the page from our web server. (In some cases, knowing the name of the user's computer can be useful in identifying the user for security purposes.)
UserHostAddress	Returns the IP address of the machine requesting our page.
UserLanguages	Tells us what language settings the browser has configured.

As usual, the syntax we use to access these commands is:

```
Request.PropertyName
```

Now let's put a couple of these properties to use.

Try It Out – Checking the Browser

In this example, we'll create a variation on our containment.aspx example from the last chapter. This web form will look at what version of Internet Explorer we're using, and suggest we upgrade if we're not using version 6 or later.

1. Open up your editor and type in the following code:

```
<%@ Page Language="c#" %>
<script Language="c#" runat="server">
  void Page_Load(object source, EventArgs e)
  {
    if (!(IsPostBack))
    {
      if (Request.Browser.Browser == "IE")
      {
        if (Request.Browser.MajorVersion < 6)
        {
          MyLabel.Text = "Time to upgrade Internet Explorer!";
        }
        else
        {
          MyLabel.Text = "Your copy of Internet Explorer is up to date.";
```

```
          }
      }
      else
      {
          MyLabel.Text = "You're not using Internet Explorer";
      }
    }
  }
</script>
<html>
  <body>
    <asp:Label id=MyLabel runat="server" Text=""/>
  </body>
</html>
```

2. Save this file as `browsercheck.aspx`.

3. Open up your browser and view the file. If you're using Internet Explorer 6, you'll see this:

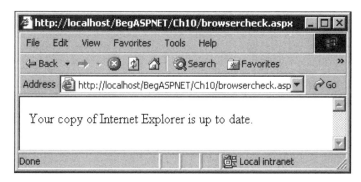

Otherwise you'll get a message telling you it's time to upgrade!

How It Works

Let's deal with the HTML first. At the end of our code is a simple ASP.NET label control called `MyLabel`:

```
<html>
  <body>
    <asp:Label id=MyLabel runat="server" Text=""/>
  </body>
</html>
```

When ASP.NET runs the page, it will fire the load event on the page. This will cause the `Page_Load` event handler we added in the script block to be executed:

```c#
<%@ Page Language="c#" %>
<script Language="c#" runat="server">
  void Page_Load(object source, EventArgs e)
  {
```

Once the page is loaded, the first thing we want to do, is check to see if the page has been posted back, or whether it's the first time it has been accessed. We use the `IsPostBack` method here to check that, just as we did when we created `navigator.aspx`, previously:

```c#
if (!(IsPostBack))
{
```

We've already discussed the `Browser` property, but here we're using two objects within the `Browser` property: `Browser` and `MajorVersion`. `Browser` is used to return the name of the browser, and `MajorVersion` returns the version number of the browser being used. So then, firstly, we check to see if the name of the browser is given as IE:

```c#
if (Request.Browser.Browser == "IE")
{
```

and, if it is, we check to see what the version number is:

```c#
if (Request.Browser.MajorVersion < 6)
{
```

If the version number is less than 6, we politely suggest to the user that they upgrade. If not, we tell the user that it's up to date. In both cases, we tell the user by setting the `Text` property of the `MyLabel` control that we created at the start of the page:

```c#
  MyLabel.Text = "Time to upgrade Internet Explorer!";
}
else
{
  MyLabel.Text = "Your copy of Internet Explorer is up to date.";
}
}
```

On the other hand, the user might not be using Internet Explorer, in which case, we tell them that!

```c#
else
    {
      MyLabel.Text = "You're not using Internet Explorer";
    }
  }
}
</script>
```

Response Object

Just as the `Request` object lets us see the incoming HTTP Request, the `Response` object provides access to the HTTP Response that is going to be sent back to the requesting web browser. This response includes the HTML for the requested page:

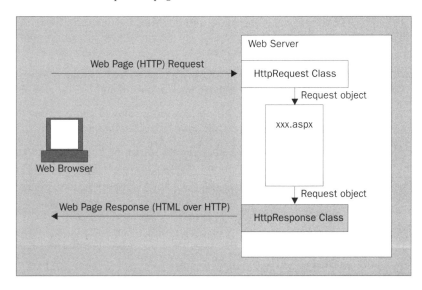

The `Response` object is of the type `HttpResponse`. The `HttpResponse` class provides a range of properties and methods for us to use, including the `Write()` and `Redirect()` methods that we've used in previous examples.

When ASP.NET is running the code in our pages, it gradually builds up the HTML that will be sent back to the browser. ASP.NET has what's called a **buffer**; as the HTML is generated, it is placed in the buffer. Normally the HTML is held in the buffer so that it isn't sent to the browser until the page finishes executing; however, we can change that behavior if we want. (In most cases, it's **not** useful to change this behavior, but we're going to do it here in order to illustrate an important point about ASP.NET performance.) The `Response` object is where we tell the page buffer what we want it to do; it's our way of managing what gets sent back to the web browser, and how and when it is sent.

Here are some of the most useful properties and methods on the `HttpResponse` class:

Property	Description
`Buffer`	The default value of this property is `True`, which means the page is buffered and sent in one block. If we set it to `False`, the Response will be sent piecemeal along the wires as and when each piece is generated. Sending the HTML in pieces like this is much slower than using the buffer, but it means the site visitor has the chance to see some HTML before the page has finished executing (which is useful if your user might be left waiting for a long piece of code to be compiled.

Table continued on following page

Property	Description
ContentType	With this property, we can set the type of data we're sending back. This setting specifies what's called a **MIME type**. (MIME, or **Multipurpose Internet Mail Extensions** is a way of identifying the different kinds of resources that Internet services like the Web and e-mail can transfer. An HTML page is represented with the MIME type text/html. A GIF image with image/gif and so on). The details of how this works aren't important for most browsers, however.
Cookies	The use of this property is how we save visitors' settings to their hard drive. We'll look at cookies in detail later in the chapter.
Clear()	If we call this method, the buffer will be emptied and the contents discarded, but we can continue and add more HTML to it if we want to.
Flush()	When we call this method all the HTML in the buffer is sent to the web browser, but we can continue creating HTML.
End()	This command is terminal; it sends all the HTML from the buffer and our page stops executing. It's useful if we want to end page execution and ensure we don't send anything else across to the web browser.
Redirect()	We've seen this method in action already; it redirects the user to another page.
	Note that one important rule with Redirect is that no HTML is allowed to already have been sent to the browser. You can ensure that this is the case by explicitly not outputting any HTML, or by turning on buffering and not sending the contents of the buffer (don't use Flush or End!). ASP.NET will produce an error if you attempt to use Redirect when HTML has already been sent to the browser.
Write()	We've seen this method in action too; it just writes a string to the HTML stream, if buffering is turned on, it'll write to the buffer and wait to be sent later.
WriteFile()	This method is exactly the same as Write, except it writes the contents of a file to the HTML output stream.

Let's look at an example page that uses some of these methods and properties so we can see, in more concrete terms, what the Response object lets us do.

Try It Out – HTML Buffering

In this example we'll create a page that we can use to see what effect buffering has on our pages. By default, buffering is turned on, but we'll see what happens when we turn it off.

1. Open up your editor and type in the following code:

```
<%@ Page Language="c#" %>
<html>
  <body>
    <%;
```

```
        for (int i = 0; i < 50; i++)
        {
          Response.Write(" X");
        }
      %>
    </body>
</html>
```

2. Save this file as `buffer.aspx` in your web site.

3. Open up your browser and view the file. You'll see this:

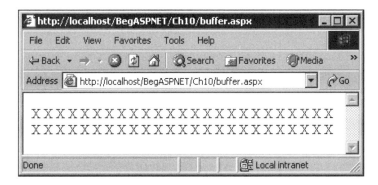

Notice that the page contents appear quickly, and in one go.

4. Now add the marked line of code to turn off buffering:

```
<%@ Page Language="c#" %>
<html>
  <body>
    <%;
    Response.Buffer = false;
    for (int i = 0; i < 50; i++)
    {
      Response.Write(" X");
    }
    %>
  </body>
</html>
```

5. Now reload the page in your web browser. You'll find that the page no longer appears in one burst, but as a trickle of HTML as each of the Xs appears. You'll also see that it is much, much slower.

If you find that your machine doesn't seem much slower the second time, try increasing the 50 value in the code sample.

How It Works

To start with, we created a `for` loop which loops our integer variable `i` 50 times:

```
<%@ Page Language="c#" %>
<html>
  <body>
    <%;
    for (int i = 0; i < 50; i++)
    {
      Response.Write(" X");
    }
    %>
  </body>
</html>#
```

Then we turned buffering off by setting the `Response.Buffer` object to `false`:

```
Response.Buffer = false;
```

With buffering switched on, ASP.NET will collect the entire HTML document that makes up the page, before sending it back to the server. The advantage of this approach is that the performance of building the page up using the code we write on the page remains relatively constant. ASP.NET asks for the HTML that makes up page, it gets the HTML, and then it passes it back to IIS, and tells IIS to send it back to the browser. When we first tried `buffer.aspx`, we saw it loaded quickly.

> **With buffering switched off, ASP.NET passes the text to IIS character-by-character. This means that it will take longer to physically process the page from top to bottom. On most web sites, you get better performance with buffering switched on, as it takes more processing power and system resources to build the page incrementally than it does to send it all back down to the client in one go.**

Let's look at another example that uses the `Response` object.

Try It Out – Response.WriteFile()

In this example, we'll create a page that displays the contents of a text file that's located in the same folder as our ASP.NET page.

1. Open up your editor and type in the following code:

```
<%@ Page Language="c#" %>
<html>
  <body>
    <H2>Response.WriteFile()</H2>
    <%
    string FileName;
```

```
      //make sure the text file is in the correct place.

      FileName = Request.PhysicalApplicationPath + "file.txt";
      Response.WriteFile(FileName);
      %>
   </body>
</html>
```

2. Save this file as `writefile.aspx` in your web site.

3. Create a file called `file.txt` in the root folder of the application that `writefile.aspx` is in (if you are using the physical directory we set up in Chapter 1, we're talking about the `BegASPNET` folder), and type this code into it:

```
<B>this text has come from file.txt</B>
```

4. Open up your browser and view the `writefile.aspx` file. You'll see this:

We can see that the text from `file.txt` has appeared in our page.

How It Works

The `PhysicalApplicationPath` property of `Request` returns the path that the web site is actually installed on. We take this path, and tack the name of our file onto the end of it, in this case `"file.txt"`:

```
<%
string FileName;
FileName = Request.PhysicalApplicationPath + "file.txt";
```

Once we have a filename, we pass it over to the `WriteFile` method:

```
Response.WriteFile(FileName);
%>
```

This method opens the file, reads its contents, and inserts the contents of the file into the HTML that makes up the page.

Server Object

The Page class also gives us access to a property called Server that returns an object of the type HttpServerUtility. This class defines a general-purpose web-related toolbox that includes some very useful bits of functionality.

Here are some of the most useful methods and properties:

Member	Description
MachineName	This read-only property returns the Windows name of the machine that ASP.NET is running on.
ScriptTimeOut	This property gets, and sets, the amount of time before an ASP.NET page times out; this will happen if the code takes an extraordinary amount of time to execute. The default setting for the ScriptTimeOut property is 90 seconds. It's generally not necessary to change this value, but if your web site is generating huge pages, or ones that take an enormous amount of time to generate, you may need to extend it.
HtmlEncode()	This method takes a string, and encodes it so it can be displayed in a browser. Browsers can display most text without conversion, but there are some characters, particularly '<' and '>' that, because they are used in HTML code, will be interpreted as HTML, and not shown correctly. In HTML, if we want to display a '<' we use < and to display '>' we use >. If we wrote the string <EEEK!>, it would appear blank in a browser, because it would read it as an <EEEK> HTML tag, which doesn't exist. If we pass that string through HtmlEncode(), it will return <EEEK!> which will be displayed as <EEEK!> in a browser.
HtmlDecode()	This method is the exact opposite of the HtmlEncode() method. It takes HTML encoded characters like > and converts them to normal characters like '>'.
MapPath()	This method takes a **virtual path** (a web address without the server name) like /webapp/myfile.aspx, and returns the exact location of that file on the physical disk, for example C:\InetPub\wwwroot\webapp\myfile.aspx.

Member	Description
UrlEncode()	This method is used when we want to pass a string in a web address (URL). For example, if we wanted to use the URL, page.aspx?command=stand & stare, we'd get into difficulties, because URLs cannot include spaces, and characters like '?' and '&' have special meanings. URLs expect these characters to be encoded, for example spaces are converted to '+'s. If we pass our parameter stand & stare through UrlEncode, it returns stand+%26+stare, which has converted the spaces to '+'s and the '&' to '%26'.
UrlDecode()	We use this method to take parameters passed to us across URLs, and convert them to normal strings again. For example, the string stand+%26+stare would be UrlDecoded as stand & stare.

These encode and decode methods can be quite hard to grasp, so let's look at an example that uses them both. This example is a good demonstration of how **not** to build web sites using ASP.NET, but it'll demonstrate admirably how these methods work!

You'll probably find in day-to-day work that the objects we use to build ASP.NET applications automatically deal with encoding issues to the degree that we physically won't need to call these methods ourselves.

Try It Out – Using Server.UrlEncode()

In this example, we'll create a pair of pages, the second of which generates a birthday card using the name and age passed from the first. The first page just shows an HTML link that passes the name and age parameters on the URL to the second page.

1. Open up your editor and type in the following code for our first page:

```
<%@ Page Language="c#" %>
<html>
  <body>
    <%
    string Name = "Sniff";
    string Age = "23";
    %>
    <a href="birthday2.aspx?name=<% Response.Write(Name); %>&age=<%
    Response.Write(Age); %>">Click here</a>
  </body>
</html>
```

Notice how the page uses an <a> tag, into which we squirt the values for Age and Name using Response.Write(). (The <a>, or 'anchor' tag places a link on the browser that we can click to visit a different page.) The href property is an HTML control used to specify or receive a URL. So here, we use the href property to specify that the following is a URL, which also tells us that we're passing the two parameters as a GET request. Effectively, the URL that IE will go to when we click on the link is: birthday2.aspx?age=23&name=Sniff.

2. Save this file as `birthday1.aspx`.

3. Open up your editor again, and type in the following for our second page:

Notice how we create two variables called `Name` and `Age`, and then set them to the two parameters passed as part of the `GET` request with the `QueryString` property on the `Request` object:

```
<%@ Page Language="c#" %>
<html>
  <body>
    <center>
      <%
      string Name = Request.QueryString["Name"];
      string Age = Request.QueryString["Age"];
      %>
      <h1>Happy Birthday <% Response.Write(Name); %></h1>
      <h3>May the next
      <% Response.Write(Age); %>
      years be as good!</h3>
    </center>
  </body>
</html>
```

4. Now save this page as `birthday2.aspx`.

5. Call up the `birthday1.aspx` page – you'll see a single link that says click here. If you roll over the link, you'll see that it points to …/birthday2.aspx?age=23&name=Sniff.

6. Click on the link to navigate to `birthday2.aspx` and you'll see this:

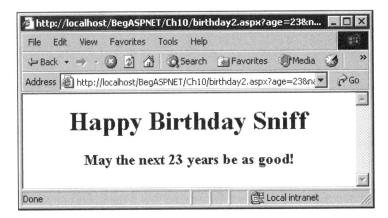

The screenshot demonstrates that we have successfully passed our two parameters (Name and Age) across to the second page, using the QueryString property of the Request object to access the parameter's values (23 and Sniff). It looks like the application works fine – or does it?

7. Open up birthday1.aspx again and change the name from "Sniff" to "Sniff & Jack", like this:

```
<%@ Page Language="c#" %>
<html>
  <body>
    <%;
    string Name = "Sniff & Jack";
    string Age = "23";
    %>
    <a href="birthday2.aspx?name=<% Response.Write(Name); %>&age=<%
    Response.Write(Age); %>">Click here</a>
  </body>
</html>
```

8. Open up birthday1.aspx in your browser again and refresh the page so the HTML link reflects the change we have made. If you click the link now, you'll see this:

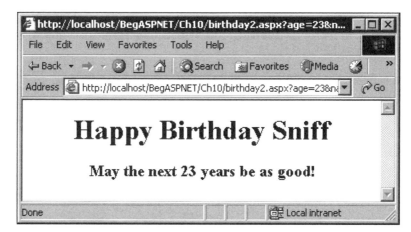

This is the same as we had before! What's going on? The reason relates to the bit of our HTML link that looks like this:

```
.../birthday2.aspx?age=23&name=Sniff & Jack
```

Our second page is interpreting that as age=23, name="Sniff", Jack="" and there's also a risk of further confusion, as our URL includes spacing – which is not allowed. This isn't what we want at all; we don't want spaces, and we want the final & to be sent as part of the Name parameter, not interpreted as a divider between parameters. The solution to this is to URL-encode the Name and Age values using the UrlEncode() method before we create the HTML link.

9. Change the code by adding the marked lines below; let's also change the age to use another illegal character, to make sure that's encoded correctly too:

```
<%@ Page Language="c#" %>
<html>
  <body>
    <%;
    string Name = "Sniff";
    string Age = "twenty three";
    Age = Server.UrlEncode(Age);
    Name = Server.UrlEncode(Name);
    %>
    <a href="birthday2.aspx?name=<% Response.Write(Name); %>&age=<%
    Response.Write(Age); %>">Click here</a>
  </body>
</html>
```

Open `birthday1.aspx` in your browser again, and refresh the page. If you roll over the link you'll find it has changed:

```
/birthday2.aspx?age=twenty+three%3f%3f&name=Sniff+%26+Jack
```

Notice how the query '?' has been converted to `%3f`, while the ampersand '&' has been converted to `%26`. These character codes are directly supported by URLs, so this link will now work. Let's try it; click the link, you should see this:

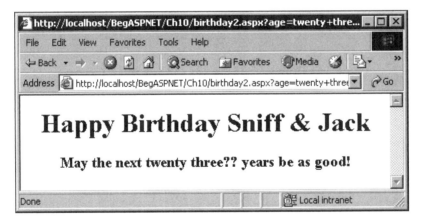

How It Works

We've explained the code as we've gone along this time, but to sum up, the `UrlEncode()` method will examine each character in a string to ensure it is in a form that can be correctly transmitted as part of a URL. As a bonus, ASP.NET automatically decodes the URL string at the other end, so we don't need to explicitly use `UrlDecode()` in `birthday2.asp`.

Let's continue this example, and look at the `HtmlEncode()` method of the `HttpServerUtility` class – as accessible through the `Server` object – to display characters used in HTML code in the browser.

1. Open up `birthday1.aspx`, and make the change shown:

```
<%@ Page Language="c#" %>
<html>
  <body>
    <%;
    string Name = "<Sniff> & <Jack>";
    string Age = "twenty three";
    Age = Server.UrlEncode(Age);
    Name = Server.UrlEncode(Name);
    %>
    <a href="birthday2.aspx?name=<% Response.Write(Name); %>&age=<%
    Response.Write(Age); %>">Click here</a>
  </body>
</html>
```

2. Now open `birthday1.aspx` up in your browser again, and hit **Refresh**.

3. Now click on the link, here's what you'll see:

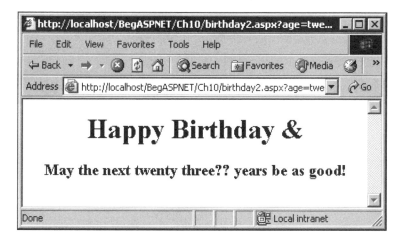

4. As you can see, we have a new problem: the `Name` parameter isn't appearing correctly, and only the '&' is visible.

5. Open up `birthday2.aspx` and make the changes marked:

```
<%@ Page Language="c#" %>
<html>
  <body>
    <center>
      <%
      string Name = Request.QueryString["Name"];
      string Age = Request.QueryString["Age"];
      Name = Server.HtmlEncode(Name);
      Age = Server.HtmlEncode(Age);
      %>
      <h1>Happy Birthday <% Response.Write(Name); %></h1>
      <h3>May the next
      <% Response.Write(Age); %>
      years be as good!</h3>
    </center>
  </body>
</html>
```

6. Now refresh `birthday2.aspx` in your browser; you'll see this:

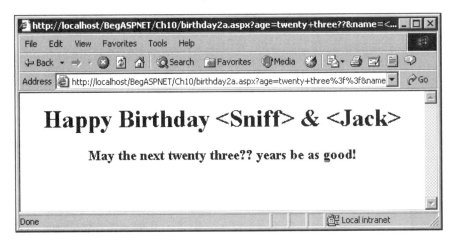

How It Works

We altered the code we created in `birthday1.aspx`, by changing our name values to:

```
string Name = "<Sniff> & <Jack>";
```

But when we clicked on our link, the names didn't appear. The reason for this is that the browser attempted to treat `<Sniff>` and `<Jack>` as HTML tags, rather than text. As a rule, when a browser doesn't understand a tag it will ignore it – the principle behind this being that the browser believes some new HTML tag has been introduced that it doesn't know about, so it decides to display the page as best it can.

In HTML, if we want to display a 'less than' symbol (<) on the page, we have to use a special syntax, and type `&lt;`. As luck would have it, `HtmlEncode()` can do all this for us. So we added the following lines to `birthday2.aspx`:

```
Name = Server.HtmlEncode(Name);
Age = Server.HtmlEncode(Age);
```

and our new name values were printed on the screen.

Let's see what has happened as a result of our tinkering. If we use our browser and select View Source, we can see that the HTML for the first line of our page looks like this:

```
<h1>Happy Birthday &lt;Sniff&gt; &amp; &lt;Jack&gt;</h1>
```

Each of the '<' and '>' characters have been encoded in such a way that they are properly displayed by the browser, rather than interpreted as HTML tags.

`HtmlEncode()` is especially useful if visitors to your web site are typing text into forms, and you want to display it on a page. For example, if you had a guestbook on your site where people can leave messages, you probably want any '<' and '>' characters displayed rather than interpreted as HTML to prevent people messing with your site, and putting pictures and their own HTML code into your guestbook.

State Handling

One of the ways that web servers manage to handle thousands of users each minute is by implementing what's known as 'stateless connections'. Whenever you ask a browser to return a page, image or other resource, the following happens:

1. You connect to the server.

2. You tell it what page, image, or other item you want.

3. It sends you the resource you ask for.

4. The server disconnects you and forgets everything about you.

It's this 'forgets everything' bit that's important. If a web server tried to watch you for twenty minutes as you moved from page to page on a popular web site, like Amazon or MSN, you'd need a server the size of a house to store the information. Instead, web servers treat every request they get in an unassociated manner, that is two consecutive Requests from you are treated as two, separate, unassociated Requests.

State management is a trick that allows the web server to make some determinations about who you are, where you have already been on the site and what you've done. Simply, the server and browser work together and use a tiny piece of memory or disk space that gives the ASP.NET pages running on the server enough information to go away and find out who you are, if it needs to.

ASP.NET provides a range of features to help us manage the **state** (persistence) of various elements of our web applications. What do we mean by state? Let's have a look at some examples of where we see state used in web sites:

❑ If our web site uses our company telephone number quite a lot, it would be very useful to be able to store it somewhere so that it's easily accessible to all the pages in our web site. It would also be handy to store it centrally so that if (when!) the number changes, we can update it in one place and be confident the change will be reflected across the web site.

❑ When we use a web site and add items to our shopping basket, we expect the contents of the basket to be retained as we shop. The state of our basket needs to be stored during our visit to the web site as we move around the site.

❑ When we log onto most web sites, we expect not to have to log on each time we come back. The fact that we have logged in before and should be allowed in without being asked to log in again has been stored to achieve this.

❑ When we fill in a form on a web site, we expect the web site to keep the information we entered so we don't have to enter it again.

As you can see, state is widely used, but there are a variety of different types of state that are being used.

Although there are quite a few, they're not hard to work with and all the difficult stuff has been done for us, even more so with ASP.NET than with previous versions of ASP.

Some of the questions we'll look at in the following sections are:

❑ What is the scope of each type of state? Does it apply to each user, across the whole web site, or is it just for one visit to the web site by one person?

❑ Where is the state stored? Is it in the user's browser, or in our web server's memory, or in a file or database somewhere?

❑ How do we change states? If we wanted to empty a shopping basket, how do we do that?

Application State

Sometimes we want to store a piece of information in such a way that it's always easily accessible by any page of the web site. This is what `Application` state is for; a central, site-wide store of variables that we can get at from any page.

We make use of it by using an object instantiated from the `HttpApplicationState` class. We get at the object using another property of the `Page` class (just like `Response` and `Request`). The property is called `Application`; in terms of the code we write to use application state, it's pretty minimal.

Words can make the `Application` object sound complex, so let's look at an example that will show you that in practice it's pretty straightforward.

Try It Out – Using Application State

Let's look at an example web site where we have a company telephone number (555 1234), that we want to store centrally, and in such a way that any page viewed by any visitor can access it and display it.

1. Open up your editor and type the following:

```
<%@ Page Language="c#" %>
<html>
  <body>
    <% Application["CompanyTelephone"] = "555 1234"; %>
    <b>Application state changed successfully</b>
  </body>
</html>
```

2. Save the file as `application1.aspx` in your web site.

3. Open your editor again and type the following into a new page:

```
<html>
  <body>
    <b>Company Telephone =
    <%
       Response.Write(Application("CompanyTelephone"))
    %>
    </b>
  </body>
</html>
```

4. Save this page as `application2.aspx`.

5. Call up `application1.aspx` in your browser and you'll see this:

6. Now open `application2.aspx` in your browser:

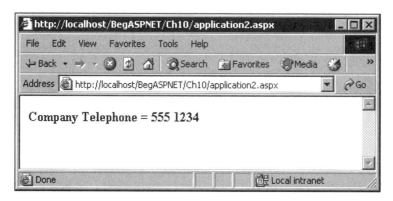

How It Works

As you can see, we were able to view the company telephone number from our browser window, even when the code that generated the window didn't contain the information. We were able to do this using this statement:

```
<%
    Response.Write(Application("CompanyTelephone"))
%>
```

This statement is saying, "Tell me the value of the `CompanyTelephone` application state."

Now, initially we set the telephone number in the application state using this statement:

```
<% Application["CompanyTelephone"] = "555 1234"; %>
```

Here, we are referencing the `Application` property of the `Page` object, and passing the parameter, `CompanyTelephone`. What this command is saying is "Please create me a new state variable called `CompanyTelephone` and set it to 555 1234." The `Application` object is a container for all the application state variables we set; it is a collection object.

Initial Configuration for Application State

You may be wondering about the fact that to set the company telephone number to "555 1234" we had to open a page. Surely on a real web site, opening a page to set up some information every time we start Internet Information Server is going to be rather irritating! Actually, there's a more realistic problem with this approach than just "being irritated". Imagine our Web server experiences a power failure in the middle of the night – the computer turns off and turns back on again. IIS automatically starts when the computer starts, but unless we visit the page part of our site (in this case the phone number), it won't work properly. We'd have to remember to check the site periodically, and if the information appeared to be missing, we'd have to open the page to set everything up.

A much better approach is to configure the application state when our web site starts up, which is where the `global.asax` file comes in. This file contains code that is executed in response to certain events; in this case the most useful event is one that's fired when the web application starts (that is, when the first visitor hits the site). Let's continue our example:

1. Open up your editor and type the following:

```
<script language = "c#" runat = "server">
  void Application_OnStart()
  {
    Application["CompanyTelephone"] = "555 4321";
  }
</script>
```

2. Save the file as `global.asax` in your application folder. The file must be in the root of a web application, which in this case means the topmost folder (`BegASPNET`).

Because we have created a new `global.asax` file, the web application restarts behind the scenes to take our changes into effect. When a web application starts up, ASP.NET looks for a `global.asax` file, and if it finds one, it looks for a function called `Application_OnStart()`. If it exists, the code inside the procedure is executed. In our case, this means that when our web site starts up, the company telephone number is set to our new number, *555 4321*.

3. Open `application2.aspx` in your browser, and you'll see that without using `application1.aspx`, our `CompanyTelephone` application state has been set correctly to the new phone number, *555 4321*:

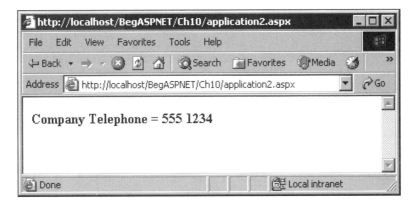

With the `Application` object, making changes to small pieces of information like this is much easier; the data is centralized and easily accessible by any of our ASP.NET pages using the `Application` object.

As you can see in the diagram below, the `Application` state is accessible from all the pages within a web application, and it is initially configured using the `global.asax` file:

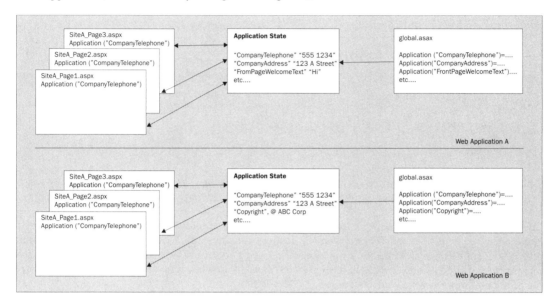

Note that if your web server contains more than one web application, each one has its own application state store and its own `global.asax` file.

If we find ourselves needing to alter the application state from within an ASP.NET page, we need to consider what happens if two pages attempt to make a change at the same time. (The nature of a web site is such that it can handle many requests at once and, as the chances of two or more pages being Requests at a given moment are not zero, we have to accommodate this eventuality.) It's possible that one will overwrite the changes made by the other in a way that we do not expect, or that cannot be predicted. Because of this, when we alter application state from an ASP.NET page, we use a pair of methods on the `Application` object called `Lock()` and `Unlock()` like this:

```
Application.Lock();
Application("SomeGlobalCounter") = <value>;
Application.UnLock();
```

This structure ensures that no two pages can alter the application state at the same time.

Using Application State

Here are a few suggestions for using `Application` state.

❑ Use it for frequently used data. The `Application` state is designed for information that will be used widely across your web site. If you have a piece of information that is only used occasionally, you're better off storing that in a file on disk, which you access when you need to. There's a file called `web.config` that will fulfill this purpose admirably in most cases and you'll see more about that in Chapter 19.

- ❏ Don't go overboard with the number of pieces of information you put in the application state. Be aware that information in the application state is held in memory, so your web server will use up more memory for each state you add.

- ❏ The `Application` object is a collection object; this means it is an object that contains a group of other objects, like the `QueryString` property. The upshot of this is that you can, if you need to, store objects within the `Application` object, not just simple textual information.

- ❏ If you're making heavy use of the `Application` object, keep a list somewhere of the items you have stored in it, so when you're writing pages you know what information you already have easy access to.

- ❏ If your site starts getting high traffic volumes, you'll generally find fewer performance problems if you use the `web.config` file instead of the `Application` state (again, see Chapter 19 for more information).

Session State

When a web site uses a shopping basket, where is that data stored? The shopping basket is a great example for how we use `Session` state. A session is a single visit to a web site, and normally includes visits to a number of pages. A session ends when the person has not viewed a page on the site for a certain period of time. The default 'timeout' is twenty minutes, in other words, if the user hasn't visited a page on the site within twenty minutes, the session ends. We use session state to manage information that we want to be available while someone is using our web site, and which is specific to that particular person. Each session usually represents an individual user, but some people may have two browsers open, and so have two sessions running.

Here are some examples of where we might use session state:

- ❏ Shopping basket – a list of items the web site visitor has decided to buy. The list is maintained throughout their visit to the web site.

- ❏ Visitor name – many sites personalize pages on the basis of the current user's identity. If we have a database of users, and we know who our visitor is, we can add details we hold about the person to the session, so that our pages can easily access it. A common candidate for this is the person's name.

- ❏ Visitor settings – if someone visits our site and specifies a preference that affects how pages are displayed, it often makes sense to keep this type of information in the session.

In the diagram below, we can see that there are multiple session states, one for each active session:

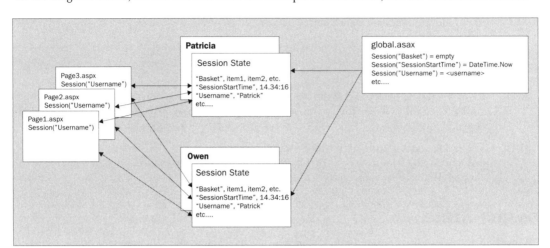

We can see that every page in the site has access to the session for the current user, which holds details specific to that session including, for example, the name of the person, the contents of their shopping basket, and the time the session started. We can also see that when a session starts (that is, when someone first opens a web page on our site) the global.asax file sets up the session, just as it did with the Application state. In this example, we set the shopping basket to be empty, we use the current time (DateTime.Now) to set the start of the session time, and we set up the username (probably from a database).

We work with session state in much the same way as we do with application state. The session is accessible through a property of the Page object called Session that returns an object of type HttpSessionState.

Here are some of the more commonly used methods and properties of the HttpSessionState class:

- ❑ Abandon() – this method ends the current session. All information in the session is cleared, and if the person visits a page subsequently, a new session will be created for them. (This is useful for "resetting" things so that the user is effectively given a brand-new session.)

- ❑ Clear() – this method removes all the information from the session state, but does not end the session.

- ❑ IsNewSession – this property returns True if the session was created when the user accessed the current page. This might be useful in cases when a session needs to be initialized with some data before it can be used.

- ❑ TimeOut – this property gets and sets the period of idle time in minutes before a session expires. By default this value is set to twenty minutes; that is after twenty minutes during which the person has not accessed a page their session will end.

In addition to these properties, we can also use the `Session` object just like the `Application` object. For example, to store a person's name in our session, we use a statement like this:

```
Session["Name"] = "Owen Blacker";
```

To read information out of the session, we use a statement like this:

```
VisitorsName String;
VisitorsName = Session["Name"];
```

Let's look at an example page that uses session state.

Try It Out – Using Session State

In this example, we'll build a simple page that mimics some of the characteristics of a shopping basket. Our page will show the number of items in the basket, and we'll have two buttons: one to add an item to the basket and another to empty the basket. For the sake of simplicity, we won't track the items in the basket, just the count of the number of items.

1. Open up your editor and type the following:

```
<%@ Page language="c#"%>
<script Language="c#" runat="server">
  void EmptyClick(object sender, EventArgs e)
  {
    Session["BasketCount"] = 0;
  }
  void AddClick(object sender, EventArgs e)
  {
    if (Session["BasketCount"] != null)
    {
      int i = (int)Session["BasketCount"];
      i++;
      Session["BasketCount"] = (object)i;
    } else {
      Session["BasketCount"] = 1;
    }
  }
</script>

<html>
  <body>
    <form id="BasketForm" method="post" runat="server">
      <asp:Button id="Empty" OnClick="EmptyClick" runat="server"
                                                  Text="Empty"/>
      <br />
      <asp:Button id="Add" OnClick="AddClick" runat="server" Text="Add"/>
      <br />
      Basket items : <%=Session["BasketCount"]%>
      <br />
    </form>
  </body>
</html>
```

When the `EmptyClick` function executes, it uses the highlighted statement to set the `BasketCount` session variable to zero. When the `AddClick` function executes, it increments the number of items in our basket by one.

2. Save the file as `session.aspx` in your web site.

3. Open your browser, and view `session.aspx`; you'll see this:

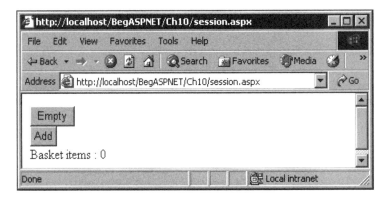

Click the Add button; the page will reload and you'll see this:

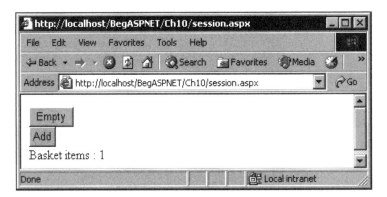

4. Click the Add button again, and you'll see that the number of items in the basket has increased. You'll also notice that if you refresh the page, the count of the number of items in the basket will remain the same; the information is stored in the session, and will persist between refreshes. The session information is only lost if you close the browser or leave it inactive for more than twenty minutes.

5. Now click the **Empty** button so we can see the `EmptyClick` function functioning. Once `EmptyClick` has executed, the page looks like this:

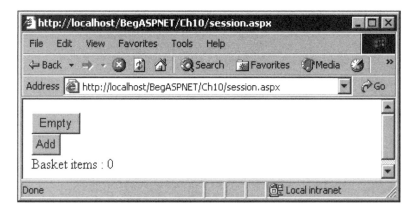

How It Works

In this page, we have a button to add an item to our basket (**Add**), we have a button to empty our basket (**Empty**), and a `Response.Write()` statement, `<%=Session["BasketCount"]%>`, that displays the number of items in our basket. Both the buttons have defined `OnClick` attributes that specify the functions that are called when we click the buttons:

```
<%@ Page language="c#"%>
<script Language="c#" runat="server">
  void EmptyClick(object sender, EventArgs e)
  {
    Session["BasketCount"] = 0;
  }
  void AddClick(object sender, EventArgs e)
  {
    if (Session["BasketCount"] != null)
    {
      int i = (int)Session["BasketCount"];
      i++;
      Session["BasketCount"] = (object)i;
    } else {
      Session["BasketCount"] = 1;
    }
  }
</script>
```

The `EmptyClick` function resets the session variable `BasketCount` to zero. We could have used `Session.Abandon()` or `Session.Clear()` to empty the basket, although both of these methods would clear every other session variable, which may not be what we want. It's better to identify the session variables you want to clear, and clear them explicitly, rather than deleting the whole lot (use a scalpel, not a broadsword!)

The `AddClick` function increments the `BasketCount` by one. Whichever button is pressed, the results are rendered to the page by retrieving the session value:

```
<form id="BasketForm" method="post" runat="server">
  <asp:Button id="Empty" OnClick="EmptyClick" runat="server"
                                              Text="Empty"/>
  <br />
  <asp:Button id="Add" OnClick="AddClick" runat="server" Text="Add"/>
  <br />
  Basket items : <%=Session["BasketCount"]%>
  <br />
</form>
```

Initial Configuration for Session State

Just as with application state, we can configure our web site to add information to the session when it begins, to do this we use the `global.asax` file again. So, for example, if we wanted to add a message to the session when it first starts, we do it by adding code like this to `global.asax`:

```
<script language = "c#" runat = "server">
  void Session_OnStart()
  {
  Session["Message"] = "Buy some of our products, Bill!";
  }
</script>
```

On any page, we can then use a statement like this to coax our visitors into spending their hard-earned cash:

```
<%=Session["Message"]%>
```

This statement produces the following output:

```
Buy some of our products, Bill!
```

Using Session State

The session store is designed for storing information about each session, which, in real terms, usually relates to each web site visitor. As with the application store, use the **session store** for regularly accessed information. Each session uses up memory, so it's a bad place to store information that you're not making good use of. Just as with the `Application` object, you can, if you wish, store objects inside the `Session` object.

By default each session usually lasts twenty minutes after a period of no activity, and there's roughly one session for each person at your site; this means sessions can create heavy memory demands if there are a lot of people visiting your site. As a general rule, don't put large amounts of information in the session, because your web server will grind to a halt when it gets busier.

Remember that if you extend the timeout duration for a session, your web server is likely to need more memory, as it will be storing each session for longer.

Cookies

A **cookie** is a small piece of information that relates to a specific user, and usually also relates to a specific web site. Cookies are a way of storing information relating to a user and a web site for longer periods of time than with a session. Cookies are also different in that the state is stored on the user's hard drive (usually with the web browser software in a folder called Cookies); remember that with session state, the information is stored on the web server.

Here are some examples of where cookies are used:

❑ User preferences – if a user specifies a preference on a web site, it often makes sense to store that preference using a cookie on the user's hard drive. If we store it in a session, it'll be lost when their session times out, and they will be forced to specify the preference again when they return. Alternatively, we could store the preference in a database, and load it into the session when the user comes to the site, but cookies are often easier, especially for smaller web sites.

❑ Sign in and 'remember me' – you've almost certainly been to a web site where you've had to sign in, and it had a checkbox labeled something like remember me. If you check the box, next time you come to the site you won't have to sign in. What happens here is the web site places a cookie on the user's hard drive, which includes enough information so that the next time they come back in, they are signed in behind the scenes and don't have to do it manually.

❑ Pop-up windows – many web sites open a small window when you visit their site showing an advert or promotion. Most companies are aware of the irritation these can cause, so the more responsible ones tend to display the window once and write a cookie to the user's hard drive. When the visitor returns to the site it checks for the cookie; if the cookie exists it does not show the advert again.

How Do Cookies Work?

On your PC, there is a set of cookie files that have been placed there by your web browser software at the request of web sites that you have visited. On Windows 2000, Internet Explorer cookies are stored in `C:\Documents and Settings\<username>\Cookies\`. Look in this folder now. You'll find hundreds! But how did they get there?

When your web browser sends an HTTP Request to the web server, it replies with an HTTP Response, including the HTML for the page. In addition to that content, we can add cookie data to the HTTP Response, which the browser software will dutifully save to disk for us. You can see this process in the upper half of the diagram overleaf, Request 1:

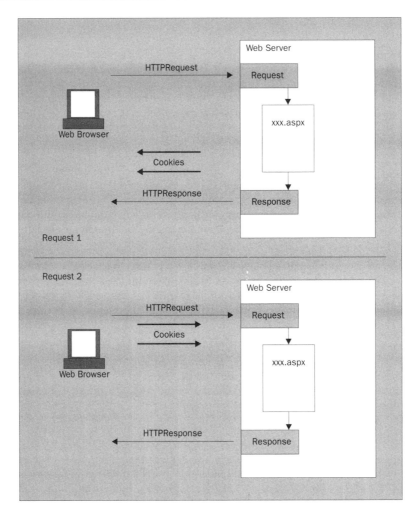

When we request another page from the web server (Request 2), whether it is a few seconds later or a few days later, the cookie data will be loaded from our hard drive by the web browser into the HTTP Request. The result of this is that if we save cookie data to a visitor's hard drive, we get sent that data each time they come back to our web site. This is an important point – cookies persist outside of the timeout period for the session, or even when the browser is closed. To get rid of them, we as web site owners have to tell the browser to delete them or, as a user, we can delete them manually.

You probably won't be surprised to hear that we set the cookie state using the Response object, and we read the existing cookie state using the Request object. Let's look at an example and see these objects working their magic.

Try It Out – Using Cookies

In this example, we're going to put together a page for which the visitor can specify the background color. Once they have chosen a background color, the color is stored as a cookie, and so our page will use that setting for all future visits.

1. Open up your editor and type the following:

```
<%@ Page Language="c#"%>
<html>
  <body>
    <form id="CookieForm" method="post" runat="server">
      <asp:DropDownList id=MyDropDownList runat="server"/>
      <asp:button id=MyButton runat="server" OnClick="Click"/>
    </form>
  </body>
</html>
```

In this page, we've created a form that holds a drop-down list and a button. We'll configure the list so that it will display a series of colors for us to choose for the page background, and the button will save a cookie containing our choice. We can see that the button is wired up with an OnClick attribute, so when it's clicked, the Click() function will be called. We'll see that in a moment.

2. Add the following code to the page; it sets the name of the button, and also adds three colors to the drop-down list:

```
<%@ Page Language="c#" %>
<script Language="c#" runat="server">
  void Page_Load(object source, EventArgs e)
  {
    if (!(IsPostBack))
    {
      MyButton.Text = "Save Cookie";
      MyDropDownList.Items.Add("Blue");
      MyDropDownList.Items.Add("Red");
      MyDropDownList.Items.Add("Gray");
    }
  }
</script>
<html>
  <body>
    <form id="CookieForm" method="post" runat="server">
      <asp:DropDownList id=MyDropDownList runat="server"/>
      <asp:button id=MyButton runat="server" OnClick="Click"/>
    </form>
  </body>
</html>
```

3. Now we add the interesting code, the code that saves our cookie:

```csharp
<%@ Page Language="c#" %>
<script Language="c#" runat="server">
  void Page_Load(object source, EventArgs e)
  {
    if (!(IsPostBack))
    {
      MyButton.Text = "Save Cookie";
      MyDropDownList.Items.Add("Blue");
      MyDropDownList.Items.Add("Red");
      MyDropDownList.Items.Add("Gray");
    }
  }
  public void Click(object sender, EventArgs e)
  {
    HttpCookie MyCookie = new HttpCookie("Background");
    MyCookie.Value = MyDropDownList.SelectedItem.Text;
    Response.Cookies.Add(MyCookie);
  }
</script>
<html>
  <body>
    <form id="CookieForm" method="post" runat="server">
      <asp:DropDownList id=MyDropDownList runat="server"/>
      <asp:button id=MyButton runat="server" OnClick="Click"/>
    </form>
  </body>
</html>
```

4. Save the file as `cookie1.aspx` in your web site.

5. Open `cookie1.aspx` in your browser, and you'll see this:

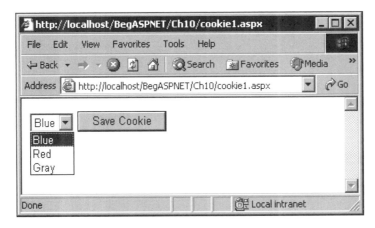

6. Now let's create a page that uses the cookie we've safely stored away on the user's machine. Create a new page in your editor, and type the following:

```
<%@ Page Language="c#" %>
  <script Language="c#" runat="server">
    void Page_Load(object source, EventArgs e)
    {
      Response.Cache.SetExpires(DateTime.Now);
    }
    string GetBackground()
    {
      return Request.Cookies["Background"].Value;
    }
  </script>
  <html>
    <body bgcolor="<% Response.Write(GetBackground()); %>">
    <asp:label id="message" runat="server" />
    </body>
  </html>
```

7. Save the second page as `cookie2.aspx`.

8. Open `cookie1.aspx` in your browser, select a color and then open `cookies2.aspx`.

You'll find that whatever color you choose on `cookie1.aspx` is reflected by the background color of `cookie2.aspx`. The `cookie2.aspx` file is making use of the `Background` cookie, which is being sent to it by the web browser every time it sends an HTTP Request.

9. Now close down your web browser. Restart it, and go to `cookie2.aspx`; you'll find that the background color has successfully been read from the cookie. This is where cookies differ from sessions – they're designed to store information for a much longer period.

How It Works

The first ASPX page saves the cookie. The code for the `Click` function that gets called when the user clicks the **Save Cookie** button is:

```
public void Click(object sender, EventArgs e)
{
  HttpCookie MyCookie = new HttpCookie("Background");
  MyCookie.Value = MyDropDownList.SelectedItem.Text;
  Response.Cookies.Add(MyCookie);
}
```

The function does three things. Firstly, it creates an object from the `HttpCookie` class, and passes a name for the cookie as a parameter; it is effectively saying, "Create me a cookie and call it 'Background'." In the next line, we use the `Value` property of the `cookie` object to specify the value for the `Background` cookie. Finally, in the last line of the function, we add the new cookie to the HTTP Response using the `Response` object, and its `Cookies` property. When the web browser receives our HTTP Response, it will write the cookie information to the hard disk.

The second ASPX page is where we actually read the cookie. In this page, we have added a statement to the `<body>` tag that squirts the color setting from the `Background` cookie into the `bgcolor` attribute of the `<body>` tag. To get the background color from the cookie, we used the `Cookies` property on the `Request` object, which returns an object of the type `HttpCookieCollection`. This class represents a set of cookies, and we access a single cookie with this syntax: `Request.Cookies("cookie name")`. This returns the cookie with that name, and then to retrieve its value, we use the `Value` property on the end of the statement:

```
<html>
  <body bgcolor="<% Response.Write(GetBackground()); %>">
  <asp:label id="message" runat="server" />
  </body>
</html>
```

The `GetBackground()` function looks up the `Cookies` property of the `Request` object, which represents a set of cookies, and we access a single cookie with this syntax: `Request.Cookies["cookie name"]`. This returns the cookie with that name, and to retrieve its value, we use the `Value` property of the individual cookie. This is then returned from the function:

```
string GetBackground()
{
  return Request.Cookies["Background"].Value;
}
```

We have also added a `Page_Load()` function, which has a single function call; it uses the `SetExpires` method on the `Cache` object, which is returned by `Response`. The `SetExpires` method takes a `DateTime` as a parameter, and ensures that the web browser does not cache the page after that time. What this statement is doing is ensuring that our browser does not keep a copy of the page, so that when we select different background colors using `cookies1.aspx`, the changes are reflected when we open up `cookies2.aspx`. If you have pages in a web site that you do not want the browser to cache, this is how you do it:

```
void Page_Load(object source, EventArgs e)
{
  Response.Cache.SetExpires(DateTime.Now);
}
```

Shelf Life – How Long Do Cookies Last?

You may be wondering how long cookies last for; well, they last for as long as we like. For example, if we wanted to set our background configuration up so it lasted for thirty days, we'd create a `TimeSpan` object to represent the period of thirty days. When we pass four parameters to `TimeSpan`'s constructor, it interprets that as days, hours, minutes, and seconds, hence we're using `30,0,0,0`.

To implement this, you would modify the code in `cookie1.aspx` (where the cookie was first created) like so:

```
public void Click(object sender, EventArgs e)
{
   DateTime dt = DateTime.Now;
   TimeSpan ts = new TimeSpan(30,0,0,0);
   HttpCookie MyCookie = new HttpCookie("Background");
   MyCookie.Value = MyDropDownList.SelectedItem.Text;
   MyCookie.Expires = dt + ts;
   Response.Cookies.Add(MyCookie);
}
```

Sessions and Cookies

In Chapter 3 we looked at persistence, and you saw how HTTP is a stateless protocol, which means state information is not preserved between pages. This means, for example, that if we request a page and then straight away request another, the web server has no way of knowing that the two requests are from the same person. It could try using the machine (IP) address of the computer, but these tend to change, so that method is pretty unreliable.

The stateless nature of HTTP doesn't affect application state, because the state information is the same for all the people using the site, and it doesn't affect cookies, because we save information to the visitor's hard drive. However, this statelessness does affect sessions; in fact on the basis of HTTP being stateless, sessions shouldn't be possible at all. So how does the web server know that the first Request and the second Request came from the same person?

The answer is that even though session information, such as a visitor's name, is stored in the web server, every session also has a **Session ID** that is stored as a cookie on the visitor's machine. A session ID is a unique code that identifies the session on the server. This is what allows sessions to be maintained across multiple pages; cookies allow us to store state, and use it, even with the stateless HTTP protocol.

When we create a session using our web browser, each request we make for a page includes the cookie containing our session ID. When the web server sees the session ID, it hooks up all our session variables because it knows who we are. When our session expires, the web server simply ignores the incoming session ID.

One final point about the difference between session state and cookies is that we can only store simple text information in a cookie, whereas, we can store any type of information (including objects) within the `Session` object.

Summary

We started off this chapter with a look at the .NET Framework from a high level, including a brief overview of some of the most commonly used namespaces before directing our focus towards the namespaces most specific to Internet development, `System.Web` and `System.Web.UI`.

We saw how the `Response` and `Request` objects represent HTTP Requests and Responses, and how those objects are accessible from the `Page` object, whose properties and methods are accessible to all our pages automatically. We also looked briefly at how the `Browser` object helps us find out about the web browser our web site visitor is using, as well as looking at using methods like `UrlEncode()` and `HtmlEncode()` that are provided by the `Server` object.

Finally, we covered state management in .NET – how, and where, we can store state. We looked at application state, which is available to our whole web application, and we looked at session state, which is provided for each person's visit to our web site. We also learned about cookies and how to explicitly save them to a visitor's computer, and how they are used to implement sessions.

Exercises

1. Explain the role of the `Page` class in ASP.NET and describe what sort of things we can do with it.

2. Write an ASP.NET page that returns the Windows name of your computer and the URL of the page that you are visiting.

3. (a) Write an ASP.NET page that prompts a user to enter a value for the radius of a circle then calculates its area (Area = *(radius)^2) and another ASP.NET page that also prompts the user to enter the length of the radius and then calculates the circumference (circumference = 2* *radius). Both pages should access the value of (pi; 3.142) stored in application state.

(b) Repeat the above example storing the value of (pi) in `global.asax`.

4. Using session variables implement a shopping cart that lets you add up to five items from a dropdown listbox and displays:

(a) The total number of items selected

(b) A list of all the items in the cart

There should also be a means of emptying all the items contained in the cart.

Create an ASP.NET page that contains textboxes in which a user can enter their name, address, and telephone number. Using cookies, display this information on a separate ASP.NET page.

Objects and Structured Data

From the last couple of chapters you should have a pretty good idea of how objects make it easier to write large modular programs, and use chunks of predefined functionality from a completely separate block of code, which may even be in a different file. We're now going to link up this discussion of objects to our understanding of data types (from Chapter 4) by considering some of the more structured forms of data that objects help us to work with.

In the course of this chapter, we're going to look at **collections**. In simple terms, these are objects designed to hold collections of other objects (hence the name) together in a single unit; they also implement a number of standard methods that we can use to work with those contained objects. The .NET Framework features a number of very useful collection objects, and we'll be taking a look at some of them shortly.

What is a Collection?

The term **collection** refers to a special sort of object that lets us bundle other objects inside it and work on them either individually, or as a group. Of course, we can do this already to some extent – we have already used objects as class properties – so what's new? The most noticeable difference is in flexibility: when we're defining class properties, we have to specify exactly what properties we're going to call (and, implicitly, how many of them there are) within the class definition. That's generally not the case with a collection – in fact, we can start off with a completely empty collection object, and subsequently add or delete as many records as we need.

The other difference is one of internal organization. When we use objects as properties, we lock ourselves into a very rigidly defined structure, effectively hard-wiring everything into the class definition. Objects contained within collections (which we refer to as **elements** of the collection) are far more loosely associated, and need only be connected by the fact that they're all held within the same unit. Therefore, they're much more flexible and able to meet your own particular needs.

Different Types of Collection

The organization (if there is any) of the contained objects depends on the particular variety of collection you're using.

The simplest type is just a bunch of objects grouped together in no particular order – this is often referred to as a **set**. A set that consists of {object1, object2, object3, object4} is functionally equivalent to a set consisting of {object3, object2, object4, object1} – order is not important here.

Note that each object in a set must be unique – since there is no built-in structure, we'd have no way to tell the difference between two identical objects.

A collection in which objects are stored in a particular sequence is known as a **list**. We can specify positions at which to add or remove new objects within the sequence, and the list is free to expand or decrease in size. Since the list has a well-defined order, the elements do not need to be unique. Here's an example of a list, in this case a list of author names:

Author Name	Index Value
Ollie	0
John	1
Juan	2
Chris	3

Let's say that we wanted to add another author called Chris to this list. By default, the name will be added to the end of the list; however, we can specify that we want it added as the second element (index = 1), in which case the list becomes:

Employee Name	Index Value
Ollie	0
Chris	1
John	2
Juan	3
Chris	4

As you can see, the index values of all subsequent names in the list have changed automatically.

A **map** collection stores objects in **key/value** pairs: one of these objects uniquely identifies the pair (the **key**), while the other object contains the information we wish to store (the **value**). The role of the key is much the same as the index in a list or array, in that it uniquely identifies a particular element. However, unlike an index, a key does not need to be an integer, but can be any type of object at all.

Since we use the key to uniquely identify an object pair within the map collection, we cannot duplicate any keys within the map.

When we want to retrieve information from a map, we locate the relevant pair by looking up the appropriate key. Consider the directory of books shown below:

ISBN	Book Title
1861007345	Beginning ASP.NET 1.0 with C#
1861007035	Professional ASP.NET 1.0 SE
1861007442	ASP.NET Namespace Reference with C#

Every book has a unique ISBN, so it would be most convenient if we could get the book title by using its ISBN. In this case we would use the ISBN as a key to retrieve the book title.

Other types of lists include:

❑   **stacks** – lists in which new objects are always added to the end of the list, and removed from the end of the list (a 'last in, first out' system). This is analogous to a pile of papers – the first one you put down remains at the bottom of the stack, and isn't exposed until you've moved all your other papers off it again.

❑   **queues** – lists in which new objects are always added to the end of the list, and removed from the beginning of the list (a 'first in, first out' mechanism – like waiting in line for a movie ticket).

Arrays as Collections

Much of our discussion of collections may sound strangely familiar – elements, indexes, objects grouped together as a single unit; these are all characteristics of the arrays we looked at back in Chapter 4. In fact, arrays represent another variety of collection object, albeit quite a rigidly structured one.

We might think of a one-dimensional array (an array containing just one value per index) as a pre-populated fixed list, since it has all of the properties of a list collection described above, except that its elements are initialized when we create it, and its size is fixed – once we have defined it we cannot add new elements to it. Like lists, we use a unique index value to reference a particular element within an array. However, the value of a particular element in an array does not change unless we've manipulated that element directly. With lists, adding or removing objects can affect the placement (and index value) of other objects. This is a consequence of the ability of lists to fluctuate in size.

All the examples we worked through in Chapter 4 were quietly making use of the three main methods defined by the System.Array class:

❑   CreateInstance – Initialize a new instance of the System.Array class

❑   SetValue – Set the value of an element at a specified index

❑   GetValue – Get the value of an element at a specified index

Let's consider a very simple use of an array:

```
string [] AnimalArray = new string[4];

AnimalArray[0] = "Dog";
AnimalArray[1] = "Cat";
AnimalArray[2] = "Elephant";
AnimalArray[3] = "Lion";
AnimalArray[4] = "Cat";

string strAnimal = AnimalArray[2];
```

We start off by instantiating a one-dimensional array of type string, with a dimension length of 4 (remember that as the first element in our dimension is of index 0, defining a length of 4 actually gives us 5 elements). As we'd expect, this calls the class constructor (which instantiates an empty `Array` object called `AnimalArray`); it also calls the `Array.CreateInstance` method, which *initializes* the array by instantiating each of the elements in it. We could rewrite the first line as:

```
Array AnimalArray = Array.CreateInstance(GetType(String), 4);
```

Note that `CreateInstance` is a shared method (see Chapter 9 for more on shared methods), so we call it on the `Array` class rather than on our `AnimalArray` object. The first parameter we specify corresponds to the object type we wish to use for each element in the array. In this case, it should be an array of strings, so using `GetType()`, we specify the string type as the parameter.

The second parameter is the length of the 0th order index – the fact that we don't specify any more parameters indicates that we only require an array with one dimension.

When we assign values to elements in the array, we're implicitly using the `SetValue` method on the array. We could rewrite our first assignment as:

```
AnimalArray.SetValue("Dog", 0);
```

Likewise, we retrieve the third element (index = 2) for assignment to the `strAnimal` string variable by using the `GetValue` method:

```
strAnimal = AnimalArray.GetValue(2);
```

So, having said all this, we could rewrite our whole sample as follows:

```
Array AnimalArray = Array.CreateInstance(GetType(string), 4);

AnimalArray.SetValue("Dog", 0);
AnimalArray.SetValue("Cat", 1);
AnimalArray.SetValue("Elephant", 2);
AnimalArray.SetValue("Lion", 3);
AnimalArray.SetValue("Cat", 4);

string strAnimal = AnimalArray.GetValue(2);
```

It certainly doesn't make our code any more concise, but it does help to illustrate that we're working with a collection object, and making well-defined method calls on that object throughout. In the course of this section, we're going to take a look at some of the other methods implemented by the `Array` class, and see how they can make our lives easier.

Try It Out – A Simple Array Example

First though, we're going to turn our code snippet into an ASP.NET page. Note that we've reverted to using shorthand, indexed, notation when declaring the array and assigning element values, as we're not going to modify these in subsequent examples. However, we've left `GetValue` as an explicit method call, so that it's easier to compare with the other calls we're going to make:

1. Create a file called `animal_array.aspx` in your test directory, and enter the following code:

```
<%@Page Language="c#" %>
<script runat="server" Language="c#">
  void Page_Load()
  {
    string[] AnimalArray = new string[5]
                      { "Dog", "Cat", "Elephant", "Lion", "Cat"};
    MyLabel.Text = AnimalArray.GetValue(2).ToString();
  }
</script>
<html>
  <asp:label id="MyLabel" runat="server" />
</html>
```

2. Call up `animal_array.aspx` from your web browser, and predictably enough, you'll see this:

435

How It Works

Most of this code should be quite familiar to you. As usual, we include a `Page` directive, open a `<script>` block and specify a `Page_Load` procedure containing code to be called when the page is called up and loaded into memory. Inside this procedure, we place the array code we discussed earlier on; the only difference is that we assign the array element to `MyLabel.Text`, the `Text` property of a the `MyLabel` control, which we specify in the presentation block at the end of the listing.

When we call up the page, the code in `Page_Load` is executed, the third element in `AnimalArray` is assigned to `MyLabel.Text`, after explicitly converting it to a string:

```
MyLabel.Text = AnimalArray.GetValue(2).ToString();
```

and the presentation code (that is, the label control) is rendered in the browser.

Let's use this simple example to look at a few of the other things we can do with arrays.

Searching an Array

Say we wanted to find out which element in our array contains a specific value. The `Array` class provides us with another shared method called `IndexOf`, which returns an integer representing the first occurrence of a value in a specified array. For example, to find out which element contains the first occurrence of the string `"Cat"`, we might use the expression:

```
Array.IndexOf(AnimalArray, "Cat");
```

In our example, this would return the integer value 1. We can extend this slightly by adding an extra integer parameter, which specifies an index from which to start searching. For example, if we said:

```
Array.IndexOf(AnimalArray, "Cat", 2);
```

the search would commence at array index number 2, and return the index of the **next** `"Cat"` element in the array, namely 4. Finally, note that the shared method `LastIndexOf` will return the index of the **final** occurrence of the specified string. We might therefore use the expression:

```
Array.LastIndexOf(AnimalArray, "Cat");
```

Which will return the value 4.

We can use these features together to step through each occurrence of `"Cat"` elements in an array as follows:

Try It Out –Searching an Array

We're going to extend our `animal_array.aspx` page so that it lists all the occurrences in our array of the specific element that we want to find, in this case the string `"Cat"`:

1. Open up your editor and modify the code as highlighted below:

```
<%@Page Language="c#" %>
<script runat="server" Language="c#">
  void Page_Load()
  {
    int intCounter = -1;
    string[] AnimalArray = new string[5]
              { "Dog", "Cat", "Elephant", "Lion", "Cat"};
    do
    {
      intCounter = Array.IndexOf(AnimalArray, "Cat", intCounter+1);
      MyText.InnerHtml += "AnimalArray[" + intCounter + "]<br/>";
    } while (intCounter != Array.LastIndexOf(AnimalArray, "Cat"));
  }
</script>
<html>
  The string "Cat" occurs in the following elements:
  <br/>
  <div id="MyText" runat="server" />
</html>>
```

2. Save the file and call it up from your browser:

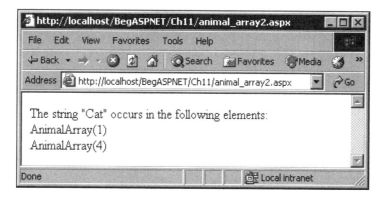

437

How It Works

The first line we add to our sample declares an integer that we're going to use to keep track of our search progress through the array. We initialize its value as –1, for reasons that will become apparent shortly:

```
int intCounter = -1;
```

Once we've set up the array, we start a do...while loop to search for elements and output their indexes. The first line of code within this loop uses the Array.IndexOf method to search for an instance of "Cat" on our animal array, starting at index intCounter+1. We've initialized intCounter to –1, so the search begins at AnimalArray(0) as we require – but why use –1 and intCounter + 1 in the first place? Bear with us just a moment more, and all will be explained.

```
do
{
    intCounter = Array.IndexOf(AnimalArray, "Cat", intCounter+1);
```

We've assigned the result of our search (which, as we already know, is the integer 1) to our intCounter variable (so intCounter now equals 1), which we now use to generate a message in the MyText HTML control:

```
MyText.InnerHtml += "AnimalArray[" + intCounter + "]<br/>"
```

Assuming this isn't the final instance of a "Cat" element in the array, we want to execute the last two lines of code again. At last it's time to explain the intCounter + 1 issue – this time, we want to search from AnimalArray(2) onwards, otherwise we're simply going to find AnimalArray(1) all over again. If you **don't** add 1 here, you'll find that your program loops round infinitely (or at least until the process times out) finding exactly the same element, each every time, and never getting any further.

Our new search proceeds from AnimalArray(2) and ought to find another "Cat" at AnimalArray(4), thus returning the value 4 for assignment to intCounter:

```
intCounter = Array.IndexOf(AnimalArray, "Cat", intCounter+1);
```

Once again, we add the information to our presentation control:

```
MyText.InnerHtml += "AnimalArray(" + intCounter + ")<br/>";
```

The while statement at the end of the loop specifies that when intCounter has any value other than that of the last index of "Cat", the loop should continue:

```
    } while (intCounter != Array.LastIndexOf(AnimalArray, "Cat"));
}
</script>
```

Of course, now that `intCounter` is 4, it's equal to the last index value, and the loop ends. We then use the same presentation code to display our results:

```
<html>
  The string "Cat" occurs in the following elements:
  <br/>
  <div id="MyText" runat="server" />
</html>
```

Working on Multiple Elements in an Array

There are various other `Array` methods that we can use to work on several elements at once. In particular, we can rearrange the order of elements in an array using the methods `Reverse` and `Sort`. To reverse the order of the elements in our `AnimalArray`, we'd simply use:

```
Array.Reverse(AnimalArray);
```

Likewise, to sort the elements into order, we'd just say:

```
Array.Sort(AnimalArray);
```

Now, wait just a moment. We're currently dealing with an array of strings, and it's not too hard to see how we can arrange them into some kind of order – given that all characters correspond to a specific numerical code (as defined by the Unicode standard) a case-sensitive alphabetical sort is the obvious one.

> **In fact, the precise manner in which .NET sorts strings will depend on factors such as the language you're using and the alphabetical conventions of your culture. It is possible to specify both of these attributes, but a full discussion of this is beyond the scope of the book. In our examples, we assume that the language and culture conventions in place are EN-US.**

Likewise, there's not much of an issue if we're sorting `integers`, dates, or other numerically based types. However, it gets a little murkier if you start considering arrays of other objects. How do we sort an array of arrays, for example? At this point, we could go into the details of how .NET determines how a specific type of object should be sorted, but it's a little beyond the scope of the book. Suffice to say, you can sort `enum`, `string`, and `version` type objects, along with any objects that are inherently numeric, but not much else.

If you want to make your own objects sortable in this way, you'll need to employ some relatively advanced techniques, and you may want to check out Professional ASP.NET 1.0 SE *(Wrox Press, ISBN 1-86100-703-5) to read more about this.*

Try It Out – A Simple Array List Example

In order to demonstrate our new ability to rearrange array elements, we're going to update our last example so that it displays the full array in a drop-down list. In order to populate it, we're going to use the `foreach` technique that was introduced in Chapter 6:

1. Copy the last sample code into a file called `sorted_array.aspx` in your test directory, and add the following code:

```
<%@Page Language="c#" %>
<script runat="server" Language="c#">
  void Page_Load()
  {
    string[] AnimalArray = new string[5]
                { "Dog", "Cat", "Elephant", "Lion", "Cat" };
      foreach (string strAnimal in AnimalArray)
    {
      MyDropDownList.Items.Add(strAnimal);
    }
  }
</script>
<html>
<form id="Form1" method="post" runat="server">
<asp:dropdownlist id="MyDropDownList" runat="server" />
</form>
</html>
```

2. Call up `sorted_array.aspx` from your web browser, and you should see this:

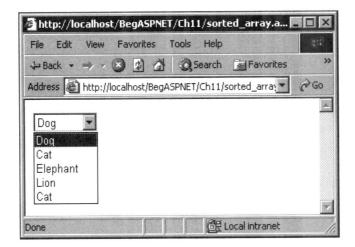

3. Now we'll update our code so that our drop-down list shows all the animals in reverse order. Open up your editor and add a single line as shown below:

```
...
  {
    string[] AnimalArray = new string[5]
                { "Dog", "Cat", "Elephant", "Lion", "Cat" };
    Array.Reverse(AnimalArray);
       foreach (string strAnimal in AnimalArray)
       {
...
```

4. Save the file again, and call it up from your browser – you should now see this:

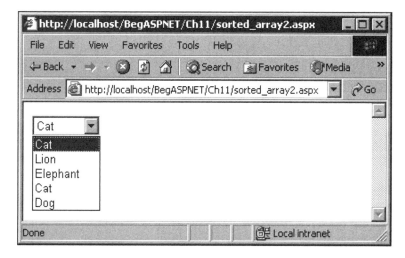

5. Now we'll update our code so that our drop-down list shows all the animals sorted in alphabetical order. Open up your editor and modify the same line, as shown below:

```
    ...
  {
    string[] AnimalArray = new string[5]
                { "Dog", "Cat", "Elephant", "Lion", "Cat" };
    Array.Sort(AnimalArray);
       foreach (string strAnimal in AnimalArray)
       {
...
```

6. Save the file again, and call it up from your browser – you should now see this:

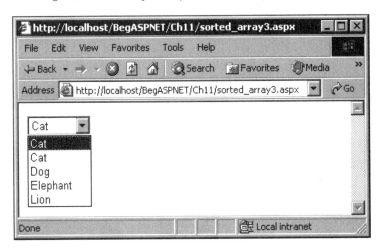

How It Works

Basically, we use a foreach statement to cycle through our array's elements and use the string they contain (that we defined as strAnimal in the first piece of new code we added) to populate a drop-down list:

```
foreach (string strAnimal in AnimalArray)
{
  MyDropDownList.Items.Add(strAnimal);
}
```

Remember that we were introduced to the foreach statement in Chapter 6, where we saw how it could be used to iterate through the elements in an array. As we're going to see later on, it can be used on all other collection objects in precisely the same way.

The order in which the elements appear in the drop-down list depends upon the order in which they're stored. So before the drop-down list is populated, we call the shared method Reverse() on the Array class to reverse the order in which the elements are stored, and, later, Sort() to arrange them alphabetically.

Data Binding

Another feature of all collections is that we can specify them as data sources by just adding a pair of statements. If you make the following changes to the code in the sample file sorted_array.aspx, for example, you'll see that the page looks the same as it did in our earlier examples:

```
  ...
  string [] AnimalArray = new string[5]
                            {"Dog","Cat","Elephant","Lion","Cat"};
  MyDropDownList.DataSource = AnimalArray;
  MyDropDownList.DataBind();
  ...
```

The first new line that we have added simply instructs the dropdown server control where to get its data from – in this case, the array. The second line binds the control to (that is, configures it to actually make use of) the specified data source. In this case, it simply applies the array elements to the items in the drop-down list.

Pros and Cons of Working with Arrays

Arrays are a very popular way to group elements together and there are some good reasons for that. However, as we noted earlier, arrays also have some distinct limitations. Let's take a look at how arrays measure up:

Benefits of Arrays

❑ **Easy to use**. Arrays really are very easy to use, and are present in almost every programming language – if you have done any programming before you will almost certainly have come across them. One of the reasons arrays are so widespread is that they are used to implement simple linear lists.

❑ **Fast to alter elements**. Arrays are just a consecutive list of items so altering one of the items is extremely fast and pretty easy, as we can easily locate any element.

❑ **Fast to move through elements**. Because an array is stored contiguously in memory, it's quick and easy to cycle through the elements one by one from start to finish.

❑ **We specify the type of the elements**. You'll notice that when we create an array, we can define it as a string array, or an integer array, or whatever. In fact, you can create an array to hold any type of object, and .NET will ensure that you only add objects of that type to the array. This benefit is not present with many other types of collection where you can add a mixture of objects of different types to the same collection.

Limitations of Arrays

❑ **Fixed size**. Once you have created an array, it will not automatically resize if you try to add more items onto the end of it. Although you can use the ReDim statement to change the size of an array's dimension, it is slow for large dimensions, and the fact that you have to perform the operation explicitly is far from ideal. Sometimes it's useful to have a list that just resizes, as we need it to.

❑ **Inserting elements is difficult**. If we wanted to add an element between two existing elements, it can be quite challenging. Firstly we may have to increase the size of the array to make space, but we then have to move all the elements up one so we have a gap for our new element. Arrays are just not designed to have new elements inserted in the middle.

443

Getting More from Collections

All in all, arrays are quite simple to understand, and very easy to use. However, we often need to find different ways to group items together – it all depends on what we need to do with them. The examples we've seen so far only really hint at the flexibility that collections can offer us – there's a lot more to come:

❑ A collection can contain an **unspecified** number of related objects (the elements in that collection).

❑ Elements of a collection need only be **related** by the fact that they exist in the collection.

❑ Elements of a collection do not have to share the same **data type**.

❑ An object's **position** in the collection can change whenever a change occurs in the collection as a whole; therefore, the position of any specific object in the collection can vary.

Given the number of different features that collections offer, you probably won't be surprised to discover that .NET provides a namespace called `System.Collections`, that contains quite a few collection classes that we can use in our applications; some of these are frequently used, others less often. In the next section of this chapter, we're going to spend some time looking at a few of the most useful ones:

❑ `ArrayList`

❑ `Hashtable`

❑ `SortedList`

Although the .NET Array type is not defined within the `System.Collections` namepace, it is nevertheless a bona fide collection. Since arrays are so widely used (playing an integral part in virtually all .NET code) the `Array` class sits in the first-level namespace, `System.Array`.

ArrayList

The `System.Collections.ArrayList` class is a special array that provides us with some functionality over and above that of the standard `System.Array`. Most importantly, we can dynamically resize it by simply adding and removing elements. Let's see how an `ArrayList` measures up:

Benefits of ArrayList

❑ **Supports automatic resizing**. When we create an `ArrayList`, we do not need to specify the array bounds; that is, we do not need to know at the start how big the collection is going to be. As we add elements, the array automatically ensures there's enough space for the new element. If there isn't enough space, .NET doubles the size of the `ArrayList` before adding the new element.

❑ **Flexibility when inserting elements**. With an array, we have a blank set of element spaces (we define the number of elements the list will contain at the beginning), and we can set each one to contain our chosen values. With `ArrayList`, we start with a collection with no elements, and we add them as we choose. In addition to this, we can do something that is pretty hard with arrays, we can insert elements at any chosen position in the collection.

❑ **Flexibility when removing elements**. In an array we can set any item to be blank (0 or " "), but we can't remove it entirely unless we shift all the elements above it down a place. But with ArrayList we can completely remove elements very easily.

❑ **Easy to use**. How easy ArrayList is to use is depends on your point of view, but given that it has some pretty intuitively named methods and properties, and they represent something we are all familiar with (items in a list), I think it's fair to say they are easy to use. You'll see later that there's a little bit more to creating an ArrayList object than an array, and the way we add elements is a little different as well, but that doesn't make it more difficult to work with.

Limitations of ArrayLists

❑ **Performance and Speed**. Given that the ArrayList control seems to offer so much more than arrays, you may be wondering why we bother using arrays at all – the reason is simply a matter of speed. The flexibility of an ArrayList comes at a cost, and since memory allocation is a very expensive business (in performance terms at least), the fixed structure of the array makes it a lot faster to work with.

We create objects from the ArrayList class in the usual way:

```
ArrayList myArrayList = new ArrayList();
```

We're using the new keyword since we are creating a new instance of the ArrayList object. As you can see, we don't need to specify how large it should be. Once we have an empty ArrayList object, we can use the Add() method to add elements to it.

Note that each new item is added to the end of the collection:

```
myArrayList.Add("Dog");
myArrayList.Add("Cat");
myArrayList.Add("Elephant");
myArrayList.Add("Lion");
myArrayList.Add("Cat");
```

Although the syntax for using ArrayLists is a little different from arrays, they are really quite similar to use.

Try It Out – Using an ArrayList

Let's update our animals drop-down list so it uses an ArrayList instead of an array as its data source.

1. Open up your editor and enter the following code, much of which is similar to our previous examples:

```
<%@Page Language="c#" %>
<script runat="server" Language="c#">
  void Page_Load()
  {
    ArrayList AnimalArrayList = new ArrayList();
    AnimalArrayList.Add("Dog");
```

445

```
      AnimalArrayList.Add("Cat");
      AnimalArrayList.Add("Elephant");
      AnimalArrayList.Add("Lion");
      AnimalArrayList.Add("Cat");
      MyDropDownList.DataSource = AnimalArrayList;
      MyDropDownList.DataBind();
}
</script>
<html>
<form id="Form1" method="post" runat="server">
  <asp:dropdownlist id="MyDropDownList" runat="server" />
</form>
</html>
```

2. Save the file as `arraylist1.aspx` in your test folder, and call it up in your browser:

3. Now add a single line to the code as highlighted below:

```
ArrayList AnimalArrayList = new ArrayList();
AnimalArrayList.Add("Dog");
AnimalArrayList.Add("Cat");
AnimalArrayList.Add("Elephant");
AnimalArrayList.Add("Lion");
AnimalArrayList.Add("Cat");
AnimalArrayList.Add("Platypus");
MyDropDownList.DataSource = AnimalArrayList;
MyDropDownList.DataBind();
```

4. Open up the page again, and you'll see that the new item has been added to the drop-down list:

How It Works

All we're doing that's new here is to use an `ArrayList` to hold our list of animals instead of using a standard array, as we've done before. We begin by instantiating it as `AnimalArrayList`:

```
ArrayList AnimalArrayList = new ArrayList();
```

Note that we don't specify a length for the new `ArrayList`, and nor do we specify an element object type. This is because the elements will be assigned dynamically (as and when we need them) and can be of any type.

Next we use the object's `Add` method to add strings as elements:

```
AnimalArrayList.Add("Dog");
AnimalArrayList.Add("Cat");
AnimalArrayList.Add("Elephant");
AnimalArrayList.Add("Lion");
AnimalArrayList.Add("Cat");
```

Finally, we specify `AnimalArrayList` as a data source for the drop-down list, and bind the data:

```
MyDropDownList.DataSource = AnimalArrayList;
MyDropDownList.DataBind();
```

This is enough to get our sample up and running. When we add an extra element in Step 3:

```
AnimalArrayList.Add("Platypus");
```

We see the effect of the dynamic sizing – we have an additional element in the `ArrayList` without having to have made the collection any longer. If we did this with an array and it was not long enough to hold the additional item, we'd see an error.

Some More ArrayList Techniques

Just like a standard array object, `ArrayList` provides the methods: `IndexOf()`, `Reverse()`, and `Sort()`. It also provides a property called `Count` (which is equivalent to the `Array` object's `Length` property; it lists the number of elements in the collection) and a few more very useful methods, some of which we're going to take a brief look at now.

Inserting Elements into an ArrayList

As we've seen, it's very simple to use the `Add()` method to add an item to the end of an `ArrayList`:

```
AnimalArrayList.Add("Platypus");
```

If, on the other hand, we want to insert the item into the middle of the list (in the example below, this is location 2), we can use `Insert()` as follows:

```
AnimalArrayList.Insert(2,"Platypus");
```

Using this in place of `Add()` in our last example, our list would wind up looking like this:

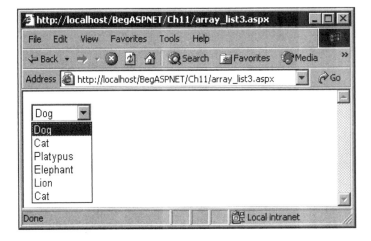

Removing Elements from an ArrayList

As an `ArrayList` makes it possible to insert items anywhere in the collection, it will probably come as no surprise that we can remove any element as well. Notice that when we talk about removing an element from an `ArrayList`, we're not just emptying an element (as we would if we set an array element equal to `nothing`) – we're literally destroying the element, and shortening the length of the array list.

To remove our Platypus element, we have two choices:

❑ We can either remove the element by specifying its index:

```
AnimalArrayList.RemoveAt(2);
```

❑ Or we can remove it using its content:

```
AnimalArrayList.Remove("Platypus");
```

Note that if a collection contains more than one matching element, only the first one (sequentially) will be removed.

Try It Out – Inserting and Removing Elements in an ArrayList

1. Make a copy of our previous code sample and name it `arraylist2.aspx`.

2. Make the alterations highlighted below:

```
<%@Page Language="c#" %>
<script runat="server" Language="c#">
  void Page_Load()
  {
    ArrayList AnimalArrayList = new ArrayList();
    AnimalArrayList.Add("Dog");
    AnimalArrayList.Add("Cat");
    AnimalArrayList.Add("Elephant");
    AnimalArrayList.Add("Lion");
    AnimalArrayList.Add("Cat");
    AnimalArrayList.Add("Platypus");
    AnimalArrayList.Insert(1,"Chicken");
    AnimalArrayList.Remove("Cat");
    AnimalArrayList.RemoveAt(0);
    MyDropDownList.DataSource = AnimalArrayList;
    MyDropDownList.DataBind();
  }
</script>
<html>
<form id="Form1" method="post" runat="server">
  <asp:dropdownlist id="MyDropDownList" runat="server" />
</form>
</html>
```

3. Call up the page in your browser, and you'll see this:

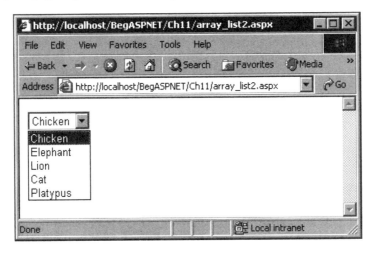

How It Works

All we've done here is to perform three additional operations on the `AnimalArrayList` object. We start by inserting the string "Chicken" as the second element (`index = 1`):

```
AnimalArrayList.Insert(1,"Chicken");
```

All subsequent elements now move along one place. We then remove the first instance of the string "Cat":

```
AnimalArrayList.Remove("Cat");
```

All subsequent elements now move back down an index place. Finally we remove the element with `index = 0`:

```
AnimalArrayList.RemoveAt(0);
```

The dog is banished, and the chicken takes pride of place at the top of the list. We've added one item and removed two, so we've ultimately shortened our list by one.

Hashtable

Earlier in the chapter, we described how map collections operate by bundling up objects as key-value pairs; the `System.Collections.Hashtable` class provides us with precisely this functionality. In some respects, the `Hashtable` object is quite similar to `ArrayList`, except that we don't have to use a numerical index – in fact we can use a variety of object types for the key (or index), and virtually any kind of object at all for the value.

For example, if we wanted to use country codes (such as US and UK) as settings in our page, we might want to discover the actual name of the relevant country, perhaps to display as text on the page. Here's an example of a `Hashtable` object that stores country codes and the full name of the country, in which we're using a string as both the key (country code) for the elements and also the element values (country name).

```
UK    United Kingdom
US    United States
DE    Germany
```

Let's take a look at the pros and cons of using the `Hashtable` object.

Benefits of Hashtable

❑ **Key-Value elements**. Each element in a `Hashtable` contains more information than an element in an `Array` or an `ArrayList`; it's smarter. The `Hashtable` object is less about storing information in a list, and more about doing lookups from one piece of data to another (as in our country code example above).

❑ **Inserting elements**. When we use a `Hashtable`, we're free to add as many pairs of key-value elements as we want. You'll remember we found that with plain old arrays, we specify how large they are upfront, and it's hard to extend beyond that size, but with the `Hashtable` object (as with `ArrayList` objects) there's no limitation like that, we just keep on adding items.

❑ **Removing elements**. Just as we can add items, we can remove items from `Hashtable` objects very easily too. Like an `ArrayList`, the `Hashtable` does the work of storing the key-value pairs in memory for us.

❑ **Fast Lookup**. The `Hashtable` collection provides very fast lookup.

Limitations of Hashtables

❑ **Performance and Speed**. Although the lookup speed is very quick, each time we add and remove items from a `Hashtable`, .NET has to do quite a bit of work in order to keep its lookup mechanism optimized. This work ultimately makes `Hashtable` objects rather slower to update than `ArrayList` objects.

❑ **Keys must be unique**. Generally this isn't a problem. For example with our country name lookup, there's only one country name for US, but if we had a `Hashtable` object full of names matched to e-mail addresses, we might find that some people have more than one e-mail address. We can't add more items to the collection because we're only allowed one key for the person's name. There is a solution to this though. There are collections in .NET where we can store one key and several values, generally the most useful of which is `NameValueCollection`.

❑ **No useful sorting**. The items in a `Hashtable` are actually sorted internally, to make it easy for the `Hashtable` to find objects very quickly, but it's not done by using the keys or the values, so for our purposes, the items may as well not be sorted at all.

Using a Hashtable

We create a `Hashtable` object from the `Hashtable` class, just like an `ArrayList` or any other Framework object:

```
Hashtable myHashtable = new Hashtable();
```

Once we've created it, we can then add the key-value pairs. Remember that the key is like an index for the entry, and the value is the data we're storing. We store each element using the `Add()` method:

```
myHashtable.Add["UK"], "United Kingdom");
myHashtable.Add["US"], "United States");
myHashtable.Add["DE"], "Germany");
```

This syntax works fine, but it's often tidier to use this simplified way of writing the same thing:

```
myHashtable["UK"] = "United Kingdom";
myHashtable["US"] = "United States";
myHashtable["DE"] = "Germany";
```

This syntax is much easier to read and makes use of a shortcut that .NET has built in. It does exactly the same thing, but there's much less typing, and it's a lot easier to read too. To read an element out, we just specify the key, and the value is returned:

```
string CountryName = myHashtable["DE"];
```

This will output the value **Germany**. Be aware that the keys are **case-sensitive**, so if we had written the following, we would have seen a blank result:

```
string CountryName = myHashtable["de"];   ' blank result, incorrect case
```

Sometimes, it's useful to be able to wander through our `Hashtable` object looking at each item and using the key and value data that it contains. Perhaps we want to display all the key-value pairs, or we want to run through some checks on them. Since it's a collection, we're able to use a `foreach` loop to do just this.

Let's look at an example page that cycles through the elements in our country codes `Hashtable`.

Try It Out – Moving through a Hashtable

In this example, we're going to build a page that displays a list of countries in a drop-down list. We're going to do it in such a way that when the page is submitted, the result we get back is a country code, and not the country name. What we're doing here is presenting user-friendly names, while behind the scenes we're using standard ISO country codes that are more efficient for our application to process.

1. Open up your editor and enter the following code:

```
<%@Page Language="c#" debug="true"  %>
<script runat="server" Language="c#">
  void Page_Load(object source, EventArgs e)
  {
    Hashtable myHashtable = new Hashtable();
    myHashtable["UK"] = "United Kingdom";
    myHashtable["US"] = "United States";
    myHashtable["DE"] = "Germany";
    if (!(Page.IsPostBack))
    {
      foreach (DictionaryEntry Item in myHashtable)
      {
        ListItem newListItem = new ListItem();
        newListItem.Text = Item.Value.ToString();
        newListItem.Value = Item.Key.ToString();
        myDropDownList.Items.Add(newListItem);
      }
    }
  }
  void Click(object source, EventArgs e)
  {
    myLabel.Text = myDropDownList.SelectedItem.Value;
  }
</script>
<html>
  <form runat="server">
    <asp:dropdownlist id="myDropDownList" runat="server" />
    <asp:button id="myButton" runat="server" text="OK" Onclick="Click" />
    <br /><br />
    <asp:Label id="myLabel" runat="server" text="" />
  </form>
</html>
```

2. Save it as `hashtable1.aspx` in your test directory, call up the page in your browser, and select a country from the drop-down list. Hit **OK**, and the page will refresh to show you the corresponding country code. Assuming we selected **Germany**, we'll see this:

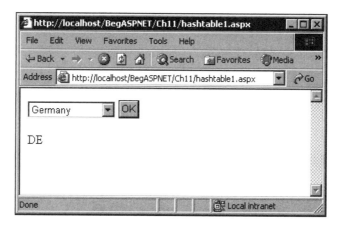

How It Works

When the page is loaded for the first time, we declare our `Hashtable` object, along with a `DictionaryEntry` object that we shall use shortly to hold key-value pairs:

```
script runat="server" Language="c#">
  void Page_Load(object source, EventArgs e)
  {
    Hashtable myHashtable = new Hashtable();
```

We define specific elements in the `Hashtable` using country codes as keys, and corresponding country names as values:

```
myHashtable["UK"] = "United Kingdom";
myHashtable["US"] = "United States";
myHashtable["DE"] = "Germany";
```

As long as we're not making a `Postback` request (meaning this is the first time the page has loaded), we then use `foreach` to cycle through the key-value pairs in myHashtable, using the `Item` variable as our placeholder. For each item, we create a new `ListItem` object to hold the pair of objects, and assign them as an entry in the dropdown control:

```
if (!(Page.IsPostBack))
  {
    foreach (DictionaryEntry Item in myHashtable)
    {
      ListItem newListItem = new ListItem();
      newListItem.Text = Item.Value.ToString();
      newListItem.Value = Item.Key.ToString();
      myDropDownList.Items.Add(newListItem);
    }
  }
}
```

Notice that we assign each item value (the country name) to the `Text` property of the list item (so as to be displayed on the list) while the item key is assigned to the corresponding `Value` property.

Next, we define an event handler to assign the `Value` property (of whichever item is currently selected in the drop-down list) to the `Text` property of the label control `myLabel`. This is how we'll present it on the browser:

```
    void Click(object source, EventArgs e)
  {
    myLabel.Text = myDropDownList.SelectedItem.Value;
  }
</script>
```

Finally, we have our presentation code – we create a form, in which we place a drop-down list, a button control (which we can use to trigger a call on `Click`), and the label `myLabel` to display the selected item value:

```
<html>
  <form runat="server">
    <asp:dropdownlist id="myDropDownList" runat="server" />
    <asp:button id="myButton" runat="server" text="OK" Onclick="Click" />
    <br /><br />
    <asp:Label id="myLabel" runat="server" text="" />
  </form>
</html>
```

When we click the button, we initiate a postback, and the button's `OnClick` event triggers the `Click` procedure, which assigns the appropriate country code to the label control. The refreshed page then shows the selected country code.

Note that if our `Hashtable` population code wasn't inside the `if` conditional block (the first part of which checks to see if the page has been posted to itself, it would be executed every time we triggered a postback, and the drop-down list would grow by three entries each time.

SortedList

A `SortedList` is another collection that stores key-value pairs, in which we can not only insert and remove items at will, but also rely on the items being usefully ordered. In fact it's really just like a `Hashtable` object whose elements are automatically sorted according to key. Just like `ArrayList` and `Hashtable`, the `SortedList` class lives in the `System.Collections` namespace.

Since the items in a `SortedList` are always stored in a well-defined order, we can reference elements using an index – in effect we get the best aspects of a `Hashtable` object (the ability to use key-value pairs) along with the best aspects of an `ArrayList` (the ability to sort the items). Remember however that the items in a `SortedList` are sorted on the **key**, and not on the value.

`SortedList`, then, is most useful when we have to sort a list of key-value pairs for which the ordering of the key is what matters, rather than the order of the values. For example, we might use a sorted list to hold entries in a dictionary:

Key	Value
amaryllis	an autumn-flowering South African bulbous herb (*Amaryllis belladonna* of the family *Amaryllidaceae*, the amaryllis family) widely grown for its deep red to whitish umbellate flowers; also : a plant of any of several related genera (as *Hippeastrum* or *Sprekelia*)
armadillo	any of a family (*Dasypodidae*) of burrowing edentate mammals found from the southern U.S. to Argentina and having the body and head encased in an armor of small bony plates

Table continued on following page

Key	Value
artichoke	a tall composite herb (*Cynara scolymus*) like a thistle with coarse pinnately incised leaves; also **:** its edible immature flower head which is cooked as a vegetable

Source: Merriam-Webster Online, Collegiate Dictionary (www.m-w.com)

We create and use a `SortedList` collection just like we do a `HashTable`. Remember we have to use the `new` keyword when we create the object. Adding items to a sorted list is exactly the same as with a `Hashtable`, the only difference being that each item is automatically inserted in the correct position in the list, according to the key-based sort order.

Try It Out – Using a SortedList

We're now going to modify our last example to present a list of words in alphabetical order, and display their definitions on request.

1. Create a new file called `sortedlist.aspx` in your test directory, and enter the following code:

```
<%@Page Language="c#" debug="true"  %>
<script runat="server" Language="c#">
  void Page_Load(object source, EventArgs e)
  {
    SortedList mySortedList = new SortedList();
    mySortedList["armadillo"]="any of a family ... small bony plates";
    mySortedList["amaryllis"]=
                "an autumn-flowering ... Hippeastrum or Sprekelia]";
    mySortedList["zebra"]="any of several fleet ... white or buff";
    mySortedList["artichoke"]=
                "a tall composite herb ... cooked as a vegetable";
    if (!(Page.IsPostBack))
    {
      foreach (DictionaryEntry Item in mySortedList)
      {
        ListItem newListItem = new ListItem();
        newListItem.Text = Item.Key.ToString();
        newListItem.Value = Item.Value.ToString();
        myDropDownList.Items.Add(newListItem);
      }
    }
  }
  void Click(object source, EventArgs e)
  {
    myLabel.Text = myDropDownList.SelectedItem.Value;
  }
</script>
<html>
  <form runat="server">
    Pick a word from the list:
    <asp:dropdownlist id="myDropDownList" runat="server" />
    <asp:button id="myButton" runat="server" text="OK" Onclick="Click" />
    <br /><br />
    <b>Definition: </b>
    <asp:Label id="myLabel" runat="server" text="" />
  </form>
</html>
```

2. Now call up the page from your browser, and expand the drop-down list. Note that the words are listed in alphabetical order, even though we didn't add them that way in the code:

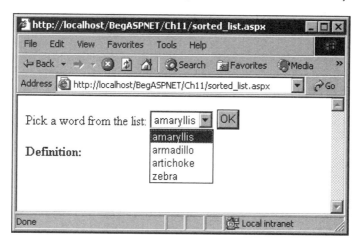

3. Select one of the words from the list, and hit **OK**. You'll now see a screen like this (with an abbreviated dictionary definition):

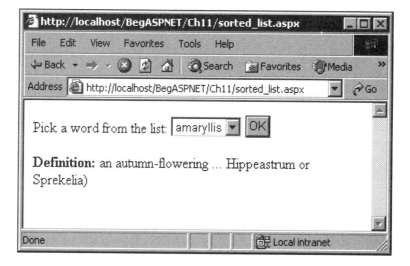

How It Works

We simply substitute a `SortedList` collection for the `HashTable` used in our previous example, and assign some new 'dictionary entry' elements, using word-definition pairs as key-value elements:

```
void Page_Load(object source, EventArgs e)
{
SortedList mySortedList = new SortedList();
```

```
mySortedList["armadillo"]="any of a family ... small bony plates";
mySortedList["amaryllis"]=
                "an autumn-flowering ... Hippeastrum or Sprekelia]";
mySortedList["zebra"]="any of several fleet ... white or buff";
mySortedList["artichoke"]=
                "a tall composite herb ... cooked as a vegetable";
```

We cycle through elements – which are already in alphabetical order – in the SortedList and for each one, we assign the key (word) to the Text property of a drop-down list element, and the associated value (definition) to the corresponding Value property:

```
if (!(Page.IsPostBack))
{
  foreach (DictionaryEntry Item in mySortedList)
  {
    ListItem newListItem = new ListItem();
    newListItem.Text = Item.Key.ToString();
    newListItem.Value = Item.Value.ToString();
    myDropDownList.Items.Add(newListItem);
  }
}
```

Besides a couple of additions to the presentation code, that's pretty much all that's new here. We display the text, drop-down list, button, and label, and once again use the button's OnClick event to trigger the Click procedure.

Summary

Collections are objects that are specifically designed to hold collections of other objects together as a unit. They feature standard methods with which to manipulate and organize their bundled elements, which may be worked on individually or as a group. These elements are only loosely associated by the fact that they're held in the same collection – consequently they're far more flexible than most other data structures.

Arrays are in fact a very rigidly structured type of collection. It's therefore quite straightforward to perform relatively complex operations – such as searching and sorting on element values (by means of shared method calls on the System.Array class). Since we can use collections as data sources for server controls, we can therefore bind arrays to such controls and show the contents of their elements on a web page without much effort at all.

An **ArrayList** is a flexible variation on the standard array, which we can dynamically resize by simply adding and removing elements at any position. Its flexibility comes at the cost of slightly higher system overheads than those incurred by a standard array, and reduced performance.

A `Hashtable` is similar to the `ArrayList`, but doesn't require the use of a numerical index. Rather it bundles up elements as key-value pairs, and sorts them internally based on their keys – it's therefore very efficient to do key-based lookups on elements in a `HashTable`. However, it also means that `HashTables` are less efficient than other collections when it comes to adding and removing elements.

A `SortedList` is another collection that stores elements as key-value pairs. In this case, we can also rely on the items being usefully ordered by key, and can therefore reference its elements using a numerical index.

All these other collections are defined in the `System.Collections` namespace.

Exercises

1. Describe a situation in which you would use each of the following and state why that choice is the best:

   ❑ Arrays
   ❑ Arraylists
   ❑ Hashes
   ❑ Sorted lists

2. Create an array with the following items:

   `Dog, Cat, Elephant, Lion, Frog`

   Display it in a drop-down list alongside another drop-down list that gives options on how the array is sorted.

3. Bind a drop-down list to an array containing five colors, then create a submit button that displays a line of text in the selected color when clicked.

4. Using a `Hashtable`, display a list of user names in a drop-down list with a submit button that displays the corresponding user ID when pressed. On the same page add two textboxes in which a user can enter new user names and IDs into the `Hashtable`.

   The newly created user name should appear in the drop-down list box, and the corresponding user ID should be displayed when the Submit button is clicked.

5. Create an ASPX page that takes a value entered via a textbox and searches for it in this sorted list:

```
mySortedList("armadillo")="any of a family ... small bony plates";
mySortedList("amaryllis")="an autumn-flowering ... Sprekelia)";
mySortedList("zebra")="any of several fleet ... white or buff";
mySortedList("artichoke")="a tall composite herb ... cooked as a vegetable";
mySortedList("aardvark")="a large burrowing ... termites and ants";
```

   The results of the search should be displayed on the page.

Reading from Data Sources

Data is the lifeblood of business, and being able to write ASP.NET pages that can access, display, manipulate, and modify information from external sources is an essential skill for an ASP.NET developer. So far we have learned how to create dynamic pages that come alive with interaction, but when it comes to deploying pages that are actually useful for a business we will need to be able to work with data. Just about any practical work on the Web will involve reading from and writing to various data stores. This may be as simple as providing a list of retail outlets, or as complex as processing an online order, but the common thread is that of using a web client – usually a browser – as an interface to a data source.

The .NET Framework includes a set of data access technologies – called ADO.NET – that make it easy for us to connect to data sources, access their data, display it, and even alter it. In this chapter we will introduce the main objects that make up ADO.NET, and look at how and when we might want to use them. You will see that it is not necessary to study ADO.NET data connections in any great depth to start getting results.

By the end of this chapter you will be able to create pages with several different methods of accessing information from a database, and ways of displaying this data. In the following chapter, we will see how to modify that data – add, change, and delete records, and we will see the important role played by XML in data access with .NET.

Understanding Modern Databases

Almost all useful applications need to be able to store and retrieve data. We have already discussed ways of using simple files for this purpose. While this approach is perfectly adequate for many simple applications, it has certain inherent limits in terms of design, performance, and scalability. The solution is to use databases, and in the following section we're going to consider this in detail. In particular, we will investigate the following topics:

- ❑ The advantages of databases over ordinary file systems
- ❑ Relational databases
- ❑ The core concepts behind relational data

As a programmer, one of the first decisions you'll have to make when creating even the simplest real-world application is what type of **data storage model** to use: in other words, how is your application going to store its data?

A simple comma-delimited file is all very well for small amounts of data, but it's not very well suited if you have information about a thousand customer orders and you need to find everything that a particular client has ordered. You'd have to search through all one thousand entries to find a match. By organizing data in a different way, we would save time and effort in implementing the kind of functionality necessary to do this. This is where databases come into their own.

A **database** is a collection of data that's been organized in such a way that its contents can easily be accessed and manipulated. Using a few well-established rules, you can determine how best to organize your data, and make it much easier to work with.

A **relational database management system** (**RDBMS**) provides software that's used to store, retrieve, and modify data in a database. An important component of an RDBMS is **metadata**, which describes the organization and nature of data. This metadata is frequently referred to as a **schema**. This will contain information about such things as the **tables** and **columns** in which data is contained, the relationships between tables, and so on. In essence, it describes a model of how our data will be structured. Getting the right data model is an important first step towards implementing an effective database.

Data Models

At its simplest, a database arranges data in **tables**, each of which contains one or more **columns**, and any number of **rows**. Each row in a table comprises a data **record**, which contains one or more **fields** of information (one for each **column**).

> **For all practical purposes, the term 'row' is synonymous with 'record', while 'column' is synonymous with 'field'. This is useful to bear in mind when visualizing tables.**

Suppose you keep a list of your site's users. The simplest method of achieving this would be to create a single table that records both user information and log data. It might look something like this, consisting of five columns (or fields) and a series of rows (or records). Each time new information is added to this table, a new row would be added:

User ID	User Name	User Country	Referring Page	Last Access
1	Jake Manning	United Kingdom	`www.wrox.com`	2003-09-05
2	Ewan Buckingham	United Kingdom	`www.microsoft.com`	2003-06-20
1	Jake Manning	United States	`www.gotdotnet.com`	2003-04-12

User ID	User Name	User Country	Referring Page	Last Access
2	Ewan Buckingham	United Kingdom	`www.wrox.com`	2003-04-21
3	Alessandro Ansa	Italy	`www.wrox.com`	2003-06-21
2	Ewan Buckingham	United Kingdom	`www.ASPToday.com`	2003-06-20

Normalization and Relational Databases

Take a closer look at the table above. The structure of the table is inefficient, because a visitor's information is recorded into the table *every* time they make a visit. Because of this duplication, values in fields like User Country and User Name are **redundant** (they are repeated).

Such redundancy is undesirable in a database. Why? Let's have an example. Say user Ewan decides to move to the United States. In order to update the table, *every one* of his records would have to be modified to include his address country. This is on top of the fact that every copy of his details takes up precious space on our hard drive.

Furthermore, if a clerk's finger slipped and entered Eqan for the last record, the table will not find both records in a search for Ewan. Redundancy is terribly inefficient, potentially wasting resources and impairing the performance of a database. Clearly, this will increase as a database becomes larger.

The notion of database **normalization** was developed to reduce data redundancy as much as possible. Normalization is the process of breaking up the data into several tables, so as to eliminate redundancy. For example, we could split the table above into a user information table and a log table:

User ID	User Name	User Country
1	Jake Manning	United States
2	Ewan Buckingham	United Kingdom
3	Alessandro Ansa	Italy

User ID	Referring Page	Last Access
1	`www.wrox.com`	2003-09-05
2	`www.microsoft.com`	2003-06-20
1	`www.gotdotnet.com`	2003-04-12

Table continued on following page

User ID	Referring Page	Last Access
2	`www.wrox.com`	2003-04-21
3	`www.wrox.com`	2003-06-21
2	`www.ASPToday.com`	2003-06-20

Notice how the original table splits naturally into these two new tables. This is because the original table provided data about two distinct things (or entities**): users and login sessions.**

Each new table contains data concerning just one entity. Although an entity is not strictly defined, you can consider it as one kind of object (person, place, thing, or type of concept). Common types of tables would represent data about such things as persons, orders, inventory items, and so on. This split of entities (and different types of information) into tables is an important element of the normalization process.

Having split our table up into entities, we can now take another step in the normalization process. Each entity must have (at least) one **unique** field. This is a field that will be unique for each row, and so will provide a way of identifying a particular row. Because of the unique nature of this field, each entry in it uniquely identifies each record in the table. This is important, because this can then be used to unambiguously refer to a specific record in the table. The field used to identify records is called the **primary key**.

Although you may have more then one field with unique values, only one primary key is named per table.

For example, in the user table we should use the User ID field as a primary key because it contains unique values. However, in our table, the User Name field also contains unique values. Which field should we pick to be the primary key? Well, there are several reasons why the User Name field will create problems. User names can change – if a user gets married for instance. Also, two different users might share the same name, which would mean this it would not uniquely identify them. The ID values are assigned by us, so we can ensure that they are unique, making them a far better choice for a primary key.

Let's review the benefits of normalization. Because we have grouped the user information into one table and the access log entries into another, the process of modifying a user's details becomes much more simple – we only have to modify one record in the user table.

Note that both the user table and the access log table both contain User ID fields. This is essential if we are to be able to associate particular users with particular visits to the site. It is via this field that the tables are *related*, and it is this that ensures that our simple database is now a **relational** database.

We can **join** information from the related tables in order to find answers to **complex queries**. For instance, we might want to find user information about users who have come from a particular site. Let's say we wanted to find out the nationality of the user that came from the gotdotnet site.

We know that it's Jake – that is, Jake Manning from the United States. The following figure shows the way in which the relation between the two tables can enable us to retrieve this information:

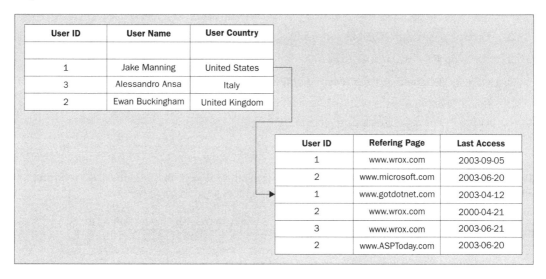

To summarize, the basic rules of normalization are:

- ❑ Minimize redundant data in individual tables

- ❑ Create a separate entity table for each set of related data

- ❑ Specify a unique field in each table to act as the primary key

Examples of **Relational Database Management Systems** (**RDBMS**) include commercial products such as Microsoft SQL Server, Access, Oracle, and Informix, as well as freely available systems such as MySQL and PostgreSQL.

For more information about Relational Databases see Beginning SQL Programming *(ISBN 1-86100-180-0 published by Wrox Press)*

Having introduced databases and how they work, we are now going to take a look at the technology that comes with the .NET Framework for accessing data from ASP.NET pages – ADO.NET.

ADO.NET

ADO.NET is the name for a group of object classes provided by the .NET Framework for interacting with data from data stores. Note that we specifically use the term **datastore** instead of **database**. This broader term includes the non-database containers of information, such as an XML file, as discussed later.

The ADO.NET objects provide ways of interacting in complex ways with many types of data – not only data stored in databases, but also data stored in e-mail servers, text files, application documents such as Excel, and XML data. Some common data sources include:

❑ Enterprise-strength RDBMS such as Oracle, Microsoft SQL Server, and IBM DB2

❑ Desk-top RDBMS such as Access

❑ Comma-delimited or fixed-length text files

❑ Spreadsheet files, such as Excel

❑ Microsoft Exchange Server 2000 data, such as e-mail

❑ XML-based data

This list is not fixed. The structure of ADO.NET connections is such that providers, drivers, and adapters can be written for data source formats that we haven't even imagined yet.

ASP.NET also makes formatting data on a web page easier than with Classic ASP. The `DataGrid`, which we will encounter later on in the chapter, creates most of the HTML tags for us. Furthermore, ADO.NET provides tools to work with data in an XML format.

When working with ADO.NET we actually work with a **disconnected** set of data. When a web site visitor requests data, a connection is made and the data is transferred, after which the connection is closed.

The user can then make changes to the data, but these will not be immediately updated in the source – we have to reopen the connection before updating the database with the changes made by the user. If we didn't use this disconnected model, then we would have to keep connections open until the end of the session for each user. On the Web, where there may be thousands of concurrent users, keeping a connection open for each user uses up resources. Using disconnected data makes our applications a lot more efficient and able to handle greater workloads: that is, they will be more **scalable**.

Bear in mind that in this book we discuss two very different kinds of connection:

❑ The connection between the browser and the IIS web server, most commonly via dial-up modem through an ISP or from a corporate desktop through the enterprise connection to the Internet.

❑ The connection between our Web Server to our Data Source. Typically, the data connection runs over the Local Area Network (LAN) between the Web Server and the Server hosting the data source. In the case of a small web application where the Web Server and data are on the same machine, the connection merely runs from one process to the other.

There are not specific names for these two kinds of connections, but you should be able to tell by context which one that we are discussing.

So, ADO.NET provides us with various ways to pull in data from diverse sources, and reduces the amount of code needed to do so. On the other hand, we still need to learn how to work with the ADO.NET objects and SQL, as well as having a firm understanding of the data source with which we are working. Let's take a closer look now at how ADO.NET communicates with the data store.

.NET Data Providers

To be able to get data from a data store you need some way to talk to the data store. This is a bit like talking to someone who speaks another language: you need a translator. The **.NET Data Provider** does that translation job for us.

Supplied with .NET are two data providers:

❑   The SQL Server .NET Data Provider, which only talks to Microsoft SQL Server version 7 or higher. Since this provider only needs to talk to one database it's optimized and extremely fast.

❑   The OLEDB .NET Data, which sits on top of OLEDB, allowing us to talk to any data store for which there is an OLEDB Provider. This means almost every data source other than Microsoft SQL Server.

A ODBC .NET Data is also available as a download from Microsoft (it does not ship with ADO.NET). You can get the 900 Kb file at www.msdn.microsoft.com/downloads; select .NET Framework and then select ODBC .NET Data Provider.

This gives us a structure like so:

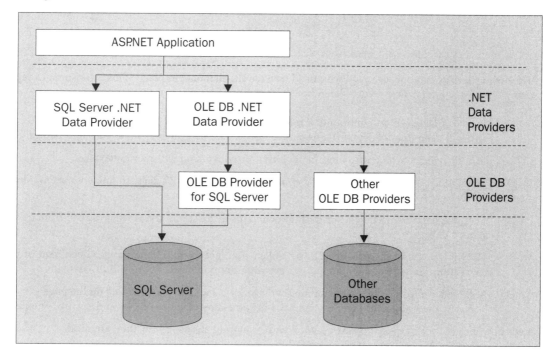

Note that the Data Provider for OLEDB has the extra OLEDB layer to go through, making it slightly, but not significantly, slower than the SQL Server provider that can access the data store directly.

Data providers are made up of four core objects, the `Connection` object, the `Command` object, the `DataReader`, and the `DataAdapter`. We will now take a look at how they work together.

ADO.NET Objects

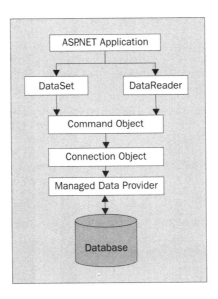

To work with data on your web page you need to have six elements in place. There are some exceptions and alternatives, but for now try to remember these:

- ❑ Source of Data – most commonly a relational database such as SQL Server, Oracle or Access. You will need to understand the basic structure of the data such as table and field names.

- ❑ Data Provider – which provides the facilities for conversing with our data store.

- ❑ ADO.NET `Connection` object – a conduit for your ASP.NET page to talk with a Provider or Driver.

- ❑ ADO.NET `Command` object – a tool that contains instructions about what to read from or say to your data.

- ❑ ADO.NET `DataReader` or `DataSet` object – a place to hold data that has been read or is to be written. These two objects support very different outcomes, as we will discuss later.

- ❑ ASP.NET controls – objects run at the server to format and display the data on the page – primarily the `<asp:DataGrid>` control, but sometimes also the `<div>` and `<span>` elements.

Let's now take at look at these objects in detail with examples showing how they are used.

The Connection Object

The ADO.NET `Connection` object is used to connect to a data source – it represents the actual connection between the data source and the data consumer. The **connection string** contains the information we need to connect to the actual store of data. It is made up of three parts, although there are differences between the different Providers and Drivers.

❑   The first specifies the kind of Provider or Driver that we want to use.

❑   The second specifies which database to use.

❑   The last section usually contains security information such as the user's name and password. These can come from the web page's visitor or may simply be an ID representing the web server and therefore not specific for any one visitor.

The three most common strings you will come across are those for Access, SQL Server, and the direct SQL Server .NET Data Provider connection. For Access, use the Jet Provider (*Jet* refers to the data engine within Access):

```
"provider=Microsoft.Jet.OLEDB.4.0;data source=MyDrive:MyPath/MyFile.MDB"
```

The standard OLEDB string for a database in a Microsoft SQL Server (all on one line):

```
"provider=SQLOLEDB.1;server=MyServerName;database=MyDatabase;initial
catalog=MyCatalog;uid=MyUserID;pwd=MyPassword"
```

The .NET Data Provider for Microsoft SQL Server has a similar syntax (note that there is no specification of a `provider`)

```
"server=MyServerName;database=MyDatabase;uid=MyUserID;pwd=MyPassword"
```

The syntax of the SQL provider connection string is different from other connection strings:

❑   The arguments are separated by semicolons

❑   Some argument names have a space in them (for example: `initial catalog`), which looks odd but is correct

❑   Quotes are not used around each argument value. Rather a pair of double quotes goes around the entire string

Once we have created the connection object and provided a `Connection` string, we can actually use the object. The two most frequently used methods are `Connection.Open()` and `Connection.Close()`. Between these two commands we can use the connection. Now, let's try setting up a connection.

> **ADO.NET has additional syntax for connection to other data stores. These are discussed in detail in *Beginning ASP.NET Databases using C#*, ISBN 1-86100-741-8.**

Connecting to Northwind

We will be connecting to "Northwind", a sample database of a small fictional company that comes with Access and Microsoft SQL Server. In this chapter we will restrict ourselves to reading and displaying data. We'll cover manipulating it in the next one.

You will first need to make sure that Northwind is installed. If you don't already have it, it's available with the code download from **www.wrox.com**. The code samples in this chapter assume that it has been placed at:

```
C:\BegASPNET\Ch12\Northwind.mdb
```

You might find it useful to repeat the Try It Out *sections in this chapter using a data source of your own creation. Once you've created the connection string, your main changes will be in the Field and Table names.*

Try It Out – Connecting to the Northwind Database in Access 2000

We're going to start our practical examples small, since there's a lot of ground to cover, and many ADO.NET objects to introduce. Here, we're only going to work with one of them, and focus on the simple mechanics of establishing a connection to a database.

1. Confirm that you have a copy of the `Northwind.mdb` file in `C:\BegASPNET\Ch12`.

2. Save the following code as `oledb_connection.aspx`. You can type it, or download from **www.wrox.com**.

```
<%@ Import Namespace="System.Data" %>
<%@ Import Namespace="System.Data.OleDb" %>
<script Language="c#" runat="server">
  void Page_Load()
  {
    string strConnection = "Provider=Microsoft.Jet.OleDb.4.0;";
    strConnection += @"Data Source=C:\BegASPNET\Ch12\Northwind.mdb";
    data_src.Text = strConnection;
    OleDbConnection objConnection = new OleDbConnection(strConnection);
    try
    {
      objConnection.Open();
      con_open.Text="Connection opened successfully.<br />";
      objConnection.Close();
      con_close.Text="Connection closed.<br />";
    }
    catch (Exception e)
    {
```

```
            con_open.Text="Connection failed to open.<br />";
            con_close.Text=e.ToString();
        }
    }
</script>
<html>
  <body>
  <h4>Testing the data connection
  <asp:label id="data_src" runat="server"/></h4>
  <asp:label id="con_open" runat="server"/><br />
  <asp:label id="con_close" runat="server"/><br />
  </body>
</html>
```

3. Call up the page in your browser, and you should see the following result:

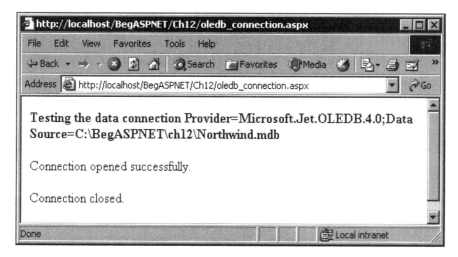

4. Now modify the connection string as follows:

```
string strConnection = "Provider=Microsoft.Jet.OleDb.4.0;";
strConnection += @"Data Source=C:\BegASPNET\Ch12\NonExistent.mdb ";
data_src.Text = strConnection;
```

5. Call up the page again, to see how it handles the invalid file reference in the connection string:

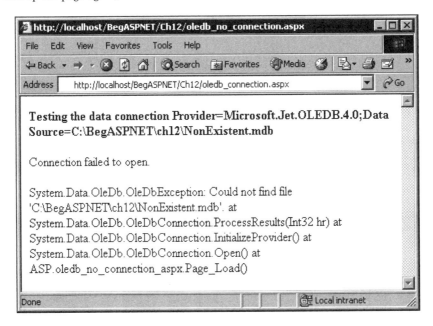

How It Works

Since this is our first look at Northwind, lets review a few facts about Access that impact on our ADO.NET pages. The MDB file used by Access stores all the information required to fully define the Northwind database, including both data and metadata (structure). Including the metadata and organizing the data into structured blocks makes Access files much more efficient then text files. The data within Northwind is properly normalized as per the rules we discussed earlier in the chapter. As we mentioned earlier, internally Access uses Microsoft's JET Engine to perform reading and writing to the data.

Our code begins with a couple of declarations, which import all the extra namespaces we require:

```
<%@ import Namespace="System.Data" %>
<%@ import Namespace="System.Data.Oledb" %>
```

The System.Data.Oledb namespace contains a class definition for OledbConnection, which we use to create a connection object for linking our code to the specific data source we're interested in. While we don't explicitly use any of the classes in the System.Data namespace at this stage, they underlie most of the data access functionality we will use, so it's good practice to import it nevertheless.

Next, we define a connection string, strConnection, which specifies the data provider we want to use (in this case the Microsoft JET engine) and the data source we want to use (the Northwind.mdb file we copied earlier):

```
<script Language="c#" runat="server">
  void Page_Load()
  {
    string strConnection = "Provider=Microsoft.Jet.OleDb.4.0;";
    strConnection += @"Data Source=C:\BegASPNET\Ch12\Northwind.mdb";
```

You can type the strConnection text all on one line, but it has been concatenated here to accommodate the size of paper in the book.

We include a little diagnostic display by assigning the connection string to the data_src label's text property so we can show it on the finished page. But its main purpose is to provide an argument when we create an OledbConnection object:

```
    data_src.Text = strConnection;
    OleDbConnection objConnection = new OleDbConnection(strConnection);
```

Note that we can use this syntax to instantiate the connection object because the OledbConnection class supports a constructor method that assigns a specified string parameter to its ConnectionString property. We could just as well have said:

```
    OleDbConnection objConnection = New OleDbConnection();
    objConnection.ConnectionString = strConnection;
```

> *Be careful not to confuse a string and an object with similar names. The **Connection** is an ADO.NET Object while the **connection string** is a variable containing the object's arguments. The string is quite long so we've built it into a variable called strConnection. We then created the Connection object and named it objConnection. The connection string (strConnection) is used to provide the information for making the connection with the connection object (objConnection).*

The next block of code sits inside a try...catch block, so that we can catch any exceptions that occur as a result of attempting to connect to the database. For now, we simply open the connection and close it again. If an exception is thrown in the course of the process, the catch clause picks it up, and uses the con_open and con_close labels to tell us what went wrong:

```
    try
    {
      objConnection.Open();
      con_open.Text="Connection opened successfully.<br />";
      objConnection.Close();
      con_close.Text="Connection closed.<br />";
    }
    catch (Exception e)
    {
```

```
            con_open.Text="Connection failed to open.<br />";
            con_close.Text=e.ToString();
        }
    }
</script>
```

Finally, we have the HTML from which the page is rendered, including the three ASP.NET label controls we mentioned earlier:

```
<html>
  <body>
  <h4>Testing the data connection
  <asp:label id="data_src" runat="server"/></h4>
  <asp:label id="con_open" runat="server"/><br/>
  <asp:label id="con_close" runat="server"/><br/>
  </body>
</html>
```

That's pretty straightforward – there's not much to show for it yet, but we have at least established a connection. Before we move on, let's take a quick look at what changes we'd need to make in order to access the same Northwind example in a SQL Server database.

Try It Out – Connecting to the Northwind Database in SQL Server 2000

As we've already discussed, the mechanics of connecting to a SQL Server database aren't that different from connecting to Access. We simply need to use a different class of connection object, and different parameters in the connection string:

1. Make a copy of the previous ASPX sample and rename it `sql_connection.aspx`.

2. Make the following amendments to the connection specification – of course, you'll need to use appropriate values for your server name (and possibly the user ID and password):

```
<%@ Import Namespace="System.Data" %>
<%@ Import Namespace="System.Data.SqlClient" %>
<script Language="c#" runat="server">
  void Page_Load()
  {

    string strConnection = "user id=sa;password=;";
    strConnection += "initial catalog=northwind;server= YourSQLServer;";
    strConnection += "Connect Timeout=30";

    data_src.Text = strConnection;

    SqlConnection objConnection = new SqlConnection(strConnection);

    try
    {
      objConnection.Open();
      con_open.Text="Connection opened successfully.<br />";
      objConnection.Close();
```

```
        con_close.Text="Connection closed.<br />";
      }
      catch (Exception e)
      {
        con_open.Text="Connection failed to open.<br />";
        con_close.Text=e.ToString();
      }
    }
  </script>
  <html>
  ...
  </html>
```

Note that this code will not work if your instance of SQL Server has been set up to use only Integrated Login. In that case, you'll need to replace user ID and password parameters with Integrated Security=SSPI.

3. Call up the page in your browser, and you should see the following result:

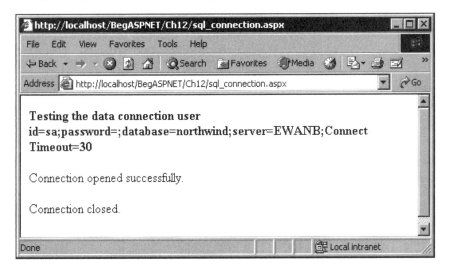

4. Now, once again, break the connection string by providing an invalid password:

```
    void Page_Load()
    {
      string strConnection = "user id=sa;password=;";
      strConnection += "initial catalog=northwind;server= YourSQLServer;";
      strConnection += "Connect Timeout=30";
```

5. Call up the page again, to see how it handles the invalid password in the connection string:

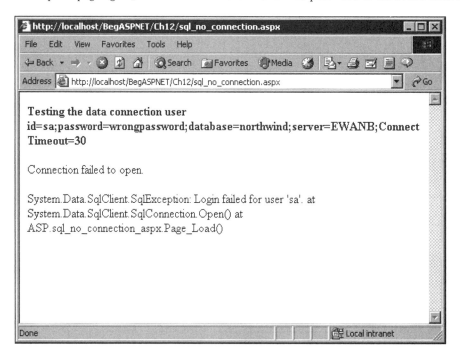

How It Works

This example demonstrates the flexibility of ADO.NET. We have connected to a completely different data source, SQL Server, yet very little of our code has had to change. The only real difference between this *Try It Out* and the last is that we used a `SqlConnection` object instead of an `OledbConnection` object and the connection string pointed to a different database. We will see more of `SqlConnection` later in the chapter. Let's now take a look at some more ADO.NET objects.

The Command Object and DataReader

Simply connecting to a data source is not enough, we also need to be able to read it and make modifications to it. The ADO.NET `Command` object contains the instruction we want to apply to the database. We can use its `ExecuteReader()` method to create a `DataReader` that displays the results of our query in a table.

Before we begin using the `Command` object we need to learn how to communicate with a relational database management system so that we can do things like create databases and tables, and save, retrieve, or update data. All of these tasks can be achieved using a standard language called **SQL**, or **Structured Query Language**. There is a SQL standard called ISO SQL–99, which defines the syntax that almost all databases understand. There are some modifications and extensions to ISO SQL–99 that are used by each RDBMS vendor, but the basic concepts and commands are always the same.

SQL Queries

SQL statements or **commands** are sent to a database engine. Some SQL statements ask for all the records that meet certain criteria. For example, we might ask the engine to retrieve records containing "John" as the first name. Other SQL statements don't return a result set. Instead they are commands that tell the database engine to do something. For example, to "delete all records that contain John as the first name".

There are four fundamental types of SQL statements:

❑   SELECT: used to **retrieve** data from one or more tables

❑   DELETE: used to **delete** data from a table

❑   INSERT: used to **add a new record** into a table

❑   UPDATE: used to **change** existing data in a record of a table

The typical form of a SELECT query, which retrieves records from a table, looks like this:

```
SELECT LastName, FirstName FROM User WHERE FirstName = 'John'
```

Take a closer look at the FROM and WHERE clauses in the query. The query returns any record **FROM** the User table **WHERE** the value of the FirstName field is John. Here's a sample of the output:

```
Simpleton John
Smith John
Thomas John
```

> *You can learn how to write more complex statements in the book* Beginning SQL Programming, *published by Wrox Press ISBN 1-86100-180-0*

After we have written our SQL statement we need to pass it to the Command object as a string, so it can then be applied to the database. We can set the SQL query string as a parameter to the Command object when we create it. We can then pass the SQL statement the Connection object as a parameter so that it knows how to find the database:

```
string strSQL = "SELECT LastName, FirstName FROM User";
OleDbConnection objConnection = new OleDbConnection(strConnection);

OleDbCommand objCommand = new OleDbCommand(strSQL, objConnection);
```

After our connection has been made and the Command object has applied the query to the database, we need a way of displaying the results. Fortunately, the Command object has an ExecuteReader method that creates an object called the DataReader – an ADO.NET tool for displaying data on pages. The DataReader is simple to use; it accepts data from the ExecuteReader method and then allows you to loop through its contents and put the information onto the page. (But be sure to read the next few *Try It Out* sections because we will show you a much better way to achieve the same goal later in this chapter.)

Try It Out – Reading Data with the DataReader

Our first try at displaying data in an ASP.NET page will be very simple. We will read the names of the employees from Northwind and display them in a list on the page.

1. Create a file called `datareader.aspx` in your test directory, and enter the following code. The shaded code is different from our last *Try It Out*, so you can start with a copy of the file and modify as follows

```
<%@ Import Namespace="System.Data" %>
<%@ Import Namespace="System.Data.OleDb" %>
<script Language="c#" runat="server">
void Page_Load()
{
  string strConnection = "Provider=Microsoft.Jet.OleDb.4.0;";
  strConnection += @"Data Source=C:\BegASPNET\ch12\Northwind.mdb";
  data_src.Text = strConnection;
  string strSQL = "SELECT FirstName,LastName FROM Employees";
  string strResultsHolder = "";
  OleDbConnection objConnection = new OleDbConnection(strConnection);
  OleDbCommand objCommand = new OleDbCommand(strSQL, objConnection);
  OleDbDataReader objDataReader = null;
  try
  {
    objConnection.Open();
    con_open.Text="Connection opened successfully.<br>";
    objDataReader = objCommand.ExecuteReader();
    while (objDataReader.Read() == true)
    {
      strResultsHolder += objDataReader["FirstName"];
      strResultsHolder += " ";
      strResultsHolder += objDataReader["LastName"];
      strResultsHolder += "<br/>";
    }
    objDataReader.Close();
    objConnection.Close();
    con_close.Text = "<br/>Connection closed.<br/>";
    divListEmployees.InnerHtml = strResultsHolder;
  }
  catch (Exception e)
  {
    con_open.Text = "Connection failed to open successfully.<br/>";
    con_close.Text = e.ToString();
  }
}
</script>
<html>
  <body>
  <h4>Reading data from the connection
  <asp:label id=data_src runat=server/> with the DataReader object.</h4>
  <asp:label id=con_open runat=server/><br>
  <div id="divListEmployees" runat="server">list will go here</div>
  <asp:label id=con_close runat=server/><br>
  </body>
</html>
```

2. Call up the file in your browser and you should see the following:

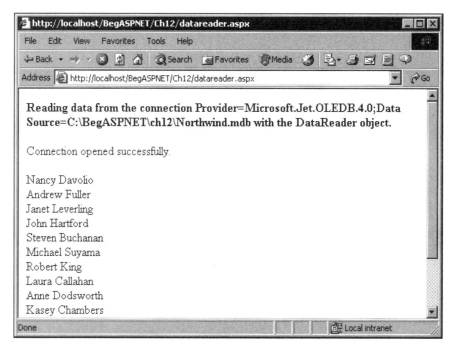

Reading data from the connection Provider=Microsoft.Jet.OLEDB.4.0;Data Source=C:\BegASPNET\ch12\Northwind.mdb with the DataReader object.

Connection opened successfully.

Nancy Davolio
Andrew Fuller
Janet Leverling
John Hartford
Steven Buchanan
Michael Suyama
Robert King
Laura Callahan
Anne Dodsworth
Kasey Chambers

How It Works

As usual, we start by importing the namespaces that will allow us to use the ADO.NET objects we need:

```
<%@ import Namespace="System.Data" %>
<%@ import Namespace="System.Data.Oledb" %>
```

Instead of making our statements very long and confusing (especially in the limited confines of the printed page), we put several strings into variables, namely:

❑ strConnection – A connection string describing the provider we want to use and where to find the required database

❑ strSQL – A description of the data we want from the database (the SQL Statement)

❑ strResultsHolder – A list of employees names extracted from the database

So, we set up three string variables to hold the connection string, the query string, and the results we're going to get back from the query:

```
void Page_Load()
{
    string strConnection = "Provider=Microsoft.Jet.OleDb.4.0;";
    strConnection += @"Data Source=C:\BegASPNET\ch12\Northwind.mdb";
    data_src.Text = strConnection;
    string strSQL = "SELECT FirstName,LastName FROM Employees";
    string strResultsHolder = "";
```

We now need three ADO.NET objects with which to query the database:

❑   A Connection object – that links our code to the data source specified in the connection string by means of an OLEDB provider

❑   A Command object – that holds and issues the SQL query against that data source

❑   A DataReader object – that holds and exposes the structured data records that it returns

Here's how we instantiate them:

```
OleDbConnection objConnection = new OleDbConnection(strConnection);
OleDbCommand objCommand = new OleDbCommand(strSQL, objConnection);
OleDbDataReader objDataReader = null;
```

Now that we've done our preparation, we are ready to fly into action. We open up a connection, and use the ExecuteReader method on our Command object to execute the strSQL query – the results are then stored in the DataReader object:

```
try
{
    objConnection.Open();
    con_open.Text = "Connection opened successfully.<br>";
    objDataReader = objCommand.ExecuteReader();
```

Once the data is in the DataReader, we use a loop to walk through each of the records and read the names of each employee into our results string. We read data from the DataReader into our results string, and apply some basic formatting along the way:

```
while (objDataReader.Read() == true)
{
    strResultsHolder +=objDataReader["FirstName"];
    strResultsHolder +=" ";
    strResultsHolder +=objDataReader["LastName"];
    strResultsHolder +="<br/>";
}
```

Now that we are done with using our ADO.NET objects, we close them. This frees up memory and improves the scalability of the site (that is, its ability to handle more simultaneous users). Notice, though, that we don't need to close the Command object because it is not 'opened' like the DataReader and Connection.

```
objDataReader.Close();
objConnection.Close();
```

> *In ASP.NET we do not have to set 'object=nothing' like we did in older ASP versions. This 'garbage collection' is now done automatically because this is .NET Managed code. However, in some scenarios setting the object to nothing will free up resources sooner than waiting for the automatic clean up.*

Now we have a full list of names in the variable strResultsHolder and we are trim and clean with all our ADO.NET objects closed. Our final step is to set the string built in strResultsHolder as the value of the text property of the <div> control. Note that since the string includes HMTL (albeit just   and <br />) we must apply it to the InnerHTML property rather than the InnerText property:

```
divListEmployees.InnerHtml = strResultsHolder;
```

Next we take care of any exceptions that may have been thrown:

```
catch (Exception e)
{
  con_open.Text= "Connection failed to open successfully.<br/>";
  con_close.Text = e.ToString();
}
}
</script>
```

Finally , we specify the required presentation elements, primarily a <div> element that we've called divListEmployees where the results of our database query are shown. As with all ASP.NET controls, check that you have included the runat attribute set to "server":

```
<html>
  <body>
  <h4>Reading data from the connection
  <asp:label id=data_src runat=server /> with the DataReader object.</h4>
  <asp:label id=con_open runat=server /><br>
  <div id="divListEmployees" runat="server">list will go here</div>
  <asp:label id=con_close runat=server /><br>
  </body>
</html>
```

Simple Data Binding

Data binding means linking a data source to a data consumer. In this book our consumer will be an ASP.NET Web Form control such as a label, textbox, or datagrid. If we want to display data from a database using a server control then we have to bind it to the database first. So far we've learned how to connect to a datastore, send a command to the store, and retrieve the data. When we get the data out of the database we know how to loop through the records and display them as simple text. In the past if we wanted to do anything more sophisticated with the data, like displaying it in a table, we were stuck with writing a lot of code. But with ASP.NET there are ways in which we can handle this data and do fancy things to it using the `<asp:datagrid>` server control. All we need to do is bind it to the data source and we can use it to do the following:

❏ Automatically format the output into a table for presentation on the page without having to loop through the records

❏ Enhance the formatting of the table with hyperlinks, format headers and footers, and alternate colors for each row

❏ Sort the data in the table

We will see more of the `DataGrid` and data binding in Chapter 13, but for now let's take a look at how we can use it along with the `Command` object to extract and display information from a database in a pleasing way, and with less code.

Try It Out – Using the DataGrid

In this example we will use the `Command` object's `ExecuteReader` method to make a page that shows the `Lastname`, `City`, and `Country` for each employee of Northwind. However, unlike the previous example where we had to manually loop through the rows, this example uses the `DataGrid` control and data binding:

1. Create a new file called `execute_reader.aspx`, and enter the following code:

```
<%@ Import Namespace="System.Data" %>
<%@ Import Namespace="System.Data.OleDb" %>
<script Language="c#" runat="server">
  void Page_Load()
  {
    string strConnection = "Provider=Microsoft.Jet.OleDb.4.0;";
    strConnection += @"Data Source=C:\BegASPNET\ch12\Northwind.mdb";
    string strSQL = "Select LastName, City, Country from employees;";
    OleDbConnection objConnection = new OleDbConnection(strConnection);
    OleDbCommand objCommand = new OleDbCommand(strSQL,objConnection);
    objConnection.Open();
    dgEmps.DataSource =
            objCommand.ExecuteReader(CommandBehavior.CloseConnection);
    dgEmps.DataBind();
  }
</script>
<html>
  <body>
    <h2>Using ExecuteReader to create a table</h2>
```

```
    <asp:datagrid id="dgEmps"
        runat="server"
        CellPadding="3"
        Font-Name="arial"
        Font-Size="8pt"
        HeaderStyle-BackColor="#dcdcdc"
        HeaderStyle-ForeColor="blue"
    />
  </body>
</html>
```

2. Test the page in your browser.

How It Works

The code starts no differently from our previous page. We begin by importing namespaces so we can find and use our ADO.NET objects, and there's no difference in connection or SQL strings, or in the creation of our `Connection` and `Command` objects. Note, however, that we don't create a `DataReader` object directly:

```
<%@ Import Namespace="System.Data" %>
<%@ Import Namespace="System.Data.OleDb" %>
<script Language="c#" runat="server">
  void Page_Load()
  {
    string strConnection = "Provider=Microsoft.Jet.OleDb.4.0;";
```

```
strConnection += @"Data Source=C:\BegASPNET\ch12\Northwind.mdb";
string strSQL = "Select LastName, City, Country from employees;";
OleDbConnection objConnection = new OleDbConnection(strConnection);
OleDbCommand objCommand = new OleDbCommand(strSQL,objConnection);
```

Now we encounter a change from prior exercises. Once we've taken care to explicitly open a `Connection` we fill the `DataGrid` control with the results returned by the `Command.ExecuteReader` method, and then we perform the binding:

```
    objConnection.Open();
    dgEmps.DataSource =
            objCommand.ExecuteReader(CommandBehavior.CloseConnection);
    dgEmps.DataBind();
  }
</script>
```

Finally we have the `<html>` section that contains the `DataGrid` server control where we apply a bit of formatting to make our table easier to read:

```
<html>
  <body>
    <h2>Using ExecuteReader to create a table</h2>
    <asp:datagrid id="dgEmps"
        runat="server"
        CellPadding="3"
        Font-Name="arial"
        Font-Size="8pt"
        HeaderStyle-BackColor="#dcdcdc"
        HeaderStyle-ForeColor="blue"
    />
  </body>
</html>
```

You can see that not only do you have to write less code to get the data, but that you don't have to loop through the rows. That's because the `DataGrid` takes care of this for you, creating an HTML table and the row elements for each row in the data.

The `DataReader` is an extremely efficient way of extracting and displaying data from a database. It has been optimized for this task. However, it pays for this efficiency by cutting back on other functionality. There are several limitations:

❑   It provides read-only access – you cannot change data using a `DataReader`

❑   It is forward-only – you can not navigate around the set of data

If you need to overcome the above limitations then you need to use more complex objects – namely the `DataSet` and `DataTable`. We'll look at changing data in the next chapter, but here we will use these other objects to display data without altering it.

The DataSet and DataTable Objects

ADO.NET works with disconnected data. It makes a copy of the data in the database for us to work with and then updates the database after we have finished. The `DataSet` represents the data in the database, and unlike the `DataReader` it can hold several tables and the relationships between them, navigate among those records, and even change data back in the data source. There are four ADO.NET objects at our disposal when working with a `DataSet`:

- ❏ `DataSet`: The central object we deal with is the `DataSet`, which can contain multiple tables and establish ad hoc relationships between them. These relationships associate a row in one table with another row in a different table.

- ❏ `DataTable`: This structure holds the actual data in a set of rows and columns.

- ❏ `DataAdapter`: This modifies and passes results from the `Connection` into the `DataSet`. The `DataAdaptor.Fill` method copies the data into the `DataSet`, and the `DataAdaptor.Update` method copies the data in the `DataSet` back into the data source.

- ❏ `DataView`: This represents a specific view of the `DataTables` held in the `DataSet`. It produces a description of the records and columns you want to read from the entire `DataSet`.

Let's look at these diagrammatically:

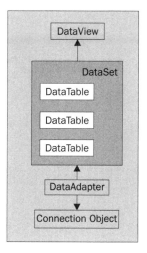

The flow of data is similar to the data reader. We get our data from a RDBMS or other data source by using a .NET Data Provider (see the section above on connections for more details). But in this case the data flows out of the `DataConnection` and through the `DataAdapter` that modifies the formatting of the data so that it fits in a .NET `DataSet`. From a `DataSet` it is possible to build a `DataView` that provides a specific subset of the data, with an optional sort. Last, we display the data in the HTML section using a `asp:DataGrid` server-side control.

Try It Out – Reading Data into a Table

We're now going to modify our last example so that the first and last names of the Northwind employees are presented neatly in an HTML table, using a `DataSet` object and a `DataGrid` control to save us from having to loop through the records.

1. Start off by creating a file called `datagrid.aspx`, and add the following code:

```
<%@ Import Namespace="System.Data" %>
<%@ Import Namespace="System.Data.OleDb" %>
<script Language="c#" runat="server">
  void Page_Load()
  {
    string strConnection = "Provider=Microsoft.Jet.OleDb.4.0;";
    strConnection += @"Data Source=C:\BegASPNET\ch12\Northwind.mdb";
    data_src.Text = strConnection;
    string strSQL = "SELECT FirstName, LastName FROM Employees";
    DataSet objDataSet = new DataSet();
    OleDbConnection objConnection = new OleDbConnection(strConnection);
    OleDbDataAdapter objAdapter =
                        new OleDbDataAdapter(strSQL, objConnection);
    objAdapter.Fill(objDataSet, "Employees");
    DataView objDataView = new DataView(objDataSet.Tables["Employees"]);
    dgNameList.DataSource=objDataView;
    dgNameList.DataBind();
  }
</script>
<html>
  <body>
  <h4>Reading data from the connection
  <asp:label id="data_src" runat="server"/> to the DataGrid control.</h4>
  <asp:datagrid id="dgNameList" runat="server" /><br />
  </body>
</html>
```

2. Use your browser to call up the file and you should see the following:

How It Works

This page starts out just the same as our previous `DataReader` example – the two strings that we create and fill serve the same functions as before. The first specifies the provider and database we want to use. The second holds the description (as a SQL statement) of the data we want to read from the database:

```
string strConnection = "Provider=Microsoft.Jet.OleDb.4.0;";
strConnection += @"Data Source=C:\BegASPNET\ch12\Northwind.mdb";
data_src.Text = strConnection;
string strSQL = "SELECT FirstName, LastName FROM Employees";
```

We now start creating our ADO.NET objects, and begin to depart from our `DataReader` example. The first difference appears when we create a `DataSet` object in place of the string we used previously to store our result set. This is so that we can retain the full structure of the data returned from the database:

```
DataSet objDataSet = new DataSet();
```

487

We must also create a `DataAdapter` that will allow the data from our database to be modified for our result set:

```
OleDbConnection objConnection = new OleDbConnection(strConnection);
OleDbDataAdapter objAdapter = new OleDbDataAdapter(strSQL, objConnection);
```

When the `DataAdapter` is created it takes two arguments:

❑ The query string that will define the exact set of data we want from the database (described by the variable `strSQL`)

❑ The `Connection` object (`objConnection`)

We now instruct the `DataAdapter` to output all its data to the `DataSet` object, and to give the newly created table the name "Employees". It is important for this table to have a well-defined name since `DataSet` objects can contain multiple tables and create ad hoc relationships between them:

```
objAdapter.Fill(objDataSet, "Employees");
```

ADO.NET lets us create various **views** of the information within a `DataSet`. This allows us, for example, to add several tables to a page, giving each its own set of columns and records as determined by various views. In our case we just want to view the entire `Employees` table as created in the last line:

```
DataView objDataView = new DataView(objDataSet.Tables["Employees"]);
```

Now that we have the desired view of our data tucked away safely in our `DataSet` within the ASP.NET code, we can focus on displaying that on the page. The next line establishes that the `DataGrid` control should get its data from the `DataView` object, we then call the `DataBind` method, which is actually responsible for assigning data to the 'name list' grid control, and results in its actually being displayed on the page:

```
    dgNameList.DataSource=objDataView;
    dgNameList.DataBind();
    }
</script>
```

In the `DataReader` we created a `<div>` HTML control in the presentation block to hold our output, but here we use a `datagrid` server control to create an HTML table:

```
<html>
  <body>
  <h4>Reading data from the connection
  <asp:label id="data_src" runat="server"/> to the DataGrid control.</h4>
  <asp:datagrid id="dgNameList" runat="server" /><br />
  </body>
</html>
```

Note that ASP.NET actually sends out a grid appropriate to the requesting device. So if the visitor was using a WAP phone or PDA the result may not actually be an HTML table.

To summarize our basic `DataTable` *Try It Out*, we want to keep in mind six points:

1. To display a table, we use a `DataGrid` control rather then a `<div>`

2. We need to create three ADO.NET objects: `Connection`, `DataSet`, and `DataAdapter`. In this example we also use the optional `DataView`

3. The `DataSet` holds structured data in `DataTables`, and can store multiple tables and relationships between them

4. The `DataAdapter` conducts data through the `Connection` object and reformats it to fit into a `DataSet`

5. The `DataView` brings together a set of columns and records from the `DataSet`

6. After the `DataView` is created we have to set the `DataGrid`'s source to the `DataView` and bind the data

We'll look at `DataGrids` again when we take a thorough look at ASP.NET's server controls in Chapter 14.

Microsoft SQL Server and ADO.NET

Microsoft has paved the way to optimize ADO.NET objects for various data sources, and we've seen that we can use the Data Provider for OLEDB to talk to an Access database. In addition to three of the objects used in the previous examples (`OleDbConnection`, `OleDbCommand`, and `OleDbDataAdapter`), Microsoft also produced siblings to each of these objects that are optimized for Microsoft SQL Server. They are named, logically enough, `SQLConnection`, `SQLCommand`, and `SQLDataAdapter`. Because these objects are optimized for Microsoft SQL Server they do not need to contain code to accommodate the differences between various other data sources. The SQL set of objects is both faster and less consuming of resources. In the future we might see additional ADO.NET objects that are optimized for the data sources of other vendors.

> **Only use the SQL Server .NET Data Provider objects when your data source is Microsoft SQL Server version 7.0 or higher.**

In order to use the SQL objects you must first import the namespace containing them. So your page must begin with:

```
<%@Page Language="C#"%>
<%@ Import Namespace="System.Data" %>
<%@ Import Namespace="System.Data.SqlClient" %>
<html>
```

Also, note below the different syntax in the connection string. You do not use a provider, so there is no "provider=" clause, instead we use "server=".

```
strConnection = "user id=sa;password=;database=northwind;server=Gateway;";
```

You can obtain a free trial version of SQL Server 2000, which is valid for 120 days, as a download from Microsoft or on the CD included with the *Beginning SQL Programming* text mentioned earlier in the chapter. Another option is to use the Microsoft Data Engine for SQL server. If you have a licensed copy of a Microsoft development tool such as Access or Visual Studio, you can get MSDE free from Microsoft. An equivalent product is available with the same restrictions for SQL Server 2000 called SSDE. Both can be downloaded from the Microsoft site: search for MSDE or SSDE. Alternatively, you can learn the ideas by studying this code without actually running it.

Try It Out – ADO.NET SqlClient Objects

We will use the SQL Server version of ADO.NET objects to create a list of names and hire dates of the Northwind Employees. Start by creating a new page named DataTableBasicUsingSQLObjects.aspx in your test direction.

1. Type or download the following code:

Note that when you specify strConnection you should use the name of your own Microsoft SQL server.

```
<%@Page Language="c#"%>
<%@Import Namespace="System.Data" %>
<%@Import Namespace="System.Data.SqlClient" %>
<html>
<head>
  <title> WROX Beginning ASP.NET - Data - Data Table <br/>
          Using Microsoft SQL Objects</title>
</head>
<body>
  <h2>Display of Data in a Table (Grid) Using SQL Objects</h2>
  Northwind Employees:<hr/>
  <asp:datagrid id="dgrEmployees" runat="server" />
  <script Language="c#" runat="server">
  void Page_Load()
  {
    // First we will set up variables to hold two strings
    string strSQL = "SELECT FirstName,LastName FROM Employees;";
    string strConnection = "server=mySQLServer;";
    strConnection += "database=Northwind;uid=sa;password=;";
    DataSet objDataSet = new DataSet();
    SqlConnection objConnection = new SqlConnection(strConnection);

    // Create new DataAdapter using connection object and select statement
    SqlDataAdapter objDataAdapter =
                          new SqlDataAdapter(strSQL, objConnection);

    // Fill the dataset with data from the DataAdapter object
```

```
      objDataAdapter.Fill(objDataSet, "Employees");

      // Create a DataView object for the Employees table in the DataSet
      DataView objDataView = new DataView(objDataSet.Tables["Employees"]);

      // Assign the DataView object to the DataGrid control
      dgrEmployees.DataSource = objDataView;
      dgrEmployees.DataBind();    // and bind [display] the data;
   }
</script>
</body>
</html>
```

2. Save the page and open it your browser. You should see the same list of employees as you did when using Northwind data in Access:

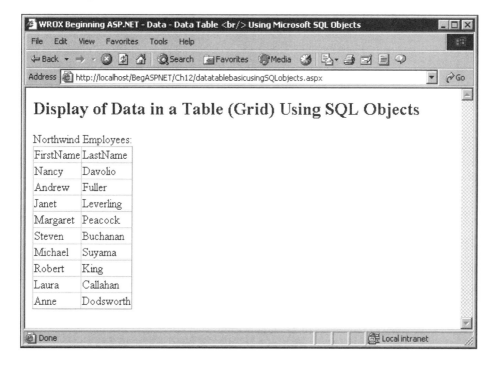

How It Works – ADO SQL Objects

Remember that our objective here is to list the employees from Northwind in Microsoft SQL Server. We could make the connection using OLEDB but in this Try It Out we will use the more efficient ADO SQL objects.

491

We start by importing a different namespace, the one holding the names of ADO's SQL objects:

```
<%@Page Language="c#"%>
<%@Import Namespace="System.Data" %>
<%@Import Namespace="System.Data.SqlClient" %>
```

There is no change from the OLEDB technique we studied earlier, until we have to create the string that will provide the connection details. Instead of using a driver or provider we just identify our server and database.

```
// First we will set up variables to hold two strings
string strSQL = "SELECT FirstName,LastName FROM Employees;";
string strConnection = "server=mySQLServer;";
strConnection += "database=Northwind;uid=sa;password=;";
```

And when we create our connection we instantiate a SQLConnection and SQLDataAdapter rather then their OLEDB equivalents, as below:

```
DataSet objDataSet = new DataSet();
    SqlConnection objConnection = new SqlConnection(strConnection);

    // Create new DataAdapter using connection object and select statement
    SqlDataAdapter objDataAdapter = new SqlDataAdapter(strSQL, objConnection);
```

The remainder of the code is no different from when using the OLEDB flavor of the objects.

The take-home message is simple. If your data is stored in Microsoft SQL Server version 7 or later (including 2000) then your ASP.NET data pages will be more efficient by using the SQL version of the ADO objects.

Catching Errors

As we'll see later, in Chapter 17, the .NET Framework provides ASP.NET with many useful methods of finding, and dealing with, errors. We're going to look at one, simple, method now, to see how we can deal with exceptions in our databases.

Let's first consider some of the things that can go wrong:

❑   Code contains references to an ADO.NET object that does not exist

❑   Code (or user) asks for data that does not exist, such as a person with last name "zzz"

❑   Code tries to connect with an improper connection string

❑   Code contains references to columns or tables that do not exist

❑   Code (or user) does not supply the correct User ID or Password

❑   Code uses a SQL statement of incorrect syntax

❑   The Web Server can not communicate to the data source because of a network problem

The key to using the C# structured error handling, is to understand which of these errors will be caught, and which will have to be resolved using other tools. You might be surprised at what is not caught. Internal errors, such as mistyping an ADO.NET object's name (point1 above), will result in a compilation error, whereas situations where no data exists for a specific WHERE clause (point2) result in no error – you just get no records returned. However, if you supply a faulty connection string, you will get a run-time error which must be handled using try...catch.

Try It Out – Reading Data into a Table with Error-Trapping

In this exercise we will add a simple error-catching routine. Then we will make some specific errors to see what is and is not trapped.

1. Create a new file called datatable_errorcheck.aspx and enter the following code. You can save time by starting with your datagrid.aspx page.

```
<%@ Import Namespace="System.Data" %>
<%@ Import Namespace="System.Data.OleDb" %>
<script Language="c#" runat="server">
  void Page_Load()
  {
    string strConnection = "Provider=Microsoft.Jet.OleDb.4.0;";
    strConnection += @"Data Source=C:\BegASPNET\ch12\Northwind.mdb";
    data_src.Text = strConnection;
    string strSQL = "SELECT FirstName, LastName FROM Employees;";
    DataSet objDataSet = new DataSet();
    OleDbConnection objConnection = new OleDbConnection(strConnection);
    OleDbDataAdapter objAdapter =
                       new OleDbDataAdapter(strSQL, objConnection);
    try
    {
      objAdapter.Fill(objDataSet, "Employees");
      DataView objDataView = new DataView(objDataSet.Tables["Employees"]);
      dgNameList.DataSource = objDataView;
      dgNameList.DataBind();
    }
    catch (OleDbException objError)
    {
      if (objError.Message.Substring(0,21) == "Login failed for user")
      {
        divErrorReport.InnerHtml = "Problem with Log-in";
      }
      else if (objError.Message.Substring(0,19) == "Could not find file")
      {
        divErrorReport.InnerHtml =
                    "We could not find the MDB file that you asked for";
      }
      else
      {
        divErrorReport.InnerHtml =  "<br />message - " + objError.Message;
        divErrorReport.InnerHtml += "<br />source - " + objError.Source;
      }
```

```
    }
  }
</script>
<html>
  <body>
  <h4>Writing data from the connection
    <asp:label id="data_src" runat="server"/>
    to the DataGrid control with error checking.</h4>
  <div id="divErrorReport" runat="server"> </div>
  <asp:datagrid id="dgNameList" runat="server" /><br />
  </body>
</html>
```

2. Save the page and take a look at it in your browser. Assuming there are no errors in the code, it should look almost exactly the same as the datagrid.aspx page from the *Try It Out* named *Reading Data into a Table*.

3. Now let's try introducing some deliberate errors – we might add a request for the employees' middle names:

```
string strSQL = "SELECT FirstName,MiddleName,LastName FROM Employees;";
```

4. Or we might specify a non-existent database as in the line change below:

```
strConnection += @"Data Source=C:\BegASPNET\ch12\Bogus.mdb";
```

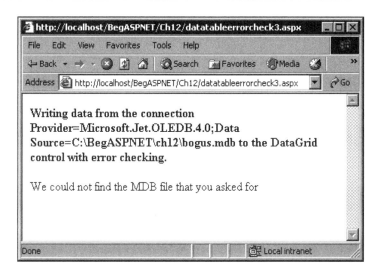

How It Works

The code starts the same as in the last few pages, so let's skip down to where we begin to declare our objects.

```
string strConnection = "Provider=Microsoft.Jet.OleDb.4.0;";
strConnection += @"Data Source=C:\BegASPNET\ch12\Northwind.mdb"
data_src.Text = strConnection;
string strSQL = "SELECT FirstName, LastName FROM Employees;";
DataSet objDataSet = new DataSet();
OleDbConnection objConnection = new OleDbConnection(strConnection);
OleDbDataAdapter objAdapter =
                    new OleDbDataAdapter(strSQL, objConnection);
```

Now we start a section of code that will either fully execute all lines without problems or execute none of them and give us the `catch` code instead.

```
try
{
  objAdapter.Fill(objDataSet, "Employees");
  DataView objDataView = new DataView(objDataSet.Tables["Employees"]);
  dgNameList.DataSource=objDataView;
  dgNameList.DataBind();
}
```

Now we write code that will be executed if there is a problem in any of the `try` section lines. We check for several possible starting strings in the error message. If we find a match then we assign a specific error message text to the `<DIV>` named `divErrorReport`. If we don't find a match then we just display the error that is provided by ADO.NET:

```
catch (OleDbException objError)
{
  if (objError.Message.Substring(0,21) == "Login failed for user")
  {
     divErrorReport.InnerHtml = "Problem with Log-in";
  }
  else if (objError.Message.Substring(0,19) =="Could not find file")
  {
    divErrorReport.InnerHtml =
                    "We could not find the MDB file that you asked for";
  }
  else
  {
    divErrorReport.InnerHtml =  "<br />message - " + objError.Message;
    divErrorReport.InnerHtml += "<br />source - " + objError.Source;
  }
}
```

The remainder of the page simply displays our results (or error).

Summary

Having learned the basics of ASP.NET theory and the techniques to interact with users, the next most important skill is the ability to work with data. ASP.NET uses ADO.NET, a suite of objects which allow a language such as VB.NET or C# to interact with data. ADO.NET is compatible with almost any kind of data through a long list of available providers and drivers. However, generally we are working with relational data.

The basic ADO.NET tools include the `Connection` object, `Command` object, and either a `DataSet` or a `DataReader`, with a `DataAdapter`.

Connection strings provide information to the `Connection` object about which data source to access, and how to work with that source. Connection strings have an odd syntax for their argument so be careful to enter them exactly as provided.

`Command` objects tell ADO.NET how to connect and read information from the data store. The data then actually resides in a `DataSet`. When using `DataSet` utilize the `DataAdapter` to format the data correctly for the `DataSet`. Alternatively the data can be passed through a `DataReader` that works more quickly by not actually holding the data.

Although SQL statements are not required by ADO.NET they are generally used as the fastest and most efficient way to get the job done. If you are using Microsoft SQL Server as your data source then you can then use a special set of ADO.NET objects that are optimized for that brand of RDBMS. Don't forget to import the namespace and be mindful of the connection string syntax.

If you only need to read (not write) data and you can get it in its final form with your SQL statement (no further sorting or filtering) then you can improve your page's performance by using the `Command.ExecuteReader`. This method fills your `DataGrid` without taking the time or memory space to create, stock, and read a `DataSet`.

In this chapter we covered the theory of ADO .NET and the techniques to read data. In the next chapter we learn to take user input and write that to our data store.

Exercises

1. Explain how the process of normalization helps us optimize databases.

2. Rewrite this section of code using the relevant connection object and namespace so that it can be used to connect to a SQL Server database, and modify the connection string accordingly:

```
string strConnection = "Provider=Microsoft.Jet.OLEDB.4.0;";
strConnection += @"Data Source=C:\begASPNET\ch12\Northwind.mdb";
OleDbConnection objConnection = new OleDbConnection(strConnection);
```

3. Write an ASP.NET page that uses the connection object to connect to the Northwind database and displays the following information using a `datagrid`:

a. The address, city, contact name, and telephone number of all suppliers

b. The names and addresses of all the German customers

c. Connect to Northwind and fill a `DataSet` with the Company Name and Contact Name fields of the suppliers table, create a `DataView` of the suppliers table and bind it to an `<asp:datagrid>` server control to display the results.

d. Repeat the above exercise, but this time bind the `DataGrid` to the `DataSet` instead.

e. Now fill the same `DataSet` with the First Names and Last Names of the Employees table as well and create another `<asp:datagrid>` to display the results so that both tables appear on one page.

4. Connect to a SQL Server database using the `SqlConnection` object including a `try...catch` block that traps login failures and incorrect connection strings.

Manipulating Data Sources

In the previous chapter we focused on the underlying theory of ADO.NET and on reading data. We covered this first because that's what we do most of the time in ASP.NET pages – display data. We saw the use of the `DataSet`, `DataReader`, and `DataView` objects, as well as how data binding can enable ASP.NET Server Controls to easily display data.

Of course, showing the data isn't the end of the story, as we often have to update it too. So, in this chapter we talk about how to change data in the data store by creating, editing, and deleting information. We'll look at two different ways of modifying data (using SQL statements and using the methods of the ADO.NET objects). In particular we'll be covering:

❑   The `DataSet`, `DataTable`, and `DataRow` objects

❑   Creating new records

❑   Changing existing records

❑   Deleting records

❑   Working with XML in ADO.NET pages, namely reading from an XML file into a `DataSet` object and writing from a `DataSet` object into an XML file.

You may think the last of these doesn't quite fit into this chapter, but one of the underlying principles of ADO.NET is its tight integration with XML. As we've already looked at XML in Chapter 5 we won't consider it again here. Instead we'll focus on methods of updating an XML file using ADO.NET objects, and see just how easy it is.

Disconnected Data

In the previous chapter we mentioned that ADO.NET is based on a disconnected architecture – once the data has been read we disconnect from the data source. This happens for two main reasons:

❏ **Database connections are resource hungry**. Keeping a connection open means it uses more resources (such as memory) on the database server. Database connections are also often limited in number, so keeping a connection open means one less connection available for someone else. The ideal is to use the server's resources for the least amount of time – get in, get the data, get out.

❏ **Application architecture**. In previous versions of ASP you might have built applications utilizing component technologies such as Microsoft Transaction Server MTS or COM (COM+ Services, as these are called in Windows 2000). This has meant we've often had to pass data around the various components, and in these cases the data is disconnected from the data source. For the loosely coupled architectures that .NET brings to the world, the disconnected model is perfect.

The whole idea of disconnected data is that it's not only more efficient for the database, but it also allows us to build better applications using components. This sort of architecture is usually quicker to implement, more robust, and more maintainable. However, it doesn't come without problems:

❏ **How do we actually update the data?** Any changes we make will be made to the disconnected data, and not to the original data source, so how do we get those changes back into the original data source?

❏ **What happens if someone else updates the same data?** It's not unusual for two people to want to update the same data, at the same time, and if they are both disconnected, what happens when one person updates the data source, followed by the other? Does the edit for the first person get overwritten?

We'll be concentrating on the first of these two problems, discussing the various ways in which data can be updated. The second topic is far more complex, and beyond the scope of the book – if you're interested in finding out about how ADO.NET can help us deal with problems like this, you may like to refer to *Professional ASP.NET 1.0 Special Edition* (Wrox Press, ISBN 1-86100-703-5), or '*Professional ADO.NET*' (Wrox Press, ISBN 1-86100-527-X*)*.

Methods of Updating Data

ADO.NET offers two main methods for changing data in your data store.

❏ In the first technique we use **methods** of ADO.NET objects to update the data, usually after finding the correct record first.

❏ In the second technique we create an **SQL statement** that fully describes the writing operation that we want to perform. We then direct ADO.NET to execute that statement on the data source.

The second of these techniques requires knowledge of SQL (Structured Query Language). We'll come back to this later in the chapter, but for now, let's concentrate on ADO.NET's features.

DataSets and DataTables

In the previous chapter our use of data was limited to the `DataReader` and `DataSet` objects. While the `DataReader` gave us the best performance, it was limited to retrieving data based upon a single table, query, or stored procedure. The `DataSet`, on the other hand, had the advantage of being able to deal with multiple sets of data. Here's a quick refresher of the `DataSet` in action. Consider the following code, which will display the employees in a data grid:

```csharp
<%@ Import Namespace="System.Data" %>
<%@ Import Namespace="System.Data.OleDb" %>

<script language="C#" runat="server">
  void Page_Load(object sender, EventArgs e)
  {
    string strConnection;
    string strSQL;
    DataSet objDataSet = new DataSet();
    OleDbConnection objConnection = null;
    OleDbDataAdapter objAdapter = null;

    // Set the connection and query details
    strConnection = "Provider=Microsoft.Jet.OLEDB.4.0; ";
    strConnection += @"Data Source=C:\BegASPNET\ch13\Northwind.mdb";
    strSQL = "SELECT FirstName, LastName FROM Employees;";

    // Open the connection and set the command
    objConnection = new OleDbConnection(strConnection);
    objAdapter = new OleDbDataAdapter(strSQL, objConnection);

    // Fill the dataset with the data
    objAdapter.Fill(objDataSet, "Employees");

    // Bind the data grid to the data
    dgNameList.DataSource = objDataSet.Tables["Employees"].DefaultView;
    dgNameList.DataBind();

    // Now do another one
    strSQL = "SELECT CategoryName, Description FROM Categories";
    objAdapter = new OleDbDataAdapter(strSQL, objConnection);
    objAdapter.Fill(objDataSet, "Categories");
    dgCategoryList.DataSource = objDataSet.Tables["Categories"].DefaultView;
    dgCategoryList.DataBind();
  }
</script>
<html>
  <body>
  <asp:DataGrid id="dgNameList" runat="server" />
  <br /><br />
  <asp:Datagrid id="dgCategoryList" runat="server" />
  </body>
</html>
```

The important point to notice here is these lines:

```
objAdapter.Fill(objDataSet, "Employees");
. . .
objAdapter.Fill(objDataSet, "Categories");
```

This is where we place the data from the command that fetches the data into the DataSet. The second argument is the name we want this data to have when it is stored in the DataSet. If this isn't supplied (it's optional), then the name used will be that of the source table (in our example code this is the same).

The reason we give it a name is that a DataSet can contain more than one DataTable. Each DataTable is held as part of the Tables collection, which allows us to store multiple sets of data within a DataSet:

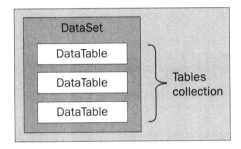

We're only going to use a single DataTable in this chapter, but the technique works the same no matter how many you have.

To access an individual table in a DataSet, we use the Tables collection. For example, assume we have a DataSet populated with data (as in our previous code sample). If we have named the data when we pass it to the DataSet, we can reference it easily when we want it later:

```
DataTable objEmps;
DataTable objCats;

// Later on in code...
objEmps = objDataSet.Tables["Employees"];
objCats = objDataSet.Tables["Categories"];
```

The name is also used when mapping tables within the DataSet to each other, but we're not going to be looking at this here.

The DataRow Object

In the same way that a DataSet can consist of many tables, a DataTable can consist of many rows, one for each row of data retrieved from the original data source. Each of these rows is represented by a DataRow object, and is held within the DataRowCollection collection:

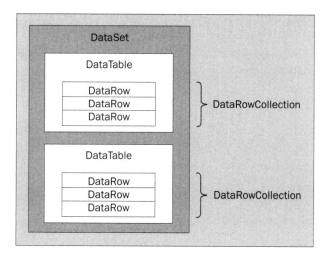

So the data is actually accessed through the DataRow object. We could use the following code to extract a single value (FirstName) from the first row (Rows(0)):

```
DataTable objTable;
string strFirstName;

objTable = objDataSet.Tables["Employees"];
strFirstName = objTable.Rows[0]["FirstName"];
```

> Notice that the **DataRowCollection** collection is zero based – so index **0** refers to the first row, index **1** refers to the second row, and so on.

The name we pass into the Item collection is the name of the column containing the data we want to extract. If we want to extract a single value for another field in the same row, we use the following code:

```
strLastName = objTable.Rows[0]["LastName"];
```

Let's now look at an example that enables us to modify data within a DataTable.

Try It Out – Adding, Changing, and Deleting Rows

We'll be conducting this *Try It Out* in stages, showing you three simple ways to manipulate the data held in a table.

> *You will need to ensure that you've got a copy of the **Northwind** database in your*
> `C:\BegASPNET\ch13` *directory for these examples to work.*

1. First of all, we will simply access some data from our database and display it. Create a new file called `EditingData.aspx` (or download it from **www.wrox.com**), and enter the following code:

```
<%@ Import Namespace="System.Data" %>
<%@ Import Namespace="System.Data.OleDb" %>

<script Language="c#" runat="server">

  void Page_Load(object sender, EventArgs e)
  {
    string strConnection, strSQL;
    DataSet objDataSet = new DataSet();
    OleDbConnection objConnection = null;
    OleDbDataAdapter objAdapter = null;
    OleDbCommandBuilder objBuilder = null;

    // Set the connection and query details
    strConnection = "Provider=Microsoft.Jet.OleDb.4.0;";
    strConnection += @"Data Source=C:\BegASPNET\ch13\Northwind.mdb";
    strSQL = "SELECT FirstName, LastName FROM Employees;";
    objConnection = new OleDbConnection(strConnection);
    objAdapter = new OleDbDataAdapter(strSQL, objConnection);
    objAdapter.Fill(objDataSet, "Employees");
    dgNameList1.DataSource = objDataSet.Tables["Employees"].DefaultView;
    dgNameList1.DataBind();

    // ----------------------------------------------------------------
    // Marker 1

    // ----------------------------------------------------------------
    // Marker 2

    // ----------------------------------------------------------------
    // Marker 3
  }

</script>
<html>
 <body>
  <table width="100%">
   <tr>
    <td>Original Data</td>
```

```
      <td>Data with new Row</td>
      <td>Data with edited Row</td>
      <td>Data with deleted Row</td>
    </tr>
    <tr>
      <td valign="top"><asp:DataGrid id="dgNameList1" runat="server" /></td>
      <td valign="top"><asp:DataGrid id="dgNameList2" runat="server" /></td>
      <td valign="top"><asp:DataGrid id="dgNameList3" runat="server" /></td>
      <td valign="top"><asp:DataGrid id="dgNameList4" runat="server" /></td>
    </tr>
  </table>
 </body>
</html>
```

> The Marker 1, 2, and 3 comments will help us add code as we expand this example.

2. Now browse to the newly created file. You should be presented with the following:

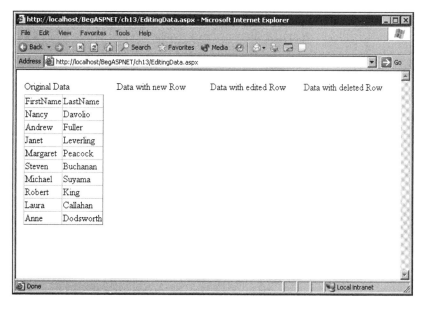

This is little different from some of the examples you saw in the previous chapter, but we'll use it as a foundation on which to build some more sophisticated functionality.

3. Now switch back to your editor, and add the following code at `Marker 1`. This will add another row to the `DataTable`, which will be displayed in another grid.

```
DataTable objTable = objDataSet.Tables["Employees"];
DataRow objNewRow = objTable.NewRow();
objNewRow["FirstName"] = "Norman";
objNewRow["LastName"] = "Blake";
objTable.Rows.Add(objNewRow);

// Bind the data grid to the new data
dgNameList2.DataSource = objTable.DefaultView;
dgNameList2.DataBind();
```

4. Back in the browser, hit the **Refresh** button (or *F5*) to see the new updated page:

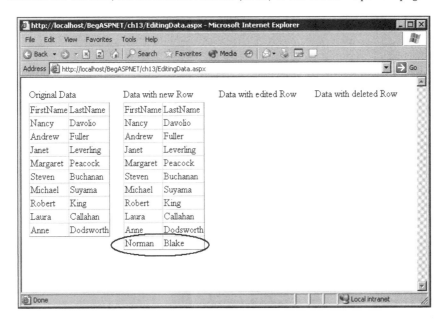

As you can see, another row has been added at the end of the table.

5. Let's look at editing a row now. In your code, add the following at `Marker 2`:

```
// Find the row to change
DataRow[] objRows = objTable.Select("FirstName='Margaret' AND " +
                                    "LastName='Peacock'");
objRows[0]["FirstName"] = "John";
objRows[0]["LastName"] = "Hartford";

// Bind the data grid to the new data
dgNameList3.DataSource = objTable.DefaultView;
dgNameList3.DataBind();
```

6. Back in the browser, hit the **Refresh** button (or *F5*) to see the new page:

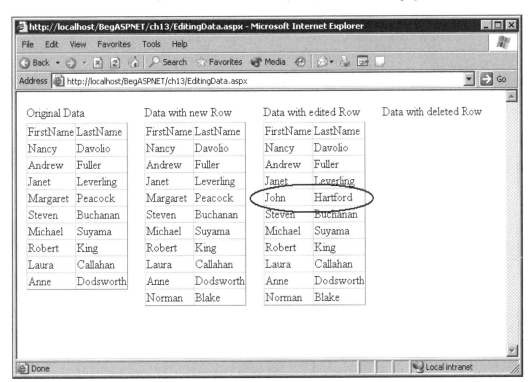

You can see that the row for **Margaret Peacock** has been changed to **John Hartford**.

7. Let's make the last addition to the code, by adding the following at `Marker 3`. This will delete a row:

```
  // The Rows collection is 0 indexed, so this removes the sixth row
objTable.Rows[5].Delete();

// Bind the data grid to the new data
dgNameList4.DataSource = objTable.DefaultView;
dgNameList4.DataBind();
```

8. In the browser, hit the **Refresh** button (or *F5*) to see the new page:

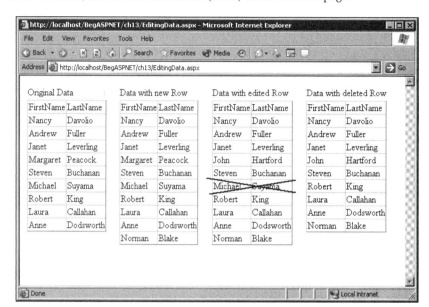

Here you can see that the row for **Michael Suyama** has been deleted, and doesn't appear in the fourth table.

Let's see how all of this code works. We don't need to examine the code that gets the data from the database, or binds it to the grid, as it's essentially the same as code used in the previous chapter. What we need to concentrate on here is how we **changed** the data. This was done by the code fragments we put in the markers.

How It Works – Adding Data

The first section of code adds a new row to the table. In order to achieve this, the first thing we do is declare two variables – one to point to the DataTable containing the data (objTable), and one to hold the data for the new row (objNewRow):

```
DataTable objTable;
DataRow objNewRow;
```

Now we use the objTable variable to point to the Employees table:

```
objTable = objDataSet.Tables["Employees"];
```

Next we use the NewRow() method of the DataTable object to create a new row:

```
objNewRow = objTable.NewRow();
```

This doesn't create a new row in the table – it just gives us a new `DataRow` object that we can add data into. We can then add this new row to the table once it is filled with data. The new row we've just created is currently empty, so we need to add some details to it. The rows in our table only hold first and last name information, but if you have tables with more columns, then you can fill in their values in exactly the same way:

```
objNewRow["FirstName"] = "Norman";
objNewRow["LastName"] = "Blake";
```

Now that we've filled in the details we need to add the new row to the existing table. Using the `NewRow()` method only creates a new row for us – we have to add it to the table ourselves. This isn't done automatically as ADO.NET doesn't know what we want to do with the new row, so it leaves us to make the choice. Recall the diagram earlier in this chapter, which showed how each `DataTable` has a `DataRowCollection` collection. This collection has an `Add` method, into which we pass the `DataRow` we want to add to the table:

```
objTable.Rows.Add(objNewRow);
```

Now we have our new row in the table, so all that's left to do is bind the table to the second `DataGrid` on the page, allowing us to see the results:

```
dgNameList2.DataSource = objTable.DefaultView;
dgNameList2.DataBind();
```

One thing to remember is that we are still disconnected from the database. This means that if your database has constraints (such as forcing the first and last names to have values), these constraints won't be enforced when adding the data to the `DataSet`. It's only when you update the original data store (which we'll see how to do later) that this becomes an issue. You can also create constraints on the `DataSet`, but we won't be covering that here.

How It Works – Editing Rows

First, we use the `Select` method of the table to find the row we want, and populate the `DataRow`:

```
objRows = objTable.Select("FirstName='Margaret' AND LastName='Peacock'")
```

The string we pass in is the same as a SQL WHERE clause.

We then update the data for the selected row. There could be many rows returned by the `Select` method, so we index into the array. In our case we know there will only be one row returned:

```
objRows[0]["FirstName"] = "John";
objRows[0]["LastName"] = "Hartford";
```

509

It isn't necessary to use the Select method, since you can edit the data directly, but using this method here makes it clear which row we are editing. If you prefer, you could just index into the Rows collection, using the following code:

```
DataRow objRow = objTable.Rows[3];

objRow["FirstName"] = "John";
objRow["LastName"] = "Hartford";
```

In this code we point the objRow DataRow at the row we are going to edit, by indexing into the Rows collection:

```
DataRow objRow = objTable.Rows[3];
```

> *It's important to note that the Rows collection (like other collections) is zero-based, so this line of code refers to the **fourth** row.*

Once the row variable is pointing to the correct row we can simply update the values for the appropriate columns:

```
objRow["FirstName"] = "John";
objRow["LastName"] = "Hartford";
```

Now that the data has been changed we can bind the data to a new grid so we can see the results:

```
dgNameList3.DataSource = objTable.DefaultView;
dgNameList3.DataBind();
```

> *Another method of finding rows is to use the Find method on the Rows collection. This method requires that primary keys are present.*

How It Works – Deleting Rows

Deleting a row from a table is a simple operation – we just use the Delete method of the DataRow object. In the code below we index into the Rows collection (each member of which is a DataRow) by specifying the row number as the index:

```
objTable.Rows[5].Delete();
```

> *Once more, remember the Rows collection is zero-based – this removes the sixth row.*

And once again we bind the data to a new grid:

```
dgNameList4.DataSource = objTable.DefaultView;
dgNameList4.DataBind();
```

Like the editing code, which we discussed earlier, we could have used the `Select` method of the table to return the rows we want to delete.

Updating the Original Data Source

You can see from the code shown above how simple changing data is. The one thing you have to remember is that we are dealing with **disconnected data**. The `DataSet` has not retained a connection to the original database, so any changes we have made are only reflected in our `DataSet` (you can easily see this by hitting the **Refresh** button on the browser (*F5*): on subsequent refreshes the original data is always the same). Other people using the database will not be able to see our changes.

This is one of the big problems of using disconnected data, but it's not so big a problem that you have to worry about it too much: ADO.NET was designed with disconnected data in mind, and provides simple ways for us to push our data back into the original data store. Part of this mechanism is the `Command` object, which was briefly introduced in the previous chapter. To understand more about how the `DataSet` and the original data store are synchronized, we need to look at the `Command` objects in more detail. We need to see how we can generate commands that will perform our updates on the data store.

There's a lot of theory to get through before we can actually perform an update, but it's not complex, and it's important to go through this so you can understand what's happening – just bear with us for a while.

The Command Object

In the previous chapter we used a `Command` object to provide a link between the `Connection` and the `DataAdapter`, enabling SQL commands to be run. To perform simple actions with ADO.NET you don't need to know much about the command objects, but there are some properties that will be required if you want to customize the update process. These properties are:

Property	Description
`Connection`	A `Connection` object containing the details of the connection to the data store.
`CommandText`	The text of the command to be run.
`CommandType`	The type of command, such as an SQL `string` or the name of a stored procedure. This can be one of:
	`Text`, to indicate a text string (this is the default),
	`TableDirect`, to indicate the name of a table,
	`StoredProcdure`, to indicate the name of a stored procedure.
`Parameters`	A collection of `Parameter` objects, for use with commands that require parameters to be passed to the data store.

Like some of the other objects in ADO.NET, there are two types of `Command` object:

❑ `OleDbCommand`, for use with OLEDB data stores

❑ `SqlCommand`, for use only with SQL Server

> *A third type of `Command` object, for ODBC, is available as part of the ODBC Data Provider, used to access ODBC data sources. This may be downloaded from http://msdn.microsoft.com/downloads/sample.asp?url= /msdn-files/027/001/668/msdncompositedoc.xml.*

In the previous chapter we showed a `Command` being used like this:

```
OleDbCommand objCommand = new OleDbCommand(strSQL, objConnection);
```

This created a new `Command` object, passing in a SQL `string` and a `Connection` object. This has the effect of setting the `CommandText` property to the SQL string that is passed in, and the `Connection` property to the `Connection` object that is also passed in.

The DataAdapter Object

Having explained the `Command` object in a little more detail, it's now time to see where this fits into the `DataAdapter`. Let's first look at a line of code we used earlier the chapter:

```
OleDbDataAdapter objAdapter = new OleDbDataAdapter(strSQL, objConnection);
```

Here we create a new `OleDbDataAdapter`, passing in an SQL string and a `Connection` object, much the same as we did for the `Command` object example. So what's the difference between the `Command` object and the `DataAdapter` object? Well, the `Command` is designed to run a command, and the `DataAdapter` is designed to provide a storage space for multiple commands, which provide two-way interaction between the actual data store and the `DataSet`.

Firstly we have to have a `Command` to fetch the data from the data store. Then we need a separate one to update the data, another to insert new data, and finally one to delete data. It's not possible to use the same command for each of these, because the syntax differs for each one. Remember how, in the previous chapter, we mentioned the following SQL statements?

❑ `SELECT`: used to retrieve data from a database

❑ `DELETE`: used to delete data from a database

❑ `INSERT`: used to insert data into a database

❑ `UPDATE`: used to update data in a table

To run any of these types of SQL queries we need to use a `Command` object, but since there are four possible types of command, we need a way to store those multiple commands.

The DataAdapter Command Objects

The `DataAdapter` has four properties that hold `Command` objects for just this purpose – the storing of commands to perform the different types of fetch and update operations to be run against the data store. The diagram below should make this clear:

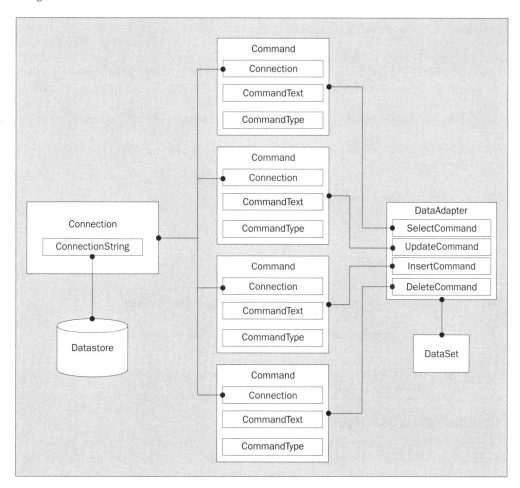

Four of the key properties of the `DataAdapter` are :

Property	Description
`SelectCommand`	The `Command` used when data is fetched from the data store
`UpdateCommand`	The `Command` used when the data store is to be updated
`InsertCommand`	The `Command` used when data is to be inserted into the data store

Table continued on following page

Property	Description
DeleteCommand	The Command used when data is to be deleted from the data store

Each of these properties is a Command object, and therefore contains the properties of the Command object, such as CommandText and CommandType.

This is important because it's these Command objects that are used whenever data is transferred to and from the data store. The good news is that you don't always have to create these yourself. For example, let's consider the DataAdapter line of code again:

```
OleDbDataAdapter objAdapter = new OleDbDataAdapter(strSQL, objConnection);
```

Have you noticed that we didn't explicitly create a Command object for this, but the command still works? Here's what happens:

1. A Command object is automatically created for us.

2. The command text (strSQL) is assigned to the CommandText property of the Command object.

3. The Connection object (objConnection) is assigned to the Connection property of the Command object.

4. The CommandType property of the Command object is set to Text.

5. The Command object is assigned to the SelectCommand of the DataAdapter.

So, under the covers, ADO.NET is doing a lot of work for us. Where this gets really clever is that the other Command objects can be generated too.

The CommandBuilder Object

To enable ADO.NET to generate the commands for updates, insertions, and deletions, we use the CommandBuilder object. This object uses details from the SelectCommand property of the DataAdapter to work out what the SQL statements should be for the other commands, and creates a Command object for us. It's pretty simple to use, so let's give it a go, and then we'll look at the code in more detail later.

Try It Out – Auto-Generated Commands

1. In your editor, create a new file called CommandObjects.aspx, and add the following code:

```
<%@ Import Namespace="System.Data" %>
<%@ Import Namespace="System.Data.OleDb" %>

<script Language="c#" runat="server">
```

```
    void Page_Load(object sender, EventArgs e)
    {
      string strConnection, strSQL;
      DataSet objDataSet = new DataSet();
      OleDbConnection objConnection = null;
      OleDbDataAdapter objAdapter = null;
      OleDbCommand objCommand = null;
      OleDbCommandBuilder objBuilder = null;

      // Set the connection and query details
      strConnection = "Provider=Microsoft.Jet.OleDb.4.0;";
      strConnection += @"Data Source=C:\BegASPNET\ch13\Northwind.mdb";
      strSQL = "SELECT EmployeeID, FirstName, LastName FROM Employees";

      // Open the connection and set the command
      objConnection = new OleDbConnection(strConnection);
      objAdapter = new OleDbDataAdapter(strSQL, objConnection);

      // Create the other commands
      objBuilder = new OleDbCommandBuilder(objAdapter);
      objAdapter.UpdateCommand = objBuilder.GetUpdateCommand();
      objAdapter.InsertCommand = objBuilder.GetInsertCommand();
      objAdapter.DeleteCommand = objBuilder.GetDeleteCommand();

      // Now display the CommandText property from each command
      lblSelectCommand.Text = objAdapter.SelectCommand.CommandText;
      lblUpdateCommand.Text = objAdapter.UpdateCommand.CommandText;
      lblInsertCommand.Text = objAdapter.InsertCommand.CommandText;
      lblDeleteCommand.Text = objAdapter.DeleteCommand.CommandText;
    }
</script>
<html>
 <body>
  <table border="1">
   <tr>
    <td>Command</td>
    <td>CommandText</td>
   </tr>
   <tr>
    <td>SelectCommand</td>
    <td><asp:Label id="lblSelectCommand" runat="server" /></td>
   </tr>
   <tr>
    <td>UpdateCommand</td>
    <td><asp:Label id="lblUpdateCommand" runat="server" /></td>
   </tr>
   <tr>
    <td>InsertCommand </td>
    <td><asp:Label id="lblInsertCommand" runat="server" /></td>
   </tr>
   <tr>
    <td>DeleteCommand</td>
    <td><asp:Label id="lblDeleteCommand" runat="server" /></td>
   </tr>
  </table>
 </body>
</html>
```

515

2. Save the file and view it in your browser:

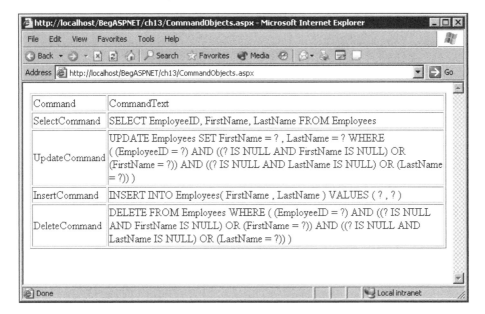

Here you can see that the SQL statements to perform updates, inserts, and deletions have been created for us. Let's see how this works:

How It Works

Initially, as usual, we have the variable declarations. You've seen most of these before, but notice the new one at the end, for the `OleDbCommandBuilder` – it's this object that will build the SQL commands for us:

```
string strConnection, strSQL;
DataSet objDataSet = new DataSet();
OleDbConnection objConnection = null;
OleDbDataAdapter objAdapter = null;
OleDbCommand objCommand = null;
OleDbCommandBuilder objBuilder = null;
```

Next comes the connection string:

```
strConnection = "Provider=Microsoft.Jet.OleDb.4.0;";
strConnection += @"Data Source=C:\BegASPNET\ch13\Northwind.mdb";
```

And now the SQL string to select the data:

```
strSQL = "SELECT EmployeeID, FirstName, LastName FROM Employees"
```

> One important thing to notice is that we have now included the **EmployeeID** column. This is a requirement for the **CommandBuilder**, since commands cannot be auto-generated unless a primary key field is available.

Now we create the connection and data adapter, in the same way as we have previously:

```
objConnection = new OleDbConnection(strConnection);
objAdapter = new OleDbDataAdapter(strSQL, objConnection);
```

Here comes the clever bit: we create a new OleDbCommandBuilder object, and pass into it the DataAdapter we are using. The command builder accessed the appropriate SelectCommand from the DataAdapter, from which it will build the commands:

```
objBuilder = new OleDbCommandBuilder(objAdapter);
```

Once the CommandBuilder has been created, we can use the GetUpdateCommand, GetInsertCommand, and GetDeleteCommand methods to build the appropriate commands. We set the associated properties of the adapter to these:

```
objAdapter.UpdateCommand = objBuilder.GetUpdateCommand();
objAdapter.InsertCommand = objBuilder.GetInsertCommand();
objAdapter.DeleteCommand = objBuilder.GetDeleteCommand();
```

Now we just display the CommandText property of each of the four command objects:

```
lblSelectCommand.Text = objAdapter.SelectCommand.CommandText;
lblUpdateCommand.Text = objAdapter.UpdateCommand.CommandText;
lblInsertCommand.Text = objAdapter.InsertCommand.CommandText;
lblDeleteCommand.Text = objAdapter.DeleteCommand.CommandText;
```

Let's look at these statements in a little more detail, just so you can understand what they are doing.

The SelectCommand object

This doesn't need much explanation, but it's worth reiterating the point that for the command builder to generate the other commands you need a key field. That's why we've included the EmployeeID. It needs this because key fields help us to uniquely identify rows:

```
SELECT EmployeeID, FirstName, LastName FROM Employees
```

The UpdateCommand Object

The `UpdateCommand` uses the SQL `UPDATE` statement. This comprises three main parts:

❑ The `UPDATE` keyword, which is followed by the table name.

❑ The `SET` keyword, which identifies the fields to be updated. This is similar to setting variables, only we use the name of the field and the value it is to be set to. The question marks are placeholders, which ADO.NET automatically replaces with the value to be updated.

❑ The `WHERE` clause, which filters the rowset. This enables us to make sure that the correct row is updated.

```
UPDATE Employees
SET FirstName = ? , LastName = ?
WHERE ( EmployeeID = ? AND FirstName = ? AND LastName = ? )
```

The InsertCommand Object

The `InsertCommand` uses the SQL `INSERT` statement. This comprises three main parts:

❑ The `INSERT INTO` keywords, which are followed by the table name.

❑ The field names to be inserted. These are surrounded by parentheses.

❑ The `VALUES` keyword, followed by the placeholders for the values to be inserted.

```
INSERT INTO Employees
( FirstName , LastName )
VALUES  ( ? , ? )
```

The DeleteCommand Object

The `DeleteCommand` uses the SQL `DELETE` statement, which comprises two main parts:

❑ The `DELETE FROM` keywords, followed by the table name.

❑ The `WHERE` clause, which filters the rowset. This allows us to make sure that the correct row is deleted.

```
DELETE FROM Employees
WHERE ( EmployeeID = ? AND FirstName = ? AND LastName = ? )
```

The DataAdapter.Update Method

At this stage we've been through two examples that show how to change the data within a `DataSet`, and how to generate commands that will update the data store. What we need to do now is combine the two, and add the command that actually update the data store with our changes. For this we will use the `Update` method of the `DataAdapter`.

This example requires files to be updated. If it does not run as anticipated, check back to Chapter 1 and ensure your Security settings have been configured correctly.

Try It Out – Synchronizing the Data Store

1. Create a new file called `Synchronize.aspx`, containing the following. There's quite a bit of code here, so you might prefer to download this sample from the Wrox site (www.wrox.com). The first section fills a `DataSet` and binds it to a `DataGrid`:

```csharp
<%@ Import Namespace="System.Data" %>
<%@ Import Namespace="System.Data.OleDb" %>
<script Language="c#" runat="server">
  void Page_Load(object sender, EventArgs e)
  {
    string strConnection, strSQL;
    DataSet objDataSet = new DataSet();
    OleDbConnection objConnection = null;
    OleDbDataAdapter objAdapter = null;

    // Set the connection and query details
    strConnection = "Provider=Microsoft.Jet.OleDb.4.0;";
    strConnection += @"Data Source=C:\BegASPNET\ch13\Northwind.mdb";
    strSQL = "SELECT EmployeeID, FirstName, LastName FROM Employees;";

    // Open the connection and set the command
    objConnection = new OleDbConnection(strConnection);
    objAdapter = new OleDbDataAdapter(strSQL, objConnection);

    // Fill the dataset with the data
    objAdapter.Fill(objDataSet, "Employees");

    // Bind the data grid to the data
    dgNameList1.DataSource = objDataSet.Tables["Employees"].DefaultView;
    dgNameList1.DataBind();
```

2. The rest of the `<script>` block to `synchronize.aspx` manipulates the data:

```csharp
// Add a new row to the table
    DataTable objTable = null;
    DataRow objnewRow = null;
    objTable = objDataSet.Tables["Employees"];
    objnewRow = objTable.NewRow();
    objnewRow["FirstName"] = "Norman";
    objnewRow["LastName"] = "Blake";
    objTable.Rows.Add(objnewRow);

    // Add another new row. We'll be deleting the one above later.
    // We can't delete existing rows from the database because of
    // referential integrity (every employee also has Orders)
    objnewRow = objTable.NewRow();
    objnewRow["FirstName"] = "Kasey";
    objnewRow["LastName"] = "Chambers";
    objTable.Rows.Add(objnewRow);
```

519

```
    // Bind the data grid to the new data
    dgNameList2.DataSource = objTable.DefaultView;
    dgNameList2.DataBind();

    // Edit an existing row in the table
    DataRow objRow = null;

    // The Rows collection is 0 indexed, so this changes the fourth row
    objRow = objTable.Rows[3];
    objRow["FirstName"] = "John";
    objRow["LastName"] = "Hartford";

    // Bind the data grid to the new data
    dgNameList3.DataSource = objTable.DefaultView;
    dgNameList3.DataBind();

    // Delete a row from the table
    // The Rows collection is 0 indexed, so this removes the second row from
    // the end
    objTable.Rows[objTable.Rows.Count - 2].Delete();

    // Bind the data grid to the new data
    dgNameList4.DataSource = objTable.DefaultView;
    dgNameList4.DataBind();

    // Generate the update commands
    OleDbCommandBuilder objBuilder = null;
    objBuilder = new OleDbCommandBuilder(objAdapter);
    objAdapter.UpdateCommand = objBuilder.GetUpdateCommand();
    objAdapter.InsertCommand = objBuilder.GetInsertCommand();
    objAdapter.DeleteCommand = objBuilder.GetDeleteCommand();

    // Update the data store
    objAdapter.Update(objDataSet, "Employees");

    // Refresh the data in the DataReader and bind it to a new grid
    // to prove that the data store has been updated
    strSQL = "SELECT EmployeeID, FirstName, LastName FROM Employees";
    objConnection.Open();
    OleDbCommand objCmd = new OleDbCommand(strSQL, objConnection);
    dgUpd.DataSource =
               objCmd.ExecuteReader(CommandBehavior.CloseConnection);
    dgUpd.DataBind();
  }
</script>
```

3. Now finish off `synchronize.aspx` with the `<html>` code:

```html
<html>
 <body>
  <table width="100%">
   <tr>
    <td>Original Data</td>
    <td>Data with new Row</td>
    <td>Data with edited Row</td>
    <td>Data with deleted Row</td>
   </tr>
   <tr>
    <td valign="top"><asp:DataGrid id="dgNameList1" runat="server" /></td>
    <td valign="top"><asp:DataGrid id="dgNameList2" runat="server" /></td>
    <td valign="top"><asp:DataGrid id="dgNameList3" runat="server" /></td>
    <td valign="top"><asp:DataGrid id="dgNameList4" runat="server" /></td>
   </tr>
  </table>
  <hr />
  Data fetched from database after the update:<br/>
  <asp:DataGrid id="dgUpd" runat="server"/>
 </body>
</html>
```

4. Save the code and view the page in your browser:

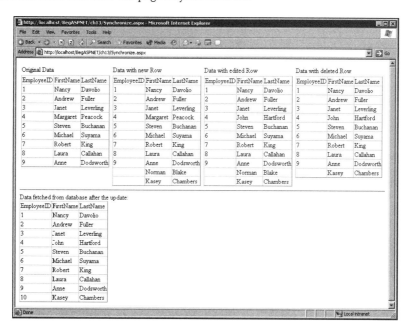

The top half of the screen shows the changes within the `DataSet`, before these changes are sent back to the data store. This is slightly different from our previous example. For new data we've actually added two rows, which allows us to delete one of them. If we delete any of the existing rows we'll get an error when we try to update the data store, because the `Northwind` database has rules to stop certain types of deletes. One such rule prevents `Employees` being deleted if they have any `Orders` associated with them (otherwise if the `Employee` were deleted, their `Order` would be left hanging). In the standard `Northwind` database all `Employees` have `Orders`, so we have to create our own in order to demonstrate a deletion.

You should also notice that there is no number in the `EmployeeID` field for the new rows. This is because this field is an `AutoNumber` field in the database, and it's the database that generates this number. Since we haven't yet updated the database there's no number – in other words we are looking at our **proposed** data changes before they are applied.

Once we've done the updates to the `DataSet`, we update the database. The bottom table of our output shows the data retrieved from the database. You can see that the changes we've made are now reflected in the data. Our new row now has an `EmployeeID`, and the row we added and then deleted never made it into the database. If you click the **Refresh** button on your browser you'll see the ID and the new record remain.

Now let's look at how this all works.

How It Works

Much of the code, we don't need to look at in detail, as it is the same as the previous examples. Let's first look at the addition of the two rows. The code is the same for adding the second row as it is for the first row – you just use the `NewRow` method of the table to create a new row and then `Add` it to the `Rows` collection:

```
objTable = objDataSet.Tables["Employees"];
objnewRow = objTable.NewRow();
objnewRow["FirstName"] = "Norman";
objnewRow["LastName"] = "Blake";
objTable.Rows.Add(objnewRow);

objnewRow = objTable.NewRow();
objnewRow["FirstName"] = "Kasey";
objnewRow["LastName"] = "Chambers";
objTable.Rows.Add(objnewRow);
```

For the deletion we've stated that we can't delete existing rows, so we decide to delete the first new row that we've added:

```
objTable.Rows[objTable.Rows.Count - 2].Delete();
```

This line of code shows another property of the `Rows` collection – `Count`. This identifies the number of items in the collection – in our case it's the number of rows in the table. We want to delete the second from last one so we subtract two from the count (remember that the collection is zero-based, so the last item is `Count – 1`).

Finally we synchronize the database with our changes, using the Update method of the DataAdapter:

```
objAdapter.Update(objDataSet, "Employees");
```

This method takes two arguments. The first is the DataSet that contains the changes to be sent back to the database, and the second is the name of the DataTable, within the DataSet, that contains the changes.

> **Remember that a DataSet can contain more than one DataTable, so it's very important that we get the right one.**

Referential Integrity

Referential Integrity is the term given to the way tables are related to each other and ensuring that the integrity of the data preserves those relationships. For example, Customers have Orders. It's logical that you can't have an Order without a Customer, so you can't add an Order without having an associated Customer. Likewise, you can't delete a Customer if they have orders because then there would be Orders without a Customer (these Orders would then be orphaned).

Referential integrity can be enforced within the database, within ADO.NET, or within both. In our examples, we're relying on the database to provide this, which is why when we show the deletion of Customers we make sure that we add one first. That way we not only know that there won't be any orders, but that we won't be deleting any existing data.

Updating Data – Summary

At this stage we've covered the basics of updating data, so let's just recap a few important points before we continue:

❑ The DataSet uses disconnected data, so changes are only made to the local DataSet, until we call the Update method of the DataAdapter.

❑ A DataSet can contain many DataTables, held in the Tables collection.

❑ Each DataTable has a Rows collection containing DataRow objects, one for each row in the table.

❑ To edit values you just change the fields directly. There is no need to use methods to start and stop editing.

❑ To insert rows into the DataSet you use the Add method of the Tables collection. To generate the new row to be added you use the NewRow method of the DataTable.

❑ To delete rows from the DataSet you use the Delete method of the Rows collection.

❑ To synchronize the database you must create the UpdateCommand, InsertCommand, and DeleteCommand objects. You can do this manually or use the CommandBuilder object to do this for you.

❑   If you use the `CommandBuilder` object, the `SelectCommand` it uses as a template must contain a key field.

❑   You use the `Update` method of the `DataAdapter` to synchronize the `DataSet` and the database.

Let's now take a brief look at using SQL directly.

Using SQL

We've already used SQL directly, to fetch data from a database using a `SELECT` statement. We're not going to talk about SQL in detail, since that's really outside the scope of this book, but what we need to do is look at how SQL can be used to update databases, either directly, or by the use of stored procedures.

Adapting the DataAdapter Commands

In the previous example we used the `CommandBuilder` to generate `Command` objects and their associated SQL commands. You've seen that this is an extremely easy technique, but what you may not realize is that you can change what that `CommandBuilder` generates – or even create it yourself.

For example, consider this code:

```
OleDbCommandBuilder objBuilder = new OleDbCommandBuilder(objAdapter);
objAdapter.UpdateCommand = objBuilder.GetUpdateCommand();
objAdapter.InsertCommand = objBuilder.GetInsertCommand();
objAdapter.DeleteCommand = objBuilder.GetDeleteCommand();
```

It's the same code we used previously. If you want to change the SQL for a particular command you could do this:

```
objAdapter.InsertCommand.CommandText = "INSERT INTO . . .";
```

Or, if you didn't want to use the `CommandBuilder`, you could create the `Command` objects directly:

```
OleDbCommand objCommand = new OleDbCommand();
objCommand.Connection = objConnection;
objCommand.CommandText = "INSERT INTO . . .";

objAdapter.InsertCommand = objCommand;
```

There's nothing to stop you doing this, although the `CommandBuilder` does save some typing. However, since it has to generate the SQL commands while the program is running there's a slight performance hit over manually creating the commands.

Using Stored Procedures

Another option is to use stored procedures instead of SQL statements. A stored procedure is a batch of SQL statements that are stored on the database server and given a name. You can then call this stored procedure just by its name (similar to the way we use subroutines in code), rather than having to retype the SQL. Another advantage is that most databases compile stored procedures, so they are generally more efficient than written SQL statements. In Microsoft Access, a **Query** is equivalent to a stored procedure.

Let's consider the `Northwind` database query called `Sales By Category`. The SQL for this is:

```
SELECT DISTINCTROW Categories.CategoryID, Categories.CategoryName,
                   Products.ProductName,
                   Sum([Order Details Extended].ExtendedPrice) AS ProductSales
FROM Categories INNER JOIN
         (Products INNER JOIN
             (Orders INNER JOIN [Order Details Extended]
                 ON Orders.OrderID = [Order Details Extended].OrderID)
             ON Products.ProductID = [Order Details Extended].ProductID)
         ON Categories.CategoryID = Products.CategoryID
WHERE (((Orders.OrderDate) Between #1/1/1997# And #12/31/1997#))
GROUP BY Categories.CategoryID, Categories.CategoryName, Products.ProductName
ORDER BY Products.ProductName;
```

Don't worry about the SQL – you don't need to know how it works, just that it's rather complex. Having this in your ASP.NET page not only makes the page harder to read, but it's also not a great design choice. After all, this is SQL, and the database is best at handling SQL so why not store it in the database? This is where stored procedures of queries come in, as they store long and complex SQL statements, allowing us to refer to them simply by name.

To use this stored procedure in place of a normal SQL statement you have to set the `CommandText` and `CommandType` properties. Let's give this a go:

Try It Out – Using Stored Procedures

1. Create a new file called `StoredProcedure.aspx`, and add the following code:

```
<%@ Import Namespace="System.Data" %>
<%@ Import Namespace="System.Data.OleDb" %>
<script Language="c#" runat="server">
  void Page_Load(object sender, EventArgs e)
  {
    OleDbConnection objConnection = null;
    OleDbCommand objCmd = null;
    string strConnection = "Provider=Microsoft.Jet.OleDb.4.0;";
    strConnection += @"Data Source=C:\BegASPNET\ch13\Northwind.mdb";
    // Create and open the connection object
    objConnection = new OleDbConnection(strConnection);
    objConnection.Open();
    // Create the Command and set its properties
    objCmd = new OleDbCommand();
```

```
      objCmd.Connection = objConnection;
      objCmd.CommandText = "[Sales by Category]";
      objCmd.CommandType = CommandType.StoredProcedure;
      dgSales.DataSource = objCmd.ExecuteReader(CommandBehavior.CloseConnection);
      dgSales.DataBind();
    }
</script>
<html>
  <body>
    <h2>Using a stored procedure</h2>
    <asp:datagrid id="dgSales" runat="server" />
  </body>
</html>
```

2. Now save the changes, and view the file from your browser:

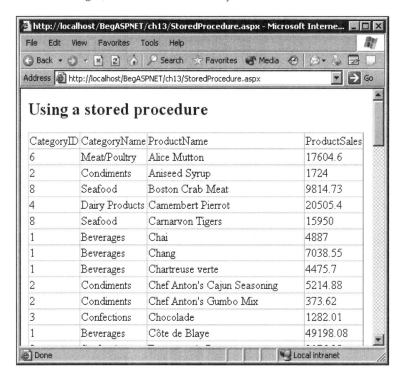

How It Works

Let's just look at the bit of code that's new:

```
objCmd = new OleDbCommand();
objCmd.Connection = objConnection;
objCmd.CommandText = "[Sales by Category]";
objCmd.CommandType = CommandType.StoredProcedure;
```

Here we create a `Command` object and then set the properties directly. We use the name of the stored procedure as the `CommandText` property (putting the square brackets around the name, which Access requires if the name has spaces in it), and setting the `CommandType` to `StoredProcedure`. You don't have to do anything else to use stored procedures.

Direct SQL Commands

Using the `DataSet` is a great way of dealing with disconnected data, but there are times when you don't need it. For example, consider a registration form on a web site to allow you to register for access to the site. This might offer you the chance to add a user name and password. In this case you wouldn't need a `DataSet` since all you are doing is adding one row. It makes more sense to run a SQL command directly.

Try It Out – Direct SQL Commands

1. Create a new file called `DirectSQL.aspx` and add the following code:

```
<%@ Page Debug="true" %>
<%@ Import Namespace="System.Data" %>
<%@ Import Namespace="System.Data.OleDb" %>

<script language="C#" runat="server">

  void Page_Load (Object sender, EventArgs e)
  {

    OleDbConnection objConnection = null;
    OleDbCommand objCmd = null;
    String strConnection, strSQL;

    strConnection = "Provider=Microsoft.Jet.OleDb.4.0;";
    strConnection += @"Data Source=C:\BegASPNET\ch13\Northwind.mdb";

    // Create and open the connection object
    objConnection = new OleDbConnection(strConnection);
    objConnection.Open();

    // set the SQL string
    strSQL = "INSERT INTO Employees (FirstName , LastName ) " +
    "VALUES ( 'Beth' , 'Hart' )";
```

```
        // Create the Command and set its properties
        objCmd = new OleDbCommand(strSQL, objConnection);

        // execute the command
        objCmd.ExecuteNonQuery();

        lblStatus.Text = "Command run";

    }

</script>

<html>
  <body>
    <h2>Using SQL directly</h2>
    <asp:Label id="lblStatus" runat="server"/>
  </body>
</html>
```

2. Now save the changes and open this page from your browser window. All you'll see is some text saying that the command has been run, and the new row has been added. Open the database to prove this:

	Employee ID	Last Name	First Name	Title
⊞	1	Davolio	Nancy	Sales Representative
⊞	2	Fuller	Andrew	Vice President, Sales
⊞	3	Leverling	Janet	Sales Representative
⊞	4	Hartford	John	Sales Representative
⊞	5	Buchanan	Steven	Sales Manager
⊞	6	Suyama	Michael	Sales Representative
⊞	7	King	Robert	Sales Representative
⊞	8	Callahan	Laura	Inside Sales Coordinator
⊞	9	Dodsworth	Anne	Sales Representative
⊞	10	Chambers	Kasey	
⊞	11	Hart	Beth	
✳	(AutoNumber)			

Let's see exactly what the code does.

How It Works

Much of the code we've already seen before, such as setting the connection details. We'll only look at the important bit, starting with the SQL statement. This is a SQL INSERT statement, which inserts a new row into the database (not the DataSet – remember we're not using a DataSet here). We're going to insert the name **Beth Hart** (I just happen to be listening to her CD as I write!):

```
        strSQL = "INSERT INTO Employees ( FirstName , LastName )" & _
                 VALUES ( 'Beth' , 'Hart' )"
```

Next we create the `Command` object using this SQL string and the `Connection` object:

```
objCmd = new OleDbCommand(strSQL, objConnection);
```

Finally we use the `ExecuteNonQuery` method of the `Command`. This method is designed specifically for this type of SQL statement, where no results are returned. We are telling the database directly that we want to add the new row, and that there is no data to return. This saves ADO.NET having to build any objects to hold data:

```
objCmd.ExecuteNonQuery();
```

You can also run `UPDATE` and `DELETE` statements this way.

Using SQL – Summary

We've come to the end of our short discussion of using SQL directly. This is a topic that has far more to offer, but is really outside the scope of this book. However, we've shown that you can use the `CommandBuilder` object to have the SQL statements generated for you automatically, so you don't need to learn SQL in depth to use these great ADO.NET features.

If you wish to learn more about SQL then there are plenty of books covering this subject. For example, Wrox Press has a *Beginning SQL* (ISBN 1-86100-180-0) book for just this purpose.

Now we'll take a short look at XML and how it's used within ADO.NET.

XML

We're not going to delve too much into XML here (it was first introduced in Chapter 5), as what we want to cover is the interaction between the ADO.NET objects and XML. Previous incarnations of ADO have allowed some interaction with XML, but it has always felt as though it was a feature added on due to public demand. The ADO.NET objects on the other hand have been designed with XML in mind, and you've got the opportunity to deal with XML data as though it came from a database. This means that you don't have to learn complex ways of handling XML – you can use the same methods you've already learned in this chapter.

Try It Out – Writing out to XML Files

In this example we'll extract the Employees from the database and save the details as an XML file.

This example also requires write permissions. Check back to the Security section of Chapter 1 if it does not work as anticipated.

1. Create a new file called `WritingXML.aspx` and add the following code:

```csharp
<%@ Import Namespace="System.Data" %>
<%@ Import Namespace="System.Data.OleDb" %>

<script language="c#" runat="server">

  void Page_Load(Object sender, EventArgs e)
  {
    String strConnection, strSQL;
    DataSet objDataSet = new DataSet();
    OleDbConnection objConnection = null;
    OleDbDataAdapter objAdapter = null;

    // set the connection and query details
    strConnection = "Provider=Microsoft.Jet.OLEDB.4.0; ";
    strConnection += "Data Source=" + Server.MapPath("Northwind.mdb");
    strSQL = "SELECT FirstName, LastName FROM Employees;";

    // open the connection and set the command
    objConnection = new OleDbConnection(strConnection);
    objAdapter = new OleDbDataAdapter(strSQL, objConnection);

    // fill the dataset with the data
    objAdapter.Fill(objDataSet, "Employees");

    objDataSet.WriteXml(Server.MapPath("Employees.xml"));

    Response.Write("<a href='Employees.xml'>View XML file</a>");

  }

</script>
```

Notice that there's no HTML in this page – just ASP.NET code.

2. Now save the changes and view the page from your browser. All you'll see is the link pointing to the newly generated XML file.

3. Click the link to view the file:

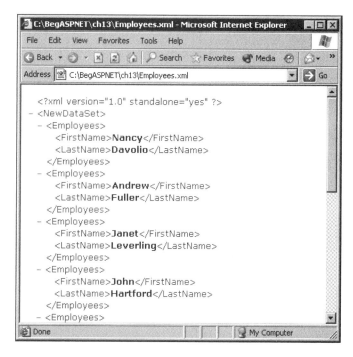

Here you can see that a standard XML file has been produced. Let's see just how easy it is.

How It Works

The only line we need to concern ourselves with here is the one that writes the file. All of the others we've seen several times before:

```
objDataSet.WriteXml(Server.MapPath("Employees.xml"));
```

There are two things to note here. The first is that we use the WriteXml method of the DataSet, which extracts the information from the DataSet, formats it into XML, and writes it to the specified location. The second is the use of Server.MapPath, which produces a file path pointing at the current application directory. This means that the XML file will be written into the directory that is configured as the **application root directory**. You could easily substitute a fixed path here.

That's all you have to do – just one line of code!

Note that there's a corresponding method WriteXmlSchema that writes out the XML Schema, which is the definition of what the XML contains.

Try It Out – Reading from XML files

Reading from XML files is just as easy as creating them – let's give it a go:

1. Create a new file called `ReadingXML.aspx`, and add the following code:

```
<%@ Import Namespace="System.Data" %>
<%@ Import Namespace="System.Data.OleDb" %>
<script Language="c#" runat="server">
  void Page_Load(object sender, EventArgs e)
  {
    DataSet objDataSet = new DataSet();
    objDataSet.ReadXml(Server.MapPath("Employees.xml"));
    dgEmployees.DataSource = objDataSet.Tables[0].DefaultView;
    dgEmployees.DataBind();
  }
</script>
<html>
  <body>
  <asp:DataGrid id="dgEmployees" runat="server" />
  </body>
</html>
```

2. Make sure you have viewed the `WritingXML.aspx` file. This ensures that the XML file we want to read in has been created.

> **If you don't do this an error will occur as the file will not be found.**

3. Open `ReadingXML.aspx` from your browser:

How It Works

There's even less to this code than previously, since we're not dealing with a database. First we define a new `DataSet`, into which we'll put the XML:

```
DataSet objDataSet = new DataSet();
```

Then we use the `ReadXml` method of the `DataSet` to read in the specified XML file. We use `Server.MapPath` again to ensure that the file is picked up from the application directory:

```
objDataSet.ReadXml(Server.MapPath("Employees.xml"));
```

Because the XML file is well-formed, the `DataSet` can infer the column names when it creates a `DataTable` in the `DataSet`.

Finally we bind the data to a `DataGrid`. In previous examples we indexed into the Tables collection using the name of the table. That was because we specified the name when we filled the `DataSet`. However, here we are not specifying the name, so we just pick the first entry:

```
dgEmployees.DataSource = objDataSet.Tables[0].DefaultView;
dgEmployees.DataBind();
```

As with `WriteXML`, there is a corresponding `ReadXmlSchema` method to read in an XML Schema. It's important to note that this schema isn't used for validation – it's used purely to infer the structure of the fields created.

XML into Strings

The `DataSet` also has two methods that allow you to extract the XML information into a string. For example:

```
string strXML, strSchema;

strXML = objDataSet.GetXml();
strSchema = objDataSet.GetXmlSchema();
```

This allows you to pass the XML data to components that only support XML in string format.

XML in a DataSet

One thing that's important to note is that once you load XML into a `DataSet`, you can treat it in the same way that we treated data in any of the other examples earlier in the chapter. A `DataSet` is a `DataSet`, no matter where the data originated. You can modify it as though it were relational (as though it came from a database), and then save it back to an XML file.

The great thing about this is that you only have one set of techniques to learn, which means you can be much more productive. If you are suddenly handed an XML file and told to integrate that into your application, you don't have to learn all of the specifics (and there are lots of them) for handling XML documents – you can just use the `DataSet`.

This next example will help illustrate this:

Try It Out – Editing XML Data

1. Create a new file called `EditingXML.aspx`, and add the following code:

```
<%@ Import Namespace="System.Data" %>
<%@ Import Namespace="System.Data.OleDb" %>
<script Language="c#" runat="server">
  void Page_Load(object sender, EventArgs e)
  {
    DataSet objDataSet = new DataSet();
    // Read in the XML file
    objDataSet.ReadXml(Server.MapPath("Employees.xml"));

    // Show it in a grid
    dgEmployees1.DataSource = objDataSet.Tables[0].DefaultView;
    dgEmployees1.DataBind();

    // Modify a row
    objDataSet.Tables["Employees"].Rows[0]["FirstName"] = "Bob";
    objDataSet.Tables["Employees"].Rows[0]["LastName"] = "Dylan";

    // Add a new row to the table
    DataTable objTable = null;
    DataRow objNewRow = null;
    objTable = objDataSet.Tables["Employees"];
    objNewRow = objTable.NewRow();
    objNewRow["FirstName"] = "Norman";
    objNewRow["LastName"] = "Blake";
    objTable.Rows.Add(objNewRow);

    // Save it to a new file
    objDataSet.WriteXml(Server.MapPath("Employees2.xml"));

    // Read in the new file
    DataSet objDataSet2 = new DataSet();
    objDataSet2.ReadXml(Server.MapPath("Employees2.xml"));

    // Show it in another grid
    dgEmployees2.DataSource = objDataSet2.Tables[0].DefaultView;
    dgEmployees2.DataBind();
  }
</script>
<html>
 <body>
```

```
  <table>
   <tr>
    <td valign="top"><asp:DataGrid id="dgEmployees1" runat="server" /></td>
    <td valign="top"><asp:DataGrid id="dgEmployees2" runat="server" /></td>
   </tr>
  </table>
 </body>
</html>
```

2. Save the file, and browse to it in your browser:

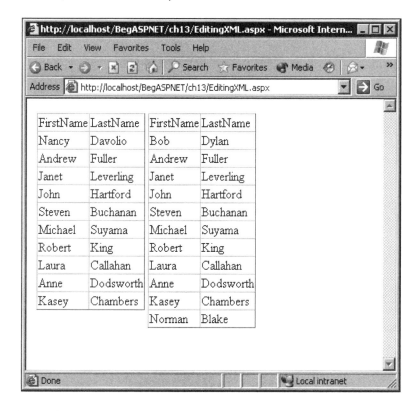

Notice that the first row has changed, and that a new row has been added.

How It Works

Let's look at the code for this to see what we've done. First we create a `DataSet` and load an XML file into it.

```
DataSet objDataSet = new DataSet();

objDataSet.ReadXml(Server.MapPath("Employees.xml"));
```

535

We use the `Server.MapPath` technique to ensure that the XML file comes from the same location as the web page.

Now we display the file in a data grid:

```
dgEmployees1.DataSource = objDataSet.Tables[0].DefaultView;
dgEmployees1.DataBind();
```

Once displayed in the grid, we start to modify the data. First we edit the first row, changing both columns:

```
objDataSet.Tables["Employees"].Rows[0]["FirstName"] = "Bob";
objDataSet.Tables["Employees"].Rows[0]["LastName"] = "Dylan";
```

Now we add a new row – this is the same technique we used before.

```
DataTable objTable = null;
DataRow objNewRow = null;
objTable = objDataSet.Tables["Employees"];
objNewRow = objTable.NewRow();
objNewRow["FirstName"] = "Norman";
objNewRow["LastName"] = "Blake";
objTable.Rows.Add(objNewRow);
```

Once the data has been changed we save it to a new XML file. We could have saved it to the same file, but using a different one allows us to compare the two if we want to:

```
objDataSet.WriteXml(Server.MapPath("Employees2.xml"));
```

Finally we read in the new file and display it in a new grid:

```
DataSet objDataSet2 = new DataSet();
objDataSet2.ReadXml(Server.MapPath("Employees2.xml"));

dgEmployees2.DataSource = objDataSet2.Tables[0].DefaultView;
dgEmployees2.DataBind();
```

This really reinforces the point that you can use the `DataSet` to manipulate XML files. This method may not be perfect for every XML file, but in many cases it works fine.

What to Study Next

ADO.NET is a huge topic, and we clearly cannot cover it all here. Luckily there is plenty of information available on web sites and in books. The documentation supplied with the .NET Framework has a great set of samples covering ADO.NET and its use, so make sure you read them, as well.

Sure you're a developer, and developers don't do documentation, but believe me it is worth it – reading a little of this stuff will go a long way to increasing your understanding and skills. The Wrox book *Professional ASP.NET 1.0 Special Edition* (ISBN 1-861007-03-5) also has several chapters devoted to the more advanced study of ADO.NET.

In particular, topics that are worth learning more about are:

❑ **The SQL Language**. Even if you don't use it a great deal it's worth having a solid understanding, as it makes developing data sites far easier. I recommend *Beginning SQL* from Wrox Press (ISBN 1-86100-180-0) to get you started.

❑ **Data binding and templating**. To show how the DataGrid control can be customized to provide a better look. There's a small section on this in the next chapter.

❑ **Concurrency**. So you can deal with update errors when you synchronize your DataSet with the database. The Wrox Press book *ASP.NET Distributed Data Applications* (ISBN 1-861-492-3) covers this in detail.

Summary

This chapter has continued the ADO.NET story, looking at changing data. We've seen that disconnected data raises problems, but that these problems can be overcome. Changing data within a DataSet is extremely easy, and synchronizing these changes with the database only requires one line of code. We've also looked at the synchronization process, seeing how there are four commands to manage our changes. You have the choice as to whether you let ADO.NET manage these commands for you, or you customize them yourself using your own SQL statements. This gives you the best of both worlds: a simple approach that's also flexible.

We've also looked at running SQL commands directly, without using a DataSet. It's important to remember that however great the DataSet is for handling disconnected data, there are times when it simply isn't required.

Finally we looked at the simple ways in which XML files can interact with DataSets, to provide us with a single set of objects for dealing with both relational and XML data.

Now it's time to look at the ASP.NET Server Controls in detail, to see how they can make the creation of web pages easier, and with a lot less code than we've previously been used to.

Exercises

1. What do we mean by 'disconnected data' and why is it so important?

2. Load a DataSet with the Shippers table from Northwind and add the following data into the DataSet using a DataTable:

❑ Company Name: FastShippers

❑ Phone: (503) 555-9384

537

3. Using the `CommandBuilder` object, update the `Northwind Shippers` table with the new information held in the `DataSet`.

4. Using direct SQL commands, change the phone number of FastShippers to (503) 555-0000 and display the updated table in a `DataGrid`.

    a.   Generate a DataSet from this XML file and bind it to a `DataGrid` to display it:

```
<?xml version="1.0" standalone="yes" ?>
 <NewDataSet>
    <books>
       <bookName>Beginning ASP.NET 1.0 with VB.NET</BookName>
       <ISBN>1861007337</ISBN>
    </books>
    <books>
       <BookName>Professional ASP.NET 1.0 SE</BookName>
       <ISBN>1861007035</ISBN>
    </books>
    <books>
       <BookName>ASP.NET Programmer's Reference </BookName>
       <ISBN>1861007450</ISBN>
    </books>
 </NewDataSet>
```

    b.   Add a new book of your choice to the `Dataset`.

    c.   Delete the entry for Beginning ASP.NET 1.0 programming and display the `DataSet` in a `DataGrid`.

ASP.NET Server Controls

By now, you should be fairly comfortable with the object-oriented approach used by the .NET Framework to create ASPX pages. Throughout this book, we've used a few of the most popular server controls (the `Button` and `Label` controls for example), however we haven't explored their characteristics in great detail – now's our chance! This chapter will present you with in-depth coverage of ASP.NET server controls (also known as Web Server Controls) and provide numerous details and examples illustrating their usage. Throughout this chapter, the phrase 'ASP.NET server controls' will refer to that specific group of controls derived from the `System.Web.UI.WebControls` base class.

ASP.NET server controls are reusable components that can perform the same work as traditional HTML controls, but have the additional benefit of being **programmable objects**. In other words, they can be programmatically accessed, just like any other .NET object or class, respond to events, get/set properties, and do all the other things objects do. If you were to suspect, by their nomenclature, that these controls perform their processing on the server, you would be absolutely correct.

Like HTML tags, but with a stronger adherence to XML tag syntax, ASP.NET server controls are also declared using a tag syntax. The following example declares an ASP.NET Button control and assigns values to three of the control's properties:

```
<asp:Button id="SampleButton" runat="server" Text="I'm A Sample Button!"/>
```

One of the unique qualities of ASP.NET server controls is that, even though their tag syntax is different from HTML's, every ASP.NET server control is rendered to standard HTML after being processed on the server, thus abstracting the functionality of the entire HTML control set. Additional ASP.NET server controls provide the ability to render rich web content – for example, a `Calendar` control for displaying dates, a `DataGrid` control for displaying data, as well as other controls, which we will explore throughout this chapter.

Here's a summary of the topics we will cover in this chapter:

- ❏ A review of the syntax and benefits of ASP.NET server controls

- ❏ A brief recap of the `System.Web.UI.Page` lifecycle

- ❏ Using a variety of ASP.NET server controls on a web form

- ❏ Using validation controls – you'll learn some techniques for validating user input in a web form

- ❏ Introducing data rendering controls – a brief introduction to this very powerful group of controls for displaying data

- ❏ A complete application that allows you to incorporate your own schedule of events within the context of an ASP.NET `Calendar` control

In the past, the way we would create a web page might vary, but it would almost always involve the embedding of various HTML tags in our pages – perhaps some client-side scripting to handle event processing, or validate form input, and some text to make up the overall content of the page. Additionally, the advanced developer would often be required to write pages in a manner that supported a variety of browser types and capabilities, thus mixing in special-case code, and even client-side validation, which added an additional layer of development complexity that was often difficult to maintain.

We'll be focusing most of our attention on four broad categories of ASP.NET server controls:

- ❏ **Basic controls** – (sometimes referred to as **intrinsic** controls) this category of controls correspond to their HTML counterparts. Examples include the `Button`, `ListBox`, and `TextBox` controls.

- ❏ **Data-list controls** – controls used for binding and displaying data from a data source, such as the `DataGrid` and `DataList` controls.

- ❏ **Rich controls** – these controls have no direct HTML counterparts. Rich controls, like the `Calendar` control, are made up of multiple components, and the HTML generated will typically consist of numerous HTML tags (as well as client-side script) to render the control in the browser.

- ❏ **Validation controls** – for example, the `RequiredFieldValidator`, which can be used to ensure proper data input within a web form.

By the end of this chapter, you will be able to create your own web forms that utilize a variety of the ASP.NET server controls available. You will be exposed to the variety of ASP.NET control properties available to you as a web developer, which can be used to tailor the look or functionality of the various controls. You will also learn to write event handlers for the various events raised by ASP.NET server controls.

Other Types of Controls

Let's briefly talk about two other types of control categories that you should be aware of

❑   HTML Server Controls

❑   User Controls

HTML Server Controls

HTML server controls correspond directly to various HTML tags, and are defined within the `System.Web.UI.HtmlControls` namespace. These controls derive their functionality from the `System.Web.UI.HtmlControls.HtmlControl` base class. Microsoft provides this suite of HTML server controls for a couple of reasons:

❑   Some web developers may prefer to work with the HTML-style of control that they're used to

❑   Developers can convert existing HTML tags to HTML server controls fairly easily, and thus gain some server-side programmatic access to the controls

The following HTML tag declaration is, believe it or not, a fully qualified HTML server control that can be accessed programmatically on the server within your web form's code:

```
<INPUT id="MyHTMLTextBox" type="text" name="MyHTMLTextBox" runat="server">
```

What makes this a programmable HTML server control? Simply the reference to `runat="server"`. In this example, using `runat="server"` ensures that the .NET Framework will convert the HTML tag into a corresponding `HtmlInputText` object (there is an HTML server control object for every corresponding HTML tag). We also add `id="MyHTMLTextBox"`, to provide a unique name of the object so that we can reference it in our server-side code.

Like ASP.NET server controls, HTML server controls offer a variety of features, which include:

❑   **Programmatic Object Model** – you can access HTML server controls programmatically on the server using all the familiar object-oriented techniques. Each HTML server control is an object and, as such, you can access its various properties and get/set them programmatically.

❑   **Event Processing** – HTML server controls provide a mechanism to write event handlers in much the same way you would for a client-based form. The only difference is that the event is handled in the server code.

❑   **Automatic Value Caching** – when form data is posted to the server, the values that the user entered into the HTML server controls are automatically maintained when the page is sent back to the browser. The "magic" behind this functionality is the result of a property called `ViewState`, which all ASP.NET server controls inherit.

❑   **Data Binding** – it's possible to bind data to one or more properties of an HTML server control.

❑ **Custom Attributes** – You can add any attributes you need to an HTML server control. The .NET Framework will render them to the client browser without any changes. This enables you to add browser-specific attributes to your controls.

❑ **Validation** – you can actually assign an ASP.NET validation control to do the work of validating an HTML server control. Validation controls are covered later in this chapter.

One reason you might consider using HTML server controls in your own web form pages is to leverage an existing HTML page's HTML tag or code base. For example, let's say you have an existing HMTL page that you would rather not re-write from scratch, but still would like to write some server-side code to access various properties of the various controls on the page. Converting an existing HTML page's controls to HTML server controls is simple: you just add the `runat="server"` attribute within the tag declaration of the HTML control. You must also add a unique `id` property value to the control declaration so that you can reference the object in your server-side code. For example:

```
<INPUT id="Button1" type="button" value="Button" name="Button1" runat="server">
```

HTML Server Controls vs. ASP.NET Server Controls

Given that Microsoft has provided two distinct categories of server controls (HTML and ASP.NET), with both sets of controls sharing some degree of overlapping functionality, you may be a bit confused as to which set of controls you should use within your web forms. The short answer is simply this: **you can use both**! It's perfectly OK to mix the usage of HTML server controls and ASP.NET server controls within your web forms – using one set of controls does not restrict you to that control type. Despite the overlap in functionality, there are some clear distinctions between these controls that you should be aware of when developing your ASP.NET web form pages (we'll be covering the ASP.NET behaviors listed below throughout this chapter):

Control Feature	HTML Server Control Behavior	ASP.NET Server Control Behavior
Control Abstraction	HTML server controls provide a one-to-one mapping with a corresponding HTML tag and offer no real abstraction.	ASP.NET server controls offer a high level of abstraction – in other words, they don't necessarily map to any existing HTML control. For example, an ASP.NET `Calendar` server control has no single HTML control equivalent – it's actually made up from a collection of several controls. As such, you will often hear the phrase **rich control** associated with many ASP.NET server controls, since their functionality is typically the result of a combination of several other controls.
Object Model	HTML server controls utilize a very HTML-centric object model. Additionally, the HTML attribute convention is not strongly typed.	ASP.NET server controls provide a consistent and type-safe programming model. All ASP.NET server controls inherit a set of base properties and methods (such as `ForeColor`, `BackColor`, `Font`, and so on).

Control Feature	HTML Server Control Behavior	ASP.NET Server Control Behavior
Target Browser	HTML server controls do not automatically detect the capabilities of the browser loading the page. It's up to you to make sure the HTML controls you use are compatible with the browsers that might be consuming your page!	ASP.NET server controls automatically detect the client browser requesting the page and render the controls based on the browser's capabilities.
How the Control Renders	HTML server controls provide you with complete control over what gets rendered and sent to the client browser. This is primarily due to the fact that however you declare the HTML control is how it will render. The only exception to this is the associated client-side script that gets automatically generated.	ASP.NET server controls provide a higher level of abstraction in terms of how the controls are rendered. In other words, when you use ASP.NET server controls, you leave the details of rendering up to the object. Naturally, the properties you choose to set for the control may play a roll in controlling how and what is actually rendered. But the bottom line here is that you don't have as much control over the rendered output. However, most developers will conclude that the delegation of the messy rendering details is a welcome relief! Naturally, if you really do want or need full control over the output you can always use inheritance and override any of the output methods of any control.

User Controls

User controls, as you might guess, are controls that you write yourself. They should not, however, be confused with yet *another* category of controls, **Custom Controls**, which are not covered in this book. (For more information on Custom Controls, see Wrox's *Professional ASP.NET Server Controls* ISBN 1-86100-564-4) You can think of User Controls as reusable groupings of several ASP.NET server controls, HTML, text, client-side script, or even server-side code to handle events and perform server-side processing. For example, suppose we're creating several pages for a site that all need to share the same header at the top of the page (or anywhere in the page for that matter). Rather than duplicate the same links, formatting, HTML, controls, and so on, in every single page, we could simply create a User Control that contained the content we desired for our header in all our pages. Each page need only declare our header User Control at the top of the page to share the common header formatting and/or code logic. The benefits of this are significant – changing the content and/or server-side code in our User Control, changes it for every page that uses it!

User Controls are created much the same way as Web Form pages (using any text editor or IDE like Visual Studio .NET), with one very important distinction – User Controls **cannot** contain a <form> tag declaration. We'll consider User Controls in more detail in the next chapter.

Now let's get into the substance of this chapter – ASP.NET Server Controls.

ASP.NET Server Controls

ASP.NET server controls are the building blocks for creating ASP.NET web forms. Like their HTML counterparts, ASP.NET server controls provide all the basic controls necessary for building web forms (Button, ListBox, CheckBox, TextBox, and many more), as well as a collection of rich controls (controls with several functions – we'll look at them later on), like the Calendar and DataGrid controls. The various control families are categorized and discussed later in this section, along with many mini-examples to demonstrate syntax and other features. At this point though, you might be wondering what benefits there are, if any, to using ASP.NET server controls instead of standard HTML controls. Here are a few of the benefits ASP.NET server controls offer us:

❑   Rich Object Model

❑   Automatic Browser Detection

❑   Properties

❑   Events

Rich Object Model

ASP.NET server controls draw from the rich features of the .NET Framework. As such, they inherit their base methods, properties, and events from either the System.Web.UI.WebControls.Control or System.Web.UI.WebControls.WebControl base classes. As you may recall from previous chapters, inheritance is a key feature of object oriented-design and programming. When instantiating an ASP.NET server control, you're really creating an instance of an object that gives you access to the properties, methods, and events of its base class and interfaces.

Automatic Browser Detection

ASP.NET server controls detect client browser capabilities, and create the appropriate HTML and client-side script for the client browser. In other words, ASP.NET pages, and the controls within them, are compiled and 'served up' meaning they're not merely static text files. For example, consider the following ASP.NET button control declaration:

```
<asp:Button id="SampleButton" runat="server" Text="My Button"/>
```

When this control is processed on the server, the resultant HTML generated for both Netscape and Internet Explorer will be pretty much the same:

```
<input type="submit" name="SampleButton" value="My Button" id="SampleButton" />
```

However, depending on the type of browser and its limitations and capabilities, as well as the type of ASP.NET control being rendered, there may in fact be a difference in the HTML generated. In the case of a simple button control, the significance is not immediately apparent – just about any browser today will be able to render a standard button. However, the benefits for the developer are substantial once **events**, **properties**, and **validation** come into play, as these are all factors that affect how the ASP.NET control is generated for the client browser. The bottom line here is that the HTML/script rendered for the different browsers (IE, Netscape, Opera) is all handled by the ASP.NET server control and, by and large, the developer is freed from having to worry too much about client browser capabilities and/or limitations.

Properties

All ASP.NET controls share a common set of base properties, as well as their own class-specific properties. These properties allow you to change the look and even the behavior of the control. Throughout this chapter, you will be exposed to a variety of properties for the various ASP.NET server controls. Some of the more common base-class properties shared by all ASP.NET server controls include:

❑   BackColor – the background color of the control. The possible values for all color properties can be ascertained by referencing the .NET Framework's Color structure properties in the SDK Documentation (or by using ILDasm). For example, AliceBlue, AntiqueWhite, or even a hexadecimal value like #C8C8C8.

❑   ForeColor – the foreground color of the control.

❑   BorderWidth – the width of the border of the control, in pixels.

❑   Visible – if set to True (the default for all controls) the control will be displayed. If set to False, the control will be hidden. This property is useful for when you want to hide a particular control on the web form. For example, if you were obtaining details from a user, and in one box, they had declared their nationality as British, you might want to hide another box that asks them for their Social Security Number, while displaying a third that asks for their National Insurance Number.

❑   Enabled – whether on not the control is enabled. If set to False, the control will appear grayed out, and will not process or respond to events until its Enabled property is set to True.

❑   Height – the height of the control in pixels.

❑   Width – the width of the control in pixels.

❑   ToolTip – hover text displayed dynamically on mouse roll-over. Typically used to supply additional help without taking up space on the form.

❑   Font-Size – the size of the control's font.

These properties are merely an abbreviated listing; many more common properties are available. To see these, have a look at the SDK Documentation. An important thing to note is that not all browsers support all the possible property settings. However, you needn't worry too much about this because, when ASP.NET server controls are rendered, the output generated for the target browser will generally be suitable for that browser, whatever its capabilities or limitations are.

The following is an example of an ASP.NET Button server control with several of the common base class properties assigned, to give the it a rather *distinctive* look:

```
<asp:Button id="MyButton" runat="server" Text="I'm an ASP.NET server control
Button!"
  BackColor="purple"
  ForeColor="white"
  BorderWidth="4"
  BorderStyle="Ridge"
  ToolTip="Common Properties Example!"
  Font-Name="Tahoma"
  Font-Size="16"
  Font-Bold="True"
/>
```

When rendered and displayed in the client browser, this ASP.NET Button server control will look something like this:

I'm an ASP.NET server control Button!

The HTML generated for this control (for Internet Explorer 6.0) looks like this:

```
<input type="submit" name="MyButton" value="I'm an ASP.NET server control Button!"
id="MyButton" title="Common Properties Example!" style="color:White;background-
color:Purple;border-width:4px;border-style:Ridge;font-family:Tahoma;font-
size:16pt;font-weight:bold;" />
```

Have a go yourself – to look at the HTML, just select View | Source from the IE browser.

Events

ASP.NET server controls support the ability to assign event handlers in order to execute programmatic logic in response to whatever events a given ASP.NET server control may raise. As we saw in Chapter 3, an event handler is essentially the code you write to respond to a particular event. For example, a Button control raises an OnClick event after being clicked, a ListBox control raises an OnSelectedIndexChanged event when its list selection changes, a TextBox control raises an OnTextChanged event whenever its text changes, and so on.

Events and event handlers are extremely useful to us as web developers, because they provide a mechanism for responding dynamically to events in our web pages. For example, let's say we were asked to write a page that contained a button that listed the current date and time to the latest second. For demonstration purposes, when the user clicks on the button, we would like the date and time to be displayed as the button's new text. To achieve this result, we'll need to "wire up" an event handler for our button control.

Try It Out – Creating an Event Handler

1. The first step is to declare the ASP.NET button control. To do this, type the following text into your code editor:

```
<form id=SampleEvent method=post runat="server">
  <asp:Button id="CurrentTimeButton" runat="server"
      Text="Click for current time..." OnClick="UpdateTime" />
</form>
```

2. Save this file as `EventHandler.aspx`.

If you run this code in your browser right now, you'll see the following error message:

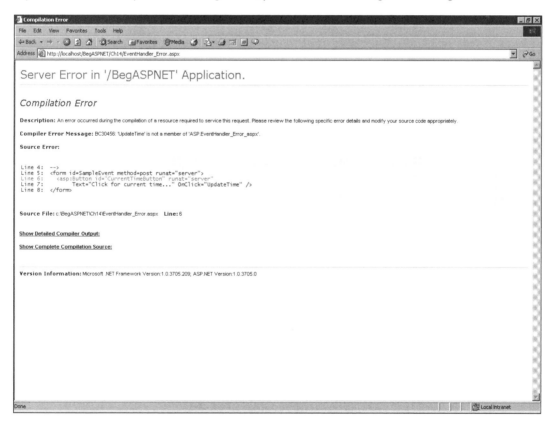

We get this error because we have not yet defined our `UpdateTime` event handler. Let's do this now:

3. Open up `EventHandler.aspx`, and amend the code by adding the following opening section:

```c#
<script language="c#" runat="server">
  public void UpdateTime (Object sender, System.EventArgs e)
  {
    // Perform custom logic here - update the button text with current time
    CurrentTimeButton.Text = DateTime.Now.ToShortTimeString();
  }
</script>


<form id=SampleEvent method=post runat="server">
  <asp:Button id="CurrentTimeButton" runat="server"
      Text="Click for current time..." OnClick="UpdateTime" />
</form>
```

4. Now if you run the code in your browser, you'll see the button we created, and when you click on it, you'll see the current time – cool!

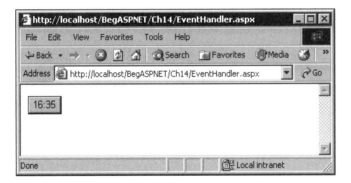

How It Works

In this example, a `CurrentTimeButton` server control is declared, and its corresponding `Text` property is set to "Click for current time...":

```
<asp:Button id="CurrentTimeButton" runat="server"
    Text="Click for current time..." OnClick="UpdateTime" />
```

Additionally, we've assigned the name of our custom event handler, `UpdateTime`, to the `OnClick` event method for this button control.

> *The `OnClick` event method for the `Button` control is essentially a placeholder, which can be assigned the name of a method (which we write, and in this case is `UpdateTime`) to perform the processing when that particular event is raised. The method name we assign to the `OnClick` handler must conform to the required 'method signature' (same number or arguments, same types, same return value) defined by the event method.*

We then defined our custom `UpdateTime` event handler to update the button text with the current time as follows:

```
public void UpdateTime (Object sender, System.EventArgs e)
{
  // Perform custom logic here - update the button text with current time
  CurrentTimeButton.Text = DateTime.Now.ToShortTimeString();
}
```

All we are doing here is first establishing the `UpdateTime` function, and then assigning to the `Text` property of our `CurrentTimeButton` the value `DateTime.Now.ToShortTimeString()`. This is basically saying, "When the `UpdateTime` function is triggered, display the current time in the text property of `CurrentTimeButton`, which is a string data type."

Page Lifecycle

Although this topic is covered elsewhere in this book, it's worthwhile to review the `System.Web.UI.Page` object's lifecycle, in the context of ASP.NET server controls. Specifically, we will briefly review how the ASP.NET `Page` class loads, processes events, and closes down. When designing a web form, you are really referencing the base functionality of the ASP.NET `Page` class. As such, the `Page` class offers its own methods, properties, and events to the form. When loading a web form for the first time, you might, for example, want to preload the `Page` object's server controls with values from a database, or set property values to various server controls on the page dynamically. The following listings provide an overview of the various methods that are commonly overridden in your ASPX `Page` object implementation, which allow you to perform processing during the various stages of the `Page` object's lifetime.

Page_Load

The `Page_Load` method is a virtual method (recall that a virtual method of an object is one which you can override) of the `Page` class, which means it can be (and often is) overridden in the `Page` class implementation. The `Page_Load` method is invoked anytime the ASPX page is requested – in other words, when the page is loaded for the first time, or refreshed. The following is an example implementation of the `Page_Load` method:

```
void Page_Load(object sender, EventArgs e)
{
  if(!(Page.IsPostBack)
  {
  //First time page loads -
  //perform initialization here!
  }
}
```

The most interesting part of the above listing is the reference to the `Page` class's `IsPostback` property. The `IsPostback` property is significant because this property can be used to distinguish whether a page is being loaded for the very first time, or if it's being loaded as the result of what is commonly referred to as a **Postback** – in other words, if a `Button` server control was clicked, an `OnClick` event would be raised and the form data would be posted *back* to the server – hence the term postback. We have seen this method several times in the past few chapters.

The most common uses for implementing the `Page_Load` method in your ASPX pages are to:

❑ Check whether this is the first time the page is being processed, or to perform processing after it is refreshed

❑ Perform data binding the first time the page is processed, or re-evaluate data binding expressions on subsequent round trips to, for example, display the data sorted differently

❑ Read and update control properties

Event Handling

The second part of a page's lifecycle is the event handling stage. After an ASPX page is loaded and displayed, additional event handlers will be invoked when control events are raised. For example, after a user clicks an ASP.NET `Button` control, the `OnClick` event will be raised, thus posting the event to the server. If an event handler is written and assigned to process the `OnClick` event for that particular control, it will be invoked whenever the `Button` control is clicked.

Not all controls perform this type of automatic "posting back" to the server when an event is raised. For example, the `TextBox` control does not, by default, post back notification to the server when its text changes. Similarly, the `ListBox` and `CheckBox` server controls do not, by default, post back event notifications to the server every time their selection state changes. For these particular controls, their `AutoPostBack` property (which can be set to either `True` or `False`) would need to explicitly be set to `True` in the control's declaration (or set programmatically within the code) to enable automatic postback of events/state changes to the server for processing.

> *If you create an ASP.NET server control that performs server-side processing whenever the control's state changes (such as when a `CheckBox` is checked) and you don't seem to be getting the results you expect, check if the control has an `AutoPostBack` property, and if so, set it to `True`. This property typically defaults to `False` if not explicitly declared when the control was defined. We'll take a closer look at the `AutoPostBack` property in action in the Try It Out section that follows.*

Page_Unload

`Page_Unload` serves the opposite purpose to the `Page_Load()` method. The `Page_Unload()` method is used to perform any cleanup just prior to the page being unloaded. It is a virtual method of the `Page` class, which can be implemented. You would want to implement the `Page_Unload()` method in cases where any of the following actions needed to be performed:

❑ Closing files

❑ Closing database connections

❑ Any other cleanup or discarding of server-side objects and/or resources

The following is an example skeleton implementation of the `Page_Unload` method:

```
void Page_Unload(object sender, EventArgs e)
{
  //Perform any cleanup here
}
```

One thing to note is that the unloading of a page doesn't happen when you close the browser or move to another page. The `Page_Unload()` event happens when the page has finished being processed by ASP.NET, and before it's sent to the browser.

Try It Out – "Oh To Travel, Travel, Travel"

OK, let's get right into this, and do something neat with ASP.NET server controls. In this section, we'll put together a single web form, `travel.aspx`, that allows us to book a flight from New York to London with only a couple clicks of the mouse! OK, so it will only be a demo – we won't actually book anything (sigh). We will, however, get some experience building a web form that uses a variety of ASP.NET server controls.

Also, because the code is quite bulky we'll break with tradition slightly and discuss what we're doing a little in the *Try It Out* section so you can keep up with things. As usual we'll consider the important aspects of the code afterwards in the *How It Works* section, as well.

1. Open your code editor and add the following starter lines to layout the framework for this ASPX page, and save it as `Travel.aspx`:

```
<%@ Page Language="c#" %>
<%@ Import Namespace="System.Drawing" %>

  <script language="c#" runat="server">

  </script>

<html>
<head></head>
  <body>
    <h1>Travel: New York to London</h1>
      <form id="TravelForm" method="post" runat="server">

      <!-- Flight Info -->

      <!-- BOOK IT BUTTON SECTION & FEEDBACK -->

      </form>
  </body>
</html>
```

In this first code block, since we'll be referencing the .NET Framework's Color structure in our code, we needed to add an Import directive referencing the System.Drawing namespace at the top of this page. The remainder of the code consists of the <script></script> tag sections (where we will insert our code for this page), and the two HTML tags to set up our page.

2. In this step, we're going to add some flight date boxes to the page. We're using the ASP.NET panel control to serve as our container for the various controls on our simulated tab. The panel control is a visual tool to display a box, within which other controls can be rendered. You will also be introduced to two new control types, RequireFieldValidator and CustomValidator – these are validation controls, their purpose, and behavior, will be examined in more detail shortly, but as you may notice, they are declared just like any of the other server controls we've worked with. Add the following lines:

```
<!-- Flight Info -->
    <asp:panel id="Panel" runat="server" Width="504px" Height="89px"
    BackColor="Wheat">Departure Date:
    <asp:TextBox id="flightDepartureDateTextBox" runat="server"
    Width="80px" Height="22px"/>Return Date:
    <asp:TextBox id="flightReturnDateTextBox" runat="server"
     Width="80px" Height="22px"/></br>
    <asp:RequiredFieldValidator id="validateFlightDepartureDate" runat="server"
    ErrorMessage="Please enter a valid Departure Date.  "
    ControlToValidate="flightDepartureDateTextBox" />
    <asp:RequiredFieldValidator id="validateFlightReturnDate" runat="server"
    ErrorMessage="Please enter a valid Return Date."
    ControlToValidate="flightReturnDateTextBox" />
    <asp:CustomValidator id="validateFlightDates" runat="server"
    ControlToValidate="flightDepartureDateTextBox"
    OnServerValidate="ValidateTravelData" />
    </asp:panel>
```

Now let's talk about those validation controls we declared above: two RequiredFieldValidator controls, and a CustomValidator control. These controls will serve to force the user to enter a value into the Departure Date and Return Date TextBox controls. The CustomValidator control will raise an OnServerValidate event, and call our ValidateTravelData method, which will perform the work of validating that the date entries make sense logically (for example, the departure date can't be later than the return date). The RequiredFieldValidator control ensures that something is entered into the field, so the user can't skip an entry.

3. The next control we'll add to this form is the bookTheTripButton, which will serve to post the form data to the server, and the feedbackLabel label control, which will serve to provide instructions, and offer feedback in the event of an invalid data entry. Add the following lines:

```
<!-- BOOK IT BUTTON SECTION & FEEDBACK -->
    <p>
    <asp:Button id="bookTheTripButton" runat="server" Text="Book This Trip"
                              OnClick="bookTheTripButton_Click" />
```

```
      </p>
      <p>
      <asp:Label id="feedbackLabel" runat="server" BackColor="Wheat"
                 Font-Bold="True" Text=
                 "Select your options, then click the 'Book This Trip' button!" />
      </p>
```

4. Recall from Step 2 that we added two `RequiredFieldValidator` controls and the `CustomValidator` control. In this section, we'll write the event handler for the `OnServerValidate` event and the `ValidateTravelData` method, to validate our dates and their logic. Add the following lines between the script tags:

```
<script language="c#" runat="server">
protected void ValidateTravelData(object source,
                        System.Web.UI.WebControls.ServerValidateEventArgs args)
  {
     // Since we have a bit to validate, assume that the entry is invalid....
     args.IsValid = false;
     DateTime departDate, returnDate;
     feedbackLabel.ForeColor = Color.Red;
     try
     {
         departDate = DateTime.Parse(flightDepartureDateTextBox.Text);
     }
     catch (Exception ex)
     {
         feedbackLabel.Text = "Invalid data entry: Departure Date is invalid. " +
                             "Enter a valid date, for example:  07/17/2002";
         return;
     }
     try
     {
         returnDate = DateTime.Parse(flightReturnDateTextBox.Text);
     }
     catch (Exception ex)
     {
         feedbackLabel.Text = "Invalid data entry: Return Date is invalid. " +
                             "Enter a valid date, for example:  07/17/2002";
         return;
     }
     // Verify that the departure date is less than the
     // return date - no same day trips in this system!
     if (departDate >= returnDate)
     {
         feedbackLabel.Text = "Invalid data entry: The Departure Date must be " +
                             "earlier than the Return Date and no same-day " +
                             "returns for this travel package!";
         return;
     }
     // Verify that the departure date is not in the past or today!
     if (departDate < DateTime.Now)
```

```
      {
          feedbackLabel.Text = "Invalid data entry:  The Departure Date cannot " +
                                "be in the past or today!";
          return;
      }
      // Everthing is valid - set the IsValid flag...
      args.IsValid = true;
  }
</script>
```

5. The final step in this `travel.aspx` example is to write an event handler for the `bookTheTripButton`'s `OnClick` event. Add the following lines to your `<script>` block, after the lines we just added:

```
<script language="c#" runat="server">
...
  private void bookTheTripButton_Click(object sender, EventArgs e)
  {
    // Has the page been validated for all data entry?
    if (!(Page.IsValid))
    {
      return;
    }
    // We're all set - book the flight!
    DateTime departDate, returnDate;
    departDate = DateTime.Parse(flightDepartureDateTextBox.Text);
    returnDate = DateTime.Parse(flightReturnDateTextBox.Text);
    feedbackLabel.ForeColor = Color.Black;
    feedbackLabel.Text = "Success!  Your trip from Chicago to London " +
                         "will depart on the " + departDate.ToLongDateString() +
                         " and return on the " + returnDate.ToLongDateString();
  }
</script>
```

6. If you load `travel.aspx` in your browser, you should see something like the following page:

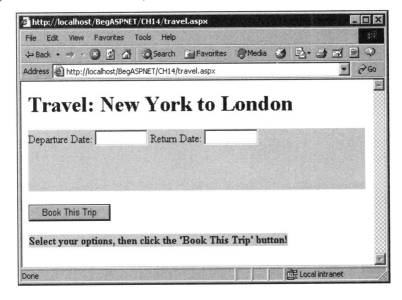

How It Works

In the `<!-- Flight Info -->` section of `travel.aspx`, we begin by creating the `panel` and set its color, width and height properties. Within the panel tag declaration, we then declare our **Departure Date** and **Return Date** text boxes, again specifying their size:

```
<asp:panel id="Panel" runat="server" Width="504px" Height="89px"
                         BackColor="Wheat">Departure Date:
<asp:TextBox id="flightDepartureDateTextBox" runat="server"
                    Width="80px" Height="22px"/>Return Date:
<asp:TextBox id="flightReturnDateTextBox" runat="server"
                        Width="80px" Height="22px"/></br>
```

Then we go on to validate the **Departure Date** and **Return Date** `TextBox` entries. After we established our `RequiredFieldValidator` controls, we added a `CustomValidator` control to our page – the event handler we assigned to the `OnServerValidate` event property was `ValidateTravelData`:

```
<asp:CustomValidator id="validateFlightDates" runat="server"
ControlToValidate="flightDepartureDateTextBox"
OnServerValidate="ValidateTravelData" />
```

This method is invoked when the form is posted back to the server. In this example, we're concerned about the data entries in the **Departure Date** and **Return Date** `TextBox` controls. We already know that the user entered something – the `RequiredFieldValidator` controls handled that task. However, we still don't know if the dates the user entered were valid – this will be the work of our `CustomValidator` method handler, `ValidateTravelData`. Let's review the pertinent sections from Step 4.

The first thing we do is to set the `IsValid` property of the `args` argument (a `ServerValidateEventArgs` object) to `false`:

```
args.IsValid = false;
```

We're being pessimistic here, but until we validate everything, we can't be sure that the data is OK. Next, we declare two variables of type `DateTime`:

```
DateTime departDate, returnDate;
```

We perform the work of getting the user's date input within a `try` block, so we can catch exceptions (we met this is Chapter 12, and it's discussed in detail in Chapter 17):

```
try
{
    departDate = DateTime.Parse(flightDepartureDateTextBox.Text);
}
catch (Exception ex)
{
    feedbackLabel.Text = "Invalid data entry: Departure Date is invalid. " +
                        "Enter a valid date, for example:  07/17/2002";
    return;
}
```

The `Date` object's static `Parse` method is called to pass the user's **Departure Date** entry. An exception will be thrown under two conditions: a `null` date (no date entered), or a malformed, or incorrect date entered; one that doesn't meet the criteria of the `DateTime` datatype. The `flightReturnDateTextBox` is similarly validated:

```
try
{
    returnDate = DateTime.Parse(flightReturnDateTextBox.Text);
}
catch (Exception ex)
{
    feedbackLabel.Text = "Invalid data entry: Return Date is invalid. " +
                        "Enter a valid date, for example:  07/17/2002";
    return;
}
```

If an exception is thrown, we provide the user with some feedback text, via the `feedbackLabel` that we created in the `<!-- BOOK IT BUTTON SECTION & FEEDBACK -->` part of our code file. We then promptly return the execution to the program that called this function, so it is ready for the user to have another go. Try entering **Today** as your departure date, and **Tomorrow** as your return date, for example, and you'll see this:

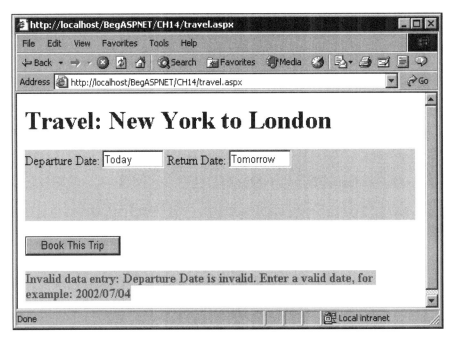

But even after it's confirmed that the user entered two valid dates, there's still some more work to do. The next validation ensures that the departure date entered is earlier than the return date:

```
// Verify that the departure date is less than the
// return date - no same day trips in this system!
if (departDate >= returnDate)
{
    feedbackLabel.Text = "Invalid data entry: The Departure Date must be " +
                         "earlier than the Return Date and no same-day " +
                         "returns for this travel package!";
    return;
}
```

The code for this section is pretty straightforward, using just an `if` statement, which sends a feedback message if the departure date is greater then the return date. The code then returns to the state it was in before the validation control was called. Just to make things even more robust, we validate that the departure date is not in the past, using the same technique:

```
// Verify that the departure date is not in the past or today!
if (departDate < DateTime.Now)
{
    feedbackLabel.Text = "Invalid data entry:  The Departure Date cannot " +
                         "be in the past or today!";
    return;
}
```

If we were to attempt to book our trip from New York to London without entering anything into the **Departure Date** and **Return Date** boxes, the assigned `RequiredFieldValidator` controls would kick into action and display a message to the user:

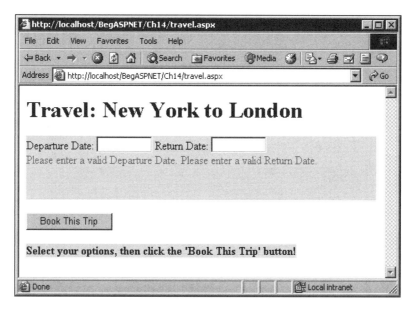

As you may have noticed, date validation involves a little work – but it's worth the effort! The nice thing about this implementation is that we didn't need to restrict the user to a particular date format for their data entry. Sure, we suggested a format like yyyy/MM/dd, but the user could have entered "10/31/2002" or even "October 31, 2002" – this is because we called the Date.Parse method, which automatically takes into account the client culture and date format.

Let's have a quick look at the button function of the web form. The button itself is very simple – we just give it some text and define its OnClick event as bookTheTripButton_Click:

```
<p>
<asp:Button id="bookTheTripButton" runat="server" Text="Book This Trip"
          OnClick="bookTheTripButton_Click" />
</p>
```

When the button is clicked, it sends the form information back to the server, which then processes all the server controls we have used. If our page validates correctly (if args.IsValid = True) our bookTheTripButton OnClick event is triggered:

```
private void bookTheTripButton_Click(object sender, EventArgs e)
  {
    // Has the page been validated for all data entry?
    if (!(Page.IsValid))
    {
      return;
    }
    // We're all set - book the flight!
    DateTime departDate, returnDate;
    departDate = DateTime.Parse(flightDepartureDateTextBox.Text);
    returnDate = DateTime.Parse(flightReturnDateTextBox.Text);
    feedbackLabel.ForeColor = Color.Black;
    feedbackLabel.Text = "Success!  Your trip from Chicago to London " +
                         "will depart on the " + departDate.ToLongDateString() +
                         " and return on the " + returnDate.ToLongDateString();
  }
```

In the end, when all the dates and logic are validated, our trip from New York to London will be booked with a simple click of the mouse – great!

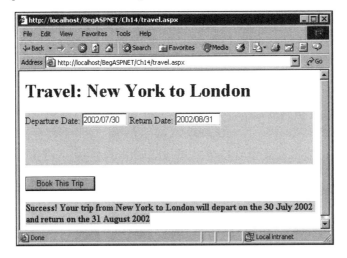

Control Families

ASP.NET server controls can be grouped into four basic family types: **Intrinsic**, **Validation**, **Rich**, and **Data-Rendering** controls. These control families are fairly broad and are based primarily on the function or purpose of the control.

When designing a web form, you'll often need to ask yourself two questions: "What do I need to display?" and "How am I going to display it?" Once you're familiar with the various controls and what they do, it's relatively easy to know which ASP.NET server controls you'll need to get the job done. When you create ASP.NET pages, you are free to mix and match all kinds of different controls within your pages, including standard HTML controls.

Intrinsic Controls

These are controls that correspond directly to HTML commands, such as `Button`, `Checkbox`, `DropDownList`, and `TextBox`. We are familiar with these controls now, as we've been using them throughout the book, so we won't spend any more time explaining how they all work, but here is a list to remind you of which controls fall into this group:

Control	Purpose
Button	General-purpose button – you typically write an `OnClick` event handler
CheckBox	Single checkbox
DropDownList	Drop-down listbox – a.k.a. "combo box", for selecting from a list of items
Hyperlink	Corresponds to the HTML `<a></a>` tag for displaying a hyperlink
Image	Display, an image file, GIF, JPG, other image file
Label	Provides a way to display text on a page corresponds to the HTML `<span>` tag
ListBox	Provides a scrollable list of items; single or multiple selection
Panel	Corresponds to the HTML `<DIV>` tag – typically serves as a container for other controls
RadioButton	Single radio button, similar to a checkbox, except you must handle deselect programmatically
Table	An HTML table
TableCell	Cell within a table
TableRow	Row within a table
TextBox	Textbox – single or multiple lines

Validation Controls

We gained some exposure to validation controls previously in this chapter – their purpose and value should be somewhat evident by now. To wax philosophical, we might conclude that the worth of any given web form could be measured by the accuracy of the data it was designed to collect. If the data is bogus, with values that are missing, out of range, or simply meaningless, the users of your site will probably complain pretty quick! The intent of validation controls is to help alleviate the problem of invalid data entry, and to make the task of validating a bit easier for developers.

Validation controls also exemplify how ASP.NET server controls, in general, abstract common tasks for us. Without validation controls, we would typically need to write our own client-side validation code (for example, client-side JavaScript) – but oh, at what a cost in terms of time, re-writing for every page, and not to mention managing all that manually written client-side code! But by using validation controls within ASP.NET web forms, our work is greatly simplified, and although validation involves a bit of overhead and some thought (for instance, what type validation control to use and some knowledge of how to implement it) the benefits include an easier code base to maintain, better control of our interface and what data gets passed to our servers and, arguably, a better experience for our users or customers. For example, if we wrote a logon form that collects a user's name and password, the process of validating that these fields were entered before passing the data on to the server is almost trivial using the `RequiredFieldValidator` control.

Since we've already seen some validation controls in action in `Travel.aspx`, take a look through the complete list of validation controls below to get an idea of what is possible:

Control	Purpose
`CompareValidator`	Compares a user's entry against a constant value (less than, equal, greater than, and so on).
`CustomValidator`	Checks the user's data entry using validation logic from a custom method that you write – processed on the server or the client.
`RangeValidator`	Checks that a user's entry is between specified lower and upper boundaries. Check ranges within pairs of numbers, alphabetic characters, and dates. Boundaries can be expressed as constants, or as values derived from another control.
`RegularExpressionValidator`	Checks that the entry matches a pattern defined by a regular expression. This type of validation allows you to check for predictable sequences of characters, such as those in social security numbers, e-mail addresses, telephone numbers, postal codes, and IP addresses.
`RequiredFieldValidator`	Ensures that the user does not skip an entry.

Rich Controls

Rich controls are controls are compound in nature, and provide extended functionality. In other words, "rich" controls are typically combinations of two or more simple or "intrinsic" controls that form a single functional unit – for instance, an `AdRotator` control. Another distinguishing trait of these controls is that they don't have a direct correlation to any single HTML control, although they do in fact render to HTML when displayed in the client browser.

Control	Purpose
AdRotator	Displays advertisement banners on a web form. The displayed ad is randomly changed each time the form is loaded or refreshed.
Calendar	Displays a one-month calendar for viewing/selecting a date, month, or year.
CheckBoxList	Multiple-selection checkbox group. Can be dynamically generated with data binding (we'll come to this shortly).
ImageButton	Provides a clickable image with (optional) access to the clicked coordinates for supporting image-map functionality.
LinkButton	Hyperlink-style button that posts back to the page of origin.
RadioButtonList	Mutually exclusive radio button group. Can be dynamically generated with data binding.

The nice thing about this family of "Rich Controls" is that they are just as easy to use as the other ASP.NET server controls. They may boast more features and properties, but the basic way to define them and interact with them programmatically is exactly the same as for all ASP.NET server controls. We haven't seen much of these yet, so let's look at a couple to see how they're used.

Calendar

One of the simplest and most practical uses for this control is to allow a user to select a particular date. It's even possible, via the `SelectionMode` property, to configure the control to allow the user to select a range of dates. The `Calendar` control has many properties, and we'll list a few here that are of particular interest:

FirstDayOfWeek=[Default|Monday|Tuesday|Wednesday|Thursday|Friday|Saturday|Sunday]

Notable here is the `FirstDayOfWeek` property – this enables you to choose which day of the week your calendar starts from, and we will use this property in the example at the end of this chapter. Some calendars default to Sunday as the first day of the week – for business purposes, however, it's typically more practical to view the week starting from Monday. A nice feature!

SelectionMode=[None|Day|DayWeek|DayWeekMonth]

By default, the `Calendar` control's `SelectionMode` defaults to `Day`. This is useful when you want your user to select a single day. However, you can select multiple days by setting the `SelectionMode` property to either `DayWeek`, which will allow you to select a single day or an entire week, or `DayWeekMonth`, which will allow you to select a single day, an entire week, or the entire month.

```
SelectMonthText="HTML text"
SelectWeekText="HTML text"
```

The `Calendar` control's `SelectMonthText` and `SelectWeekText` properties allow you to customize the HTML – use these properties if you're really going for a customized look.

You need not define all of the properties of the ASP.NET `Calendar` control to display the control. In fact, the following declaration will create an ASP.NET `Calendar` server control that looks OK and displays quite nicely:

```
<asp:Calendar id="MyCalendarControl" runat="server" />
```

When delivered to the client browser, the result is an HTML calendar that enables you to navigate through the various days, months, and years. Try it for yourself:

≤		July 2001				≥
Mon	Tue	Wed	Thu	Fri	Sat	Sun
25	26	27	28	29	30	1
2	3	4	5	6	7	8
9	10	11	12	13	14	15
16	17	18	19	20	21	22
23	24	25	26	27	28	29
30	31	1	2	3	4	5

Have a look at the HTML that your ASP.NET produced to create this page – over 100 lines of code, consisting of HTML and JavaScript, were generated to produce this, and you wrote only a single line!

The ASP.NET `Calendar` control is extremely feature-rich. Refer to the ASP.NET documentation for complete details on this control.

LinkButton

The `LinkButton` control is functionally very much like the `Button` control. What distinguishes this control, though, is that when rendered in the client browser, it looks like a traditional hyperlink. The `LinkButton` object's functionality is dependent upon how the `OnClick` event handler is implemented. The following is an example of a `LinkButton` declaration:

```
<html>
  <body>
    <form runat="server">
```

```
        <asp:LinkButton id="WroxLinkButton" runat="server"
          Text="Visit the Wrox Press Home Page"
        />
      </form>
    </body>
  </html>
```

In this example, the `Text` property is set, and the `OnClick` event is assigned the name of the method handler, `OnWroxLinkButtonClick`. When displayed in the browser, this particular `LinkButton` will look like this:

<u>Visit the Wrox Press Home Page</u>

If we added the following event handler for an `OnClick` event to our link button:

```
<script language="c#" runat="server">
  public void OnWroxLinkButtonClick(object sender, EventArgs e)
  {
    Response.Redirect("http://www.wrox.com")
  }
</script>
```

and an `OnClick` event to our link button:

```
<html>
  <body>
    <form runat="server">
      <asp:LinkButton id="WroxLinkButton" runat="server"
        Text="Visit the Wrox Press Home Page"
        OnClick="OnWroxLinkButtonClick"
      />
    </form>
  </body>
</html>
```

we end up at the Wrox web site! Try it for yourself.

So what's the advantage of using a `LinkButton` control over a standard hyperlink? Well, because this is a button rather than a standard hyperlink, when it is clicked we can perform any additional server-side processing before performing the expected task. For example, in the above example, rather than just redirecting the user to the Wrox home page, we could have added code to add an entry in a database to track that this user was interested in such a link.

Data Rendering Controls

These controls are extremely feature-rich (they have numerous properties to choose from) and greatly simplify the work of displaying a variety of data, particularly database-related data. The definition of "data" in the context of these controls is very broad. It could include database records, an `ArrayList`, an XML data source, and even our own custom collection objects containing custom class instances.

Before we look at the controls themselves, we need to understand two important concepts:

❑ **Data Binding.** This is the term used to describe the process of associating information in a data store (which could be anything from a database table, to an `ArrayList` object) with a server control. Binding data to our server control is a two-step process in ASP.NET – first we must assign our server control's `DataSource` property to the data we want to bind to. Second, we must call our control's `DataBind` method. You will see several examples of this process throughout the remaining examples in this chapter.

❑ **Templates.** This is a way to define the various layout elements of a particular control, to describe how the data is displayed in the browser. The `DataGrid` and `DataList` have default templates, so you only need to create templates if you want to change the default look.

Now let's look at those controls:

Control	Purpose
DataGrid	Creates a multi-column, data-bound grid. This control allows you to define various types of columns, both to lay out the contents of the grid and to add specific functionality (edit button columns, hyperlink columns, and so on).
DataList	Displays items from a data source using templates. You can customize the appearance and contents of the control by manipulating the templates that make up its different components.
Repeater	The `Repeater` control is a data-bound list that renders a row for every row in the data source. You define the appearance of the `Repeater` rows using templates. The `Repeater` control does not have any built-in selection or editing support.

These controls are very powerful and it is beyond the scope of this book to examine all of their features. However, the sections that follow should serve to give you a solid foundation for working with these types of controls.

DataGrid

The `DataGrid` control provides a wealth of functionality for displaying data in columns and rows and provides a plethora of properties to control the layout of your grid. The control's use of **template** properties make it particularly wellsuited for defining the overall look and feel of the display elements. For example, you could alternate the colors for the rows of data being displayed. We will learn more about defining and using templates when we examine the `DataList` control. Some useful properties for the `DataGrid` control include:

❑ AllowSorting: enables you dynamically sort and re-display the data based on a selected column. For example, if you had a table containing your employee's surnames and salaries, enabling sorting would allow you to sort your table according to either column.

❑ AllowPaging: the ability to view subsets of the data called by the DataGrid control on different pages. The number of items displayed on the page is determined by the PageSize property.

❑ AlternatingItemStyle: the style (such as background color) of every other item listed.

❑ FooterStyle: the style of the footer at the end of the list (if any).

❑ HeaderStyle: the style of the header at the beginning of the list (if any).

❑ ItemStyle: the style of individual items. If no AlternatingItemStyle is defined, all the items will render with this style.

To use the DataGrid control, you declare it like the other server controls we've seen (using the <asp:DataGrid> start tag and </asp:DataGrid> end tag), set the relevant properties, define the columns in your table, and then apply the relevant template for those columns. Within the template tags, you include the information the template must be applied to – pay special attention to the unique data binding syntax used:

```
<asp:DataGrid id="EventData"
   AllowSorting="true"
     <Columns>
       <asp:TemplateColumn HeaderText="Column1">
         <ItemTemplate>
           <%# Container.DataItem("ShortDesc") %>
         </ItemTemplate>
       </asp:TemplateColumn>

       <asp:TemplateColumn HeaderText="Column2">
         <ItemTemplate>
           <%# Container.DataItem("DetailDesc") %>
         </ItemTemplate>
       </asp:TemplateColumn>
     </Columns>
   </asp:DataGrid>
```

We'll see the DataGrid control in action in the last *Try It Out* of this chapter.

DataList

The DataList control is useful for displaying rows of database information (which can become columns in DataGrid tables) in a format that you can control very precisely using **templates** and **styles**. Manipulating various template controls changes the way your data is presented. The DataList control enables you to select and edit the data that is presented. The following is a listing of some supported templates:

Template	Purpose
ItemTemplate	Required template that provides the content and layout for items referenced by DataList.
AlternatingItemTemplate	If defined, this template provides the content and layout for alternating items in the DataList. If not defined, ItemTemplate is used.
EditItemTemplate	If defined, this template provides editing controls, such as textboxes, for items set to 'edit' in the DataList. If not defined, ItemTemplate is used.
FooterTemplate	If defined, the FooterTemplate provides the content and layout for the footer section of the DataList. If not defined, a footer section will not be displayed.
HeaderTemplate	If defined, this provides the content and layout for the header section of the DataList. If not defined, a header section will not be displayed.
SelectedItemTemplate	If defined, this template provides the content and layout for the currently selected item in the DataList. If not defined, ItemTemplate is used.
SeparatorTemplate	If defined, this provides the content and layout for the separator between items in the DataList. If not defined, a separator will not be displayed.

The DataList control is declared like all other ASP.NET server controls. Within the body of its tag declararation we will declare the templates – it is between the tags of these tempates that we can add other controls or formatting for our data. Naturally, we will need to assign the DataSource property of DataList control, then call the DataBind method to initiate the binding process. The following provides a shell implementation for our first DataList control declaration:

```
<asp:DataList id="DataList1" runat="server">
    <FooterTemplate>
      'Items to be affected by this template
    </FooterTemplate>
    <SeparatorTemplate>
      'Items to be affected by this template
    </SeparatorTemplate>
</asp:DataList>
```

If you use the `DataList` control to set up a column in a grid, you can set additional templates within that column by using the `DataGrid` control. Refer to the ASP.NET documentation for more information.

Repeater

The `Repeater` control is very similar to the `DataList` control with one very important distinction: the data displayed is always **read only** – you cannot edit the data being presented. It is particularly useful for displaying repeating rows of data. Like the `DataGrid` and `DataList` controls, it utilizes templates to render its various sections. The templates it uses are generally the same as the ones used with the `DataList` control, and the syntax is also the same. We'll see an example of the `Repeater` control in action in the next *Try It Out.*

Well, we've now looked at almost everything we're going to in this chapter. All that is left to do is to bring everything together in two exercises, the first of which creates a dynamic calendar, and the second uses the `EditItemTemplate` to create an editable table of information.

Try It Out – MyCalendar

In the previous sections of this chapter, you were exposed to many of the most common ASP.NET server controls, including the `Calendar` control. Many web sites, particularly personal home pages, share information regarding upcoming events. For example, a local soccer team might have a web site that displays the team's game schedule for the players, parents, coaches, and so on, or a band might display an online calendar to share all upcoming gigs for their fans. In either case, the ability to render intuitive and familiar calendar-related events or appointments on a web page is a requirement.

Because of the centrality of the calendar to many situations, we've decided to base this *Try It Out* around the `Calendar` control. We're not going to try to replicate the advanced features of a desktop calendaring tool, such as Microsoft Outlook though. The object of our application will be to share some key dates and appointments on the Web, in the context of a familiar calendar.

To flesh this out a little, here's a mini-specification of some of the features we'll be implementing for the `MyCalendar` application:

❑ The `Calendar` control should read our calendar data from an XML file (we'll be using the XML file as a data source). This will make it easy to update and change the calendar data, without ever having to change the ASPX file. Because of this, none of our appointments or events will be hard-coded within the ASPX page itself.

❑ We'd like to be able to see several events within a day.

❑ While we obviously want to see the title of an event or appointment on the calendar, we also want to see some additional information (for example, a detailed description of the event and the start and end times). To enable this, when we click on the event link, a listing of all details should appear.

❑ Although the `Calendar` control defaults to Sunday as the first day of the week, we want the first day of the week to be Monday.

❑ Weekends should display in a slightly different shade (so we know they're coming!), as should days that are part of the previous or next month.

Since we're taking all our information from an XML file, let's begin by looking at the XML that we're going to use.

The XML Source – MyCalendar.xml

The source XML file we shall use will contain only the basic information we want display in the `Calendar` control. It's worth noting that you will need to ensure `MyCalendar.xml` has write permissions on the web server you deploy to because we will be dynamically updating the contents of this file later in this chapter. The `MyCalendar.xml` file, as with all the listings throughout this book, is available for download on **www.wrox.com**. The following excerpt of the `MyCalendar.xml` file is provided, just to show you the XML format used, as well as some of the sample data:

```
<MyCalendar>
  <Event>
     <ShortDesc>Concert at the Riverfront</ShortDesc>
     <DetailDesc>4th of July celebration. Bring stand and a jacket.</DetailDesc>
     <EventDate>2002/07/04</EventDate>
     <StartTime>9:30PM</StartTime>
     <EndTime>11:00PM</EndTime>
  </Event>
  <Event>
     <ShortDesc>CCT Rehearsal - Brigadoon</ShortDesc>
     <DetailDesc>Community Theatre orchestra rehearsal - bring mutes.</DetailDesc>
     <EventDate>2002/07/14</EventDate>
     <StartTime>3:30PM</StartTime>
     <EndTime>6:30PM</EndTime>
  </Event>
</MyCalendar>
```

The elements of this XML file are fairly straightforward:

- ❏ `MyCalendar` – the root element. XML requires a single root element to contain the child elements.

- ❏ `Event` – basically serves as the main parent for each group of elements.

- ❏ `ShortDesc` – a short description of the event.

- ❏ `DetailDesc` – a detailed description of the event – could be random notes, comments, or thoughts.

- ❏ `EventDate` – the date on which the event occurs. The format for this particular entry is in the date format of **yyyy/MM/dd**. This will serve to eliminate any ambiguity between various local date formats and is also a requirement for our code to dynamically select and display only those events for a given date.

- ❏ `StartTime` – the time the event starts.

- ❏ `EndTime` – the time the event ends.

The rest of the XML file is very similar to this excerpt – it merely contains information that we are going to reference in our `MyCalendar.aspx` file. Let's take a look at this now.

The Web Form – MyCalendar.aspx

The following is the complete listing of the `MyCalendar.aspx` web form implementation. You'll declare the various ASP.NET server controls used in this web form, as well as the corresponding code and event handlers, in a series of incremental steps. Because the example is a long one, we'll discuss much of what is going on as we go through it. At the end, further analysis and discussion will be provided in the subsequent *How It Works* section.

1. Download `MyCalendar.xml` from **www.wrox.com**, and save it in the Chapter 14 folder of your `BegASPNET` virtual directory.

2. Create a new file, called `MyCalendar.aspx`, save it in the same folder as `MyCalendar.xml`, and add the following lines, which will serve as a starting point for creating the page's ASP.NET server control objects, as well as the corresponding code and event handlers:

```
<%@ Page Language="c#" %>
<%@ Import Namespace="System.Data"%>
<%@ Import Namespace="System.IO" %>

<html>
<head>
<script language="c#" runat="server">

</script>

</head>
<body>

</body>
</html>
```

3. Add the following code between the `<body>` tags:

```
<body>
<h1>My Calendar</h1>
  <form id="MyCalendarForm" method="post" runat="server">
    <p align="center">
      <asp:Calendar id="MyCalendar" runat="server"
        SelectedDate="2002/07/17"
        VisibleDate="2002/07/01"
        FirstDayOfWeek="Monday"
        DayNameFormat="Full"
        ShowDayHeader="True"
        ShowGridLines="True"
        ShowNextPrevMonth="True"
        ShowTitle="True"
        nextprevstyle-backcolor="DodgerBlue"
        nextprevstyle-forecolor="White"
```

```
                nextprevstyle-font-bold="True"
                nextprevstyle-font-size="Large"
                TitleFormat="MonthYear"
                TitleStyle-BackColor="DodgerBlue"
                TitleStyle-ForeColor="White"
                TitleStyle-Font-Size="Large"
                TitleStyle-Font-Bold="True"
                dayheaderstyle-backcolor="DodgerBlue"
                dayheaderstyle-forecolor="White"
                daystyle-horizontalalign="Left"
                daystyle-verticalalign="Top"
                daystyle-font-size="Small"
                SelectedDayStyle-Font-Bold="True"
                selecteddaystyle-horizontalalign="Left"
                selecteddaystyle-verticalalign="Top"
                selecteddaystyle-font-size="Small"
                selecteddaystyle-forecolor="Red"
                TodayDayStyle-HorizontalAlign="Left"
                TodayDayStyle-VerticalAlign="Top"
                todaydaystyle-backcolor="White"

                OnDayRender="MyCalendar_DayRender"
                OnSelectionChanged="MyCalendar_SelectionChanged">

          </asp:Calendar>
      </p>

  <p align="center">
      <asp:label id="SelectedDate" runat="server" font-size="Large" />
  </p>

    <asp:panel id="DailyDetailsPanel" runat="server">
        <asp:Repeater id="DailyEventDetailRepeater" runat="server">
          <HeaderTemplate>
          <p align="center">
          <table border="1" width="100%">
          <table style="color:Black;border collapse:collapse;">
            <tr style="color:White;background-color:DodgerBlue;
                       font-weight:bold;">
              <td><b>Event</b></td>
              <td><b>Description</b></td>
              <td><b>Start Time</b></td>
              <td><b>End Time</b></td>
            </tr>
          </HeaderTemplate>
          <ItemTemplate>
            <tr style="background-color:White;">
              <td><%# DataBinder.Eval(Container.DataItem, "ShortDesc") %></td>
              <td><%# DataBinder.Eval(Container.DataItem, "DetailDesc") %></td>
              <td><%# DataBinder.Eval(Container.DataItem, "StartTime") %></td>
              <td><%# DataBinder.Eval(Container.DataItem, "EndTime") %></td>
            </tr>
```

```
                </ItemTemplate >
                <AlternatingItemTemplate>
                  <tr style="background-color:Gainsboro;">
                    <td><%# DataBinder.Eval(Container.DataItem, "ShortDesc") %></td>
                    <td><%# DataBinder.Eval(Container.DataItem, "DetailDesc") %></td>
                    <td><%# DataBinder.Eval(Container.DataItem, "StartTime") %></td>
                    <td><%# DataBinder.Eval(Container.DataItem, "EndTime") %></td>
                  </tr>
                </AlternatingItemTemplate>
                <FooterTemplate>
                </table>
                </p>
                </FooterTemplate>
              </asp:Repeater>
            </asp:panel>

        </form>
    </body>
```

In this step, we're adding the main visual component of the page – the ASP.NET `Calendar` control. Since the `Calendar` control will be responding to events, it's declared within the context of a `<form>` tag. The numerous properties defined here will serve not only to give the `Calendar` control a unique look, but will also affect its behavior. For example, the `FirstDayOfWeek` property is set to `"Monday"`. If you have a look through the other properties we're defining here, you'll find they're pretty self-explanatory. You should also take note of the style templates declared – `TodayDayStyle`, `DayStyle`, `NextPrevStyle`, `DayHeaderStyle`, `TitleStyle`, `WeekendDayStyle`, and `OtherMonthDayStyle`. These style templates provide us with a great deal of control over how our calendar will look.

> *A couple things to note so far: the `SelectedDate` and `VisibleDate` properties are hard-coded for demonstration purposes only – this is discussed in more detail in the* How It Works *section to follow.*

We assigned event handlers for the `OnDayRender` and `OnSelectionChanged` events just before the style template tag definitions. These will be explained in detail later in this section:

```
<body>
...
        OnDayRender="MyCalendar_DayRender"
        OnSelectionChanged="MyCalendar_SelectionChanged">
...
      </asp:Calendar>
      </p>
    </form>
</body>
```

4. We now add a `Label` control to the page, which will later serve to provide some date selection feedback to the user, regarding the currently selected date. Add these lines after the declaration of the `Calendar` control, and just before the `</form>` end tag:

```
<body>
...
    <p align="center">
    <asp:label id="SelectedDate" runat="server" font-size="Large" />
    </p>
    </form>
</body>
```

5. The final visual components used in this example consist of two controls: the `Panel` and `Repeater` controls. When a user selects a date from the calendar, the `OnSelectionChanged` event (for which we assigned the handler in Step 2) will be raised by the `Calendar` control. This will enable us to gather a `DataSet` of all daily events and bind them to the `Repeater` control. The ASP.NET `Panel` control serves as a container for the `Repeater` control, and will be used to control the visibility state of the `Repeater` elements (when the `Panel` control's `Visible` property is set to `false`, all corresponding child controls, like the `Repeater` control, are also hidden).

The code we're adding here sets up the `Repeater` control (within the panel control) and establishes the properties of the templates, which will be used to display our information. Insert the following ASP.NET `Panel` and `Repeater` control declarations before the final `</form>` end tag:

```
<body>
...
    <asp:panel id="DailyDetailsPanel" runat="server">
      <asp:Repeater id="DailyEventDetailRepeater" runat="server">
        <HeaderTemplate>
        <p align="center">
        <table border="1" width="100%">
        <table style="color:Black;border collapse:collapse;">
          <tr style="color:White;background-color:DodgerBlue;font-weight:bold;">
            <td><b>Event</b></td>
            <td><b>Description</b></td>
            <td><b>Start Time</b></td>
            <td><b>End Time</b></td>
          </tr>
        </HeaderTemplate>
        <ItemTemplate>
          <tr style="background-color:White;">
            <td> <%# DataBinder.Eval(Container.DataItem, "ShortDesc") %> </td>
            <td> <%# DataBinder.Eval(Container.DataItem, "DetailDesc")%> </td>
            <td> <%# DataBinder.Eval(Container.DataItem, "StartTime") %> </td>
            <td> <%# DataBinder.Eval(Container.DataItem, "EndTime") %> </td>
          </tr>
        </ItemTemplate >
```

```
            <AlternatingItemTemplate>
              <tr style="background-color:Gainsboro;">
                <td> <%# DataBinder.Eval(Container.DataItem, "ShortDesc") %> </td>
                <td> <%# DataBinder.Eval(Container.DataItem, "DetailDesc")%> </td>
                <td> <%# DataBinder.Eval(Container.DataItem, "StartTime") %> </td>
                <td> <%# DataBinder.Eval(Container.DataItem, "EndTime") %> </td>
              </tr>
            </AlternatingItemTemplate>
            <FooterTemplate>
            </table>
            </p>
            </FooterTemplate>

        </asp:Repeater>
      </asp:panel>
    </form>
</body>
```

6. At this point, all the visual components used in `MyCalendar.aspx` have been declared and set up. Over the next few steps, we will add the method and event handler code implementations between the `<script>` and `</script>` tags of the page. Add the following code for the `Page_Load` method implementation:

```
<script language="c#" runat="server">
```

```
protected void Page_Load(object sender, EventArgs e)
  {
    if (!(IsPostBack))
    {
      ShowDailyEvents();
    }
  }
```

```
</script>
```

In this listing, the `IsPostback` property is checked to see if this is the first time the page has been loaded – if so, a method, `ShowDailyEvents`, is called, which will perform the work of binding and displaying the daily event data in the `Repeater` control. We'll define `ShowDailyEvents` shortly.

7. The `Calendar` control in this page declares an event handler for the `OnSelectionChanged` event that we added in Step 2. Remember that in Step 2 the name of the event handler we assigned was `MyCalendar_SelectionChanged`. The implementation for this event handler should be added between the `<script>` and `</script>` tags, and below the `Page_Load` method we just added, as follows:

```
<script language="c#" runat="server">
...
public void MyCalendar_SelectionChanged(object sender, EventArgs e)
```

```
    {
      ShowDailyEvents();
    }

</script>
```

When the user clicks a new date on the calendar control (thus triggering the OnSelectionChanged event), the MyCalendar_SelectionChanged event handler will call the ShowDailyEvents method. So this is almost functionally identical to our Page_Load implementation, above.

8. In order to display our custom calendar events within the Calendar control, we must write a method that loads the data from MyCalendar.xml into a DataSet object. This is implemented as follows (again, add this code between your <script> and </script> tags, below the event handler we just added):

```
<script language="c#" runat="server">
...
  protected DataSet LoadMyCalendarData()
  {
    string sourceXml = Server.MapPath("MyCalendar.xml");
    if (!(File.Exists(sourceXml)))
    {
      return null;
    }
    DataSet cachedDataSet = (DataSet)Session["MyCalendarData"];
    if (cachedDataSet != null)
    {
      return cachedDataSet;
    }
    DataSet dataSet = new DataSet();
    try
    {
      dataSet.ReadXml(sourceXml);
      Session["MyCalendarData"] = dataSet;
    }
    catch (Exception e)
    {
      SelectedDate.Text = e.Message;
      dataSet = null;
    }
    return dataSet;
  }
</script>
```

The key points to observe from this listing are that we first check to see if our calendar data file (MyCalendar.xml) exists. If it doesn't exist on the server file system, we won't be able to display any of our custom calendar data in the Calendar or Repeater controls. Note also that we use the Session object to determine if we've already loaded (or cached) this DataSet object – if so, we can use it and optimize our code slightly. We'll discuss this more in the *How It Works* section. The part of the code in the try block loads the XML data into a DataSet object via the ReadXml method (which enables the XML in the file to be read). The Catch block checks that LoadMyCalendarData does return something when it is called, as it is possible that nothing could be returned, particularly if MyCalendar.xml is an improperly formatted XML document.

9. We are able to display our own data within the calendar by implementing an event handler for the Calendar control's OnDayRender event, which is raised each time a visible day in the calendar is being rendered. The MyCalendar_DayRender method (remember we introduced this in Step 3) renders the Calendar control's Cell display by utilizing our own helper method, GetEventsDataSet, which as the name implies, gathers for us a DataSet comprising only the event rows that match the date on the calendar we're rendering. It is implemented as follows, and is to be placed, once again, within the <script> and </script> tags:

```c#
<script language="c#" runat="server">
...
protected void MyCalendar_DayRender(object sender, DayRenderEventArgs e)
  {
    if (e.Day.IsOtherMonth)
    {
       e.Cell.BackColor=System.Drawing.Color.FromName("Gainsboro");
    }
    else
    {
      if (e.Day.IsWeekend)
      {
        e.Cell.BackColor=System.Drawing.Color.FromName("PaleGoldenrod");
      }
      else
      {
         e.Cell.BackColor=System.Drawing.Color.FromName("LightGoldenrodYellow");
      }
    }
    DataSet dataSet = LoadMyCalendarData();
    if (dataSet == null)
    {
      return;
    }
    foreach (DataRow zRow in dataSet.Tables[0].Rows)
    {
      DateTime compareDate = GetSafeDate(zRow["EventDate"].ToString());
      if (compareDate == e.Day.Date)
      {
        // Event matches date criteria - display it...
        MyCalendarEventData myEventData = new MyCalendarEventData();
```

```
              myEventData.ShortDesc = zRow["ShortDesc"].ToString();
              myEventData.DetailDesc = zRow["DetailDesc"].ToString();
              myEventData.StartTime = zRow["StartTime"].ToString();
              myEventData.EndTime = zRow["EndTime"].ToString();
              Label dailyEventLabel = new Label();
              dailyEventLabel.Text = "<br />" + myEventData.ShortDesc;
              e.Cell.Controls.Add(dailyEventLabel);
          }
        }
    }
</script>
```

10. The next section implements the method, `ShowDailyEvents`, that we referenced in Steps 5 and 6. This method's task is to display the detailed information for all events (the detailed event description, the start time, the end time, and so on), based on the currently selected day in the calendar. This detailed display of calendar data will actually be rendered via a `Repeater` control, and will be displayed below the calendar. In this way, we'll have a bit more room on our page to display the detailed information about the selected day's events, which would normally be too verbose to display in within `Calendar`'s day cell. Add the following lines between the `<script>` and `</script>` tags:

```
<script language="c#" runat="server">
...
protected void ShowDailyEvents()
  {
    DateTime d = MyCalendar.SelectedDate;
    DataSet dataSet = LoadMyCalendarData();
    if (dataSet == null)
    {
      return;
    }
    ArrayList aEvents = new ArrayList();
    foreach (DataRow zRow in dataSet.Tables[0].Rows)
    {
      DateTime compareDate = GetSafeDate(zRow["EventDate"].ToString());
      if (compareDate == d)
      {
        // Event matches date criteria - display it...
        MyCalendarEventData myEventData = new MyCalendarEventData();
        myEventData.EventDate = d;
        myEventData.ShortDesc = zRow["ShortDesc"].ToString();
        myEventData.DetailDesc = zRow["DetailDesc"].ToString();
        myEventData.StartTime = zRow["StartTime"].ToString();
        myEventData.EndTime = zRow["EndTime"].ToString();
        aEvents.Add(myEventData);
      }
    }
    // Bind to the Repeater control...
    DailyEventDetailRepeater.DataSource = aEvents;
    DailyEventDetailRepeater.DataBind();
```

```
      if (aEvents.Count > 0)
      {
        DailyDetailsPanel.Visible = true;
        SelectedDate.Text = "Events For " + d.ToLongDateString();
      }
      else
      {
        DailyDetailsPanel.Visible = false;
        SelectedDate.Text = "No Events Scheduled For " + d.ToLongDateString();
      }
    }

</script>
```

11. Because the `MyCalendar.xml` data source file could conceivably contain an invalid date entry in its `EventDate` XML element tag, we'll add the following helper method to our page to guarantee that a non-null `DateTime` object is always returned, regardless of the date value obtained from the source XML:

```
<script language="c#" runat="server">
...
  private DateTime GetSafeDate(string proposedDate)
  {
    // Returns a non-null DateTime even if proposed date can't be parsed
    DateTime safeDate;
    try {
      safeDate = DateTime.Parse(proposedDate, DateTimeFormatInfo.InvariantInfo);
    } catch (Exception e) {
      Response.Write("<!-- Failed to parse date: " + e.Message + " -->");
      safeDate = DateTime.MinValue;
    }
    return safeDate;
  }
</script>
```

12. In this step, we add a `MyCalendarEventData` class implementation. This class serves as a container for the various data elements that make up our own custom calendar event data:

```
<script language="c#" runat="server">
...
  public class MyCalendarEventData
  {
    private string m_ShortDesc;
    private string m_DetailDesc;
    private DateTime m_EventDate;
    private string m_StartTime;
    private string m_EndTime;
    public string ShortDesc
    {
```

```
      get {
        return m_ShortDesc;
      }
      set {
       m_ShortDesc = value;
      }
    }
    public string DetailDesc
    {
      get {
        return m_DetailDesc;
      }
      set {
        m_DetailDesc = value;
      }
    }
    public DateTime EventDate
    {
      get {
        return m_EventDate;
      }
      set {
        m_EventDate = value;
      }
    }
    public string StartTime
    {
      get {
        return m_StartTime;
      }
      set {
        m_StartTime = value;
      }
    }
    public string EndTime
    {
      get {
        return m_EndTime;
      }
      set {
        m_EndTime = value;
      }
    }
  }
</script>
```

13. Once you've completed all the steps for entering the controls and code, you should be able to load the `MyCalendar.aspx` file into your browser. You should see the following display served up after the page loads:

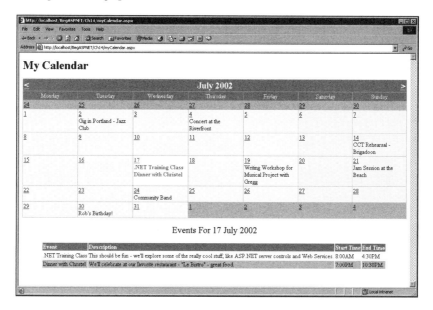

How It Works

The first step in creating the `MyCalendar.aspx` web form was to define what we wanted it to do, which was this: given a custom XML file with various calendar event data (`MyCalendar.xml`), load each of the event items in an ASP.NET `Calendar` control. In Steps 1 through 4, above, we basically created an ASPX page that defined three different ASP.NET server controls: `Calendar`, `Repeater`, and `Panel`.

Calendar Implementation Details

The `Calendar` control serves as the primary visual interface for the user. We set a host of properties to customize the look of the control – see Step 2 for details. The first question you might be wondering is, why does the `Calendar` control default to July 2002, and why is the date July 17, 2002 selected by default? It comes down to the following code:

```
<asp:Calendar id="MyCalendar" runat="server"
   SelectedDate="2002/07/17"
   VisibleDate="2002/07/01"
```

The `SelectedDate` property is used to set the date that the calendar will default to when first opened. The `VisibleDate` property sets the month of the calendar that is visible, for example, defining the date `"2002/08/01"` will make the month August of 2002 visible.

As previously mentioned, the SelectedDate and VisibleDate properties were set this way for demonstration purposes only, since the entries in the MyCalendar.xml file only have calendar data for this particular time span.

When we declared the Calendar control, we assigned event handlers for two of the Calendar control's events:

```
<asp:Calendar id="MyCalendar" runat="server"
...
    OnDayRender="MyCalendar_DayRender"
    OnSelectionChanged="MyCalendar_SelectionChanged">
...
```

The MyCalendar_DayRender event is invoked whenever the Calendar control begins to display a day that will be visible, and the MyCalendar_SelectionChanged event is invoked when a new date is selected.

Our Calendar control displays six weeks' worth of data; the days representing the month being displayed, as well as a share of days from the previous and next months. In order to give our Calendar control a unique look, we implemented a bit of logic to determine if the day being rendered was part of another month (IsOtherMonth), a weekend day (IsWeekEnd), or if the day is part of the month being displayed. The logic for displaying the various Calendar Cell color formatting is demonstrated in this code fragment (from Step 9 of the previous *Try It Out* section):

```
protected void MyCalendar_DayRender(object sender, DayRenderEventArgs e)
    {
    if (e.Day.IsOtherMonth)
    {
        e.Cell.BackColor=System.Drawing.Color.FromName("Gainsboro");
    }
    else
    {
        if (e.Day.IsWeekend)
        {
            e.Cell.BackColor=System.Drawing.Color.FromName("PaleGoldenrod");
        }
        else
        {
            e.Cell.BackColor=System.Drawing.Color.FromName("LightGoldenrodYellow");
        }
    }
    ...
    }
```

In using the DataSet from the Session object, we don't need to load the MyCalendar.xml file from scratch each time the Calendar control renders a day item. Keep in mind that the Calendar control renders 6 weeks' worth of days, which amounts to 42 calls (6 weeks times 7 days in a week) to the LoadMyCalendarData method on a single page load – so even though the LoadMyCalendar method is being invoked numerous times, it's **optimized** to use the cached DataSet stored in Session ("MyCalendarData").

The code to render the `MyCalendar.xml` data to a specific `Cell` within the `Calendar` control is fairly straightforward. We loop through all the rows in our `DataSet` object's default `Table` and compare with the date the `Calendar` control is currently rendering – if the dates are the same, we have some work to do. Remember that each row represents a single event, and each time a day is rendered we have to see if that day matches any of the events. Otherwise, we loop through to the next item. When we encounter a match, we actually add the content to the `Calendar` object's `Cell` property, by creating a new `Label` object, setting its display properties, and adding it to the `Cell` object's `Controls` container:

```
protected DataSet LoadMyCalendarData()
  {
    string sourceXml = Server.MapPath("MyCalendar.xml");
    if (!(File.Exists(sourceXml)))
    {
       return null;
    }
    DataSet cachedDataSet = (DataSet)Session["MyCalendarData"];
    if (cachedDataSet != null)
    {
       return cachedDataSet;
    }
    DataSet dataSet = new DataSet();
    try
    {
      dataSet.ReadXml(sourceXml);
      Session["MyCalendarData"] = dataSet;
    }
    ...
  }
```

Repeater Control Implementation Details

The sole reason for implementing a `Repeater` control is to display the specific `MyCalendar.xml` event details that correspond to the currently selected day in the calendar. The details of an event or an appointment could contain quite a bit of information, so trying to put it all into a single `Cell` object of the `Calendar` control probably wouldn't look all that great. Displaying a short description (`ShortDesc`) in the `Calendar` control's `Cell` and relegating the detailed description (`DetailDesc`) and any additional information to the `Repeater` is prudent.

The mapping of the `MyCalendar.xml` data to the `Repeater` control is handled by the `ShowDailyEvents` method, which is invoked when the page first loads, and also as a result of an `OnSelectionChanged` event posted by the `Calendar` control. This event is automatically raised when the user changes the day (or month) selected. Recall from Step 10 that we declared a class, `MyCalendarEventData`. This contained various `Private` members and corresponding `Public` properties, which served as a container for the data extracted from the `MyCalendar.xml` file:

```
public class MyCalendarEventData
  {
    private string m_ShortDesc;
```

```
    private string m_DetailDesc;
    private DateTime m_EventDate;
    private string m_StartTime;
    private string m_EndTime;
    public string ShortDesc
    {
      get {
        return m_ShortDesc;
      }
      set {
       m_ShortDesc = value;
      }
    }
  . . .
```

There are at least two reasons for going through the effort of creating this class. The first is purely related to object-oriented design. In the event that the MyCalendar.xml file changes, or if new elements are added, it's good practice to have an object, like MyCalendarEventData, to map the new values to. This way, we would only have to make the changes under the relevant sections of our XML file – the method that calls these sections would still work.

The second reason is interrelated with the first, but is actually more practical: we can bind MyCalendarEventData objects to any data rendering control, like a Repeater control (which we did in Steps 8 and 9).

This brings us back to the ShowDailyEvents method. When invoked, this method performs a similar set of tasks to the MyCalendar_DayRender method, with a key difference: it renders all the matching events for a given day to the Repeater control, not the Calendar control. The ShowDailyEvents method proceeds to loop through all the DataRow objects in the DataSet object's default table in order to build an ArrayList of MyCalendarEventData objects. We need to do this because the DataSet contains all events, and not just those for the selected day. So, we build an ArrayList containing just those events for the selected day, as you can see in the code we added in Step 9:

```
    protected void ShowDailyEvents()
    {
      . . .
      foreach (DataRow zRow in dataSet.Tables[0].Rows)
      {
        DateTime compareDate = GetSafeDate(zRow["EventDate"].ToString());
        if (compareDate == d)
        {        // Event matches date criteria – display it...
          MyCalendarEventData myEventData = new MyCalendarEventData();
          myEventData.EventDate = d;
          myEventData.ShortDesc = zRow["ShortDesc"].ToString();
          myEventData.DetailDesc = zRow["DetailDesc"].ToString();
          myEventData.StartTime = zRow["StartTime"].ToString();
          myEventData.EndTime = zRow["EndTime"].ToString();
          aEvents.Add(myEventData);
        }
      }
```

```
      // Bind to the Repeater control...
      DailyEventDetailRepeater.DataSource = aEvents;
      DailyEventDetailRepeater.DataBind();
  ...

    }
```

The significance of storing the matching MyCalendarEventData objects in the aEvents variable (an ArrayList containing just those events for the selected day) is that we can bind this sub-set of records to the DailyEventDetailRepeater object to generate a detailed listing of the events for the selected day.

The final details concerning the Repeater control implementation deal with display issues. For some days, there may be no specific events. As such, when the user clicks on a particular day Cell link of the Calendar control that has no related events, we implement the following code to toggle the visibility of the Panel control (which contains the DailyEventDetailRepeater object):

```
    protected void ShowDailyEvents()
      {
        ...
      if (aEvents.Count > 0)
      {
        DailyDetailsPanel.Visible = true;
        SelectedDate.Text = "Events For " + d.ToLongDateString();
      }
      else
      {
        DailyDetailsPanel.Visible = false;
        SelectedDate.Text = "No Events Scheduled For " + d.ToLongDateString();
      }
    }
```

The SelectedDate object is a Label control that is not declared within the DailyDetailsPanel declaration, and therefore will not be affected when the DailyDetailsPanel.Visible property is changed. The DailyEventDetailRepeater control's visibility status, however, will correspond to whatever the DailyDetailsPanel.Visible property is. This is a nice feature to use, especially when you want to control the visibility state of a group of controls with one single property change.

Editing the Data Using Templates

In Chapter 13 we looked at updating data in DataSets, and in this chapter we've looked at using the grids and templates. One of the most powerful features behind ASP.NET is the templating architecture, which allows us to define a different set of controls depending upon the actions of the user. For the DataGrid and DataList we can use the EditItem template we saw earlier to automatically display different controls when the user wishes to edit some data.

Let's look at a simple example to see how this works:

Try It Out – Using the EditItem Template

1. Create a new file called `EditItemTemplate.aspx`, and add the following HTML elements and ASP.NET server controls. Don't worry about it looking long and complex – we'll explain it after we've seen what it does:

```
<html>
  <body>
    <form runat="server">
      <asp:Label id="ErrorMessage" runat="server" /><br/>
      <asp:LinkButton OnClick="DEDR_Add" Text="Add new event"
          runat="server"/><br/>
      <asp:DataGrid id="EventData"
          AutoGenerateColumns="false" width="100%" runat="server"
          OnEditCommand="DEDR_Edit"
          OnUpdateCommand="DEDR_Update"
          OnCancelCommand="DEDR_Cancel"
          OnDeleteCommand="DEDR_Delete">
        <HeaderStyle ForeColor="White" BackColor="DodgerBlue"
                    Font-Bold="true"/>
        <ItemStyle BackColor="White"/>
        <AlternatingItemStyle BackColor="Gainsboro"/>
        <Columns>

          <asp:TemplateColumn HeaderText="Date">
            <ItemTemplate>
              <%# DataBinder.Eval(Container.DataItem, "EventDate") %>
            </ItemTemplate>
            <EditItemTemplate>
              <asp:TextBox id="txtEventDate" Size="25";
                    Text='<%# DataBinder.Eval(Container.DataItem,"EventDate") %>'
                    runat="server"/>
            </EditItemTemplate>
          </asp:TemplateColumn>

          <asp:TemplateColumn HeaderText="Event">
            <ItemTemplate>
              <%# DataBinder.Eval(Container.DataItem, "ShortDesc") %>
            </ItemTemplate>
            <EditItemTemplate>
              <asp:TextBox id="txtShortDesc" Size="25";
                    Text='<%# DataBinder.Eval(Container.DataItem,"ShortDesc") %>'
                    runat="server"/>
            </EditItemTemplate>
          </asp:TemplateColumn>

          <asp:TemplateColumn HeaderText="Description">
            <ItemTemplate>
              <%# DataBinder.Eval(Container.DataItem, "DetailDesc") %>
            </ItemTemplate>
            <EditItemTemplate>
```

```
                  <asp:TextBox id="txtDetailDesc" Size="50"
                     Text='<%# DataBinder.Eval(Container.DataItem, "DetailDesc") %>'
                        runat="server"/>
               </EditItemTemplate>
            </asp:TemplateColumn>

            <asp:TemplateColumn HeaderText="Start Time">
               <ItemTemplate>
                 <%# DataBinder.Eval(Container.DataItem, "StartTime") %>
               </ItemTemplate>
               <EditItemTemplate>
                  <asp:TextBox id="txtStartTime" Size="7"
                        Text='<%# DataBinder.Eval(Container.DataItem, "StartTime") %>'
                        runat="server"/>
               </EditItemTemplate>
            </asp:TemplateColumn>

            <asp:TemplateColumn HeaderText="EndTime">
               <ItemTemplate>
                 <%# DataBinder.Eval(Container.DataItem, "EndTime") %>
               </ItemTemplate>
               <EditItemTemplate>
                  <asp:TextBox id="txtEndTime" Size="7"
                        Text='<%# DataBinder.Eval(Container.DataItem, "EndTime") %>'
                        runat="server"/>
               </EditItemTemplate>
            </asp:TemplateColumn>

            <asp:TemplateColumn>
               <ItemTemplate>
                  <asp:LinkButton CommandName="Edit"    Text="Edit"
                        runat="server"/>
                  <asp:LinkButton CommandName="Delete" Text="Delete"
                        runat="server"/>
               </ItemTemplate>
               <EditItemTemplate>
                  <asp:LinkButton CommandName="Cancel" Text="Cancel"
                        runat="server"/>
                  <asp:LinkButton CommandName="Update" Text="Update"
                        runat="server"/>
               </EditItemTemplate>
            </asp:TemplateColumn>
         </Columns>
     </asp:DataGrid>
     </form>
   </body>
</html>
```

587

2. Now add the following to the top of this page:

```csharp
<%@ Import Namespace="System.Data" %>
<%@ Import Namespace="System.IO" %>
<%@ Import Namespace="System.Globalization" %>
<script Language="c#" runat="server">
  void Page_Load(object sender, EventArgs e)
  {
    if (!(Page.IsPostBack))
    {
      EventData.DataSource = LoadMyCalendarData();
      EventData.DataBind();
    }
  }


  protected DataSet LoadMyCalendarData()
  {
    string sourceXml = Server.MapPath("MyCalendar.xml");
     if (!(File.Exists(sourceXml)))
     {
        return null;
     }
    DataSet cachedDataSet = (DataSet)Session["MyCalendarData"];
    if (!(cachedDataSet == null))
    {
        return cachedDataSet;
    }
    DataSet dataSet = new DataSet();
    try
    {
       dataSet.ReadXml(sourceXml);
       Session["MyCalendarData"] = dataSet;
    }
    catch (Exception e)
    {
       ErrorMessage.Text = e.Message;
       dataSet = null;
    }
    return dataSet;
  }

  void DEDR_Edit(object sender, DataGridCommandEventArgs e)
  {
     EventData.EditItemIndex = Convert.ToInt32(e.Item.ItemIndex);
     EventData.DataSource = LoadMyCalendarData();
     EventData.DataBind();
  }

  void DEDR_Update(object sender, DataGridCommandEventArgs e)
  {
     DataSet dataSet  = LoadMyCalendarData();
```

```
        int row = Convert.ToInt32(e.Item.ItemIndex);
        TextBox EditText = null;
        EditText = (TextBox)e.Item.FindControl("txtShortDesc");
        dataSet.Tables[0].Rows[row]["ShortDesc"] = EditText.Text;
        EditText = (TextBox)e.Item.FindControl("txtDetailDesc");
        dataSet.Tables[0].Rows[row]["DetaiLDesc"] = EditText.Text;
        EditText = (TextBox)e.Item.FindControl("txtEventDate");
        dataSet.Tables[0].Rows[row]["EventDate"]= EditText.Text;
        EditText = (TextBox)e.Item.FindControl("txtStartTime");
        dataSet.Tables[0].Rows[row]["StartTime"] = EditText.Text;
        EditText = (TextBox)e.Item.FindControl("txtEndTime");
        dataSet.Tables[0].Rows[row]["EndTime"] = EditText.Text;
        dataSet.WriteXml(Server.MapPath("MyCalendar.xml"));
        Session["MyCalendarData"] = null;
        EventData.EditItemIndex = -1;
        EventData.DataSource = LoadMyCalendarData();
        EventData.DataBind();
    }

    void DEDR_Cancel(object sender, DataGridCommandEventArgs e)
    {
      EventData.EditItemIndex = -1;
      Session["MyCalendarData"] = null;
      EventData.DataSource = LoadMyCalendarData();
      EventData.DataBind();
    }

    void DEDR_Delete(object sender, DataGridCommandEventArgs e)
    {
      DataSet dataSet = LoadMyCalendarData();
      int row = Convert.ToInt32(e.Item.ItemIndex);
      dataSet.Tables[0].Rows[row].Delete();
      dataSet.WriteXml(Server.MapPath("MyCalendar.xml"));
      Session["MyCalendarData"] = null;
      EventData.EditItemIndex = -1;
      EventData.DataSource = LoadMyCalendarData();
      EventData.DataBind();
    }

    void DEDR_Add(object sender, EventArgs e)
    {
      DataSet dataSet = LoadMyCalendarData();
      DataRow newRow;
      newRow = dataSet.Tables[0].NewRow();
      newRow["ShortDesc"] = "";
      newRow["DetailDesc"] = "";
      newRow["EventDate"] = "";
      newRow["StartTime"] = "";
      newRow["EndTime"] = "";
      dataSet.Tables[0].Rows.Add(newRow);
      dataSet.WriteXml(Server.MapPath("MyCalendar.xml"));
      Session["MyCalendarData"] = null;
```

```
        EventData.DataSource = LoadMyCalendarData();
        EventData.DataBind();
        EventData.EditItemIndex = EventData.Items.Count - 1;
        EventData.DataSource = LoadMyCalendarData();
        EventData.DataBind();
    }
</script>
```

3. Save the page as `EditItemTemplate.aspx` and view it from your browser:

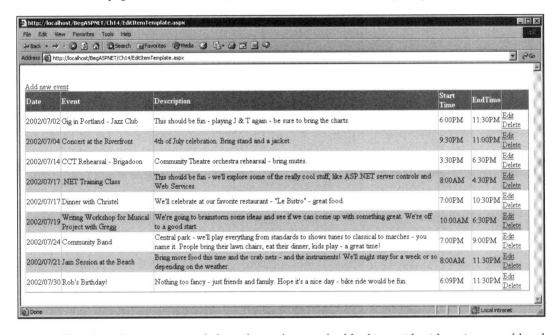

There's nothing very special about this – it's a standard looking grid, with options to add and edit data.

4. Now hit the Edit link for the first row:

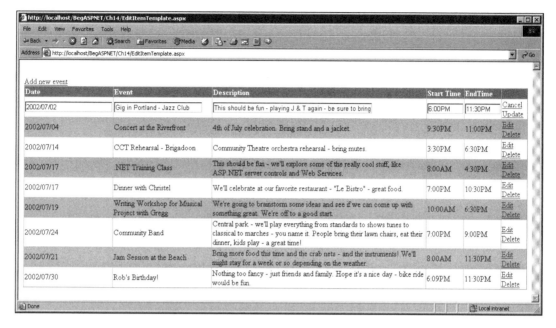

Notice how the row has changed – instead of just text, we now have textboxes allowing us to edit the text. The links in the last column have also changed; now indicating we can either cancel the changes, or update the data with our changes.

5. Try making some changes to the text and hitting the Cancel button. Notice how the changes you typed in are ignored. Try the Edit link again and this time hit the Update link – the changes are now saved.

6. Try the Add new event link:

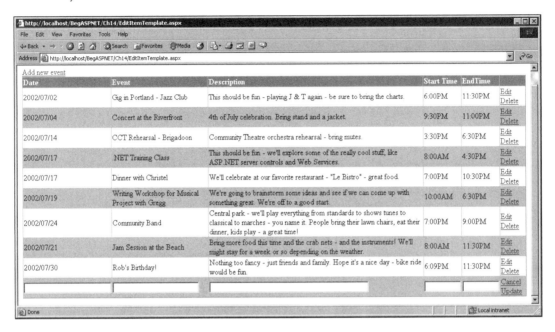

Notice how an extra row has been added, with empty values for you to type in the new data. Try pressing Cancel, and you see that the empty row disappears. Add another row and this time press Update to save the changes:

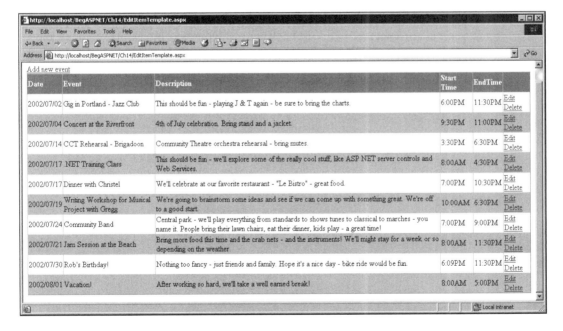

7. For the row you have just added, press the Delete link to test this function out.

Let's see how all of this works.

How It Works

Let's first look at the controls. We start with the server form, and a label to be used for displaying any error messages that might occur:

```
<html>
  <body>
    <form runat="server">

      <asp:Label id="ErrorMessage" runat="server" /><br/>
```

Next we add a LinkButton, which is used as the link that adds new rows to the data. You could use an ordinary button here, but I think this looks neater:

```
<asp:LinkButton OnClick="DEDR_Add" Text="Add new event"
     runat="server"/><br/>
```

Now we start on the DataGrid. The first thing to note is that we have set the AutoGenerateColumns attribute to false, telling the DataGrid not to generate any columns automatically. One of the great features of the DataGrid is that when you bind data to it, it cycles through the rows and columns of the data and generates the HTML table accordingly. In this example, we don't want that, as we want to create the columns ourself:

```
<asp:DataGrid id="EventData"
     AutoGenerateColumns="false" width="100%" runat="server"
```

Also on the DataGrid are some command properties. The DataGrid understands the concept of editing data, and has some special properties that allow us to tell it which event procedures are to be run when a set command is selected. You'll see how these commands are defined a little later:

```
OnEditCommand="DEDR_Edit"
OnUpdateCommand="DEDR_Update"
OnCancelCommand="DEDR_Cancel"
OnDeleteCommand="DEDR_Delete">
```

Next we define some style properties of the DataGrid object. We could have done this using the attributes of the grid itself, but I thought it would be worthwhile showing a different way to do it. For example, we could do this:

```
<asp:DataGrid id="EventData"
     HeaderStyle-ForeColor="White" HeaderStyle-BackColor="DodgerBlue"/>
```

593

There's no difference in the way the two methods of declaring these attributes work, so you can pick a style that you prefer. All we are doing here is defining the style properties for the various templates (the Header, Item, and AlternatingItem):

```
<HeaderStyle ForeColor="White" BackColor="DodgerBlue"
             Font-Bold="true"/>
<ItemStyle BackColor="White"/>
<AlternatingItemStyle BackColor="Gainsboro"/>
```

Now comes the bit where we define our columns. Remember that it's we who are defining them, not the grid. For each column we are going to use a TemplateColumn (this is just a column type that allows you to customize the layout of controls in the column), denoting that the column is to have a template applied. Earlier in the chapter you saw some code like this:

```
<asp:DataList id="DataList1" runat="server">
    <FooterTemplate>
      'Items to be affected by this template
    </FooterTemplate>
    <SeparatorTemplate>
      'Items to be affected by this template
    </SeparatorTemplate>
</asp:DataList>
```

This defined a template and then, within the template, the columns. The DataGrid works the other way round, defining the columns first, and then the templates within each column. This is sensible because the grid is inherently columnar. So, we have our first template column, with some text to be placed in the header:

```
<Columns>
  <asp:TemplateColumn HeaderText="Event">
```

Now, for this new column, we define the templates, the first being the ItemTemplate, which just shows the data:

```
<ItemTemplate>
  <%# Container.DataItem("ShortDesc") %>
</ItemTemplate>
```

The line in the template is an advanced form of data binding. You've seen how we use the DataSource property of a server control (such as a DataGrid or Repeater) to identify where the data comes from. When you are defining the columns yourself, you need to specify which fields in the data are shown. To do this we have to refer to the Container, since this is where the data is stored. In our case the Container is the DataSet that the grid is bound to. We use the DataItem collection to point to a specific item – it's ShortDesc in the example above, but it could be the name of any field. ASP.NET knows this is advanced databinding because we have surrounded the binding details with <%# and %>. This is very similar to the <% ... %> ASP tags, but it's the # that is the important bit – it's this that switches on the binding features.

The grid will automatically put the HTML table tags (the TR and TD tags) in for us, so all we have to do is output the data using the databinding syntax described above. For the EditItemTemplate, which comes into effect when we are editing this row, we need some way to type in text, so we use a TextBox. In this case, we set the Text property of the textbox to contain the data that we showed in the ItemTempate:

```
<EditItemTemplate>
  <asp:TextBox id="txtShortDesc" Size="25"
       Text='<%# Container.DataItem("ShortDesc") %>'
       runat="server"/>
</EditItemTemplate>
</asp:TemplateColumn>
```

So that's the definition of one column. It's a TemplateColumn with two templates: one for just displaying the data, and one for editing the data. The ItemTemplate is normally used, until the row is put into edit mode (you'll see how in a while). When this happens ASP.NET automatically displays the EditItemTemplate for the selected row.

The other columns are exactly the same as this, just getting their data from different columns in the data set. The final column is different, however, as it's here that we have our edit links. Again there are two templates. For the ItemTemplate we have a link to **Edit** and a link to **Delete**. When we are in edit mode (the EditItemTemplate) we want different buttons – to **Update** and **Cancel**. I've again used LinkButtons as I think they look nicer in this example, but you could easily use standard buttons:

```
<asp:TemplateColumn>
  <ItemTemplate>
    <asp:LinkButton CommandName="Edit"   Text="Edit"
         runat="server"/>
    <asp:LinkButton CommandName="Delete" Text="Delete"
         runat="server"/>
  </ItemTemplate>
  <EditItemTemplate>
    <asp:LinkButton CommandName="Cancel" Text="Cancel"
         runat="server"/>
    <asp:LinkButton CommandName="Update" Text="Update"
         runat="server"/>
  </EditItemTemplate>
</asp:TemplateColumn>
```

The key thing about this is the CommandName property, which identifies which command this button is associated with. Remember how when we defined the grid we identified event procedures with commands – well it's these commands that we were defining the procedures for. So the button with CommandName="Edit" will call the event procedure defined by OnEditCommand="DEDR_Edit".

Now let's look at the code. When the page is first loaded, we use the LoadMyCalendarData routine to load the calendar details from the XML file. This is exactly the same routine as we used earlier in the MyCalendar.aspx example, so we won't look at that again here.

Now let's look at the event procedures for editing, starting with the one for directly editing an entry. This is run when we select the Edit link, and its job is to tell the grid which row is being edited. It does this by setting the `EditItemIndex` property on the grid. Whenever this is set to a row, the `EditItemTemplate` for that row is displayed instead of the `ItemTemplate`. To identify the correct row, we use the arguments of the event procedure – these arguments are defined by ASP.NET, and provide information on which object called the event, along with various other sorts of information. In this case, the other information is the index number of the row that we are editing, as defined by the `ItemIndex` property. This is provided automatically by ASP.NET – because we have the link button in a row on the grid, whenever that link button is pressed the index number is supplied to the event procedure, thus allowing us to identify the correct row. As soon as the `EditItemTemplate` appears, we can make our changes:

```
    void DEDR_Edit(object sender, DataGridCommandEventArgs e)
{
    EventData.EditItemIndex = Convert.ToInt32(e.Item.ItemIndex);
    EventData.DataSource = LoadMyCalendarData();
    EventData.DataBind();
}
```

To update a row, we have to extract the data we have inserted into the textboxes on the row. We once again obtain the current row number, and this will be used to index into the rows in the `DataSet`:

```
  void DEDR_Update(object sender, DataGridCommandEventArgs e)
    {
      DataSet dataSet  = LoadMyCalendarData();
      int row = Convert.ToInt32(e.Item.ItemIndex);
```

To find the information in the `DataSet` textboxes, we have to use the `FindControl` method. Although we have given our textboxes names, because they are used within a grid, these names could be ambiguous. So, when generating a grid, ASP.NET uses this name as part of a unique name for the controls on the grid. Because we don't know what the rest of this unique name is, we have to use `FindControl` to find the correct control. Once we have found the row, we then update the data in the `DataSet`:

```
    TextBox EditText = null;
    EditText = (TextBox)e.Item.FindControl("txtShortDesc");
    dataSet.Tables[0].Rows[row]["ShortDesc"] = EditText.Text;
    EditText = (TextBox)e.Item.FindControl("txtDetailDesc");
    dataSet.Tables[0].Rows[row]["DetaiLDesc"] = EditText.Text;
    EditText = (TextBox)e.Item.FindControl("txtEventDate");
    dataSet.Tables[0].Rows[row]["EventDate"]= EditText.Text;
    EditText = (TextBox)e.Item.FindControl("txtStartTime");
    dataSet.Tables[0].Rows[row]["StartTime"] = EditText.Text;
    EditText = (TextBox)e.Item.FindControl("txtEndTime");
    dataSet.Tables[0].Rows[row]["EndTime"] = EditText.Text;
```

At this stage the `DataSet` has been updated, but the data hasn't been written back to the XML file, so we use `WriteXml` to write the file out to disk:

```
      dataSet.WriteXml(Server.MapPath("MyCalendar.xml"));
```

When we initially read the XML we placed it in `Session` state, to save having to read it again. However, now that the data has changed it needs to be reloaded into the `Session`, so we remove the copy currently in the `Session`:

```
Session["MyCalendarData"] = null;
```

We then set the `EditItemIndex` of the grid to –1, which takes the grid out of edit mode. When this happens the `EditItemTemplate` is no longer used, and the row reverts back to using the `ItemTemplate`:

```
EventData.EditItemIndex = -1;
```

Finally, we reload the data into the grid:

```
EventData.DataSource = LoadMyCalendarData();
EventData.DataBind();
}
```

That takes care of changing existing data, but what about canceling changes? When in edit mode, we have the **Cancel** link, which calls the following procedure. This is quite simple, first setting the `EditItemIndex` to –1, to take the grid out of edit mode. We then invalidate the `Session` state, and reload the data. Strictly speaking we don't always need to invalidate the `Session` variable here. For example, when editing a row, the changes are only available as part of the form – it's the **Update** procedure that updates the `DataSet`. So, we could just rebind to the cached data, which hasn't changed. However, when we add a row, we do update the `DataSet` – in this case just rebinding wouldn't work – we actually have to invalidate the `Session` state, and reload the data from the file:

```
void DEDR_Cancel(object sender, DataGridCommandEventArgs e)
{
  EventData.EditItemIndex = -1;
  Session["MyCalendarData"] = null;
  EventData.DataSource = LoadMyCalendarData();
  EventData.DataBind();
}
```

To delete a row, we just have to identify the row number selected (using the `ItemIndex`), and then use this to delete the selected row in the `DataSet`. Once it is deleted, we write the data to the XML file and invalidate the `Session` data because the data has changed:

```
void DEDR_Delete(object sender, DataGridCommandEventArgs e)
{
  DataSet dataSet = LoadMyCalendarData();
  int row = Convert.ToInt32(e.Item.ItemIndex);
  dataSet.Tables[0].Rows[row].Delete();
  dataSet.WriteXml(Server.MapPath("MyCalendar.xml"));
  Session["MyCalendarData"] = null;
```

We then take the grid out of edit mode, and rebind the data:

```
EventData.EditItemIndex = -1;
EventData.DataSource = LoadMyCalendarData();
EventData.DataBind();
}
```

Adding data is slightly different from the other methods of changing data, because there is no specific Add command. What we have to do is add the row to the DataSet, and then rebind the data. First we load the data from the Session:

```
void DEDR_Add(object sender, EventArgs e)
{
    DataSet dataSet = LoadMyCalendarData();
```

Then we use the NewRow method of the table to create a new row object:

```
DataRow newRow;
newRow = dataSet.Tables[0].NewRow();
```

Now we have the new row, we can initialize the data for it. In this case, we're simply setting each item to an empty string – for your own use, you could initialize the date/time items to the current date/time:

```
newRow["ShortDesc"] = "";
newRow["DetailDesc"] = "";
newRow["EventDate"] = "";
newRow["StartTime"] = "";
newRow["EndTime"] = "";
```

Once the data is set, we add the new row the to the table:

```
dataSet.Tables[0].Rows.Add(newRow);
```

Now we save the data to its file, invalidate the Session, and reload it:

```
dataSet.WriteXml(Server.MapPath("MyCalendar.xml"));
Session["MyCalendarData"] = null;
EventData.DataSource = LoadMyCalendarData();
EventData.DataBind();
```

Now the data is reloaded, we set the EditItemIndex of the new row, so that the row is put into edit mode. You don't have to do this, but it saves the user from having to click the Edit link on the new row. We use the Items collection of the DataGrid to identify how many rows it has. The Count property tells us how many rows, and since the rows are indexed from 0, we subtract 1 from this count, and then rebind the data (thus forcing the switch of templates):

```
          EventData.EditItemIndex = EventData.Items.Count - 1;
          EventData.DataSource = LoadMyCalendarData();
          EventData.DataBind();
      }
  </script>
```

That's all there is to it. It seems a lot, but there's not actually much code. The key things to remember are:

- ❏ Use `Button` or `LinkButton` controls to provide the edit commands

- ❏ Link these edit command buttons with event procedures using the `On...Command` attributes of the `DataGrid`

- ❏ Set the `EditItemIndex` to the required row and rebind the data to put the grid into edit mode

- ❏ Set the `EditItemIndex` to –1 to cancel from edit mode

This example used an XML file, but in each of the event procedures that updated data you could easily update a database. This could be done by either using the built-in commands of the `DataSet`, or by issuing SQL commands directly.

AutoGenerating the Columns

As an alternative solution to writing the column information yourself, you can let the `DataGrid` do most of the layout for you. In our code above we used the `AutoGenerateColumns` attribute to tell the grid **not** to automatically create columns from the bound data. That enabled us to provide the exact layout we required. However, if you let the grid generate the columns, you can also add columns using the `Columns` tag. The following code shows how this is done – it lets the grid handle the columns for the data, while we add the extra columns for the edit links.

```
<asp:DataGrid id="EventData"
        AutoGenerateColumns="true"
        width="100%" runat="server"
        OnEditCommand="DEDR_Edit"
        OnUpdateCommand="DEDR_Update"
        OnCancelCommand="DEDR_Cancel"
        OnDeleteCommand="DEDR_Delete">

    <HeaderStyle ForeColor="White" BackColor="DodgerBlue"
                Font-Bold="true"/>
    <ItemStyle BackColor="White"/>
    <AlternatingItemStyle BackColor="Gainsboro"/>

    <Columns>
      <asp:TemplateColumn>
        <ItemTemplate>
          <asp:LinkButton CommandName="Edit"    Text="Edit"
              runat="server"/>
          <asp:LinkButton CommandName="Delete" Text="Delete"
```

599

```
                    runat="server"/>
      </ItemTemplate>
      <EditItemTemplate>
        <asp:LinkButton CommandName="Cancel" Text="Cancel"
              runat="server"/>
        <asp:LinkButton CommandName="Update" Text="Update"
              runat="server"/>
      </EditItemTemplate>
    </asp:TemplateColumn>
  </Columns>
</asp:DataGrid>
```

This would create a grid like that we saw in the previous `EditItemTemplate.aspx` example.

One issue with automatically generated columns is that the column headings will be the same as the names of the columns, rather than some alternative text of our choosing. In the long run, I think defining your own templates is better, as you have finer control over what your data will look like.

The `EditItemTemplate` technique is also available with the `DataList`, which is particularly useful when you require a more free-form approach to your layout, as opposed to the more columnar layout of the grid. Whichever way you choose to display your data, templating makes it really easy.

Summary

This chapter introduced a variety of ASP.NET server controls available to use within any web form. Numerous examples were provided to illustrate how to use ASP.NET server controls within an ASPX page, as well as specific examples for working with these controls programmatically. By now you should have a good basic understanding of ASP.NET server controls, including:

❏ The syntax for declaring an ASP.NET server control

❏ The benefits of ASP.NET server controls, such as the rich object model, automatic browser detection, a variety of properties, events, and reusability

❏ The various ASP.NET server control families (intrinsic, validation, rich, and data rendering controls)

ASP.NET server controls derive their methods, properties, and events from the various classes and objects that make up the .NET Framework and provide an object-oriented way to write dynamic web forms. All ASP.NET server controls are declared using same tag element naming conventions, similar to well-formed XML, and provide a uniform way to declare properties, and assign event handler methods.

Some insight into the ASP.NET page lifecycle, in relation to ASP.NET server controls was provided. The `Page` object's `Page_Load()` and `Page_Unload()` methods were explained to provide a context for when and why these methods are implemented. We also covered the basics of event handling as related to the `Page` object's `IsPostback` property.

The ASP.NET validation controls covered in this chapter, and the examples herein, should serve to open a gateway to understanding the tools you have at your disposal for creating web forms that are capable of validating data. Although we only scratched the surface of the possibilities of the various data rendering controls, such as the `DataGrid`, `DataList`, and `Repeater`, you should be able to see their advantages in rendering a variety of types of data.

Exercises

1. Describe the pros and cons of ASP.NET Server Controls and HTML controls, and describe situations in which you might use both of them.

2. Firstly, modify the `travel.aspx` file you created to change the font of the text in each control to Arial. Then, add three checkboxes to the page to allow the user to choose whether they want to have a window seat, to travel first class, or to receive a vegetarian meal. Update your confirmation message to include this information.

3. Have a go at creating some templated controls. Create an ASP.NET page that has a drop-down box to select either a book, computer game, or DVD. Then customize what appears below:

    ❑   If the user selects a book, display a textbox for the ISBN, a textbox for the title, a textbox for the publisher, and a button to submit the query.

    ❑   If the user selects a game, display a textbox for the title of the game, a textbox for the platform, and a submit button.

    ❑   If the user selects a DVD, display a textbox to enter the title, a textbox for the region, and a submit button.

    Display a confirmation message to include the details entered.

4. Convert the textboxes used in the previous question to either drop-down boxes or listboxes, and bind their data source to an XML file containing a list of books, games, or DVDs, together with their associated details.

    As an additional exercise, you might want to add a section to the page to add extra items to the list of books, games, and DVDs, and use validation controls to ensure that the information to be added is of the correct type, and that all the fields have been entered correctly.

Reusable Code for ASP.NET

So far, most of the ASP.NET pages we've built have been quite specialized and self-contained. We've put a lot of functionality into each one, and only really retained the benefits of our hard work from one page to another by copying the entire contents into a new ASPX page.

It should come as no surprise to discover that this isn't really an ideal way to write functionality-rich web sites – particularly not if you're on a salary and expected to deliver results before the next millennium. For that reason, we're now going to look at how to write reusable code for ASP.NET. Note that we're not just talking about objects here (although, yet again, objects play a crucial role in the story) but about code **components**: totally independent files that encapsulate groups of useful functionality.

In the course of this chapter, we're going to look at two specific ways to use components in ASP.NET:

❑   User controls – a Web Form that is encapsulated in a reusable Server Control

❑   Code behind – used for separating HTML user interface design (color, aesthetics, and so on) from page code

First though, we're going to take a careful look at what we mean when we talk about components, and consider the various advantages they offer us.

Encapsulation

When we first met objects in Chapter 8, we discussed how they are essentially a software construct that bundles together data and functionality. We define a few very specific interfaces on an object so that we can use the functionality it contains, for example, by creating methods and properties that we can access programmatically.

By hiding away absolutely everything that doesn't concern task-specific usage of an object, we hide implementation details from the consumer, making it a lot easier to plug it together robustly with other objects. This makes it far easier for large teams of developers to build complex applications that don't fall prey to lots of low-level weaknesses.

The crucial information we need to make an object is held in the class definition, and any code with access to this class should be able to instantiate an instance of our class, and store this in an object. The way in which the object works is encapsulated, so that only the public methods and properties are available to the programmer.

In a similar way, a component is a set of reusable code that is stored in such a location that it is accessible by many applications. Like an object, it encapsulates functionality, but the difference is that while an object is an implementation unit, a component is a deployment or packaging unit. A component could be a single class, or it could hold multiple class definitions.

All the code we've written so far has been held in specific ASPX pages. So, what's the point in having all this wonderful reusable code if we can only get at it from within a single page?

> **We need to break out our reuseable code into a separate component that we can reference from our ASPX pages.**

A component packages up a set of classes and interfaces in order to isolate and encapsulate a specific set of functionality, and can provide a well-specified set of publicly available services. It is designed for a specific purpose rather than for a specific application.

Components

A component is a self-contained unit of functionality, with external interfaces that are independent of its internal architecture. In other words, it's a bunch of code that's been packaged up as a black box that can be used in any number of different applications as required.

An example of componentization that we're all familiar with is Microsoft Windows. If you spend a lot of time working with Windows, you're almost certain to have come across (or at least heard of) DLL files – Dynamic Link Libraries. Many of these files contain components that define most of the functionality you're likely to come across in Windows, including that of any applications you've installed.

Note that DLLs are classified as system files, which are hidden by default. They can only be seen in Windows Explorer if your Folder Options are set to 'Show hidden files and folders'.

For example, every time you fire up an instance of Internet Explorer, you're actually running a small program called iexplore.exe, which accesses numerous DLLs that reside in your system directory (if you have Windows 2000 running on your C: drive, this will probably be C:\WinNT), and most of the browser's functionality is defined inside these files. This directory also contains the file explorer.exe, which is the executable for Windows Explorer. You might note that both these applications feature an identical Address bar, where you type in the URL of a website, or the path to a local directory – this user interface element has been implemented once, packaged inside a component, and is now being used by both programs.

What's more, if you enter the URL for a web page in the Windows Explorer address bar, you can view that page and even browse the Web in the main pane without having to use `iexplore.exe` at all. Likewise, you can use `iexplore.exe` to view and browse your files, simply by entering a file path in the address bar.

What we can deduce from this is that either there's a lot of duplication between the two EXE files, or the two sets of browser functionality are actually implemented as standalone components that can be accessed by both applications. In fact, it is down to the components.

Another case to consider is the Microsoft Office suite, which features many components that are shared among the individual Office applications, and throughout Windows itself. For example, there is a component that handles the **Save As** dialog as used by Word, Excel, Outlook, and the rest – this is why the **Save** dialog looks the same, no matter which application you run it from. This component is actually a Windows component, but the Office package makes use of it whenever you save or load a file. You can also use this from any other application that will let you save or load files, Internet Explorer for example, or even Notepad. In this component there's probably some code that has the presentation code for all of the buttons, and some logic that understands what to do when you click on those buttons (for example, show the contents of a different directory in the main window in the middle of the dialog).

Throughout this book, we've been using the `aspnet_isapi.dll`, which has been working away behind IIS to process all of our ASP.NET pages. When IIS spots that someone is requesting a page with the extension `.aspx`, it uses this component to process it and communicate with the .NET Framework.

> *The DLLs in these examples are examples of COM DLLs. The .NET DLL differs slightly in what it contains, but the concept of componentization is the same, whatever the underlying technology.*

Why use Components?

You should be starting to build up a picture of components as small, self-contained nuggets of functionality that can potentially make life a lot simpler when it comes to building any sort of non-trivial application. In this respect, they are similar to objects, but a component is reuseable code whose behind-the-scenes functionality is encapsulated away, so that only certain interfaces are available to the programmer. It can contain one or more class definitions, from which objects can be created, and which can be used for behind-the-scenes code. So, what are the benefits of using components?

- ❏ An individual component is a lot simpler than a full-blown application. It is restricted to a set of pre-defined functionality.

- ❏ As components are self-contained, we can seamlessly upgrade (or fix) them simply by replacing one component with another that supports the same interfaces (methods, properties, and so on).

- ❏ Since using components is a good way of dividing our application into serviceable chunks, sometimes the functionality a component contains may be reusable elsewhere. We might even make it available to other programmers, or incorporate some of their components into our own applications.

Ultimately, components reduce the amount of code you write and make your code easier to maintain – once you've written one, you can reuse it over and over again within as many different applications as you like. Moreover, you can even obtain components from third-party component vendors, which is becoming a very popular way to enhance the functionality of ASP.NET sites. If, for example, you need components that utilize the drawing capabilities of .NET to their limit, and your existing knowledge does not cover this, you can consider looking for a third-party solution that you can bolt into your application.

Applying Component Theory to our Applications

Let's look at how componentization relates to our application models. So far in this book, we've created ASP.NET pages that do all sorts of things, from working with information input via a form, through to connecting to a database and working with data. Throughout, we've encouraged you to keep your code separated into distinct blocks – namely dynamically generated content (ASP.NET code) and presentation (HTML and various controls) – so that it's easy to change the way a page **looks** without affecting what it **does**. Also consider that raw content is most likely to be stored in a database, and that most of our code serves to provide a framework of logical operations between that and the presentation code.

Let's look at an example. Imagine that a team of developers are creating a web site that sells books. One set of developers would probably be concerned with the look, feel, and ease of use of the site. They'd be responsible for the public image of the company on the Web, so they'd be most concerned with design, color, and usability. These are our **designers**, and they're probably using HTML and perhaps some graphics tools like Flash for fancy loading screens. There would probably also be another set of developers whose main interests lay in providing nifty blocks of code that did cool things when you clicked a button, or that validated the information entered into a form by the customers. These **developers** might also be responsible for generating the code required for connecting to the database of different books, and preparing the information on individual titles for display on the site. The designers would then make use of that information and display it in an aesthetically pleasing fashion.

If we were to constantly use ASP.NET pages that had all of the code and HTML on the same page, it would be awkward for both sets of people to work on the site at once. Simple mistakes could easily be made as people overwrote each other's code. Also, every page would have to be handmade, and code would have to be copied, pasted, and amended as appropriate. If you made one change to the functionality of your site, you'd have to remember to make that change to all the appropriate pages. However, if you could separate out the HTML and design-focused code from the ASP.NET code blocks, and then reuse bits of that code, it would be much easier to update a single piece of code to change functionality – every page that used it would be automatically updated.

If we work in this way then everyone is happy – Web Designers get to play with color and layout as much as they like, and the ASP.NET developers can fine-tune their code without altering the look and feel of the site.

In this chapter, we'll look at two ways of dividing code into reusable sections, user controls and code behind. In the next chapter, we'll take this one step further, and look at compiled components and custom server controls.

We're now going to move on to look at user controls, which are the first application of this code-separation concept that we'll be meeting.

User Controls

When the ASP.NET team first devised the concept of user controls, they were called pagelets. A term that many people disliked. They were later renamed, but I feel that the term pagelet, which implies a mini-page, was a good descriptive term for these controls.

User controls are web forms encapsulated into a reusable control. They are used to hold repetitive blocks of code that many of the pages in a web site need. For example, consider the Microsoft web site: each page has the same header style – a menu bar and a logo. This is a very common feature for a lot of web sites; even our own www.wrox.com has this kind of style:

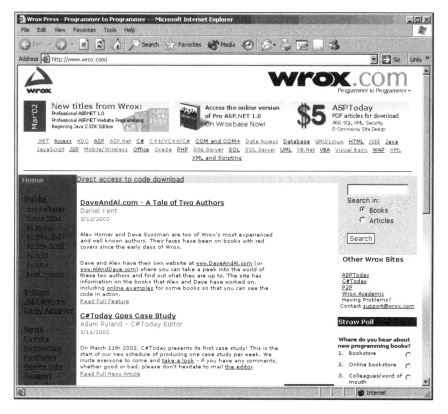

The Wrox site has the same kinds of menu bars at the top, left-hand side, and right-hand side of the screen at all times. These panes, panels or frames, depending on what you call them, and how you code them, are just one example of the types of things that user controls can provide programmatically.

Instead of having to copy and paste over chunks of repeated code to provide the header on all of our pages, we can create a simple **user control** that will have this code inside it, ready to be used. It's a way of accessing the same functionality over and over again throughout an application.

*If you ever programmed with ASP 3.0, you'll probably be familiar with **include files**. User controls are similar to include files, but because ASP.NET is different from ASP 3.0, these controls are now created and used in a different manner and include advanced features such as caching.*

User controls can also do a lot more than simply produce headers and footers. We can give these controls the ability to look and behave a bit like ASP.NET Server controls. We can code properties so that our control can adapt depending on which attributes have been set on it. Anywhere on a site where many pages have similar blocks of functionality, we can use a user control to provide a repository for these repetitive code blocks. Take, for example, a user login control. This control could be created as a user control, using a couple of textboxes and labels. Another example would be a menu control that applies different formatting to a link representing the page currently being viewed, or even displays a submenu for that page. A user control is saved with an `.ascx` file extension, and can be called from any of the ASP.NET pages in our application using just two lines of code. The main principle of user controls is that we could essentially cut out a portion of code from our ASP.NET page and paste it into a user control, where it would work just fine – just as long as the ASP.NET page knows where to find the code, and where to put it.

When Should we use User Controls?

Let's take a look at a few pros and cons so we can identify when we should be using a user control in our applications.

User controls are ideal for:

❑ Repetitive elements on pages like headers, menus, login controls, and so on

❑ Reducing the amount of code per page by encapsulating those repetitive elements into user controls

❑ Improving performance of your pages by making use of the caching functionality available to user controls to cache frequently-viewed data

However, some situations aren't ideal for using user controls. These include:

❑ Separating presentation HTML from the code blocks (ideal for using code behind, which we'll meet later in this chapter)

❑ Encapsulating business logic in a reusable package (ideal for pre-compiled assemblies, which we'll meet in the next chapter)

❑ Creating a control that can be reused more widely than in just your application (ideal for custom server controls, which we'll meet in the next chapter)

It's time to start looking at code. In this, and the next chapter, we'll be looking at creating custom reusable elements to our ASP.NET pages, showing how these elements can all be plugged together with a minimum of fuss to produce a very clean ASPX file, hiding the advanced functionality within reusable components. Let's start by taking a look at an example showing user controls in action:

Try It Out – Our First User Control

We'll start with a very basic example to show the theory, then we'll take a look at a more complex example.

1. Open up your editor and enter the following code, which forms our user control. Save this code as `SimpleUserControl.ascx`.

*Note the different file extension – `.ascx`, **not** `.aspx`.*

```
<%@ Control Language="c#" %>

<b> Hello, I'm a user control, </b>
```

2. Next, open up your editor again and enter the following code:

```
<%@ Page Language="c#" %>
<%@ Register TagPrefix="WroxUC" TagName="SimpleControl"
                              Src="SimpleUserControl.ascx" %>

<html>
<head>
<title>Simple User control Example</title>
</head>
<body>
    <form runat="server">
        <p>
            <WroxUC:SimpleControl id="MySimpleControl" runat="server" />
            and I'm text in an ASPX page.
        </p>
    </form>
</body>
</html>
```

3. Save this file as `SimpleUserControl.aspx` – this is our ASPX page. Now, run this file as normal from your browser and you should see the following:

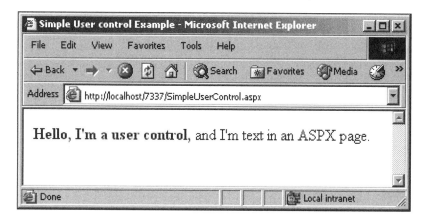

How It Works

We've started with a fairly simplistic example that displays text from two different sources. Let's take a look at the code.

Our simple user control only has two lines of code:

```
<%@ Control Language="c#" %>

<b> Hello, I'm a user control, </b>
```

The first line of code tells the compiler that this is a control, written in C#. The next line is a simple line of HTML that renders some text in bold.

Let's take a look at the **consumer** of our ASCX user control, our `SimpleUserControl.aspx` page:

```
<%@ Register TagPrefix="WroxUC" TagName="SimpleControl"
                               Src="SimpleUserControl.ascx" %>
```

The first line is where we declare that we're using a user control. This tag must appear at the top of your page, before any HTML code, in order for it to work. We set two attributes of the `Register` tag:

❑   The `TagPrefix` attribute

❑   The `TagName` attribute

The `TagPrefix` is the collective name for our group of controls. The `TagName` is the name of this specific control. For example, if we are using an ASP.NET textbox control on an ASPX page, we use the syntax `<asp:textbox />`. The `TagPrefix` in this case is the bit before the colon; for an ASP.NET textbox, this is **<asp:...>**, and the `TagName` in this case follows the colon, and is **<...:textbox>**. In our example, we are defining our `TagPrefix` as `WroxUC`, and our `TagName` as `SimpleControl`, so that when we come to use our control, we call it using `<WroxUC:SimpleControl />` as we'll see below. We could have a whole library of `WroxUC` tags, each identified by different `TagNames` in our code. The final part of our line is where we specify the source file of our user control. ASP.NET expects this to be in the same place as our ASP.NET file. If this is not the case, then the relative or absolute path must be entered here.

The next section of our page is simple HTML:

```
<html>
<head>
<title>Simple User control Example</title>
</head>
<body>
  <form runat="server">
    <p>
```

This code simply starts off the main section of our page. The next line is where we insert our user control:

```
<WroxUC:SimpleControl id="MySimpleControl" runat="server" />
```

Here we can see the `WroxUC:SimpleControl` syntax we discussed earlier – we make use of the `TagName` and `TagPrefix` that we assigned earlier to call our user control. We then assign an `id` to our control and a `runat="server"` directive, as we would include on any ASP.NET control.

The last part of our control is basic HTML:

```
        and I'm text in an ASPX page.
      </p>
    </form>
  </body>
</html>
```

We include our line of text that forms the second half of the visual element in our page, then we close up all of the open tags on the page.

That's it! Now, let's move on to a slightly more functional example of a user control in action.

Try It Out – Simple Header Control Example

We're going to have a go at creating a simple user control that forms a header for our web site. In our example, we've used an image, called `logo.gif`. This file is available for download, along with the rest of the code for the book, from **www.wrox.com**, but you could substitute any small image of your choice.

1. Open up your editor and enter the following code:

```
<%@ Control Language="c#" %>

<table style="background-color:#cc0033" width="100%" cellpadding="10"
                                                cellspacing="0">
    <tr>
        <td width="10%"">
            <img src="logo.gif" align="left" />
        </td>
        <td width="60%"> <font face="verdana,arial" size="4" color="yellow">
            <asp:label id="WelcomeMessage" runat="Server"
                            >Welcome to the Wrox shop!</asp:label></font>
        </td>
        <td width="30%">
            <font face="verdana,arial" size="2" color="lightyellow"
                                > Select your Language:<br />
            <asp:DropDownList id="LanguageList" runat="Server"
                            OnSelectedIndexChanged="DropList_Changed"
                            AutoPostBack="True"/>
            </font>
        </td>
    </tr>
```

```
    </table>

    <script runat="server">

      Hashtable Languages = new Hashtable();

      public void Page_Load()
      {
        Languages.Add("English", "Hello, and welcome to the shop");
        Languages.Add("French", "Bonjour, et bienvenue a le magasin");
        Languages.Add("Spanish", "Buenas Dias, e bienvenido a la tienda");
        Languages.Add("German", "Guten Tag, und wilkommen ins geschaeft");

        if (!Page.IsPostBack)
        {
          LanguageList.DataSource = Languages.Keys;
          Page.DataBind();
        }
      }

      public void DropList_Changed(object sender, EventArgs e)
      {
        WelcomeMessage.Text = (String)
                            Languages[LanguageList.SelectedItem.Text];
      }

    </script>
```

2. Save this file as header.ascx

3. Now open up your editor again and enter the following code into a new file, which will form
our ASP.NET web form:

```
<%@ Page Language="c#" %>
<%@ Register TagPrefix="WroxUC" TagName="Header" Src="header.ascx" %>

<html>
<head>
  <title>User Control Examples</title>
</head>

<body>
    <form runat="server" method="post">
        <WroxUC:Header id="MyHeader" runat="Server" />
        <h3>The Multi-Lingual Control Example </h3>
    </form>
</body>
</html>
```

4. Save this file as `main.aspx` and view it in your browser:

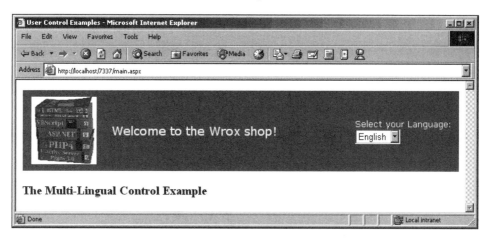

How It Works

Our header control has some basic functionality for changing the welcome text according to which language is selected in the drop box. Let's start going through the code step by step, looking at our user control:

```
<%@ Control Language="c#" %>

<table style="background-color:#cc0033" width="100%" cellpadding="10"
                                                    cellspacing="0">
    <tr>
        <td width="10%"">
            <img src="logo.gif" align="left" />
        </td>
```

The beginning portion of our control is fairly simple – we're starting out by creating a layout using an HTML table. The first table cell in our table holds our logo.

```
        <td width="60%"> <font face="verdana,arial" size="4" color="yellow">
            <asp:label id="WelcomeMessage" runat="Server"
                                >Welcome to the Wrox shop!</asp:label> </font>
        </td>
```

The second table cell in our header holds our welcome text, in the format of the text attribute of an `<asp:label...>` control.

```
        <td width="30%">
            <font face="verdana,arial" size="2" color="lightyellow"
                                    > Select your Language:<br />
            <asp:DropDownList id="LanguageList" runat="Server"
                    OnSelectedIndexChanged="DropList_Changed"
```

613

```
                              AutoPostBack="True"/>
                   </font>
               </td>
           </tr>
       </table>
```

The third and final table cell contains our drop-down box with our language selection options in it. We've included a couple of attributes on our drop-down list so that whenever the selection in this box changes, an **event** is fired. This event will be handled in the code later on in this control, but we tell our control to look out for the `DropList_Changed` event handler to provide the code to work with this event. The last thing we include is an attribute to force a postback once the selection changes, thereby firing the event whenever the user changes their mind about which language they prefer.

The next section of our code is the script to accompany our control. Let's look through this step by step:

```
<script runat="server">

  Hashtable Languages = new Hashtable();

  public void Page_Load()
  {
    Languages.Add("English", "Hello, and welcome to the shop");
    Languages.Add("French", "Bonjour, et bienvenue au magasin");
    Languages.Add("Spanish", "Buenas Dias, e bienvenido a la tienda");
    Languages.Add("German", "Guten Tag, und wilkommen ins geschaeft");
```

We need to create a set of options and values for our drop box and for our label control. We've used a **hashtable** in this example (we met hashtables in Chapter 12 earlier in this book), which, you may recall, is a great way of storing key-value pairs of data. In our example, the key is the first item in the list (the language), and the value is the translated text. We've put our hashtable in the `Page_Load` event handler in our code, so that each time the page is loaded, the hashtable exists and is ready to use.

```
      if (!Page.IsPostBack)
      {
```

The next section of our code is where we populate our drop-down listbox with data. The first line tells the compiler to only populate our box the first time the page is loaded. We don't want to repopulate with more data each time the page is loaded, so this line ensures that this section of code is only run once:

```
        LanguageList.DataSource = Languages.Keys;
        Page.DataBind();
      }
    }
```

We then give our drop-down box (with an ID of `LanguageList`) its `Datasource` attribute, which in our case is the `Keys` section of our hashtable (called `Languages`). We then call the `DataBind` method on our page, which performs our binding to our droplist, then we close this function.

The next function is where we handle the change event on our drop-down list:

```
public void DropList_Changed(object sender, EventArgs e)
{
    WelcomeMessage.Text = (String)
                        Languages[LanguageList.SelectedItem.Text];
}

</script>
```

We take the value of the item currently selected in our drop-down listbox (the text that details which language we'd prefer our message to be in), and we use this value to find out the value in the hashtable that corresponds to this key. We then place the value portion of our pair in the text attribute of our `WelcomeMessage` label control.

Moving on to our ASPX page, we have the following code:

```
<%@ Register TagPrefix="WroxUC" TagName="Header" Src="header.ascx" %>
```

Again, we start with the line of code that tells our page that whenever we see the `WroxUC TagPrefix` in combination with the `Header TagName`, we are to use the code in the `header.ascx` user control:

```
<html>
<head>
  <title>User Control Examples</title>
</head>

<body>
    <form runat="server" method="post">
        <WroxUC:Header id="MyHeader" runat="Server" />
        <h3>The Multi-Lingual Control Example </h3>
    </form>
</body>
</html>
```

The rest of our code is simple HTML again, with one line of code in the middle:

```
...
    <WroxUC:Header id="MyHeader" runat="Server" />
...
```

This single line of code is all we need in our ASPX page to use our user control's functionality in our page.

615

This is a great example of encapsulating functionality into a user control. We have a clean ASPX page with a single line of code linking to our control, and a single line of code implementing our control. Any ASPX page in an application can access this same control the same way, without worrying about the code in the control itself.

Let's take a look at a slightly different type of control now. This is a control that shows a list of books on promotion.

Try It Out – Creating a Featured Items List Control

This example will create another reuseable user control for showing a list of books from a `WroxShop` database. This database is available for download from **www.wrox.com** as `WroxShop.mdb`.

1. Open up your editor and type in the following code:

```
<%@ Control Language="c#" %>
<%@ import Namespace="System.Data" %>
<%@ import Namespace="System.Data.OleDb" %>

<asp:label id="FeaturedBooksLabel" runat="server"/>

<script language="c#" runat="server">

void Page_Load()
{
  string ConnectString = "Provider=Microsoft.Jet.OLEDB.4.0;Data " +
                         " source=c:\\begaspnet\\ch15\\WroxShop.mdb";
  string SQLString = "SELECT Title, ISBN FROM Books";

  OleDbConnection MyConnection = new OleDbConnection(ConnectString);
  OleDbCommand MyCommand = new OleDbCommand(SQLString, MyConnection);
  MyConnection.Open();

  OleDbDataReader MyDataReader = MyCommand.ExecuteReader();

  string ResultString =
   "<table><tr><td class='datatablehead'>Today's Featured Books:</td></tr>";

  while (MyDataReader.Read())
  {
    ResultString += "<tr><td class='datatable'>";
    ResultString += "<a href='http://www.wrox.com/ACON11.asp?ISBN=";
    ResultString += MyDataReader["ISBN"] + "' target='new'>";
    ResultString += MyDataReader["Title"] + "</a>";
  }

    ResultString += "</table>";

  FeaturedBooksLabel.Text = ResultString;

  MyDataReader.Close();
  MyConnection.Close();
}
</script>
```

2. Save this file as `featuredbooks.ascx`. Next, open up your `main.aspx` file and add the following highlighted lines of code:

```
<%@ Register TagPrefix="WroxUC" TagName="Header" Src="header.ascx" %>
<%@ Register TagPrefix="WroxUC" TagName="FeaturedBooks"
                              Src="FeaturedBooks.ascx" %>

<html>
<head>
  <title>User Control Examples</title>
  <link rel="stylesheet" type="text/css" href="style.css">
</head>

<body>
  <form runat="server" method="post">
    <WroxUC:Header id="MyHeader" runat="Server" />
    <br />
    <table>
      <tr>
        <td width="70%" valign="top">
          This is the Wrox Shop, where you can find out more about
          Wrox books. The links on the left take you to a page on
          the Wrox site where you can find out more details about
          each title.
        </td>
        <td width="30%">
          <WroxUC:FeaturedBooks id="MyFeaturedBooks" runat="server" />
        </td>
      </tr>
    </table>
  </form>
</body>
</html>
```

3. Save this as `main2.aspx`. You may have noticed we referred to a CSS file in our code – for completeness, we've included the code for this file here, but we're not going to be examining it in detail because it's outside the scope of this book (see Chapter 5 for a quick introduction to CSS):

```
body {
font-family:verdana,arial;
}

td.datatablehead {
Background:#d0d0d0;
font-family:Verdana,arial;
font-size:x-small;
font-weight:bold;
text-align:left;
}

td.datatable {
```

```
Background:#f0f0f0;
font-family:Verdana,arial;
font-size:x-small;
}

a {
text-decoration:none;
color:#000080;
font-family:Verdana,arial;
font-size:x-small;
}
```

4. Save this file as `style.css` in the same directory as your other files, and open `main2.aspx` in your browser:

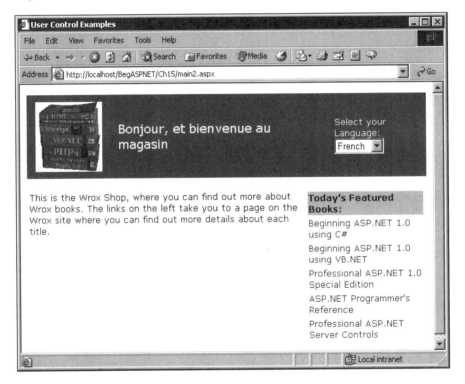

How It Works

In this example we created a second control and added this to our front page in a similar way to before. Let's start by looking at our new control:

```
<%@ import Namespace="System.Data" %>
<%@ import Namespace="System.Data.OleDb" %>
```

Our first two statements should be relatively familiar from our work in the data access chapters earlier in the book. We are importing the namespaces that are necessary for working with data from an Access database, using the `Oledb` connection method:

```
<asp:label id="FeaturedBooksLabel" runat="server"/>

<script language="c#" runat="server">

void Page_Load()
{
  string ConnectString = "Provider=Microsoft.Jet.OLEDB.4.0;Data " +
                         "Source=c:\\begASPNET\\Ch15\\WroxShop.mdb";
  string SQLString = "SELECT Title, ISBN FROM Books";
```

Our first few lines of code specify a connection string to our database, which in our case is a small Access database called `Wroxshop.mdb` (available for download from www.wrox.com). We then enter the details of the SQL statement for obtaining the required data from our database:

```
OleDbConnection MyConnection = new OleDbConnection(ConnectString);
OleDbCommand MyCommand = new OleDbCommand(SQLString, MyConnection);
MyConnection.Open();

OleDbDataReader MyDataReader = MyCommand.ExecuteReader();
```

We're using a `DataReader` in our code to obtain data from the database. We create a new connection using the connection string, before executing the SQL statement. We create a new `OledbDataReader` object, called `MyDataReader`, and a string called `ResultString`, which will be used for holding the output of our reader. We open the connection, and connect the `MyDataReader` object to the resulting rowset.

To start work on our table we simply add the HTML table information to the `ResultString` string:

```
string ResultString =
  "<table><tr><td class='datatablehead'>Today's Featured Books:</td></tr>";
```

We then loop through the contents of the `MyDataReader` and enter the values obtained from each row and column of the table into the `ResultString` string using the concatenation += syntax:

```
while (MyDataReader.Read())
{
  ResultString += "<tr><td class='datatable'>";
  ResultString += "<a href='http://www.wrox.com/ACON11.asp?ISBN=";
  ResultString += MyDataReader["ISBN"] + "' target='new'>";
  ResultString += MyDataReader["Title"] + "</a>";
}
```

The remainder of our script block closes up the HTML table, and outputs the contents of `ResultString`:

```
ResultString += "</table>";

   FeaturedBooksLabel.Text = ResultString;
```

We then close up the `MyDataReader`, and the `MyConnection` objects to free up resources, and close up our code:

```
   MyDataReader.Close();
   MyConnection.Close();
}
</script>
```

And that's it for our control. Let's move on and look at the new lines of code in our ASPX page:

```
<%@ Register TagPrefix="WroxUC" TagName="FeaturedBooks"
                                Src="FeaturedBooks.ascx" %>
```

Our first line of code references our second control in exactly the same way as before, and assigns it the same `TagPrefix`, but a different `TagName`:

```
<link rel="stylesheet" type="text/css" href="style.css">
```

The next line is a simple line of code to import the stylesheet for our page to help display the page's output more clearly:

```
<body>
  <form runat="server" method="post">
    <WroxUC:Header id="MyHeader" runat="Server" /><br />
    <table>
      <tr>
        <td width="70%" valign="top">
          This is the Wrox Shop, where you can find out more about
          Wrox books. The links on the left take you to a page on
          the Wrox site where you can find out more details about
          each title.
        </td>
```

The next section of new code is plain and simple HTML again, and we're creating another table. The first cell contains some text for the reader. The second cell contains our book list control:

```
        <td width="30%">
          <WroxUC:FeaturedBooks id="MyFeaturedBooks" runat="server" />
        </td>
      </tr>
    </table>
  </form>
</body>
</html>
```

We then close up the table, and page, as before.

We're not going to look at how the CSS works in detail, but there are many more books you can look at if you want to know more about CSS. You could try Wrox Press's *HTML 4.01 Programmer's Reference,* ISBN 1-86100-533-4.

Next, we're going to move on to look at code behind, and how we can better divide up our code into manageable sections.

Code Behind

When we were creating simple forms in Chapter 3, we simply created textboxes and worked with buttons that sent data on a round trip to the server. We later enhanced these forms by adding code that handles validating our input, and so on. We had to put all of the extra code to enable validation in small functions at the bottom of our pages to avoid cluttering up our presentation code. There is a cleaner way of doing this, however, which is to move all of this code into a **code-behind** file.

A code-behind file can be used to store all of the script blocks of an ASP.NET page. While it's perfectly possible to include this in the same page as the presentation HTML code, separating out the script blocks is a good way to cleanly separate presentation from the code. The presentation code remains all in one ASPX file (or, if you've got a couple of user controls for repetitive presentation elements, it can reside in part in ASCX files), and the code-behind code lives in a language-specific file, for example, .cs for a C# code-behind file, or .vb for a Visual Basic .NET code-behind file. The ASPX file is the central point for the application, and it is from here that we reference the code-behind file, and any user controls.

Code-behind files are easy to deploy – all you need to do is copy over the code-behind file along with the ASPX page. We can even compile our code-behind files into an assembly if we want to reuse the functionality contained within them over more than one page or application. We'll look at compilation in more detail in the next chapter.

A code-behind file can be written in any .NET-compatible language, so we could write our code in C# (as we have throughout this book so far) or we could use VB.NET, or JScript.NET, for example. We'll take a brief look at this concept in the next chapter, when we talk about .NET assemblies – don't worry if you haven't got any experience with the other languages, as we'll stick with C# for this chapter, and the majority of the next.

> It's worth noting that if you have Visual Studio .NET, Web Forms applications are always created with a code-behind file, instead of placing your code on the same page. In addition, code-behind files in Visual Studio .NET are named the same as the ASPX page, with an additional .cs or .vb on the end of the filename. For example, MyPage.aspx would have an associated C# code-behind page named MyPage.aspx.cs.

Let's take a look at a simple example of a code-behind file:

Try It Out – Our First Code-Behind File

In this example we're going to create a very simple Web Form with a textbox and a button, and we'll give this simple arrangement some extra functionality by adding a code-behind file.

1. Create a file called `SimpleCodeBehind.cs`, and enter the following code:

```
using System;
using System.Web.UI;
using System.Web.UI.WebControls;


public class MyCodeBehind : Page
{
  public TextBox name;
  public Label message;

  public void SubmitBtn_Click(object sender, EventArgs e)
  {
    message.Text = "Hello " + name.Text;

  }
}
```

2. Next, save the following code as `SimpleCodeBehind.aspx` in the same directory:

```
<%@ Page Inherits="MyCodeBehind" Src="SimpleCodeBehind.cs" %>

<html>
<head>
    <title>Simple Code-Behind Page</title>
</head>
<body>
    Please enter your name then click the button below:
    <br />
    <br />
    <form action="CodeBehind1.aspx" method="post" runat="Server">
        <asp:textbox id="name" runat="Server" />
        <asp:button id="Button1" onclick="SubmitBtn_Click" runat="server"
                                                text="ClickMe!" />
        <br /><br />
        <asp:label id="message" runat="Server" />
    </form>
</body>
</html>
```

3. Call up the `SimpleCodeBehind.aspx` in your browser, and follow the instructions provided. You should then see a result like the one shown below:

How It Works

This example did a very basic job of passing information from the ASPX page to the C# page and back again. We input a name into a textbox on the ASPX page, the C# code-behind file took this name and passed it into a string along with some text, and then outputted this string to a label control that was sitting almost invisibly on our page. Let's look at the stages step by step so that we can fully-understand this process:

```
<%@ Page Inherits="MyCodeBehind" Src="SimpleCodeBehind.cs" %>
```

This line of code is essential when working with code behind. The first part of the statement tells us that we want to inherit from the `MyCodeBehind` class. We met inheritance in Chapter 9, but to quickly recap, this effectively says "Find me the `MyCodeBehind` class and use its functionality in the page." The second part of this statement tells us where to find the class – in this case, we've stored this class in our `SimpleCodeBehind.cs` file. It's worth noting that we can only use one of these declarations per ASPX page:

```
<html>
<head>
  <title>Simple Code-Behind Page</title>
</head>
  <body>
    Please enter your name then click the button below:
    <br />
    <br />
    <form action="CodeBehind1.aspx" method="post" runat="Server">
      <asp:textbox id="name" runat="Server" />
      <asp:button id="Button1" onclick="SubmitBtn_Click" runat="server"
                                              text="ClickMe!" />
```

```
            <br /><br />
            <asp:label id="message" runat="Server" />
        </form>
    </body>
</html>
```

The rest of this ASP.NET page is a simple Web Form with a `textbox`, a `button`, and a `label` control. These controls are exactly the same as the controls we first met in Chapter 3 – there's nothing particularly special about them. Let's move on to our code-behind file and see how this works. You'll notice that the syntax in this file looks different from the sort of code we've been using so far – this is because this is a purely C# file, not an ASP.NET Web Form. This code doesn't necessarily have to be used in a Web Form – we could even use this code as part of a Windows Form.

```
using System;
using System.Web.UI;
using System.Web.UI.WebControls;
```

This first block of code lays the foundation for our code-behind file. These three lines of code import important namespaces from the .NET Class Library. These namespaces are used to access all of the functionality of ASP.NET pages. These are actually loaded by default in any ASP.NET page, though we never get to see this ourselves because it's all done behind the scenes. As we saw in Chapter 2, these namespaces provide us with easy access to the classes that they contain. When we wish to make use of one of their classes, we can simply refer to the class by name, instead of having to type out the full path including all of the namespace.

```
public class MyCodeBehind : Page
{
```

The next line of code assigns a name to the class in the code-behind file. If you remember, the first line in our ASP.NET page mentioned `MyCodeBehind` – well, this is what the ASP.NET page is looking for. The second part of this line means that we are inheriting from our ASP.NET `Page` object. We'll look at inheritance in more detail shortly, but all we need to know now is that this means "Take the `Page` class, combine it with the one defined below, and call it `MyCodeBehind`." Essentially, both of the `Inherits` statements in the two files are like a kind of glue – they make the two files stick together as if they were one single file. This statement is essential when working with code behind on an ASP.NET page.

```
    public TextBox name;
    public Label message;
```

These two lines are simply variable declarations, and they mimic the names of the controls on the ASP.NET page.

```
    public void SubmitBtn_Click(object sender, EventArgs e)
    {
        message.Text = "Hello " + name.Text;
    }
```

We then move on to the business of our code-behind file. This block of code is where the action happens. We are creating a subroutine to react to a `Click` event of our **Click Me!** button. We take the value held in our textbox that was entered by the user, and add that to the string of text we want, building a welcome message, then we change the `text` attribute of our `label` control to display our welcome message, thus displaying our message on the screen.

This example was very simple, and it doesn't really show off the capabilities of the code-behind style of coding to its fullest; however, it does illustrate the principle of encapsulation. We can use this technique to encapsulate a lot of logic to deal with user input, thereby separating out the jobs of the designer and the programmer, which is one of the goals of ASP.NET.

Using Code Behind

Code behind can be used on any ASPX page with a `<script...>` block on it. We can cleanly move the code portion of our page out to the code-behind file.

> *If you use or intend to use Visual Studio .NET, you will notice that this is the default behavior. Using code behind is good practice since it cleanly separates presentation from code – using it outside of the Visual Studio .NET environment is optional, but it's still a good idea.*

All we need to do to move our code is make sure we reference the code-behind file from our ASPX page using that single line at the top of the page, then in our accompanying code-behind file, we enter the code that formerly resided in the script block, along with some `Imports` statements, so that the appropriate class libraries are referenced to ensure our code runs as intended. There's also couple of extra things we may have to add, as we'll see in the next example.

We can apply the principle of code behind to our user controls in exactly the same way as we can to normal ASPX pages. We'll take a look at an example of this in action, since we've only really been using `<script>` blocks in this chapter in our user controls, and not in our ASPX pages:

Try It Out – Separating Presentation from Code in a User Control

For this example, we'll be working with the `main2.aspx` and `header.ascx` files that we used earlier in the chapter.

1. Open up your editor and enter the following code (note that a lot of this code is the same as `header.ascx`, so you can copy and paste the un-highlighted lines from the earlier file if you prefer):

```
using System;
using System.Web.UI;
using System.Web.UI.WebControls;
using System.Collections;

public class HeaderClass : UserControl
{
   Hashtable Languages = new Hashtable();
   public DropDownList LanguageList;
   public Label WelcomeMessage;
```

```
public void Page_Load()
{
  Languages.Add("English", "Hello, and welcome to the shop");
  Languages.Add("French", "Bonjour, et bienvenue a le magasin");
  Languages.Add("Spanish", "Buenas Dias, e bienvenido a la tienda");
  Languages.Add("German", "Guten Tag, und wilkommen ins geschaeft");

  if (!Page.IsPostBack)
  {
    LanguageList.DataSource = Languages.Keys;
    Page.DataBind();
  }
}

public void DropList_Changed(object sender, EventArgs e)
{
  WelcomeMessage.Text = (String) Languages[LanguageList.SelectedItem.Text];
}
}
```

2. Save this file as `header_CB.cs`. This is the code-behind file for our user control. Now, open up your editor, and enter the following code (again, this is based on `header.ascx`, so you may want to copy over the un-highlighted lines of code, making sure not to copy over the `<script...>` and `</script>` tags and everything between them – that code now resides in our code-behind file and we don't want duplication):

```
<%@ Control inherits="HeaderClass" src="header_CB.cs"  %>
<table style="background-color:#cc0033" width="100%" cellpadding="10"
                                                       cellspacing="0">
  <tr>
    <td width="10%"">
      <img src="logo.gif" align="left" />
    </td>
    <td width="60%"> <font face="verdana,arial" size="4" color="yellow">
      <asp:label id="WelcomeMessage" runat="Server">
        Welcome to the Wrox shop!
      </asp:label> </font>
    </td>
    <td width="30%">
      <font face="verdana,arial" size="2" color="lightyellow">
      Select your Language:<br />
      <asp:DropDownList id="LanguageList" runat="Server"
                OnSelectedIndexChanged="DropList_Changed" AutoPostBack="True"/>
      </font>
    </td>
  </tr>
</table>
```

3. Save this file as `header_CB.ascx`. Now open up `main2.aspx`, and amend the following highlighted line of code at the top of the file:

```
<%@ Page Language="c#" %>
<%@ Register TagPrefix="WroxUC" TagName="Header" Src="header_CB.ascx" %>
<%@ Register TagPrefix="WroxUC" TagName="FeaturedBooks"
                                        Src="featuredbooks.ascx" %>
```

4. Save this as `main3.aspx`. Now, open up `main3.aspx` in your browser and you should see the following:

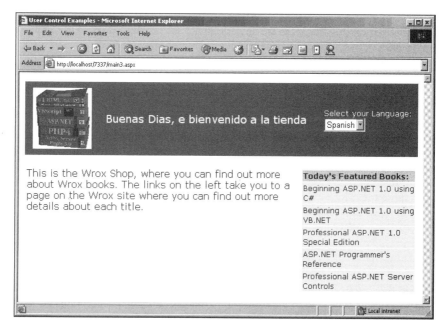

How It Works

All we've done in this example is effectively copy out all of the code in the `<script>` block from our user control and paste it into a code-behind file, tweaking a few bits along the way. The end result looks the same, but behind the scenes we're using the code-behind version of our header, not the original.

Let's start our discussion with our code-behind file, `header_CB.cs`:

```
using System;
using System.Web.UI;
using System.Web.UI.WebControls;
using System.Collections;

public class HeaderClass : UserControl
{
```

This first block of code is different from the beginning of our original control `header.ascx`. This block of code is now in a C# file, not in script blocks. We start off by importing all of the namespaces we need. We then have to declare a class to contain our code – we've called ours `HeaderClass`, and it inherits from the `UserControl` class. This statement of inheritance must be included for all code-behind files for user controls.

```
public DropDownList LanguageList;
public Label WelcomeMessage;
```

We add a couple of public variables that correspond to the controls on our header, which is essential when returning data to these controls.

The rest of the code is exactly the same as the code that once resided within that `<script>` block on our original header control, so we won't be looking at how that works here.

Let's take a quick look at the changes to the ASCX file:

```
<%@ Control inherits="HeaderClass" src="header_CB.cs"  %>
```

We've added one line of code to the top of our user control, and removed the block of script. The line of code shown above is where we indicate that the code to accompany the user control is stored in a code-behind file. The @ `Control` directive has two parameters that we need to set here: the first is the `inherits` statement, with which we identify which class we're using, the second is the location of our code-behind source file. The rest of the control is unchanged.

Moving on to the final section, which is our ASPX page:

```
<%@ Register TagPrefix="WroxUC" TagName="Header" Src="header_CB.ascx" %>
```

We've amended the line at the top of our control to indicate that we want to work with the code-behind version of our header, and not the original header. The rest of this page is exactly the same as before.

Now we'll return to the concept of inheritance one final time, so we can expand our knowledge before we go any further.

Inheritance

Inheritance is a feature of object-oriented programming that is at the very center of the C# language. In our examples above, we created two files, and told them both to inherit from each other. In basic terms, that means we told them to "make use of the functionality in both files as if they were one". However, we can make use of inheritance in even better ways than this.

Imagine we define a class for a generic car. This class could have the following characteristics, as we saw earlier in the book:

The Car Class	
Properties:	Color
	Gear
	Model
Methods:	ChangeGear()
	Ignition()
	IsRunning()

Our car is very simplistic, but the general concepts that it embodies are common to all cars. Every car can move, every car has an engine that starts, and every car has a door that can be opened (except if you live in Hazard County). On top of this, all cars have a color, make, and model. But what if we were to have a class for off-road vehicles or sports cars? Let's take a look at the sort of characteristics we could define here:

Off-Road Car Class		Sports Car Class	
Properties:	Color	**Properties:**	Color
	Gear		Gear
	Model		Model
	FourWheelDriveEngaged		TopDown
Methods:	ChangeGear()	**Methods:**	ChangeGear()
	Ignition()		Ignition()
	IsRunning()		IsRunning()
	Engage4WheelDrive()		LowerTop()
	Disengage4WheelDrive()		RaiseTop()

In our off-road class, we've introduced a FourWheelDriveEngaged property, which is a bool. This property reflects the status of the four-wheel drive feature of the car, which we can either engage or disengage using the two new methods. In our sports car class, we have a similar situation, except that we're raising or lowering the top depending on the weather.

If we were coding these kinds of classes, we could copy and paste from our original definition into two new classes. However, this isn't very efficient, and tends to be error-prone. Instead, since our car class contains characteristics common to all kinds of cars, including off-road and sports cars, we are able to **inherit** from this **base class**, which contains the common characteristics, and **extend** this class by adding the appropriate methods and properties to form two new classes in a minimum of effort. Our new classes benefit from having less code, and they also benefit from reusing code that has been thoroughly tested elsewhere. You don't actually need to see what the code for the base class does under the covers – someone else could code the base car class, and you could go off and extend this functionality to cover your specific implementations.

The only limitation to inheritance is that you can only inherit from one class at a time. You cannot, therefore, define a Sports Utility Vehicle (SUV) class that inherits both from the Off-Road Car class and the Sports class. You need to create a separate class specifically for this class of car. This is designed to reduce errors and simplify coding. For example, our sports car may move in a totally different way from our off-road car – it may have a manual gear change lever, instead of being an automatic, so you'd have to worry about a clutch somewhere in the equation. If our SUV tried to move, and it had somehow managed to inherit from both classes, it could get very confused. Fortunately, this situation doesn't happen because of the fact that we're prevented from doing this. If you do try, you'll probably end up with an error message.

> *Note that this applies only to implementation inheritance. There is another form of inheritance called interface inheritance, but we'll not be covering this here. This is handled differently when it comes to multiple inheritance. If you're interested in getting knee-deep in inheritance, and OO concepts in general, then you might want to read* Professional C#, 2nd Edition, *ISBN 1-86100-704-3.*

The concept of inheritance applies well to the concepts we'll be meeting again in the next chapter.

Summary

In this chapter we have introduced two methods of encapsulating sections of code into separate files, to keep our code as maintainable as possible:

❑ User Controls, which are designed to hold code for sections of ASPX files that are repeated on numerous pages in a site

❑ Code behind, which is designed for containing all of the script code in our page in one file, leaving the ASPX file purely for the HTML and control placement to be done by designers

These two methods are relatively straightforward, and are simply methods of moving code into different areas to improve readability, reduce complexity, and reduce errors caused by mixing presentation and script.

In this chapter we also discussed inheritance from an implementation perspective, and talked about inheriting and extending from a class.

In the next chapter, we'll move on to looking at more advanced methods of encapsulating code functionality into reusable components, namely .NET Assemblies and Custom Server Controls.

Exercises

1. Explain what a User Control is, and under what circumstances you'd use User Controls in your pages.

2. Think of a scenario where using a User Control is beneficial, and explain what kind of controls you might have in that situation. Explain which parts of your code could be separated out into a code-behind file, and why you would do this.

3. Create a User Control that produces a user login control. You'll need to ask the users for a User ID, which will be an e-mail address, and they'll need to enter their password.

4. Add some very basic validation to the control to check that they've entered a value in the e-mail address box, and to check that the password field has a value in it too, also checking that the e-mail address is a valid e-mail address, and the password is exactly eight characters, with no spaces. Next, create a simple Web Form that displays this control on the page. Test your code to see if the validation is being performed correctly.

As an additional exercise, you may want to write some code that connects to a database, and retrieves the user's details, provided the e-mail address and password that are entered match up with the records in the database. This would be useful for retrieving information on a customer's previous orders, and so on.

.NET Assemblies and Custom Controls

In the previous chapter we met User Controls and code behind as two different ways to break up our code into manageable sections. These two methods could be used for encapsulating commonly used chunks of ASP.NET code, and for separating out the script sections of our page into separate files. In this chapter, we'll be concentrating on some more advanced techniques of componentization, namely, creating .NET Assemblies and Custom Server Controls.

.NET Assemblies are components containing a collection of classes, encapsulated into a compiled assembly. They can be written in any .NET-compliant language, and are pre-compiled into a DLL file. The ASPX page then references this file to gain access to the functionality contained in it.

Assemblies can be used to contain any kind of functionality we require. They can be used, for example, to store a set of classes relating to accessing and working with data, all compiled into one file, or they can even store a custom server control, which is designed to render a custom user interface component that can be used on an ASPX page as easily as an ASP.NET DataGrid control. An assembly is a .NET construct that contains reusable functionality required in your applications, and applies to all kinds of .NET applications, not just Web Forms.

> **.NET Assemblies are groups of related classes and interface definitions encapsulated in a compiled file that can be accessed programmatically from ASP.NET Web Forms, Windows Forms, or any .NET application.**

We'll take a closer look at what assemblies are and how they're created after we consider why and when we'd want to use them.

Three-Tier Application Design

Let's take the concept of separation of content from presentation one step further. Once we've separated the elements of an application into distinct purpose-specific categories, often referred to as layers, it becomes much easier to structure them efficiently. In many respects, everything we've said in the book so far about structured code has served as a preparation for what we're about to do – breaking out this 'application logic' code into separate components that we can use both here and elsewhere. So, in traditional application design terms, we ultimately have our ASP.NET pages to deal with the top **presentation layer**, a database to store our content in a bottom **data layer**, and components that sit in between to marshal the flow of data between them – these components provide the core logic of our application, and are usually referred to collectively as the **application logic layer**:

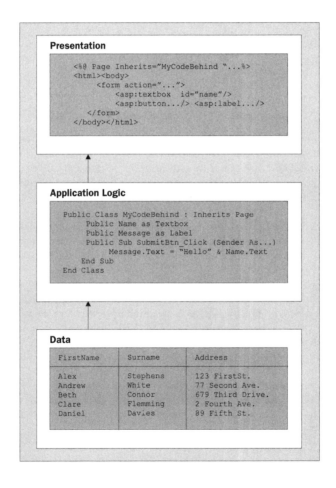

The diagram represents the three layers we've just described – in fact, an application built using this sort of architecture is known technically as a **3-tier application**. So, how do these fit together? Our user might click a button on a travel-related web site that says "Show me all available hotels in Gran Canaria", which, in a two-tier situation, would call a class in one of our application logic components that connected to the database and queried it for all hotels matching the criterion. In a 3-tier scenario, this application logic may talk to data logic that, in turn, talks to the database. In either case, we're looking for hotels in Gran Canaria, but we could expand this to match hotels available on a certain date, or hotels of a certain style.

The three tiers in generic 3-tier applications can be broken down as follows:

❑ **Data** – This could be any type of data store, for example, a database, an XML file, an Excel work sheet, or even a text file

❑ **Application Logic** – Also known as business logic, this contains all the code that we use to query the database, manipulate retrieved data, pass data to the user interface, and handle any input from the UI as well

❑ **Presentation** – This comprises all our user interface code, containing a mixture of static HTML, text and graphics, User Controls, and server controls

So how does this relate to the concepts we've met so far, and how do assemblies and server controls fit into the mixture?

ASP.NET Application Design

User Controls are used to encapsulate frequently used sections of ASP.NET code into separate files to improve manageability, and make it easier to reuse code within one application. In the previous chapter, we chose to use code-behind files to hide the code that processed our Web Form. Taking this a bit further, we could have the following situation:

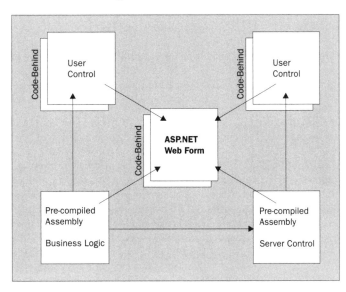

In this structure, each ASPX page can have a code-behind file and each User Control (ASCX) can have a code-behind file. These User Controls can be used by any of our ASP.NET pages. We can create business logic components stored in assemblies that can be used by any of our User Controls, ASP.NET pages, or Custom Server Controls. We can also create Custom Server Controls that can be used again by any of our User controls or ASP.NET pages. Our application logic can reside in our assemblies, code-behind files, ASP.NET pages, Server Controls, or User Controls, so traditional 3-tier application design is a little more tricky. Once you decide how you're going to structure your application, however, the process becomes much clearer.

Firstly, you need to decide what part of your code does what. One scenario is that you keep your ASPX files purely for HTML and control elements. You then use code-behind to handle OnClick events for any buttons, or OnChange events for selections, and so on. You can then apply exactly the same process to the User controls, separating presentation and code as appropriate. Then you create assemblies that will plug in to your ASPX and ASCX that contain all of your data connectivity code, and the code to process your data. Finally, server controls could also make use of data-handling classes from another assembly, so you're left with a very interlinked but compact model. This process is entirely up to you.

> *You could, theoretically, keep all of your code in ASPX pages, but, this isn't recommended, given the benefits that encapsulating functionality into different components can bring to your applications.*

Since we've looked at the user interface design using ASPX and ASCX files, and we've seen how we can encapsulate page logic into a code-behind file, let's now move on to looking at how we can encapsulate some of our application logic into a .NET **assembly**.

.NET Assemblies

An assembly is a logical grouping of functionality contained in a physical file. Assemblies are designed to solve the problem of versioning and make your code extremely simple to deploy. An assembly consists of two main parts:

❑   **The assembly manifest** – which contains the assembly metadata. This can be thought of as a table of contents that describes what's in the assembly and what it does, including the version number and culture information. It is generated when the assembly is compiled.

❑   **The MSIL code** (Microsoft Intermediate Language) – The source code (pre-compilation) is written in a .NET language, for example, C#, or VB.NET. This source code is then translated at compile time into MSIL code, which is the language that .NET uses to communicate.

In the remainder of the chapter, we'll look at some examples of what can be put into assemblies. We'll look at everything from a very basic component, through to a component containing classes that can be used to work with data. We'll also look at a simple custom server control that renders its own custom user interface. We'll do this by writing code in C#, compiling it into DLLs using the C# compiler (csc.exe) and calling it from our applications. We'll also look at how we can create an assembly in a different language that can be used in exactly the same way, so the language difference is transparent in the end result.

The DLLs we'll be creating will have a namespace declaration, and contain one or more classes encapsulating our functionality. This criterion applies to .NET DLLs in general.

For our first ASP.NET Assembly, we'll create a component with just one method – the `SayHello` method.

Try It Out – Our First ASP.NET Component

Let's have a go at creating our first ASP.NET component.

1. First, open up your editor and type in the following code:

```
namespace WroxComponents {

  public class HelloCS {

    public string SayHello() {

      return "Hello World - I'm a C# component!";

    }
  }
}
```

2. Save this file as `MyFirstComponent.cs` in your `C:\BegASPNET\Ch16` directory. *We won't be using this code just yet, but we'll be using it in the next couple of exercises.*

How It Works

This is a very simple component; so let's take a brief look at what it does:

```
namespace WroxComponents {
```

The first line qualifies all of the following classes into a namespace, which we'll use to corral together related components under a single banner, which is how the .NET namespaces are grouped, as we saw in the previous chapter. We'll be using the same namespace for each of our components – as long as each method name in each component is unique, this is a good way of combining specific groups of functionality. Once our component is compiled, other pages and applications can import this namespace, and all the classes it contains can easily be accessed. It doesn't matter which DLL contains each class, since ASP.NET automatically loads all the classes contained in the `/bin` directory when the application is started.

```
public class HelloCS {
```

The next line declares the class in our namespace, which we're calling `HelloCS`. Once we have imported our `WroxComponents` namespace in an ASPX page, we will be able to access the `HelloCS` class from within our ASP.NET page.

```
        public string SayHello() {

      return "Hello World - I'm a C# component!";

    }
```

The next few lines are where our method is coded. We declare our function, in this case called `SayHello()`, and we say that it will return a string. By declaring this function as `Public`, we're making this available to the outside world as an interface. We'll be able to call a `SayHello()` method on any object derived from this class once we're in our ASPX page. We're going to be really simplistic and explicitly tell our function to return the text "Hello World – I'm a C# component!" whenever the method is called, but in a more complex component, you can obviously do a lot more than this, as we shall see later.

```
    }
  }
```

The last lines of code in our component simply close up the class declaration and the namespace declaration.

This component must now be **compiled**, and the compiled version of the component must be saved to the `bin` directory of your web application. If there's not one there already, you'll need to create one yourself. Previously, when using COM, any components created had to be registered with the system registry. With .NET, all we need to do is save our files in the right place, compile them, and away we go.

Let's take a closer look at what we mean by 'compile' before we move on to compiling our component.

What is Compilation?

When we create an ASP.NET page, we write code using an editor, and save our code as an ASPX page somewhere on our system. When that ASPX page is requested, the code is compiled into **Intermediate Language (IL)** behind the scenes when the page is first run, and stored in a cache until the web server is restarted, or until the page (the ASPX file) has been changed in some way (for example, if you added some code and re-saved the file). The cached Intermediate Language code is then **Just-In-Time (JIT)** compiled into native machine code at run time.

When we use an ASP.NET page, we suffer a performance hit the first time the page is accessed because the page has to be compiled to IL, then JIT compiled. Once the page has been accessed once, the process of accessing the page is much quicker because all that needs to be done then is for the JIT compiler to run. However, when we create a .NET assembly, we do the compilation to IL in advance, saving us from even more of this performance hit. This means that components are slightly faster than an ASPX page the first time a page is run – though subsequent page hits will perform about the same. Our compiled assembly is more discrete than the raw source code we put into it – it's much harder now to simply look through the code and see how the classes are structured in the assembly without using a specialist tool – simply opening the DLL in Notepad will display gibberish, so alternative methods have to be used to see the code in its true form (although we'll not be looking into this in detail here because this is outside the scope of this book).

Now let's move on to compiling our first component.

Try-It-Out – Compiling our First ASP.NET Component

In order to compile our component, we need to create a file that will perform this compilation for us by running a series of specified commands.

1. Type the following into a new file called `CompileMyFirstComponent.bat`, and save this in our `C:\BegASPNET\Ch16` folder:

```
set indir=C:\BegASPNET\Ch16\MyFirstComponent.cs
set outdir=C:\BegASPNET\bin\MyFirstComponent.dll

csc /t:library /out:%outdir% %indir%
pause
```

2. Save the `CompileMyFirstComponent.bat` file on your system and then double-click it to run the commands. You should see the following text appear on your screen:

```
C:\WINNT\System32\cmd.exe                                    _ □ ×

C:\BegASPNET\Ch16>set indir=C:\BegASPNET\Ch16\MyFirstComponent.cs

C:\BegASPNET\Ch16>set outdir=c:\BegASPNET\bin\MyFirstComponent.dll

C:\BegASPNET\Ch16>csc /t:library /out:c:\BegASPNET\bin\MyFirstComponent.dll C:\B
egASPNET\Ch16\MyFirstComponent.cs
Microsoft (R) Visual C# .NET Compiler version 7.00.9466
for Microsoft (R) .NET Framework version 1.0.3705
Copyright (C) Microsoft Corporation 2001. All rights reserved.


C:\BegASPNET\Ch16>pause
Press any key to continue . . .
```

We'll examine how this works in just a moment. However, if you received any kind of error messages when you ran this command, and the output looked different from what we can see above, double-check your code to make sure it's typed in correctly (especially the spacing in the `.bat` file because DOS is very picky about this).

If this doesn't solve your problem, and if you're getting an error message that reads **System Cannot find file csc.exe** then you will need to check that your environment variables are configured correctly. There is a tutorial on how to do this available with the code download from www.wrox.com.

How It Works

So, what did this do? Well, let's take a look at what's been created, and then we'll look at the compilation batch file in more detail.

If you browse your hard drive in the normal way and look at the `C:\BegASPNET\bin` directory, you'll notice that there's a new file in here – `MyFirstComponent.dll`. This is our compiled assembly, ready for use:

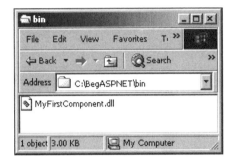

Let's take a look at the compilation batch file that we created, and go through it step by step. Firstly, here's the code we entered:

```
set indir=C:\BegASPNET\Ch16\MyFirstComponent.cs
set outdir=C:\BegASPNET\bin\MyFirstComponent.dll

csc /t:library /out:%outdir% %indir%
pause
```

Let's start at the beginning:

```
set indir=C:\BegASPNET\Ch16\MyFirstComponent.cs
```

This first part of the file creates an alias for the path to the C# file that we created earlier (`MyFirstComponent.cs`), which is our source file. Our path is the complete path to our file, including directory, filename, and extension:

```
set outdir=c:\BegASPNET\bin\MyFirstComponent.dll
```

The next part of our file creates an alias for the path to the file we're creating in the compilation process, which is `MyFirstComponent.dll`. We include the name that the file will assume once it's compiled:

```
csc /t:library /out:%outdir% %indir%
```

Finally we get to the actual compile command. The first part of the command is the name of the C# compiler – `csc.exe`. The next provides additional information that the compiler needs:

```
csc /t:library /out:%outdir% %indir%
```

This is what's known as a **switch** or an **option**. We're telling the C# compiler that when it compiles, we want it to produce a **library** file, or assembly, and not an executable. If we'd not included this switch, a default value would have been used instead – which would have attempted to produce an executable.

> *Attempting to create an executable file in this situation would have failed since EXE files must be coded so that they have a method called* main *in them, that is called when the EXE is called. Our code doesn't have this method in it, so we would see an error.*

Then we come to the last two parts of our statement. Firstly:

```
csc /t:library /out:%outdir% %indir%
```

The first part of this is another option that we're passing in to the compiler, telling it where to put our compiled file. This is where we use the alias we created earlier that points to the path where we're creating the component, and includes the name of the component itself. We're telling our compiler to create our output file, MyFirstComponent.dll, and place it in the bin directory:

```
csc /t:library /out:%outdir% %indir%
```

The last option in this section refers to our other alias, which simply tells the compiler where to get the source code that we're going to compile from.

The last statement, pause, tells the operating system to wait for the user to press a key before closing the command-prompt window that's popped up. This gives us the chance to watch and see what happens before the window disappears so we can be assured that our code executed correctly, or if not, we can read the error message.

It's worth noting that we could have simply typed in the complete command in one line, like this:

```
csc /t:library /out:c:\BegASPNET\bin\MyFirstComponent.dll C:\BegASPNET\MyFirstComponent.vb
```

We built the command up in several steps for simplification. Manually creating aliases for each of the paths and splitting these out from the main compile command, helps to simplify the compilation process if we need to amend any of the options. This is particularly useful for more complex compilations.

When we're working with batch files, there are several options available to us other than those we've already met. When we compiled our component, we used the /t parameter to specify the type of output the compiler would create – in our case, we used /t:library switch to produce a DLL library file. This option, a shortened form of /target, can also take the following arguments:

Option	Effect
/target:exe	Tells the compiler to create a command-line executable program. This is the default value, so if the /target parameter is not included, an EXE file will be created.

Table continued on following page

641

Option	Effect
`/target:library`	Tells the compiler to create a `DLL` file that will contain an assembly consisting of all of the source files passed to the compiler. The compiler will also automatically create a manifest for this assembly.
`/target:module`	Tells the compiler to create a `DLL`, but not to create a manifest for it. This means that in order for the module to be used by the .NET Framework, it will need to be manually added to an assembly using the Assembly Generation tool (`al.exe`). This tool allows you to create the assembly manifest information manually, and then add modules to it.
`/target:winexe`	This tells the compiler to create a Windows Forms application. This is not covered in this book. (For more information about Windows Forms, you can refer to *Professional Windows Forms, ISBN 1-86100-554-7*, or *Professional C#, ISBN 1-86100-704-3*.)

There are two other compilers supplied by default with the .NET Framework, which are used to compile VB .NET and JScript components. These compilers are in the same directory as the `csc.exe` *compiler, and are called* `vbc.exe` *and* `jsc.exe`, *respectively. They take the same parameters.*

Accessing a Component from within an ASP.NET Page

It's time to look at accessing our compiled component from an ASP.NET page. So far, we've got a simple component that contains code that displays Hello World – I'm a component! We're going to access this from a simple ASP.NET page.

Try It Out – Using a Compiled Component

1. Let's start work on our ASP.NET page. Fire up your editor and type the following code:

```
<%@ Import Namespace="WroxComponents" %>

<html>
<head><title>My First Component Example</title></head>
<body>

Our component says: <br /> <br />

<asp:Label id="label1" runat="server" />

<script language="c#" runat="server">

void Page_Load(Object sender, EventArgs e)
{
  HelloCS CSComponent = new HelloCS();
  label1.Text = CSComponent.SayHello();
```

```
    }

</script>

</body>
</html>
```

2. Save this as `UseMyFirstComponent.aspx` in your `C:\BegASPNET\Ch16` folder, and view it in your browser:

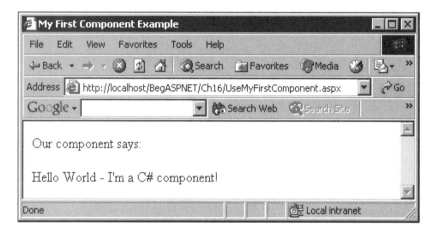

How It Works

Let's take a look through our ASP.NET page:

```
<%@ Import Namespace="WroxComponents" %>
```

Our first line refers to the namespace that we declared in our component. If you refer back to the component, you'll remember that we had the following lines of code:

```
namespace WroxComponents {
...
}
```

This is what we are referring to here. The namespace declaration is different from the class declarations in that a namespace can contain more than one class. These classes can then be referenced with the notation namespace.class, but if you use the Import Namespace command, you can simply refer to the class by name. It's a form of shorthand, and is exactly the same as the syntax we used in the previous chapter when we imported System.Web.UI and similar namespaces. They act as shortcuts to commonly used classes. If we had used a code-behind file in conjunction with our ASPX, the namespace would have to be imported into the code-behind file.

ASP.NET loads all the assemblies that reside within the /bin directory, when an application is started by default, so the only thing any ASP.NET page has to do to reference these assemblies is refer to the namespace in which the required classes reside.

> *There are also ways of enabling us to make use of assemblies stored elsewhere on our system. We'll look at these later in the chapter.*

So, going back to our ASP.NET page:

```
<html>
<body>

Our component says: <br /> <br />
```

We use plain and simple HTML to put some text on the screen so that we can compare this with the output of our component.

```
<asp:Label id="label1" runat="server" />
```

Our next line of code creates a label, which we will use to display the output of our component logic. In our case, we know that we're expecting some text, and the Label control is a great placeholder for text.

```
<script language="c#" runat="server">

void Page_Load(Object sender, EventArgs e)
{
```

We open a script block that states that we'll be writing our code in C# and we want to run this block on the server. We then declare a function that will run when the page loads.

```
    HelloCS CSComponent = new HelloCS();
    label1.Text = CSComponent.SayHello();
```

We instantiate a new instance of our HelloCS class by creating an object, in this case called CSComponent. This object now has all the functionality of our class available to it as its own methods and properties. In our case, it has only one method – the SayHello() method. The second line of code shown above changes the value of the Text property of the label1 control to display the output of the SayHello() method of our CSComponent object.

```
    }

    </script>

    </body>
    </html>
```

The remainder of our code finishes off our example. We close our function, and `script` block. All that remains then is to close the web page correctly with closing `</body>` and `</html>` tags.

> *No doubt some of you will be using Visual Studio. Creating and using an assembly in Visual Studio is a little different from the command-line method. However, since Visual Studio is such a vast product, and since we've already discussed how we can compile components from the command line, we'll not be looking at compiling components from Visual Studio .NET in here. If you'd like to know more about Visual Studio, you might want to look at* Professional Visual Basic .NET, *ISBN 1-86100-716-7, or* Professional C#, *ISBN 1-86100-704-3, which cover Visual Studio .NET development in detail.*

XCopy Deployment

If you've ever played around with Windows in detail, you've probably heard of the **Registry**. The Registry is a database that holds all the information about your computer, hardware, setup, and software. It provides Windows with a way of locating DLL files, or components. In this sense, it's a bit like the Yellow Pages of your computer. Any traditional DLL that is created has to have an entry in the Registry so that the computer can locate it when it's needed. This process is called **Registration**. With basic ASP.NET components, there's no longer any need to do this – all we need to do is have the right directory in the right place, and ASP.NET will know where to look and what to do with it.

When we created our DLL, we had to place our compiled component into a `/bin` directory. This is a subdirectory of our web application, or virtual directory.

> **Any time you need to use an assembly with .NET web applications, the easiest way is to place your assembly in a `/bin` directory, and your ASP.NET application will then be able to use it.**

In the good old days of DOS, copying from one location to another was done with a command called `xcopy`: hence the term `xcopy` deployment.

When a component is created, it can be accessed by any web pages in that application space. All you need to do is include an `<%@ Import Namespace ... >` declaration in your code to import the functionality in the component and you're away. If, however, you need to alter the functionality in the component in any way, all you need to do is go back to your original source file, alter the code, and recompile it. Once that process is complete, the new component will be used by any web site hits that require it. This is totally different from the scenario faced by ASP developers, who had to stop and start their web application to update components, thereby losing uptime for the duration of the process.

When a change is made to a component, ASP.NET allows any requests that are currently executing to complete, and directs all new incoming requests to the new component, so the users of a site barely notice any change.

Accessing Assemblies in Other Locations

In our previous example, we stated that all we needed to do to access our assembly was to place it within the /bin directory in the root of our web application. But what if we wanted to use an assembly in another location?

ASP.NET has a default configuration setup so that each application we create knows how to access its required functionality. Occasionally, we may want to override or alter this default functionality to tailor it more to our specific application configuration. We can accomplish this using a file called web.config, which resides within the root of our web application, directing our pages to find the required components.

web.config is an XML-based file that specifies important configuration information that every ASP.NET application will need. It can store everything from information on debug settings and session state timeout values, to references and ASP.NET components. Being XML-based it's human-readable, and this makes it very easy to add, remove, and change settings. Any changes to configuration that we make are instantaneous; they take effect as soon as the file is saved.

Let's take a quick look at an example of a web.config file:

```
<configuration>
  <system.web>
    <sessionState timeout="10" />
    <compilation>
      <assemblies>
        <add assembly="AssemblyName" />
      </assemblies>
    </compilation>
  </system.web>
</configuration>
```

*A quick word of warning – web.config files are **case-sensitive**, so all the tag names must be typed in with care.*

This simple configuration file sets the session state timeout of a page to be 10 minutes, and it references an assembly called AssemblyName. We'll be meeting web.config again in Chapter 19, so we're not going to look into it in much more detail here. The important feature to note is the <add assembly="AssemblyName" /> tag. Here, AssemblyName refers to the assembly we require that resides outside of the bin directory. For example, we could, reference System.Data if we wanted to use the classes within the System.Data namespace on a regular basis throughout our application.

Writing Code in Other Languages

Since the .NET Framework is happily language-agnostic, we can write our components in any .NET-compiled language we like. Throughout this book, we've been writing code in C#. Indeed, our first component in this chapter was written in C#. Now we'll look at that first component again, but this time written in VB.NET, and show how easy it is to work with any language to create your components.

Try It Out – Writing a Component in VB.NET

> Although this example is written in VB.NET, don't panic if you've never looked at VB .NET code. It's just for exemplary purposes and, as we'll see, there are a lot of similarities between the two languages since they have to follow the same rules in order to both be .NET- compliant.

1. Start by opening up your editor and enter the following code. Save the file as CSharpComponent.vb:

```
Namespace WroxComponents

  Public Class HelloVB

    Public Function SayHello() As String

      Return "Hello World - I'm a VB.NET component!"

    End Function

  End Class

End Namespace
```

2. Now open up your editor, and enter the following code, in a new file:

```
set indir=C:\BegASPNET\ch16\VBComponent.vb
set outdir=c:\BegASPNET\bin\VBComponent.dll

vbc /t:library /out:%outdir% %indir%
pause
```

Save this file as CompileVBComponent.bat in your C:\BegASPNET folder.

3. Double-click this batch file and you should see the following:

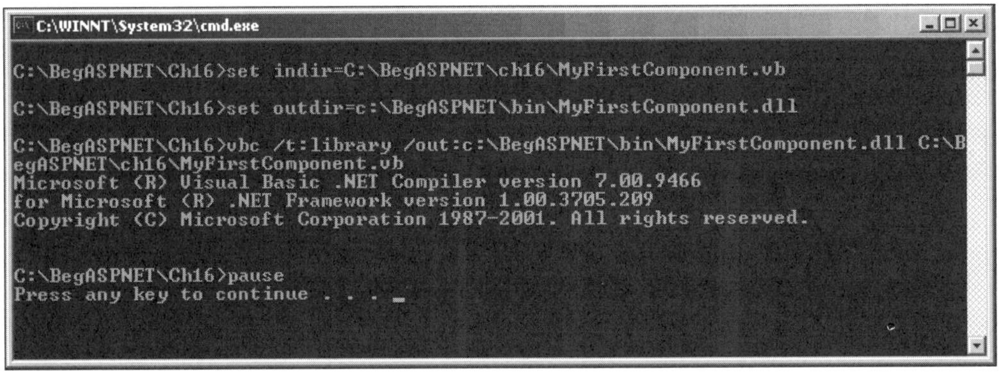

4. Next, open up `UseMyFirstComponent.aspx`. Amend the file by inserting the highlighted lines as shown below, and save it as `MultiLingualComponent.aspx`:

```
<%@ Import Namespace="WroxComponents" %>

<html>
<head><title>My First Component Example</title></head>
<body>

Our component says: <br /> <br />

<asp:Label id="label1" runat="server" />
<br /><asp:Label id="label2" runat="server" />

<script language="c#" runat="server">

void Page_Load(Object sender, EventArgs e)
{
  HelloCS CSComponent = new HelloCS();
  HelloVB VBComponent = new HelloVB();

  label1.Text = CSComponent.SayHello();
  label2.Text = VBComponent.SayHello();
}
</script>

</body>
</html>
```

5. Now, open up `MultiLingualComponent.aspx` in your browser:

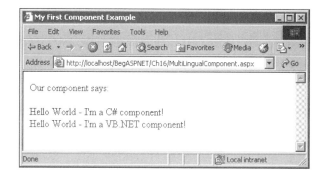

How It Works

The VB.NET code is very straightforward. First we declare the namespace that is to be imported into the ASP.NET page and then the name of the class:

```
Namespace HelloWorldVB
   Public Class HelloVB
```

Next we define the class's single function, which is enclosed in a `Function...End Function` block:

```
      Public Function SayHello() As String
         Return "Hello World - I'm a component in VB!"
      End Function
```

Like the C# example presented earlier, all we do is return a message string.

Finally, as is characteristic of VB.NET code, we explicitly close our class and namespace like so:

```
   End Class
End Namespace
```

Now, let's briefly look at the new lines encountered in our ASP.NET page.

We add an extra `Import` statement at the top of our ASP.NET page to reference our new component, in a very similar way to the previous examples.

```
<%@ Import Namespace="HelloWorldVB" %>
```

We need to add a line break and another label, which we'll use to store the output of our component, just as we did with the C# component:

```
<br /><asp:Label id="label2" runat="server" />
```

Finally, we call out to the component in exactly the same way as we did before, and output the message to our new label control:

```
HelloVB Component2 = new HelloVB();
label2.Text=Component2.SayHello();
```

In this short page, we are actually referencing two components: one originally written in VB, one originally written in C#, and they've both been integrated seamlessly into our page. We could have written other 'Hello World' components in other languages, and the results would be the same. This is one of the coolest features of .NET, and it's one that many developers will grow to love. Imagine, a C# developer, working on a project alongside a Visual Basic .NET developer, and a JScript .NET developer – each could write components to be used in the same ASP.NET pages, with no need to worry about which language the original component code was written in, as long as it has been compiled into Intermediate Language. The only way this is possible is to have a compiler that is supported by the Common Language Runtime. The .NET Framework only includes a handful of compilers by default (C#, VB.NET, and JScript), but compilers for a lot more languages are likely to emerge over time.

Data Access Components

A common use for components is to contain code for accessing data, or application logic. Our previous example of using an assembly didn't exactly push the boundaries very far, so in this next example, we're going to be slightly more adventurous and include some code to work with a database.

In the following example, we will create a component that connects to the Authors table in the WroxShop Access database we used in the previous chapter. We will create a namespace with one class, the WroxAuthors class, which has the following methods and property:

Method	GetAuthorsByBook	Queries the database for a list of authors on each book and returns a DataSet
Method	GetBooks	Queries the database to find a list of available books and returns a DataSet
Property	DatabaseConnection	Creates a connection to the database

Again, we've limited the functionality in the component for reasons of simplicity, but you can extend this much further to include methods that add or delete records from the database and much, much, more.

In this example we will be connecting to a database, running a query against that database, then displaying selected records in an ASP.NET `DataGrid` control on an ASP.NET page.

1. Make sure that you have a copy of the `WroxShop` database that we used in the previous chapter in your `C:\BegASPNET\Ch16` code directory. (This database is available for download from **www.wrox.com**.)

2. Enter the following code into a new file:

```csharp
using System;
using System.Data;
using System.Data.OleDb;

namespace WroxComponents
{

  public class WroxAuthors
  {
    private string m_DSN;

    public WroxAuthors(string DSN)
    {
      m_DSN = DSN;
    }

    public DataSet GetAuthorsByBook (string ISBN)
    {
      string SQLString =
              "SELECT Authors.AuthorFirstName, Authors.AuthorSurname " +
              "FROM Authors LEFT JOIN Books ON " +
              "Authors.Book = Books.Title WHERE (((Books.ISBN)='" + ISBN +
              "'));";

      OleDbConnection myConnection = new OleDbConnection(m_DSN);
      OleDbDataAdapter myDataAdapter =
                          new OleDbDataAdapter(SQLString, myConnection);

      DataSet authorsByBook = new DataSet();
      myDataAdapter.Fill(authorsByBook);

      return authorsByBook;
    }

    public DataSet GetBooks ()
    {
      string SQLString = "SELECT * FROM Books";

      OleDbConnection myConnection = new OleDbConnection(m_DSN);
      OleDbDataAdapter myDataAdapter =
                          new OleDbDataAdapter(SQLString, myConnection);
```

```
        DataSet Books = new DataSet();
        myDataAdapter.Fill(Books);

        return Books;
    }
  }
}
```

3. Save this file as `WroxAuthors.cs`. Then, open up your editor and enter the following code, which will form our compilation file. Save this as `C:\BegASPNET\CompileWroxAuthors.bat`.

```
set indir=C:\BegASPNET\Ch16\WroxAuthors.cs
set outdir=c:\BegASPNET\bin\WroxAuthors.dll
set assemblies=System.dll,System.Data.dll,System.Xml.dll

csc /t:library /out:%outdir% %indir% /r:%assemblies%
pause
```

4. Double-click this file, and you should see the following output:

5. We're going to use an ASPX page called `WroxAuthors.aspx` with a code-behind file called `WroxAuthorsCB.cs`. Enter the following code, which will form the ASPX page:

```
<%@ Page Language="cs" debug="true" src="WroxAuthorsCB.cs"
                            Inherits="WroxAuthorsCB"%>
<html>
<head><title>Wrox Authors by Book</title></head>
<body>

Please select a book: <br /> <br />

<form Method="Post" runat="Server">
```

```
    <P>
      <asp:DropDownList id="DropDownList1" runat="server" />
      <asp:Button id="Button1" runat="server" Text="Submit" />
    </P>
    <P>
      <asp:DataGrid id="DataGrid1" runat="server"
        Font-Name="Verdana,arial,helvetica"
        Font-Size="10pt"
        CellSpacing="2"
        CellPadding="2"
        HeaderStyle-BackColor="silver" />
    </P>
  </form>

</body>
</html>
```

6. Save this file as `WroxAuthors.aspx`.

7. Now, fire up your editor again and enter the following code. This will form our code-behind file:

```csharp
using System;
using System.Web.UI;
using System.Web.UI.WebControls;
using WroxComponents;

public class WroxAuthorsCB : Page
{
    public DropDownList DropDownList1;
    public Button Button1;
    public DataGrid DataGrid1;

  public void Page_Load(object Sender, EventArgs e)
  {
    string ConnectString = "provider=Microsoft.Jet.OLEDB.4.0;data source=" +
                "C:\\BegASPNET\\Ch16\\WroxShop.mdb";

    WroxAuthors WroxAuthorsList = new WroxAuthors(ConnectString);

    if (!(Page.IsPostBack))
    {
      DropDownList1.DataSource = WroxAuthorsList.GetBooks();
      DropDownList1.DataValueField="ISBN";
      DropDownList1.DataTextField="Title";
      DropDownList1.DataBind();
    }
    else
    {
      DataGrid1.DataSource = WroxAuthorsList.GetAuthorsByBook
        (DropDownList1.SelectedItem.Value);
      DataGrid1.DataBind();
    }
  }
}
```

8. Save this file as `WroxAuthorsCB.cs`.

9. Finally, view `WroxAuthors.aspx` in your browser. Select a book from the drop-down list, hit Submit, and you should see something like this:

How It Works – The Component

We've got a lot to get through here, so let's start off with our component:

```
using System;
using System.Data;
using System.Data.OleDb;
```

As shown above, our next three lines of code import all the standard namespaces that are used when working with data from a non-SQL Server data source in ASP.NET. We met these previously in Chapters 12 and 13. We only need to import these namespaces in the code-behind file.

```
namespace WroxComponents
{
```

We declare that in this example we are again using the same namespace for our classes called `WroxComponents`. When we build our ASP.NET page we will import the `WroxComponents` namespace so we can use the functions on this code-behind page.

```
public class WroxAuthors
{
```

Our class in this example is called `WroxAuthors`, and this is the template from which we'll create an object.

```
private string m_DSN;
```

The next line creates a private variable, which is a variable that our ASP.NET pages **can't** access, but anything within this component **can** access. This variable is used inside the component to pass in the value of the DSN – the data source information – when called by the main ASP.NET page.

```
public WroxAuthors(string DSN)
{
  m_DSN = DSN;
}
```

We create a function that will form our public property. This property accepts the value of a DSN, and when we set this property from our ASP.NET page, we must pass in the DSN for our database. The DSN is handled here, where it's value is passed to our private variable m_DSN. This is essential when we connect to our database. We'll see how we use this when we look at our code-behind page.

```
public DataSet GetAuthorsByBook (string ISBN)
{
string SQLString =
         "SELECT Authors.AuthorFirstName, Authors.AuthorSurname " +
         "FROM Authors LEFT JOIN Books ON " +
         "Authors.Book = Books.Title WHERE (((Books.ISBN)='" + ISBN +
         "'));";

   OleDbConnection myConnection = new OleDbConnection(m_DSN);
   OleDbDataAdapter myDataAdapter =
                       new OleDbDataAdapter(SQLString, myConnection);
```

Our next section of code is where we create our method, `GetAuthorsByBook`. This method is used to query the database to find out which of the authors have written on a specific book, identified by the parameter `ISBN`, which is implicitly selected by the user at runtime using a drop-down box control. (The dropdown box lists book names, but our function has the corresponding ISBN passed to it because the ISBN for a book will always be strictly unique.) We create a string variable that holds our lengthy SQL query string, called `SQLString`, which contains three concatenated lines of information. Our next two lines of code are where we create our `SQLConnection` object, as we saw in the previous chapters, and our `DataAdapter`. The `DataAdapter` is where we enter the details of our query, which include the contents of the `SQLString` variable and the details of the connection, which we will execute on the database once we try to fill our `DataAdapter`.

```
DataSet authorsByBook = new DataSet();
myDataAdapter.Fill(authorsByBook);

return authorsByBook;
}
```

These two lines populate our new `DataSet` with information via the `OleDbDataAdapter`; we then finish this method by setting the `return` value.

```
public DataSet GetBooks ()
{
  string SQLString = "SELECT * FROM Books";
```

```
OleDbConnection myConnection = new OleDbConnection(m_DSN);
OleDbDataAdapter myDataAdapter =
                    new OleDbDataAdapter(SQLString, myConnection);
```

The next section is similar to the previous section. We are creating a function that obtains a list of books from the `Books` table of our `Wroxshop` database so that our users can choose one of them. We again create a new variable called `SQLString` to hold the database query string, since the last one we used only existed within the scope of the previous function. This time, `SQLString` will hold a slightly different query string.

```
    DataSet Books = new DataSet();
myDataAdapter.Fill(Books);

return Books;
    }
  }
}
```

The next lines of code start off by creating a `DataSet` and filling it with the output of the `OleDbDataAdapter` – the output of the `MyDataAdapter` is the result of our query. We then set our `return` value to be a `Dataset` of books, before closing the function, the class, and finally, the namespace.

The ASPX page

Since we're using a code-behind file alongside our ASPX page, we won't need to add the `<% Import Namespace ... %>` declaration at the top of our ASPX to work with our compiled class. The first line of code is where we specify our code-behind page.

```
<%@ Page Language="cs" debug="true" src="WroxAuthorsCB.cs"
                          Inherits="WroxAuthorsCB"%>
```

We reference the code-behind file that we'll be using for this page, and we also declare the language for our page. The `src` attribute specifies the file containing the classes, and the `Inherits` statement refers to the class we wish to inherit from.

```
<html>
<head><title>Wrox Authors by Book</title></head>
<body>

Please select a book: <br /> <br />
```

The next lines of code are fairly simple and are completely HTML-based.

```
<form Method="Post" runat="Server">

  <P>
    <asp:DropDownList id="DropDownList1" runat="server" />
    <asp:Button id="Button1" runat="server" Text="Submit" />
```

```
    </P>
    <P>
      <asp:DataGrid id="DataGrid1" runat="server"
        Font-Name="Verdana,arial,helvetica"
        Font-Size="10pt"
        CellSpacing="2"
        CellPadding="2"
        HeaderStyle-BackColor="silver" />
    </P>
  </form>

  </body>
  </html>
```

This block of code is where our form is laid out. Encapsulating these controls in one form binds them together, so that the compiler knows that hitting the Submit button will post back the values of any controls with a `runat="server"` tag on them. The first two controls are our drop-down box and button. The box will display the list of books from which a user can choose. The button fires the postback. The last control in this section is an ASP.NET `DataGrid` control, like we met in Chapter 14. This control will be used to store the results of our query. We've applied some basic formatting to this grid control as a reminder of how simple it is to style our output.

The Code-Behind File

```
using System;
using System.Web.UI;
using System.Web.UI.WebControls;
using WroxComponents;
```

The first lines of code shown above import all the necessary namespaces, along with one extra namespace – this is the namespace containing our components, so we need to reference it here by name, as shown in the fourth line above. This is the namespace we declared at the top of the component we created.

```
public class WroxAuthorsCB : Page
{
    public DropDownList DropDownList1;
    public Button Button1;
    public DataGrid DataGrid1;
```

We declare our class here, inherit from the `Page` object, and create three public variables corresponding to the three controls on our Web Form.

```
public void Page_Load(object Sender, EventArgs e)
{
    string ConnectString = "provider=Microsoft.Jet.OLEDB.4.0;data source=" +
                              "C:\\BegASPNET\\Ch16\\WroxShop.mdb";

    WroxAuthors WroxAuthorsList = new WroxAuthors(ConnectString);
```

657

The next few lines are where it starts to get really interesting. We have a script block with a `Page_Load` event handler. In this event handler, the first thing we do is create the connection string that points to our database. Next, we instantiate a new instance of our class into the `WroxAuthorsList` object, and pass in the connection string as a parameter.

This connection string applies to the database we used in the previous chapter, so you'll need to make sure this database is available for use and resides within the Ch16 *folder.*

```
if (!(Page.IsPostBack))
{
  DropDownList1.DataSource = WroxAuthorsList.GetBooks();
  DropDownList1.DataValueField="ISBN";
  DropDownList1.DataTextField="Title";
  DropDownList1.DataBind();
}
```

This `if` statement is very useful to us. When we first load the page, when we're ***not*** posting back to the server, we only need to concern ourselves with the first part – this part populates our drop-down list with a list of books, using the parameters specified in the component. We identify the `DataSource` as being our `DataSet` that we obtained from our component, and then we set two values on our `DropDown` box. We are binding to the `ISBN` field of our table, but we're displaying the `Title` field, so we're binding to unique data, and displaying data in a more human-readable form – we don't expect everyone else to memorize ISBNs. Finally, we bind our data to the drop-down list.

Note that if we'd not included this if *statement, our list would be re-populated on every page refresh, duplicating the existing data in the list. You may want to try this out for yourself to see how it affects the output – simply remove the* if *block, and let the code run each time.*

```
else
{
  DataGrid1.DataSource = WroxAuthorsList.GetAuthorsByBook
                         (DropDownList1.SelectedItem.Value);
  DataGrid1.DataBind();
}
```

In the second part of our `DataGrid` control, we react to a postback by a user, and pass in the `DataSource` attribute for our `DataGrid`. We bind this data source to our grid.

```
  }
}
```

Finally, we close up our file in the usual way.

This chapter isn't meant to be a tutorial in ADO.NET. If you're unsure about this works, please refer back to Chapters 12 and 13 of this book.

Custom Server Controls

ASP.NET pages revolve around the concept of Server Controls. Control-based development is the new 'Big Thing', as you may have gathered by now. In Chapters 14 and 15, we discussed how to use the built-in HTML Server Controls, the ASP.NET Server Controls, and we saw how to create our own User Controls for reuse in our Web Forms. Now we're going to look at what ASP.NET Custom controls are, how they differ from User Controls and Business Objects, and how these are created.

What are Custom Controls?

Custom Controls are very similar to business logic components in their design – they contain classes and are compiled. However, the main difference between a Custom Control and a business logic component is that a Custom Control generates a visible user interface, while a business logic component doesn't. When we place a Server Control on our page, we can see it and hopefully interact with it.

How are Custom Controls Different from User Controls?

Custom Controls inherit from the `System.Web.UI.Control` namespace, and are compiled. These controls can combine the functionality of several other pre-existing Server Controls (in which case they are referred to as **composite controls**), or create new controls from the ground up. They are fully compiled and have no UI code contained in an ASPX page as all rendering is controlled programmatically. They are designed to provide functionality that can be reused across many applications for example, a tree view control for representing file systems or XML file structures. User Controls are simply partial ASP.NET pages that link to our main ASP.NET page. Custom Controls are meant to be more easily reuseable.

> *If you use Visual Studio .NET, you'll notice a difference between these two types of controls. Whereas a user control **does not** display fully in design view, and you can't set properties on this control via the property tab, a custom control **can** be coded to work with Visual Studio .NET so that you see a visual representation of the rendered page at designtime and you are able to make use of the property toolbox to work with the control at designtime.*

How are Custom Controls different from Business Objects?

While a Business Object is designed to hold application logic, such as database connection information, or the code to produce a dataset based on a query, custom controls are designed to produce viewable output. They are compiled to make it easier to deploy components on other systems or applications. They can also inherit from other assemblies and business objects themselves, yet their visual appearance is all coded by hand. A lot of functionality that is taken for granted when working with existing ASP.NET Server Controls, such as the ability for a control to maintain its visual state (known as its viewstate) across a postback has to be coded by hand. This does mean a lot of coding when you get into advanced controls, but it gives the developer a very powerful reusable tool that works the way you want, rather than having to hack about to produce a less-than-ideal solution.

Let's have a go at creating a simple Custom Control, and displaying it in a very simple ASP.NET page.

Try It Out – Our First ASP.NET Custom Control

We're going to create a very simple Custom Control that will output some text to our ASP.NET Web Form.

1. Fire up your editor and enter the following code:

```
using System;
using System.Web.UI;

namespace WroxControls
{
  public class WelcomeControl : Control
  {
    protected override void Render (HtmlTextWriter writer)
    {
      writer.Write("<h2>Welcome to the Wrox Shop - we cater for all your " +
                                      "ASP.NET needs</h2>");
    }
  }
}
```

2. Save this as `MyCustomControl.cs`.

3. Open your editor once again, and enter the following code:

```
Set indir=C:\begaspnet\Ch16\MyCustomControl.cs
Set outdir=c:\begaspnet\bin\MyCustomControl.dll
Set assemblies=System.dll,System.Web.dll

csc /t:library /out:%outdir% %indir% /r:%assemblies%
pause
```

4. Save this file as `CompileMyCustomControl.bat` in your `C:\BegASPNET\Ch16` directory.

5. Run the batch file and you should see the following:

6. Finally, open up your editor once more and enter the following code:

```
<%@ Register TagPrefix="CustomControl" Namespace="WroxControls"
                            Assembly="MyCustomControl" %>

<html>
<head><title>Custom Control Example</title></head>
<body>

   <CustomControl:WelcomeControl runat="server" />

</body>
</html>
```

7. Save this file as `MyCustomControl.aspx`, then view it in your browser:

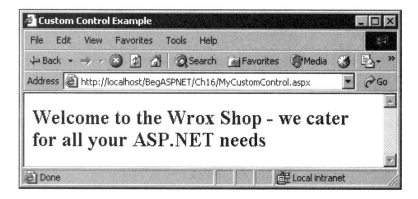

How It Works – The Control

We created a simple control with very limited output to demonstrate custom controls. Let's take a look at how we put it together:

```
using System;
using System.Web.UI;
```

Our `using` statements are included at the beginning of our file as usual.

```
namespace WroxControls
{
```

Our namespace declaration comes next; we're calling our namespace `WroxControls`.

```
   public class WelcomeControl : Control
   {
```

Our next line creates a class called `WelcomeControl`. We are then inheriting from the `Control` class of the `System.Web.UI` namespace.

This is an important part of Custom Control development, because all Custom Controls must inherit from this namespace. This class provides a lot of basic functionality behind the scenes that any control needs in order to work.

```
protected override void Render (HtmlTextWriter writer)
{
```

We're creating one method in our class. There are a couple of new terms in here, which you're probably unfamiliar with. There is a method in the `Control` class called `Render`. What we're doing here is altering how that method works by **overriding** its functionality with our own functionality. While we don't want to go too far into the world of C# programming here, you need to know that this statement is required to provide the output we specify, instead of the default output from the `Control` class. We will be using an `HtmlTextWriter` to display the output of our control.

The only difference between this example and the previous one is that the control is rendering (writing) the text directly while our previous tests required a `label` control to return the text of our components. This means our controls have the ability to be used by Windows Forms applications, as well as Web Forms applications.

```
writer.Write("<h2>Welcome to the Wrox Shop - " +
             "we cater for all your ASP.NET needs </h2>");
```

We call the `Write` method of our `HtmlTextWriter` to produce output on our page. In this case it is a simple piece of H2-style HTML text.

```
        }
    }
}
```

We finish off our control by closing the function, the class, and the namespace.

The Batch File

```
Set indir=C:\begaspnet\Ch16\MyCustomControl.cs
Set outdir=c:\begaspnet\bin\MyCustomControl.dll
Set assemblies=System.dll,System.Web.dll

csc /t:library /out:%outdir% %indir% /r:%assemblies%
pause
```

In a similar way to the previous make files, we set aliases for our input and output directories, as well as for the assemblies we need to reference to complete the compilation. We compile the file in the same way as before using the `csc` command.

The ASPX page

```
<%@ Register TagPrefix="CustomControl" Namespace="WroxControls"
                     Assembly=" MyCustomControl " %>
```

Our first line is where we reference our control so that our page knows where to look. We set a
TagPrefix as we did with our User Controls; however, we do not set a TagName – we'll see why in a
moment. We specify that the namespace we're using is the WroxControls namespace, and that we're
using the MyCustomControl assembly.

```
<html>
<head><title>Custom Control Example</title></head>
<body>

  <CustomControl:WelcomeControl runat="server" />

</body>
</html>
```

The last few lines on our page include one line of interest. This is where we place our control on the
page. We call it by the TagPrefix we set earlier, followed by the class name we specified in the
control. We specify a runat="server" attribute and close the tag. Hey presto! – We've just used our
first Custom Control.

How It All Fits Together

We're going to use one last example to incorporate the concepts we've learned over the course of these
two chapters. We'll be using quite a few files from the previous chapter in here, so make sure the
following files are available in your application directory (they're available from www.wrox.com):

```
featuredbooks.ascx
header_CB.ascx
header_CB.vb
logo.gif
style.css
```

All we'll be working on here is an ASPX page. Let's take a look at the code, before moving on to look at
the output.

Try It Out – Putting it all Together – The Componentized Wrox Shop Site

This example incorporates some User Controls, some codebehind, a business object, and a Custom
Control – quite a handful, but not terribly complicated – as we'll see. We're going to show how the
reusable elements we've coded up in the last two chapters can be 'plugged' together to form a small site of
sorts. The actual page that combines all of these elements is fairly small and simple, yet the components it's
referring to all provide different types of functionality. Here's a list of the files we'll be using:

Section	Files
Frontend	`WroxShop.aspx`
Header control	`Header_CB.ascx` and the associated code-behind file, `Header_CB.cs`; the header User control also makes use of an image file called `logo.gif`
Welcome message	`MyCustomControl.dll` – our custom Server control
Featured books list	`FeaturedBooks.ascx` – another User Control
Author list	`WroxAuthors.dll` – our component that contains data-access functionality

Let's start putting it together:

1. Enter the following code and save it as `WroxShop.aspx` in your application directory:

```
<%@ Page Language="c#" src="WroxAuthorsCB.cs" Inherits="WroxAuthorsCB"%>
<%@ Register TagPrefix="WroxUC" TagName="Header" Src="header_CB.ascx" %>
<%@ Register TagPrefix="WroxUC" TagName="FeaturedBooks" Src="FeaturedBooks.ascx"
%>
<%@ Register TagPrefix="CustomControl" Namespace="WroxControls"
Assembly="MyCustomControl" %>

<html>
<head>
  <title>Welcome to the Wrox Shop</title>
  <link rel="stylesheet" type="text/css" href="style.css">
</head>

<body>
  <form runat="server" method="post">
    <WroxUC:Header id="MyHeader" runat="Server" /><br />
    <CustomControl:WelcomeControl runat="server" />
    <table>
      <tr>
        <td width="70%" valign="top">
          This is the Wrox Shop, where you can find out more about
          Wrox books. The links on the left take you to a page on
          the Wrox site where you can find out more details about
          each title.<br /><br />


          Select a book to find out more: <br /> <br />

          <p>
            <asp:DropDownList id="DropDownList1" runat="server">
            </asp:DropDownList>
            <asp:Button id="Button1" runat="server" Text="Submit">
```

```
          </asp:Button>
        </p>
        <p>
          <asp:DataGrid id="DataGrid1" runat="server"
            Font-Name="Verdana,arial,helvetica"
            Font-Size="10pt"
            CellSpacing="2"
            CellPadding="2"
            HeaderStyle-BackColor="silver">
          </asp:DataGrid>
        </p>

      </td>
      <td width="30%" valign="top">
        <WroxUC:FeaturedBooks id="MyFeaturedBooks" runat="server" />
      </td>
    </tr>
  </table>


  </form>
</body>
</html>
```

2. Save the file, then open up your editor one last time and enter the following code:

```csharp
using System;
using System.Web.UI;
using System.Web.UI.WebControls;
using WroxComponents;

public class WroxAuthorsCB : Page
{
    public DropDownList DropDownList1;
    public Button Button1;
    public DataGrid DataGrid1;

  public void Page_Load(object Sender, EventArgs e)
  {
    string ConnectString = "provider=Microsoft.Jet.OLEDB.4.0;data source=" +
                              "C:\\BegASPNET\\Ch16\\WroxShop.mdb";

    WroxAuthors WroxAuthorsList = new WroxAuthors(ConnectString);

    if (!(Page.IsPostBack))
    {
      DropDownList1.DataSource = WroxAuthorsList.GetBooks();
      DropDownList1.DataValueField = "ISBN";
      DropDownList1.DataTextField = "Title";
      DropDownList1.DataBind();
    }
    else
    {
      DataGrid1.DataSource = WroxAuthorsList.GetAuthorsByBook
        (DropDownList1.SelectedItem.Value);
      DataGrid1.DataBind();
    }
  }
}
```

3. Save this file as `WroxShopCB.cs` in the same directory, then view `WroxShop.aspx` in your browser:

How It Works – The ASPX page

We've basically combined a lot of the components we've developed over the course of these two chapters and displayed them on one page. Since we've already looked at how these components worked, we'll not be going into too much detail here. Let's dive in quickly:

```
<%@ Page Language="c#" src="WroxAuthorsCB.cs" Inherits="WroxAuthorsCB"%>
<%@ Register TagPrefix="WroxUC" TagName="Header" Src="header_CB.ascx" %>
<%@ Register TagPrefix="WroxUC" TagName="FeaturedBooks"
                                      Src="FeaturedBooks.ascx" %>
<%@ Register TagPrefix="CustomControl" Namespace="WroxControls"
                                      Assembly="MyCustomControl" %>
```

The top of our file references our code-behind file, our header control, our featured books control, and our custom welcome message control.

```
<html>
<head>
  <title>Welcome to the Wrox Shop</title>
  <link rel="stylesheet" type="text/css" href="style.css">
</head>

<body>
```

We have some HTML that references a style sheet to provide some consistency in presentation.

```
<form runat="server" method="post">
  <WroxUC:Header id="MyHeader" runat="Server" /><br />
  <CustomControl:WelcomeControl runat="server" />
```

We include two controls – our header control, and our welcome message Custom Control, at the top of our page.

```
<table>
    <tr>
      <td width="70%" valign="top">
        This is the Wrox Shop, where you can find out more about
        Wrox books. The links on the left take you to a page on
        the Wrox site where you can find out more details about
        each title.<br /><br />
```

The next part of our page is similar to the page we used to display our FeaturedBooks.ascx User Control. The first cell in the table is actually the same as before, pretty much, then we add the code we used with our WroxAuthors component, so we can find out who wrote on each book.

```
        Select a book to find out more: <br /> <br />

      <p>
        <asp:DropDownList id="DropDownList1"
                             runat="server"></asp:DropDownList>
        <asp:Button id="Button1" runat="server"
                           Text="Submit"></asp:Button>
      </p>
      <p>
        <asp:DataGrid id="DataGrid1" runat="server"
          Font-Name="Verdana,arial,helvetica"
          Font-Size="10pt"
          CellSpacing="2"
          CellPadding="2"
          HeaderStyle-BackColor="silver">
        </asp:DataGrid>
      </p>
    </td>
```

The DataGrid appears exactly the same as earlier in the chapter, with some simple styling applied.

```
      <td width="30%" valign="top">
        <WroxUC:FeaturedBooks id="MyFeaturedBooks" runat="server" />
      </td>
    </tr>
</table>
```

Our second table cell holds our FeaturedBooks User Control, which we saw in the previous chapter.

Finally we finish off our ASP.NET page with some HTML closing tags.

The Code-Behind file

A very quick look through the codebehind again doesn't reveal anything too new – in fact, it's very similar to the codebehind in the previous example:

```
using System;
using System.Web.UI;
using System.Web.UI.WebControls;
using WroxComponents;
```

We import all of our namespaces.

```
public class WroxAuthorsCB : Page
{
    public DropDownList DropDownList1;
    public Button Button1;
    public DataGrid DataGrid1;
```

We create our class, and declare some public variables.

```
    public void Page_Load(object Sender, EventArgs e)
    {
        string ConnectString = "provider=Microsoft.Jet.OLEDB.4.0;data source=" +
                "C:\\BegASPNET\\Ch16\\WroxShop.mdb";

        WroxAuthors WroxAuthorsList = new WroxAuthors(ConnectString);
```

We create the connection string for our database, and instantiate a new instance of our `WroxAuthors` class, passing in the connection string.

```
        if (!(Page.IsPostBack))
        {
          DropDownList1.DataSource = WroxAuthorsList.GetBooks();
          DropDownList1.DataValueField="ISBN";
          DropDownList1.DataTextField="Title";
          DropDownList1.DataBind();
        }
        else
        {
          DataGrid1.DataSource = WroxAuthorsList.GetAuthorsByBook
            (DropDownList1.SelectedItem.Value);
          DataGrid1.DataBind();
        }
```

In the same way as we did earlier, we specify the fields to be bound to our `DropDownList`, so that the list of books is displayed as intended.

```
  }
}
```

Finally, we close up the class, and we're done!

Summary

In this chapter we have continued the thread from the previous one, and discussed creating .NET Assemblies that can be used to store classes that handle business logic, or Custom Server Control code. We've looked at:

❑   How to compile a .NET assembly

❑   How to use classes contained in a compiled assembly on a page

❑   How to encapsulate business logic into a compiled component

❑   How to use User Controls, code-behind, business objects, and Custom Controls on the same page

We've not gone into too much detail with regard to Custom Controls, since this is a vast and complex area. If you're serious about this field and would like to know more, you might like to read *Professional ASP.NET Server Controls*, ISBN: 1-86100-564-4.

Exercises

1. Explain the benefits of using Components, and what sorts of things we should encapsulate in a .NET assembly. When should we use compiled `.dll`s instead of code-behind files and User Controls?

2. What is business logic? Give an example of the sort of code that can be described as business logic, and talk about how this code can be reused elsewhere.

3. Create a new component that converts from imperial units to metric and back again. You'll need four methods: Celsius to Fahrenheit temperatures, Fahrenheit to Celsius, Kilometers to Miles, and Miles to Kilometers. You'll need the following data:

❑   Fahrenheit temperature = Celsius temperature * (9/5) + 32

❑   Celsius temperature = (Fahrenheit temperature - 32) * (5/9)

❑   1 Mile = 1.6093 Kilometers (to 4 decimal places)

❑   1 Kilometer = 0.6214 Miles (to 4 decimal places)

4. Create an ASP.NET page that uses this functionality. One example might be a page about holiday destinations. Users in other countries might want to know distances in metric instead of imperial, or temperatures in Celsius, rather than Fahrenheit.

5. Additionally, you might want to access this functionality from a completely different type of site, for example, one that has some scientific purpose that requires unit conversion, a route planner that will provide results in both miles or kilometers, or a weather site that needs to provide today's temperatures in both Celsius and Fahrenheit. A completely different situation would be a cookery site that displayed instructions for cooking a meal in an oven set to either Celsius or Fahrenheit temperatures.

Debugging and Error Handling

One of the fundamental truths of organized systems is that the more complex they become, the more likely they are to go wrong. While most of the examples we've looked at so far in this book have been quite simple, the principles behind OOP and the .NET Framework are aimed at making it easier for you to build larger and more complex systems.

Once you have planned and created your program, the steps involved in ensuring that your code runs smoothly at all times can be broken down into two main categories:

❑   **Debugging** – No matter how much painstaking attention to detail we give to our code, rest assured that mistakes will occur. We can minimize the ill effects of those mistakes by identifying the portions of our code that are most prone to errors and by adhering to good coding practices that facilitate troubleshooting.

❑   **Error Handling** – Even if we produce flawless code, there is no guarantee that everything will operate smoothly at run time. There is always the potential for many things to go wrong. Problems may occur in the operating environment, such as network connection failures or power failures. There may be problems with unexpected data types or the data may not have been properly prepared. Third-party programs may return unexpected data. Good programming practices dictate that we anticipate as many problems as possible before they occur so that we may apply a graceful solution.

This chapter will provide information to help you identify problems, fix them, and prevent them from occurring in future. Specifically, we'll look at the following topics:

❑   Good coding practices

❑   What can go wrong: the different types of errors that can occur

❑   Locating errors in the page

❑   Tracing

❑   Exceptions

❑ Handling Exceptions

❑ Handling errors

❑ Notifying and logging any errors that have occurred

A Few Good Habits

Whether you're an expert developer or a beginner, you can significantly reduce the probability of an error occurring by adopting some very straightforward habits. Finding an error in your application is not a cause for panic – it is an indication that an effective error handling strategy is needed. This chapter will provide you with the information you need to design and implement an effective error handling strategy.

Before we go into detail about the different kinds of errors that may afflict your beautiful code, let's talk about how you may reduce the time and effort required to identify and fix an error.

❑ **Understand your code** – The most important factor in finding a cause for an error is to understand the code. Make clean distinctions in your code between server- and client-side functionality. Compartmentalize presentation, business, and data layers. Adopt and consistently use naming conventions. Write headers for methods that explicitly state their purpose. Give variables meaningful names. These habits will go along way to producing self-documenting code. If sections or routines in your code are still unclear after these practices have been implemented then document some more. Clear and concise code will be an invaluable asset when it is time to locate where, and understand why, an error has occurred.

❑ **Identify where it might break** – Before even loading the page and testing its functionality, identify the potential problem areas. For instance, say you have developed a page that communicates with a database and pulls a set of records. You must create a connection to the database, formulate a query, and then execute that query to retrieve the records. Connecting to the database or the execution of the query may throw an error. We will discuss different kinds of errors later in this chapter, which will assist you in looking out for potential problems at an early stage.

❑ **Amend identified error conditions** – Once you have identified areas that could break within your page, the next step is to make sure the page is as stable as possible under the conditions that could lead to an error. Remember the old adage, 'an ounce of prevention is worth a pound of cure'.

So what can we learn from the above three steps? Mistakes in your code are not the end of the world. What matters is how quickly you can identify them and provide a fix. With that in mind, let's start with a look at the types of habits that we should cultivate.

Good Coding Practice

It may not be feasible to expect perfect, totally error-free programs, but there are some precautions we can take to reduce or avoid the most common mistakes.

Format your Code

This is quite an obvious and straightforward step. Although it won't ensure an error free program, this will really help to improve the readability of your code, either for yourself or for others. Formatting your code will help you to find many kinds of errors more quickly. The following example lays out some code, we will be using later, in two different ways. See the difference for yourself:

```
<html>
<head>
<title>Syntax Error Example </title>
</head>
<body>
<form method="post" action="sytntaxerror.aspx" runat="server">
<asp:TextBox id="txtQuantity" runat="server" />
</form>
</body>
</html>

<html>
  <head>
   <title>Syntax Error Example </title>
  </head>
  <body>
    <form method="post" action="sytntaxerror.aspx" runat="server">
    <asp:TetBox id="txtQuantity" runat="server" />
    </form>
  </body>
</html>
```

Structure your Code

Use functions in your code to implement specific tasks. This is even more important for tasks that are used several times in your applications. For instance, consider a situation when you need to format the display of a date. The database might store a date in the form "CCYYMMDD", whereas you need to display it on the screen as "MM/DD/CCYY". You could then create a function, such as the one shown below:

```
public string FormatDate(string CCYYMMDD)
{
  int intYear, intMonth, intDay;
  intYear = left(CCYYMMDD,4);
  intMonth = mid(CCYYMMDD,5,2);
  intDay = right(CCYYMMDD,2);
  return (Cstr(intMonth) &"/"& Cstr(intDay) &"/"& Cstr(intYear));
}
```

If you need to format the display of your date at different places in your program, you can simply call this function to format the display, rather than writing the whole process over and over again. Not only does this save us time; if there's an error in the code (or we need to change it) we only need to change our code once.

Comment your Code

This is another effective and simple technique. This technique also aids readability of the code. Believe me, code you have written will look extremely confusing, even to you, after a period of time (maybe a few weeks or months). Writing comments in your code will help you remember exactly what your code is doing, which will be invaluable when you try to debug the it after a period of time. Look again at the method from the section above:

```
//****************************************************************************
public string FormatDate(string CCYYMMDD)
//*Purpose: convert date from CCYYMMDD format to MM/DD/CCYY format
//*Input:    String   date in the format CCYYMMDD
//*Returns: String   string that represents a date in the format MM/DD/CCYY
//****************************************************************************
{
  int intYear, intMonth, intDay;
  intYear = left(CCYYMMDD,4);
  intMonth = mid(CCYYMMDD,5,2);
  intDay = right(CCYYMMDD,2);
  return (Cstr(intMonth) &"/"& Cstr(intDay) &"/"& Cstr(intYear));
}
```

The example above may seem excessive for such a little method. But the small investment in time that it takes to adequately comment your code will pay huge dividends when it is time to revisit that code. Also, habits such as writing method headers and providing general comments facilitate the reuse of code.

Try to Break your Code

This can be a more difficult task than expected. It is often difficult for the developer of an application to anticipate all the unusual things a user might attempt to do with the application. So when it is time to test your application try to think like a user with little or no computer savvy. We can break down our testing strategy into two main approaches:

❑ **Being nice to your program** – Supply your program with legal values, or values that your program is designed to expect and handle. For instance, if your program contains an age field, supply only numbers, not letters. Watch how your program behaves – does it respond as you expect it to with the legal values you're supplying it?

❑ **Try to break your program** – This is the fun part. Supply your program with illegal values. For instance, provide string values where integers are expected. This ensures that your program handles all illegal values appropriately. Depending upon the kind of data you are expecting in your program, you might have to do anything from a simple numeric or alphabetic check to a validity check (such as inserting invalid dates into a date field). If your program spans several pages then surf to some of the pages out of the expected sequence.

All these techniques can be used to help standardize and improve the readability of your code. A great many basic errors can be avoided in this way. However, even if you do apply all these suggestions, your code still can't be guaranteed bug-free. Let's take a look at some of the specific errors that may plague us.

How and from where do Errors Arise?

The errors that occur in an ASP.NET page can be grouped into four categories, as given below:

❑ **Parser errors** – These occur because of incorrect syntax, or bad grammar, within the ASP.NET page.

❑ **Compilation errors** – These are also syntax errors, but they occur when using statements that are not recognized by the language compiler, rather than ASP.NET itself. For example, using If (capital 'I') instead of if, or not providing a closing bracket to a for loop, will result in a compilation error. The difference between the parser error and compilation error is that the parser error occurs when there is a syntax error in the ASP.NET page, whereas the compilation error occurs when there is a syntax error within the C#, VB.NET, or JScript.NET code block.

❑ **Configuration Errors** – These occur because of the incorrect syntax, or structure, of a configuration file. In a nutshell, an ASP.NET configuration file is a text file, in XML format containing a hierarchical structure that stores application-wide configuration settings. There can be one configuration file for every application on your web server. The web configuration files are named web.config. We'll be discussing web.config files, in Chapter 19, so we won't delve into them any further until then.

❑ **Run-time errors** – As the name implies, these are errors that are not detected during compilation or parsing, but are caught during execution. For example, when the user enters letters into a field expecting numbers, and your program assigns the user entry to an integer variable, you will get a run-time error when the code tries to execute.

Now let's take a look at some specific examples that fall into the above categories.

Syntax Errors

As the name suggests, this type of error occurs when there is a problem in the syntax of the code. These types of errors fall under the parser and compilation error categories. This will, most likely, be the first type of error that you'll encounter when developing ASP.NET pages. It might occur for one of the following reasons:

❑ A typo or bad grammar in the code syntax. For example, instead of typing <asp:textbox> for creating a text boxcontrol in your page, you type <asp:textbx>. The browser shows an error.

❑ Incorrect code syntax. For instance, when creating a text boxcontrol, we might forget to close the tag as shown below:

```
<asp:TextBox id="txtName" runat="server">
```

When it should actually be:

```
<asp:TextBox id="txtName" runat="server" />
```

❑ Combining or splitting keywords between languages. This is an error that I make quite a lot. If you've been coding in another language and come back to coding in C# you might forget brackets, or type keywords in the wrong case.

677

❑ **Not closing a construct properly.** This error occurs if we forget to close a construct, such as a `for` loop, or a nested `if` statement. Take a look at this, for example:

```
if condition1 {
 //do this
}
else condition2 {
   //do this
   if condition2a {
    //do this
   }
   else {
   //do this
}
```

Did you catch the error in the above code? We're missing a close-bracket. Imagine how difficult it would be to spot this if we had the above code block set amongst hundreds of other lines of code.

Try It Out – Syntax Error

1. Use your favorite editor to type the following lines of code. Let's make a spelling mistake (or typo) when creating the textbox control, as shown below:

```
<html>
  <head>
    <title>Syntax Error Example </title>
  </head>
  <body>
    <form method="post" action="sytntaxerror.aspx" runat="server">
    <asp:TetBox id="txtQuantity" runat="server" />
    </form>
  </body>
</html>
```

2. Save this file as `syntaxerror.aspx` and load the file using a browser. We're expecting to see a textbox in the browser, as shown in the figure below:

But what we actually see is:

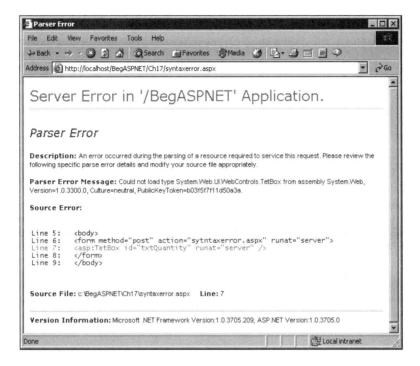

How It Works

As the error message clearly states, the ASP.NET parser points to Line 7, and asks us to check the details. When we look through the line, we can see that we have a spelling mistake: Tetbox, which should, of course, be TextBox. If you correct the spelling, and re-run the code, you'll get the expected result.

Errors of this kind are very common, and are usually quick and easy to fix, since the error message provides a detailed breakdown of the error and the line on which it occurs.

Logical Errors

The second type of error is the 'Logical Error', and unfortunately, they are relatively difficult to find and fix. These types of errors will become apparent during run time. As the name implies, this kind of error occurs due to a mistake in the programming logic. The following are some of the more common reasons for this type of error:

❑ **Division by zero** – This is an infamous error that has been around since the days of valve-based computers. This error occurs when your program ends up dividing a number by zero. But why in the world are we going to divide a number by zero? In most cases, this occurs because the program divides a number by an integer that should contain a non-zero number, but for some reason, the variable contains a zero.

❏ **Type mismatch** – Type mismatch errors occur when you try to work with incompatible data types, and inadvertently try to add a string to a number, or store a string in a date data type. It is possible to avoid this error by explicitly converting the data type of a value before operating on it. We will talk about variable data type conversion later in this chapter.

❏ **Incorrect output** – This type of error occurs when you use a function that returns a different output from that which you are expecting in your program.

❏ **Use of a non-existent object** – This type of error occurs when you try to use an object that was never created, or an attempt to create the object failed.

❏ **Mistaken assumptions** – This is another common mistake that we make, which could be corrected during the testing phase (if one exists). This type of error occurs when the programmer uses an incorrect assumption in the program. For instance, a program that adds withdrawal amounts to a current balance, instead of subtracting them.

❏ **Processing invalid data** – This is type of error occurs when the program is accepting invalid data. An example of this would be a library checkout program that accepts a book's return date as February 29th, 2003, in which case, you may not have to return the book for a while!

While this is far from being an exhaustive list of possible logical errors, it should give you a feel for what to look out for when testing your code.

Try It Out – Generate a Run Time Error

1. Enter the following code:

```csharp
<%@ Page Language="c#" Debug="true" %>
<script Language="c#" runat="server">
  void CompleteOrder(object sender, EventArgs e)
  {
    if (txtQuantity.Text != "")
    {
      if (Convert.ToInt32(txtQuantity.Text) == 0)
      {
        lblOrderConfirm.Text = "Please provide a Quantity greater than 0.";
      }
      else if (Convert.ToInt32(txtQuantity.Text) > 0)
      {
        lblOrderConfirm.Text = "Order Successfully placed.";
      }
    }
    else
    {
      lblOrderConfirm.Text = "Please provide an Order Quantity.";
    }
  }
</script>
<html>
  <head>
    <title>Manual Trapping Example</title>
  </head>
```

```
<body>
  <form method="post" action="manualtrapping.aspx" runat="server">
    <asp:Label text="Order Quantity" runat="server" />
    <asp:TextBox id="txtQuantity" runat="server" />
    <br />
    <asp:Button id="btnComplete_Order" Text="Complete Order"
                                       onclick="CompleteOrder"
                                       runat="server"/>
    <br />
  <asp:Label id="lblOrderConfirm" runat="server"/>
  </form>
</body>
</html>
```

2. Save the file as runtimeError.aspx.

3. View the runtimeError.aspx file using the browser. Provide a non-numeric value to the order quantity textbox, and click the **Complete Order** button. The following figure shows the result:

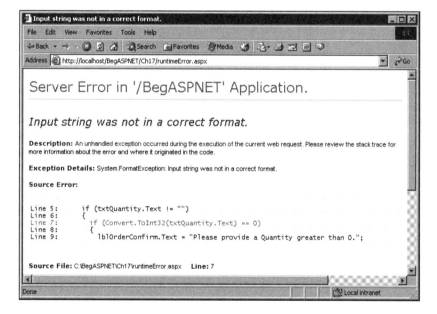

How It Works

Our control block validates input for null values and for numeric values that are equal to or less than zero. It does not validate input for other nonnumeric input values. The code generated a run-time error when the Convert function tried to convert a non-numeric entry to an integer field.

Let's take a closer look at validating user input.

Trapping Invalid Data

Testing your code by supplying both legal and illegal values is necessary for the proper functioning of your program. Your program should return expected results when provided with legal values, and handle errors when supplied with illegal values. In this section, we'll talk about ways to handle the illegal values supplied to your program. We have two objectives here:

❑ Prevent the occurrence of errors that may leave you with many disgruntled users

❑ Prevent your program from accepting and using illegal values

There are two main techniques that we can use to fulfill these objectives: manual trapping and validation.

Manual Trapping

When building our application we could create error traps to catch illegal values before they get into the page processing, where they might halt the execution of the page or provide invalid results. How do we block illegal values from sneaking in to page processing? Let's develop a page that accepts order quantity from the user.

Try It Out – Catching Illegal Values

1. Type the following code into your editor:

```
<%@ Page Language="c#" Debug="true" %>
<script Language="c#" runat="server">
  void CompleteOrder(object sender, EventArgs e)
  {
    if (txtQuantity.Text != "")
    {
      if (!(Char.IsNumber(txtQuantity.Text,0)))
      {
        if (txtQuantity.Text.Substring(0,1) != "-")
        {
          lblOrderConfirm.Text =
                    "Please provide only numbers in Quantity field.";
        }
        else
        {
          lblOrderConfirm.Text =
                    "Please provide a Quantity greater than 0.";
        }
      }
      else if (Convert.ToInt32(txtQuantity.Text) == 0)
      {
        lblOrderConfirm.Text = "Please provide a Quantity greater than 0.";
      }
      else if (Convert.ToInt32(txtQuantity.Text) > 0)
      {
        lblOrderConfirm.Text = "Order Successfully placed.";
      }
    }
  }
```

```
      else
      {
          lblOrderConfirm.Text = "Please provide an Order Quantity.";
      }
  }
  </script>

  <html>
    <head>
      <title>Manual Trapping Example</title>
    </head>
    <body>
      <form method="post" action="manualtrapping.aspx" runat="server">
        <asp:Label text="Order Quantity" runat="server" />
        <asp:TextBox id="txtQuantity" runat="server" />
        <br />
        <asp:Button id="btnComplete_Order" Text="Complete Order"
                                    onclick="CompleteOrder"
                                    runat="server"/>
        <br />
        <asp:Label id="lblOrderConfirm" runat="server"/>
      </form>
    </body>
  </html>
```

2. Save the file as `manualTrapping.aspx`.

3. Now load this file using your browser. The following figure shows the result of providing an order quantity of `10`:

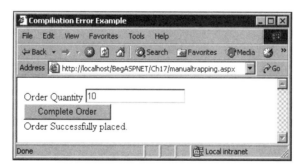

Try supplying different values to the order quantity textbox and verify if the page behaves as expected.

How It Works

First point to notice is that we have added an extra directive to our page calls:

```
<%@ Page language="C#" Debug="true" %>
```

This will enable us to view detailed error messages throughout the course of the chapter. We will discuss how it works within the course of this chapter.

683

We are using two label controls, one textbox control, and one button control. The first label control is the label for the order quantity textbox:

```
<asp:Label text="Order Quantity" runat="server" />
```

The second label control is to display the message "lblOrderConfirm" after processing the order:

```
<asp:Label id="lblOrderConfirm" runat="server"/>
```

The textbox accepts an entry from the user for the order quantity:

```
<asp:TextBox id="txtQuantity" runat="server" />
```

The button calls the CompleteOrder procedure when clicked:

```
<asp:Button id="btnComplete_Order" Text="Complete Order"
        onclick="CompleteOrder"
        runat="server"/>
```

Within the CompleteOrder function, we create a series of checks to avoid illegal values. First we check for no entry to the textbox:

```
if (txtQuantity.Text != "")
{
  ...
else
{
  lblOrderConfirm.Text = "Please provide an Order Quantity.";
}
```

which is followed by the numeric check and checks to ensure the quantity is greater than zero:

```
if (!(Char.IsNumber(txtQuantity.Text,0)))
{
  if (txtQuantity.Text.Substring(0,1) != "-")
  {
    lblOrderConfirm.Text =
                "Please provide only numbers in Quantity field.";
  }
  else
  {
    lblOrderConfirm.Text =
                      "Please provide a Quantity greater than 0.";
  }
}
else if (Convert.ToInt32(txtQuantity.Text) == 0)
{
  lblOrderConfirm.Text = "Please provide a Quantity greater than 0.";
}
```

Finally, there is code to accept the order:

```
else if (Convert.ToInt32(txtQuantity.Text) > 0)
{
  lblOrderConfirm.Text = "Order Successfully placed.";
}
}
```

Using Validation Controls

The second technique is to use one or more of the different validation controls provided by ASP.NET. (Refer back to Chapter 14 for a detailed discussion about using validation controls.)

Validation controls are used to validate user input. For instance, you could use the `RequiredFieldValidator` control to ensure that users enter a value to a textbox. By doing this, you could avoid run-time errors that occur because of your program using a `null`, while it is expecting an entry from the user.

By using one of the many validation controls provided by ASP.NET, which are listed below, you could present the users with a message informing them about the incorrect value supplied, and the value your program is expecting. This prevents the program from processing an illegal value, and developing an error.

Let's look at an example to demonstrate how to use these controls. In the following *Try It Out*, we'll use the `RequiredFieldValidator` to ensure that the user provides a value for the `Order Quantity` field:

Try It Out – Using RequiredFieldValidator

1. Open `manualtrapping.aspx` from the previous exercise, and make the following changes to second half of it:

```
<form method="post" action="manualtrapping.aspx" runat="server">
    <asp:Label text="Order Quantity" runat="server" />
    <asp:TextBox id="txtQuantity" runat="server" />
    <asp:RequiredFieldValidator ControlToValidate="txtQuantity"
        runat="server"
        ErrorMessage="Please enter a value in the Order Quantity Field">
    </asp:RequiredFieldValidator>
    <br />
    <asp:Button id="btnComplete_Order" Text="Complete Order"
                                    onclick="CompleteOrder"
                                    runat="server"/>
    <br />
    <asp:Label id="lblOrderConfirm" runat="server"/>
</form>
```

2. Save this file as `usingvalidationcontrol.aspx`.

3. Use your browser to open `usingvalidationcontrol.aspx`. When you try to complete the order without entering anything, you're presented with the following request:

How It Works

In this example, we have used a `RequiredFieldValidator` control. The `ControlToValidate` property is used to specify the control we are validating:

```
<asp:RequiredFieldValidator ControlToValidate="txtQuantity" runat="server"
```

In this case, we are validating the order quantity textbox. The `ErrorMessage` property is used to provide an error message when the user does not enter a value to the order quantity field:

```
ErrorMessage="Please enter a value in the Order Quantity Field">
```

System Errors

These are errors that are generated by ASP.NET itself. They may be due to malfunctioning code, a bug in ASP.NET, or even one in the Common Language Runtime. Although you could find this type of error, it is usually not possible to fix the problem – particularly if it is an ASP.NET or CLR error.

Other errors that can be placed in this category are those that arise due to the failure of a web server or component, a hardware failure, or a lack of server memory.

When an error does occur in an ASP.NET page, the details about the error are sent to the client. Don't worry though, ASP.NET by default shows detailed error information only to a **local client**.

A local client is a client running on the same machine as the web server. For instance, if you create the ASP.NET examples from this book on a machine running a web server, and access them using a browser on the same machine, then the browser is a local client.

The fact that ASP.NET sends detailed information about errors to local clients is actually very helpful to the developer during the development phase.

Finding Errors

OK, so we adopted the good coding practices listed earlier in our program, and used different techniques to trap the invalid data, now why are we still talking about finding errors? Even after taking the above precautions, our program might still end up in an error page. It could be because we did not cover all possible error scenarios in our testing, (point the fingers at the testers), or another program did not behave as expected (refer it to the other team) or worse, the server administrators did not set up the server right (blame it on the network administrators). However well you plan ahead, it is always difficult, if not impossible, to catch every bug in advance. So what do we do if our well-constructed code still doesn't work? We will discuss this topic next.

Let's go back to the local client scenario. ASP.NET displays a **callstack** when a run-time error occurs. What is a call-stack? A call-stack contains a series of procedure calls that lead up to an error. Before you do this, we suggest you delete (or rename) any `web.config` files residing with your samples, as otherwise all errors generated will be handled by this file.

Let's create a page that leads up to a run-time error.

Try It Out – Viewing the Call-Stack

1. Type in the following code:

```
<%@ Page Language="c#" Debug="true" %>
<script language="c#" runat="server">
  void CreateRunTimeError()
  {
    int[] array = new int[5];
    int arrayIndex = 5;
    array[arrayIndex] = 5;

    Response.Write("This should never be reached");
  }
</script>

<%
  CreateRunTimeError();
%>
```

2. Save this file as `callstack.aspx`.

3. Open this file in your browser. You should see something like the following (as long as you have deleted `web.config`):

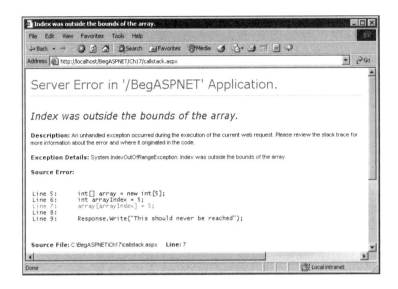

How It Works

In the block of code we entered, we set up an array of five elements, numbered from 0 to 4, and tried to access an element with the number 5, that is an element beyond the end of the array:

```
int[] array = new int[5];
int arrayIndex = 5;
array[arrayIndex] = 5;
```

When we ran this code, an error was generated when the program tried to execute an integer data type containing a string. We were presented with the error page above. The error page contains different sections, such as **Exception Details** (we'll discuss exceptions shortly), **Source Error**, **Stack Trace** and so on. The **Stack Trace** contains the callstack, which says that the value we are trying to assign to an integer variable is not valid. If you look through the callstack, you can see the series of procedures that led to the exception.

The information provided under the **Source Error** section is useful in locating the line in which the error occurred. The display of this information is controlled by the **Debug mode**.

Debug mode

If `Debug` mode is enabled, then the **Source Error** section of the error message is displayed as part of the error message, which pinpoints the location in the code that created the error. If `Debug` mode is disabled, then the **Source Error** section is not displayed.

Now the question is: where and how can you set the value to `Debug` mode?

It can be set in two different places. The first place should be familiar as we have used it twice already within this chapter. You can set it at every page within the `Page` directive, as shown:

```
<%@ Page Debug="true" %>

<%@ Page Debug="false" %>
```

If the Debug mode is set like this, at the page level, the setting is applied **only** to that specific page. (That was easy).

Let's return to our previous example, and disable the Debug mode at the page level:

Try It Out – Disable the Debug Mode

1. Open the callstack.aspx file, and change the following line at the top of the page:

```
<%@ Page Language="c#" Debug="false" %>
```

2. Save the file as debugmode.aspx, and access the page using the browser. You will see an error page that looks like the one below:

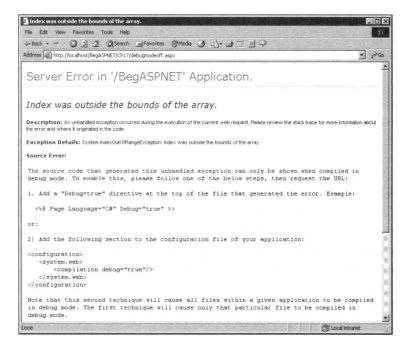

How It Works

We disabled the Debug mode in our callstack.aspx by adding the following line at the top of the page:

```
<%@ Page Language="c#" Debug="false" %>
```

Then when we ran our new file in the browser, we saw a new error message. In this error message, under the **Source Error** section, there are instructions to enable the Debug mode for displaying the source code that generated the exception, but the actual source code is not there.

As mentioned a moment ago, there are two ways to set the Debug mode. The second way is to set it at the **application level**, using the <compilation> configuration section in the configuration file (see Chapter 19).

Setting the debug mode at the application level will display the **Source Error** section in the error message for all the files under the application. This has a performance overhead though, so before moving your application to a production environment, make sure you disable the Debug mode.

Tracing

When developing an application, we execute the page at different levels of that development, and for effective debugging we always need to see the values assigned to variables and the state of different conditional constructs at different stages of execution. In earlier versions of ASP, developers used the ubiquitous Response.Write statement to display this information. The downside of doing this is that when completing the application development, the developer has to go to every page, and either comment, or remove, the Response.Write statements they created for testing purposes. ASP.NET, however, provides a new feature to bypass all of this, using the Trace capability.

The tracing feature provides a range of information about the page, including request time, performance data, server variables, and most importantly, any message added by the developers. It is disabled by default. Similar to the Debug mode, tracing can be either enabled or disabled at either the page or application level. We'll now discuss these levels, and tracing itself, in more detail.

Page-Level Tracing

Tracing can be enabled at the page level to display trace information using the Page directive's Trace attribute, as shown below:

```
<%@ Page Trace = "true" %>
```

or:

```
<%@ Page Trace = "false" %>
```

When tracing is enabled, the trace information is displayed after the page's contents. Let's create a simple ASP.NET page with a textbox and a label control, and enable tracing at the page level.

Try It Out – Enabling Trace at the Page Level

1. Open your code editor and type in the following code:

```
<%@ Page Trace="true"%>
<html>
  <head>
    <title>Page Level Tracing</title>
```

```
      </head>
      <body>
        <form method="post" action="pageleveltracing.aspx" runat="server">
        <asp:label text="Name" runat="server" />
        <asp:textbox name="txtName" runat="server" />
      </form>
    </body>
  </html>
```

2. Save this file as `pageLevelTracing.aspx`, and view it using your browser. The following figure shows how this file should look:

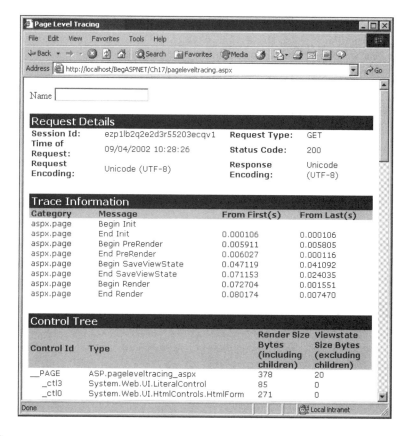

How It Works

First of all we enabled the page trace with the line:

```
<%@ Page Trace="true"%>
```

And we then created a textbox with some text beside it. What we got was the textbox, plus a whole load of tracing!

We're now going to look at each section of the trace output to get a fuller understanding of what we're looking at here:

- ❑ **Request Details** – This section contains information pertaining to the page request, such as the Session ID for the current session, the request type (whether it is GET or POST), the time at which the request was made, and the encoding type of the request among others as shown in below:

Request Details			
Session Id:	eyouok55ijut2jbxwdbahu55	Request Type:	GET
Time of Request:	6/17/2001 12:34:25 AM	Status Code:	200
Request Encoding:	Unicode (UTF-8)	Response Encoding:	Unicode (UTF-8)

- ❑ **Trace Information** – This is the section in which the actual trace information is displayed. It is also the section were the messages written by developers are displayed. As shown below, this section displays the category, the message, and the times since the first message was displayed and the most recent message was displayed:

Category	Message	From First(s)	From Last(s)
aspx.page	Begin Init		
aspx.page	End Init	0.006500	0.006500
aspx.page	Begin PreRender	0.006642	0.000142
aspx.page	End PreRender	0.006764	0.000122
aspx.page	Begin SaveViewState	0.007932	0.001168
aspx.page	End SaveViewState	0.009137	0.001205
aspx.page	Begin Render	0.009264	0.000128
aspx.page	End Render	0.010613	0.001349

- ❑ **Control Tree** – This section displays details about the different controls used in the page. The details include the ID provided for the control and, the type of control used among others, as shown in the figure below:

Control Id	Type	Render Size Bytes (including children)	Viewstate Size Bytes (excluding children)
__PAGE	ASP.pageleveltracing_aspx	341	20
ctrl3	System.Web.UI.LiteralControl	87	0
ctrl0	System.Web.UI.HtmlControls.HtmlForm	233	0
ctrl4	System.Web.UI.LiteralControl	3	0
ctrl1	System.Web.UI.WebControls.Label	17	0
ctrl5	System.Web.UI.LiteralControl	3	0
ctrl2	System.Web.UI.WebControls.TextBox	49	0
ctrl6	System.Web.UI.LiteralControl	4	0
ctrl7	System.Web.UI.LiteralControl	21	0

- ❑ **Cookies Collection** – This section displays all cookies used in the page. The figure below shows only the SessionID since it is the only member of the cookie used in our page:

Name	Value	Size
ASP.NET_SessionId	eyouok55ijut2jbxwdbahu55	42

❑ **Headers Collection** – This section displays the various HTTP headers sent by the client to the server, along with the request as show below:

Headers Collection	
Name	**Value**
Connection	Keep-Alive
Accept	image/gif, image/x-xbitmap, image/jpeg, image/pjpeg, application/vnd.ms-powerpoint, application/vnd.ms-excel, application/msword, */*
Accept-Encoding	gzip, deflate
Accept-Language	en-gb
Host	localhost
User-Agent	Mozilla/4.0 (compatible; MSIE 6.0; Windows NT 5.0; .NET CLR 1.0.3705)

❑ **Server Variables** – This section displays all the members of the Server Variables collection as shown below:

Server Variables	
Name	**Value**
ALL_HTTP	HTTP_CONNECTION:Keep-Alive HTTP_ACCEPT:image/gif, image/x-xbitmap, image/jpeg, image/pjpeg, application/msword, */* HTTP_ACCEPT_ENCODING:gzip, deflate HTTP_ACCEPT_LANGUAGE:en-us HTTP_HOST:ajoys-mobile HTTP_USER_AGENT:Mozilla/4.0 (compatible; MSIE 6.0b; Windows NT 5.0; .NET CLR 1.0.2728; .NET CLR 1.0.2901)
ALL_RAW	Connection: Keep-Alive Accept: image/gif, image/x-xbitmap, image/jpeg, image/pjpeg, application/msword, */* Accept-Encoding: gzip, deflate Accept-Language: en-us Host: ajoys-mobile User-Agent: Mozilla/4.0 (compatible; MSIE 6.0b; Windows NT 5.0; .NET CLR 1.0.2728; .NET CLR 1.0.2901)
APPL_MD_PATH	/LM/w3svc/1/root/Chapter9
APPL_PHYSICAL_PATH	d:\inetpub\wwwroot\Chapter9\
AUTH_TYPE	
AUTH_USER	
AUTH_PASSWORD	
LOGON_USER	
REMOTE_USER	
CERT_COOKIE	
CERT_FLAGS	
CERT_ISSUER	

Now that we've introduced the information displayed in the trace page, let's talk about techniques you can use to write your own message to the **Trace Information** section, and get updates on what's going on behind the scenes as your code is executed.

Writing to the trace log

Each ASP.NET page provides an object called `Trace` that can be used to write messages to the trace log. There are two methods that can be used to write messages to the trace log:

❑   `Trace.Write`

❑   `Trace.Warn`

Note, though, that the messages are only displayed when tracing is enabled.

Both of these methods are used to write messages to the trace log, but when using the `Trace.Warn` method, the messages are displayed in red. You may want to use `Trace.Warn` for writing unexpected results, or incorrect values, for variables in your program, to highlight them. Let's create an example that shows the usage of these two methods.

693

Try It Out – Writing to the Trace Log

1. Type the following code into your code editor:

```
<%@ Page Trace="true"%>
<script Language="c#" runat="server">
  void WriteToTrace()
  {
    // This is where messages are written to Trace Log
    // Syntax as follows:
    // Trace.Write ["Category", "Message to be displayed"];
    // Trace.Warn ["Category", "Message to be displayed"];
    int intCounter=1;
    Trace.Write("FirstCategory", "Variable is initialized");
    while (intCounter > 10)
    {
        intCounter++;
    }
    if(intCounter < 10)
    {
        Trace.Warn("ErrorCategory", "Value of intCounter is not incrementing");
    }
  }
</script>
<%
  WriteToTrace();
%>
```

2. Save this file as `writetotrace.aspx`, and then open it in your browser. The message we wrote using the `Trace.Warn` method is displayed in red:

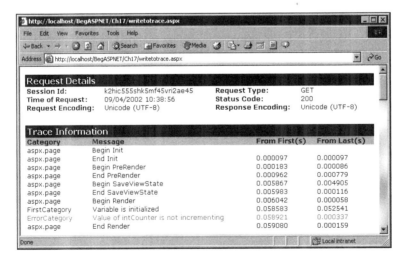

How It Works

The first thing we do is declare `intCounter` (which we're using as a label) as an integer data type, and assign it a value of 1:

```
int intCounter=1;
```

We write a message to the trace log, which says our variable has been initialized:

```
Trace.Write ("FirstCategory", "Variable is initialized");
```

The next three lines of code constitute a loop, so that while `intCounter` is greater than 10, it will have 1 added to it:

```
while (intCounter > 10)
{
  intCounter++;
}
```

This looks like a programming error, because we initialized `intCounter` to 1, so it cannot be greater than 10. We then introduce our `Trace.Warn()` statement that displays a warning message if `intCounter` is less than 10 (which it is):

Which is what we want because, in order for the loop to work, `intCounter` must be greater than 10:

```
if(intCounter < 10)
{
    Trace.Warn("ErrorCategory",
               "Value of intCounter is not incrementing");
}
```

Note that we've specified category information in both the `Write()` *and* `Warn()` *methods.*

Application-Level Tracing

As we said earlier, tracing can also be enabled, or disabled, at the application level, in which case the tracing information for all the pages under the application is affected.

The application-level tracing setting can be overridden by setting the trace at the page level. For instance, if tracing is enabled at the application level, and a page within this application disables tracing at the page level, then the tracing information will not be displayed for that page.

Application level-tracing is set using the <trace> section in the configuration file we discussed earlier (web.config). The following is an example of the <trace> section:

```
<configuration>
  <system.web>
    <trace enabled="false" requestLimit="10" pageOutput="false"
    traceMode="SortByTime" localOnly="true" />
  </system.web>
```

```
</configuration>
```

The use of tracing in `web.config` is discussed in more detail in Chapter 19.

Trace.axd

When application-level tracing is enabled, the trace information is logged to `trace.axd`. This file can be accessed using the URL for your application, followed by `trace.axd` – for example:

http://yourwebservername/applicationname/trace.axd

The following figure shows how the `trace.axd` file looks in the browser:

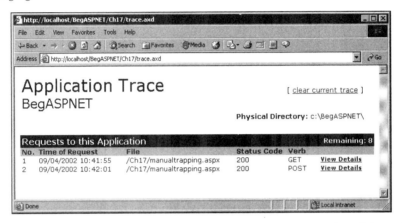

You can see that `trace.axd` provides a summary of each page we requested, and for each page displayed there is a hyperlink, which will take you to the trace information page for that particular screen.

Handling Errors

So we've looked at what kind of errors can occur, how to avoid them, and how to find them if things do go wrong; but what if the errors just won't go away? Annoyingly, it happens. Don't worry, though, there is a way of dealing with this – we can use an error handling technique to catch them, and even though we can't write a wonder program to fix all bugs on the fly, we can let users know that there is a bug, and not to worry if things don't look right. In this section, we will talk about different error handling techniques that can be used to catch errors, and make our life – and the user's life – easier.

On Error Goto...?

If you are coming from a Visual Basic background, you might be asking yourself whether you can use an syntax like `On Error Resume Next` in C#, and the short answer is no, you cannot. C#'s in-built error handling syntax is based on structured exception handling, the topic of the next section of this chapter. Structured exception handling in C# does not allow you just to skip the line of code producing the error and proceed with the next one. Such a function is OK for a script-based application such as a traditional ASP page, but for the object-oriented world of C# and ASP.NET, you need something more robust. Structured exception handling also largely replaces the crude error handling offered by `On Error Goto Label` syntax as well. C# also does not have any equivalent to the Visual Basic `Err` object.

Structured Error Handling

We have already come across structured exception handling in this book wherever we have actually needed it. The main areas where it was discussed are:

❑ In Chapter 4, we used it to deal with situations where conversion between data types might fail and generate a run-time error.

❑ In Chapter 9, we mentioned it as a means of dealing with situations where conversion between object types might fail and generate a run-time error.

❑ In Chapter 12, we used it when dealing with databases. Run-time errors can occur for many reasons including the unavailability of the database, trying to access a non-existent data field, or trying to update a read-only data field.

In all cases we referred forward to this point in the book, which is where we look more closely at how we implement error handling. However, to provide the most complete picture of what C# error handling can achieve, we are going right back to first principles, starting with a definition.

So what do we mean by structured exception handling? Well, it means applying a code structure to error handling, just as you do with other operations such as logical comparisons and loops, using, in the case of C#, the ubiquitous curly brackets. This is opposed to the old way of doing things using `On Error...` and similar syntaxes, which is "unstructured". The following list shows the sequence of events that take place when using structured exception handling:

1. Execute one or more lines of code in a group.

2. This might execute without an error, or it might generate different kinds of errors.

3. If errors are generated, depending on which error occurs, a corresponding handler, which you will have defined, will be called. If there is no error, no handler will be called.

4. You might also have defined a generic handler, which will handle any errors for which you did not define a specific handler.

From this we can see that there are two important things that need to be done if you want to use structured error handling effectively:

❏   The first is to create a group of lines, or block of code

❏   The second, and most important, is to create handlers for the different kinds of errors that could occur when the code block is executed

Before launching into this subject, we need to introduce the concept of exceptions.

Exceptions

An **exception** is any error condition or unexpected behavior that occurs during the execution of a program and consequently disrupts the normal flow of instructions – in fact, the term is just shorthand for 'exceptional event'. If an error occurs within a method call, the method creates an exception object and hands it off to the runtime system – this object contains information detailing the type of exception that was raised and the state of the program at the time.

> **Depending on whether the exception originates from the program itself or from the CLR, you may or may not be able to recover from the exception. While you can recover from most application exceptions, you can seldom recover from a runtime exception.**

The exception event is **thrown** to the code that calls the event, which can either catch it (resolve the problem), or pass it on up to the code that called that code, and so on up the invocation stack. If it reaches the top of the stack without being caught by a handler along the way, the program will crash. Before talking about how to handle exceptions, we'll briefly introduce you to the exception object, and its properties.

The Exception Class

The .NET Framework provides a System.Exception class, which acts as the base class for all exceptions. The Exception class contains properties that inform our understanding of the exception. The following list summarizes the different properties within Exception class:

Property	Description
StackTrace	This property contains the stack trace (which shows the sequence of nested procedure calls your program has executed). This can be used to determine the location of the error occurrence.
Message	This property contains the message about the error.
InnerException	This property is used to create and store a series of exceptions during exception handling. For example, imagine if a piece of your code threw an exception. The exception, and its handler, could be stored in the InnerException property of that handler. You could then reference the exception, see how it was handled, and, based on that information, perhaps create a more effective handler. This can be very useful when you are reviewing the execution of a piece of troublesome code. InnerException can also be used to store an exception that occurred in a previous piece of code.

Property	Description
Source	This property contains information about the application that generated the error.
TargetSite	This property contains information about the method that throws the exception.
HelpLink	This property is used to provide the URL for a file containing help information about the exception that occurred.

The two important exception classes that inherit (derive methods and properties) from `System.Exception` are `ApplicationException` and `SystemException`. The `SystemException` class is thrown by the runtime, and the `ApplicationException` class is thrown by an application.

Having explained a little about what exceptions are, let's look some actual code that makes structured exception handling possible.

Using try...catch...finally

The general C# syntax for error handling is as follows:

```
try
{
    // statement or statements which might fail at runtime
}
catch (Exception e)
{
    // error handing block
}
catch
{
    // optional second error handling block
}
finally
{
    // Code must be run regardless of what happens above
}
```

Let's explain what each block means.

The `try` block contains all the code that might cause a run-time exception. This can be a single line of code, or multiple lines. There is not much more to say on this as there are no parameters to consider, neither are there any limitations on what you can wrap in a `try` block. However, a `try` block by itself is not valid code and immediately after the closing brace you must have a `catch` (or `finally`) block to handle any exceptions that would be raised. Therefore the code construct that fulfils the minimum requirements for structured exception handling would look like this:

```
try
{
    // statement or statements which might fail at runtime
```

```
   }
   catch (Exception e)
   {
      // error handing block
   }
```

We have seen many instances of this type of structure earlier on in this book. However, there is more.

Multiple catch Blocks

A `try` block can be followed by more than one `catch` block. We said in our bulleted list earlier on that you can write error handlers that respond to different types of error as well as a general purpose error handler, which is able to deal with any error at all. In C# this is achieved by stacking `catch` blocks one after the other. If an exception is thrown from the `try` block then the code will pass the `Exception` object created down the chain of `catch` blocks until there is a match, or if there is no match then the exception is passed to the .NET runtime and you will get an unhandled exception error page as we saw earlier.

> Note that like all code blocks in C#, any variables declared in the block are locally scoped so if you want variables to be available to **try**, **catch**, and **finally** blocks, they must be declared before the **try** block starts.

Let's illustrate what I mean using some pseudo-code:

```
try
{
   // Error generated here, Exception object created
}
catch (SystemException e)
{
   // If Exception type matches SystemException, then this code is run
}
catch (Exception e)
{
   // If Exception type matches Exception, then this code is run
}
// If Exception doesn't match either SystemException or Exception, then code
// execution is aborted
```

One important thing to note here is that only one `catch` block is executed at any one time, and this is the very first one that matches the exception object type being thrown. Therefore you have to be careful when implementing more than one handler. The more specific error handler should always come before any general error handler. We have already mentioned three of the many types of `Exception` object: `Exception`, `ApplicationException`, and `SystemException`, the last two of which derived from the first. The correct sequence for the catch blocks is as follows:

```
try
{
  // Error generated here, Exception object created
}
catch (SystemException s)
{
  // If Exception type matches SystemException, then this code is run
}
catch (Exception e)
{
  // If Exception type matches Exception, then this code is run
}
```

The catch block dealing with objects of the derived class, SystemExeception, comes first and the catch block dealing with the base Exception object last. If you reversed the two, you would find that the code will not compile:

```
try
{
  // Error generated here, Exception object created
}
catch (Exception e)
{
  // If Exception type matches Exception, then this code is run
}
catch (SystemException se)
{
  // If Exception type matches SystemException, then this code is run
}
```

Why is this code wrong? The reason is that the catch block that is executed as the result of an error is the very first one that matches the exception object type. The first catch block in the above code would thus be called for *any* .NET exception that is thrown, including system exceptions. In other words, if a SystemException is thrown, it will be caught by the catch (Exception e), because it is first in the list, and derived exception types can be caught by error handlers matching the base type Exception. Therefore the second, more specific error handler can never be executed: it is unreachable code, which the compiler will flag up as an error.

So the rule is that you place all error handlers in order, from the most specific to the least specific. So does that mean that code blocks preceded with catch (Exception e) always come last in the set? Well, no – you can define a catch block that is even more general that this one. The catch (Exception e) block can deal with any .NET-related exception but it cannot deal with any exceptions thrown by objects outside .NET, such as from the Windows operating system. To trap any error at all, regardless of its origin, C# allows you to use a catch with no parameter at all:

```
catch
{
  // Code here
}
```

As this type of `catch` block is as general as you can get, it has to be placed at the very end of a sequence of `catch` blocks.

What You Can Put in a catch Block

There is no limit to what you can put in a `catch` block. Normally, you would generate some message to output to the user that something exceptional had occurred or write the information to an error log. Alternatively, you could add some recovery code to deal with the error and bring the application back to a normal state, without the user even knowing that anything happened at all. In most cases you will want to make use of the contents of the exception object that was created when the exception was thrown. The general `Exception` object only provides general information on an error, which may or may not be useful to you. A more specific exception object using one of the derived classes would contain more specific information about the error that would make it easier to deal with. For this reason, it is always best to include as many specific error handlers as you deem reasonable, when you know beforehand what kind of exceptions are likely to occur. We saw this in Chapter 12 when we covered data access using OLE DB – we used a `catch` block matching the `OleDbException` object that would be thrown as the result of any data access failure. We could have used the `catch (Exception e)` syntax, but this error handler would have discarded any OLE DB-specific information that we might have wanted.

This example would print out the contents of the `Message` property of an `IndexOutOfRangeException` object:

```
catch (IndexOutOfRangeException e)
{
    Response.Write (e.Message)
}
```

The general-purpose error handler should only be used if you do not know what type of exception is likely to occur, or as a catch-all error handler for any unlikely exceptions. You can also use this error handler if you are only outputting a simple error message:

```
catch (Exception e)
{
    Response.Write("You must type your name in the box");
}
```

Here the compiler may complain that you are not using the `Exception` object e (which you don't have to). If you want to eliminate this compiler warning altogether you can use the ultimate general-purpose error handler:

```
catch
{
    Response.Write("You must type your name in the box");
}
```

Because the latter error handler receives no error information at all, you cannot retrieve any error-specific information.

And finally

The `finally` block, if defined, will be executed either after the error has been handled, or after the code in the `try` block has been executed, depending on whether an error occurred or not. The `finally` block is typically used to do cleanup tasks, such as releasing resources, closing objects, and so on. The syntax is very simple:

```
finally
{
    // Clean-up code here for example calling Close() on previously opened objects
    // for example database connections
}
```

Generating Exceptions using throw

Up until now we have assumed that we only handle exceptions that are thrown by the .NET runtime and that we create error handlers that are matched to the various exception objects that could be produced. We have even considered exceptions that are thrown by code outside the control of the .NET runtime. However we can take control of the exception generation process ourselves my manually generating an exception in response to a given set of conditions. Any code can be configured to generate an exception, and the syntax for doing this is as follows:

```
if (something happens)
{
    throw new Exception("An error has occurred");
}
```

What happens here is that the exception is generated whenever the above condition evaluates to `true` and will contain the terse message "An error has occurred". If left as is, the program execution will immediately terminate, therefore the code containing the `throw` statement could be enclosed in a `try` block and followed by an appropriate `catch` block as we have seen before. However, this need not be the case. The above statement could well be included in a function without any `try` and `catch` blocks defined at all. This means that the function call must itself be placed in a `try` block and the code calling the function must take responsibility for handling any error that could be generated by the function. Say we have a function like this:

```
double MayThrowError(double a, double b)
{
    if(b == 0)
    {
        throw new DivideByZeroException();
    }
    return a/b;
}
```

Here if we pass zero as the second parameter we will get an exception that is not handled in the function itself, and must be handled by the calling code. Because you know what type of exception will be thrown – you created it in the first place – you can implement a `catch` block that matches it:

```
try
{
  double result = MayThrowError(50,0);
}
catch (DivideByZeroException dbz)
{
    Response.Write(dbz.Message);
}
```

However, you might not have created the function containing the `throw` statement, but have called it from an external class, and it is conceivable that you will not know that the chosen function actually throws an exception until you get one! Therefore it is normal for the documentation for a class to inform you whether an exception could be thrown by a function, and if so, what kind. If you should go on to create a function for general use that can throw an exception then you should inform your potential users of this to prevent them from receiving a nasty surprise.

There is a second way of manually generating exceptions, which we explained back in Chapter 4. The `checked` keyword, when applied to a statement that can fail, makes sure that a runtime exception is thrown which might otherwise be suppressed or an alternative action taken. We saw this when considering overflows of variable types, but it can be applied to other potential problem areas such as data type conversions. If you use `checked` in your code, you must also use `try...catch` blocks.

Try It Out – Using try...catch...finally

1. Open up your editor and add this code:

```
<script Language="c#" runat="server" >
  void StructuredErrorHandling ()
  {
    try
    {
      int [] array = new int[9];
      for(int intCounter=0; intCounter <= 9; intCounter++)
      {
        array[intCounter] = intCounter;
        Response.Write("The value of the counter is:" + intCounter +
                                                "<br>");
      }
    }
    // Handler for index out of range exception
    catch (IndexOutOfRangeException ex)
    {
        Response.Write("Error Occurred"+ "<br>" + ex.ToString() + "<br>");
    }
    // Handler for generic exception
    catch (Exception e)
    {
        Response.Write("Generic Error Occurred" + "<br>");
    }
    finally
    {
```

```
        Response.Write("The Page Execution is completed" + "<br>");
    }
  }
</script>
<%
  StructuredErrorHandling();
  Response.Write("Function call completed" + "<br>");
%>
```

2. Save this file as `structurederrorhandling.aspx`, and load it into your browser. The following figure shows the result:

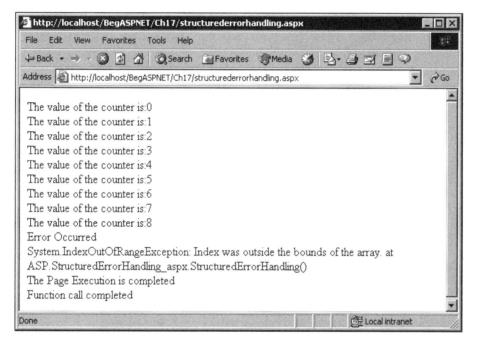

How It Works

In the function, the `try` block encloses all the code we want to execute. We create an integer array and we attempt to loop through it:

```
void StructuredErrorHandling ()
{
  try
  {
      {
    int [] array = new int[9];
    for(int intCounter=0; intCounter <= 9; intCounter++)
    {
      array[intCounter] = intCounter;
      Response.Write("The value of the counter is:" + intCounter +
```

```
                                                             "<br>");
    }
  }
```

Note we have made a deliberate mistake in the code, in that we are attempting to loop through ten elements in an array where there are only nine. An exception will be thrown.

There are two `catch` blocks defined, one for the expected `IndexOutOfRangeException` object:

```
catch (IndexOutOfRangeException ex)
{
   Response.Write("Error Occurred"+ "<br>" + ex.ToString() + "<br>");
}
```

and one generic catch-all handler, which should not be executed in this code, but is there just as a precaution:

```
catch (Exception e)
{
    Response.Write("Generic Error Occurred" + "<br>");
}
```

The `finally` block is there just to confirm that it was actually run:

```
finally
{
    Response.Write("The Page Execution is completed" + "<br>");
}
```

At the end, once the function has been called, a line is sent to inform the user that the whole function is complete:

```
Response.Write("Function call completed" + "<br>");
```

Nested try Blocks

Structured exception handling can be extended to allow for multiple levels of error handling using nested `try` blocks. This enables you to exert more control over the error handling process than can be achieved using a single `try` block. There are two things you can do with nested `try` blocks that may not be achievable using just one. You can modify the type of exception thrown, and you can enable different types of exception to be handled in different places in your code. The syntax for implementing nested `try` blocks looks like this:

```
try
{
  // main code block [1]
  try
  {
    // code block that needs closer attention [2]
  }
  catch (SystemException se)
  {
    // [3]
  }
  catch (ApplicationException ae)
  {
    // [4]
  }
  finally
  {
  }
  // more code
}
catch
{
  // [5]
}
finally
{
}
```

This is a very simplified representation as there are only two `try` blocks (there can be any number of them). The inner block has two `catch` blocks and a `finally` block, the outer one has one `catch` block and a `finally` block.

This is how it works. If the code at the point marked **[1]** fails, then the catch block marked **[5]** will be called upon to handle it. This corresponds with the behavior already outlined for a single `try` block; a failure occurring before the inner `try` block starts will not even be aware that the inner `try` block exists, as all code from the point where the exception occurs is ignored.

If, however, the code in the inner `try` block fails, marked by **[2]**, then control passes to `catch` blocks **[3]** or **[4]**, which will process the error. Then the inner `finally` block is executed and the code execution continues as normal until the end of the outer `try` block whereupon the outer `finally` block is executed. This is all well and good, but what if none of the inner `catch` blocks can handle the error? What happens then? Well, the .NET runtime will keep looking for a handler to deal with the exception generated. It will run the code in the inner `finally` block before leaving the outer `try` block (passing over any code that occurs after the end of the inner `try` block). The set of `catch` blocks following the outer `try` block are examined for a match and, if there is one, then the code for that particular `catch` block is executed. If even at this point there is no match, then the outer `finally` block is run and control passes to the .NET runtime.

So what happens if the code in the `catch` blocks **[3]** and **[4]** fails? We have not considered this before in this section, but code can fail even in error handlers! If failure occurs in either of these two blocks, then the first place the .NET runtime will look for an error handler is any `catch` block associated with the outer `try` block, that is block **[5]**.

This passing around of exception objects between catch blocks can actually be used to our advantage. We have said before that the benefit of using nested try blocks is that you can modify the exception that was originally thrown. You might want to do this because the exception object that was thrown might not be the root cause of the problem, hence you might want to look at other possibilities. So if you have code like that shown below and an ApplicationException is thrown, it will be caught by the appropriate catch block. However, on further investigation, you might find that the real problem lies with a missing file and so you can generate a new exception dealing with this situation using throw. In the code, the line marked in bold achieves this. The new exception is thrown with an appropriate message as well as a reference to the original ApplicationException stored in the InnerException property:

```
try
{
  // main code block [1]
  try
  {
    // code block that needs closer attention [2]
  }
  catch (SystemException se)
  {
      // [3]
  }
  catch (ApplicationException ae)
  {
    if (something happens)
    {
    // [4]
      throw new FileNotFoundException("File does not exist", ae);
    }
  }
  finally
  {
  }
  // more code
}
catch
{
  // [5]
}
finally
{
}
```

If, however, you want to manually rethrow an exception from a catch block without modifying it, then you can use the throw keyword by itself:

```
catch (ApplicationException ae)
{
  if (something happens)
  {
  // [4]
    throw;
  }
}
```

What this does is pass control back to the outer `try` block where its can be dealt with by any of its associated `catch` blocks. This method enables the same exception to be handled by more than one error handler.

You might be thinking that this is all a bit complicated, but nested `try` blocks are actually more common than you realize. This is because nested `try` blocks do not have to be in the same code block at all; they don't even have to be in the same class. The fact is that when you call a function `A()` from within a `try` block, that function itself might include a `try` block of its own. Any exception thrown by `A()` that is not handled by `A()` will be caught by the error handlers in your code. The point I am trying to make here is that `A()` might not be defined in your class at all – it might be a .NET Framework base class function; the rules for passing exceptions around are handled by the .NET Framework and so are not dependent on the way the code is structured. Indeed it is possible for code written in Visual Basic .NET to throw an exception is then handled by code written in C#.

Handling Errors Programmatically

We can now handle errors using `try...catch` blocks, but there is still a possibility that some exceptions will sneak through. ASP.NET provides us with yet two more methods that can be used to handle any 'unaccounted for' errors, and provide a friendly message to the user, instead the default runtime error screen.

The two methods are:

❑   `Page_Error` method

❑   `Application_Error` method

Page_Error method

The `Page` class provides this method. Refer to the section called *The Page Class* in Chapter 10 for more information on the `Page` class and its members.

The `Page_Error` method can be used to handle errors at the page level. Every time an unhandled exception occurs, this event gets called. To see how it works, let's take our previous example and modify it to use the `Page_Error` method.

In the above example, we created an error by storing a string to an integer datatype, and we used the `try` statement to handle exceptions. This time, we'll just use the `Page_Error` method to handle the exception.

Try It Out – Using Page_Error

1.   Open the code file, `structurederrorhandling.aspx`, and make the following adjustments:

```
<script Language="c#" runat="server">
  void PageLevelErrorTest()
  {
    // Remove opening try
    int[] array = new int[9];
    for(int intCounter=0; intCounter <= 9;intCounter++)
    {
        array[intCounter] = intCounter;
        Response.Write("The value of the counter is:" + intCounter + "<br>");
    }
    // Remove catch and finally blocks
  }
  void Page_Error(object sender, EventArgs e)
  {
    Response.Write("Error occurred: " + Server.GetLastError().ToString());
    Server.ClearError();
  }
  void Page_Load()
  {
    PageLevelErrorTest();
  }
</script>
```

2. Save the file as `PageLevelError.aspx`, and open it in your browser. You should see something like this:

How It Works

We already know about the first half of this code, as it is the same as for the previous example. However, it's the `Page_Error()` function that we're interested in:

```
void Page_Error(object sender, EventArgs e)
```

Within the `Page_Error()` method, we write a message to the user to say that an error has occurred, and get detailed error information from the server using the `GetLastError()` method of the `Server` object:

```
Response.Write("Error occurred: " + Server.GetLastError().ToString());
```

Refer to the ASP.NET core objects section in Chapter 10 for more information on the `Server` object and its members.

After displaying the message, we free up the server by using the `ClearError()` method of the `Server` object.

The `Page_Error()` method is called whenever an unhandled exception is thrown within the page. This method could be used to catch the error, log the error to a log file, notify the administrator of the error using e-mail, or store the error information to a database. We will talk about this in a moment, in the *Notification and Logging* section.

Application_Error Method

This is the other method that can be used to handle any 'un-accounted for' errors. The `Application_Error()` method is similar to the `Page_Error()` method, in that, if it is enabled, it is called whenever an unhandled exception is thrown, but from any page under the application. This method is part of the `global.asax` file. Another similarity with the `Page_Error()` method, is that `Application_Error()` can also be used to log the errors to a log file, notify an administrator using e-mail, or store the error information to a database.

The following example shows the usage of this method:

```
void Application_Error(object sender, EventArgs e)
{
  //Handle the Error
  //Provide code to log the error or send an email
}
```

Notification and Logging

In this section, we are going to talk about the techniques that are used to log errors to the Windows event log, and notify a site manager or administrator of the occurrence of the error.

Customized Error Messages

The next question is, what if the development server is on a different machine? Well, ASP.NET allows you to specify whether you want the detailed message to be displayed on the local client, remote clients, or both. You can specify this information using the `<customErrors>` section in the web configuration file, `web.config` (see Chapter 19 for more details). As I said earlier, we'll discuss `web.config` later in the book; for now, just create a new file in your application folder called `web.config`, so that you can get used to using it in this chapter. The following example shows a sample setting for the `<customErrors>` section:

```
<configuration>
  <system.web>
    <customErrors defaultRedirect="userError.aspx" mode="On">
    <error statusCode="404" redirect="PagenotFound.aspx" />
  </customErrors>
  </system.web>
</configuration>
```

> *Note that all settings in `web.config` have to be enclosed with `<configuration>` and `<system.web>` tags. Also make sure that you copy the upper and lower case of this code exactly, as `web.config` is case-sensitive.*

As shown above, the `<customErrors>` configuration section has two attributes. The first is the `defaultdirect` attribute, and specifies the URL for the page to be redirected to when an error occurs. The above configuration setting will redirect the user to a default error page, `userError.aspx`, when an error occurs.

The second attribute is the `mode` attribute, which takes three values: `On`, `Off`, and `RemoteOnly`. The value, `On`, specifies that the custom error is enabled, so the users will be redirected to the custom error page specified in `defaultdirect` attribute. The value `Off` specifies that the custom error is disabled, so the users will not be redirected to a friendly error page. The value `RemoteOnly` specifies that only remote clients should be redirected to the custom error page, not local clients; this is the default setting.

The `<customError>` configuration section contains a sub-tag, `<error>`, and this is used to specify error pages for different errors. In the above example, I have specified `PagenotFound.aspx` page as the error page when error HTTP 404 occurs. You could provide multiple `<error>` sub-tags for different error codes.

Let's create the two friendly error pages, `userError.aspx` and `PagenotFound.aspx`, specified in the configuration file.

Try It Out – Creating Error Pages

3. First of all, make sure the `<customErrors>` section in your web configuration file matches the code example above and is saved in the application root.

4. Now we'll create the `userError.aspx` page. Open up your editor, and enter the following code:

```
<html>
  <head>
  <title> Friendly Error Page</title>
  </head>
  <body>
  <h2> An error has occurred in executing this page. Sorry for the
inconvenience. The site administrator is aware of this error occurrence.</h2>
  </body>
</html>
```

5. Next we'll create the `PagenotFound.aspx` page. Enter the following code:

```
<html>
  <head>
  <title> Friendly Error Page</title>
  </head>
  <body>
  <h2> Sorry, the resource you are requesting is not available. Please verify the
address. </h2>
  </body>
</html>
```

6. Before testing this page, if you are using a local client to view the pages, then change the `mode` setting in the `<customErrors>` section of your `web.config` file to `On` from `RemoteOnly`. Otherwise, you will still see the detailed error message, instead of the friendly error message page. Don't forget to change the `mode` setting before moving the files to a production environment.

7. Now, load the `RuntimeError.aspx` file, using your browser. The following figure shows the result:

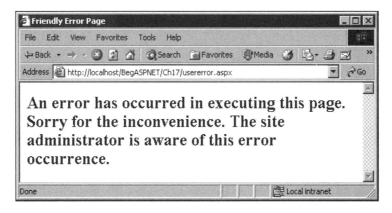

What we see in this figure is the `userError.aspx` *file and not the detailed error message showing the runtime error.*

713

8. Now, try to access a file that does not exist in your application folder. Something like `thispagedoesntexist.aspx`. The following figure shows the result of accessing a file that is not found in the application:

What we see is the `pagenotfound.aspx` file, with the friendly error message and not the default page-not-found message from the web server.

How It Works

We began by making sure that the `<customErrors>` section in the web configuration file pointed to the correct file. Specifically, that the default error page displayed was `userError.aspx`, and the error page for status code 404 was `PagenotFound.aspx`:

```
<customErrors defaultRedirect="userError.aspx" mode="RemoteOnly">
 <error statusCode="404" redirect="PagenotFound.aspx" />
</customErrors>
```

Once we had done this, we inserted our own text into the `userError.aspx` and `PagenotFound.aspx` files. Then we checked that `<customErrors>` was set to On, so that our new error pages were sent to the local browser, enabling us to view them when we triggered them by using files containing mistakes.

In the above example, we saw how we could redirect users to a friendly error page using the different attributes in the `<customErrors>` section of `web.config`. By doing this, the users are redirected to the same friendly error page when an error occurs in any page in the application. There is a way to redirect users to different friendly error pages based on which page the error has occurred on, though. This is done by using the `ErrorPage` property in the `Page` directive, as shown below:

```
<% @ Page ErrorPage="ErrorPage.aspx" %>
```

For instance, if you have this directive in `runtimeerror.aspx`, then the users will be redirected to `ErrorPage.aspx` when an error occurs in `runtimeerror.aspx`.

Now let's go back to the local client scenario. ASP.NET displays a **callstack** when a runtime error occurs. What is a callstack? A callstack contains the series of procedure calls that lead up to an error. Before you do this, we suggest you delete the `web.config` file as otherwise all errors generated will be handled by this file.

Writing to the Event Log

So we now know that any exceptions that are not handled can call the `Application_Error` and `Page_Error` methods. There is another step we can take in handling these unforeseen errors, which involves finding out their occurrence, as this could provide vital clues as to how we handle them in the future.

For instance, say a customer who is ordering a few items from your online shopping center receives an error that the order could not be completed. The site manager should be able to see that an error has occurred, so they can take steps to avoid this error in the future.

To achieve this, errors can be logged in to the Windows event log, which can then be reviewed on a periodic basis. Depending on the nature of the application, the event log could be reviewed every hour, day, or week.

System.Diagnostics Namespace

The tool that the .NET Framework provides for us here is the `System.Diagnostics` namespace, which contains classes that can be used for reading and writing to event logs. Before using the class for accessing event logs, we have to import the `System.Diagnostics` namespace into the program, as shown below:

```
<%@ Import Namespace="System.Diagnostics" %>
```

This line goes at the very top of your code page.

EventLog class

The class that we will use to read and write to the event log is the `EventLog` class. Using this class, we can create a new log, or write entries to an existing log.

First of all, you need to create a log that you can write to, and then you need to specify an event **Source**. A source is a string identifying an individual entry to the log. Creating an event source opens some space in the log for the entry to be recorded. The `CreateEventSource` method can be used to create both a source and a log. In the following example, we create a log called `MyApplicationLog`, and a source called `MyApplicationSource`.

To actually write an entry to the log, we use the `WriteEntry` method, and, as in our last example, provide detailed error information by using the `GetLastError()` method of the `Server` object.

Try It Out – Writing to the Windows Error Log

1. Type the following code into your code editor:

```
<%@ Import Namespace="System.Diagnostics" %>
<script Language="c#" runat="server" >
  void EntrytoLog()
  {
```

```
    int[] array = new int[9];
    for(int intCounter=0; intCounter <= 9;intCounter++)
    {
        array[intCounter] = intCounter;
        Response.Write("The value of the counter is:" + intCounter + "<br>");
    }
}
void Page_Error(object sender, EventArgs e)
{
    string errorMessage = "Error occurred" + Server.GetLastError();
    Server.ClearError();
    string LogName = "MyApplicationLog";
    string SourceName = "MyApplicationSource";
    if (!(EventLog.SourceExists(SourceName)))
    {
        EventLog.CreateEventSource(SourceName, LogName);
    }
    // Insert into Event Log;
    EventLog MyLog = new EventLog();
    MyLog.Source = SourceName;
    MyLog.WriteEntry(errorMessage, EventLogEntryType.Error);
}
</script>
<%
 EntrytoLog();
%>
```

2. Save this file as `entrytolog.aspx`, and load it in your browser. After the page has loaded, you will see the following:

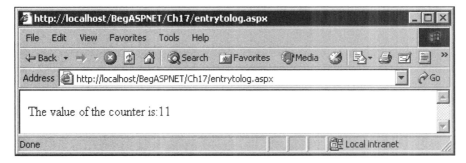

3. However it's not really the display we interested in, but the fact that it has written to a log. To view the contents of the log, open the Event Viewer. The following figure shows the Event Viewer on my machine:

> To open the **Event Viewer**, click **Start** from the Windows tool bar, then select **Settings**. Click **Control Panel** and the **Control Panel** window appears. Double-click on the **Administrative Tools** icon. This will launch the **Administrative Tools** window. Double-click on the **Event Viewer** icon to open the **Event Viewer** window.

4. In the event viewer, you will see **MyApplicationLog** listed under the **Name** column, after **System Log**. Double-click **MyApplicationLog** to open it, and you will see the **Error** entry that we made. The figure below shows the entry:

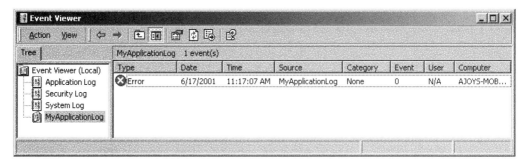

5. Double-click on the **Error** entry to open the **Event Properties** window, as shown in the figure below. This shows the date and time the entry was made, and the description we provided using the `WriteEntry` method:

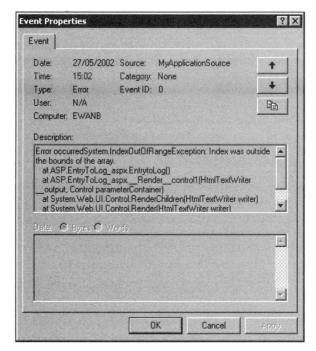

How It Works

As before, the main function in the code creates an array of 9 elements and attempts to loop through 10. After this, we create the `Page_Error()` function, open it by typing our `errorMessage` variable as a string, and supplying it with a line of text to display, along with error information from the server, before erasing the error from the server:

```
void Page_Error(object sender, EventArgs e)
{
  string errorMessage = "Error occurred" + Server.GetLastError();
  Server.ClearError();
```

Next we define the name of our log, and this particular source, but before creating them, we check to see if the source already exists:

```
string LogName = "MyApplicationLog";
string SourceName = "MyApplicationSource";
if (!(EventLog.SourceExists(SourceName)))
{
    EventLog.CreateEventSource(SourceName, LogName);
}
```

If the source does not already exist, then we proceed to create the log object and set the Source property before writing out the error message:

```
// Insert into Event Log;
EventLog MyLog = new EventLog();
MyLog.Source = SourceName;
MyLog.WriteEntry(errorMessage, EventLogEntryType.Error);
```

In the above example, we have used the EventLog class to make an entry to the log file using the Page_Error() method. Alternatively, you could use this class within the Application_Error() method in global.asax. Doing this will create an entry to the log files for any unhandled errors occurring throughout all the pages within the application.

Mailing the Site Administrator

In our last example, we made an entry to a log file after the occurrence of an error. In the real world this log file could be reviewed at regular intervals, perhaps by a web site manager or administrator. However, this may not be prudent for certain applications. Depending on the nature of the application, the manager or administrator may need to be informed of an error right away. To do this, we could notify the site administrator by sending an e-mail with the details of the error as soon as it happens.

System.Web.Mail Namespace

The .NET Framework provides a namespace with a set of classes to do this. The System.Web.Mail namespace contains three classes that can be used to create and send an e-mail using SMTP:

❑   MailMessage

❑   MailAttachment

❑   SmtpMail

Before using these classes in our page, we need to import the System.Web.Mail namespace, just as we did with the System.Diagnostics namespace in the last example. Let's look at our three classes in more detail.

MailMessage

The `MailMessage` class provides properties that are used to create an e-mail. The following table lists the name and purpose of some of the more commonly used members of this class:

Name	Use
From	This property is used to specify the sender's e-mail address.
To	This property specifies the recipient's e-mail address.
Subject	This property specifies the subject line for the e-mail message.
Body	This property is used to set the body of the e-mail message.

The syntax when using this class looks like this:

```
mailMessage.From = "senders email address";
mailMessage.To = "recipients email address";
mail.Message.Subject = "subject line";
mailMessage.Body = "body of email message";
```

MailAttachment

This class contains members that are used to create an attachment that is to be sent with the e-mail message.

SmtpMail

This class provides properties that are used to send an e-mail using the SMTP Service. The method we are interested in, at the moment, is the `Send` method of this class. This method is used to send an e-mail, and the code looks like this:

```
SmtpMail.Send(mailMessage);
```

To show you how a working piece of code, based on the `System.Web.Mail` namespace, would look, we have modified the previous example to send an e-mail, instead of writing to the log file:

```
<%@ Import Namespace="System.Web.Mail" %>
<script language="c#" runat="server" >
  void sendMailTest()
  {
    int[] array = new int[9];
    for(int intCounter=0; intCounter <= 9;intCounter++)
    {
        array[intCounter] = intCounter;
        Response.Write("The value of the counter is:" + intCounter + "<br>");
    }
  }

  void Page_Error(object sender, EventArgs e)
  {
```

```
        string errorMessage = "Error occurred" + Server.GetLastError();
        Server.ClearError();

        // Create an email message
        MailMessage newMail = new MailMessage();
        newMail.From = "fromaddress@yourserver.com";
        newMail.To = "administrator@yourserver.com";
        newMail.Subject = "Error Occurred";
        newMail.Body = errorMessage;
        // send the mail to the administrator.
        SmtpMail.Send(newMail);
    }
</script>
<%
  sendMailTest();
%>
```

This code allows e-mail to be sent to the administrator of the server in the event of an error being generated.

Summary

In this chapter, we talked about error handling techniques that can be used when developing ASP.NET applications.

We discussed the different kinds of errors that can occur, techniques for handling errors (including the new tracing features), handling exceptions using unstructured and structured error handling, and finally, techniques to log the error messages to a log file and notify the site administrator through e-mail.

We saw that adopting good coding practice helps to reduce the number of errors in your code, and that time spent in testing helps us create handlers for recurring errors before the application is moved to the production environment.

Using different error handling techniques helps us to develop applications with fewer bugs, which are, therefore, more successful and competitive.

Web Services

In the days before the Internet started to find its way into every corner of our lives, whenever we wanted to research a subject, the chances are we'd have visited a library to find a book on the topic, possibly visited another library for some more specialized literature, and browsed the relevant periodicals to find the latest articles. While this is still quite possible (if you like that sort of thing), it's usually not necessary. Now that the Internet connects computers containing all sorts of different data sources, it frequently provides us with a one-stop shop for whatever information we might need. In a sense, the Internet has become a 'virtual library' for web users.

Web developers face a similar situation. Over the years, we created isolated web applications that were essentially islands unto themselves. Each island became larger and larger, and in its wake, we would often produce large amounts of redundant logic. To overcome this, many developers began using technologies (such as COM and DCOM) that would allow them to build code components once and bundle them up so they could be shared by multiple applications, by multiple developers, even between multiple machines.

However, in practice these components were usually very difficult to work with, since they had to be physically distributed and then explicitly registered on each new user's machine. It was possible to share logic around, but it was far from easy.

At the same time, the Web was achieving credibility (not to mention ubiquity) as a useful and reliable medium for the exchange of human-readable information. The logical next step was to use the same infrastructure to pass around information that was specifically designed for machines to consume – not just GET and POST statements, and simple HTTP headers, but complex data and procedure calls, such as you'd expect to be passed around within an application.

The ASP.NET Web Services model provides us with a simple, straightforward way to do precisely this. Since the Internet has given us a standard method of communication across a global network, web developers can use it to share application logic and therefore reduce the overall amount of code duplication. Not only do we need to create less logic, but we can also build upon it and extend it. They also provide us with the ability to easily access information from different sources. As we'll see, Web Services truly make the Web a 'virtual library' of ready-made code for developers.

This chapter will introduce you to ASP.NET Web Services. These are easy to create and use, and possess a programming model that will be very familiar to anyone who has already worked with ASP.NET. It's also a concept that programmers of all levels can learn quickly.

By the end of this chapter, you will have learned:

❑   What a Web Service is and its role in the .NET Framework

❑   How to create and use a Web Service

❑   How to describe a Web Service's behavior using WSDL

❑   How users can discover which Web Services are available using UDDI

❑   What you need to consider when building a Web Service

Now, let's jump straight into the world of Web Services!

What is a Web Service?

Technically speaking, a Web Service is a component of programmable application logic that can be accessed using standard web protocols, meaning, it's quite similar to the components we considered earlier on in the book. The big difference is that it lets us access all of its functionality via the Web. In principle, anyone who can browse the Web can see and use a Web Service.

Think of a Web Service as a black box resource that accepts requests from a consumer (an application running on the web client), performs a specific task, and returns the results of that task.

Currently the term, 'Web Service', is something of a buzzword within the sphere of software development, thanks to a number of new protocols that have opened up the scope of what we can expect Web Services to do. XML plays a central role in all these technologies, and these **Web Services** are something you can expect to hear a great deal about, both now and well into the future.

> **Most of the time, you'll find that when people talk about Web Services, they're referring to Web Services that use XML. This is now so prevalent that many people believe that all Web Services use XML by definition.**
>
> **Microsoft calls its Web Services technology *XML Web Services*. However, note that almost all Web Services technologies are based on XML protocols. Throughout this chapter, we will be discussing Microsoft's XML Web Services.**

If we use an XML Web Service, we can assume the results will be returned as some kind of XML document, with information that's explicitly structured and self-describing. It's therefore quite straightforward to write a program that interprets these results and perhaps even uses the results to formulate a new submission.

As we're going to see, ASP.NET makes it very easy to build XML Web Services, and just as easy to use them – ultimately you only need to reference the Web Service in your code, and you can use it just as if it were a local component. As with normal components, you don't need to know anything about how the service functions, only the tasks it can do, the type of information it needs to do them, and the type of results you'll be getting back.

We can use Web Service methods to do just about anything from adding two numbers together, to writing information to a database. The logic they use can be as simple or as complex as we need it to be.

Let's create a simple Web Service to demonstrate just how easy it is:

Try It Out – Creating our First Web Service

In this example, we'll make a Web Service that takes a string input and returns a greeting that includes whatever name we've specified in the input.

1. Create a new file, called `greetings.asmx`, and enter the following code:

```
<%@ WebService Language="c#" Class="Greetings"%>
using System.Web.Services;
public class Greetings
{
  [WebMethod]
  public string Hello(string strName)
  {
    return "Hello, " + strName + ". Have a great day!";
  }
}
```

2. Open the file in your browses and you should see something like this:

Just below the Hello hyperlink, this page will also include a warning message about using the default namespace of http://tempuri.org. It will also display how to use the Web Service directly from SOAP, from HTTP GET, and from HTTP PUT requests. We'll discuss the implications of this warning in the *How It Works* section in just a moment.

3. Click on the bulleted Hello hyperlink – this is the name of the method we defined in our Greetings class above. A new page will be displayed that allows us to enter a name:

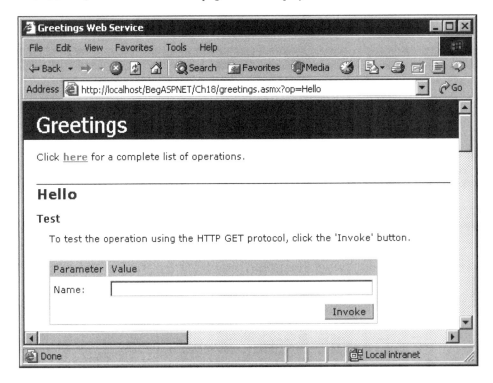

4. Enter your name in the textbox adjacent to the parameter Name, and hit the Invoke button to call our Web Service's Hello method. The following result should now appear in a new browser window (note the XML format):

That's it! We've now demonstrated that the Web Service is working on our local machine. Now let's consider what it's actually doing:

How It Works

First of all, we can see from the following line that our Web Service is written in C#. We also declare our class name as `Greetings`, which will be important when a consumer wants to use it:

```
<%@ WebService Language="c#" Class="Greetings"%>
```

Our next line gives us access to objects that are needed to build a Web Service:

```
using System.Web.Services;
```

Now, we have some logic to actually define the Web Service's functionality:

```
public class Greetings
{
  [WebMethod]
  public string Hello(string strName)
  {
    return "Hello, " + strName + ". Have a great day!";
  }
}
```

Within the `public class Greetings` declaration (notice the name here matches the one in the `WebService` declaration), we define a `Hello` function that simply returns a string based on the parameter `strName`. We prefix this method declaration with a `[WebMethod]` attribute – this is how we specify that it's to be exposed as a web method, making the function visible to the outside world.

With just a few lines of code, we've created a functioning Web Service. We didn't need to specify a format for the result, or write any code to handle any network connections. We didn't even have to register it on the client – all we needed to know was the URL.

To conclude this *Try It Out*, we'd just like to touch upon the warning message that appeared on the first page of the Web Service. It looked something like this:

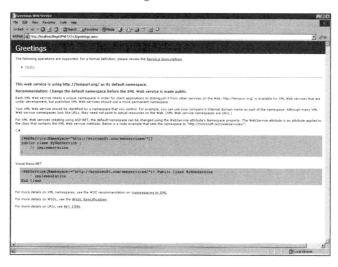

Just below the Hello hyperlink, the page includes a warning message about using the default namespace of http://tempuri.org. If we do not make a practice of changing this namespace, our Web Service will be organized within the `tempuri.org` namespace, which can become difficult to manage if there are multiple developers on a project.

We discussed namespaces in detail back in Chapter 10; but we'll recap a little for you here. A namespace allows us, as developers, to organize our programming components into categories. For instance, imagine we have multiple Web Services that perform various tasks for specific parts of an application. If we were working on a 'Purchasing' module for an accounting system, we could specify a `Purchasing` namespace within all of our Web Service files pertaining to purchasing-related tasks.

That way, if we, in Purchasing, have a Web Service called `Reporting` and Joe, in Accounts Receivable, has a similarly named service, we can declare our namespace in applications that use it as `Purchasing.ReportingWS` while Joe can declare `AccountsReceivable.ReportingWS` and the two will not conflict.

Now, let's take a quick look at how this works in a bit more detail. How are the requests and responses sent to and from a Web Service?

HTTP, XML, and Web Services

We've already introduced you (back in Chapter 3) to the basic mechanism by which information is passed back and forth across the Web, so that we can pop a URL in our browser's address bar and request a web page from a remote server. We've also pointed out that ASP.NET Web Services rely on the same mechanism – namely the HTTP Request-Response system. All the information that we submit to a Web Service is sent as an HTTP Request. Likewise, any information we get back from the Web Service is sent as an HTTP Response:

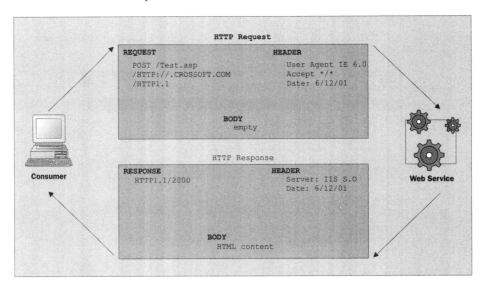

We've already seen that a typical Web Service operates by accepting input from a consumer and using it to produce a result that is sent back to the consumer as XML. When a consumer makes use of a Web Service's logic, it takes the form of an HTTP Request – that's why it's so easy to access from a web browser, which is tailor-made for such requests.

This HTTP Request consists of packets of information that are sent to the Web Service (wherever it may reside). These packets contain:

❑ Vital information such as the Web Service's URL and the fact that we're submitting a Request (that is, initiating a data exchange that requires a Response, rather than simply Responding to someone else's Request)

❑ Details of the amount of information being sent

❑ The type of document we require back from the Web Service

❑ Information about the consumer, the request date, general configuration statistics, and the data itself

The Web Service will return an HTTP Response with:

❑ A return address for the consumer, and the fact that it's submitting a Response and so doesn't expect any further action from the recipient

❑ A success or failure status code indicating whether or not the Web Service received a valid Request from the consumer

❑ Configuration information

❑ Any appropriate data

We can transmit HTTP Requests and Responses between a Web Service and a consumer as many times as we like, depending on how the interaction between the two has been designed.

So, how exactly does our submitted data get wrapped up in this bundle of HTTP information? As we know from Chapter 3, there are two ways to submit information within an HTTP Request, using the GET and POST methods respectively – let's give them each a quick recap:

HTTP GET

This is the simplest way to send data to the client, and probably the most familiar to users of the Web. Simple, unstructured information is bundled in with the page as a sequence of **name-value pairs**. These pairings are a simple way to combine all the values into a single string. We can use the `Request.QueryString` collection in our ASP.NET code to access these name-value pairs on the server.

When we tested our `Greetings.Hello` web method just a moment ago, the built-in testing mechanism provided by ASP.NET used HTTP GET to submit the string `Abigail` to the Web Service. Here's the actual GET request that our browser used to access the Web Service when we tested it a moment ago:

```
GET /BegASPNET/Ch18/greetings.asmx/Hello?Name=Abigail HTTP/1.1
Host: localhost
```

It specifies the GET method, states the page we've requested (including the virtual directory path) along with our query string, and declares that it has structured the Request according to version 1.1 of HTTP. It then states the name of the host to which it wants the request submitted, in this case the local machine. The resource requested is:

```
/BegASPNET/Ch18/greetings.asmx/Hello?Name=Abigail
```

and using this path along with the Host value, we have a full URL:

```
localhost/BegASPNET/Ch18/greetings.asmx/Hello?Name=Abigail
```

The corresponding Response simply specifies the content type we're returning (text/xml) along with the character set and content length. The body of the Response then contains the XML we saw earlier:

```
HTTP/1.1 200 OK
Content-Type: text/xml; charset=utf-8
Content-Length: 112


<?xml version="1.0" encoding="utf-8"?>
<string xmlns="http://tempuri.org/">
Hello, Abigail. Have a great day!</string>
```

> **Notice that the Response contains our desired message within a string, which is the return type specified in the function.**

The Response from the server is a 200 message, which is HTTP's success message.

Another common return code is 404, which indicates 'File not found'. Our HTTP Response from the server can also tell us information such as the web server software, the number of bytes to expect, content type, and the type of cookie that will be set.

Note that it's very easy to make a new request to our Web Service by simply editing the query string in the browser's address bar. You might like to try calling up your page again as follows:

```
http://localhost/BegASPNET/Ch18/greetings.asmx/Hello?strName=my%20fine%20fellow
```

HTTP POST

While HTTP GET uses the end of the URL to pass its information from resource to resource, HTTP POST uses the body of the transmission to carry the same name-value pairs. We can retrieve these values using the Request.Form collection in ASP.NET. Using POST means a less-cluttered URL, as well as slightly tighter security, since manipulating the name-value pairs is no longer as easy as typing in the address bar.

Below is an example of an equivalent POST message being sent to the web server:

```
POST /BegASPNET/ch18/greetings.asmx/Hello HTTP/1.1
Host: localhost
Content-Type: application/x-www-form-urlencoded
Content-Length: 15

Name=Abigail
HTTP/1.1 200 OK
```

This time, the Request specifies the POST method before stating the page we've Requested and the HTTP version. It states the host name and content type (usually this is `application/x-www-form-urlencoded`) and the content length, which now tells the server how many bytes' worth of name-value pairs to expect. This is all followed by the name-value pairs themselves, which are placed on a separate line. The corresponding Response from the web server is exactly the same as we saw when using the GET method, returning a simple XML document in the Response body, along with the result that our web method placed inside a `<string>` element.

That's all well and good so far as it goes, but it's still rather limited. Since we ultimately want to use these web methods to replace various local method calls in our applications, we surely need to be able to pass more than strings and integers – what about passing things like data sets and other complex objects?

This is where XML really comes into its own. As we've established, XML plays a vital role in Web Services, as it allows us to send simple, structured, self-describing data between many different computer platforms and setups.

Web Services therefore use XML to describe data sent from the consumer as well as that being returned. It can also be used to describe the parameters a Web Service expects, and how to find information on Web Services available to consumers on the Internet.

We'll look into this topics in more detail a little later in this chapter.

While XML is very easy to read and understand, which is handy when we debug our code, it can often be verbose since even the simplest of data exchanges require a significant amount of description (since we are exchanging all types and structures of data, we must cater to the lowest common denominator). With a common protocol (HTTP/ HTTPS, or even SMTP) and a common language (XML) that transcends individual machine platforms and operating systems, you should begin to see what a potentially powerful tool Web Services can be.

Simple Object Access Protocol (SOAP)

The **Simple Object Access Protocol** provides an effective way to call all sorts of remote functions. It wraps up any call-specific information inside an XML element (a **SOAP envelope**) and frees us from most of the structural limitations imposed by the HTTP methods we looked at earlier. Here's what a SOAP envelope looks like:

```
POST /BegASPNET/Ch18/greetings.asmx HTTP/1.1
Host: localhost
Content-Type: text/xml; charset=utf-8
```

```
Content-Length: length
SOAPAction: "http://tempuri.org/Hello"

<?xml version="1.0" encoding="utf-8"?>
<soap:Envelope
    xmlns:xsi="http://www.w3.org/2001/XMLSchema-instance"
    xmlns:xsd="http://www.w3.org/2001/XMLSchema"
    xmlns:soap="http://schemas.xmlsoap.org/soap/envelope/">
  <soap:Body>
    <Hello xmlns="http://tempuri.org/">
      <Name>Abigail</Name>
    </Hello>
  </soap:Body>
</soap:Envelope>
```

As we can see, the submitted string value `Abigail` is held in a `<Name>` element (identifying the specific parameter being specified in the web method call) and this is nested within a `<Hello>` element (identifying the name of the method we're calling). Admittedly, at this stage it hardly looks more complex than our previous Requests, but that's largely due to the fact that we're only passing a single string value, once we start sending more data, things will change.

Aside from being somewhat more explicit about our Request, this approach allows us to submit data in a well-defined structure. Even if we wanted to submit a huge array of complex data objects, the flexibility inherent within this SOAP envelope means that we could. What's more, although the SOAP Request is submitted as part of an HTTP POST Request, you can see that it's totally separate and self-contained.

> *One consequence of this is that we're not tied to HTTP as a transport protocol – for example, it's quite possible to send this envelope to the Web Service via SMTP (that is, simply e-mail it to the Web Service). While this is a fascinating and extremely useful option, it's beyond the scope of this book. If you're interested in finding out more, I suggest you check out* Professional ASP.NET 1.0 Special Edition *(Wrox Press, ISBN 1-86100-703-5).*

The SOAP response takes a similar form:

```
HTTP/1.1 200 OK
Content-Type: text/xml; charset=utf-8
Content-Length: length

<?xml version="1.0" encoding="utf-8"?>
<soap:Envelope
    xmlns:xsi="http://www.w3.org/2001/XMLSchema-instance"
    xmlns:xsd="http://www.w3.org/2001/XMLSchema"
    xmlns:soap="http://schemas.xmlsoap.org/soap/envelope/">
  <soap:Body>
    <HelloResponse xmlns="http://tempuri.org/">
      <HelloResult>Hello, Abigail. Have a great day!</HelloResult>
    </HelloResponse>
  </soap:Body>
</soap:Envelope>
```

We can see explicitly that the Response string is the result of a call to the `Hello` method. Again, this result could just as easily take the form of some sort of structured data, and isn't tied into the HTTP response in any way.

When we come to actually **use** Web Services within our ASP.NET logic, it's important to recognize that SOAP is the protocol that they'll use by default. Although at first sight it seems a little more bulky than the other options, it's the only mechanism that makes it possible to use web methods directly, flexibly, and seamlessly from within our code.

Building an ASP.NET Web Service

We've already defined what a Web Service is and seen one in action. We've introduced some of the ways in which data can be sent between a Web Service and a consumer using XML and HTTP. Now we'll take a more detailed look at how we put a Web Service together. We'll also start to explore the enormous range of possible uses we can find for Web Services.

As we've seen, we can define a Web Service by simply writing a few lines of code and placing them in an IIS virtual directory, inside a file with an ASMX extension. This extension tells IIS to use the `aspnet_isapi.dll` and lets the ISAPI filter know that we're going to define a Web Service. We can create this just like a standard ASP.NET page, using anything from a text-based editor like Notepad to a full-blown integrated development environment like Visual Studio .NET.

A Web Service definition contains four essential parts:

- ❑ Processing Directive
- ❑ Namespaces
- ❑ Public Class
- ❑ Web-callable methods

Let's take a look at each of these, in turn:

Processing Directive

Within our empty ASMX file, which is the required file type for an ASP.NET Web Service page, we must let the web server know that we're creating a Web Service. To do this, we enter a directive at the top of our page:

```
<%@ WebService Language="language" Class="classname"%>
```

As we know, this sort of statement appears at the top of an ASP.NET source file to tell the .NET Framework about any settings or constraints that should be applied to whatever object is generated from the file. In this case, the directive tells the compiler the language in which we've written the Web Service, and the name of the class in which it is defined. This class might reside in the same file (as it will in this example) or within a separate file (which must be in the `\bin` directory immediately beneath the Web Application root in which the Web Service lives).

Namespaces

Just as is possible with an ASPX page, we can make use of other files' logic within our ASMX page by specifying appropriate namespaces. In this case, we can use the C# import directive using:

```
using System.Web.Services;
```

Web Services require us to import this namespace as an absolute minimum, as it contains the classes needed for Web Services to handle network connection issues and other OS-related tasks.

Public Class

Now we define a public class that acts as a container for the methods in our Web Service:

Note that the name of this class is effectively the name of the Web Service, and should therefore correspond to the Class value we specified in the processing directive.

```
public class ClassName
{
    ...
}
```

Essentially, we're just defining an object whose methods we're going to expose over the Web. This will ultimately allow us to make remote method calls over the Internet that, to our server, will look like method calls to the same machine that the consuming application resides on.

Web Methods

The methods that we expose for consumption over the Internet are known as **web-callable methods** or simply **web methods**. By definition a Web Service will expose one or more web methods – of course it can have other non-web methods as well, and these can be protected as needed so that consumers cannot use them directly. The syntax varies slightly depending upon which language is used, but they all tend to follow a similar structure; in C# it is the following:

```
[WebMethod] public string Hello(string strName)
```

> We place the **WebMethod** declaration only before functions we wish to expose to consumers. Those without this declaration cannot be seen.

The WebMethod attribute can take parameters of its own where you can set various properties, which modify the activity of the attribute. This allows us to customize our web methods in various ways; for example, we can use CacheDuration to set the number of seconds for which the WebMethod will cache its results. If a consumer requests a result from the web service, WebMethod will retrieve the cached copy of these values instead of retrieving them from the original source for the time specified:

```
[WebMethod(CacheDuration:= 5)]
public string Hello(string strName)
{
   ...
```

> For more information on **WebMethod** attributes, such as **CacheDuration**, please
> visit: **www.microsoft.com/library/default.asp**, and use the search.

Creating web methods accounts for the majority of the work when building a Web Service. As we
mentioned earlier, it is possible to include more than one web method in an ASMX file, as we'll see in
our next example.

Try It Out – Creating a Web Service with Multiple Web Methods

This Web Service contains four web methods that convert inches to centimeters, centimeters to inches,
miles to kilometers, and kilometers to miles, respectively.

1. Create a new file called `MeasurementConversions.asmx` and enter the following:

```
<%@ WebService Language="c#" Class="MeasurementConversions"%>
using System.Web.Services;
public class MeasurementConversions : System.Web.Services.WebService
{
  [WebMethod(Description="Convert Inches to Centimeters")]
  public decimal InchesToCentimeters(decimal decInches) {
    return decInches * 2.54m;
  }
  [WebMethod(Description="Convert Centimeters to Inches")]
  public decimal CentimetersToInches(decimal decCentimeters) {
    return decCentimeters / 2.54m;
  }
  [WebMethod(Description="Convert Miles to Kilometers")]
  public decimal MilesToKilometers(decimal decMiles) {
    return decMiles * 1.61m;
  }
  [WebMethod(Description="Convert Kilometers to Miles")]
  public decimal KilometersToMiles(decimal decKilometers) {
    return decKilometers / 1.61m;
  }
}
```

2. Call it up in your browser and you should see something like this:

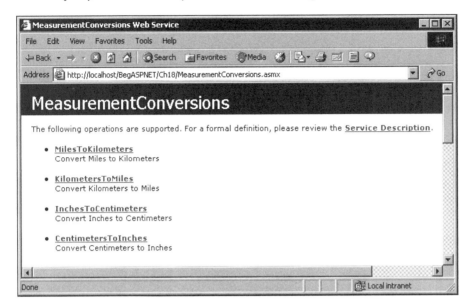

We'll break off here for a moment, to look at the code. We'll pick up again afterwards to consider the testing of our Web Service.

How It Works

In our example, we've created a Web Service that converts between Imperial (UK) measurements and Metric measurements. Now let's look at the code.

The first line tells us that the file is a Web Service written in C#. We have a class name of MeasurementConversions that will be used by consumers to make reference to our Web Service:

```
<%@ WebService Language="c#" Class="MeasurementConversions"%>
```

Next, we import the namespace that allows us to refer to Web Service objects without using fully qualified names:

```
using System.Web.Services;
```

We then name our class to match the processing directive class name. When we are ready to make remote calls to our Web Service through a consumer, we'll need to know this:

```
public class MeasurementConversions : System.Web.Services.WebService
{
```

Finally, we have the actual web methods. These are separate functions that can be called within a Web Service to return a result. In the first, we pass a value in inches as a `decimal` value and will receive a `decimal` value in centimeters using the standard conversion formula. The second receives a `decimal` in centimeters and converts it to inches in the same manner:

```
[WebMethod(Description="Convert Inches to Centimeters")]
public decimal InchesToCentimeters(decimal decInches) {
  return decInches * 2.54m;
}
[WebMethod(Description="Convert Centimeters to Inches")]
public decimal CentimetersToInches(decimal decCentimeters) {
  return decCentimeters / 2.54m;
}
```

The third and fourth web methods perform similar conversions from miles to kilometers and kilometers to miles, respectively:

```
[WebMethod(Description="Convert Miles to Kilometers")]
public decimal MilesToKilometers(decimal decMiles) {
  return decMiles * 1.61m;
}
[WebMethod(Description="Convert Kilometers to Miles")]
public decimal KilometersToMiles(decimal decKilometers) {
  return decKilometers / 1.61m;
}
}
```

We've now created a complete Web Service using the **processing directive**, adding **namespaces**, and creating our **Web methods**. Now the big question is "How do we know it works?" It's time to put it through its paces.

Testing your Web Service

As we saw earlier, the creators of ASP.NET have come up with a great way to test Web Services. All you need is an Internet connection and a browser. In the browser address window, just enter the URL of the Web Service in this format:

http://[path]/[webservice].asmx

The first time our Web Service is accessed, the code will compile on the web server and a new browser window will appear containing some very helpful diagnostic information. This Web Service Description page allows us to impersonate a consumer and enter input values to send to the Web Service. As we view the page, we can see information about the Web Service:

❑ Names of the Web Service's web-callable functions

❑ Request Parameters – the names of all the inputs that the Web Service expects a consumer to supply

❑ Response Type – the data types of the result sent by the Web Service to a consumer (such as `int`, `string`, `long`, and so on)

❑   Fields to enter test values

You'll also see the following message at the top of the test page:

> The following operations are supported. For a formal definition, please review the Service Description.

The Service Description is a comprehensive technical description of all the functionality exposed by the Web Service. We'll be taking a closer look at it later on in the chapter.

Try It Out – Browse to the Conversions Test Page

So, what happens when we test it our `MeasurementConversions` Web Service?

1. Open your browser, and call up the ASMX page from the appropriate test directory:

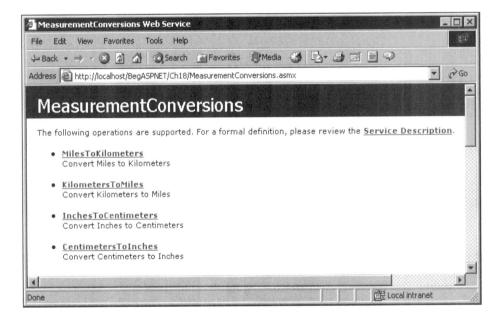

2. Click on the MilesToKilometers hyperlink:

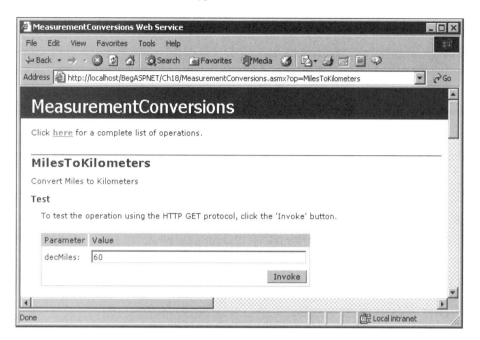

3. Enter a test value in the decMiles value field, of 60.

4. Press Invoke, and a new browser window appears containing our result in kilometers in XML format:

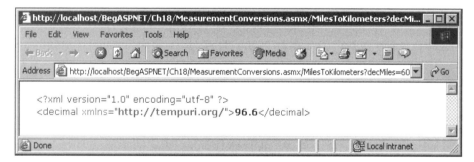

5. In the original page, click on the word here in the hyperlink at the top of the test page, and you'll return to the original test screen. You can now repeat this procedure for the other methods shown on the page.

How It Works

When we browse to our test page we see a screen containing the name of our Web Service and, underneath it, a list of the methods that it exposes. These method names are hyperlinks.

When we click on MilesToKilometers, the web method test section will appear in the browser window. We are given the name of the parameter, decMiles, and an associated field to enter our test value in.

> *Remember from our example that the data type for MilesToKilometers is a* decimal. *This is the value that our MeasurementConversions Web Service expects from a consumer.*

Once the value is entered, we can press the Invoke button to execute the web method. We are impersonating a consuming application when we do this. When we enter the test value 60, it is passed using HTTP as a request to the MilesToKilometers web method. The value will be multiplied by 1.61 and returned as a decimal. As we've discussed earlier, the result is in XML.

You might say "Sure, our test page tells us what the Web Service's expectations are. But how would a consumer know what they are?"

In the next section, we discuss how to know what a Web Service requires, what it produces, and how a consumer can communicate with it.

Using your Web Service

As we've learned, it's essential for consumers to know what parameters to send to a Web Service and what values they should expect it to return. To accomplish this, we use a Web Service Description Language file or **WSDL**. This is an XML file that sets out how interaction between a Web Service and its consumer will occur.

The impact of this WSDL standard is enormous. Because it is able to define all the interactions of a Web Service, regardless of whether the service is running on Windows, Linux, Unix, or any other platform, and whether it is written in ASP.NET, Java, or something else entirely it is little short of revolutionary!

This means that in future we won't need to concern ourselves with whether our services, or languages, are cross-platform compatible, but can instead concentrate on the real issue of writing robust, functional code – WSDL will take care of declaring the interaction for us.

For instance, if a Web Service expects two specific parameters and returns a single value, the WSDL defines the names, order, and types of each input and output value. Since we know where to find the Web Service using its URL, we don't need to know the physical location, nor the internal logic of the Web Service. With WSDL, we have all the information we need to begin making use of the Web Service functionality within our own applications. It's really that simple!

> **WSDL is the result of several recent improvements to cross-platform standards. At the time of this writing, the WSDL 1.1 specification is currently being reviewed for adoption by the W3C (the World Wide Web Consortium), the Internet technology standards governing body.**

Let's take a quick look at what a WSDL contract looks like using our `MeasurementConversion` Web Service:

1. Open up your browser and enter the path:

http://localhost/BegASPNET/ch18/MeasurementConversions.asmx

As before, you'll see the following page:

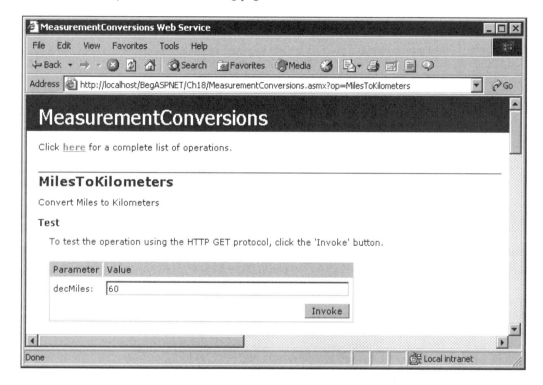

2. Now, click on the Service Description hyperlink at the top of the page:

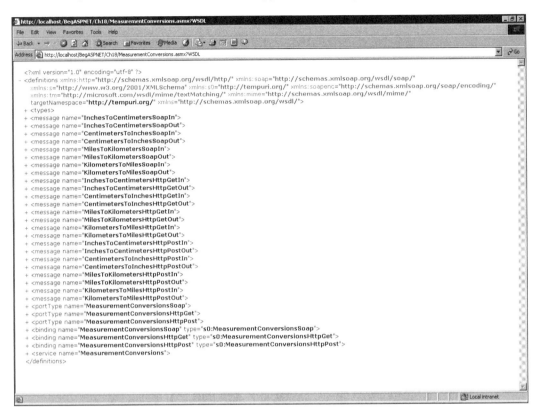

As you can see, there's a lot of information in here (and this is just the collapsed view!). Our web method message names are there and the various HTTP GET, HTTP POST, and SOAP message structures are laid out. These message formats contain the requirements for a consumer to know what parameters are needed to communicate with a Web Service using each message structure.

At the top, the following declaration indicates that the WSDL file is in XML format:

```
<?xml version="1.0" encoding="utf-8" ?>
```

Below that declaration is the <definitions> element, which contains various namespaces. Most of these namespaces make reference to SOAP, which we discussed earlier. These must be included in the file in order for SOAP to work correctly:

```
<definitions xmlns:s="http://www.w3.org/2001/XMLSchema"
  xmlns:http="http://schemas.xmlsoap.org/wsdl/http/"
  xmlns:mime="http://schemas.xmlsoap.org/wsdl/mime/"
  xmlns:tm="http://microsoft.com/wsdl/mime/textMatching/"
```

```
xmlns:soap="http://schemas.xmlsoap.org/wsdl/soap/"
xmlns:soapenc="http://schemas.xmlsoap.org/soap/encoding/"
xmlns:s0="http://tempuri.org/" targetNamespace="http://tempuri.org/"
xmlns="http://schemas.xmlsoap.org/wsdl/">
```

The <types> element, that comes next, defines each of the data types that the Web Service expects to receive and return after completion. This is very complex, and almost a science in itself. It is written in XML Schema Definition language, or XSD. You can't see the definitions in our screenshot as its section, like the others, is collapsed. All you need to do is click on the node in Internet Explorer in order to view them.

After this, we have the various one-way transmissions, from a consumer to our Web Service and back again. Our web method message names are in here and the various HTTP GET, HTTP POST, and SOAP message structures are laid out.

For example, when we expand the message element, we can see the `InchesToCentimeters` web method message structures for SOAP:

```
<message name="InchesToCentimetersSoapIn">
  <part name="parameters" element="s0:InchesToCentimeters" />
</message>
<message name="InchesToCentimetersSoapOut">
  <part name="parameters" element="s0:InchesToCentimetersResponse" />
</message>
```

There are corresponding elements of its HTTP GET and HTTP POST methods. In short, we've got all of the information we need in this file to communicate with our Web Service.

Now that we've discussed the process of building and communicating with XML Web Services in detail, let's create something a bit more complex. Our next example will accept a value, and return a result using ADO.NET to retrieve data from an Access database.

Try It Out – ISBN Search Web Service

We'll create a Web Service that returns the title of a book, based on an ISBN that the consumer provides. This will allow our librarian to add a function on the library's web page to enable users to search by consuming our Web Service.

This particular service will access a database of books. The database contains information on ISBN and book titles. Once the details are received from the database, the results will be inserted into a `DataReader` and returned to the consumer in XML.

This example uses the Access database `Library.mdb`, which you can download along with the code samples for this book from **www.wrox.com**. You should ensure that the file is in the same path as the Web Service that you create.

1. Create a new file in Notepad called `ISBN.asmx`.

2. Add the processing directive and `using` statements to the beginning of the file:

```
<%@ WebService Language="c#" Class="ISBN" %>
using System.Web.Services;
using System.Data;
using System.Data.OleDb;
```

3. Web Service-enable this program by adding this code:

```
public class ISBN : System.Web.Services.WebService
{
  [WebMethod]
  public string BookDetail(string strIsbn)
  {
    return GetBookDetails(strIsbn);
  }
}
```

4. Enter the following code directly following the `BookDetail` web method. This function performs the database lookup and returns the book title string:

```
private string GetBookDetails(string strIsbn)
{
    OleDbDataReader objLibraryDR = null;
    OleDbConnection objLibraryConn = null;
    OleDbCommand objLibraryCmd = null;
    string strConn = "Provider=Microsoft.Jet.OLEDB.4.0;Data Source=" +
                                Server.MapPath("Library.mdb") + ";";
    string strSQL = "SELECT Title FROM Books WHERE ISBN = '" + strIsbn +
                                                          "'";

    string strBookTitle;
    objLibraryConn = new OleDbConnection(strConn);
    objLibraryCmd = new OleDbCommand(strSQL, objLibraryConn);
    objLibraryConn.Open();
    objLibraryDR =
            objLibraryCmd.ExecuteReader(CommandBehavior.CloseConnection);
    if (objLibraryDR.Read())
    {
       strBookTitle = objLibraryDR[0].ToString();
    }
    else
    {
       strBookTitle = "Book not found in the database";
    }
    objLibraryDR.Close();
    return strBookTitle;
}
}
```

5. Once we have completed this code entry, we can test our Web Service: Save the file, then browse to http://localhost/BegASPNET/Ch18/isbn.asmx.

6. Within the Isbn field, enter the ISBN 1861007345. A new browser window will appear containing the following XML:

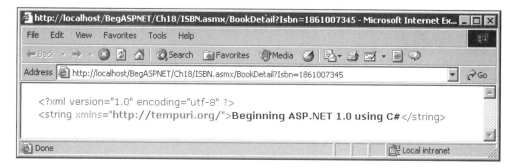

How It Works

Our Web Service provides what is technically known as a 'level of abstraction'. This means that the code to do the work of finding our information isn't taken care of by the web-callable method `BookDetail`. Instead, `BookDetail` calls another, internal, function that we, as consumers, can't see. This function, `GetBookDetails`, does the work of finding the book information and then returns it to `BookDetail`. In turn `BookDetail` returns it to us:

```
[WebMethod]
public string BookDetail(string strIsbn)
{
  return GetBookDetails(strIsbn);
}

private string GetBookDetails(string strIsbn)
{
  ...
}
```

We do this because the job of the `GetBookDetails` function remains the same, regardless of which source is making the request. The same function may be called from a non-Web-Service source, and we certainly wouldn't want to maintain two separate functions that do the same thing, the difference being only the `[WebMethod]` declaration.

We're using ADO.NET to connect to the `Library.mdb` database, retrieve a book title from its `Books` table based on the ISBN, and store it in a `string` variable.

Keeping the data request simple, we define a connection string (`Conn`), and then open the connection to the database (with `LibraryConn`):

```
objLibraryConn = new OleDbConnection(strConn);
objLibraryCmd = new OleDbCommand(strSQL, objLibraryConn);
objLibraryConn.Open();
```

Using the `LibraryCmd` object, we execute the query for a specific ISBN, placing the results in the `LibraryDr` DataReader:

```
objLibraryDR =
        objLibraryCmd.ExecuteReader(CommandBehavior.CloseConnection);
```

We then check whether a row was returned, by calling the `Read` method of our `DataReader`, `LibraryDr`. If it returns `true`, we take the first column (column zero, the `Title` column of the database) from the `DataReader` and place it into `BookTitle`. Otherwise, if it returns `false`, we know that the book was not found, and we place a 'not found' message in the title value. Then we close our `DataReader` and return the book title string:

```
if (objLibraryDR.Read())
{
    strBookTitle = objLibraryDR[0].ToString();
}
else
{
    strBookTitle = "Book not found in the database";
}
objLibraryDR.Close();
return strBookTitle;
```

> For more information on working with data sources, please refer to Chapters 12 and 13.

Consuming a Web Service

Now, we've created some Web Services from start to finish using a variety of technologies. The next step is to understand how to include this functionality within a consumer application. To do this, we must first create an interface that will allow the consumer to see all of the web-callable methods and properties exposed by the Web Service. This saves us the headache of ensuring our parameters are the correct type and from having to create our own protocol request and response handlers. We refer to this interface as a Web Service **proxy**.

How does a Proxy Work?

A proxy resides on the consumer's machine and acts as a relay between the consumer and the Web Service. When we build a proxy, we use a WSDL file (the source of which we'll examine below) to create a map that tells the consumer what methods are available and how to call them. The consumer then calls the web method that is mapped in the proxy, which in turn, makes calls to the actual Web Service over the Internet. The proxy handles all of the network-related work and sending of data, as well as managing the underlying WSDL so the consumer doesn't have to. When we reference the Web Service in the consumer application, it looks as if it's part of the consumer application itself.

Let's take a look at a diagram that illustrates this process:

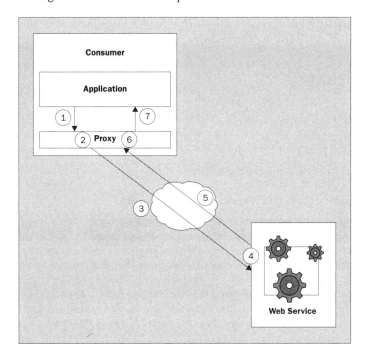

The procedure works as follows:

1. The application executes a function in the proxy code, passing any appropriate parameters to it, without being concerned that the proxy is going to call a Web Service.

2. The proxy receives this call, and formulates the request that will be sent to the Web Service, using the parameters the consumer has specified.

3. This function call is sent from the proxy to the Web Service. This call can be within the confines of the same machine, across a Local Area Network (LAN), or across the Internet. The method of calling remains the same.

4. The Web Service uses the parameters provided by the proxy to execute its web-callable function and build the result in XML.

5. The resulting data from the Web Service is returned to the proxy at the consumer.

6. The proxy parses the XML returned from the Web Service to retrieve the individual values generated. These values may be as simple as integers and strings, or they may define more complex data types.

7. Your application receives the expected values from the proxy function, completely unaware that they resulted from a Web Service call.

747

In order to make use of a Web Service from an ASP.NET page, our proxy must be created and compiled appropriately. Creating a proxy to a Web Service using the .NET Framework tools is very straightforward. These tools make use of WSDL to create a proxy, built in the language of your choice. To demonstrate this, we'll create a new ASP.NET application with which we'll access our new ISBN Web Service.

Creating a Proxy

Building a proxy is a two-step process:

- ❏ Generate the proxy source code
- ❏ Compile the proxy into a run-time library

We'll take a look at how to do this in the following example:

Try It Out – Accessing the ISBN Web Service from an ASP.NET Page

In this example, we will build the proxy and a simple page for retrieving book titles from our ISBN Web Service, demonstrating how quickly we can have our Web Service applications up and running.

We'll assume that you've already configured the Windows environment variable PATH so that it includes a directory path to the executable csc.exe. If not, you should refer to the document *'Configuring your Environment Variables'* available for download with this book's code samples from www.wrox.com.

You'll now need to follow the same process to add a PATH to another file called wsdl.exe. The exact location of this file will depend on how you've installed ASP.NET, and what version you're using. You should be able to find it by using the Windows' search under the directory C:\Program Files. Once you've got it, add the appropriate path to your PATH environment variable and you're ready to proceed (this is also covered in the download PDF if you need a reminder).

1. Navigate to the directory in which your isbn.asmx file resides, and execute this statement (the spaces are important, please type carefully):

```
> wsdl /l:cs /o:ISBNProxy.cs http://localhost/BegASPNET/Ch18 /ISBN.asmx?WSDL /n:ISBNService
```

You should see results something like this:

```
Microsoft (R) Web Services Description Language Utility
[Microsoft (R) .NET Framework, Version 1.0.3705.0]
Copyright (C) Microsoft Corporation 1998-2001. All rights reserved.

Writing file 'ISBNProxy.cs'.
```

We've created our proxy in C# (by specifying the /l:cs parameter), and defined the namespace ISBNService. By selecting a namespace, we will be able to reference our proxy class from within our consuming application.

2. Now let's compile our new proxy code – note that this statement must be entered in full on a single line:

```
> csc /out:ISBNProxy.dll /t:library /r:system.web.dll,system.dll,
system.xml.dll,system.web.services.dll,system.data.dll ISBNProxy.cs
```

You should see something like this after execution:

```
Microsoft (R) Visual C# .NET Compiler version 7.00.9466
for Microsoft (R) .NET Framework version 1.00.3705
Copyright (C) Microsoft Corporation 2001. All rights reserved.
```

3. We'll need a binaries directory for our proxy DLL, so unless you have one already, navigate to the directory you're using as the application root (if you're following the steps that we suggested earlier in the book, this will be C:\BegASPNET), create a folder in it called bin, and copy the newly-created ISBNProxy.dll over from the original test directory.

Now that we have a proxy class, and we've moved it to the correct position, we're ready to make use of our ISBN Web Service from within an ASP.NET page. We'll call the page BookInfo.aspx, and use it to call the web-callable function BookDetail in ISBN.asmx. By using a proxy, our reference to the function's namespace will appear as if it were a function within the same page.

4. Create the BookInfo.aspx file in your test directory, and enter the following code:

```
<%@ Page Language="c#" Debug="true"%>
<%@ Import namespace="ISBNService" %>
<script Language="c#" runat="server">
private void RetrieveBook(object sender, EventArgs e)
{
  ISBNService.ISBN ws = new ISBNService.ISBN();
  lblBookTitle.Text = ws.BookDetail(txtISBN.Text);
}
</script>
<html>
  <body>
    <form id="Form1" method="post" runat="server">
      <asp:TextBox id="txtISBN" runat="server"></asp:TextBox>
      <asp:Button id="Button1" runat="server" Text="Submit"
                OnClick="RetrieveBook"></asp:Button><br />
      <asp:Label id="lblBookTitle" runat="server" Width="152px"
                Height="23px"></asp:Label>
    </form>
  </body>
</html>
```

5. Save the file and call it up in your browser. You should see something like this:

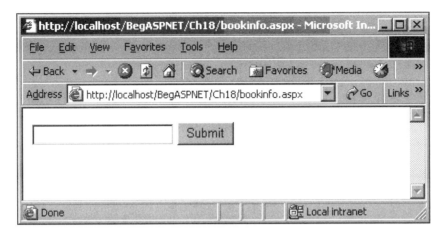

6. Enter an ISBN that we know is in the Books table, like 1861003129:

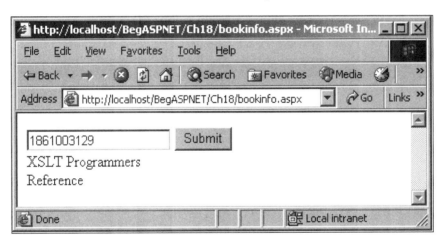

7. Now try an ISBN that you know will not be found, to ensure the proxy is actually working:

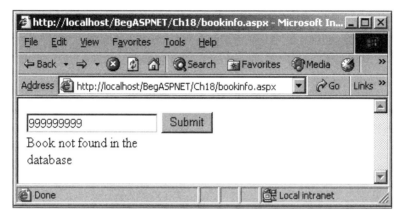

How It Works

When we compiled our proxy to create the `ISBNProxy.dll`, we needed to place it in a `\bin` directory, beneath our application root, as the .NET Framework expects to find our DLLs there:

```
> csc /out:ISBNProxy.dll /t:library /r:system.web.dll,system.dll,
system.xml.dll,system.web.services.dll,system.data.dll ISBNProxy.cs
```

We made use of Web Form controls on our ASP.NET page. These controls, `<asp:TextBox>`, `<asp:Label>` and `<asp:Button>`, make up our simple mini-form that makes a very specific call to the `BookDetail` function.

Upon clicking the Submit button, the `RetrieveBook` event fires, as we specified in the `OnClick` attribute of `<asp:Button>`:

```
<asp:Button id="Button1" runat="server" Text="Submit"
                              OnClick="RetrieveBook" /></asp:Button>
```

Within our `RetrieveBook` function, first of all, we create an instance of the proxy that we'll be using:

```
ISBNService.ISBN ws = new ISBNService.ISBN();
```

Then it's simply a matter of calling the `BookDetail` function of the `ws` object. With a single line of code, we pass the string contents of `txtISBN.Text` to the Web Service and receive the book title, placing that string into the label `lblBookTitle.Text`:

```
lblBookTitle.Text = ws.BookDetail(txtISBN.Text);
```

Once again, this example proves the simplicity and power of Web Services.

Web Service Discovery

As you begin to build Web Service-integrated applications, it will become increasingly important to locate services that provide the functions you need. Universal Description, Discovery, and Integration (UDDI) allows you to do this.

Whenever an industry initiative gains the support of several large industry players, it will likely become mainstream. For this reason, UDDI is positioned to dominate the Web Service discovery field in the future. The UDDI service (which is accessible from http://uddi.microsoft.com or http://www-3.ibm.com/services/uddi/) lets businesses register themselves and list their existing Web Services at no charge. Anyone can browse and search the UDDI database for a service that may suit their needs. UDDI provides information such as contact details (address, phone number, e-mail address, web site), business details (DUNS number and industry sector), and a discovery URL for each service. WSDL is a key component of the UDDI project.

Using http://uddi.microsoft.com/visualstudio/, you can search for businesses that provide Web Services, select the WSDL appropriately, and build your proxies:

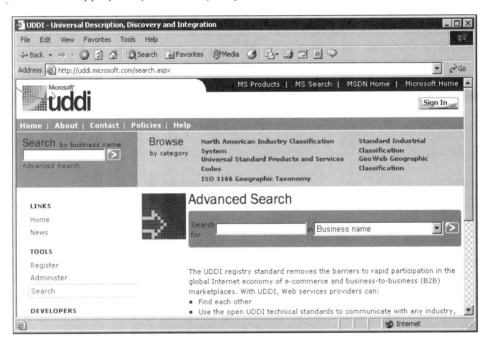

Securing a Web Service

Whether your Web Service is made available on a subscription basis or is completely free to the public, it is important to consider security. The reasons for securing Web Services can range from simple usage logging to strict access control. If your Web Service provides a very useful feature (of course it will!), it's helpful to keep track of who's using it. While you can log the usage of a Web Service that provides privileged information, more stringent security measures should be taken to make sure that the use of your Web Service is consistent with your purposes.

There are many options for securing web applications and services. Here we'll discuss some of the most common techniques. These methods are not mutually exclusive, and can be combined to provide a higher level of security.

Username-Password Combination or Registration Keys

By requiring either a username and password pair or a registration key code as an input parameter, you can provide a way to track which consumers are using your Web Service. A simple database table or XML file containing each username-password pair or registration key code is all that's required to provide this kind of security. Considering that no authentication of the consumer takes place in this scenario, it is very simple for the client to share the username and password (or registration key) with others. A simple "Here, have my password, and you can use this Web Service too" is all that's needed to compromise your security. However, when the data provided by the Web Service is not sensitive or proprietary in nature, this security method provides us with a quick and effective option.

Let's examine how we might apply this type of security to our ISBN Web Service.

Try It Out – Securing a Web Service with Username-Password

We will be using the `security.mdb` database, provided with the code for this book, which can be downloaded from www.wrox.com. This contains a very simple `Users` table consisting of usernames and passwords. Ensure this database is in the same path as the `isbn.asmx` file we created earlier. All our security will do is attempt to match details from the user with an entry in the `Security` table.

1. Re-open the ISBN Web Service in Notepad (`isbn.asmx`), and make the following modifications to the `BookDetail` web method:

```
...
   [WebMethod]
   public string BookDetail(string strIsbn, string strUsername,
                            string strPassword)
   {
     OleDbDataReader objSecurityDR = null;
     OleDbConnection objSecurityConn = null;
     OleDbCommand objSecurityCmd = null;
     string strConn = "Provider=Microsoft.Jet.OLEDB.4.0;Data Source=" +
                      Server.MapPath("Security.mdb") + ";";
     string strSQL = "SELECT Username FROM Users WHERE username = '" +
                     strUsername + "' AND password = '" + strPassword + "'";
     objSecurityConn = new OleDbConnection(strConn);
```

```
        objSecurityCmd = new OleDbCommand(strSQL, objSecurityConn);
        objSecurityConn.Open();
        objSecurityDR =
                objSecurityCmd.ExecuteReader(CommandBehavior.CloseConnection);
        if (objSecurityDR.Read())
        {
           objSecurityDR.Close();
           return GetBookDetails(strIsbn);
        }
        else
        {
           objSecurityDR.Close();
           return "Login to library failed.";
        }
    }
    ...
```

2. Save the result as `ISBNSecurity.asmx`.

Notice that we haven't made any changes to `GetBookDetails()`, as the core functionality of retrieving the book title from the database hasn't changed. Our goal in this scenario is to provide a gatekeeper that prevents access to the internal logic if the consumer's username and password pair is not found in the database.

Browse to the Web Service to test this newly applied security. The only entry in the security table should have the username **librarian** and the password **secret**. This is the only user that is permitted to access our Web Service:

You can add more registered users by modifying the `Security` table.

How It Works

We have used nearly the same logic validating the login as we previously used in `GetBookDetails()` to look up a book. By adding this logic to the web-callable `BookDetail` function, we completely prevent access to the internal `GetBookDetails()` function if the login fails. Upon a failure to login correctly, we return a simple string:

```
        return "Login to library failed.";
```

If the username and password combination is successfully located in the database, the result of the `GetBookDetails()` function is returned just as before.

Secure Sockets Layer (SSL)

The most common method of securing information on the Web is the Secure Sockets Layer (SSL). When you make an online purchase, you'll typically see a lock or key icon displayed in the browser's status bar to let you know you're communicating safely. Information passed between the browser and the web site travels in an encrypted form. In the case of Web Services, applying SSL ensures that the data traveling between the consumer and endpoint is encrypted, and thus, difficult to intercept.

The beauty of SSL is that it has no affect on the integrity of the data provided by your Web Service. When a value is returned to the consumer it remains the same, regardless of the encryption used in its transportation. The only downside is that it does have an effect on the overall performance of your site, as there is more processing required. You can get more information about verifying your identity for use with SSL from a Certificate Authority like Verisign (www.verisign.com).

IP Address Restriction

Maintaining an IP address list of all registered users can help us control the use of a Web Service. This approach presents a number of potential issues, the greatest being the never-ending maintenance of IP address ranges for each client. IP address restriction can take place at both hardware and software levels. A hardware application of this security typically involves firewall restrictions to specific IP addresses. Restricting IP access using software security often involves keeping a database table of clients and another with associated IP addresses.

Each time a Web Service is accessed, we can get the requestor's IP address (using the HTTP headers) and confirm that it exists in the security tables. If a match is located, the Web Service executes normally. Another option for software-based IP-address security is at the web-server level. Most web-server software permits any number of IP addresses to be restricted or enabled. Within IIS, it's as simple as selecting the properties of a given site and changing the IP restrictions. Since maintaining IP addresses of clients can be terribly cumbersome, as well as overly restrictive (if a consumer's IP address changes frequently), this option is generally not recommended.

Other Considerations

Web Services are bringing about a major paradigm shift, not seen since the early days of the Internet. Because of this, it's important to recognize that these new conveniences have their own set of advantages and disadvantages. While we won't talk about all the ways to avoid these pitfalls (which would require a book in itself), we will consider some of key issues.

If you want more detailed information, you might like to consider Professional ASP.NET Web Services *(1-86100-545-8), also published by Wrox Press.*

Network Connectivity

A few years ago, the idea of calling a remote function and retrieving a value from it seemed unlikely. Now that we have Web Services this newfound ability to use, or purchase, a given function from any organization on the Web causes us to think about the issue of Internet connectivity. It's important to realize that not only must your company's Internet connection be reliable, but now we must rely on your Web Service provider's connection to be reliable as well. Furthermore, if a Web Service requires any additional Internet resources, its service vendor's network must also be stable. There are many potential failure points in this arrangement. Often, this can be compounded if a Web Service provider hesitates, or refuses, to disclose who their providers are, since they don't want you going direct to them!

Asynchronous Method Calls

Since SOAP can be transported using SMTP (the e-mail protocol), we can write Web Services that make use of asynchronous method calls. Asynchronous communication is a sort of disconnected, two-way interaction that doesn't require an immediate response. Most programming deals with synchronous communication, where you call a function and wait for it to complete and return a value:

```
Distance_To_Rome = DistanceBetween("Los Angeles", "Rome", "meters");
```

In a situation like this, our application will not continue until the DistanceBetween function completes its logic and returns a value, which is placed in Distance_To_Rome. While this suits our needs most of the time, it is not always appropriate, especially when dealing with web programming. Batch processing, application speed, and anticipated disconnections are three situations where we may wish to consider the possible advantages of asynchronous communication. The great news is that your Web Service need not be tailored specifically for synchronous or asynchronous communication; this is the duty of the proxy.

The following C# code snippet illustrates how we might implement asynchronous function calls, using events:

```
...
DistanceBetween("Los Angeles", "Rome", "meters");
...
public void DistanceBetween_CalculationComplete(int Distance)
{
  Distance_To_Rome = Distance;
}
...
```

If our application contains code such as this, we will issue a request to DistanceBetween to calculate the distance between two cites, and then move on with our code. When the DistanceBetween object completes its calculation, it fires the CalculationComplete event, which allows us to handle the returned value, without making the rest of the application wait.

Because we can call a remote function without the need for immediate response (without breaking an application), our applications can support longer time intervals and handle poorer network conditions, such as dial-up situations. In the case of SMTP, the SOAP request is packaged in an e-mail format and delivered to a mailbox on the server, just as if it was an e-mail composed and addressed to another individual. The specification for SOAP over SMTP defines a process of retrieving this message from the mail server, executing the function required, and mailing the SOAP results again to the consumer, again using SMTP.

Service Hijacking (or Piggybacking)

Once your Web Service is available to the public, you may attract a client who is particularly interested in the service you provide. They're so interested, in fact, that they consider wrapping your powerful Web Service inside of their own and representing it as their own product. Without security safeguards in place (and legal documents as well), a client may repackage your Web Service as if it were their own function, and there's no way for you to detect that this is being done (though you may become suspicious by examining your usage log when your client who occasionally uses your Web Service suddenly shows an enormous increase in activity). Given the level of abstraction that Web Services provide, it would also be nearly impossible for any customers of your unethical client to know who really owns the functionality.

Some organizations use a combination of usage logging and per-use charges. In my opinion, a cleverer way to avoid piggybacking is by using false data tests. We could create an undocumented function within our Web Service that creates a result that only our logic could produce. We would able to determine whether this code is really ours and the client is piggybacking our Web Service or if the client is truly using its own logic. An example of implementing a false data test would be a Web Service that provides book information for a given ISBN. As in our ISBN Web Service, we may return some arbitrary details if a certain ISBN is provided and is not associated with a real book. If ISBN "ABCDEFGHI" were entered, special codes or copyright information could be sent as the resulting book title. We could then test this on the piggybacking company we suspect is stealing our Web Service. Since this hidden functionality would not be published, it would provide a great way to prove that a company was reselling your Web Service's logic without your legal approval.

Provider Solvency

Since the Web Service model is a viable solution, you're probably eager to add its functionality to your core information systems and mission-critical applications. As Web Services become more and more interdependent, it becomes increasingly necessary to research the companies from whom you consume Web Services. You'll want to make sure these providers appear to have what it takes to remain in business. UDDI goes a long way towards helping you with this research by providing company information for each registered Web Service provider (including their DUNS number). In the business world, nothing seems to impact and force sweeping changes more than insolvency, and if you find yourself in the unfortunate circumstance of lost functionality due to a bankrupt Web Service provider, you'll realize how painful the hurried search for a new vendor can be (with little room to bargain with your ex-service's competitors). Although the initial work can be a bit tedious, it is important to know, as far as you can, whether a potential Web Service vendor will still be in business five years from now.

The Interdependency Scenario

The basis for all these and other Web Service considerations is the issue of **interdependency**. The potential exists for you to wake up any given morning, start an application that has worked for years, and find that the Web Service that it relies on is no longer available.

To some extent, thanks to the UDDI search capabilities, you can investigate and assess potential providers, but at the end of the day a degree of faith needs to be put into the services of each provider you choose to consume.

Summary

In this chapter, we've seen that a Web Service exposes its functions as a service that other applications can use. We began by discussing what a Web Service is and how one might be used. We recapped XML and HTTP and their uses within the Web Services architecture. Then we delved into the process of building Web Services, and creating and compiling a Web Service proxy. We learned how to use Web Services in an application by incorporating a defined namespace and making use of its methods. Afterwards, we covered how to discover what Web Services we have available to consume. Finally, we considered some of the ways to make a Web Service secure.

As .NET makes programmatic interfaces over the Web more commonplace, we'll gradually be able to see applications sharing and building upon the contributions made by the community of Web Service providers. Web Services will provide a powerful means of seamlessly assembling applications that can span multiple platforms and languages. For the user, a transition is on the horizon from the browser to the more specific applications that make use of Web Services. For the developer, ASP.NET Web Services will make the Internet a programmer's toolbox, with a greater assortment of tools than ever before.

Exercises

1.

    a. Explain the role of the Simple Object Access Protocol (SOAP) in web services.

    b. What is the purpose of the WSDL?

    c. How would you locate a web service that provides the functions you require?

2. Create a Web Service with a class name of `circles` that calculates the area of a circle, the circumference of a circle and the volume of a sphere. (Area = ( )r^2; Circumference = 2( )r; Volume of a sphere = 4/3 ( )r^3

3. Create a Web Service that connects to the Northwind database and returns Employee's addresses based on their last names.

4. Create an ASP.NET page containing a drop-down listbox in which a user can select names of Northwind employees to return their addresses.

5. Secure the Northwind employee Addresses Web Service so that no unauthorized users have access to it.

Configuration and Optimization

Throughout this book we've been creating ASP.NET pages that solve a variety of problems. We've looked at basic programming constructs, objects, data, and controls, to name just a few. With each of these we've looked at various ways of producing our results – some short and sharp, others long and wordy. We've only really been concerned with demonstrating the concept and the ways it can be done, not with efficiency.

In this chapter we'll be looking at how we can improve this process by increasing the performance of our pages through configuration, and through general optimization techniques. We'll also look at other aspects of optimization to improve security and user-friendliness, and to make it easier to debug and manage applications. In particular, we'll look at:

❑   The structure and function of the ASP.NET configuration files, `machine.config` and `web.config`

❑   Customization of those files to increase performance, security, and usability

❑   How to use caching to increase the performance of your server

❑   The use of tracing to debug your code without inserting additional code into it

❑   How to monitor the resources your application is taking up, and gather basic statistics about its operation

This chapter covers some fairly advanced ground, so we'll not be looking at these issues in too much detail, but hopefully we'll set you on the right path to a well-configured and highly-optimized ASP.NET site.

If you want to learn more about the advanced topics presented in this chapter, you might want to refer to Professional ASP.NET 1.0 Special Edition, *Wrox Press ISBN: 1-86100-703-5.*

Configuration Overview

ASP.NET has been designed to be easily customizable by adopting XML-based configuration files. These files can be used to configure any component of ASP.NET by editing the file in a text editor. You simply write a piece of code to explain how you'd like ASP.NET to perform a certain operation, and then configure ASP.NET to run your code instead of its built-in code.

You're not restricted to just defining configuration settings at design or run time, either. You can add or change them at any time. The new configuration settings you have supplied will simply be activated, with no loss of efficiency for the server.

In this chapter, we're going to be looking at two types of configuration file:

❑   The Machine Configuration File – `machine.config` – for machine-wide settings

❑   Application Configuration Files – `web.config` – for application-specific settings

The .NET Framework has two other configuration files, which are beyond the scope of this book. They are the Security Configuration Files (`enterprisesec.config` and `security.config`) that deal with the tiers of a web server's security policy.

Let's take a look at how we can view configuration files using Internet Explorer.

Browsing .config Files

Because the configuration files are XML documents their contents are stored in plain text, meaning that you can view them with a simple text editor. However, as you may remember from Chapter 5, if you open the document using Internet Explorer you have the ability to expand and collapse the nodes of the tree, making a large file easier to read. Let's take a look at the `machine.config` file. You can find this at the following location:

```
%SystemRoot%\Microsoft.NET\Framework\v1.0.3705\CONFIG\machine.config
```

If you **copy** this file and save it as `machine.config.xml` anywhere on your system, and then open it in your browser, you'll see your `machine.config` file displayed in the same way as an XML document:

> **Important note – do not rename the original `machine.config` – ASP.NET relies on this file for its configuration, and will not run properly without it!**

If you collapse the major nodes, you'll get a graphical display of the basic elements:

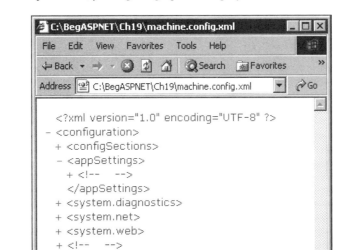

The Configuration Files

As we have already mentioned, we'll be examining two configuration files in this chapter, namely machine.config and web.config. Your system will have only one file called machine.config on it, but probably many web.config files. machine.config contains any machine-specific settings that ASP.NET needs to function, whereas web.config contains configuration information for a **specific** web application, and can override default functionality defined in the base machine.config file to provide a customized environment for each application that you produce.

The configuration sequence of events runs like this:

When a page is initialized, the information in machine.config is read. Once this has been done, ASP.NET descends to the next level of the hierarchy and reads the individual web.config files stored in your web application root directories. These files supply additional configuration information to augment, or override, settings inherited from machine.config. Then, ASP.NET will descend to the next level and read web.config files stored in your application's child directories below the root. These will be used to augment or override information given either in machine.config, or in the root web.config. Next, any web.config files in child directories below these will be read and acted on in a similar manner. This will continue until all web.config files in the tree have been processed. Some of your directories may not have a web.config file – in this case, they will inherit their settings from the closest configuration file node in the tree above them.

This can be seen more clearly by looking at the following diagram, of the virtual directories in IIS:

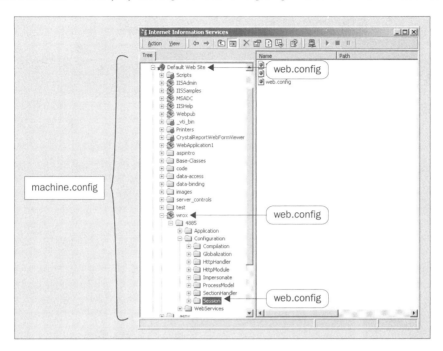

A well-structured setup would store general settings you want taken into account at a machine-wide level in the `machine.config` file, and then override them, when necessary, using `web.config` files specific to the application page or pages that need to do so. This approach is beneficial as if changes need to be made to the general structure of your application you only need to make alterations to the one `machine.config` file. Likewise, if an individual page needs special settings to function, it can be placed in a child directory with its own `web.config` file, and any changes you make there will affect just that page, and not your whole application or machine.

At run time, ASP.NET uses the information provided by the configuration files to compute the settings for each application or URL resource. The settings are then cached (see later in the chapter) to allow faster access on subsequent calls. ASP.NET can detect changes made to the configuration files while the web server is running, and will apply the altered version immediately without needing to have the server stopped or rebooted.

Configuration files are protected from unauthorized snooping because IIS is automatically configured to prevent HTTP access to them. A server error will be returned if any attempt is made to browse these files over HTTP, even if the file does not exist. You can try this for yourself by directing your browser to http://localhost/web.config, where you will see the following message:

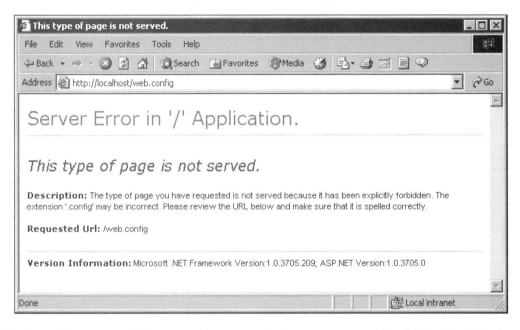

You'll get this same result if you try to browse to global.asax, or any file that has the following extensions: .ascx, .cs, .csproj, .vb, .vbproj, and .webinfo as they're set up the same way.

Configuration File Rules

We've already mentioned that our configuration files are XML-based, so now we're going to recap what that means, and how it applies to the well-formedness of these files (see Chapter 5 if you need a more in-depth discussion):

❑ They must have a single unique **root element** that encloses all other elements within it. The root element for both machine.config and web.config is <configuration>.

❑ Elements must be enclosed between corresponding start <tag> and end </tag> tags. These tags are case-sensitive so <Tag> and <tag> will be treated differently.

❑ Any attributes, keys or values must be enclosed in double quotes: <add key="data" />.

❑ Elements must be nested and not overlap.

> Be very careful when you're editing configuration files, as they affect your server's behavior – always make a backup before modifying them.

765

Configuration File Format

Now that we've refreshed our memory about the basic XML rules that apply to configuration files, let's look at the way these files are structured.

The XML structure is most noticeable in `machine.config` where all of the XML elements are declared, and their values set: `web.config` is usually smaller and ordinarily only contains a selection of settings, as it is altering elements already declared in `machine.config`.

The configuration files are structurally divided into two main areas. First there is a **declarations** section, where individual classes are defined to manipulate information. This section is delimited by `<configSections>` tags. Second, there is the **settings** section where values are assigned to the classes declared in the first section. This is delimited by `<sectionGroup>` tags.

In `web.config` files we can override the values of classes defined in the `machine.config` declarations section. Within these two main groups there are several subgroups that divide the information up into manageable chunks. The only one that we are going to worry about is the `system.web` group, which contains the ASP.NET specific material.

Here's a screenshot of the declarations section, with the `system.web` group expanded:

After all the declarations have been made, we move on to the settings section. Here we are establishing the attributes and properties of the declared classes. You don't have to define the settings for elements in the same order that you declared them in the <configSections> tags, but you must define settings for every handler you have declared or an exception will be thrown. You must also take care to ensure that all tags are properly closed and nested, and that any values specified fall within the correct range.

You should note that there is a great deal more structure and detail in these files than we've covered here. Our aim has been to give you a general idea of what these files are, and what they look like, so that when we move on to the next section you'll be able to find your way around and tune your system.

The Structure of the Configuration Files

If you look at your machine's machine.config file, you'll see that its declarations and settings are broken up into about thirty blocks of configurations. We're going to give you a quick overview of four of the most useful of these, and point out some of the simple alterations that you can make to improve the functioning of your machine.

> Note that all these changes take place in the *settings* section.

General Configuration

This section of our configuration files contains general application configuration settings, such as how long a request is processed for before it is timed out, the maximum size of a request, and whether or not to use a fully qualified URL when re-directing pages. They are contained within the <httpRuntime> tags, and occur within the <system.web> tags, that we mentioned earlier. Here's how you'd set them up in your web.config file:

```
<configuration>
  <system.web>
    <httpRuntime executionTimeout="120"
    maxRequestLength="8192"
    useFullyQualifiedRedirectUrl="false"
    />
  </system.web>
</configuration>
```

Let's look at these settings in a bit more detail:

❑ executionTimeout controls the time in seconds for which a request is allowed to try to execute before ASP.NET cancels (times out) the execution of the request. 90 seconds is the default value. If you know that a process (like a complex database query) will most likely take longer than 90 seconds to execute, you should increase this value. This is a very useful feature because if your database breaks during the code's execution ASP.NET knows how long to wait before delivering an error message – it will not wait forever.

❑ maxRequestLength specifies the maximum length of a request. 4MB is the default value. If the content requested is larger than 4MB, increase this value. If the content requested never exceeds a lesser value, use that instead. This can be a useful precaution. If your code breaks it will prevent it from dumping great quantities of data to your client, as it will stop when it hits the maxRequestLength.

Also it stops clients trying to request too much information at once and hogging all your server's processing time dealing with their requests at the expense of other users.

❑ useFullyQualifiedRedirectUrl is not often used. One example of when you need to use this parameter is when you are working with some mobile controls. It indicates whether client-side redirects are fully qualified, or whether relative redirects should be used (which is the default). Certain mobile controls require that you use fully qualified redirects.

Page Configuration

The page configuration settings give us control over the default behavior of ASP.NET pages. This can include things such as whether we should buffer output before sending it, and whether or not session state is enabled for pages within your application. The information is housed within the <pages> element in your configuration files. Here's how you'd set it up in your web.config file. All values are set to their defaults:

```
<configuration>
  <system.web>
    <pages buffer="true"
    enableSessionState="true"
    enableViewState="true"
    autoEventWireup="true" />
  </system.web>
</configuration>
```

Let's take a closer look at what these settings do:

❑ buffer indicates the code execution processing mode. When it is set to true, all code is executed before any HTML data in the page is rendered. When it is set to false, all code is rendered as it executes.

For example, you could turn off buffering if you're running a complex data query that returns results with a slight delay between each record – you could display a table line by line while the page is loading, so that the user is aware of the fact that something is happening.

- ❑ `EnableSessionState` indicates whether server `session` variables are available. The default value is `true`, enabling `session` state. To disable it set the value to `false`. We recommend that you set it to `true` only if you need to use `session` variables in your page, as disabling `session` state improves performance.

- ❑ `EnableViewState` indicates whether server controls maintain state when the page request ends. When it is set to `true` the server controls maintain state (that is they 'remember' their value). This is the default setting. If it is set to `false`, the server controls don't maintain state. Only set it to `true` if you need your controls to maintain state, as disabling it improves performance.

- ❑ `AutoEventWireup` indicates whether ASP.NET fires page events, like `Page_Load`, automatically or not. `true` is the default setting. Changing it to `false` allows custom assemblies to control the firing of page events.

*`false` is the default setting for the Visual Studio .NET IDE, as it uses an internal mechanism to control event firing. If you are **not** using VS.NET you should leave it at the default `true`.*

Application Settings

Application settings allow us to store application configuration details in configuration files without the need to write our own custom section handlers for them. The key-value pairs declared here are used to populate a table that we can access from within our applications. This is a great benefit – because configuration files cannot be read over HTTP it keeps your database connection strings, and so on, away from prying eyes while always being available. Here's how you'd set it up in `web.config`:

```
<configuration>
 <appSettings>
 <add key= "DSN"
  value="server=LSERV; uid=user; pwd=password; database=data" />
 </appSettings>
</configuration>
```

Here a key called `DSN` is being added to the table, and the values in the value section are being associated with it. We would now be able to access this information from inside our application. This is done in your ASP.NET script as follows:

```
...
  strDataSource = ConfigurationSettings.AppSettings("DSN");
...
```

Custom Errors

While every developer does their best to ensure their pages are thoroughly tested before they are deployed in a full application, errors still happen. When a page has errors that are caught during compilation by a .NET Framework compiler (remember that ASP.NET pages are compiled) ASP.NET generates a syntax error report with information about the error, and sends this information to the browser. On the other hand, if an error occurs while a page is being executed, ASP.NET sends a **Stack Trace** containing information about the error to the browser. This Stack Trace contains information about what was going on when the error occurred. While this information is convenient for the developer to debug their code, it's not something you'd want visitors to your site to see, not least because it can reveal detailed information about how your code works – potentially allowing malicious types to find loopholes and exploit them.

That aside, we don't want this information to be displayed to our users because this 'raw' information is going to disconcert them and bring the quality of our coding into question. It's spoiling our client's experience. Far better for us to make some changes to the way our application handles errors, so that user can be redirected to elsewhere on our site.

You can configure custom error pages for your application using the `<customErrors>` section of your `web.config` file, inside the `<system.web>` tags:

```
<customErrors
  defaultRedirect="url"
  mode="On|Off|RemoteOnly">
  <error statusCode="statuscode" redirect="url"/>
</customErrors>
```

❑ `defaultRedirect` indicates the default URL to redirect the browser to if an error occurs. This allows your application to recover if a page fails by sending your users elsewhere, so they're not confronted with a broken page.

❑ `mode` configures whether custom errors are `On`, `Off`, or `RemoteOnly`. `On` shows your custom error to everyone when it occurs, regardless of where they are. `Off` never shows anyone a custom error, and `RemoteOnly` shows your custom error to browsers that are not located on your server.

> **You'll need to set this to On in order to test your custom error pages (unless you've access to a browser off the server) after you're done we recommend you change it to RemoteOnly so your users will see the custom error page while you'll still get the standard error page with all the useful debugging information that it contains.**

❑ `error` subtags can appear as often as required throughout your custom error element. They are used to define special conditions above and beyond the default re-direct we set up with the `defaultRedirect` value. They are given an HTTP status code to react to and an URL to redirect to if that status code occurs. This gives you the flexibility to react to different errors differently. For example reacting to 404 Page Not Found, and 403 Access Forbidden errors differently.

The default `customErrors` configuration option for ASP.NET is `RemoteOnly`, which means that custom errors are only shown on browsers not located on the server. However no redirect page is specified in the defaults, so the redirection won't work until you set it up in `web.config`, like this:

```
<configuration>
  <system.web>
    <customerrors
      defaultRedirect = "customerror.aspx"
      mode = "RemoteOnly"
    />
  </system.web>
</configuration>
```

Performance Optimization

Some of the options we've just looked at in the previous section are used to improve your system's security (for example, using configuration files to house database connection strings) others are for user friendliness (creating customized error pages). But some are simply used to improve the speed at which your applications perform (enabling page buffering, while disabling `session` state will speed up your pages).

Now we're going to look at other ways we can make your application perform faster.

Caching

If you're working on your home PC, and it's connected to the internet via a modem, when you browse a web page for the first time, you may find that the page takes a while to load. Subsequent visits to that page may well be a lot quicker, because the page has been cached on your machine. In a similar way, if one person on a corporate network visits a web site, the page may take a while to load. But, if someone else visits the same page, depending on the settings on the network, they may find the page loads a lot more quickly because it has been cached by a network proxy. This method is also used by ASP.NET to cache frequently used portions of ASP.NET pages on the web server so they don't need to be compiled every time a page is accessed.

However, you probably don't want certain items to be cached indefinitely – for example, if you're running a news site, you want the content on your site to be refreshed at regular intervals to display any new news items. Depending on the nature of your news, you might want it to refresh every half an hour, every ten minutes, or even every minute. Any requests that get served during the cached period see the same page, but after the cache duration expires, the old cache is destroyed, and a new page is generated with updated content. Simply checking for the absence of the item in the cache causes the recreation of the data in the cache. This content is then cached for the required duration and the cycle starts again.

Setting the appropriate time period is of maximum importance. A list of cities or ZIP codes won't need a short expiration period, while a list of clients, or a product list, will need regular refreshing over relatively short periods of time. Keep in mind that anything you place in the cache consumes memory, so use this feature judiciously.

Now let's look at the different types of caching that you can set up:

Output Caching

Output Caching allows caching of any response generated by any request for any application resource. Output caching is very useful when you want to cache the contents of an entire page. On a busy site, caching frequently accessed pages for even as little as a minute can result in substantial performance gains. While the page lives in the output cache, additional requests for that page are served from the cache without recompiling and executing the code that created the page.

The complete syntax for the Output Cache is this:

```
<%@ OutputCache Duration="#ofseconds" Location="Any | Client |
   Downstream | Server | None" VaryByControl="controlname"
   VaryByCustom="browser | customstring" VaryByHeader="headers"
   VaryByParam="parametername" %>
```

Let's look at some of the most important parameters in more detail:

❑ Duration specifies the duration in seconds that the content be allowed to cache for.

❑ Location is used to specify which locations are allowed to cache the page. When set to Server, only the server running the application is allowed to cache the page. A setting of Downstream means that any intervening network proxies are allowed to cache a copy of the page. When set to Client, the browser is allowed to cache the page locally. When set to Any, any of these caches may be used.

Alternatively you could specify a setting of None, which stops caching from being used.

❑ VaryByControl allows controls to be cached on the server, so that they do not have to be rendered every time a page is requested. Using this parameter caches the control specified as it appears on the page. For example, if you have a control that displays a list of news items, these could be cached for ten minutes, simply by caching the control for that long.

❑ VaryByCustom allows you to specify whether you want to store different versions of the cache for different browser, or to vary by a specified string. If this parameter is given the value browser, different caches are created by browser name and major version, which allows you to have different cached versions of a page for different browsers. This is particularly useful for when you need to target output differently for different browsers or different devices. It allows you to specify in detail the parts of a page that you want to cache.

❑ VaryByHeader enables us to cache pages specified by different HTTP headers, using a semicolon-separated list. When this parameter is set to multiple headers, the output cache will contain a different version of the requested document for each specified header.

❑ VaryByParam allows you to vary the caching requirements by specific parameters in the form of a semicolon-separated list of strings. By default, these strings correspond to a query string value, or to a parameter sent with the POST method. When this parameter is set to multiple values, the output cache will contain a different version of the requested document for each specified value. Possible values include none,*, and any valid query string or POST parameter name.

This attribute is required when you Output-cache ASP.NET pages and/or user controls. A parser error will occur if you don't include it. If you do not want to specify a value to vary cached content by, for example, if you want the complete page cached at all times, set the value to none. If you want to have a different output cache for all possible parameters, set the value to *.

Let's have a look at how this works in a quick example:

1. Create an ASPX file containing the following code, and call it `ServerTime.aspx`:

```
<script  language="c#" runat = "server">
  string ServerTime()
  {
    return System.DateTime.Now.ToLongTimeString();
  }
</script>

The time on your web server is : <%=ServerTime() %>
```

This code displays the current time on your web server. Call it up in your browser, and verify that the code is working. After a couple of seconds, click your browser's refresh button and watch the numbers change.

2. Now add the following page directive at the top of your code:

```
<%@ OutputCache Duration="60" VaryByParam="none" %>

<script  language="c#" runat = "server">
  string ServerTime()
  {
    return System.DateTime.Now.ToLongTimeString();
  }
</script>

The time on your web server is : <%=ServerTime() %>
```

3. Save your code as `CachedServerTime.aspx` and call it up in your browser again. To begin with everything looks the same, the code displays the time as before, but when you click the refresh button the time doesn't change, it remains the same. In fact it will remain the same for 60 seconds. Try it and see!

How It Works

Our `ServerTime.aspx` code example is very simple. It runs a function called `ServerTime()` on your server to get the server's time, and then returns it formatted as a string. This returned information is then displayed to the screen using a line of HTML and some in-line ASP.NET tags:

```
<script  language="c#" runat = "server">
  string ServerTime()
  {
    return System.DateTime.Now.ToLongTimeString();
  }
</script>

The time on your web server is : <%=ServerTime() %>
```

This code does not specify that it should be cached, so the server processes it anew each time that the page is called. So, when you click your browser's refresh button, it processes the code, and gives you the newly processed result. The time changes each time as you press the refresh button.

When the page directive is added this is no longer the case:

```
<%@ OutputCache Duration="60" VaryByParam="none" %>
```

We're instructing the server to cache the output generated by our request for a period of 60 seconds. Any subsequent page requests within that period will be served with the cached version, so the time will remain the same until the cached page expires and it is processed anew. The `VaryByParam` attribute that we saw earlier is set to `none` in this example, meaning that the same page will be delivered from the cache regardless of the parameters delivered with the request (although our example is quite basic, and as a result, it doesn't have any parameters).

Fragment Caching

This allows the caching of portions of a response generated by any request that includes user controls. Sometimes it's not practical to cache an entire page, (for example, if you've got a section for advertisements on a page, or some personalization features that have to be unique to every user). In cases such as these, you may still want portions of the page to be cached, and the remainder to be generated programmatically for each user. If this is the case, it is worthwhile to create user controls for those portions that do not change, so that they can be created once and cached for a defined time period.

For example, to cache all the controls defined in an ASCX (user control) source file, just include this directive in the control itself:

```
<%@ OutputCache Duration="60" VaryByParam="none" %>
```

You don't have to place the `OutputCache` directive in the page in which the controls are called (the ASPX page). All other controls included in the ASCX will automatically be cached for 60 seconds.

If you wanted to cache each of the possible variations of your control's properties, you'd use this directive:

```
<%@ OutputCache Duration="60" VaryByParam="*" %>
```

The asterisk (*) directs the Output Cache to cache a page for every parameter property returned by your control.

Tracing

Tracing is a very useful feature of ASP.NET that lets us follow the execution of our code, and then review it afterwards (see Chapter 17 for a detailed discussion). It can help us tighten up loose coding and fix bugs. Throughout this book, when we've written code we've used either `Response.Write` or an ASP.NET `<label>` tag to print information to the screen. They're good as far as they go, but when we use them to debug our code, we're introducing additional code into our program. This is not a good thing to do, as it is often very hard to get this additional code back out again when we want to deploy our application, and it can affect the sequence of operation, meaning you have to adjust your code to accommodate it. Fortunately the `Trace.Write()` object gives us a way of avoid inserting additional code into our applications:

Let's refresh our memories with a quick example:

Try It Out – Tracing

1. Here's some code that needs debugging. Call it `TraceCode.aspx`, and save it in your `Ch19` directory within your `C:\BegASPNET` directory:

```
<script Language="c#" runat = "server">
  public int Subtract(int intFirst, int intSecond)
  {
    return intFirst - intSecond;
  }
</script>
The value of 45 minus 30 is : <%=Subtract(45, 30) %>
```

2. Run this code, to verify it's working, and you'll get this output:

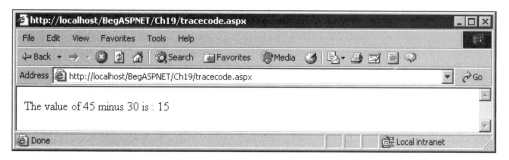

3. Now make the following changes to the code, and save it again:

```
<%@ Page trace= "true" %>
<script Language="c#" runat = "server">
  public int Subtract(int intFirst, int intSecond)
  {
    Trace.Write( " intFirst : ", intFirst);
    Trace.Write("intSecond : ", intSecond);
```

```
    return intFirst - intSecond;
  }
</script>

The value of 45 minus 30 is : <%=Subtract(45, 30) %>
```

4. When you run it the output now looks like this:

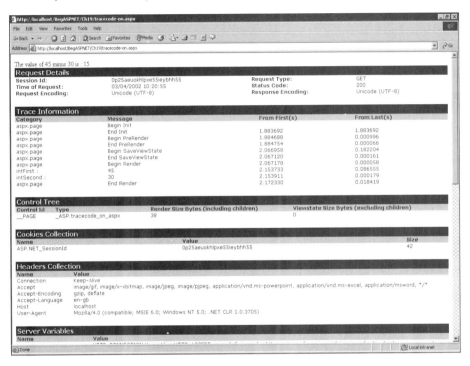

Our page is still at the top, but beneath it a large amount of trace information is now showing, including the values of our variables in the Trace Information section.

How It Works

The code we're using is very simple – there's nothing here that we've not already discussed in Chapter 17. We're displaying the returned value of a function that is being fed two values, 45 and 30.

```
<script Language="c#" runat = "server">
  public int Subtract(int intFirst, int intSecond)
  {
   return intFirst - intSecond;
  }
</script>

The value of 45 minus 30 is : <%=Subtract(45, 30) %>
```

To trace the sequence of execution, and the values being used in our code we're adding two
`Trace.Write` statements and a page directive to activate them:

```
<%@ Page trace= "true" %>
<script Language="c#" runat = "server">
  public int Subtract(int intFirst, int intSecond)
  {
    Trace.Write( " intFirst : ", intFirst);
    Trace.Write("intSecond : ", intSecond);
    return intFirst - intSecond;
  }
</script>

The value of 45 minus 30 is : <%=Subtract(45, 30) %>
```

This provides the following information, as we saw previously:

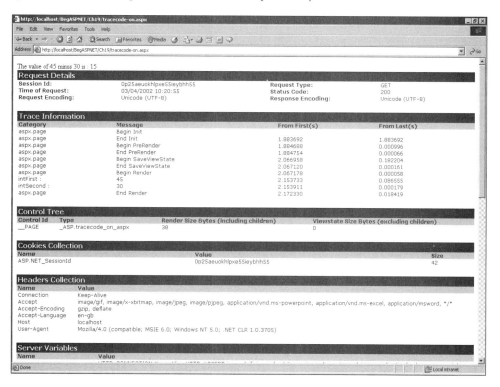

It is the Trace Information section that is of interest to us. It outlines the order in which our page's
functionality has been executed. It shows that before getting to our code, and rendering it, a number of
other ASP.NET native procedures have been run, including a PreRender, and a SaveViewState
function. We're not using state information in our page, so we might want to think about turning the
Viewstate function off as we explained earlier in the chapter to save resources and speed up our
code. The trace also confirms, as expected, that our function is using the values we gave it, 45 and 30,
for its calculations.

Trace can also be set up in your `web.config` files with code like this:

```
<configuration>
  <system.web>
    <trace
      enabled="true"
      requestLimit = "10"
      pageOutput="false"
      traceMode="SortByTime"
      localOnly = "true"
    />
  </system.web>
</configuration>
```

When we set tracing up in this way (the default value for `enabled`, inherited from `machine.config`, is `false`) we can view our trace output using a special tool called `trace.axd`. This file is a log file that can be used to store the trace results for the last page viewed. This can be called from your browser in the directory for which you have enabled tracing. This method is useful if you don't want to display the actual trace information at the bottom of your page, but want to keep a record of it in a separate file, which is overwritten each time a page is called. Setting the `pageOutput` directive back to `true` appends this information back to the bottom of your page.

You can try this out by adding this information to the `web.config` file in your application root, and then run both your ASPX file and `trace.axd` from this location:

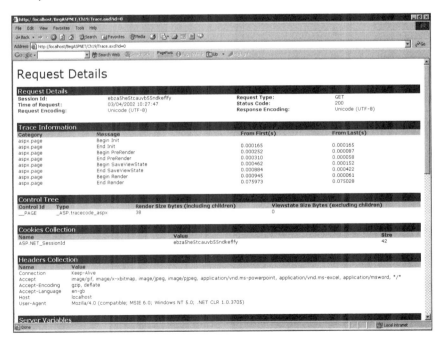

The options for the your `web.config` file are:

❑ `enabled` switches tracing on or off at the application level. When it is switched off, you can still set traces for individual pages using the page directive. By default, this is set to `false` in `machine.config`.

❑ `requestLimit` is the total number of trace requests to keep for later viewing with `trace.axd`. By default, this is set to ten.

❑ `pageOutput` allows you to decide whether you want trace information displaying on every page, as well as being available through `trace.axd`. When it is set to `true`, the tracing information will be added to every page. By default it is set to `false`.

❑ `traceMode` allows you to specify if the trace information is sorted by time or by category. If you sort by category, it will be group information based on the system and `Trace.Write()` settings. By default, this is set to `SortByTime`.

❑ `localOnly` specifies that only requests made through http://localhost/ will be allowed to see the trace information. By default it is set to `true`. This stops your users from viewing your trace information, while letting you see exactly what's going on at the same time.

You can embed `Trace.Write` statements in your code while you're debugging your pages to provide useful information when you view a trace on the page. If you turn tracing off on the page, these statements get hidden, and do not need to be removed because they do not affect the final page output. However, if you find that your application isn't actually performing as it should at a later date, all you need to do is re-enable tracing, and these statements will be used again.

Monitoring the ASP.NET Process

It's always good, especially when you're testing an application, to be able to monitor what it is doing. Information such as how long the application has been running, how much memory it's using, how many requests it has served, and so on, provide a good insight into how your server is holding up to the demands placed on it by browser requests.

The `ProcessModelInfo` class allows us to monitor part of the ASP.NET process online:

Try-It-Out – Using ProcessModelInfo

1. Save the following code as `ProcessInfo.aspx`, and run it:

```
<html>
<head>
<title>ASP.NET Process Info</title>
</head>
<body>
<script Language="c#" runat=server>
void Page_Load(object sender, EventArgs e)
{
   ProcessInfo[] history = ProcessModelInfo.GetHistory(10);
```

```
    for(int i = 0; i< history.Length; i++)
    {
        Response.Write ("<table border>");
        Response.Write ("<tr><td>ASP.NET Process Start Date and Time<td>" +
                    history[i].StartTime.ToString());
        Response.Write ("<tr><td>Process Age ( HH:MM:SS:LongDecimal )<td>" +
                    history[i].Age.ToString());
        Response.Write (
                "<tr><td>Process ID ( The same as in Task Manager )<td>" +
                    history[i].ProcessID.ToString());
        Response.Write (
                "<tr><td>Total Request Count (Requests served since the " +
                        "process started)<TD>" +
                        history[i].RequestCount.ToString());
        Response.Write ("<tr><td>Peak Memory Used ( KB ) <td>" +
                        history[i].PeakMemoryUsed.ToString());
        Response.Write ("</table>");
    }
}
</script>
</body>
</html>
```

2. You should see something like this:

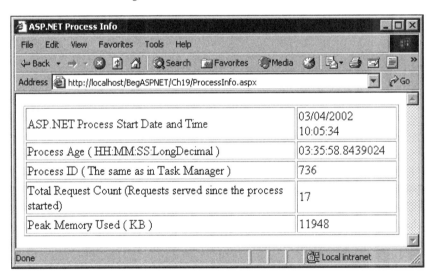

How It Works

The information that we're using here is made available through the `GetHistory` method of the `ProcessModelInfo` class. This has several properties, `StartTime`, `Age`, `ProcessID`, `RequestCount`, and `PeakMemoryUsed`, which we are displaying in our example. We're placing this information into our `history` variable here:

```
<html>
<head>
<title>ASP.NET Process Info</title>
</head>
<body>
<script Language="c#" runat=server>
void Page_Load(object sender, EventArgs e)
{
   ProcessInfo[] history = ProcessModelInfo.GetHistory(10);
```

The number of entries in our table is defined by a `for` loop that continues for as many items as there are in our `history` variable. The table itself is constructed using HTML tags:

```
for(int i = 0; i< history.Length; i++)
{
   Response.Write ("<table border>");
   Response.Write ("<tr><td>ASP.NET Process Start Date and Time<td>" +
                   history[i].StartTime.ToString());
   Response.Write ("<tr><td>Process Age ( HH:MM:SS:LongDecimal )<td>" +
                   history[i].Age.ToString());
   Response.Write (
             "<tr><td>Process ID ( The same as in Task Manager )<td>" +
                   history[i].ProcessID.ToString());
   Response.Write (
             "<tr><td>Total Request Count (Requests served since the " +
                      "process started)<TD>" +
                      history[i].RequestCount.ToString());
   Response.Write ("<tr><td>Peak Memory Used ( KB ) <td>" +
                      history[i].PeakMemoryUsed.ToString());
   Response.Write ("</table>");
   }
}
</script>
</body>
</html>
```

This can be handy information to have when you are developing your code. The **Peak Memory Used** counter is very useful, to determine whether your test file is consuming too much RAM, and the **Total Request Count** serves as a poor person's page hit counter. Oh, and if the **Process Age** reads 00:0x:xx.x then you know that whatever changes you made to your code have just crashed ASP.NET – oops!

Fear not – the development team at Microsoft did a great job of making process restarts as seamless as possible, so it shouldn't bring your entire machine crashing down, but you'll need to look at the application that caused the fault and fix it, or else your users will be getting errors.

781

Tips and Tricks

No configuration guidelines would be complete without offering a list of optimization tips. Here's a brief listing of the tips and examples included in the Microsoft QuickStart samples. If you've not got these installed, they're available from the following sites:

http://www.gotdotnet.com/quickstart/aspplus/
http://docs.aspng.com/quickstart/aspplus/default.aspx
http://aspalliance.com/quickstart/aspplus/
http://www.dotnetjunkies.com/quickstart/default.aspx

Don't worry if you don't understand them all! They're being included here so that you can refer back to them throughout your development as a programmer. Think of them as a quick reference guide, that you'll still be able to use as a refresher in the years to come.

- ❏ **Disable Session State when it is not needed**. Maintaining session state consumes memory and processing time. If you don't need to recall or modify session variables in a page, disable session state for that page.

- ❏ **Choose your Session State provider carefully**. If you are running just one web server, the fastest and most economical mode of maintaining state is In-Process. Only if you are running a web farm, on more than one machine, should you even consider using SQL Server or the State Server.

- ❏ **Avoid excessive round trips to the server**. Round tripping to the server takes time and server resources. You should only round-trip to the server when storing or retrieving data. You can program your controls to generate client-side code, and still use ASP.NET's efficient server controls. Use client-side processing to save server-processing time as much as you can.

- ❏ **Use** `Page.IsPostback` **to avoid extra work on a round trip**. You can use `IsPostback` to determine if a dataset needs to be generated, for example. Generating data is expensive, in terms of processing time. Generating one query on first access and another one on a `POST` can cost you processing time.

- ❏ **Use server controls sparingly and appropriately**. Even though server controls are very cool, and afford you incredible event-handling capabilities, for simple displays, a simple rendering using `Response.Write` will be far more efficient.

- ❏ **Avoid excessive server control viewstate**. The more data you're passing back and forth between the client and the server, the larger the viewstate gets, and the longer it takes for the more resources your consuming. Like session state, turn this feature off if you don't need to keep state on a page.

- ❏ **Use** `System.Text.StringBuilder` **for string concatenation**. When you modify a string object using the traditional concatenation methods, you add a new string object for every modification made. That adds up! The new `StringBuilder` object is much more efficient because you use one, and only one, object no matter how many modifications you perform on the string.

❑ **Use SQL stored procedures for data access**. In the .NET Framework, the `SqlConnection` class allows you to have even larger performance gains, since it can actually execute native SQL Server code. Now, not only do you gain the speed of stored procedures but, also, they are executed natively. Performance gains are estimated at 200 to 300% over `OLEDB` or `ODBC` connections!

❑ **Use `SqlDataReader` for a fast-forward, read-only data cursor**. `SqlDataReader` provides what was known in the ASP world as a 'firehose' cursor, which is much faster than other cursors available. In addition, `SqlDataReader` reads data directly from a database connection using Tabular Data Streams (TDS), and allows you to bind server controls directly to data.

❑ **Use Caching features wherever possible**. In high-traffic situations caching data can save you a lot of processing time, since the data will be served from RAM, instead of using precious processing cycles.

❑ **Enable Web Gardening for multiprocessor computers**. Hey, why encourage idleness? Enabling the use of all processors available makes sense, since the more processing power available to your applications, the more efficient your web server will be.

❑ **Do not forget to disable Debug mode**. Having a compiler watching for errors is the most expensive process that a processor can undertake! **Never** enable debugging on a production box!

Summary

In this chapter we've covered a lot of ground in the vast topic of configuration and optimization. We looked at `machine.config` and `web.config` and saw how they were structured and their settings hierarchically inherited. Then we looked in more detail at some of the specific settings within those files that you can use to improve the performance, security and user friendliness of your applications.

Next we moved on to look at how we could increase our server's performance through the use of output and fragment caching so that our pages didn't need to be compiled as frequently, before presenting an overview of how we can use the new tracing features to debug our code, while simultaneously avoiding the inclusion of redundant debugging information in our finished production code.

Finally we briefly looked at the built-in system monitoring information that we can use to assess the performance and suitability of our code, before concluding the chapter with a reference list of recommended performance optimization tips.

ASP.NET Security

As soon as you start making information available on the Web, you've got to stop and ask yourself "Who do I want to see this?" The chances are, unless you actively do something to protect your site's resources, they'll be available to anyone who cares to look for them. Unlike corporate intranets the Web is a public forum, so there are lots of people out there who could be interested in what your ASP.NET pages have to offer. You need to take considered action to prevent your pages and Web Services being used and consumed by people who you have not authorized to do so.

Fortunately there are many ways that we can control who's looking at our information. In this chapter we'll be looking at a selection of simple ways that you can use IIS in conjunction with ASP.NET to protect yourself and your company. Specifically we'll cover:

- ❑ Basic Authentication
- ❑ Integrated Authentication
- ❑ Forms Authentication
- ❑ Forms Database Authentication

What is Security?

First of all, let's discuss what security actually is:

Security is a process: it screens private property from the general pubic, and permits access based on verifying that individuals are who they claim to be, in accordance with the access permissions that you have granted them.

For example, you protect the possessions in your home by fitting a lock to your front door. Provided you only give the key to approved people you will be able to decide who has access to your property, and who does not. You could fit a further, different, lock to the door of your study, and place a second set of **access permissions** with regard to who could enter that area.

Types of Security

When you are implementing a security solution the first thing you need to consider is what type of security is going to be most appropriate for your site. This will depend on the type of resources that your exposing to users (whether your data is sensitive, or you just want to keep a track of who's viewing what) and the nature of the users that come to your site.

Many sites traditionally feature three levels of **user security**:

❑ **Anonymous Visitors** – anyone visiting the site

❑ **Registered Visitors** – users who have logged into the site with a user name and password

❑ **Administrators** – users who have logged into the site with an administrative user name and password

Having levels of user security on your site can be a very powerful tool. It allows you to grant people access to your site without giving them *carte blanche* to go anywhere they like on it.

Preventing **Anonymous** access to key areas of your site is one of the simplest ways to reduce the likelihood of people viewing information that they are not authorized to view. By restricting access to **Registered** users and **Administrators** you're drastically cutting the number of people that can view that part of your site, and preventing people just wandering in and looking around. That said, of course, some sites, such as www.usatoday.com are happy to allow anonymous access, as it is the nature of their business to let people pop in and read the newspaper without having to give details about who they are.

You should choose a level of security that is appropriate for your site, and perhaps combine several to create a complete solution. For example, www.amazon.com allows you **Anonymous** access to browse its products, but requires you to become a **Registered** user in order to place an order or request account information.

We'll be looking at user security in two parts. Primarily, we'll be covering **Authentication**, which is the process of verifying that people are who they say are. There are several different ways that you can do this, and it's the area that you, as a developer, can have most influence over. Then we'll look at **Encryption**, through the use of the **Secure Sockets Layer** (SSL) to protect the information that you are passing back and forth from eavesdroppers.

We'll finish up with a quick mention of Microsoft Passport as an alternative method of authentication that you might like to consider.

Authentication

As we've already mentioned, there are several methods of authenticating that visitors to your site have permission to access the information that they are requesting. In this chapter we'll be covering the following basic techniques:

❑ **Basic Authentication** – a simple method of verifying users. Mostly used for customization options, rather than restricting access.

❑   **Integrated Windows Authentication** – a very simple, quick, and easy means of authenticating users, but can only be used with Internet Explorer browsers higher than version 5.0.

❑   **Forms-Based Authentication** – A powerful and flexible means of taking control of the presentation of your security features to the user. We'll discuss how you can use this to authenticate user details stored both in `web.config` and in a database.

Implementing Basic Authentication

Basic Authentication is provided by Internet Information Services (IIS). When a user comes to a page protected by Basic Authentication IIS will ask the browser to collect credentials from the user. The browser then pops up a dialog box to collect a username and password. These are then passed back to the server to allow authentication.

> When using Basic Authentication, the user name, password pair is not encrypted, and is transmitted as clear text. Therefore, it can be read by anyone who intercepts the transmission. For this reason Basic Authentication is only recommended for applications where weak security is sufficient. Examples of this could be an intranet application where the outside world is excluded by other means, or an Internet application in conjunction with SSL, which we will discuss later.

When the username and password are returned from the browser they are compared with the **Windows User Account Database**. This is a list of all the users permitted to use the computer serving the pages.

You can view the users that are currently permitted on your system by right-clicking the My Computer icon, and selecting Manage. The system's accepted users are listed under Users as shown below. Right-click on the list and select New User... in order to add additional logins to your system, then select the Groups folder, right-click, and select Add to Group in order to assign your new user to a group (such as Administrators, Users, Guests, and so on).

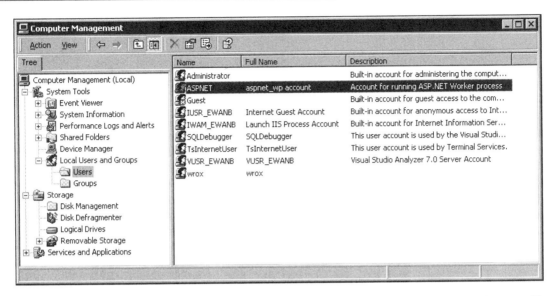

If the information provided by the client matches one of the user accounts stored, it will be authenticated by IIS and the ASP.NET page that the user requested will be called. If the authentication is unsuccessful, however, then the ASP.NET page will not be called, and an HTTP 401 – Access Denied error will be returned instead.

Programmatically, information about the logged-in user can be ascertained using the ASP.NET User property that resides in the HttpContext class of the System.Web namespace. The User object exposes an identity property, that in turn contains Name and AuthenticationType properties from which the user's details can be extracted.

We'll look at an example of how to do this now, using Basic authentication.

Try It Out – Setting Up Our Virtual Directories

All the examples in this chapter rely upon IIS in order to function correctly. They all need to be set up as virtual directories. This was covered in detail at the very beginning of this book where we explained how to create a test directory for our ASP.NET applications. Because of this we will only recap briefly here. Please follow this procedure for each of the examples.

1. Create a new folder on your server, and name it Basic; for example this could be in the test directory C:\BegASPNET\Ch20\Basic

2. Open the MMC by clicking the Start button, and under Run... entering MMC:

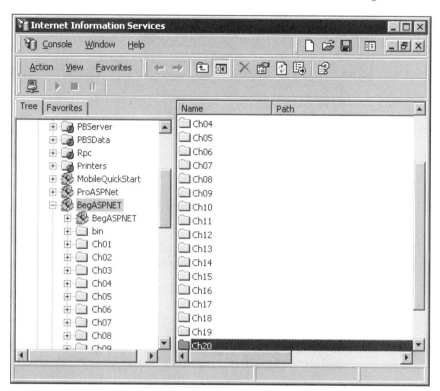

3. Call up IIS and map the folder Basic as an IIS **virtual directory**, by right-clicking on it and selecting New, then Virtual Directory. Give the new directory the name Basic (refer to Chapter 1 if you need detailed help with this Wizard).

4. That's it! You've set up your first Virtual Directory. You'll need to repeat this procedure for each of the example folders that we use throughout the chapter – just go through the same series of steps, creating a new folder for each, and giving it a new name.

In a moment, we'll move on to discuss how to setup Basic authentication on your Basic virtual directory, but before we do, a word about the options that you can set on your virtual directories:

5. In the IIS MMC right-click on your virtual directory and select Properties. You'll see the following panel:

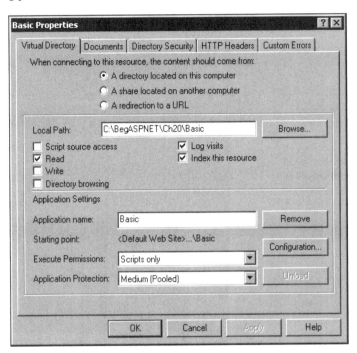

> **As we discussed in Chapter 1, it is recommended that you only allow the "Read" and "Scripts only" options in your virtual directory's Properties menu.**

- ❏ You should only check the "Execute (such as ISAPI applications or CGI)", if you are going to run web applications built on ISAPI or CGI technology. If you're going to run just ASP.NET applications then this option should be turned off to provide greater security (you're further limiting the things people can do in this portion of your site).

- ❏ Be aware that if you enable the "Write" option then, other people will be able to upload any kind of files to your server (including malicious code such as viruses) from the Web. This could potentially be very dangerous, so in virtually every situation you'll want to keep this turned off (the only time you might want to switch it on is within a secure intranet environment).

- ❏ If you enable the "Directory browsing" option, then users will be able to view the contents of the folder over the Web. This is also not desirable, as it will allow people to view the structure of your program's physical directories from the Web, and possibly even read your code and other files such as Word documents, PDF files, and so on. Couple this with "Write" permissions and you've a recipe for disaster .

Now, let's look at securing our Basic virtual directory.

Try It Out – Implementing Basic Authentication

Now that we've got our generic virtual directory waiting for us, setting up Basic Authentication takes place in three sequential steps. They are:

❑ The IIS Setup

❑ The web.config file

❑ The ASP.NET code

We'll begin at the beginning:

IIS Setup

1. Right-click on your Basic virtual directory in the IIS MMC and select the Properties tab. You'll be presented with the same panel that you saw in Step 5 of the IIS setup, earlier:

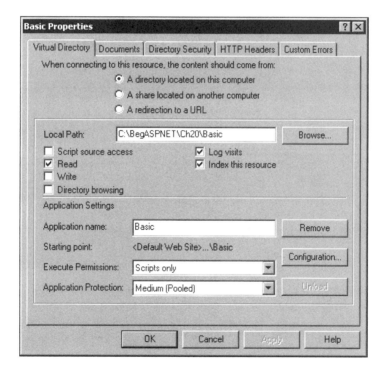

2. Select the Directory Security tab from the options along the top of the panel:

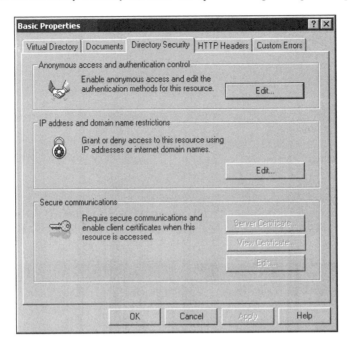

3. In the Anonymous Access... pane, click the Edit button:

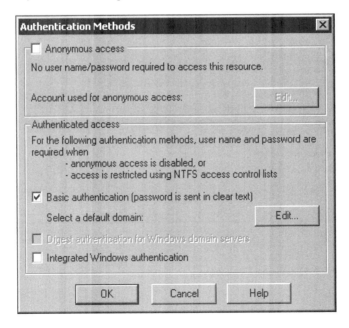

4. De-select the Anonymous access and Integrated Windows authentication checkboxes (depending on your setup, they may already be de-selected) and select the Basic authentication checkbox. When you select this option, IIS will prompt you with a warning message box:

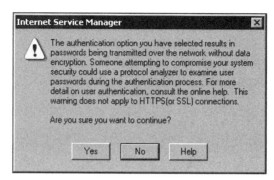

5. This is to warn you that the password will be sent as plain text over the network. Select Yes from the dialog box.

6. If you want to enter default domain information, click on the option provided and do so.

> **If you don't specify the domain name; then users will have to specify it when they log into the ASP.NET application.**

web.config

Now that we're done with IIS it's time to turn our attention to web.config.

7. Enter the following code into your text editor:

```
<configuration>
  <system.web>
    <authentication mode="Windows" />
  </system.web>
</configuration>
```

8. Save this code as web.config in the root of your application. In our example, this is C:\BegASPNET\Ch20\Basic.

The ASPX code

That's it! Basic Authentication is now configured. Of course, we'll need a default page before we can test it. We'll do that now:

1. Open up your text editor and enter the following code. Save it as `default.aspx` in your test directory:

```
<html>
<head>
  <script language="C#" runat="server">
    void Page_Load(Object Src,EventArgs E)
    {
        lblUser.Text = User.Identity.Name;
        lblType.Text = User.Identity.AuthenticationType;
    }
  </script>
</head>
<body>
    <font face="Verdana" size="4" color="navy">
    <b>Windows Authentication</b></font><hr>
    <table border=1 bordercolor="#FFFFFF" bgcolor="Silver"
    cellspacing=0 cellpadding=4>
      <tr>
        <td><b>Current Users Name</b></td>
        <td><asp:label id=lblUser runat=server/></td>
      </tr>
      <tr>
        <td><b>Current Authentication Type</b></td>
        <TD><asp:label id=lblType runat=server/></TD>
      </tr>
    </table>
</body>
</html>
```

2. Launch your browser and navigate to your test page. As it's called `default.aspx` entering http://localhost/BegASPNET/Ch20/Basic/ will be enough:

3. If your browser's not logged in, you'll receive a challenge to enter your details. Do so and click OK:

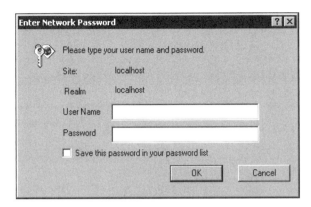

4. If you enter incorrect information you'll be confronted with an 'HTTP Status 401 – Access Denied' error:

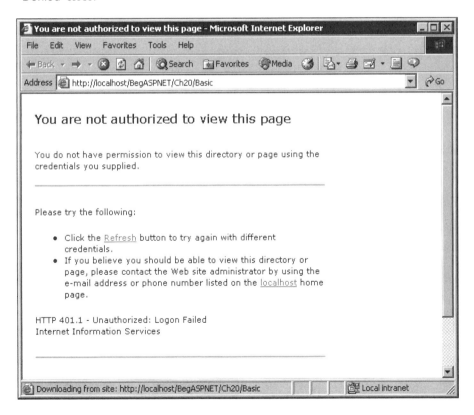

5. If you enter the correct credentials for a user recognized by your system you'll get the following display, showing the username and authentication type:

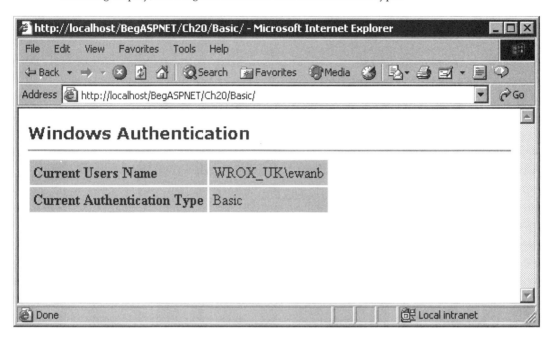

Your user has now been authenticated – we've asked them to prove who they are and, based upon their response, we've taken a decision as to whether or not we will provide content. Now let's look at what's been going on in a bit more detail.

How It Works

The following figure shows the tasks that take place when Basic Authentication is used:

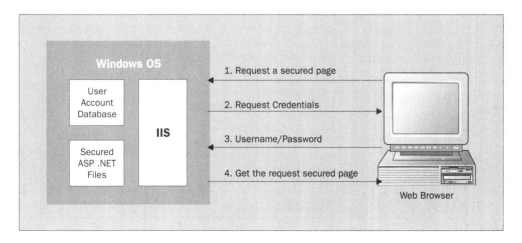

The numbers in the above figure correspond to:

1. IIS receives the request for a secure page (default.aspx) and checks to see if the file exists on the web server. If the file is not found on the server, IIS will return Error 404 (Page Not Found) back to the browser. If the file exists then, IIS will check if the browser has already logged in.

2. If the browser has **not** logged in, then IIS will challenge it for credentials. Upon receiving the challenge, the browser will then pop-up a login box for the user to enter their details in:

3. Once the username and the password are entered and the OK button clicked by the user, the encoded username and password information is sent to IIS.

4. If the credentials supplied match an entry in the Windows User Account Database, IIS will send the page that was requested back to the browser. If the credentials do not match an entry, then IIS will not serve the page, but will instead issue an HTTP 401 – Access Denied error.

The ASPX code is really very simple. We're creating a page containing two ASP.NET labels within an HTML table. Stripping away the HTML, for clarity, we're left with:

```
<script language="C#" runat="server">
  void Page_Load(Object Src,EventArgs E)
  {
      lblUser.Text = User.Identity.Name;
      lblType.Text = User.Identity.AuthenticationType;
  }
</script>

<asp:label id=lblUser runat=server/>
<asp:label id=lblType runat=server/>
```

797

As you can see, all we're doing here is using the `Page_Load` event to collect the user's `Name` and `AuthenticationType` from the `User.Identity` class, before displaying it on the screen to show that the example has worked correctly.

Weighing up Basic Authentication

That's all there is to it – quite a few steps to follow, but nothing too complex. Now, before moving on, let's consider the pros and cons of this method:

Basic Authentication has its good points:

- ❏ Easy to implement and supported by IIS
- ❏ No coding required – it's all done in the IIS MMC and a couple of lines of `web.config`
- ❏ Supported by all the modern browsers
- ❏ Supported by all **Proxy servers** and **Firewalls**

> *A Proxy Server is a system that stands between client applications (such as Internet Explorer) and the connection to the Internet (Server) and intercepts the requests to the server to see if it can action them itself, this improves performance by filtering requests that go out to the Internet.*
>
> *A Firewall is a form of access control technology, which prevents unauthorized access to information resources by placing a barrier between an organization's or individual's network and an unsecured network – such as the Internet.*

It also has its bad points:

- ❏ Username and password are sent in encoded format (clear text). The encoding is not a strong encryption and almost anybody can decode the credentials.
- ❏ Username and password are passed with every request, so they cross the network many more times than is strictly necessary to authenticate someone.
- ❏ When we use Basic Authentication the credentials will be always compared against the Windows User Account Database – we can't use it to compare the user's credentials against a database or text file instead, so every user will need to be registered on the server.

Because of these disadvantages Basic Authentication isn't really a very viable option for serious security. But if you're just looking for a simple way to secure a site against accidental access, when the sensitivity of your data isn't an issue it might be worth considering.

> *If you are interested in using Basic Authentication and would like to make it more robust, there is information available from Microsoft explaining how to configure Basic Authentication to work with Secure Sockets Layer (SSL) encryption technologies. More information can be found at:*
>
> *http://support.microsoft.com/default.aspx?scid=kb;en-us;Q290625*

Integrated Windows Authentication

Integrated Windows Authentication offers some real advantages over Basic authentication, as it uses a process called **hashing** to avoid having to send usernames and passwords over the network in clear text.

Hashing is a technique that allows you to take a piece of information, such as a password, and use a mathematical algorithm to create a representation of that password that appears vastly different from it, and at the same time has a unique one-to-one relationship with it. The server will send a small piece if information, called a **key**, across the network to the client, which will then use that key to conduct its hashing algorithm on the password value (try thinking of it as being a like an input parameter, with the subsequent hash being the output and varying in accordance with it):

Once this is done, the hashed password will be sent over the network to the server. As the server also has a copy of the password, and knows value of the key that it sent, it can also conduct the hash and compare its result with that sent from the client. This way the password itself is never sent across the network, only the hash that is valueless without knowledge of both the password and key.

Now, let's look at an example of how this works.

Try It Out – Integrated Windows Authentication

Implementing Integrated Windows Authentication is very similar to implementing Basic Authentication.

1. Begin by setting up a test directory called 'Integrated' in the manner we outlined in the *Setting Up Our Virtual Directories Try It Out* at the beginning of this chapter.

2. In the IIS MMC select the Properties option of your newly created virtual directory:

3. Then, under the Directory Security tab, select Edit in the Anonymous access and authentication control panel, and then deselect everything except the Integrated Windows authentication option:

4. Close the IIS MMC and copy across your web.config and default.aspx files from the previous example – they'll work just fine as they are.

5. Browse to the example and, if your credentials are accepted, you should see something like this:

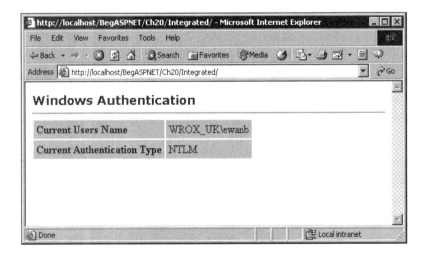

6. Alternatively, you will receive an HTTP 401 – Access Denied error if your credentials are not authenticated.

Again, this kind of authentication is quite simple to set up, with the hard work being taken care of behind the scenes by IIS. Let's have a look at that now, and see what's going on.

How It Works

The following figure shows the tasks taking place when basic authentication is used.

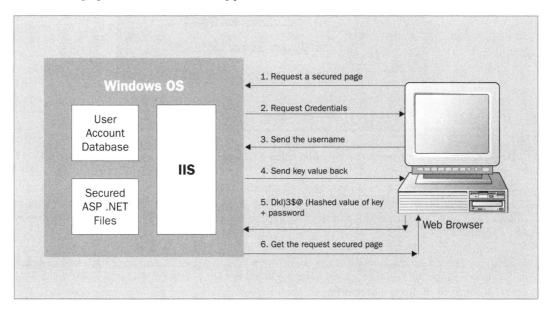

In the above diagram the following is taking place:

7. IIS receives a request for the page from the client, and checks to see if the browser has already been logged in. If the browser is logged in, it serves the page, if it is not then it issues a challenge.

8. The browser pops up a dialog, in response to the challenge, for the user to enter username and password details:

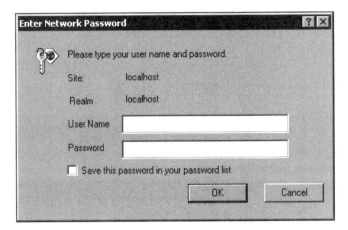

9. The browser then sends the **only** username to the server as clear text.

10. The server sends back a unique key value to the client, also as clear text.

11. The client then hashes the password, using the key value received from the server, and sends it back.

12. Upon receiving the hash from the client, the server will generate another hash based on the user's password (which it knows from the Windows User Account Database) and the key that it supplied. If the two hashes match, then IIS will authenticate the user, and serve them the page they requested. If they do not match then a HTTP 401 – Access Denied error will be served.

Weighing up Integrated Windows Authentication

Now we've seen just how easy Integrated Windows Authentication can be, let's weight up the points it has in its favor:

❑ Just like Basic Authentication, Integrated Windows Authentication is easy to set up and doesn't require any development effort – it's all done in the IIS MMC and a couple of lines in the web.config file.

❑ The user's password is never sent over the network, instead it a hash value is transmitted. So the privacy of the password is guaranteed.

The points against Integrated Windows authentication are:

❑ It is only supported by Internet Explorer Version 2.0 and above. Other browsers, like Netscape and Opera, don't support it at all.

❑ It can't work with Proxy servers.

❑ Additional TCP ports needs to be opened in the Firewall to use Integrated Windows Authentication. (Every protocol uses a port to operate. For example, Port 80 is used by the HTTP protocol.) This means it won't necessarily work 'out of the box', and may mean your server is more exposed to the outside world.

❑ Like Basic Authentication, it can only be used to verify information against the Windows User Account Database.

So Integrated Windows authentication is much more secure than Basic Authentication, but by no means perfect. It's up to the individual developer to decide if the type of protection it offers is suitable for their application (and if they can work with its restrictions).

Implementing Forms-based Authentication

The forms of authentication we've looked at so far have been fine, as far as they go, but they've got serious limitations with regard to the way they present themselves to your users and the kind of information you can use with them (all your users need accounts in the Windows User Account Database).

Forms-based Authentication is different – it is founded on cookies. When a user logs into your ASP.NET application using Forms-based authentication, ASP.NET issues an authentication cookie that will be sent back and forth between the server and client during the ensuing web requests. If the authentication cookie is **persistent** then a copy will be stored on the user's hard drive and whenever they visit your ASP.NET application again, they can be pre-authenticated based on it until the cookie expires. If the authentication cookie type is **non-persistent**, then the authentication cookie will be destroyed at the end of each browser session. In this case when they visit your ASP.NET application again, you can't pre-authenticate them and they will have to provide their credentials all over again.

You can use persistent and non-persistent cookies very flexibly. For example, if you look at www.ASPToday.com or WWW.CSharpToday.com's home page, beneath the password textbox they've placed a checkbox called 'Remember my password'. If you check this box when you log into the site it will place a persistent cookie on your local computer and will be able to pre-authenticate you on your subsequent visits to the site. If you don't check it, then a non-persistent cookie is used and you'll have to login each time you visit.

You'll be pleased to hear that forms-based authentication is also easy to implement. All we have to do is create a configuration file (web.config) and a login page to accept the credentials from the user and verify them, and a default page where we'll display the content we wish to restrict. Admittedly that's not as straightforward as the previous examples, but it's still pretty simple. Let's look at how to do it.

Try It Out – Forms-based Authentication

1. Begin by setting up a generic virtual directory, called Forms, as we showed you at the beginning of the chapter.

2. Now fire up your text editor and create following file:

```
<configuration>
  <system.web>
```

803

```
      <authentication mode="Forms">
        <forms name=".WroxDemo" loginUrl="login.aspx"
        protection="All" timeout="60" />
      </authentication>
      <machineKey validationKey="AutoGenerate"
      decryptionKey="AutoGenerate" validation="SHA1"/>
      <authorization>
        <deny users="?" />
      </authorization>
    </system.web>
</configuration>
```

3. Save the file as `web.config`.

4. Next we'll create the `login.aspx` file. In this we're going to create two ASP.NET textbox server controls. The first will accept the username from the client, the second their password. For good measure we'll also include some validation controls to make sure that the boxes are not left blank. An additional validation control will display any messages there may be from the server-side code. Finally, we'll add a button server control to allow us to submit the form using the `Login_Click` event:

```
<%@ Import Namespace="System.Web.Security " %>
<html>
<head>
<script language="C#" runat=server>
  void Login_Click(Object Src, EventArgs E)
  {
    if (Page.IsValid)
    {
      if (txtEmail.Text == "Wrox" && txtPwd.Text == "MyPass")
        FormsAuthentication.RedirectFromLoginPage(txtEmail.Text,false);
      else
        lblLoginMsg.Text = "Use Wrox as user name and password as MyPass. Please
try again";
    }
  }
</script>

</head>
<body>
<form runat="server">
<h1>Using Form based Authentication</h1><hr>
Users Name:<br />
<asp:textbox id="txtEmail" runat=server /> 
<FONT SIZE=2 COLOR="RED">*</FONT>

<asp:RequiredFieldValidator
  ControlToValidate="txtEmail"
  Display="Dynamic"
```

```
      ErrorMessage="Login name can't be empty."
      runat=server/>
<br />Password:<br />

<asp:textbox TextMode="Password" id="txtPwd" runat=server />
   <FONT SIZE=2 COLOR="RED">*</FONT>
  <asp:RequiredFieldValidator
    ControlToValidate="txtPwd"
    Display="Dynamic"
    ErrorMessage="Password can't be left empty."
    runat=server/>
<br />

<asp:Label
  id="lblLoginMsg"
  ForeColor="Red"
  Font-Name="Verdana";
  Font-Size="10"
  runat=server />
<b />

<asp:button
  id="btnLogin"
  Text="Login"
  OnClick="Login_Click"
  runat=Server />
</form>
</body>
</html>
```

> Be aware that we've hard coded our login details within this file. We've set the username
> to *Wrox* and the password to *MyPass*.

5. Finally, we'll create our trusty `default.aspx` file. This will display the username of the currently logged in user, the type of authentication that we've used, and an option for them to logout:

```
<%@ Import Namespace="System.Web.Security " %>
<html>
<head>
<script language="C#" runat=server>
  void Page_Load(Object S, EventArgs E)
  {
    lblUser.Text = User.Identity.Name;
    lblType.Text = User.Identity.AuthenticationType;
  }

  void Logout_Click(Object S, EventArgs E)
  {
```

```
        FormsAuthentication.SignOut();
        Server.Transfer("login.aspx");
    }
</script>
</head>
<body>
<form runat="server">
    <font face="Verdana" size="4" color="navy">
    <b>Forms Authentication</b></font><hr>
    <table border=1 bordercolor="#FFFFFF" bgcolor="Silver"
    cellspacing=0 cellpadding=4>
      <tr>
        <td><b>Current Users Name</b></td>
        <td><asp:label id=lblUser runat=server/></td>
      </tr>
      <tr>
        <td><b>Current Authentication Type</b></td>
        <TD><asp:label id=lblType runat=server/></TD>
      </tr>
    </table>
  <asp:button text="Logout" OnClick="Logout_Click" runat=server/>
</form>
</body>
</html>
```

6. When you request your application from the browser, you should see something like this:

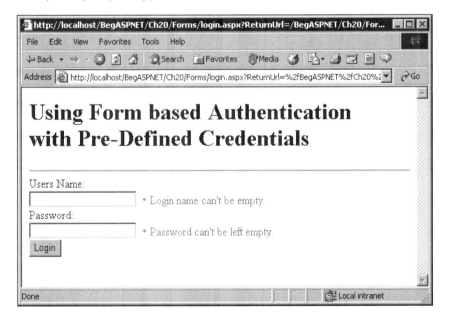

7. If you enter the login credentials incorrectly, you will receive the following (rather insecure) error message:

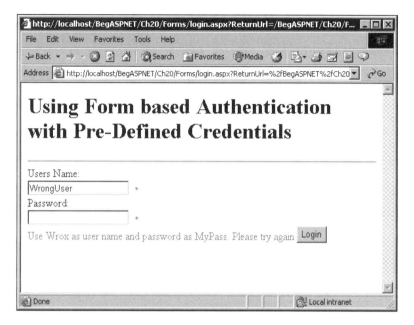

8. If you login correctly you will be granted access to the restricted page:

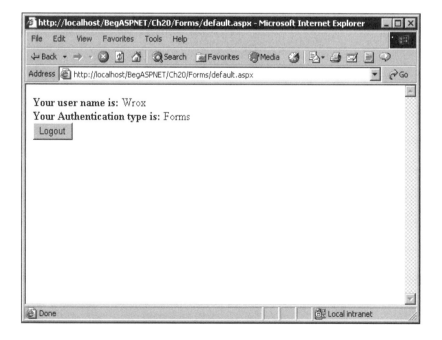

How It Works

When the browser requests the `default.aspx` file IIS checks to see if we've logged in. As we haven't, it serves us with `login.aspx` instead. It does this by first verifying if any of the authentication methods supported by IIS are present. If they are not, it passes the authentication request to the ASP.NET runtime. This then reads the `web.config` file and discovers that we're using Forms-based Authentication. The runtime will then look for the authentication cookie named in the `web.config` file (in the `name` attribute of the `<forms>` tag):

```
<authentication mode="Forms">
  <forms name=".WroxDemo" loginUrl="login.aspx"
  protection="All" timeout="60" />
</authentication>
```

In this file, we're using the `<forms>` tag to set the `Forms` authentication properties. The following table describes the possible values for the `<forms>` tag:

Tag Attribute	Description
name	Name of the authentication cookie. If you are hosting more than one ASP.NET application from your web server, make sure you give different names to each of the authentication cookies that you're using.
loginUrl	The login page to which unauthenticated users should be redirected. This `loginUrl` can be on the same server, or a different one. If the `loginUrl` is on a different server then both servers should use the same `decryptionKey` parameter in the `machineKey` tag.

Tag Attribute	Description
protection	This method is used to protect the authentication cookie. The protection tag has four possible values (`All`, `Encryption`, `Validation`, `None`).
	❑ When you set the value as 'All', both the validation and encryption will be performed against the authentication cookie to protect it. For the validation and decryption the values specified in the validationKey and decryptionKey of the machineKey tag will be used. The value "All" is the default, and suggested, value for this parameter.
	❑ When you set the value as "None", the cookie will be transferred between the client and the server as plain text and you can turn off the encryption and validation with the machineKey tag.
	❑ When you set the value as "Encryption", the cookie will be decrypted as per the value specified in the decryptionKey of the machineKey tag and the content of the cookie will not be validated.
	❑ When you set the value as "Validation", the cookie will be validated, when received from the client, as per the value specified in the validationKey of the machineKey tag and the content of the cookie will not be encrypted and decrypted.
timeout	The timeout value for the cookie to expire since the last request was made. The default value is 30 minutes.

Next, the machineKey tag configures the encryption, decryption, and validation level for the authentication cookies. These values can be set for the machine level, site level, and application level. The value can't be set for the sub-directory level. The machineKey tag supports three attributes.

Tag Attribute	Description
validationKey	Specifies the validation key to be used when validating the authentication cookie data. The possible values for this element are either "AutoGenerate" or a manually assigned key.
	The minimum and maximum length of the key should be 40 characters (20 bytes) and 128 characters (64 bytes). *AutoGenerate is the default.*

Table continued on following page

Tag Attribute	Description
`decryptionKey`	Specifies the encryption key to be used when validating the authentication cookie.

Permitted values are the same as for `validationKey`. |
| `validation` | Specifies the type of encryption used for the data validation. The possible values are `"SHA1"`, `"MD5"`, and `"3DES"`.

SHA1 and MD5 are hashing algorithms and 3DES an algorithm used to encrypt and decrypt data. |

If an authentication cookie is present, the ASP.NET runtime checks the protection element of the form tag and takes appropriate action based on its value. If the cookie is valid, the requested page will be served back to the client. If the authentication cookie is not present, or invalid, then, the runtime will transfer the browser to the login page:

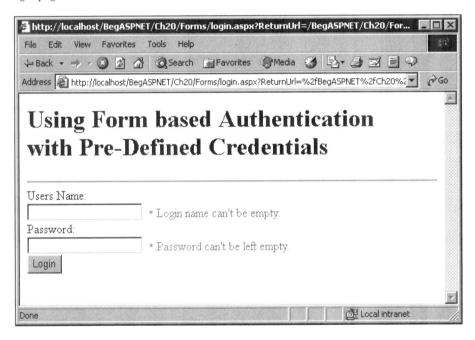

As you can see from the screenshot, the page URL holds a QueryString called "ReturnUrl" with a reference to the previous page (default.aspx) that we requested from IIS. That's how the RedirectFromLoginPage method of the FormsAuthentication class knows where to transfer the browser back to once the user is successfully logged in. When you click the login button without entering the username and password, the validation controls display their error messages (refer back to Chapter 17 for more information on this topic).

Login.aspx

Let's look at the logic in our login.aspx <script> block (we'll forgo discussion of the validation controls for simplicity – if you want to know more about them refer back to Chapter 17).

Firstly we use the Page.IsValid property to ensure that all the validation procedures have completed successfully (if they haven't we stop at this point):

```
<script language="C#" runat=server>
  void Login_Click(Object Src, EventArgs E)
  {
    if (Page.IsValid)
    {
```

Then we compare the txtEmail textbox value with the hard coded value "Wrox" and txtPwd textbox value with the hard coded value "MyPass".

```
if (txtEmail.Text == "Wrox" && txtPwd.Text == "MyPass")
```

If the values match, we call the RedirectFromLoginPage method of the FormsAuthentication class. This method takes two parameters. The first is the username and the second is whether it is a persistent cookie or not. As we've set this to false, our cookie will be non persistent.

```
FormsAuthentication.RedirectFromLoginPage(txtEmail.Text, false);
```

If the login details don't match our values, we display a message via the lblLoginMsg label to the user telling them to use "Wrox" as the user name and "MyPass" as the password:

```
else
  lblLoginMsg.Text =
      "Use Wrox as user name and password as MyPass. Please try again";
  }
 }
</script>
```

Default.aspx

Now we'll take a brief look at our `default.aspx` page:

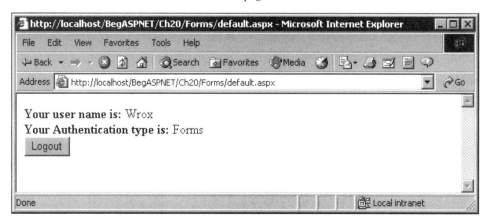

In many ways this is no different from the one that we used for the Basic and Integrated Authentication examples:

```
<<script language="C#" runat=server>
  void Page_Load(Object S, EventArgs E)
  {
    lblUser.Text = User.Identity.Name;
    lblType.Text = User.Identity.AuthenticationType;
  }
```

The only new thing here is the code for the Logout button:

```
  void Logout_Click(Object S, EventArgs E)
  {
    FormsAuthentication.SignOut();
    Server.Transfer("login.aspx");
  }
</script>
```

When we click this button the `Signout` method of the `FormsAuthentication` class is called. This will remove the authentication cookie from the client regardless of its persistence. The user is then transferred back to the login page.

Forms-based Authentication using a Database

From what we've seen of Forms-based Authentication so far, it should be obvious that it is a very flexible and secure approach to authenticating users. However our previous example had a major weakness – authentication took place against values hard-coded into the ASPX file. While this is OK for demonstration purposes, where there are only a few users, its no good for production environments.

We'll fix this weakness in our final authentication example: Forms-based Authentication using a database.

Try It Out – Authenticating against a Database

For this example you'll need to download the WroxDBAuth.mdb *database that's available with this book's code samples on* **www.wrox.com**

1. Begin by creating a directory called FormsDB, and making it into a virtual directory.

2. Place the WroxDBAuth.mdb database in a folder named DB beneath this directory (so if you're using C:\BegASPNET\Ch20\FormsDB it will be in C:\BegASPNET\Ch20\FormsDB\DB\).

3. Create a web.config file containing the following information and place it in the directory root:

```
<configuration>
  <system.web>
    <authentication mode="Forms">
      <forms name=".WroxDemo2" loginUrl="login.aspx"
      protection="All" timeout="20" />
    </authentication>
    <authorization>
      <deny users="?" />
    </authorization>
  </system.web>
</configuration>
```

4. Now, modify the login.aspx file that we used in the previous example and save it in your FormsDB virtual directory:

```
<%@ Page Language="C#" %>
<%@ Import Namespace="System.Web.Security " %>
<%@ Import Namespace="System.Data.OleDb" %>
<html>
<head>
<script language="C#" runat=server>
  void Login_Click(Object Src, EventArgs E)
  {
    if (Page.IsValid)
    {
    String strConn ="PROVIDER=Microsoft.Jet.OLEDB.4.0;DATA SOURCE=" +
                    Server.MapPath("DB\\WroxDBAuth.mdb") + ";";
    OleDbConnection Conn = new OleDbConnection(strConn) ;
    Conn.Open();

    String strSQL = "SELECT Pwd FROM Tbl_MA_Users WHERE Email = '" +
                                        txtEmail.Text + "'";
    OleDbCommand Cmd = new OleDbCommand(strSQL,Conn);

    //Create a datareader, connection object
```

```
OleDbDataReader Dr =
    Cmd.ExecuteReader(System.Data.CommandBehavior.CloseConnection);

//Get the first row and check the password.
if (Dr.Read())
{
  if (Dr["Pwd"].ToString() == txtPwd.Text)
    FormsAuthentication.RedirectFromLoginPage(txtEmail.Text, false);
  else
    lblLoginMsg.Text = "Invalid password.";
}
else
  lblLoginMsg.Text = "Login name not found.";

  Dr.Close();
  }
}
</script>

</head>
<body>
  ...
</body>
</html>
```

5. Copy over the `default.aspx` page from the previous example. It doesn't need changing for this one.

6. Now call up the file in your browser and enter the login credentials:

The login details from the database are Username = **User@MyDomain.com** and Password = **MyPass.**

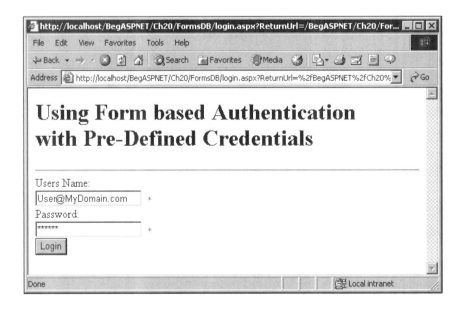

7. If you've entered the code correctly you'll be shown the `default.aspx` page:

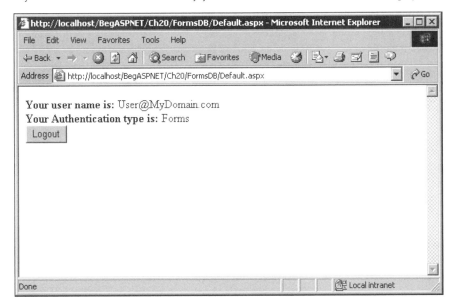

If you make a mistake you'll be shown the `login.aspx` page again, with an error message highlighted in red:

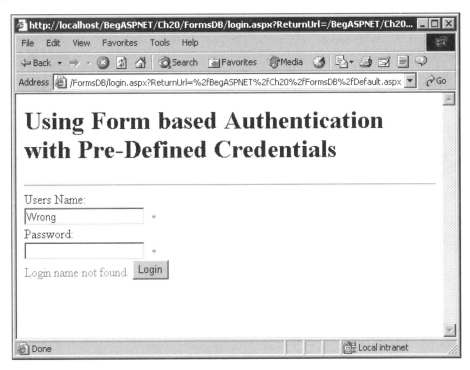

How It Works

The `login.aspx` page is the only one that has changed substantially from the previous example: We'll talk our way through it now:

First of all we're including the "`System.Web.Security`" and "`System.Data.OLEDB`" namespacess for Security and Microsoft Access 2000 data access, respectively:

```
<%@ Import Namespace="System.Web.Security " %>
<%@ Import Namespace="System.Data.OleDb" %>
```

Then in the `Login_Click` event, we're building a connection string for the Access database and declaring an OLEDB connection object to connect to the Access database and open the connection:

```
String strConn ="PROVIDER=Microsoft.Jet.OLEDB.4.0;DATA SOURCE=" +
                    Server.MapPath("DB\\WroxDBAuth.mdb") + ";";
OleDbConnection Conn = new OleDbConnection(strConn);
Conn.Open();
```

Then we're building a dynamic SQL statement into the `strSQL` variable, before creating an `OLEDBCommand` object by passing the dynamic SQL statement and the OLEDB connection object to its constructor:

```
String strSQL = "SELECT Pwd FROM Tbl_MA_Users WHERE Email = '" +
                                    txtEmail.Text + "'";
OleDbCommand Cmd = new OleDbCommand(strSQL,Conn);
```

Next, we create an `OLEDBDataReader` object and initialize it with the result of executing the `OLEDBCommand` object. We specify the `CommandBehavior` as `CloseConnection`. This is to make sure that when we close the `OLEDBDataReader` object the associated database connection will be closed:

```
OleDbDataReader Dr =
        Cmd.ExecuteReader(System.Data.CommandBehavior.CloseConnection);
```

Now we read the first record from the `OLEDBDataReader` object and compare the username and password with those entered by the user. If there are no rows in the `OLEDBDataReader` object, the e-mail address entered by the user doesn't exist in the database (if it did it would have been `SELECT`ed). So we displaying the error message "**Login name not found.**" in the label control. If, instead, the password doesn't match, we display the error message "**Invalid password.**" in the label control. If they both match we then transfer the user to the page that they originally requested:

```
if (Dr.Read())
    {
        if (Dr["Pwd"].ToString() == txtPwd.Text)
            FormsAuthentication.RedirectFromLoginPage(txtEmail.Text,
                                                    false);
        else
            lblLoginMsg.Text = "Invalid password.";
    }
    else
        lblLoginMsg.Text = "Login name not found.";
```

This concludes our authentication examples for this chapter. Hopefully they'll have given you a basic grasp of how to go about securing your content on the Web. Combining the ideas here with those in the Chapter 17 will allow you to create a flexible and secure solution for handling user's inputs and dealing with their errors.

We'll move on now to quickly consider **encryption** of data on the Web and some of its implications.

Encryption using SSL

Over the past few years there's been an explosion in the amount of business conducted over the Internet. This business, known as **e-commerce**, comprises such things as online banking, online brokerage accounts, and Internet shopping. Today you can book plane tickets, make hotel reservations, rent a car, transfer money, and buy clothes without leaving your PC.

Unfortunately this convenience doesn't come without a cost. Simply entering your credit card number on the Internet leaves you wide open to fraud as your information can be intercepted and read on route. SSL (Secure Sockets Layer) Encryption solves this problem by encrypting the information that you send over to the server (not just your credit card number, the entire message). The server then receives this information, decrypts it, and proceeds with the transaction without the fear that your personal information has fallen into the wrong hands.

In order to do this the SSL protocol is able to negotiate encryption and hashing keys, as well as authenticating servers before data is exchanged by the higher-level application. It maintains the security and integrity of the transmission channel by using encryption, authentication, and message authentication codes. SSL uses sophisticated hashing algorithms like MD5 and SHA1.

Further discussion of SSL is beyond the scope of this book, but if you would like to know more you can find out about if from a Certificate Authority such as www.verisign.com, from whom you can also buy an SSL certificate to prove your server's identity.

Finally, we'll conclude this chapter with a mention of Microsoft Passport, which has great implications for the way that online security may be conducted in the future.

Microsoft Passport Authentication

What is Microsoft Passport?

Passport authentication is a centralized online authentication service provided by Microsoft. It benefits the end user by providing a single login for all registered member sites of www.passport.com.

Why Passport?

As virtually every consumer web site online today requires a login, remembering all of them can be a nightmare. Most of the time your first choice of login name seems to already be taken and the password you'd like to use doesn't conform to the site's validation rules.

Passport aims to solve this problem by providing you with a 'virtual wallet' where you can store all your personal information (not just a password; you can store your credit card numbers, address information, phone numbers, and so on – in short everything that identifies you as a person). The idea is that you sign into Passport once, and then it takes care of authenticating you to all member sites and providing them with your information.

Technologies Supported by Passport

The Passport service uses common web technologies such as SSL, HTTP redirects, cookies, JavaScript, and strong **symmetric key encryption** (**Triple DES**).

> *Symmetric key encryption is an algorithm where the same key is used for encryption and decryption. Symmetric encryption systems are typically used for bulk data encryption.*

In brief, Passport fully supports Windows NT 4.0, 2000 and XP Operating Systems, running IIS 4/5 Web Servers with ISAPI and ASP/ASP.NET support. It will also function on most popular Unix-based operating systems. A complete list of what it needs and provides can be found at www.passport.com/business.

The Microsoft Passport service is a cookie-based authentication service. The new Microsoft Web Services model (called **.NET My Services**) uses Passport extensively. When a web request comes to your site for a secure resource your server will check for a **Passport ticket** (cookie). If this Passport ticket is not found then your server will return HTTP 302 (redirect) and redirect the user to the Passport login page (held on a Microsoft server). Once the client is logged in with the Passport service using SSL, they will be transferred back to the original requested page on your server.

> *The heart of Passport authentication is a cookie. If the client browser does not accept cookies then Passport authentication will fail.*

Summary

In this chapter we've covered a few of the most important aspects of basic ASP.NET security. We saw how to use:

❑ Basic Authentication

❑ Integrated Windows Authentication

❑ Forms-based Authentication

❑ Forms-based Authentication with a database

We also touched upon the idea of encryption and mentioned the up-and-coming technology of Microsoft Passport.

We saw how basic authentication is only really valuable for securing intranet applications where there is a low security risk and the data is not sensitive (remember the details are passed as plain text) and how Integrated Windows Authentication, with its use of hashing, is much more secure but only supported by Internet Explorer browsers.

Then, we moved on to look at how we can secure our applications flexibly using the more complex method of Forms-based security that allows us to build our own user interfaces, and how we can improve upon the basic ideas of this approach by storing the user's details in a database.

Finally, we mentioned the idea of encryption and the basic premises upon which SSL works, before finishing up by discussing the emerging technology of Microsoft Passport and .NET My Services.

This chapter has necessarily been a quick 'whistle-stop' tour, if you'd like to know about ASP.NET security in more detail you might like to consider Professional ASP.NET Security *(ISBN 1-86100-620-9) also from Wrox Press.*

Index

A Guide to the Index

The index is arranged hierarchically, in alphabetical order, with symbols preceding the letter A. Most second-level entries and many third-level entries also occur as first-level entries. This is to ensure that users will find the information they require however they choose to search for it.

D

Notes

Notes

C# Today

The daily knowledge site for professional C# programmers

Got more Wrox books than you can carry around?

Wroxbase is the new online service from Wrox Press. Dedicated to providing online access to books published by Wrox Press, helping you and your team find solutions and guidance for all your programming needs.

The key features of this service will be:

- Different libraries based on technologies that you use everyday (ASP 3.0, XML, SQL 2000, etc.). The initial set of libraries will be focused on Microsoft-related technologies.
- You can subscribe to as few or as many libraries as you require, and access all books within those libraries as and when you need to.
- You can add notes (either just for yourself or for anyone to view) and your own bookmarks that will all be stored within your account online, and so will be accessible from any computer.
- You can download the code of any book in your library directly from Wroxbase

Visit the site at: www.wroxbase.com